Contemporary Issues in
Experimental Phonetics

PERSPECTIVES IN
NEUROLINGUISTICS and PSYCHOLINGUISTICS

Harry A. Whitaker, Series Editor
DEPARTMENT OF PSYCHOLOGY
THE UNIVERSITY OF ROCHESTER
ROCHESTER, NEW YORK

HAIGANOOSH WHITAKER and HARRY A. WHITAKER (Eds.).
Studies in Neurolinguistics, Volumes 1 and 2
NORMAN J. LASS (Ed). Contemporary Issues in Experimental
Phonetics

Contemporary Issues in Experimental Phonetics

Edited by

Norman J. Lass

Speech and Hearing Sciences Laboratory
West Virginia University
Morgantown, West Virginia

Academic Press   New York   San Francisco   London   1976

A Subsidiary of Harcourt Brace Jovanovich, Publishers

The figure on page 111 is adapted from *Function of the
Human Body*, by Arthur Guyton (Philadelphia: W. B.
Saunders, 1974), p. 110. By permission.

ACADEMIC PRESS, INC.
111 Fifth Avenue, New York, New York 10003

United Kingdom Edition published by
ACADEMIC PRESS, INC. (LONDON) LTD.
24/28 Oval Road, London NW1

Library of Congress Cataloging in Publication Data

Main entry under title:

Contemporary issues in experimental phonetics.

        (Perspectives in neurolinguistics & psycho–
linguistics)
        Includes bibliographies and index.
        1.   Phonetics, Experimental.   2.   Speech.
I.   Lass, Norman L.
QP306.C754   612'.78   75-30470
ISBN 0–12–437150–7

PRINTED IN THE UNITED STATES OF AMERICA

Contents

PART IV SPEECH PERCEPTION

List of Contributors

Numbers in parentheses indicate the pages on which the authors' contributions begin.

James H. Abbs (41, 139), Speech Physiology Laboratory, Department of Speech and Hearing Sciences, University of Washington, Seattle, Washington

Daniel S. Beasley (419), Department of Audiology and Speech Sciences, Michigan State University, East Lansing, Michigan

Charles I. Berlin (327), Kresge Hearing Research Laboratory of the South and Department of Otorhinolaryngology and Biocommunication, Louisiana State University Medical Center, New Orleans, Louisiana

John F. Brandt (459), Bureau of Child Research and Department of Speech and Drama, University of Kansas, Lawrence, Kansas

Peter D. Bricker (295), Bell Laboratories, Murray Hill, New Jersey

Gerald R. Eilenberg (139), Speech Physiology Laboratory, Department of Speech and Hearing Sciences, University of Washington, Seattle, Washington

Raymond D. Kent (79), Department of Communicative Disorders, University of Wisconsin, Madison, Wisconsin

Ilse Lehiste (225), Department of Linguistics, The Ohio State University, Columbus, Ohio

Jean E. Maki (419), National Technical Institute for the Deaf, Rochester Institute of Technology, Rochester, New York

Malcolm R. McNeil (327), Audiology and Speech Pathology Service, Veterans Administration Hospital, Denver, Colorado

Larry L. Pfeifer (171), Speech Communications Research Laboratory, Inc., Santa Barbara, California

Sandra Pruzansky (295), Bell Laboratories, Murray Hill, New Jersey

June E. Shoup (171), Speech Communications Research Laboratory, Inc., Santa Barbara, California

Michael Studdert-Kennedy (243), Department of Communication Arts and Sciences, Queens College of the City University of New York, Flushing, New York, and Haskins Laboratories, New Haven, Connecticut

Hisashi Wakita (3), Speech Communications Research Laboratory, Inc., Santa Barbara, California

Donald W. Warren (105), Department of Dental Ecology, School of Dentistry, University of North Carolina, Chapel Hill, North Carolina

Richard M. Warren (389), Department of Psychology, University of Wisconsin, Milwaukee, Wisconsin

Kenneth L. Watkin (41), Speech Physiology Laboratory, Department of Speech and Hearing Sciences, University of Washington, Seattle, Washington

Preface

Contemporary Issues in Experimental Phonetics provides comprehensive coverage of a number of current research topics of importance to graduate students in experimental phonetics as well as those involved in experimental phonetics research, including speech and hearing scientists, speech pathologists, audiologists, psychologists, and linguists. All contributing authors are currently involved in original research in the areas in which they have written. They have presented an interpretive review of the literature as well as a delineation of the current unresolved issues on each topic. Moreover, they have also provided, either explicitly or implicitly, specific suggestions for further inquiry and/or general directions for future research. The emphasis throughout the entire volume is on current literature and issues.

The book contains 13 chapters, divided into four major sections: *Research Techniques*, *Speech Production*, *The Speech Signal*, and *Speech Perception*. The *Research Techniques* section contains two chapters concerned with a discussion and description of the current instrumentation systems employed in the study of speech acoustics and speech physiology, including speech analysis and synthesis techniques, techniques for the measurement of the electrical activity of the speech muscles, and techniques for the measurement of structural movement during speech production.

Three chapters are included in the second section, *Speech Production*. The first deals with models of speech production, the various problems encountered with these models, and the current status of modeling. The aerodynamic principles of speech production and the instrumentation necessary to study these principles are discussed in the second chapter. The third chapter is concerned with the peripheral physiological mechanisms of speech production, including the peripheral mechanical properties of speech motor control and the afferent feedback mechanisms involved in speech production. Also discussed are the methodological difficulties involved in the study of the physiological mechanisms underlying the oral communication process, and criticism of the methodologies employed in previous research on the role of afferent feedback mechanisms in the control of speech movements.

The Speech Signal section has two chapters. In addition to the descriptions of the speech wave types, the acoustical speech parameters, and the acoustical characterization of speech sounds, the first chapter contains a discussion of the problems of current interest in the specifications of the acoustic characteristics of speech sounds. The topic of the second chapter is the suprasegmental features of speech, including quantity, pitch, stress, and the relationship of suprasegmental and segmental speech features.

There are six chapters in the *Speech Perception* section. The first is concerned with the speech perception process, including differences between speech perception and general auditory perception, levels of processing involved in speech perception, acoustic cues to the phonetic message, problems of invariance and segmentation associated with discovering these cues, the units of speech perception, models of phonetic perception, the processing of consonants and vowels, specialized neural processes for speech perception, and the transition from acoustic feature to phonetic percept in the speech perception process. The topic of the second chapter is speaker recognition: by listening, by machine, and by visual inspection of spectrograms. Special emphasis, appropriate in this section of the book, is given to speaker recognition by listening. The third chapter presents six theories on the nature of the dichotic right ear advantage and provides data believed to be important for incorporation into a working theory of dichotic speech perception. It also contains a tabular analysis of over 300 studies on dichotic speech perception. Errors in auditory perception are discussed in the fourth chapter in an attempt to uncover and study normal perceptual mechanisms. Three interrelated phenomena are described: (1) illusory changes in repeated auditory patterns, (2) perceptual cancellation of masking, with illusory presence of obliterated sounds, and (3) perception and confusions of temporal orders within sequences of sounds. The fifth chapter deals with the measurement of temporal processing in speech perception, the effects of time and frequency alteration on perception, and some of the theoretical interpretations associated with the findings of investigations on time- and frequency-altered speech. The interrelationship of speech, hearing, and language in an understanding of the total human communication process is the topic of the last chapter. The phenomenon of pitch and how it transcends speech, hearing, and language is employed to illustrate the author's point that, ". . . to infer something about the perception of speech from data on the perception of nonspeech *is* justifiable. Speech perception *may* be predicted from the analysis of the acoustic properties of spoken utterances *and* the characteristics of the human auditory system."

Since this book is not intended to serve as a basic text, the format of the chapters is generally not didactic in style. The reader is assumed to have a basic understanding of the fundamentals of the speech and hearing mechanisms, including the acoustic, anatomic, physiological, and perceptual bases of speech and hearing.

The authors are individually responsible for the opinions expressed in their chapters. No attempt has been made to avoid differences between authors' views since this book is not an elementary text and many of the topics discussed contain issues that are presently unresolved. Despite the broad coverage of topics in experimental phonetics contained in this volume, I am aware of the omission of a number of areas which might have been included in the book. Within the self-imposed limitations of length and the purpose of the book, the inclusion of other areas was unfeasible and unnecessary.

The reader will become aware of the fact that there are numerous unresolved issues in experimental phonetics requiring further investigation. He may also disagree with some of the statements made in this volume, especially since many of the discussions center around these unresolved issues. It is hoped that this book will serve as a comprehensive review of what is actually known on the included topics as well as a stimulus for future research in those areas where the extent of our understanding is still considerably limited.

Acknowledgments

I am grateful to the 18 authors who have contributed to this book, for without them there would be no book. In addition to their skillful writing, they have shown an exceptional amount of cooperation and tolerance of my compulsive perfectionistic behavior. Special thanks are due to Professor Ilse Lehiste for her helpful comments on the organization of the book, and to Professors Daniel S. Beasley and James H. Abbs whose sound advice and encouragement have been helpful to me throughout all stages of development of the book. I would also like to express my gratitude to my former mentors, Professors J. Douglas Noll, Kenneth W. Burk, Ralph L. Shelton, and John F. Michel, whose influence on my thinking has far exceeded their expectations. And finally, to my wife, Martha, whose patience and understanding were most helpful to me during the four-year duration of this project, I am deeply indebted.

PART I

RESEARCH TECHNIQUES

chapter 1

Instrumentation for the Study of Speech Acoustics

Hisashi Wakita

Speech Communications Research Laboratory, Inc.
Santa Barbara, California

Introduction

This chapter focuses on some recently developed speech analysis and synthesis techniques for the study of acoustic phonetics. Although these techniques were developed exclusively as efficient means of speech transmission and not for the study of acoustic phonetics, it should be obvious that they do provide some powerful new tools for the acoustic phonetician.

In the study of basic acoustic phonetics, many researchers are still heavily dependent on the sound spectrograph for obtaining speech parameters, despite the fact that there now exist more efficient and accurate methods, such as the method for pitch detection and the linear prediction method for formant tracking. There seem to be several reasons for this. Perhaps one of the main reasons is that the spectrograph has been in existence for such a long period that there are many people familiar with its use, and familiar with the appearance of spectrograms. Also, the spectrograph is relatively easy to operate, and, if caution is used, speech parameters can be measured fairly accurately from the spectrograms. Another reason that many people are hesitant to use recent methods, which are usually simulated by a digital computer, is that the principles of these methods are relatively difficult to understand; many non-engineer users may not be certain about their advantages and disadvantages or about their limitations in practical applications. In addition, user-oriented hardware and/or software systems may not be readily available. Frequently when a new method is developed and published, it has not been tested in all possible difficult situations, thus leaving a gap between the method and its application by the naive user. For the researcher, development of a new technique is fruitful, but adaptation to user-oriented systems can require much more labor. Since this process has been neglected, many techniques for extracting speech parameters that have been developed in the past have never been widely used. The purpose of this chapter, therefore, is to introduce recently developed techniques and methods in the area of speech analysis and synthesis. The reader is assumed to be reasonably familiar with basic instrumentation such as microphones, amplifiers, tape recorders, and so forth, and to have a fundamental knowledge of digital computers.

Speech Model and Parameters

Speech Production Model for Analysis

Most natural phenomena in our world are so complicated that we usually do not have adequate mathematical tools to describe them in general terms. The speech event is no exception. There are not as yet sufficient mathematical tools to describe completely the human speech event, even if all the physiological processes of speech production and perception could be elucidated. In developing a method of speech analysis, we must simplify the actual speech event to the extent that existing mathematical tools can be applied to it, but not to such an extent that the essential physical properties of the event cannot be preserved satisfactorily. In some cases, a greatly simplified model of the speech event can be created by adopting very simple hypotheses and assumptions and by imposing strong constraints. Generally speaking, we consider speech production processes involving only the activities of the larynx, pharynx, and oral cavity. Obviously, this does not take into account the nasal cavity or the subglottal activities which are important for speech production. It is necessary to ignore these, however, in the analysis techniques, since they unduly complicate the model and associated mathematics.

As a simplification of the speech production process, three major factors are considered: the excitation (glottal oscillation), the transmission (pharyngeal and oral cavity configuration), and the radiation effect at the mouth. Although these factors are inseparable in the actual speech production process, the strong assumption is imposed that they are separable. Under this assumption, it becomes possible for the first time to apply some of the concepts of mathematics and engineering to modeling of the speech production process. A linear system satisfies this assumption, and most of the models for speech analysis and synthesis are linear systems. It should be realized, therefore, that limitations exist from the starting point. Yet, because of the assumption of separability of factors, we are able to describe characteristics of sounds in terms of simple parameters which can be extracted from the linear model of speech production. This assumption also allows the acoustic characteristics attributable to the excitation source, the vocal cavity, and the radiation effect to be specified. Using this basic model of the speech production process, a specific set of parameters can be extracted with a certain degree of accuracy.

Speech Parameters

Speech parameters which can be extracted include *(1)* formant frequencies and bandwidths, *(2)* fundamental voice frequency, commonly referred to as *voice pitch*, *(3)* amplitude of fundamental frequency, also known as *voice intensity, (4)* average energy, and *(5)* vocal tract shapes. For the description of phonetic values of speech sounds, the formant frequencies are most important, although recent studies provide the possibility of computing, from acoustic data, vocal tract shapes from which some articulatory features can be extracted. In speech synthesis, parameters *(1)* through *(3)* are necessary.

Speech Analysis

Introduction

Since the middle 1960s, and especially since the early 1970s, digital computers have played an extremely important role in speech research. One major use of the digital computer is the simulation of a system. This is especially helpful in the development of sophisticated analysis techniques. To provide the same development by using only electronic hardware would take an exceedingly long time. The advantages of computer simulation are that processes can be repeated exactly and that the control of parameters is easy. The only disadvantage is that in many cases the simulation cannot be accomplished in real time. After extensive study of a technique by computer simulation, it is relatively easy to replace it partly or entirely with special-purpose hardware. Since hardware implementation of a computer simulation or replacement of part of the simulation with hardware implementation (a *hybrid system*) is relatively easy, the following discussion will focus on the computer simulation of various techniques.

In the early 1960s, there were no particular developments of new analysis techniques. Those quiet days were ended by the development of the *cepstrum* technique (Noll, 1964), a method that was developed for extracting the fundamental frequency of speech sounds. It attracted many people because it provided a fresh concept for separating the periodic components from the nonperiodic components of speech sounds. Although the term *cepstrum* became widely known among speech researchers, the method itself was seldom used by them, probably because of its sophistication. The cepstrum method continued to be investigated for possible application to automatic formant analysis (Schafer and Rabiner, 1970) as well as to fundamental frequency extraction. Several years after the cepstrum method was developed, two new techniques for speech analysis and synthesis gained prominence at the Sixth International Congress on Acoustics in 1968: the *maximum likelihood* method (Itakura and Saito, 1968) and *predictive coding of speech* (Atal and Schroeder, 1968). The development of these techniques was truly epoch making, for they vastly improved efficiency, accuracy, and speed. Their merits, however, were not widely proved in the United States until 4 years later when the *PARCOR* method (Itakura and Saito, 1972) demonstrated its amazing fidelity in analysis—synthesis telephony at the International Conference on Speech Communication and Processing in 1972. Since then, the PARCOR method and the first two methods have influenced the thinking of many speech researchers and now are known popularly as the *linear prediction* method. In the meantime, Markel (1971) pointed out the similarity between the maximum likelihood method and linear predictive coding, and then developed the *inverse digital filter* method, which is more closely related to a physical model of speech production (Markel, 1971). It was then shown that the inverse digital filter method is equivalent to the PARCOR method (Wakita, 1972) and the equivalences and differences among various approaches in the linear prediction method were investigated (Makhoul and Wolf, 1972). Through the efforts of those mentioned above and others, the theoretical basis for the linear prediction method has become much better understood, and currently this technique is extensively used for formant frequency tracking and fundamental frequency extraction. It also plays an extremely important role in speech compression and automatic speech recognition. The method has attracted so much attention that in a remarkably short time it has been further developed theoretically and practically in considerable detail (Makhoul, 1975; Markel and Gray, 1976). Details of the linear prediction method will be discussed in a later section.

In discussing the development of speech analysis techniques, the contribution of the Fast Fourier Transform (FFT) algorithm (Cooley and Turkey, 1965) cannot be neglected. The development of FFT truly accelerated the improvement of computer simulation efficiency. The Fourier transform is an important mathematical tool used to obtain from time-domain acoustic speech waveforms their frequency-domain characteristics. Since the development of digital computers, an algorithm for computing the Fourier transform much more rapidly than the existing algorithms had been sought. A fast algorithm, known as the *FFT*, was revolutionary not only in the area of numerical analysis but also in various areas of research involving the use of digital computers.

In developing speech analysis methods, past efforts were exerted predominantly toward formant tracking and fundamental frequency extraction. However, there were also a few attempts to obtain articulatory information from acoustic data. There was considerable interest in the relationships between the vocal tract configuration and its formant frequency characteristics. The reason is, of course, that in some cases, the description of speech sounds in terms of articulatory features directly related to the physiological aspects of speech production is much easier and more definitive than a purely acoustic description. Despite considerable interest in this aspect of speech research (e.g., Dunn, 1950; Stevens, Kasowsky, and Fant, 1953), there was little progress in this area until Mermelstein and Schroeder (1965) developed a method for computing the shape of the vocal tract from formant frequencies. In this case, the vocal tract shape was represented in terms of the vocal tract area function in which the cross-sectional areas along the tract were represented in a distance—area diagram. The vocal tract area function indicates gross features of the vocal tract configuration but not its detailed structure. This step was, nevertheless, a breakthrough for obtaining a better understanding of speech sounds in the articulatory and frequency domains. The method was further extended by Schroeder (1967), Mermelstein (1967), and Heinz (1967). The vocal tract area function was computed by measuring the input impedance at the lips, a method which required the use of a cumbersome tube attached to the speaker's mouth. Sondhi and Gopinath (1971) have attempted to avoid this difficulty by utilizing the impulse response at the lips instead of measuring the lip impedance. This method is still being investigated. In the meantime, another possibility of computing the vocal tract area function from acoustic speech waveforms had been investigated (Atal, 1970). A milestone in this technique was the development of a method for estimating the vocal tract area function directly from speech waveforms based on the linear prediction method (Wakita, 1972). Further, it was demonstrated theoretically that the linear prediction digital filtering is a discrete solution to the wave equations (from which can be derived the well-known *Webster's horn equation*) which describes the behavior of sound pressure and volume velocity in the models used by Schroeder, Mermelstein, and others (Wakita and Gray, 1974). It is quite surprising that the linear prediction digital filter is equivalent to an acoustic tube model or a transmission line analog of the vocal tract as proposed by Kelly and Lochbaum (1962) more than 10 years ago. Yet the practical significance of the linear prediction method lies in its efficiency and accuracy in extracting speech parameters. In the following sections, the details of some of the work mentioned above will be discussed to provide a more complete understanding of recent analysis techniques. Although this research is conceptually and mathematically sophisticated, an attempt will be made to explain it in laymen's terms with few equations. In some cases, therefore, the descriptions may be inadequate from the theoretical point of view. Readers interested in more advanced knowledge are encouraged to read the original papers or other references listed in the bibliography at the end of this chapter.

Cepstrum Method

VOICE PITCH EXTRACTION

Most previous fundamental frequency extraction techniques were based on the idea of detecting the recurrent peaks in the speech waveform. A difficulty with this approach was that peaks related to the periodicity of the laryngeal voice source could not always be distinguished from peaks resulting from the resonance behavior of the supraglottal spaces. The significance of the cepstrum method is that it provides a means for separating the periodic components (the fundamental frequency and its harmonics) from the nonperiodic components (the vocal tract characteristics). To develop the theory of the cepstrum, a linear system is assumed in which the spectrum of a voiced sound can be expressed as a product of the source spectrum and the spectrum of the vocal tract resonance characteristics. Products, however, are usually more difficult to handle than sums; therefore the description of the spectrum in terms of its components is simplified formally if we take the logarithm (*log*) of the speech spectrum. The product is thereby changed to a sum, and the resulting *log spectrum* can be expressed as the sum of the log source spectrum and the log spectrum of the vocal tract impulse response. In Figure 1.1(a) an example of the log spectrum of a voiced sound is shown. Note that the log operation results in a vertical scale the units of which are decibels. The slowly varying broken line denotes the log spectrum of the vocal tract impulse response on which the logarithm spectrum of the voice source is superimposed as the ripples. These ripples correspond to the harmonics of the fundamental frequency and are equally spaced along the frequency axis. Here the question is how to get information on the fundamental frequency from the log spectrum. That is, how can the regular spacing of the ripples be measured without interference from fluctuations attributable to resonance behavior? The approach which leads to the cepstrum is to look at the log spectrum in Figure 1.1(a) as if it were an ordinary time-domain waveform. If there are two sinusoidal waves of different frequencies and amplitudes superimposed in the time domain, how can they be separated? Can the frequency of each one be determined? In

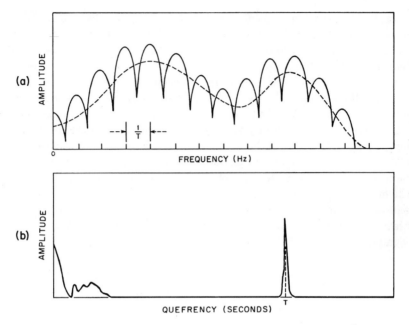

Figure 1.1   (a) Log spectrum of a voiced speech segment; (b) the cepstrum of (a). [After Noll, 1967.]

this case, taking the Fourier transform of the wave would result in two line spectra in the frequency domain, and the frequency and amplitude of each sinusoidal wave would be given by the positions and lengths of the two lines. By applying the same concept to the present problem, we may take the Fourier transform of the log spectrum (formally, an inverse Fourier transform). Since the spectrum of a log spectrum is a new quantity, it is given a new name, the *cepstrum*, formed by inverting the first four letters in *spectrum*, and the horizontal scale in the cepstrum is defined as the *quefrency* (Bogert, Healy, and Tukey, 1963) and has the unit of time. The cepstrum of Figure 1.1(a) is shown in Figure 1.1(b). Note that, since the horizontal axis denotes the time scale, the periodicity of the source spectrum appears as a sharp spike in the higher range of the cepstrum and that the slowly varying components of the vocal tract spectrum appear in the very low range. The location of the spike represents the period of the harmonic components from which the fundamental frequency is computed as the reciprocal of the period. Since the period is determined from the periodicity of the harmonics in the cepstrum method, it is possible to determine the voice pitch even for speech signals which have had the fundamental frequency component lost or filtered out, such as speech sent over a telephone line, the frequency band of which ranges between 300 Hz and 3400 Hz. In this case, the periodicity is still recovered from the regular spacing of the higher harmonics that are within the transmission band. Quite obviously, unvoiced sounds do not show any spike in the higher region of the cepstrum, and no periodicity can be determined. An example of cepstrum pitch analysis for a voiced sound is shown in Figure 1.2(a). The rapidly varying harmonic source components and the slowly varying vocal tract characteristics of the log spectrum as seen in Figure 1.2(b) are distinctly separated in the cepstrum. Changes in voice pitch are

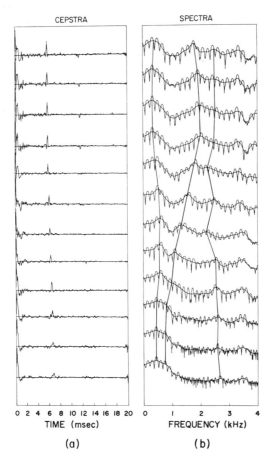

Figure 1.2 An analysis example of the cepstrum method: (a) cepstrum; (b) log spectrum. [From Schafer and Rabiner, 1970.]

clearly demonstrated by changes in the locations of spikes. The drawback of the cepstrum is that it takes a long time to compute the voice pitch by a digital computer since the computation involves taking the Fourier transform twice. However, this problem can be overcome by replacing the computer simulation with special-purpose hardware, or at least by implementing the Fourier transform with hardware.

FORMANT ANALYSIS

Since the excitation source characteristics and the vocal tract characteristics are separated in the cepstrum, the method is also effective for obtaining formant frequencies as well as the fundamental frequency of the voice. To obtain the vocal tract characteristics from the cepstrum, the source characteristics in the higher region of the cepstrum are discarded and the Fourier transform is applied to the vocal tract component in the lower range. As a result of this procedure, the slowly varying log spectrum of the vocal tract resonance characteristics is obtained, the peaks of which correspond to formant frequencies. It should be noted here that the ordinary spectrum of a speech segment also consists of the ripples corresponding to harmonics of the fundamental frequency. Thus, the vocal tract characteristics are not easily determined from it. What makes it easy to obtain vocal tract characteristics is the ability to find a smooth spectral envelope of the ordinary spectrum from which the peak frequencies can be determined. The cepstrum method makes this operation possible. A block diagram of the cepstrum method for pitch and formant frequency extraction is shown in Figure 1.3. In practice, the speech signal to be analyzed is digitized after being passed through the low-pass filter, the cutoff frequency of which is chosen as half the sampling frequency. One segment of the speech signal, normally 25—35 msec long, is passed through a filter called a *Hamming window* before the FFT is applied to it. The Hamming window is a special-purpose filter used for reducing distortion in the frequency domain. If the Fourier transform were applied to a short segment of unfiltered speech, the two ends of the segment would have discontinuities in the time domain which would cause distortion in the frequency domain. Figure 1.4 shows an example of the pitch period and formant data automatically processed from an utterance *We were away a year ago.*

When the cepstrum method was first developed, its computer simulation took a long time because of frequent use of the Fourier transform. With the development of the Fast Fourier Transform (FFT) algorithm, the situation improved appreciably, though not to the point of satisfaction. However, the recent development of real-time FFT analyzers will eliminate this drawback, at least as far as feasibility is concerned. The cost may still be a problem. Before such an implementation could be realized, another powerful analysis method, the linear prediction method, appeared.

Linear Prediction Method

LINEAR REGRESSION

In computing formant frequencies, the linear prediction method is analogous to the cepstrum method in that it is the purpose of both to obtain the smooth spectral envelopes of speech sounds. The difference is in their approaches: The linear predic-

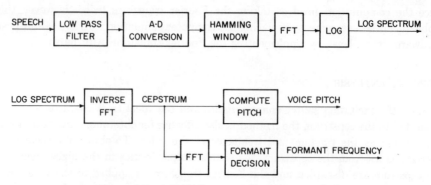

Figure 1.3   A block diagram of the cepstrum method.

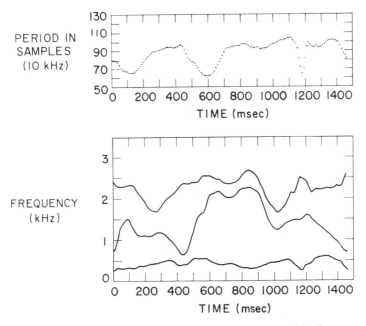

Figure 1.4 An analysis example of period data and formant data obtained by the cepstrum method. [After Schafer and Rabiner, 1970.]

tion method manipulates sampled speech data mainly in the time domain, whereas the main processing of the cepstrum method is accomplished in the frequency domain and involves using the Fourier transform three times, twice to get the cepstrum and once to get the smooth spectrum. So in terms of computer simulation of the two methods, the linear prediction method is more efficient than the cepstrum method.

To make it easier to understand the linear prediction of speech, an example of a similar concept in statistics is given: Suppose there are two statistical quantities, the highest temperature (T_i) and the number of traffic accidents (N_i) in a day during the past years. A question arises: Is it possible to estimate the number of traffic accidents by knowing the high temperature of the day (so that ambulances, doctors, hospital beds, etc., are available)? In this example, the conditional distribution of the number of traffic accidents for a given temperature is known from past data. It is also known in statistics that the best possible estimate of N_i from a given T_i, in the sense of the least squares principle, is the mean (m_i) of the conditional distribution for T_i. Thus, in this particular example, the conditional mean, m_i, can be used as the best estimate for the number of traffic accidents when the high temperature, T_i, is recorded. However, in many cases, especially those in which more than two statistical quantities are involved, it becomes more difficult to calculate the conditional mean. In such a case, by the use of past data, it is possible to determine a certain simple mathematical function which best approximates the conditional mean in the sense of the least squares principle. In this example, the aim is to determine a straight line which would give the estimate of N_i, ($\hat{N}_i$), for a given T_i. Suppose the straight line is expressed as

$$\hat{N} = \alpha T + \beta. \tag{1}$$

In Equation (1), α and β are constants and, particularly, α determines the slope of the straight line. The error e_i between the actual value N_i and the estimated value $\hat{N}_i$ is

$$e_i = N_i - \hat{N}_i. \tag{2}$$

The straight line is determined from the statistical properties of the event by observing N_i and T_i for a sufficient range of i. It is computed by applying the least squares principle so that the mean of the square errors between the actual values and the straight line becomes as small as possible. The straight line thus determined gives the best estimate of N_i for a given T_i. Of course, this best estimate is not as accurate as the actual conditional mean but is as close to it as possible with a straight line approximation. Once the formula in Equation (1) is determined from the past data, the number of traffic accidents can be predicted by ascertaining the highest temperature of a day. In this case, it is easily understood that the smaller the standard deviation of a conditional distribution, the greater the accuracy of prediction. In statistics, this method is called *linear mean square regression*, and α in Equation (1) is called the *regression coefficient* which determines the slope of the straight line.

The preceding example involves two different statistical quantities, but linear regression also can be applied to a sequence of single statistical quantities. In this case, we wonder whether it is possible, for example, to predict tomorrow's high temperature based on knowledge of today's high temperature. By letting tomorrow's temperature be N and today's temperature be T, we can use the same procedure to obtain the formula in Equation (1) for the linear mean square regression.

It will not be difficult to imagine the expansion of the concept to an n-dimensional case. In the second example, tomorrow's temperature would be predicted based on knowledge of the temperatures in the past n days. And Equation (1) would be expanded to a straight line in the n-dimensional space, even though it is difficult to conceptualize visually. The prediction accuracy will increase as the number of temperatures (n) to be used in the past is increased, as long as tomorrow's temperature is correlated with the temperature of n days ago. Thus, the highest prediction accuracy is attained by using all the past temperatures which have correlation with tomorrow's temperature.

LINEAR PREDICTION OF SPEECH

Consider an application of this concept to the speech event, using a time sequence of sampled speech. The problem is to obtain the best estimate of the next sample, $\hat{x}_n$, by observing the past M samples. In this case, the error e_n between the actual sample x_n and the estimated sample $\hat{x}_n$ is

$$e_n = x_n - \hat{x}_n. \tag{3}$$

The estimated sample $\hat{x}_n$ is computed from a straight line in M-dimensional space as an expansion of the previous example, and expressed as

$$x_n = \alpha_1 x_{n-1} + \alpha_2 x_{n-2} + \ldots + \alpha_M x_{n-M}. \tag{4}$$

Here, x_{n-1}, x_{n-2}, $\ldots$, x_{n-M} are M samples observed in the past and α_1, α_2, $\ldots$, α_M are the regression coefficients to be determined. The regression coefficients are determined in such a way that the mean square error is minimized. A time window is set through which speech events for a certain period are observed in order to determine the regression coefficients. In this case, it is assumed that the speech event during the observation is stationary. By *stationary* it is meant that the statistical distribution characteristics do not change; that is, the mean and the standard deviation of the speech event are constant during the observation. This assumption is satisfied reasonably well for time windows of approximately 10 msec duration. The computational procedure to determine the regression coefficients in an efficient manner is the kernel of the linear prediction method. However, the procedure is so technical that it has to be omitted here. It may be noted that the autocorrelation coefficients play an important role in determining the regression coefficients. The process in the linear regression method can be schematically represented as shown in Figure 1.5.

What significance do the regression coefficients α_i have in this speech production model? How are they related to formant frequencies? Here it is assumed that the spectrum of a voiced non-nasalized sound is characterized only by the frequencies and bandwidths of the peaks in its smoothed spectrum. Strictly speaking, the speech spectra of voiced non-nasalized sounds sometimes have dips that arise from the dips in the glottal wave characteristics. They are not conspicuous in most cases, and the sepctra, even in such cases, are well approximated by peaks only. By this assumption, the spectral envelope of a voiced non-nasalized sound can be represented in terms of the reciprocal of a polynomial of a certain kind, as

$$\text{Spectral envelope} = \frac{1}{\text{Polynomial } A}. \tag{5}$$

The roots of the polynomial in Equation (5) give the peak frequencies and bandwidths. Thus, the problem of determining the formant frequencies and bandwidths is reduced to the problem of determining this polynomial from speech waveforms.

The representation in Equation (5) can be interpreted as a system's input—output

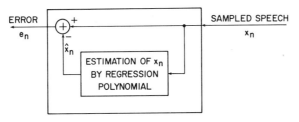

Figure 1.5   A linear regression filter.

relation. The input—output relation is represented in the frequency domain as the product:

$$\text{Speech}\left(\frac{1}{A}\right) = \text{Excitation (1)} \times \text{System transfer function}\left(\frac{1}{A}\right). \qquad (6)$$

The system as a production model is shown in Figure 1.6 (a). It is more convenient, however, to consider the system in terms of an analysis model, as shown in Figure 1.6 (b), since it is desired to determine the polynomial A from a given speech input. Since a constant in the frequency domain represents either an impulse or white noise in the time domain, the polynomial A is determined in such a way that the excitation as output becomes either an impulse or white noise.

In the linear prediction technique in which speech sounds are handled in the form of sampled data, a special type of polynomial for A in which *z-transform* notation is used is employed and expressed as

$$A = 1 + a_1 z^{-1} + a_2 z^{-2} + \ldots + a_M z^{-M}. \qquad (7)$$

Here, $a_1, a_2, \ldots, a_M$ are called the filter coefficients. By expressing the polynomial A as in Equation (7), we can prove a very important fact: *The filter coefficients a_i are identical to the regression coefficients α_i in Equation (4)!* That is, the coefficients of a polynomial which gives the best estimate of the next sample x_n are equal to the coefficients of the transfer function polynomial of an inverse filter. The prediction error is given as the output of the inverse filter. The formant frequencies and bandwidths which were sought are given by the roots of the polynomial $A = 0$. This is easily done by the use of a polynomial root-solving subroutine in the computer. However, a much easier way to obtain formant frequencies and bandwidths is to note the particular properties of the z-transform notation in Equation (7).

The z-transform notation of the inverse filter transfer function in Equation (7) represents both frequency-domain and time-domain information. To obtain the spectral envelope, $\log |A|^2$ is computed for all the frequencies of interest by substituting each frequency value into z, since z itself is a function of frequency. The result of this computation is precisely the smooth spectrum estimate; its local maxima therefore correspond to the formants. The formant frequencies and bandwidths can be measured directly from this smooth spectrum without having to solve for the roots of $A = 0$. One example of the inverse filter spectrum is shown in Figure 1.7(a),

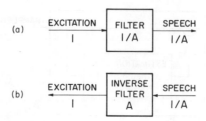

Figure 1.6 Models for the linear prediction method: (a) the production model; (b) the analysis model.

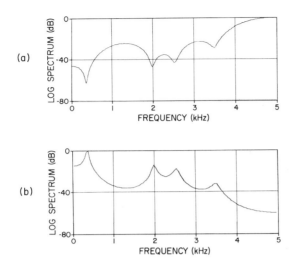

Figure 1.7 An example of the spectrum of the inverse filter: (a) An inverse filter spectrum; (b) the reciprocal of (a). [After Markel, 1972b.]

and the reciprocal of the inverse filter spectrum, shown in (b), defines the resonance structure of the input speech spectrum. In the time domain, on the other hand, the coefficients of A, $\{1, a_1, a_2, \ldots, a_M\}$ denote the sampled values of the impulse response of the inverse filter. Since the inverse filter spectrum is obtained as the Fourier transform of the impulse response of the filter, the same inverse filter spectrum as shown in Figure 1.7(a) is computed by taking the Fourier transform of a set of filter coefficients. Determination of formant frequencies and bandwidths from the spectrum is relatively easy, and some examples will be presented in a later section.

PARTIAL CORRELATION COEFFICIENT

The filter coefficient is a new speech parameter, sometimes called the *a-parameter*, that is directly related to the formant frequencies as discussed in the previous section. This relation is not the only reason that linear prediction is interesting. In the areas of speech compression and automatic speech recognition, there are, besides formant frequencies, other parameters, such as the filter coefficients themselves, which are preferred for their efficiency, especially when they are related to formant frequencies or have some other physical meaning in the speech production model of interest. One such speech parameter is the *partial correlation coefficient (PARCOR coefficient)*, which is also called the *k-parameter* or the *reflection coefficient*. This parameter is playing a most important role in the areas of speech compression and automatic speech recognition because several of its properties are particularly suitable in these areas. This parameter is obtained as an intermediate result in the computation of the filter coefficients; thus, it is indirectly related to the formant frequencies. As will be described in a later section, it is equivalent, when properly processed, to a set of acoustic reflection coefficients that determine the vocal tract area function. The partial correlation coefficient is so significant in the linear prediction method that an attempt to explain some of its physical meanings will be made, even though it is very difficult to explain clearly without considering the mathematical details.

Let us first consider the partial correlation coefficient in an easy statistical example. Suppose there is a group of pairs of beautiful sisters; let A denote the beauty of the first sister of a pair, and let B denote that of the second. The ordinary correlation between A and B for the whole group (called the *total correlation*) includes the effects of all the factors that might contribute to their beauty: Their parents are also beautiful and handsome, they exercise every morning, they use the most expensive cosmetics, and so forth. Sometimes it becomes desirable to consider the correlation between A and B in such a way that the effects of one or two of the factors are eliminated. For example, what is the correlation between A and B which does not include effects of the beauty of the parents? To answer this question, let the beauty of the mothers be C and the handsomeness of the fathers be D. By applying linear mean square regression, the best estimates of the sisters' beauties ($\hat{A}$ and $\hat{B}$), based on C and D can be computed. $\hat{A}$ and $\hat{B}$ can be interpreted as the best estimates of the contribution of C and D to A and B. Then the correlation between ($A - \hat{A}$) and ($B - \hat{B}$) represents the correlation after the effects from the parents are subtracted in the sense of the least mean square principle. The correlation thus computed is called the *partial correlation*, and is essentially the correlation between the *errors* of the estimates $\hat{A}$ and $\hat{B}$ for A and B. The partial correlation in this case is the correlation between A and B of a group of two beautiful sisters whose parents are equally beautiful. Thus, a statement such as "two sisters are beautiful because their parents are beautiful" is excluded via this partial correlation.

Now consider the concept of partial correlation in the linear prediction of speech. Suppose there are $m + 1$ speech data $x_n, x_{n-1}, \ldots, x_{n-m}$ sampled 5000 times per second. This means that speech is observed every .1 msec. If the length of the vocal tract is assumed to be 17.65 cm and the sound velocity is 35,300 cm/sec, then it takes .5 msec for the acoustic wave at the glottis to travel to the lips. Two acoustic waves are considered to exist within the vocal tract; one is propagating toward the lips, and the other is reflecting back from the lips to propagate toward the glottis. Thus, it takes 1.0 msec for a wave to propagate from the glottis to the lips and to be reflected back down the tract to the glottis. Now, attention should be directed to the wave (A) at the glottis which is about to proceed toward the lips. At the glottis, the wave A is affected by the waves reflected back toward it from various positions along the vocal tract. The most distant position from which reflected waves arrive is the lips, and therefore the wave A is affected by the past behavior of A only as far back as 1.0 msec if the higher-order reflections are neglected. The way this effect on the wave A is woven into the speech wave can be described in terms of the partial correlation between pairs of speech samples spaced 1.0 msec apart; that is, the partial correlation between x_n and x_{n-10}. Suppose the wave A has proceeded for .45 msec (1.765 cm short of the lips). At that point, it is further affected by the wave which was proceeding .1 msec ahead of the wave A and was reflected at the lips. This effect is added to the speech wave via the partial correlation between pairs of samples spaced .1 msec apart; that is, between x_n and x_{n-1}. The intervening partial correlations have similar interpretations for the effects of the reflected waves at intermediate positions in the vocal tract. In the PARCOR analysis method, one approach of the linear prediction method, the partial correlation between x_n and x_{n-1} is first computed; it represents the effect added to the wave at a point 1.765 cm from the lips. In the next stage of analysis, the partial correlation between x_n and x_{n-2} is computed by eliminating the effect from sample x_{n-1} by the use of the partial correlation between x_n and x_{n-2}. Thus, the partial correlation between x_n and x_{n-2} represents the effect woven into the wave at a point 3.53 cm from the lips. In this manner, successive stages unravel the effects accumulated into the wave at discrete points within the vocal tract. This process is illustrated in Figure 1.8. At each stage, the shaded portion represents the correlated quantity between pairs of samples; this quantity is subtracted from the original quantity at each stage of filtering. The residual signal is denoted as ε^+ and ε^-, and z^{-1} denotes a time delay corresponding to a sampling period. After subtraction of the correlated quantity at each stage, the partial correlation coefficient (k_i) to be used to determine the correlated quantity in the next stage is computed from the residual signal. The detailed structure of the inverse filter is shown in Figure 1.9. The triangles in the figure denote multipliers. From the partial correlation coefficients (k-parameters) thus computed, the filter coefficients (a-parameters) can be obtained easily by the use of a *recursive relation*. (A recursive relation is one in which successive members of a sequence can be computed from a formula that involves the computed values of the preceding members of the sequence.) This procedure is efficiently accomplished in the computer by means of a digital filter as shown in Figure 1.9.

Some previously discussed aspects of the linear prediction method are summarized here:

1. The coefficients of the transfer function polynomial of the inverse filter are

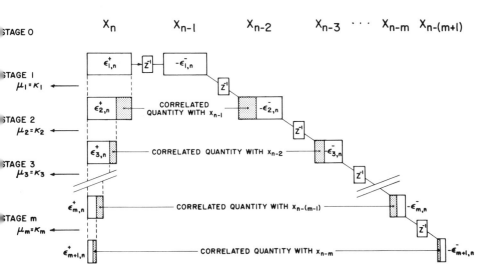

Figure 1.8 Schematic representation of the inverse filtering process. [From Wakita, 1972.]

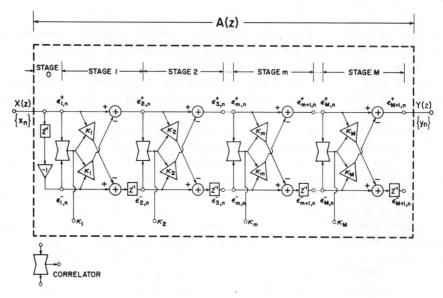

Figure 1.9   Detailed structure of the optimum inverse filter. [From Wakita, 1972.]

identical to those of the regression polynomial which give the best estimate of the next speech sample in the least mean square principle.

2. The peak frequencies in the speech spectrum are obtained either by solving for the roots of the transfer function polynomial of the inverse filter or by taking the Fourier transform of the filter coefficients.

3. The filter coefficients are obtained in a very efficient manner by using the partial correlation coefficients; these, in turn, give some physical insight into the speech production mechanism.

FORMANT ANALYSIS

Based on the discussion in the previous sections, it is easy to construct a block diagram for obtaining the peaks in the spectrum of a speech segment. Figure 1.10 shows a block diagram of the inverse filter approach. The differencing network is used to emphasize the attenuated higher-frequency components in order to attain more accurate estimation of the higher formants. As mentioned before, the autocorrelation coefficients of the speech signal are used to compute the filter coefficients. The smooth spectral envelope is then obtained by taking the FFT of the filter coefficients. An example of the smooth spectrum obtained by this analysis system and a comparison with the input spectrum is shown in Figure 1.11. In this example, the degree of the transfer function polynomial M, or the number of past data to be used for predicting the next sample, was chosen as 14. From various studies (e.g., Markel, 1972b), it was found empirically that the optimum number for M depends on the sampling frequency used to digitize analog speech. If the sampling frequency is K kilohertz, then the optimum number for M is found to be between K and $K + 4$. The next step one would

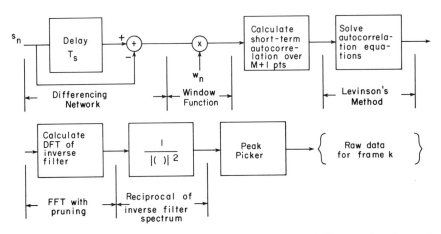

Figure 1.10 Block diagram of the inverse filter method for automatically extracting the raw data for formant trajectory estimation. [From Markel, 1972b.]

like to take is to track automatically the formant frequencies. A problem arises, however, in choosing as precisely as possible those peaks attributable to vocal tract resonances, since the peaks do not always correspond to formants. Various schemes to choose the correct peaks have been attempted (e.g., Markel, 1973; McCandless, 1974). A simple peak-picking scheme applied to the smooth spectral envelope is found to be fairly satisfactory for obtaining the formant trajectories for the first three formant

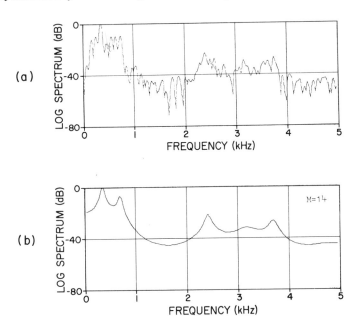

Figure 1.11 A smooth spectral envelope obtained by the linear prediction method: (a) input speech spectrum; (b) smooth spectrum. [After Markel, 1972b.]

frequencies. The three largest peaks of the speech spectrum in ascending order of frequency are defined as the formants in the peak-picking method. Although the input spectra will not produce correct results, it was found that peak picking of the inverse filter would give correct results approximately 90% of the time. This was tested on utterances chosen because they were representative of a difficult form of voiced speech having close first and second formants, close second and third formants, and fast transitions. One analysis example for such an utterance, *we were away*, is shown in Figure 1.12. Formant trajectories are quite clear even from this raw data plotting. For this analysis, a sampling frequency of 10 kHz and a polynomial of degree 14 were used. Each speech frame to be analyzed contained 256 samples (spanning 25.6 msec) and analysis was done every 16 msec. As indicated in the figure, the portion where the formant frequencies are varying rapidly can be analyzed more minutely. In that portion, the second formant is varying rapidly from a high to a low frequency. During this period, the number of analyses was tripled and then the second formant trajectory was enhanced as shown in the figure.

As can be seen from the example, the capability of formant analysis in the linear prediction method is so superb that various applications, such as a digital spectrograph, currently are being attempted in order to facilitate future research in acoustic phonetics.

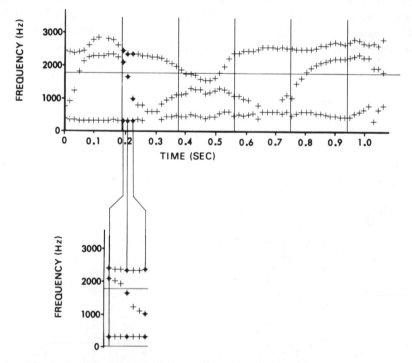

Figure 1.12 An analysis example of formant tracking: (top) the raw data output for the utterance *We were away*; (bottom) an expanded resolution analysis for the interval indicated to illustrate the tracking of a rapid F_2 transition. [From Markel, 1972b.]

VOICE PITCH EXTRACTION

As mentioned before, the linear prediction method processes the input speech so that an impulse or white noise is obtained as the residual signal. This ideal situation is actually realized as the degree of transfer function polynomial M approaches infinity. In practice, however, an optimum M was chosen to be at most the sampling frequency in kilohertz plus 4. Under this condition, the residual signal is not an impulse or white noise. The linear prediction filter can extract the slowly varying frequency characteristics attributable to the glottal wave shape, the vocal tract, and the radiation, but it cannot extract the rapidly varying characteristics attributable to the fundamental frequency and its harmonics. Thus, the residual signal still contains this information; that is, the pitch information is well preserved in the residual signal, as shown in Figure 1.13. The residual signal contains clear spikes that are separated by a pitch period. It should be noted that the spikes correspond to the peaks of the original speech waveform. Thus, the largest prediction error occurs exactly at these peaks in the speech waveform.

There are various conceivable schemes to detect the periodicity of these spikes. The simplest way is to compute the autocorrelation function of the residual signal. Two conspicuous spikes are found in the autocorrelation function at the origin and at the point, that is, one pitch period from the origin. The pitch frequency then is given by the reciprocal of the pitch period.

For those signals which do not have a fundamental frequency component (such as telephone conversations, in which the fundamental may be too low in frequency to be transmitted), the harmonic relation is still preserved in the residual signal even though the original signal does not have clear spikes in the time domain.

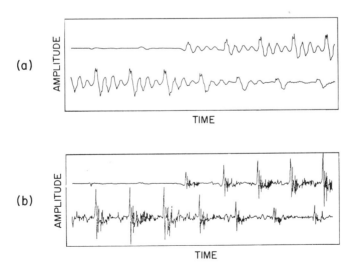

Figure 1.13 Waveforms from the segment *is*: (a) input speech; (b) residual signal. [After Markel, Gray, and Wakita, 1973.]

Although the linear prediction method was modeled for non-nasalized voiced sounds, it has been experimentally demonstrated that the method works for voiceless and nasal sounds as well, at least in analysis—synthesis schemes. The method is completely acceptable for voiceless and nasal sounds in that the peaks in their spectra are accurately extracted, although the model itself becomes physically unrealistic for these sounds since it assumes the noise sounds to be always at the glottis for voiceless sounds and assumes no separate nasal tract for nasal sounds. A particular drawback of the linear prediction method is said to be the inability to extract the spectral zeros (dips in the spectrum) attributable to the glottal waves and to the nasal tract. In addition to its computational convenience, a justification for using the linear prediction method to detect the spectral peaks is that the human ear is insensitive to the spectral zeros. Whether or not the detection of the spectral zeros is necessary and whether or not it is possible to develop an analysis technique to determine them with reasonable accuracy remain as unsolved problems.

Two recent analysis techniques have been discussed in detail. The linear prediction method, in particular, is becoming recognized as the most powerful analysis method in every respect. It is still essential to implement this technique in user-oriented analysis systems, either in software or in hardware. Otherwise, the merits of this sophisticated method as a research tool for phonetics could be lost. It also will be important for users to be able to use properly other analysis methods, depending upon the available instrumentation and the research problem that is at hand. For example, for the analysis of a small amount of speech data, the sound spectrograph still may be the most useful instrument available. On the other hand, if the voice pitch is the only parameter to be extracted, easier and faster methods, such as the autocorrelation method (Fujisaki, 1960), will suffice.

Methods for Computing Vocal Tract Area Functions

Attempts to describe speech sounds in terms of formant frequencies have been predominant in acoustic phonetics. There also has been considerable interest in the relationships between movements of articulators, such as the tongue, jaw, or lips, and the formant frequency behavior (e.g., Chiba and Kajiyama, 1941; Dunn, 1950; Fant, 1960; Öhman, 1967; Lindblom and Sundberg, 1971). It is very difficult to determine directly the formant frequencies from the positions of these articulators. Instead, the vocal tract configuration first is described in terms of an area function that is determined by the position of the articulators. Although the actual vocal tract configuration is quite irregular and complicated, it is regarded for simplicity as a nonuniform acoustic tube having a cross-sectional area that varies along its length. To compute formant frequencies from a known vocal tract shape based on the acoustic tube model was found to be relatively easy. The question that remained open was whether or not it is also possible to compute a unique vocal tract shape in terms of an area function from given acoustic data, such as formant frequencies.

Until recently, the only way to obtain a vocal tract shape was to utilize an X-ray technique supplemented by palatograms, plaster casts of the mouth, and so forth

(Chiba and Kajiyama, 1941; Fant, 1960). Drawbacks of X-ray techniques are that processing the data is laborious, and it involves guesswork and many assumptions. Yet, even today, the use of X-rays is considered to be the most reliable method for observing the vocal tract area function, since it provides a visualization of some details of the vocal tract configuration. Probably the X-ray technique and the direct measurement methods will continue for some time to be best for observing in detail the movements of articulators. On the other hand, it would certainly be convenient if there were some simple, fast, and efficient way to obtain information on the vocal tract shape, even if the information is not as fine as that obtained through the direct methods. There have been two major recent developments in this area. The first is based on the mathematical formula known as *Webster's horn equation*, which describes the behavior of the sound pressure and acoustic volume velocity of airflow within an acoustic tube. The other development is based on the linear prediction of speech. Brief descriptions of these methods are given in this section.

LIP IMPEDANCE METHOD

The development of the lip impedance method was indeed a pioneering, innovative work in the attempt to estimate vocal tract shape from acoustic measurements (Schroeder, 1967; Mermelstein, 1967). To be able to derive vocal tract shape from acoustic measurements or, eventually, from acoustic speech waveforms, had been a dream of speech researchers for a long time. The lack of an appropriate analysis technique had hindered development in this important area of speech research.

The method is based on Webster's horn equation. The vocal system is assumed to be lossless. As boundary conditions, it is assumed that the tract is closed at the glottis and open at the lips. It is known that for a given acoustic tube shape, Webster's horn equation gives not only an infinite number of resonance frequencies when the glottis end is closed and lip end is open, but also an infinite number of resonance frequencies when both ends are closed. It can be shown that at the resonance frequencies for the first boundary condition, the input impedance looking into the tube from the lip end becomes zero (this is called a *zero*), and that it becomes infinite (this is called a *pole*) at the resonance frequencies for the second boundary condition. Conversely, it is known from a theorem on the uniqueness of solutions that a unique area function must exist given a complete infinite set of resonance frequencies under both boundary conditions, that is, a complete infinite set of zeros and poles of the input impedance. In practice, however, we cannot observe an infinite number, but only the first few zeros and poles of the lip impedance. Thus, the question in this problem was whether the use of the first few zeros and poles of the lip impedance could produce a good representation of the original tube shape, if the tube length was known. A very significant finding in this method was that the coefficients in the Fourier expansion of the logarithm of an area function are related to the zeros and poles of the lip impedance and their slight perturbations. Although the method was not straightforward, this finding permitted the computation of tube shape from given lip impedance zeros and poles under the condition of known tube length. The computation starts from a uniform tube for which the zeros and poles of the input impedance can be computed easily. By perturbing the first few zeros and poles, a set of Fourier expansion coefficients is determined, from which a perturbed tube shape is obtained. This tube shape represents the first estimate of the true tube shape. Exact zeros and poles of the input impedance are then recomputed for the perturbed tube shape, and further perturbations are introduced to bring them into coincidence with the given measured values. This procedure is iterated until the computed zeros and poles become as close to the given values as possible. A preliminary test on known area functions gave reasonably good results, as shown in Figure 1.14. However, the difficulty with the method was in the measurement of the zeros and poles of the lip impedance. An impedance tube was connected to the subject's mouth, and a signal to measure the lip impedance was sent into the mouth via the tube; the subject was required to articulate without phonation. This procedure imposed a somewhat unnatural condition on the subject. Because of this difficulty, the method has not been pursued further for the study of acoustic phonetics, even though subsequently the method was somewhat improved (Paige and Zue, 1970a; Gopinath and Sondhi, 1970; Wakita and Gray, 1973, 1975). The development of this method, however, stimulated activities in this important area because for the first time it was shown that a vocal tract shape actually could be deduced from acoustic data.

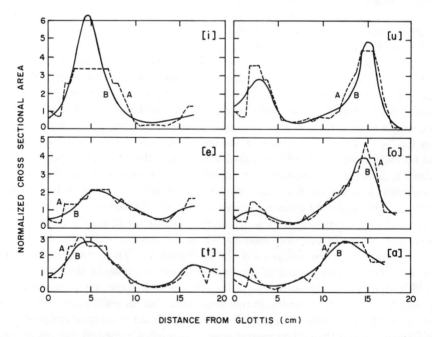

Figure 1.14   Area functions of six Russian vowels. A: X-ray derived area function. (After Fant, 1960.) B: Area function based on the lip impedance calculated from X-ray derived area function. [From Mermelstein, 1967.]

LIP IMPULSE RESPONSE METHOD

In order to avoid the drawbacks in the lip impedance method, an impulse was used to measure the acoustic impulse response at the lips (Sondhi and Gopinath, 1971). The use of an impulse eliminated the requirement of the boundary condition at the glottis, and the length information did not have to be assumed beforehand. The experimental setup is shown in Figure 1.15. An impulse generated by the source proceeds in both directions. The left-going signal is absorbed by the wedge so that no reflection takes place at this end. The right-going signal is reflected at the lips in a manner dependent upon the shape of the vocal tract. The microphone first picks up the right-going impulse, and then, after some time delay, picks up the reflected waves from the lips. Since the response dies down in a few milliseconds, rapidly recurring measurements are possible to study the dynamics of a moving vocal tract. A subject is again required to articulate without any phonation. The procedure to construct the vocal tract shape from a measured impulse response is mathematically quite complicated, and thus the details of the procedure will be omitted here. A test result obtained for a metal tube of known shape is shown in Figure 1.16. The resulting reconstruction is reasonably good even though the tube has step discontinuities.

Since this method is based on the assumption of a lossless system, the losses should be considered for the impulse response measured from the actual lossy vocal tract. Efforts for improving the method toward this direction are continuing (Sondhi, 1974).

LINEAR PREDICTION METHOD

In contrast to the previous two methods, linear prediction enables us to estimate the vocal tract area function directly from the acoustic speech waveforms. As mentioned earlier, it was proved that the mathematical procedure for computing the partial correlation coefficients is equivalent to a discrete solution for wave equations that describe the behavior of sound pressure and volume velocity inside an acoustic tube (Wakita and Gray, 1974). Thus, this theory applies to a vocal tract model in which the vocal tract is regarded as a nonuniform acoustic tube which is represented by a concatenation of cylindrical tubes of equal length. The cross-sectional area of a section denotes the average cross-sectional area of the corresponding portion of the

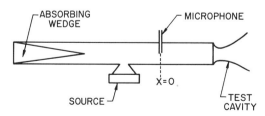

Figure 1.15 Schematic of an experimental setup for estimating vocal tract shape. [From Sondhi and Gopinath, 1971.]

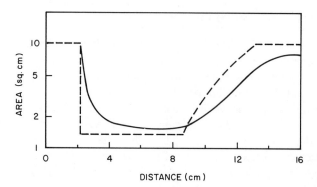

Figure 1.16 A test result of the lip impulse response method obtained for a metal tube. The dotted graph is the shape of a test cavity, and the solid graph is the reconstruction produced by the impulse response method. [From Sondhi and Gopinath, 1971.]

vocal tract. For a discrete representation of an area function like this, the reflection coefficient μ_m can be defined at the boundary between two adjacent sections whose cross-sectional areas are S_m and S_{m+1}, respectively, as

$$\mu_m = (S_m - S_{m+1})/(S_m + S_{m+1}). \tag{8}$$

This relationship between cross-sectional areas and the acoustic reflection coefficient is actually a well-known result from elementary acoustics (e.g., Hunter, 1957). The sound pressure and the volume velocity within the acoustic tube can be represented in terms of the wave proceeding toward the lips (the forward-going wave) and the wave proceeding toward the glottis (the backward-going wave). The forward- and the backward-going waves correspond to the error signals ε^+ and ε^-, respectively, in Figure 1.9 (the direction of ε^- would be inverted in a synthesis mode). Interestingly enough, the partial correlation coefficients have been shown to be equal to the respective reflection coefficients if the speech model is modified as follows. First note that the transfer function we have considered so far includes all the contributions from the glottal and radiation characteristics as well as the vocal tract characteristics. This transfer function can be expressed as the reciprocal of a polynomial A for voiced and non-nasalized sounds. In order to obtain the *true* vocal tract transfer function, a speech production model as shown in Figure 1.17(a) is considered. Through the glottal filter, an impulse train is shaped into a train of glottal waves that excites the vocal tract filter. Speech is generated after passing the output of the vocal tract filter through the radiation filter. Since the system is assumed to be linear, it can be modified into the system in Figure 1.17(b) without changing the input–output relation. The vocal tract transfer function, $1/H$, can then be computed from a knowledge of impulse train E and output X. To determine the vocal tract transfer function from a given speech segment, it may be convenient to consider the latter system in terms of an analysis mode as shown in Figure 1.17(c). X is obtained through the inverse glottal radiation filter. Then the transfer function of the inverse vocal tract filter H can be determined by applying the linear prediction method, because this method is formulated to produce the filter that, in the least squares sense, will

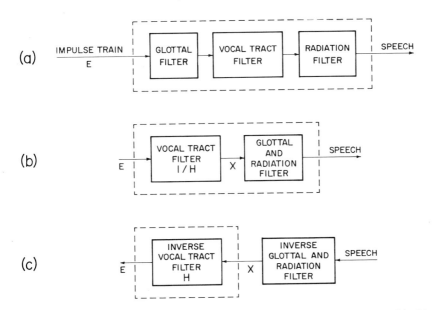

Figure 1.17 Equivalent transforms of a speech model: (a) a speech production model; (b) an equivalent transform of (a); (c) a speech analysis model based on (b).

optimally transform X into an impulse train E. The partial correlation coefficients computed for this system are identical to the reflection coefficients of the vocal tract area function. Once the reflection coefficients are known, therefore, the area function is easily computed via Equation (8). In practice, the design of an optimum inverse glottal and radiation filter is one of the major problems in using this method. However, since the glottal and radiation characteristics in this case can be assumed to be slowly varying, they can be equalized in an approximate manner. For example, if a -12 dB/octave glottal characteristic and a $+6$ dB radiation characteristic are assumed, the glottal and radiation filter will have a -6 dB/octave characteristic. Thus, the inverse glottal and radiation filter would be satisfied by a $+6$ dB/octave preemphasis of the input speech signal. In practice, it is found that this simple equalization produces very reasonable results.

Another important factor in this method is the length of the vocal tract (L). Since the sampling period (T) is chosen as the time that it takes for a sound wave to make a round trip between the ends of one of the cylindrical sections, the sampling frequency $F_s = 1/T$ must be adjusted to satisfy

$$L = \frac{cMT}{2} = \frac{cM}{2F_s} \qquad (9)$$

where M is the number of sections in the model and c is a sound velocity that is approximately 353 m/sec under normal conditions. Figure 1.18 shows examples of area functions for five American vowels extracted from recordings of a male speaker. Gross features for each vowel are fairly well extracted. Smooth spectral characteristics

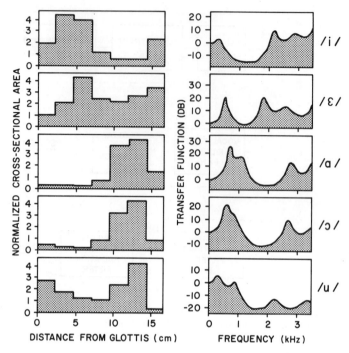

Figure 1.18 Vocal tract area functions and transfer functions obtained for five American vowels spoken by a male speaker. [From Wakita, 1972.]

of the vocal tract transfer function are shown alongside the area functions. One feature of the linear prediction method is its ability to perform simultaneous extraction of both area functions and their corresponding smooth spectral envelopes. Dynamic changes in the area functions are also obtainable by analyzing successive frames of a recording.

The study of analysis techniques for observing vocal tract shapes is relatively new, and the capabilities and limitations of the linear-prediction—acoustic-tube method remain to be examined. For example, the method might be evaluated by comparing the results with those obtained by X-ray techniques. The accuracy of the X-ray techniques, however, has not been established, since an accurate estimation of the lateral size of the vocal tract is rather difficult. Thus, the strict evaluation and comparison of these methods continues to be a problem. One study (Nakajima, Omura, Tanaka, Ishizaki, 1973), using synthetic speech generated by a vocal tract analog synthesizer, reports that the original area functions are almost completely reconstructed by the linear prediction method.

Methods for estimating the vocal tract length from given acoustic data also have been investigated (Paige and Zue, 1970b; Wakita, 1974). Continued studies in this area will be needed for better understanding of speech sounds. It also is anticipated that physiological studies of speech production will provide more information to interpret vocal tract area functions.

Speech Synthesis

Introduction

Both because of its broad applications and because of its contribution to a better understanding of speech (Flanagan and Rabiner, 1973; Wakita and Broad, 1975), speech synthesis has been studied in great detail ever since the first attempts were made in the late eighteenth century, as described by Dudley and Tarnoczy (1950). In addition to its application in analysis—synthesis telephony, speech synthesis has been used as a tool for the study of phonetics and speech perception and as a potentially practical means for giving computers the possibility of having voice outputs.

Speech synthesis provides some sort of absolute acoustic and perceptual criteria for evaluating speech parameters obtained by acoustic analysis. Speech synthesis can be extremely useful in the study of phonetics since each acoustic parameter can be controlled independently and arbitrarily. The synthesizers used in the study of acoustic phonetics are mainly formant synthesizers, also called *terminal analog synthesizers* because the behavior of formant frequencies for different sounds has been extensively studied and formant analysis techniques have been well developed. In the terminal analog synthesizer, the speech production process is represented, but not modeled, by a simple equivalent input—output relation of a filter; and the frequency characteristics of the filter usually are controlled by the use of resonant and antiresonant circuits to represent the peaks and the dips in the speech spectrum. The reason this type of synthesizer is called a *terminal* analog is that its purpose is to represent the final speech output without modeling the actual speech production processes in detail. Ideally, the synthesized speech would be made indistinguishable from humanly produced speech by a sort of technical mimicry rather than by a simulation of the human system. This type of speech synthesizer was studied and realized in hardware in the 1950s (e.g., Flanagan, 1957; Fant, 1959). The computer simulation of the terminal analog synthesizer, however, was studied in more detail in the 1960s because of the computer's capability for more precisely controlling the parameters, and because of the availability of suitable digital computers and techniques (e.g., Flanagan, Coker, and Bird, 1962; Rabiner, 1968a). The terminal analog synthesizer contributed considerably to the study of acoustic phonetics (e.g., Bell, Fujisaki, Heinz, Stevens, and House, 1961), and great efforts were exerted toward the improvement of the output speech quality. However, it remained difficult to get rid of a characteristic *machine-like* character, and skill was needed to attain satisfactory results. The development of high-quality analysis—synthesis telephony based on linear prediction, therefore, was literally revolutionary (Itakura and Saito, 1968; Atal and Hanauer, 1971; Itakura and Saito, 1972). This development showed that it is technically possible to attain, by automatic processing of speech, synthetic speech that is hardly distinguishable from the original. It also showed that it is possible to extract efficient speech parameters to produce perfect synthetic speech. The linear prediction synthesis itself has not been used actively for the study of acoustic phonetics since it is based on the use of the filter coefficients or the reflection coefficients instead of on the more familiar formant information. However, it is certain that the linear prediction analysis method could provide satisfactory analysis of data to control a new kind of terminal analog synthesizer.

In addition to the formant synthesizer, there are other types of speech synthesizers in which articulatory features are used as parameters. One simple type is called the *vocal tract analog*, in which the vocal tract configurations are controlled in terms of the area functions or their corresponding reflection coefficients (Dunn, 1950; Stevens, Kasowski, and Fant, 1953; Rosen, 1958). The more complicated forms of early vocal tract analog models were implemented by computer simulations (Kelly and Lochbaum, 1962; Matsui, Suzuki, Umeda, Omura, 1968). An even more physiologically oriented approach is represented by the *articulatory model*, in which speech is synthesized by simulating the movements of articulators such as the tongue, the jaw, the lips, and so on (Coker, 1967). In this case, the synthesis requires the articulator movements to be transformed into a vocal tract area function, even though it is very difficult to do so (Coker and Fujimura, 1966). Such a model has many advantages over other synthesis models for aiding our understanding of the speech production process because its parameters are directly related to the physiological behavior of the vocal organs, and it is thus easy to conceptualize the process itself. Unlike the formant synthesizer, which is often considered in analysis—synthesis situations, the vocal tract model and the articulatory model are considered purely in a synthesis mode. Thus, it is possible to complicate the models by implementing various factors which cannot be clearly specified in the formant synthesizer model. For instance, the acoustic losses can be attributed variously to the glottal opening, the vocal tract wall vibration, the radiation load, and so forth. Such models are particularly useful for understanding the speech production process because, indeed, they can be viewed as implementations of our theoretical models for speech processes. As synthesizers, their behavior provides a way of testing our models by experiment.

In the study of speech synthesis for voice output, the purpose is to generate natural-sounding speech from a minimum of input information. An extreme goal is to synthesize speech from written text alone. The central issue in this area is to formulate rules to generate natural-sounding speech; thus, this research area is known as speech *synthesis by rule*. This area involves all the problems of speech production, from the elucidation of the mechanics of the supraglottal part of the speech mechanism to the processes at higher levels of control. Early attempts at speech synthesis by rule were made in the 1950s (e.g., Peterson, Wang, and Sivertsen, 1958; Liberman, Ingemann, Lisker, Delattre, and Cooper, 1959) and were continued into the 1960s. Particularly, the technical improvements in the terminal analog synthesizers and in the techniques to control the synthesizers from digital computers stimulated the intensive study of rules for generating speech sentences using terminal analog synthesizers (e.g., Holmes, Mattingly, and Shearme, 1964; Mattingly, 1968; Rabiner, 1968b). For the vocal tract analog model and the articulatory model, reasonably good rules have been written, considering the present limitations on our knowledge of speech production processes (Teranishi and Umeda, 1968; Coker, Umeda, and Browman, 1973; Allen, 1973). In the following section, some aspects and problems of speech synthesis, especially in the context of digital techniques, are discussed.

Synthesis by Analysis

TERMINAL ANALOG SYNTHESIZER

The terminal analog synthesizer is particularly useful in the study of acoustic phonetics, partly because the control data can be obtained relatively easily and partly because it can be implemented easily in hardware.

The development of digital techniques facilitated study of the synthesizer itself by computer simulation, which tests new ideas and modifications effectively and efficiently. Repetition of exact synthesis conditions is also possible. That this latter condition is not to be taken for granted is illustrated by the fact that some earlier analog synthesizers had temperature-dependent speech characteristics or, because of the aging of components, never quite produce the same utterance twice even with identical control parameters. Furthermore, the computer simulation is free from the necessity for elaborate adjustments and calibrations that are required in analog circuits. Finally, the computer program itself is simple. As in the analog machine (e.g., Fant, 1960), the peaks and dips of the speech spectrum are represented by resonant and antiresonant circuits connected either in series or in parallel. A digital resonant circuit is realized in the computer by several operations of addition, multiplication, and delay. For example, a typical digital resonant circuit is shown in Figure 1.19(a). The constants e, g, and h can be computed from a given resonance frequency (F_n) and bandwidth (B_n). Its frequency characteristics are shown in Figure 1.19(b). Since the speech spectrum has three or four peaks in the frequency band of 0 to 3.5 kHz, the same number of resonant circuits are connected in series

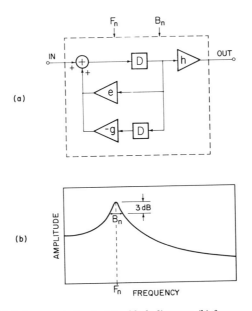

Figure 1.19   A digital resonant circuit: (a) a block diagram; (b) frequency characteristics.

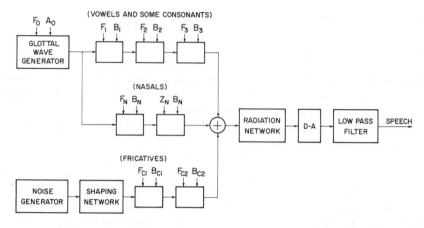

Figure 1.20   Block diagram of a digital terminal analog synthesizer.

or in parallel. Figure 1.20 shows a typical cascade-connected terminal analog synthesizer. As an excitation source, an impulse train or a train of triangular-shaped waves usually is used. In the case of an impulse train excitation, the signal is passed through a glottal-shaping filter in a later stage. Frequency and amplitude of the glottal waves are controlled according to the input data. Vowels and some of the voiced consonants are synthesized via the upper three cascade-connected resonant circuits. The center frequency and bandwidth of each resonant circuit are also controlled according to the input data. They are updated every time unit, for example, every 10 msec. For generating nasals, extra resonant and antiresonant circuits to account for the characteristics of nasals may be added parallel to the vocal tract resonances. The voiceless fricatives and the unvoiced component of the voiced fricatives are generated by exciting the fricative filter with noise. By properly operating the synthesizer with good input data, speech of fairly good quality is obtained. It takes exceptional skill, however, to generate sentences and utterances as natural as humanly produced utterances from hand-analyzed data. Yet, the terminal analog digital synthesizer is certainly a powerful tool for the study of acoustic phonetics. Its drawback is that it is not a real-time synthesizer at the moment, but this fact does not reduce its merit for acoustic phonetic study.

LINEAR PREDICTION SYNTHESIZER

In the field of analysis—synthesis transmission systems, the linear prediction method is so far the best available. The synthesizer portion of the linear prediction analysis—synthesis, however, has not been utilized yet for the study of acoustic phonetics, probably because of its short history and because it does not use formant information as its input parameters. There are two types of linear prediction synthesizers, one based on the a-parameter and the other based on the k-parameter. Since the formant frequencies and bandwidths can be converted easily into a-parameters, the synthesizer based on the a-parameter may become an alternative to the formant synthesizers.

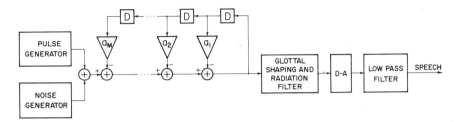

Figure 1.21 Block diagram of a linear prediction synthesizer based on the a-parameter.

The synthesizer based on the k-parameter may play an important role in future studies since the k-parameter is related to the acoustic reflection coefficient. The two linear prediction synthesizers previously mentioned are shown in Figures 1.21 and 1.22, respectively. In Figure 1.21, the transfer function of the vocal tract is realized by a digital filter shown in the middle of the figure. The filter consists of adders, multipliers, and delay units. Excitation sources are a pulse generator and a noise generator. Depending upon the sound to be generated, one of the three excitation modes is selected: the pulse generator for vowels and some of the voiced consonants (e.g., /w/, /v/, /r/, /j/, /l/), the noise generator for voiceless consonants (e.g., /f/, /θ/, /s/, /ʃ/, /p/, /t/, /k/), and a combination of the two sources for some of the voiced consonants (e.g., /b/, /d/, /g/, /z/, /ʒ/, /v/, /ð/). The output of the vocal tract filter is passed through a filter which gives effective glottal and radiation characteristics. The final speech sounds are generated by passing the output through the D–A converter and a low-pass filter. The synthesizer based on the reflection coefficients (or k-parameters) in Figure 1.22 is basically the same as the one based on the filter coefficients. The difference is in the slightly more complicated structure of the vocal tract filter, although the filter is also realized by adders, multipliers, and delay units.

VOCAL TRACT ANALOG

As mentioned before, the behavior of the sound pressure or the acoustic volume velocity within the vocal tract can be described by Webster's horn equation under certain boundary conditions. This equation also holds for describing the behavior

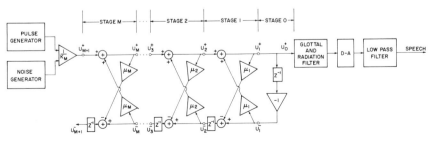

Figure 1.22 Block diagram of a linear prediction synthesizer based on the k-parameter (K_M is a constant).

of the voltage or the current within a nonuniform lossless transmission line. Thus, when the vocal tract is represented by a concatenation of a finite number of sections, each section can be realized equivalently with electrical components of inductance (L) and capacitance (C). The early vocal tract analog synthesizers were built on this concept (e.g., Dunn, 1950; Stevens, Kasowski, and Fant, 1953). With the development of digital techniques, the computer simulation of this model was studied (Kelly and Lochbaum, 1962). In this case, instead of using electrical components, the cross-sectional areas along the vocal tract were controlled in terms of the reflection coefficients.

One section of an acoustic tube representation of a vocal tract, as shown in Figure 1.23(a), can be realized by an electrical network as shown in Figure 1.23(b) or by a digital filter, as illustrated in Figure 1.23(c). Since the linear prediction digital filter was shown to be equivalent to the vocal tract analog model, these representations can

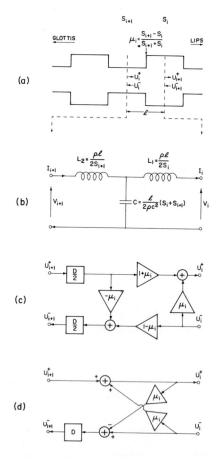

Figure 1.23 Various representations for a section of an acoustic tube: (a) a tube section; (b) an electrical network representation; (c) a Kelly–Lochbaum-type representation; (d) a linear prediction digital filter.

be realized equivalently by a linear prediction digital filter, as shown in Figure 1.23 (d). Thus, the three representations of a section of an acoustic tube are all equivalent, and the synthesizers based on these representations are equivalent to the linear prediction synthesizer based on the k-parameter (i.e., the reflection coefficient) as shown in Figure 1.22. Until the equivalence of the vocal tract analog model and the linear prediction model was shown, the problem in using a vocal tract model for synthesis was in obtaining the control data, that is, the vocal tract area functions. X-ray techniques, palatography, and so forth, plus intuition were the main tools used for estimating the area functions. Now it is anticipated that the linear prediction technique may be improved to the extent that it can provide more reliable area function data for vocal tract models.

ARTICULATORY MODEL

An articulatory domain speech synthesizer is more appealing for the phonetician than the formant synthesizer since understanding its operations is conceptually easy. It is probably better and more powerful than the formant synthesizer for gaining a better understanding of speech production and for the study of phonetics. Coker's (1967) model is a successful articulatory synthesizer. Each sound is designated in terms of a target configuration, and the movement of the vocal tract is specified by separate fast or slow motions of the articulators. These include rapid motion of the tongue tip, rapid lip closure, slow lip protrusion, slow front—back tongue motion, slow mandible motion, and slow change in the pharyngeal area. The formant frequencies are computed from the area function specified by the movements of these articulators and are passed on to a formant synthesizer for the final generation of the sounds. Word or sentence utterances are generated from sequences of separately specified target positions by controlling the times and rates of transitions between target positions.

It seems to be more difficult to obtain the control data for an articulatory synthesizer than for the vocal tract analog model. At the moment, some X-ray data are used, along with intuitions, to obtain the parameters. Some ad hoc adjustments also are required to ensure that the spectrum of the synthetic speech will match that of human speech.

A unique attempt to construct a synthesis system by combining a laryngeal model and a vocal tract analog is that of Ishizaka and Flanagan (1972). The laryngeal model used in this synthesis system considers the most essential physiological factors, such as the subglottal pressure, vocal cord tension, and rest area of the vocal cord opening. The model operates under the assumption that the vocal cords are symmetric. Each vocal cord consists of two separate horizontally movable masses. This is a step toward modeling the vocal fold as a soft tissue. The uniqueness of this system is that the two-mass laryngeal model is combined with the vocal tract analog into a single speech production system without assuming any separability between excitation source and the vocal tract. This system is particularly useful for evaluating the effects of some estimated physiological data such as the subglottal pressure during phonation and the losses due to the vocal tract wall vibration. The advantage of this model and other articulatory models over the terminal analog synthesizer and the linear prediction synthesizer is their capability for making the system more complex and for taking into account more physiologically realistic factors. This advantage results from using these models in the synthesis mode alone. However, the problem inherent in articulatory models is the lack of control data. There is no easy way to obtain articulatory movements or to convert them into a vocal tract area function that can satisfactorily control a synthesizer based on the articulatory models. Speech synthesis models, such as the formant synthesizer, are sometimes criticized for being overly simple compared with these complicated articulatory models. Here it should be noted, however, that, at our present technical level, it is almost impossible to develop an analysis—synthesis technique based on a more complicated speech production model. By sacrificing complexity, speech parameters for synthesis are obtained in an effective manner. However, this is not a matter of tradeoffs; rather, both the fine models and the simple models are needed for the study of phonetics, and they should supplement each other.

Synthesis by Rule

The central issue in generating natural-sounding speech based on rules with a minimum amount of data is the attainment of naturalness for three factors: phonetic quality (intelligibility), prosodic quality, and voice quality. In the acoustic domain, these factors are not independent but are all reflected in a mixed manner in the spectral peak locations, the overall spectral shape, its temporal variations, the fundamental frequency, and its amplitude. The phonetic quality is dependent mainly on the formant frequency information. In speech synthesis by rule, target values for the first three or four formant frequencies for each sound normally are stored. The question then becomes: Which rules govern the transitions between successive sounds?

Rules for deriving the transitions must be made so that reasonably smooth and continuous formant contours can be generated. For the terminal analog synthesizers, the rules for formant transitions can be made mechanically in the time-frequency domain, and reasonably good results have been obtained in this way (Holmes, Mattingly, and Shearme, 1964; Rabiner, 1968b). To attain improved results, it probably will be better to derive rules in the articulatory domain either from dynamic vocal tract area functions or from observations of the movements of the articulators. Although such attempts have been made with reasonably good results (Coker and Fujimura, 1966; Matsui *et al.*, 1968), the lack of proper methods for observing the articulator movements has hindered developments in this area.

In generating formant contours, the rules for assigning proper sound durations are indispensable for producing natural prosodies. Good rules for sound duration are expected to be derived from an extensive statistical study of sound durations in human speech (e.g., Lehiste, 1971; Umeda, 1972). For instance, it is known qualitatively that the durations of stressed vowels are normally longer than those of unstressed ones. The durations of certain consonants are known to be dependent upon their contexts as well as upon their positions in words (initial, medial, or final). It is not precisely known, however, how to incorporate these characteristics into duration rules in a quantitative manner to attain naturalness in this respect. It is expected that results obtained from the extensive study of individual cases can be integrated into a comprehensive set of rules for sound durations. Such data are also obviously necessary for a better understanding of how the human system determines segment durations.

Equally important and difficult are rules for voice pitch. Voice pitch is related not only to sound durations in the acoustic domain but also to various linguistic, syntactic, and semantic factors, as well as to social and emotional ones.

Voice quality is another important factor which cannot be neglected even when intelligibility and prosodic naturalness are attained. The current problem for synthesis by rule is to eliminate the machine-like quality. In the near future, it will probably become a central issue to be able freely to produce speech of either sex or of any age based on a minimum storage of data. For instance, it is not possible to synthesize realistically a female voice merely by raising the voice pitch and formant frequencies to the female regions. A recent study on synthetic female voice (Sato, 1974) points out that critical factors for generating natural-sounding female voice quality include not only the peaks in the spectral envelope (which do not always correspond to formants) but also the shape of the spectral envelope (especially its slope in the higher-frequency region). Since an impulse train was used for the source excitation in this study, this result seems to indicate that a fine control of the glottal wave characteristics is necessary for better synthesis of female voice. Thorough knowledge of glottal wave characteristics will eventually lead to a better understanding of individual voice characteristics, knowledge of which is particularly important in the area of automatic speaker identification and verification. Thus, the study of speech synthesis by rule is an integration of almost all of the branches of speech research.

The arrival of the day when a machine can read any written text as naturally as can a human is eagerly awaited. By the turn of the century, we may indeed have computers speaking to us in measured tones of reassuring condescension (Clarke, 1968), but only if our own understanding of speech has advanced correspondingly.

ACKNOWLEDGMENTS

The author acknowledges the help received from J. E. Shoup and D. J. Broad at the Speech Communications Research Laboratory, Inc.

REFERENCES

Allen, J. Speech synthesis from unrestricted text. In J. L. Flanagan and L. R. Rabiner (Eds.), *Speech synthesis*. Stroudsburg, Pennsylvania: Dowden, Hutchinson, and Ross, 1973, 416–428.

Atal, B. S. Determination of the vocal tract shape directly from the speech wave. *Journal of the Acoustical Society of America* 1970, *47*, 65 (A).

Atal, B. S., and Hanauer, S. L. Speech analysis and synthesis by linear prediction of the speech wave. *Journal of the Acoustical Society of America*, 1971, *50*, 637–655.

Atal, B. S., and Schroeder, M. R. Predictive coding of speech signals, In Y. Kohashi, (Ed.), *Proceedings of the Sixth International Congress on Acoustics.* Tokyo: Acoustical Society of Japan, 1968, C13—C16.

Bogert, B. P., Healy, M. J. R., and Tukey, J. W. The frequency analysis of time series for echoes: cepstrum, pseudo-autocovariance, cross-cepstrum and shape cracking, In M. Rosenblatt, (Ed.), *Proceedings of the Symposium on Series Analysis.* New York: Wiley, 1963, 209—243.

Bell, C. G., Fujisaki, H., Heinz, J. M., Stevens, K. N., and House, A. S. Reduction of speech spectra by analysis-by-synthesis techniques. *Journal of the Acoustical Society of America,* 1961, *33,* 1725—1736.

Chiba, T., and Kajiyama, M. *The Vowel, its nature and structure.* Tokyo: Kaiseikan, 1941.

Clarke, A. C. *2001: A space odyssey.* New York: New American Library, 1968.

Coker, C. H. Synthesis by rule from articulatory parameters. In *Proceedings of the 1967 Conference on Speech Communication and Processing.* Cambridge, Massachusetts: IEEE 1967, A9, 52—53.

Coker, C. H., and Fujimura, O. Model for specification of the vocal-tract area function. *Journal of the Acoustical Society of America,* 1966, *40,* 1271 (A).

Coker, C. H., Umeda, N., and Browman, C. P. Automatic synthesis from ordinary English text. *IEEE Transactions on Audio and Electroacoustics,* 1973, AU—21, 293—298.

Cooley, J. W., and Tukey, J. W. An algorithm for the machine calculation of complex Fourier series. *Mathematics of Computers,* 1965, *19,* 297—301.

Dudley, H., and Tarnoczy, T. H. The speaking machine of Wolfgang von Kemplen. *Journal of the Acoustical Society of America,* 1950, *22,* 151—166.

Dunn, H. K. The calculation of vowel resonances and electrical vocal tract. *Journal of the Acoustical Society of America,* 1950, *22,* 740—753.

Fant, C. G. M. Acoustic analysis and synthesis of speech with applications to Swedish. *Ericsson Technics,* 1959, *1,* 3—108.

Fant, C. G. M. *Acoustic theory of speech production.* The Hague: Mouton, 1960.

Flanagan, J. L. Note on the design of *Terminal Analog* speech synthesizers. *Journal of the Acoustical Society of America,* 1957, *29,* 306—310.

Flanagan, J. L., Coker, C. H., and Bird, C. M. Computer simulation of a formant-vocoder synthesizer. *Journal of the Acoustical Society of America,* 1962, *35,* 2003 (A).

Flanagan, J. L., and Rabiner, L. R. *Speech synthesis.* Stroudsburg, Pennsylvania: Dowden, Hutchinson and Ross, 1973.

Fujisaki, H. Automatic extraction of fundamental period of speech by auto-correlation analysis and peak detection. *Journal of the Acoustical Society of America,* 1960, *32,* 1518 (A).

Gopinath, B., and Sondhi, M. M. Determination of the shape of the human vocal tract from acoustical measurements. *Bell System Technical Journal,* 1970, *49,* 1195—1214.

Heinz, J. M. Perturbation functions for the determination of vocal tract area functions from vocal tract eigenvalues. *Speech Transmission Laboratory Quarterly Progress and Status Report.* Stockholm: Research Institute of Technology. April 1967, 1—14.

Holmes, J. N. Mattingly, I. G., and Shearme, J. N. Speech synthesis by rule. *Language and Speech,* 1964, *7,* 127—143.

Hunter, J. L. *Acoustics.* Englewood Cliffs, New Jersey: Prentice-Hall, 1957.

Ishizaka, K., and Flanagan, J. L. Synthesis of voiced sounds from a two-mass model of the vocal cords. *Bell System Technical Journal,* 1972, *51,* 1233—1268.

Itakura, F., and Saito, S. Analysis synthesis telephony based on the maximum likelihood method. In Y. Kohashi (Ed.), *Proceedings of the Sixth International Congress on Acoustics.* Tokyo: Acoustical Society of Japan, 1968, C17—C20.

Itakura, F., and Saito, S. On the optimum quantization of feature parameters in the PARCOR speech synthesizer. In *Proceedings of the 1972 Conference on Speech Communication and Processing.* New York: IEEE, 1972, 434—437.

Kelly, J. L., and Lochbaum, C. Speech synthesis. In *Proceedings of the Stockholm Speech Communication Seminar.* Stockholm: Research Institute of Technology, 1962.

Lehiste, I. Temporal organization of spoken language. In L. L. Hammerich, R. Jakobson and Z. Eberhard (Eds.), *Form and Substance.* Odense, Denmark: Akademisk Forlag, 1971, 159—169.

Liberman, A. M., Ingemann, F., Lisker, L., Delattre, P., and Cooper, F. S. Minimal rules for synthesizing speech, *Journal of the Acoustical Society of America*, 1959, *31*, 1490—1499.

Lindblom, B. E. F., and Sundberg, J. E. F. Acoustical consequences of lip, tongue, jaw and larynx movement. *Journal of the Acoustical Society of America*, 1971, *50*, 1166—1179.

Makhoul, J. Linear prediction: A tutorial review. *Proceedings of the Institute of Electrical and Electronic Engineers*, 1975, *63*, 561—580.

Makhoul, J., and Wolf, J. *Linear prediction and the spectral analysis of speech* (Rep. 2304). Cambridge, Massachusetts: Bolt, Beranek and Newman, 1972.

Markel, J. D. Formant trajectory estimation from a linear least-squares filter formulation. *SCRL Monographs 7*. Santa Barbara: Speech Communications Research Lab., 1971.

Markel, J. D. Digital inverse filtering, a new tool for formant trajectory estimation. *IEEE Transactions on Audio and Electroacoustics*, 1972, *AU—20*, 129—137.

Markel, J. D. Application of a digital inverse filter for automatic formant and Fo analysis. *IEEE Transactions on Audio and Electroacoustics*, 1973, *AU—21*, 154—160.

Markel, J. D., and Gray, A. H. *Linear prediction of speech*. Berlin: Springer-Verlag, 1976.

Markel, J. D., Gray, A. H., and Wakita, H. Linear prediction of speech—theory and practice. *SCRL Monographs, 10*. Santa Barbara: Speech Communications Research Lab., 1973.

Matsui, E., Suzuki, T., Umeda, N., and Omura, H. Synthesis of fairy tales using an analog vocal tract. In Y. Kohashi, (Ed.), *Proceedings of the Sixth International Congression Acoustics*. Tokyo: Acoustical Society of Japan, 1968, B159—B162.

Mattingly, I. G. Some rules for synthesis of general American English. *Status report on speech research*, SR-13/14. New York: Haskins Laboratories, 1968, 37—45.

McCandless, S. S. An algorithm for automatic formant extraction using linear prediction spectra. *IEEE Transactions on the Acoustics, Speech and Signal Proceedings*, 1974, ASSP—22, 135—141.

Mermelstein, P. Determination of the vocal tract shape from measured formant frequencies. *Journal of the Acoustical Society of America*, 1967, *41*, 1283—1294.

Mermelstein, P., and Schroeder, M. R. Determination of smoothed cross-sectional area functions of the vocal tract from formant frequencies. In D. E. Commins (Ed.), *Proceedings of the 5th International Congress on Acoustics*. Liege: 1965, 1a, A24.

Nakajima, T., Omura, H., Tanaka, K., and Ishizaki, S. Estimation of vocal tract area function by adaptive inverse filtering. Paper presented at the Speech Symposium of Acoustical Society of Japan, February 16, 1973, Sendai, Japan.

Noll, A. M. Short-time spectrum and *cepstrum* techniques for vocal pitch detection. *Journal of the Acoustical Society of America*, 1964, *36*, 296—302.

Noll, A. M. Cepstrum pitch determination. *Journal of the Acoustical Society of America*, 1967, *41*, 293—309.

Öhman, S. E. G. Numerical model of coarticulation. *Journal of the Acoustical Society of America*, 1967, *41*, 310—320.

Paige, A., and Zue, V. W. Computation of vocal tract area functions. *IEEE Transactions on Audio and Electroacoustics*, 1970, *AU—18*, 7—18.(a)

Paige, A., and Zue, V. W. Calculation of vocal tract length. *IEEE Transactions on Audio and Electroacoustics*, 1970, *AU—18*, 268—270.(b)

Peterson, G. E., Wang, W. S-Y, and Sivertsen, E. Segmentation techniques in speech synthesis. *Journal of the Acoustical Society of America*, 1958, *30*, 739—742.

Rabiner, L. R. Digital-formant synthesizer for speech-synthesis studies. *Journal of the Acoustical Society of America*, 1968, *43*, 822—828.(a)

Rabiner, L. Speech synthesis by rule. *Bell System Technical Journal*, 1968, *47*, 17—37.(b)

Rosen, G. Dynamic analog speech synthesizer. *Journal of the Acoustical Society of America*, 1958, *20*, 201—209.

Sato, H. Acoustic cues of female voice quality. *Transaction A of Institute of Electronics and Communication Engineers of Japan*, 1974, 57—A, 23—30.

Schafer, R. W., and Rabiner, L. R. System for the automatic analysis of voiced speech. *Journal of the Acoustical Society of America*, 1970, *47*, 634—648.

Schroeder, M. R. Determination of the geometry of the human vocal tract by acoustic measurement. *Journal of the Acoustical Society of America*, 1967, *41*, 1002—1010.

Sondhi, M. M. Model for wave propagation in a lossy vocal tract. *Journal of the Acoustical Society of America*, 1974, *55*, 1070—1075.

Sondhi, M. M., and Gopinath, B. Determination of vocal tract shape from impulse response at the lips. *Journal of the Acoustical Society of America*, 1971, *49*, 1867—1873.

Stevens, K. N., Kasowski, S., and Fant, G. An electrical analog of the vocal tract. *Journal of the Acoustical Society of America*, 1953, *25*, 734—742.

Teranishi, R., and Umeda, N. Use of pronouncing dictionary in speech synthesis experiments. In *Proceedings from the Sixth International Congress on Acoustics*, Tokyo: Acoustical Society of Japan, 1968, B155—B158.

Umeda, N. Vowel duration in polysyllabic words in American English. *Journal of the Acoustical Society of America*, 1972, 52—133(A).

Wakita, H. Estimation of the vocal tract shape by optimal inverse filtering and acoustic/articulatory conversion methods. *SCRL Monographs, 9*. Santa Barbara: Speech Communications Research Laboratory, 1972.

Wakita, H. Estimation of the vocal-tract length from acoustic data. *Journal of the Acoustical Society of America*, 1974, *55*, Supplement, J7.

Wakita, H., and Broad, D. J. Models and methods for speech synthesis. In E. L. Eagles (Ed.), *The nervous system*. Vol. 3. New York: Raven Press, 1975, 459—467.

Wakita, H., and Gray, A. H. Noniterative computation of the area function for given lip impedance. *Journal of the Acoustical Society of America*, 1973, *54*, 340(A).

Wakita, H., and Gray, A. H. Some theoretical considerations for linear prediction of speech and applications. *Preprints of the Speech Communication Seminar*. Stockholm: Speech Transmission Laboratory, KTH, 1974, *1*, 45—50.

Wakita, H. and Gray, A. H. Numerical determination of the lip impedance and vocal tract area functions. *IEEE Transactions on Acoustics, Speech, and Signal Processing*, 1975, ASSP-23, 574—580.

chapter **2**

Instrumentation for the Study of Speech Physiology

James H. Abbs   Kenneth L. Watkin

University of Washington, Seattle

Speech physiology is the study of the neuromuscular, biomechanical, and aerodynamic processes involved in the production of speech. Emphasis on the physiological aspects of speech production is relatively recent. Only in the last ten years has this area of study become sufficiently sophisticated to take a permanent position alongside more traditional avenues of speech science investigation. In part, the emergence of speech physiology represents the realization that we cannot make inferences from analysis of the acoustic signal (or from auditory impressions of that signal) to the underlying organization of speech behavior without also understanding the peripheral motor system that is involved. The present chapter is an attempt to provide potential speech physiologists with information on the kinds of data that can be obtained and the procedures and instrumentation required to do this work.

The Physiological Events of Speech Production

Prior to initiating a discussion of the various instrumental devices that have been applied to the study of speech physiology, let us look to the speech production system to evaluate the kinds of data that we can obtain as well as to review briefly the general limitations of these data. Figure 2.1 is a schematic representation of the speech production system. This representation provides a basis from which to illustrate the observable events of the speech production system and their interaction. The major components of the speech system represented in Figure 2.1 include the speech muscles, system mechanical properties, system air volumes, sound source constrictions, and system acoustic resonances. Also represented are the transfers of energy among these components. The first level of activity shown in Figure 1 is the neural

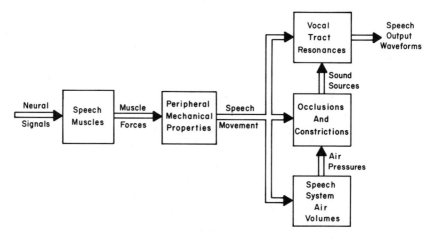

Figure 2.1 A schematic representation of the functional components of the speech production periphery. The purpose of this simplified representation is to illustrate the difficulties of interpreting measures obtained from this system, both in relation to sources of these measures and in relation to the casual influence on other variables.

input to the speech muscles. The force output of the muscle elements, in turn, acts upon the mechanical properties of the speech production apparatus. The interaction of these muscle forces and mechanical properties provides the basis for two peripheral behaviors: movement of the speech structures and/or changes in the muscle tension. These movement patterns contribute to the speech output in several ways. Speech movements modify air volumes to produce air pressures and air flow which, in turn, are the basis for generation of acoustic energy. Speech movements also control the vocal tract resonance properties and produce constrictions in the system as sites for sound generation. The movement manipulation of air volumes for pressure generation cannot be separated from the movements that control vocal tract resonance or the movements that provide sound source constrictions (except in the case of the respiratory system). The obvious point of this illustration is that these complex exchanges of chemical—electrical, electrical—mechanical, mechanical—aerodynamic, and aerodynamic—acoustic energy must be approached with considerable care if one is to contribute meaningful information concerning the speech production process.

Many pioneering studies in speech physiology involved sampling of a single set of variables. For example, several investigators observed air pressures or air flows in the supraglottal airway (Isshiki and Ringel, 1964; Arkebauer, Hixon, and Hardy, 1967; Klatt, Stevens, and Mead, 1968). In other investigations, electromyographic (EMG) techniques were employed to identify which of several muscles were active during phonetically specified behaviors (MacNeilage, 1963; MacNeilage and Scholes, 1964; Fromkin, 1966; Öhman, 1967; Huntington, Harris, and Scholes, 1968; Harris, Gay, Sholes, and Lieberman, 1968; Lubker, Fritzell, and Lindquist, 1970; Minifie *et al.*, 1974).

Unfortunately, many of these studies provide only indirect information on the physiology of speech production. Electromyographic and aerodynamic monitoring represent micro and macro poles in the specification of speech production activity. That is, muscle action potentials reflect components of single muscle force vectors contributing to the movement of a single structure, while aerodynamic changes reflect movements of the total mechanism. It would appear worthwhile to observe the mediating variable (viz., structural movement) simultaneously with EMG or air pressures and air flows to facilitate interpretation of these aerodynamic or electromyographic indices of speech system activity. Indeed, considerable ambiguity may result when one attempts to interpret aerodynamic or EMG patterns independent of other measures. For example, changes in intraoral air pressure during speech may reflect a modification of volume in either subglottal or supraglottal cavities. Likewise, electromyographic activity may be confounded by mechanical properties or distant electrical activity and thus may not reflect the true activity level of a particular muscle. Indeed, several investigators have observed movement and electromyographic variables simultaneously in attempts to determine how changes in electromyographic activity are related to structural movements (Fritzell, 1969; Abbs, 1973b; Sussman, MacNeilage, and Hanson, 1973; Gay, Ushijima, Hirose, and Cooper, 1973; Bell-Berti, 1973). We do not mean to imply by these comments that there is no place for observation of aerodynamic and/or electromyographic variables without concomitant observation of structural movement, but that in many situations in which a single variable is observed, considerable chance exists for misinterpretation. The danger of misinterpretation is particularly acute in those studies in which the experimental objective is to make inferences to the mechanisms that are involved in the control of organization of speech. In other words, the energy transfer characteristics between different components of the system are not sufficiently defined to allow one to assume that (*1*) certain movements are causally related to observed EMG, or (*2*) aerodynamic patterns are the result of particular movements. It is apparent from this discussion that the techniques and instrumentation to be presented here must be employed with caution and with an understanding of physiological processes, if they are to be useful.

The discussion of speech physiology instrumentation that follows will focus primarily upon current methods for the observation of muscle activity and structural movement during speech production. A review of recent techniques for observation and analysis of aerodynamic events during speech is provided in this volume by Warren.

Electrical Activity of the Speech Muscles

The recording of electrical activity from living tissue has been of major interest to students of physiology since Galvani's discovery that skeletal muscle provides a detectable *bioelectricity* when it is activated. This discovery proved to be largely a scientific curiosity until methods were devised to sense and record accurately these bioelectric currents of muscle contraction. The first known recording of muscles during speech was accomplished, as far as the present authors can determine, by Stetson and Hudgins (1930). Later work by Ladefoged, Draper, and Whitteridge (1958) marked the beginning of electromyography as a technique for the modern study of the speech production system.

The Origin and Nature of the Bioelectromyogram

All electrical activity in living tissue has the same common origin, namely, the cell membrane resting potential, which is the potential difference between inside and outside of an active cell. In mammalian muscle fibers at rest, this potential is approximately -90 mv. Depolarization of the muscle fiber by electrochemical changes at the motor end plate results in rapid change from this resting level to a peak potential of approximately $+20$ mv.

Muscle fibers are organized functionally in relation to their innervation. The muscle fibers innervated by a single motoneuron are termed a *motor unit*. The firing of a single motoneuron (i.e., a single motor unit) generally is considered the smallest contractile event in the activity of skeletal muscle. When a maximal suprathreshold stimulus is delivered to a single motoneuron, all the muscle fibers that are innervated by that nerve fiber are activated, and the *twitch*, as shown in Figure 2.2, is developed. This twitch response (the activation of a single motor unit) is considerably different from the smooth development of tension (and concomitant change in length) that one typically associates with voluntary contraction. If one were to apply a second stimulus pulse to the nerve fiber before the first contraction cycle was completed, the magnitude of the response would be greater than if elicited by two single stimuli. Thus, during voluntary contraction of a skeletal muscle, one means by which tension or contractile output is controlled is via the rate of motoneuron firing (Ruch, Patton, Woodbury, and Towe, 1965; Aidley, 1973). A schematic example of the relationship between nerve firing rate and the tension level of a muscle is shown in Figure 2.3.

The second means by which the contraction of a muscle is controlled is via the number of motor units that are firing. It has been suggested that the gross control of

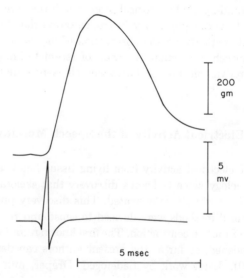

200
gm

5
mv

5 msec

Figure 2.2   The tension response of a single motor unit (upper trace) to a suprathreshold stimulus (lower trace).

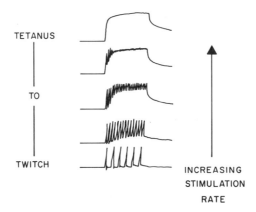

Figure 2.3 A schematic illustration of the relationship between neural firing rate and the level of tension developed by a muscle. For lower stimulus rates, the tension between impulses returns to a value near rest. However, at higher rates, there is an obvious *temporal summation* of tension, manifested most clearly in the smooth tension curve at tetanus.

muscle contraction is provided by recruitment of motoneurons, while fine control is exerted by variation in motor unit firing frequency (Lenman, 1969).

In a normal voluntary contraction, the recorded electrical activity is the result of many motoneurons (motor units) firing simultaneously, thus providing the smooth pattern of muscle force. The relationship between the activity of a single motor unit and the typical gross electromyogram is illustrated in Figure 2.4. The gross electromyogram is referred to as an *interference pattern*, reflecting the knowledge that it represents the *combined* electrical activity from many motor units which vary in their

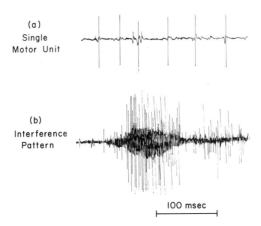

Figure 2.4 Two records of electrical activity recorded from the mentalis muscle with the same hooked-wire electrode placement and identical amplifier gain settings: (a) firing of a single motor unit recorded during a minimal voluntary contraction, using audio and visual biofeedback, and (b) an interference pattern electromyogram recorded during production of the utterance [æpæ]. Comparison of these signals illustrates the contrast in complexity between the firing of a single motor unit and the normal activity of an entire muscle.

rate, phase, and amplitude characteristics. It is obvious from comparison of the signals shown in Figure 2.4 that one generally cannot discern the firing pattern of individual motor units from the interference pattern one records during speech activities.

Most often, electrical activity in muscle is sampled by observing the potential differences between two conductors placed adjacent to one another and in the vicinity (or within) the muscle under investigation. The electrical signal reflected to these conductors from the firing of any individual motor unit is influenced by the impedance of the tissue in the conductive path between the muscle fibers (of that motor unit) and the electrode conductor, including the tissue-electrode interface impedance. It is apparent that the impedance of this conductor path is influenced by very small variations in electrode placement. Indeed, if one observes the activity of two separate electrode pairs placed in the same muscle, the recorded signals may differ considerably. Further, it has been documented that the characteristics of individual motor units (sampled under conditions of minimal contraction) will vary as a function of electrode characteristics (Basmajian and Cross, 1971).

It is clear from the preceding discussion that electromyography represents a sampling process, and only a limited number of the total muscle fibers in a muscle can be observed with a single electrode pair. To assure that the sample of muscle fiber activity is representative, one must carefully consider the electrodes to be employed and their pickup characteristics. The *conductive volume* of the tissue between members of an electrode pair will determine the magnitude of the recorded interference pattern and the number of muscle fibers that are represented. The proximity of the electrodes to those motor units which are active for a particular task will also influence the electromyographic pattern. Thus, the possibility that one is going to sample a subset of muscle activity that is unrepresentative of the total muscle always exists. These concerns lead us directly to a consideration of the various types of electrodes used for sampling speech muscle activity.

Electrodes for Speech Electromyography

A general discussion of electrodes for sampling EMG signals is reviewed in some detail by Geddes (1972), and there is no need to recount it here. However, observing the electrical activity of the speech musculature presents some special problems. First, many of the speech muscles are inaccessible through the outside skin and must be approached intraorally (Shipp, Deatsch, and Robertson, 1968; Smith and Hirano, 1968, Minifie *et al.*, 1974). The general inaccessibility of these sites often makes it difficult to verify and/or maintain electrode placements. A second difficulty peculiar to speech electromyography is related to the rapid movements of many speech structures. In particular, these rapid movements tend to dislodge electrodes or result in their migration, making comparisons of recorded muscle activity difficult before and after electrode migration occurs. In addition, movement of an electrode within a muscle itself generates an electrical pattern that may not reflect accurately the underlying bioelectric events. These *movement artifacts* are apparently caused by rapid changes in the recording field of the electrodes. A third problem in the electromyographic observation of speech muscles relates to the possibility that the recording electrodes have obtruded in such a manner as to cause compensatory modifications in the motor activity under study.

Based upon these limitations, it is obvious that electrodes for measurement of speech muscle activity must (*1*) allow for placement in confined spaces (such as the oral cavity), (*2*) be light enough to follow the movement of a muscle and yet remain in place (to minimize movement artifacts), and (*3*) be unobtrusive in relation to the speech movement activity that one is attempting to observe. The observation of speech muscle activity generally has involved either surface electrodes (one of several varieties) or implanted hooked wire electrodes, the latter being most widely used for research purposes.

Surface Electrodes

Aside from the early observations by Stetson (1951) and Ladefoged, Draper, and Whitteridge (1958), the first widespread use of electrodes in speech research involved suction cup electrodes developed at Haskins Laboratories (Lysaught, Rosov, and Harris, 1961; Harris, Rosov, Cooper, and Lysaught, 1964). These electrodes were constructed of sterling silver jewelry beads which were cut in half and attached to a short piece of brass tubing. The bead was employed as a tissue contact element for one of a bipolar electrode pair.

This electrode system was used in several pioneering studies for recording muscle activity from the lips, tongue, and soft palate. In large part, the suction electrode system has been superseded by more recent techniques. However, for the reader interested in additional information on the suction electrodes in speech research and data obtained therefrom, these are reviewed in detail by Cooper (1965).

Recently, several additional types of surface electrodes have been employed in speech electromyography. The most notable of these is the paint-on electrode (Hollis and Harrison, 1970; Allen and Lubker, 1972). Paint-on electrodes are constructed by making a paste of two parts silver powder,[1] two parts Duco cement, and two parts acetone. An initial layer of this paste or silver paint is applied to a skin area approximately 2—4 mm in diameter over the muscle that one wishes to monitor. A loop of fine wire (38—40 gauge, stripped of insulation) is placed on this initial layer of sliver paint. A second layer of paint is placed over the wire, providing a sandwich that acts as one conducting element of a bipolar electrode pair. If the skin is adequately prepared (i.e., cleaned of surface oils and moistened slightly with an electrode paste in the area of the intended placement), these electrodes provide an excellent means of recording EMG potentials of those speech muscles that can be recorded through the skin. Paint-on electrodes appear to be especially applicable to observations in clinical populations (Netsell, 1972; Marquardt, 1973).[2]

---

[1] The silver powder can be obtained from Handy and Harman, New York, New York.

[2] Micro Circuits, Inc. (New Buffalo, Michigan) provides a premixed silver paint designed especially for electrodes on human skin. We have used this electrode paint in our laboratory and feel that it is superior, in terms of subject comfort and ease of application, to the Duco cement—silver powder—acetone variety described above.

Allen, Lubker, and Turner (1973) have reported a paint-on electrode that can be attached to mucous membrane. These electrodes are similar in principle to the cutaneous paint-on variety. The primary difference is that the fine electrode wire is attached to the mucosa with a monomer adhesive (n-alkyl-2-cyanoacrylate).[3] The adhesive used in this application polymerizes in less than a minute on contact with water. Although Allen, Lubker, and Turner (1973) reported no adverse reaction from this adhesive, they caution against its extended clinical use until further studies have been conducted concerning possible inflammatory responses in the mucosa.

Another form of surface electrode that has been applied with success to some muscles is the Beckman Bio-miniature. This electrode is held in place with a double adhesive collar; its advantage is that it is available commercially and can be applied easily to some of the facial and masticatory muscles. However, owing to the large size of the Beckman electrode (10 mm in diameter), it tends to be somewhat obtrusive.

With some justification, the widespread use of surface electrodes for observation of speech muscles has been discontinued in recent years in favor of intramuscular electrodes of either the needle or hooked-wire variety. As suggested by Basmajian (1967, p. 26), "We must condemn the exclusive use of surface electrodes to study fine movements, deep muscles, the presence or absence of activity in various postures, and, in short, in any circumstances where precision is desirable." From the standpoint of the present authors, this condemnation may not be entirely appropriate, especially when one is dealing with certain well-defined muscles, even if the study of fine movements is involved. For example, Figure 2.5 shows simultaneous recordings of

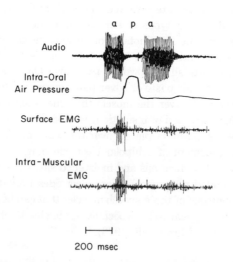

Figure 2.5 Oscillographic records of muscle activity recorded from the orbicularis oris muscle with surface electrodes (the paint-on variety) and implanted electrodes, simultaneously.

[3]This particular monomer adhesive can be obtained from Polysciences, Inc., Warrington, Pennsylvania.

the orbicularis oris muscle obtained with silver powder paint-on electrodes and with intramuscular hooked-wire electrodes. The similarity of these two recordings provides testimony for the usefulness of surface electrodes in certain applications, particularly those in which muscles lie close to the skin surface and penetration of the skin is undesirable.

Intramuscular Electrodes

As a *general* rule, we would agree with Basmajian: The use of intramuscular electrodes in speech research is certainly a step toward increased precision and specificity. For intramuscular recording in general electromyography, as noted by Basmajian (1967), the bipolar concentric needle electrode is by far the most common. These electrodes basically consist of a hypodermic needle with an insulated wire fixed in the cannula. Muscle potential differences that are found in the area between the two conductors can be amplified and recorded. Needle electrodes having only a single conductor are used when a large recording field is desirable. We generally would expect that needle electrodes would be obtrusive to normal speech muscle activity. Moreover, because of the size of these electrodes, there is likely to be a movement artifact created by the movement of the electrode within the muscle.

The intramuscular electrode which has gained the widest acceptance in speech electromyography is the hooked-wire electrode. The hooked-wire electrode consists of two fine insulated wires threaded through the barrel of a small hypodermic needle (23—30 gauge) and bent to form a *hook*. The needle itself is placed into the desired muscle, acting as an insertion vehicle to guide the wires through the intervening skin and tissue. The needle is then removed, leaving the hooked wires implanted within the muscle, that is, hooked into the muscle fibers. The specific wires employed vary from .1397 mm (36 gauge) to .0584 mm (44 gauge) in diameter. Many investigators use wire specifically designed for electrode use (i.e., platinum-iridium), while others employ common copper transformer wire or an alloy wire.[4] The platinum-iridium wire apparently has the advantage of providing a lower and more stable tissue—electrode impedance. To control the size of the recording field in the muscle, the wire pair can be twisted together to control the distance between the wires. The size of the area deinsulated on the tips of the wires also allows for some control over the size of the recording field. The construction of hooked-wire electrodes is illustrated in Figure 2.6.

The major advantage offered by hooked-wire electrodes is that the wires are flexible enough to move with most speech structures, thus minimizing movement artifact. Moreover, these thin wires cause the subject very little discomfort and thus reduce the chance of his altering his voluntary activity in response to that discomfort.

In summary to this point, Basmajian (1967) suggests that, for studies of moving structures, the hooked-wire electrodes "have proved a boon to 'kinesiological' studies

---

[4]Platinum-iridium wire can be obtained from Medwire Corporation, Mt. Vernon, New York.

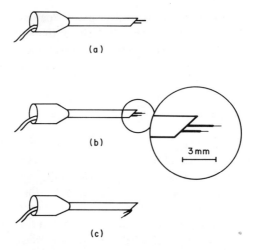

(a)

(b)

3 mm

(c)

Figure 2.6 Construction of hooked-wire electrodes: (a) insertion of the wires through the barrel of a hypodermic needle, with one wire extended approximately 2 mm beyond the other, (b) removal of the insulation approximately 1 mm back from the tip of each wire, (c) bending of the wires back along the barrel of the needle to form a hook. The difference in length between the wires is designed to reduce chances of their making contact within the muscle and thus shorting out the input to the amplifier (which results in loss of the EMG signal or transient *shorting artifacts*).

because they are: (*1*) extremely fine (and therefore painless), (*2*) easily implanted and withdrawn, (*3*) as broad in their pick-up from a specific muscle as are the best surface electrodes, and yet, (*4*) they give beautiful, sharp spikes similar to those from needle electrodes" (p. 32).

Preamplification of EMG Signals

It is advantageous to amplify EMG signals as close to the electrode pickup as possible. The low level of these signals at the electrode (from 250 μv to 2 mv) makes them particularly susceptible to radiated energy from main power lines, and the greater the distance between the electrode pickup and the first stage of amplification, the greater the influence of radiated energy. In addition, as suggested by McCleod (1973), short electrode wires minimize motion artifact. For these reasons, many electromyographers employ two stages of EMG amplification: a low-gain preamplifier near the electrode pickup and a higher-gain amplifier prior to FM recording or oscillographic display. In many cases, both of these amplifier stages are *differential*; that is, they amplify the *difference* in potential between the two input leads.

In the choice of a preamplifier for EMG, there are several specifications of major significance: (*1*) input inpedance, (*2*) bandwidth, and (*3*) common-mode rejection. Unfortunately, in any particular application, there are no firm rules for the selection of the optimal values for these parameters.

Input impedance of an EMG amplifier refers to the parallel resistance and capacitance on the input stage. Generally, it is desirable to maximize input impedance while at the same time minimizing input capacitance. Geddes (1972) recommends an amplifier input impedance that is at least 100 times larger than the electrode impedance. The electrode impedance—amplifier input impedance ratio is not functionally different from the impedance relationship between two stages of voltage circuitry. For both, it is appropriate to choose relative impedance values that minimize current flow through the input circuit. If current is allowed to flow, the electrode capacitance and input capacitance will introduce changes in the signal at higher frequencies and thus distort the bioelectric waveform; that is, not only will the input voltage be reduced in amplitude, but various frequencies of the complex waveform will be altered in their phase relations. According to Basmajian (1973), hooked-wire electrodes have a higher electrode impedance than surface or concentric needle electrodes. Hooked-wire electrodes would thus require higher values of amplifier input impedance than other electrodes.

The second variable in the choice or construction of EMG amplifiers is *bandwidth*. Unfortunately, there appears to be little agreement by electromyographers on the frequency band necessary for EMG signal recording. Moreover, one would expect that the frequency bandwidth requirements would vary as a function of the electrodes. Intramuscular electrodes are known to pick up sharper and faster potential changes than comparable surface electrodes and thus will detect higher frequency energy. Many authors suggest that the upper frequency cutoff should be approximately 10,000 Hz (Buchthal, Guld, and Rosenfalck, 1954; Fromkin, 1965; Hubler, 1967; Geddes and Baker, 1968). However, others suggest lower values: 200 Hz (Hayes, 1960), 1000 Hz (Basmajian, 1967), or 5000 Hz (Pacela, 1967). Electromyographers have been considerably more consistent in relation to lower frequency cutoff. Generally, the low-frequency roll-off has ranged from 20—40 Hz (Rogoff, Delagi, and Abramson, 1961; Fromkin, 1965; Hubler, 1967). This high-pass value appears necessary to remove low-frequency movement artifacts if they cannot be avoided in other ways. It would appear that a definitive study outlining the bandwidth of EMG from speech musculature would be worthwhile.

The third variable of importance to an adequate EMG amplifier is the common-mode rejection ratio. *Common-mode rejection* is defined as the capability of an amplifier to reject undesirable voltages that are in phase on its two inputs. Generally, such undesirable voltages are caused by the presence of electrical interference and, as such, are not of bioelectric origin. Common-mode rejection is generally expressed as the ratio of the magnitude of the in-phase voltage to the magnitude of the out-of-phase voltage required to produce the same output voltage, that is, the out-of-phase gain divided by the in-phase gain. Most modern EMG equipment has amplifier common-mode rejection ratios of at least 100,000:1. However, to optimize the common-mode rejection of a particular amplifier, the external electrode circuit must be symmetric (the electrode wires should be exactly the same length, and the impedance of the electrode—tissue interface for the two electrodes should be as similar as possible). The in-phase noise components will cancel each other on the input to the amplifier only if they are of equal amplitude and remain truly in phase. Differences in resistance and/or capacitance between the electrodes will modify this balance and reduce the cancellation.

Transformation and Quantification of EMG Signals

It is the opinion of some workers in electromyography that the "easiest and, in most cases, the most reliable evaluation is the trained observer's visual evaluation of results colored by his knowledge of the techniques involved" (Basmajian, 1967, p. 47). However, in addition to this method of evaluation, there appear to be a number of more objective techniques that have come into wide use for quantification and interpretation of EMG. Several comments are appropriate here as to the nature of such quantification and the information that can be derived from these techniques for purposes of speech research. Generally, in the study of speech muscle actions, we cannot evaluate variation in the *absolute* amplitude of activity for a single muscle. Since the amplitude will vary with electrode characteristics and exact placement, the absolute amplitude carries, by itself, little significant information. Moreover, we do not have a basis for the absolute comparison of EMG signals from two separate muscles, even if these were recorded simultaneously. Our analysis must, by virtue of these limitations, be confined to the questions of (1) whether or not there is activity present which relates in time to a certain speech gesture, and (2) whether or not that activity undergoes relative changes with corresponding changes in elicited speech movement patterns. To the extent that certain electronic or computer manipulation of EMG signals lends itself to making the latter judgments, these techniques are appropriate to the present discussion.

Frequently in speech EMG, the raw signals are rectified and filtered (smoothed). In the study of the relationship between EMG signals and the tension of muscle, several authors have shown that the average value of the smoothed and rectified EMG signal is proportional to the square root of the muscle force (Person and Libkind, 1967; Libkind, 1968). However, under conditions of isometric contraction, or where a muscle is shortening with constant velocity, the full-wave average has been shown to vary in a linear manner with muscle force (Lippold, 1952). These disparate observations may be congruent if it can be assumed that with increasing muscle force, motor units become progressively more synchronized, resulting in a disproportionate rise in the amplitude of the smoothed and rectified EMG.

As pointed out by Fromkin and Ladefoged (1966), for speech muscles, it is important that we are able to observe changes in the EMG patterns in relation to transient, short-duration speech movements. Based on the nature of these transient events, it is necessary to set the low-pass filter time constant for smoothing rectified EMG signals "relatively long compared to the duration of each spike and the time interval between spikes, but short in relation to the number of times per second the muscle activity changes in the production of a speech sound" (Fromkin and Ladefoged, 1966, p. 230). Obviously, this ideal time constant would change, depending on the muscle that was being observed and, perhaps, the nature of the experimental task. That is, the same time constant would not be optimal for all speech muscles and all speech tasks, In practice, however, one typically chooses a time constant that is appropriate for the highest rates of muscle activity change and this time constant is employed for slower activity patterns as well. Figure 2.7 illustrates the effect of various smoothing time constants (from 5 to 25 msec) upon patterns of rectified EMG.

Multiple Token Averaging of EMG Signals

At several laboratories, primarily Haskins Laboratories and the UCLA Phonetics Laboratory, digital computers have been employed to provide an average transient analysis of recorded EMG signals. These techniques, which are discussed in some detail by Cooper (1965), Fromkin and Ladefoged (1966), Gay and Harris (1971), and Port (1971), usually involve recording muscle activity for 20 or more repetitions of the same utterance. The time interval associated with each of these utterances is superimposed, either by reference to the acoustic signal or by other criteria (Fromkin and Ladefoged, 1966), and this activity is summed. In this manner, so it is suggested, the capricious aspects of muscle activity seen in individual repetitions are canceled out, and those elements of the wave that are consistently repeated are enhanced. This technique relies upon judgment as to the point in time which should be used as a reference to align various repetitions; indeed, as suggested by its proponents, misalignment may result in a general smoothing of some of the more significant aspects of the EMG signal.

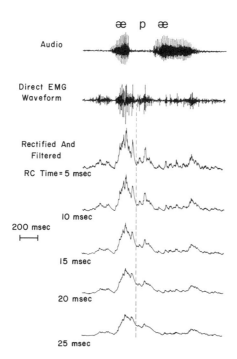

Figure 2.7   An illustration of the influence of filter time constant upon rectified and filtered (smoothed) EMG. The vertical dashed line provides a reference for a point of minimal muscle activity in the direct EMG signal. The extent to which that minimum is discernible in the rectified and filtered traces provides some indication as to the influence of the time constant upon the preservation of EMG fine structure— which may be important for the interpretation of muscle activity.

Interpretation of EMG Data from Speech Muscles

The speech literature is abundant in descriptions of the electrical activity of various speech muscles. The experimental questions surrounding the gathering of these data, however, have not always resulted in a better understanding of the nature of peripheral speech physiology, per se. For example, the flurry of speech EMG work in the early 1960s was an attempt to discover whether the muscle activity accompanying the production of certain phonemes was indicative of invarient motor commands (Harris, Schvey, and Lysaught, 1962; Harris, 1963; MacNeilage, 1963; Fromkin, 1966). Considerable work using speech EMG since that time has been concerned with the question of whether or not linguistic categories are discernible in EMG pattern variations. The answer to this question generally has been in the negative (MacNeilage, 1970).

In retrospect, these findings are not surprising. Neither the peripheral nor central aspects of speech motor control can be appreciated fully on the basis of electromyographic data alone. Workers studying other motor systems have found it imperative to incorporate into their models some approximation of peripheral mechanics to optimize understanding of movement systems' behavior. Indeed, very different EMG patterns can accompany the same movement or vice versa. As suggested by Jonsson (1973, p. 498, "The EMG analysis is only one part of the study [of the motor control of movement]. The other part of the study deals with the analysis of the movement and the forces involved in the action." He goes on to point out that "this means that all imaginable joint movements and postures have to be studied with EMG before one knows in detail the function of a muscle or the coordination pattern of the muscles acting on a specific joint." EMG can be considered a reasonable tool for speech research, if investigators are also aware of the movement or tension changes of the system under study. That is not to say that general questions concerning which muscles are active during certain speech events cannot be determined by EMG recordings, but that the specific contribution of those muscles can be evaluated best when simultaneous information is available on the force-generated output of the system. A more complete discussion of peripheral speech mechanical properties and the implications of these properties for interpretation of EMG is provided in the discussion by Abbs and Eilenberg in this volume.

Structural Movement during Speech Production

Since 1960, we have seen a renewed interest in the observation of structural movement during speech production. This renaissance, as suggested by Moll (1965), may result, in part, from the realization that inferences about the physiological aspects of speech from acoustical and perceptual analyses have certain limitations. In keeping with the purposes of the present volume, we will focus primarily on those techniques for observation of speech movements that have been employed since 1960.

Until recently, the major means for the observation of vocal tract movement during speech was radiological. Early speech researchers relied upon single-frame

X-ray fluoroscopic methods to obtain knowledge of vocal tract shapes. Since speech is a time-dependent event, more recent investigators have found the need to take motion picture X-rays (cinefluorography) of the vocal tract during speech. This latter technique involves the utilization of an X-ray source and an image intensifier to brighten the X-ray image for the motion picture camera. Most cinefluorographic systems available to the speech researcher are similar to that described by Moll (1960). Two of the more recent and significant advances made in the utilization of X-ray techniques that deserve note are (*1*) increased efficiency of data reduction and (*2*) an improved method for soft tissue visualization.

The reduction of cinefluorographic data is a tedious and time-consuming project. In fact, data reduction is one of the major drawbacks to radiological techniques. Recently, several researchers (Hayden and Koike, 1972; Mermelstein, 1973) have attempted to automate the data reduction process. One means of increasing the speed of cine data reduction was developed at the Speech Communications Research Laboratory in Santa Barbara, California by Hayden and Koike (1972). Their technique utilizes a standard single-frame advancement film projector, a Tektronix oscilloscope, and a small laboratory computer. The X-ray picture is projected onto the face of the oscilloscope. On the oscilloscope face, the computer generates up to 32 dots which can be positioned by the experimenter at various reference points on the projected X-ray display. The position of these dots for each frame is sequentially stored on magnetic tape for subsequent computer analysis and display. The development of more efficient data reduction techniques for cinefluorography has been complemented by a technique that allows more accurate soft tissue visualization.

Early speech researchers utilized gold chains and barium paste as contrast material defining articulator contours. More recently, speech researchers have been utilizing small, radiographically opaque beads (Houde, 1968) which are glued onto the surface of the soft tissue structures, using a nontoxic adhesive compound. Unlike earlier contrast materials, these beads allow an experimenter to track the movement of a particular flesh point.

More recent innovations in the observation of speech movement have involved primarily the development of on-line continuous transduction techniques. Reference to *on-line* techniques is in contrast to photographic or radiographic techniques which involve *off-line* measurement and data summary to obtain a quasi-continuous display of time—motion events.

Figure 2.8 is an oscillographic record of upper lip, lower lip, and jaw movement in both anterior—posterior and inferior—superior dimensions obtained by direct transduction. This record was available (in the form shown here) immediately following production of the utterance. The capability of obtaining records of this nature without tedious frame-by-frame tracing and/or point-by-point plotting (characteristic of photographic or cineradiographic methods) is one major advantage of on-line monitoring methods. The other major advantage is that these signals are available for FM tape storage, electronic manipulation, or direct analog-to-digital conversion for digital computer analysis and summary.

Recent attempts at direct monitoring have taken various forms. Variable resistance devices, notably strain gages, have been used to observe jaw, lip, and velar movements.

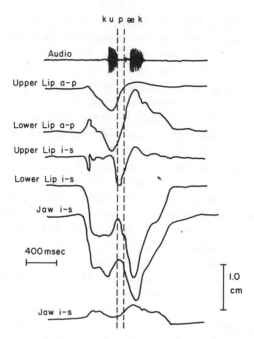

Figure 2.8 A multiple channel oscillographic record showing movements of the upper lip, lower lip, and jaw in both anterior—posterior (a—p) and inferior—superior (i—s) dimensions. The vertical dashed lines indicate the period of the acoustic silent period associated with the bilabial stop [p].

Electromagnetic and photoelectric techniques have been applied to the monitoring of the jaw, lip, thyroid cartilage, and velar movement during speech production. Ultrasonic techniques have been applied to observe pharyngeal wall and tongue movements.

Strain Gauge Techniques

Strain gauge transduction, which recently has gained acceptance in speech research, is based upon the principle of variable resistance. In the use of these techniques, structural displacement is coupled to a variable resistance strain gauge. A direct or alternating voltage is impressed across this resistance, and the voltage drop then changes in proportion to the resistance change, that is, the structural movement. A line illustration of a strain gauge (variable resistance) transducer is shown in Figure 2.9. Strain gauge techniques have been applied to the monitoring of jaw movement (Sussman and Smith, 1970a; Abbs and Gilbert, 1973), velar movement (Christiansen and Moller, 1971), lip movement (Sussman and Smith, 1970b; Abbs and Gilbert, 1973), and lip closing force (Kim, 1971).

Strain gauge transducers operate on the principle that, as a wire is stretched, it is reduced in diameter and increased in length, thus offering greater resistance to current flow. The opposite situation results when these conductors are compressed, thereby providing a resistance change proportional to applied stretch or compression

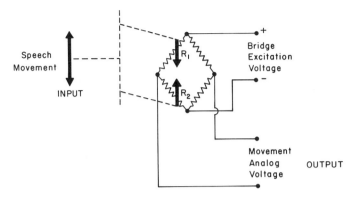

Figure 2.9 A schematic illustration of a variable resistance transducer applied to transduce speech movements. R1 and R2 are variable resistors (strain gauges) which change resistance by virtue of their being coupled mechanically to speech movements. The bridge excitation voltage is impressed across the bridge circuit. With the system at some definable point of rest, a reference position is established. From this reference position, variations in resistance due to speech movement are reflected in variations in the output voltage. This output voltage then can be amplified and analyzed as an analog of the speech movement that created the resistance changes in R1 and R2.

around some point of mechanical rest. This stretch and compression (deformation due to an applied force) is referred to as *strain* and is expressed in changes in length per unit of original length (dL/L: units of cm/cm) of the conductive material. By bonding the strain gauge element to a cantilever beam (in speech research this is generally a thin metal or plastic strip), a resistance change proportional to deformation of that strip (as a function of speech structure displacement) can be employed to modulate direct or alternating current, as shown in Figure 2.9. The end product of such a system is a voltage that varies dynamically in amplitude with structural movement.

The first step in developing a strain gauge displacement transducer is to ascertain the three-dimensional path of motion accomplished by the structure of interest. Inasmuch as the strain developed will be proportional to the movement along a single movement path, a strain gauge transducer can best transduce displacement where motion can be defined in one plane. For example, the anterior undersurface of the jaw is known to move principally (for speech) in a superior—inferior plane. Frequently, however, multidimensional forces are present because of movement across several planes. A single unidimensional cantilever, such as the one shown in Figure 2.10, provides only the confounded geometric result of these forces or displacement. For example, in order to observe inferior—superior lip movement with a simple uniform cantilever placed on the superior surface of the lower lip, movements of this structure in the anterior—posterior dimension generate forces which stress the cantilever in ways that cannot be distinguished from inferior—superior movement. One means by which these problems can be overcome is through the design of cantilever configurations that allow one to observe movements in more than one dimension. A strain gauge transducer recently developed at our laboratory allows for the observation of two-

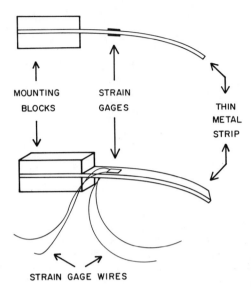

Figure 2.10   A line illustration of a strain gauge transducer constructed around a single unidimensional cantilever (the thin metal strip). As speech structures move, the strip is bent, creating stress on the strain gauges, which are bonded to the cantilever. As the cantilever is bent, conductive material of the strain gauge on the upper side is stretched, increasing its resistance. Conversely, the conductive material of the strain gauge on the lower side is compressed, decreasing its resistance. The mounting blocks provide a stable mechanical reference for the movement of the flexible end of the cantilever when force resulting from speech movement is applied.

dimensional motion (Abbs and Gilbert, 1973). This configuration is shown in Figure 2.11. A comparable transducer for observation of motion in three dimensions is feasible.

The strain gauge resistance that is most common for speech research is 350 ohms. This is the same value of resistance used for most air pressure transducers. Thus, strain gauge displacement devices generally can be employed with the bridge amplifiers used for pressure recording. In most strain gauge displacement transducers, a two-arm active bridge is employed with the two *matched* gauges physically positioned on opposite sides of the cantilever. With the gauge mirror-positioned, any temperature-dependent resistance change in the cantilever material is canceled in the bridge circuit (as illustrated in Figure 2.10).

With proper choice of strain gauge, cantilever dimensions, and cantilever material, signals in the low millivolt range can be obtained easily from strain gauge transducers. These levels are more than adequate to drive available DC amplifiers and, as noted earlier, usually will operate through existing air pressure and air flow channels in speech research systems. Calibration of these transducers requires that one have available a known and controllable mechanical displacement generator. A sinusoidal generator with variable frequency control is particularly desirable. One such device is described by Abbs and Gilbert (1973). This device allows one to check transducer velocity, acceleration, and amplitude linearity, as well as mechanical phase shift.

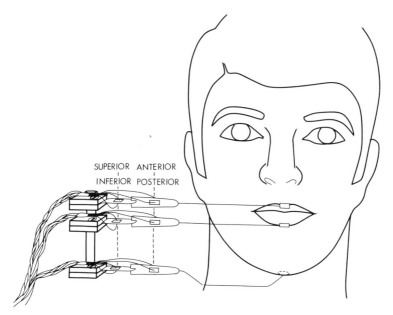

Figure 2.11 A line illustration of a two-dimensional lip and jaw transducer system. Motion of the speech structures in the anterior–posterior dimension results in stress on the vertically oriented transducers. Motion in the inferior–superior dimension results in stress on the horizontally oriented transducers. [After Abbs and Gilbert, 1973.]

Electromagnetic Techniques

Another method for observing movements during speech production employs the principle of mutual inductance. These transduction devices, referred to as *magnatometers*, have been employed to observe jaw movement in both anterior–posterior and inferior–superior dimensions. In the single dimension, one coil (either coil can be the sensor or generator) is placed on a stable reference point, and a second coil is placed on the moving structure which one wishes to observe. This configuration is shown in Figure 2.12(a). When the long axes of these two coils are oriented parallel to one another, the voltage induced in the sensor coil is inversely proportional to the cube of the intercoil distance. As noted by Hixon (1971), as long as the range of motion is small compared to the intercoil distance, the voltage-displacement proportion is essentially linear. However, to the extent that the long axes of the coils are not parallel, the voltage induced in the receiver coil may not be directly proportional to the distance between the coils. Moreover, the use of a magnetic field that has isogausian lines that are equidistant is of considerable importance. That is, a linear relationship between induced voltage and receiver-coil–primary-coil distance depends upon a magnetic field that has equal increments of density for equal increments of intercoil distance.

When one wishes to observe movements in two dimensions of this system, the generator coil is placed on the moving jaw, and sensor coils are placed on stable points both superior and posterior to the jaw (as shown in Figure 2.12(b)). The

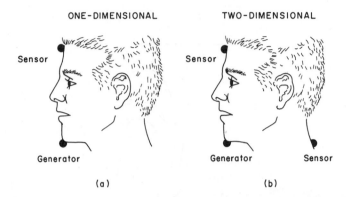

Figure 2.12 Placement of magnetometer coils for transduction of jaw movement: (a) inferior—superior movement, reflected in the distance between the generator and the single sensing coil and the voltage induced in sensing coil; (b) inferior—superior and anterior—posterior movement, reflected by the voltage induced in the coils on the forehead and back of the neck, respectively.

sensor coil, superior to the jaw, picks up induced voltages proportional to movements in the anterior—posterior dimension. These signals can be observed as two separate time—motion signals, or displayed as X and Y motion components in a two-dimensional display, such as an oscilloscope.

Photoelectric Methods

An additional means for transducing lip and jaw movements during speech production has involved attaching miniature lamps to these structures and then recording the displacement of these light sources (as the lips and jaw move) via some photosensitive technique. Lindblom and Bivner (1966) and Kozhevnikov and Chistovich (1965) attached light sources to the lips and jaw and used them to expose moving film in an oscilloscope camera. The vertical movement of the lips and jaw during speech was registered as the film was moving horizontally. To assure that the traces recorded were not contaminated by movement of the head in relation to the camera, the head was stabilized. In addition, to measure for any small head or body movements that could not be eliminated, a reference lamp was positioned on the head of the subject to record these undesirable head movements.

A modification of this technique has been reported by Ohala, Hiki, Hubler, and Harshman (1968). These authors employed photocells to transduce the moving light source to an analog voltage. In the preliminary system tested, a single articulator (either upper lip, lower lip, or jaw) could be monitored in the inferior—superior dimension. The light source, attached to the lips or teeth, was converted through a cylindrical lens to a horizontal bar of light and directed to a triangular photocell. The width of the bar of light striking the photocell was directly proportional to the jaw displacement, thus producing a voltage output that was directly proportional to inferior—superior lip movement. To overcome any variations in light intensity that might arise from anterior—posterior movements, the photocell and cylindrical lens

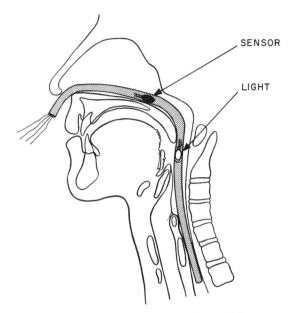

Figure 2.13 A midsagital illustration of the sensor (photocell) and light source as they are positioned in the compressible polyethylene tube. As the velopharyngeal port closes, the amount of light reflected to the photocell is reduced, and conversely. [After Ohala, 1971.]

were placed lateral to the subject. In the use of photovocalic cells, one must be aware of their spectral sensitivity and possibility of response time limitations. As pointed out by Geddes and Baker (1967), the response time of a photovocalic cell is seldom less than 5 msec and tends to increase with increased photocell size.

Another application of photocells to monitoring of speech movements involves observation of the magnitude of the velopharyngeal opening (Ohala, 1971). All the details of this technique are not available, but we know it involves placing a light source and photocell (inserted into a compressible polyethylene tube) above and below the velopharyngeal port, respectively. This device is illustrated in Figure 2.13. As the velopharyngeal port opens or closes, the light intensity striking the photocell varies in proportion to the area of opening, providing an analog voltage. The disadvantage of this technique, as pointed out by Ohala, is that the output cannot be calibrated easily, and only a relative measure of the opening between the oral and pharyngeal cavities is provided.

Ultrasonic Techniques

Different types of ultrasonic monitoring techniques have been employed in speech physiology research. Two types of ultrasonic techniques will be discussed below: pulse-echo and pulse-through transmission.

The most common ultrasonic technique employed in speech research is the pulse-echo technique. The method employs the piezoelectric effect in both the transmission and reception phases of ultrasonic transduction. To create an ultrasonic energy pulse, a crystal is briefly stimulated with a high voltage. This sudden application of a voltage results in a deformation of the crystal. Deformation of the crystal causes the material to vibrate or ring at frequencies within the megahertz range. The ultrasonic energy emitted by the sudden deformation of the crystal is directed away from the crystal by special construction of the housing encasing the crystal. An example of an ultrasonic transmitter—receiver transducer is schematically drawn in Figure 2.14. For speech research, the crystals typically are pulsed at rates ranging from 500 to 2000 sec^{-1}. The principle of pulse-echo ultrasound also involves the reflection of the ultrasonic pulse by tissue discontinuities (acoustic impedance mismatches) in the transmission pathway. When the acoustic pulse emitted by the sender encounters a tissue discontinuity, in part, the wave is reflected back toward the transmitter (see Figure 2.15). The piezoelectric effect is employed to determine the arrival of the reflected ultrasonic wave. In the echo mode, the ultrasonic system acts like a clock and monitors the transmission time of the ultrasonic pulse. Time-to-voltage conversion of the *echo* delay time results in an analog signal corresponding to the echo distance from the sender.

The pulse-echo technique has been employed most successfully for monitoring motions of the lateral walls of the pharynx. Ultrasonic processing of lateral pharyngeal wall movement during speech production is schematically presented in Figure 2.16. To monitor lateral pharyngeal wall motion during swallowing or speech, a beam of ultrasonic energy is directed mesially from the external neck wall toward the lateral margins of the pharynx (Kelsey, Minifie, and Hixon, 1969; Minifie, Hixon, Kelsey, and Woodhouse, 1970). Because of the acoustic impedance mismatch at the tissue—air interface at the lateral surface of the pharynx, the ultrasonic beam is reflected completely, back toward the transmitter.[5]

Once the ultrasonic echo has been received by the generator, it is converted into a time—amplitude display on a cathode ray tube. This type of display is called an *A-scope* display. The horizontal axis in this type of display is time; the vertical axis is amplitude. The initiation of the ultrasonic pulses at the external neck wall (*ENW* in Figure 2.16) appears as the first amplitude in the A-scope display. Echoes from the lateral wall of the pharynx (*LPW*) also appear in the form of an amplitude. The time between the initiation of the ultrasonic pulses to the echo amplitude (T_e) is proportional to the distance from the sender at the ENW to the acoustic discontinuity at the lateral wall of the pharynx. If appropriate time-to-voltage conversion circuitry is employed, the echo amplitudes may be recorded on FM tape. The FM tape records may be converted later to digital form for computer processing or displayed oscillographically as time—motion plots along with other physiological variables.

---

[5]Because of the elliptic shape of the lateral pharynx, not all of the ultrasonic energy is reflected directly back toward the transmitter. Thus, changes in the angle of incidence of the echo pulse to the transmitter may lead to a loss of signal from the lateral pharynx. This is one of the most troublesome problems when employing pulse-echo ultrasonic methods to track movement of the lateral pharynx.

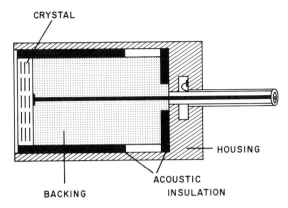

CRYSTAL

HOUSING

BACKING

ACOUSTIC
INSULATION

Figure 2.14 A schematic illustration of an ultrasonic transducer. The transducer is constructed such that the acoustic energy radiated away from the housing (to the left side of the drawing) is transmitted, while energy radiated toward the back of the transducer housing is absorbed.

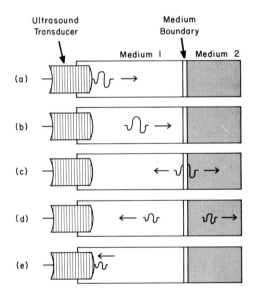

Ultrasound
Transducer

Medium
Boundary

Medium 1   Medium 2

(a)

(b)

(c)

(d)

(e)

Figure 2.15 A graphic illustration of the operation of the pulse—echo ultrasound monitoring technique. The sequence of events for one ultrasonic pulse is shown: (a) the pulse being emitted from the transducer; (b) the progression of that pulse through medium 1; (c) the arrival of the pulse at the boundary between medium 1 and medium 2, with partial refraction and partial reflection at their boundary; (d) the reflected echo pulse progressing back toward the transducer; and (e) the arrival of the echo pulse at the transducer. Knowledge of the speed of sound in medium 1 and information on the time taken to complete the transmit-to-reflection loop allows for determination of the distance between the transducer and the medium boundary.

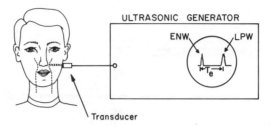

Figure 2.16 A schematic illustration of a pulse-echo monitoring system. The transducer is oriented toward the pharynx. The beam is reflected toward the transmitter. The processing unit converts the pulses sent and received into an amplitude—time display (*A-scope*). ENW is the initial ultrasonic pulse at the external neck wall; LPW is the echo received from the lateral surface of the pharynx. T_e is the oscillographic representation of the transit time of the pulses emitted from the sender.

The major problem with the pulse-echo technique is the inability of the experimenter to note precisely the point on the speech structure from which the echo is returning. The inability of the researcher employing ultrasound to specify a precise point on a structure has led to the utilization of an ultrasonic technique which permits monitoring of discrete points on speech articulators.

Pulse-through transmission employs a sender and a receiver. As shown in Figure 2.17, the ultrasonic sender transmits an acoustic pulse into the medium. The pulse is detected by a separate receiver. The distance from the transmitter to the receiver is reflected in the delay time between the transmission of the acoustic pulse and the reception of that pulse by the detector. This technique has been used successfully by Watkin and Zagzebski (1973) to monitor movement of the tongue during speech. They attached a small (3 mm diameter) piezoelectric crystal to the dorsal surface

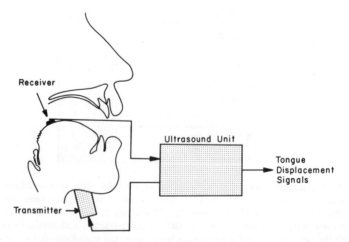

Figure 2.17 A line drawing depicting the employment of the pulse-through transmission ultrasonic technique for monitoring tongue movement in a single dimension. Notice that the ultrasonic transmitter is located below the tongue mass and coupled directly to the skin surface. The detector is affixed on the tongue surface with an adhering agent. [After Watkin and Zagzebski, 1973.]

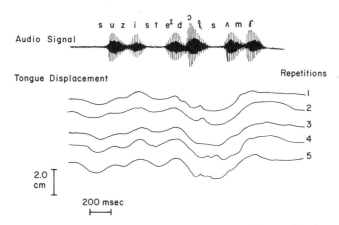

Figure 2.18 Sample data on the vertical movements of the tongue during selected speech samples. In this sample, the subject repeated the sentence *Susie stayed all summer* five times. [After Watkin and Zagzebski, 1973.] Note the similarities and dissimilarities in the patterning of tongue motion for these repeated utterances.

of the tongue to act as a detector (Figure 2.18). Samples of the type of data obtained using the through-transmission—time-motion mode are illustrated in Figure 2.19.

Recent advances in ultrasonic imaging involve the deployment of multicrystal arrays which outline the entire shape of internal body structures (Skolnick, Zagzebski, and Watkin, 1975). Such advances in nonradiographic techniques have the potential to provide three-dimensional monitoring of vocal tract movements during speech production.

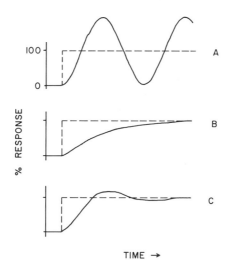

Figure 2.19 A schematic illustration of the response of a second-order system to a step function input. Dashed lines indicate the terminal amplitude of the step input. Solid lines indicate system response. Curve A is the system response when the damping is zero; curve B is the system response when the damping ratio is large; curve C is the critically damped system response.

Fundamental Instrumentation Requirements for Speech Physiology

To this point, we have focused our discussion primarily on those devices that convert speech muscle activity or movement into voltage analogs. However, the major instruments in a speech physiology laboratory, from the standpoint of cost and electronic sophistication, are those devices that amplify, store, shape, and dispaly these physiological signals. These instruments are of particular importance to a speech laboratory where on-line or direct monitoring of speech activity, as discussed in the present chapter, is employed.

Some General Precautions

When employing on-line monitoring techniques, the researcher must ensure that the voltage analogs obtained are accurate representations of the physiological events being recorded. Faithful transduction of speech events and subsequent reproductions of the resulting signals are especially important if one intends to further manipulate these signals by differentiation, integration, multiplication, subtraction, and/or addition.

The properties of any transduction system (mechanical or electrical) which will influence system response properties can be described using the equation of motion of the form:

$$F(t) = M\frac{d^2x}{dt^2} + B\frac{dx}{dt} + Kx \qquad (1)$$

or its electrical equivalent (for recording or reproduction systems):

$$V(t) = L\frac{d^2q}{Dt^2} + R\frac{dq}{dt} + \frac{q}{c}. \qquad (2)$$

In Equation (1), M is the mass, B is the coefficient of viscous damping, K is the elastic coefficient, X is the linear displacement, and t is time. In Equation (2), L is inductance, R is resistance, C is capacitance, and q is the charge. In these transduction or recording systems, the interaction of mass, viscosity, and elasticity provides the *damping ratio*:

$$\zeta = B/2\sqrt{KM}. \qquad (3)$$

One may determine the amount of damping of any electrical or mechanical system by the application of different types of forces or voltages. One of the most common forces applied to a transduction system is a step function. Utilization of the step function input provides maximum information on the damping characteristics of the system. For example, if the relative mass and the viscous and elastic properties of a system are inappropriate, the system will not accurately transduce or record the application of the step function. For example, an underdamped system responds with a rapid rise time[6] and undesirable overshoot. If the damping is zero (as indicated in

---

[6]Rise time most often has been described as the time in seconds for the amplitude to rise from 10% to 90% of its terminal value.

Figure 2.19(A)), the entire system will oscillate for a long time after the initial excitation before coming to rest. On the other hand, if the damping within a system is too great, while there is no overshoot, the rise time of this overdamped system will be very long, as illustrated in Figure 2.19(B). Most biomedical instruments are constructed to permit optimal rise time in conjunction with the smallest amount of overshoot after the application of the step force. Such a condition is called *critical damping*. If a system is critically damped, it will exhibit approximately 7% overshoot above the terminal amplitude of the applied step force (or voltage). This condition is illustrated in Figure 2.19(C).

While this general precaution applies to all transduction-recording-reproduction systems employed in speech research, it may be illustrated best by reference to observation of speech movement. Obviously, most of the physiological events of speech production are not step functions. Speech researchers have observed that some articulators may move as much as 4 cm during the speech act as well as exhibit peak velocities of 30 cm/sec and peak accelerations as high as 700 cm/sec^2. In order to accurately monitor these values in displacement, velocity, and acceleration, the researcher must be certain that the recording and transducing equipment employed has the capability of responding to these components of motion with a high degree of accuracy. Thus, if the speech physiology researcher employs a transduction system that is critically damped, he may be assured of the capability to record faithfully most speech physiological variables.

In summary, it cannot be overemphasized that these precautions apply not only to speech physiology transduction systems, but also to electronic devices which are employed to amplify, store, and display the signals obtained from these transducers. Obviously, the transduction of a speech event and the amplification, storage, display, and ultimate measurement of that event are only as faithful as the poorest component in this data acquisition analysis chain.

Amplification

The first stage of signal manipulation following transduction generally involves additional amplification, a step generally necessary to bring the transduced signal to a level where it can be stored on FM instrumentation tape or employed to drive a power amplifier for an oscillograph. We have already discussed the requirements for initial amplification of EMG signals. While the first stage of amplification provides an electrode—amplifier interface and is usually in close physical proximity to the subject, the second stage of amplification of EMG signals is less crucial in terms of input impedance or common-mode rejection. Often the same amplifier can be used for movement analogs and EMG signals. For movement signals, the amount and nature of amplification required varies with the transduction technique. For example, the signals from a strain gauge transducer range from 1.0 to 5.0 mv. Signal levels from other transduction systems, such as ultrasound, vary with the ultrasonic unit employed. Nevertheless, with either EMG or movement signals, it is generally necessary to bring the level signal to a peak-to-peak amplitude between 1.0 and 2.5 volts. This level is appropriate for driving most FM tape recorders and/or for providing a galvanometer or pen motor amplifier with sufficient voltage to provide high resolution oscillographic traces. Some control over this stage of signal amplification is desirable. For example, while most FM recorders will faithfully record and reproduce a signal of .25 volts, these recorders have an inherent noise level that does not vary as a function of input signal level. To optimize playback signal-to-noise ratio, the input signal should be substantially above this recorder noise floor. The upper limit on signal amplitude for FM recording is established by the range of frequency modulation and the frequency-to-voltage modulation ratio. That is, a signal that drives the frequency modulators outside their range will be peak-clipped on playback.

Signal Storage and Graphic Display

Following amplification, physiological signals can be stored on FM tape or played out directly on the oscillograph. While the capability for FM data storage may be considered by some to be an unnecessary convenience (and it certainly is a convenience), it is essential in many experiments. Attempting to capture transient signals at the time of their transduction on an oscillograph or oscilloscope is a difficult and harrying task. Moreover, once these signals are lost, one is prohibited from returning to them and applying additional amplification, selective filtering, and/or other forms of signal shaping. An FM recording capability also allows for off-line analysis with a digital computer, following analog-to-digital conversion. Computer averaging of EMG signals, discussed earlier, is accomplished in this manner.

FM tape recorders come with varying channel capacities and a range of frequency response characteristics. Some recorders can be purchased with 4 to 7 channels (using $\frac{1}{2}$-inch tape) and then later expanded, for additional cost, to as many as 14 channels (using 1-inch tape). Other recorders, costing far less, can be employed with $\frac{1}{4}$-inch tape, but are limited to 4 channels of recording capacity. In our experience, 7 channels is the absolute minimum number for *general* physiology research. If one has a routine experimental paradigm where the number of variables is limited, fewer channels might be appropriate. One such application might involve the routine monitoring of aerodynamic variables in a clinical evaluation of cleft palate speech. In this case, $\frac{1}{4}$-inch tape is a convenient storage for subsequent reexamination in relation to pre- and post-surgery, or pre- and post-therapy, and so forth. In many experimental situations, however, it appears that one always needs to record one more signal than the available FM recorder channel capacity.

The characteristics for FM storage of EMG signals differ little from the characteristics for their amplification. Assuming that the gain of the prerecording amplifiers is adequate, one need be concerned with the frequency and phase response of the FM recorder and its inherent signal-to-noise ratio. Some speech researchers have employed multichannel audio recorders for this purpose (Fromkin, 1965; Hubler, 1967). Such recorders seem to be quite adequate for EMG recording (since EMG signals are in the audio range), but most are limited to a capacity of four channels.

As would be expected, analogs of speech movement require a much lower frequency range than raw EMG signals. Even an upper frequency cutoff of 500 Hz does not distort components of most speech movements. However, it is particularly important that a recorder have a response down to DC. Following storage on FM tape, one can play back the recorded signals directly in real time or at a slower speed. Many investigators use a high record speed and then playback at a lower speed to increase the effective frequency response of the display or analysis system. As pointed out by Hardy (1965), this slow play back technique is particularly useful if one is using a conventional ink-writing recorder, which typically does not have frequency response that extends much above 100 Hz. Oscillograph frequency response is not commonly a problem with optical oscillographs which have galvanometers that respond to frequencies as high as 13,000 Hz. The direct-writing ink jet oscillograph is another alternative, having a high frequency cutoff of approximately 1000 Hz. Of course, if RMS circuits are employed to smooth and rectify the high-frequency signals (EMG or audio), most ink-writing oscillographs will have the requisite frequency response to produce these signals adequately.

Signal Shaping

Assuming that one is able to store the analog signals on FM tape, additional electronic manipulation can be applied off-line to assist in the data analysis. One such signal manipulation circuit that we have found worthwhile is an electronic differentiator. Figure 2.20 is an oscillographic record showing a displacement signal (Trace 1) which has been differentiated one time to provide a continuous velocity signal (Trace 2), and differentiated twice for a continuous acceleration signal (Trace 3). We have found these instantaneous, continuous displays of velocity and acceleration quite useful for interpretation of movement data (Abbs, 1973a, 1973b; Abbs and Netsell, 1973). Other such devices for manipulation of analog movement signals include signal inverters and analog subtractors. Figure 2.21 illustrates the use of these

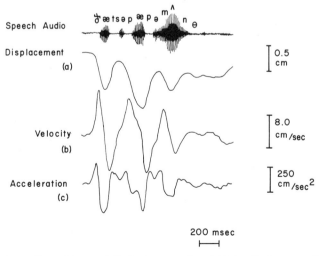

Figure 2.20 An oscillographic record displaying an analog of (a) jaw displacement, (b) jaw velocity, and (c) jaw acceleration for the utterance *that's a* [pæp] *a month.*

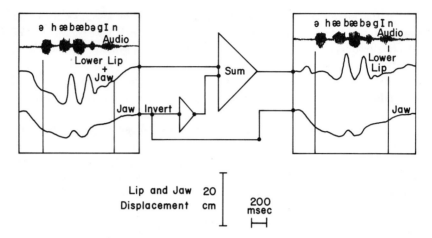

Figure 2.21   A schematic representation of off-line signal-shaping circuits being used to obtain an analog signal of the lower lip movement independent of the jaw. Note that inverting the *jaw signal* and adding it to the *lower lip + jaw signal* effectively results in subtraction of these signals.

devices in extracting the jaw component from a lower lip plus jaw signal. This particular manipulation provides an analog signal that is representative of the lower lip movement components with jaw movement components extracted. These manipulations, based upon verification of lower lip movement independent of the jaw, were accomplished on signals played back from FM tape. With an appropriate configuration of analog signal shaping circuits, one can accomplish a number of subtle manipulations that are very useful for speech physiology data analysis. Several specific examples of additional configurations which we have employed are illustrated in the Abbs and Eilenberg chapter in this volume.

Other circuits of value include a select number of sharp-skirted discrete filters. For example, if 60 Hz interference were to inadvertently become exceedingly large on a particular movement signal, one could save the data (i.e., the actual movement signal) by applying a low-pass filter with a sharp roll-off. Low-pass filters available on oscillographs typically do not have very sharp roll-off characteristics. A comparable filter with a low-pass cutoff at 75 Hz is likewise very useful in removing some of the AC variations from intraoral air pressure or air flow rate signals. In the use of these filters, the unfiltered signal is stored on FM tape and then filtered prior to display on the oscillograph.

Signal shaping circuits are also useful for the display of EMG signals. The obvious case is the smoothing and rectifying circuits mentioned previously. It also appears worthwhile, under some circumstances, to manipulate EMG signals in other ways. For example, as indicated by Abbs and Eilenberg in this volume, rectified and smoothed EMG signals sometimes can be combined to provide an approximate indication of the *net* muscle forces that are acting on a particular speech structure. Conceivably, one might wish to look at the rate of change of muscle activity; in this case, differentiation of smoothed and rectified EMG could be employed.

Off-line shaping circuits are also useful in studies of speech aerodynamics. For example, a true integrator (as indicated by Warren in this volume; Hardy and Edmonds, 1968) provides a means for obtaining measures of lung volume change. This is accomplished by integrating the air flow rate signal.

Signal Monitoring Equipment

In addition to the usual test equipment (test oscilloscopes, vacuum tube voltmeters, etc.), one additional item of electronic hardware which appears useful is a multichannel oscilloscope. The oscilloscope we are using currently for this purpose in our laboratory has eight channels and is employed to (1) monitor signals during set-up of the transduction devices and general equipment, (2) preview signals recorded on FM tape prior to oscillographic write-out, (3) provide subject *biofeedback*, and (4) observe simultaneously all channels being recorded on FM tape during an experimental run.

Some Additional Components

To optimize the use of the components discussed above, there are some additional components that fill out the instrumentation armamentarium for a flexible laboratory. The first of these components is a set of DC amplifiers with vernier control over gain and a capability for DC offset. Frequently, when one plays back signals from FM tape, they are either too large or too small in amplitude, or two signals of comparable origin have been recorded at different calibration levels, making them difficult to compare visually on the oscillographic display. In situations such as these (especially in light of the knowledge that signals recorded on FM tape must be adjusted for optimal tape signal-to-noise ratio and sometimes cannot be recorded at equivalent calibration levels), it is clearly worthwhile to have a general amplification capability. In addition, these DC amplifiers work well for many preamplification needs.

An additional item in a speech physiology laboratory, especially if the laboratory is to be used by several experimenters, is an interconnection *patch panel*. The patch panel facilitates flexible interconnection of various signal manipulation, monitoring, storage, and display devices. Generally, all inputs and outputs are hard-wired to panel jacks and are thus accessible for easy and fast interconnections. Once a patch panel is installed, one is no longer faced with the time-consuming problem of finding cables of the appropriate length and/or with the adaptive connectors to route signals through various items of connector-incompatible equipment. Moreover, if all input impedances are maximal and output impedances minimal, component interconnection problems are minor. In addition, if power driving circuits are placed at output stages of the system, impedance mismatches, if they must occur, have minimal impact. In a speech physiology system, the only place that power amplifiers are needed is in the oscillograph.

A final item of laboratory instrumentation that has proved very useful in its ap-application to speech physiology research is the small laboratory computer. Several laboratories, particularly the Phonetics Laboratory at UCLA and Haskins Laboratories, have made use of the laboratory computer for analysis and summary of physiological data. In the future, more extended use of minicomputers will be absolutely necessary to allow for faster and more accurate measurement, analysis, and summary of the deluge of physiological information that is currently accessible through the use of on-line techniques. Indeed, to this point, the ability to transduce and record physiological indices of speech production has far outdistanced any comparable ability to measure, analyze, and summarize these data. Laboratory computers also may find some application in the quantitative modeling of the physiological and biomechanical processes of speech in a manner parallel to their current use in the modeling of the acoustic aspects of speech processes.

In summary, it should be noted that most or all of the techniques discussed in the present chapter originally were developed, at least in principle, for application to the study of other physiological or physical systems. The implication to be drawn from this fact is that if we are to maintain a *state of the art* laboratory approach to the study of speech physiology, we must continue to interact with the areas of engineering and bioengineering where most of our existing techniques have originated.

REFERENCES

Abbs, J. H. The influence of the gamma motor system on jaw movement during speech: A Theoretical framework and some preliminary observations. *Journal of Speech and Hearing Research*, 1973, 52, 175–200.(a)

Abbs, J. H. Some mechanical properties of lower lip movement during speech production. *Phonetica*, 1973, 28, 65–75.(b)

Abbs, J. H., and Gilbert, B. N. A strain gage transducer system for lip and jaw motion in two dimensions. *Journal of Speech and Hearing Research*. 1973, 16, 248–256.

Abbs, J. H., and Netsell, R. A. dynamic analysis of two-dimensional muscle force contributions to lower lip movement. *Journal of the Acoustical Society of America*, 1973, 53, 295(A).

Aidley, D. J. *The physiology of excitable cells.* Oxford: Cambridge University Press, 1973.

Allen, G. D., and Lubker, J. F. New paint-on electrodes for surface electromyography. Journal of *the Acoustical Society of America*, 1972, 52, 124(A).

Allen, G. D., Lubker, J. F., and Turner, D. T. Adhesion to mucuous membrane for electromyography. *Journal of Dental Research*, 1973, 52, 391.

Arkebauer, H. J., Hixon, T. J., and Hardy, J. C. Peak intra-oral air pressures during speech. *Journal of Speech and Hearing Research*, 1967, 10, 196–208.

Basmajian, J. V. *Muscles alive—their functions revealed by electromyography* (2nd ed.). Baltimore, Maryland: Williams & Wilkins, 1967.

Basmajian, J. V. Electrodes and electrode connectors. In J. E. Desmedt (Ed.) *New Developments in electromyography and clinical neurophysiology*, Vol. 1. Switzerland: Basel, S. Karger, 1973, 502–510.

Basmajian, J. V., and Cross, G. L. Duration of motor unit potentials from fine-wire electrodes. *American Journal of Physiological Medicine*, 1971, 50, 144–148.

Bell-Berti, F. The velopharyngeal mechanism: An electromyographic study. Unpublished doctoral dissertation, City University of New York, 1973.

Buchthal, F., Guld, C., and Rosenfalck, P. Action potential parameters in normal human muscle and their dependence on physical variables. *Acta Physiologica Scandinavia*, 1954, 32, 200–218.

Christiansen, R., and Moller, K. Instrumentation for recording velar movement. *American Journal of Orthodontics*, 1971, 59, 448–455.

Cooper, F. S. Research techniques and instrumentation: EMG. *ASHA Reports*, 1965, *1*, 153—168.

Fritzell, B. The velopharyngeal muscles in speech: An electromyographic and cineradiographic study. *Acta Otolaryngolica*, 1969, Supp. 250.

Fromkin, V. A. Some phonetic specifications of linguistic units: An electromyographic investigation. *UCLA Working Papers in Phonetics*, 1965, *9*, 170—199.

Fromkin, V. A. Neuro-muscular specification of linguistic units. *Language and Speech*, 1966, *9*, 170—199.

Fromkin, V. A., and Ladefoged, P. Electromyography in speech research. *Phonetica*, 1966, *15*, 219—242.

Gay, T., and Harris, K. S. Some recent developments in the use of electromyography in speech research. *Journal of Speech and Hearing Research*, 1971, *14*, 241—246.

Gay, R., Ushijima, T., Hirose, H., and Cooper, F. Effect of speaking rate on labial and consonant-vowel articulation. *Status report on speech research*. Haskins Laboratories, 1973. SR—33, 221—227.

Geddes, L. A. *Electrodes and the measurement of bioelectric events*. New York: Wiley-Interscience, 1972.

Geddes, L. A., and Baker, L. E. *Principles of applied biomedical instrumentation*. New York: Wiley, 1968.

Hardy, J. C. Air flow and air pressure studies. *ASHA Reports*, 1965, *1*, 141—152.

Hardy, J. C., and Edmonds, T. D. Electronic integrator for measurement of partitions of the lung volume. *Journal of Speech and Hearing Research*, 1968, *11*, 777—786.

Harris, K. S. Behavior of the tongue in the production of some alveolar consonants. *Journal of the Acoustical Society of America*, 1963, *35*, 784(A).

Harris, K. S., Gay, T., Sholes, G. N., and Lieberman, P. Some stress effects on electromyographic measures of consonant articulations. *Status report on speech research*. Haskins Laboratories, 1968, SR—1, 137—151.

Harris, K. S., Rosov, R., Cooper, F. S., and Lysaught, G. F. A multiple suction electrode system. *Electroencephlography and Clinical Neurophysiology*, 1964, *17*, 698—700.

Harris, K. S., Schvey, M. H., and Lysaught, G. F. Component gestures in the production of oral and nasal labial stops. *Journal of the Acoustical Society of America*, 1962, *34*, 743(A).

Hayden, E., and Koike, Y. A data processing scheme for frame by frame film analysis. *Folia Phoniatrica*, 1972, *24*, 169—181.

Hayes, K. J. Wave analysis of tissue noise and muscle action potentials. *Journal of Applied Physiology*, 1960, *15*, 749—752.

Hixon, T. J. An electromagnetic method for transducing jaw movements during speech. *Journal of the Acoustical Society of America*, 1971, *49*, 603—606.

Hollis, R., and Harrison, B. Spray-on EMG electrodes. *American Journal of Occupational Therapy*, 1970, *24*, 28—30.

Houde, R. A. A study of tongue body motion during selected speech sounds. *SCRL Monographs, 2*. Santa Barbara: Speech Communication Research Laboratory, 1968.

Hubler, S. A high input impedance electromyography preamplifier. *UCLA Working Papers in Phonetic*, 1967, *7*, 25—34.

Huntington, D. A., Harris, K. S., and Scholes, G. N. An electromyographic study of consonant articulation in hearing-impaired and normal speakers. *Journal of Speech and Hearing Research*, 1968, *11*, 147—158.

Isshiki, N., and Ringel, R. L. Air flow during the production of selected consonants. *Journal of Speech and Hearing Research*, 1964, *7*, 151—164.

Jonsson, B. Electromyographic kinesiology—aims and fields of use. In J. E. Desmedt (Ed.), *New developments in electromyography and clinical neurophysiology*, Vol. 1. Basel, Switzerland: S. Karger, 1973, 489—501.

Kelsey, C. A., Minifie, F. D., and Hixon, T. J. Applications of ultrasound in speech research. *Journal of Speech and Hearing Research*, 1969, *12*, 564—575.

Kim, B. W., A physiological study of the production mechanisms of Korean stop consonants. Unpublished Doctoral dissertation, University of Wisconsin, 1971.

Klatt, D. H., Stevens, K. N., and Mead, J. Studies of articulatory activity and airflow during speech. In A. Bouhuys (Ed.), *Sound production in Man*. New York: Annals of the New York Academy of Sciences, 1968, 42–55.

Kozhevnikov, W. A., and Chistovich, L. *Speech: Articulation and perception*. Washington, D.C.: Joint Publications Research Service, U.S. Dept. of Commerce, No. *30*, 1965, 543.

Ladefoged, P., Draper, M., and Whitteridge, D. Syllables and stress. *Miscellaneous Phonetica*, 1958, *3*, 1–15.

Lenman, J. A. Integration and analysis of electromyography and related techniques. In J. N. Walton (Ed.), *Disorders of voluntary muscle*. Boston: Little, Brown, 1969, 121–130.

Libkind, M. S. Modelling of interference bioelectric activity. *Biophysics (Biofizika)*, 1968, *13*, 811–821 (English Translation).

Lindblom, B., and Bivner, P. O. A method for continuous recording of articulatory movement. *Quarterly Progress and status report, Speech Transmission Laboratory*, Stockholm: Royal Institute of Technology 1966, *1*, 14–16.

Lippold, O. C. The relation between integrated action potentials in a human muscle and its isometric tension. *Journal of Physiology*, 1952, *117*, 492–499.

Lubker, J. F., Fritzell, B., and Lindquist, J., Velopharyngeal function: An electromyographic study. *Quarterly Progress and Status Report, Speech Transmission Laboratory*, Stockholm: Royal Institute of Technology, 1970, *4*, 9–20.

Lysaught, G., Rosov, R. J., And Harris, K. S. Electromyography as a speech research technique with an application to labial stops. *Journal of the Acoustical Society America*, 1961, *33*, 842(A).

MacNeilage, P. F. Electromyographic and acoustic study of the production of certain final clusters. *Journal of the Acoustical Society of America*, 1963, *35*, 461–463.

MacNeilage, P. F. Motor control of serial ordering of speech. *Psychological Review*, 1970, 77, 182–196.

MacNeilage, P. F., and Scholes, G. N. An electromyographic study of the tongue during vowel production. *Journal Speech and Hearing Research*, 1964, *7*, 209–232.

Marquardt, T. P. Characteristics of speech production in Parkinson's disease: Electromyographic, structural movement, and aerodynamic measurements. Unpublished doctoral dissertation, University of Washington, 1973.

McCleod, W. D. EMG instrumentation in biomechanical studies: Amplifiers, recorders, and integrators. In J. E. Desmedt (Ed.), *New developments in electromyography and clinical neurophysiology*, Vol. 1. Basel, Switzerland: S. Karger, 1973, 511–518.

Mermelstein, P. Computer-assisted measurement system for x-ray films of the vocal tract. *Journal of the Acoustical Society of America*, 1973, *53*, 320(A).

Minifie, F. D., Abbs, J. H., Tarlow, A., and Kwaterski, M. EMG activity within the pharynx during speech production. *Journal of Speech and Hearing Research*, 1974, *17*, 497–504.

Minifie, F. D., Hixon, T. J., Kelsey, C. A., and Woodhouse, R. J. Lateral pharyngeal wall movement during speech production. *Journal of Speech and Hearing Research*, 1970, *13*, 585–594.

Moll, K. L. Cinefluorographic techniques in speech research. *Journal of Speech and Hearing Research*, 1960, *3*, 227–241.

Moll, K. L. Photographic and radiographic procedures in speech research. *ASHA Reports*, 1965, *1*, 129–139.

Netsell, R. Lip electromyography in the dysarthrias. Paper presented at the Annual Convention of the American Speech and Hearing Association, October 18–21, 1972, San Francisco, California;

Ohala, J. J. Monitoring soft palate movements in speech. *Journal of the Acoustical Society of America*, 1971, *50*, 140(A).

Ohala, J. J., Hiki, S., Hubler, S., and Harshman, R. Photoelectric methods of transducing lip and jaw movements in speech. *UCLA Working Papers in Phonetics*, 1968, *10*, 135–144.

Öhman, S. Peripheral motor commands in labial articulation. *Quarterly progress and status report, Speech Transmission Laboratory*, Stockholm: Royal Institutes of Technology, 1967, *4*, 30–63.

Pacela, A. F. Collecting the body's signals. *Electronics*, 1967, *14*, 103–112.

Person, R. S., and Libkind, M. S. Modelling of interference bioelectric activity. *Biophysics (Biofizika)*, 1967, *12*, 145—153 (English Translation).

Port, D. K. The EMG data system. *Status report on speech research*, Haskins Laboratories, 1971, SR—25/26, 67—72.

Rogoff, J. B., Delagi, E. F., and Abramson, A. S. Critical factors in electromyographic instrumentation. *Archives of Physiological Medicine and Rehabilitation*, 1961, *42*, 175—179.

Ruch, T. C., Patton, H. D., Woodbury, J. W., and Towe, A. L. *Neurophysiology*. Philadelphia: Saunders, 1965.

Shipp, T., Deatsch, W. W., and Robertson, K. A technique for assessment of deep neck muscle activity. *Laryngoscope*, 1968, *78*, 418—432.

Skolnick, L., Zagzebski, J. A., and Watkin, K. L. Two-dimensional ultrasonic demonstration of lateral pharyngeal wall movement in real time—a preliminary report. *Cleft Palate Journal* 1975, *12*, 299—303.

Smith, T. S., and Hirano, M. Experimental investigations of the muscular control of the tongue in speech. *Journal of the Acoustical Society of America*, 1968, *44*, 354(A).

Stetson, R. H. *Motor phonetics: A study of speech movement in action*. Amsterdam: North Holland Publishing, 1951.

Stetson, R. H., and Hudgins, C. V. Functions of the breathing movements in the mechanism of speech. *Arch. Ne'erl. Phon. Exper.*, 1930, *5*, 1—30.

Sussman, H. M., MacNeilage, P., and Hanson, R. Labial and mandibular dynamics during the production of bilabial stop consonants. *Journal of Speech and Hearing Research*, 1973, *16*, 385—396.

Sussman, H. M., and Smith, K. U. Transducer for measuring lip movements during speech. *Journal of the Acoustical Society of America*, 1970, *48*, 858—860.(a)

Sussman, H. M., and Smith, K. U. Transducer for measuring mandibular movements during speech. *Journal of the Acoustical Society of America*, 1970, *48*, 857—858.(b)

Watkin, K. L., and Zagzebski, J. A. On-line ultrasonic technique for monitoring tongue displacements. *Journal of the Acoustical Society of America*, 1973, *54*, 544—547.

PART II

SPEECH PRODUCTION

chapter **3**

Models of Speech Production

Raymond D. Kent

University of Wisconsin, Madison

Introduction

A model of speech production represents an attempt to account for the control of the speech production mechanism or any part of that mechanism. This definition expands somewhat upon Whitaker's (1970) minimal demand that a model of speech production account for the control of the vocal tract. Although models often have been designed with an emphasis on the supralaryngeal or vocal tract level, a complete model must recognize the interactions of the respiratory, phonatory, and vocal tract components of the speech production mechanism. The central concern of this chapter is the motor control of speech. Although problems in articulatory—acoustic conversions and auditory analysis ultimately are important to speech production, these issues are not considered in detail here. However, these topics are discussed in other chapters of this book.

The perspective taken here is that the two major control problems in the production of speech are: (*1*) the seriation of the control elements (whatever these may be), and (2) the neuromuscular, or articulatory, representation of these elements. Seriation is a category that deals with the general problem of patterning or sequencing, and probably finds its most obvious expression in the assembly of phonetic or syllabic strings. Also included in this category are certain phenomena that have been labeled as problems of articulatory timing. The category of neuromuscular or articulatory representation involves the conversion of high-level neural control elements to positions and shapes at the peripheral level.

Hence, the motor skills in the act of speaking are considered to fall into two categories, one dealing with temporal structure and the other with position or spatial structure. MacKay (1974, p. 642) posed a similar dichotomy when he wrote: "A syntax

of behaviors such as playing the piano or speaking must contain two basically different
types of rules, syntagmatic rules for specifying the order of the behavioral components,
and paradigmatic rules for specifying the form or simultaneous configuration of the
components." For example, in the case of speech, the syntagmatic rules might yield the
serial ordering of phonemes, and the paradigmatic rules might yield the articulatory
features of each phoneme in the string. The two categories of motor control, temporal
and spatial, form the expository skeleton of the present chapter.

Basic Control Strategies in Skilled Motor Behavior

Many of the recent papers on speech (and skilled movements in general) have
been concerned with one or the other of two basic dichotomies in control strategy,
viz., *open-loop versus closed-loop* and *preprogramming versus chaining*. The two
dichotomies have a thread of similarity but they are not functionally equivalent.

An open-loop control system is characterized by a control action that is *independent* of the output, whereas a closed-loop control system is characterized by a control
action that *depends* upon the output by virtue of feedback. Calibration is critical
to open-loop control systems because performance accuracy demands a known
relationship between the input and the output of the system. Accordingly, open loop
control systems assume (*1*) knowledge of the properties of the effector apparatus,
and (*2*) negligible environmental disturbances. For both man-made and natural systems, failure to satisfy one or both of these conditions usually leads to employment
of closed-loop control, which corrects for effector variance and disruptive factors by
feeding back to the controller relevant information about the output quantity.
Furthermore, closed-loop control is useful for improving the static and dynamic characteristics of the elements in a system. But the application of feedback is not without
disadvantages, and two of the most important drawbacks are a tendency toward oscillation or instability and a possible reduction in the speed of response (equivalent
to a reduction in bandwidth).

Preprogramming is opposed to chaining in somewhat the same way what open-loop
is opposed to closed-loop. Preprogramming is akin to open-loop control in that the
control exercised in the system does not rely on the output. For the purposes of this
chapter, preprogramming may be defined as "a set of motor commands that are structured before a movement sequence begins, and that allows the entire sequence to be
carried out uninfluenced by peripheral feedback" (Keele, 1968, p. 387). On the other
hand, a chaining strategy for motor sequencing assumes that the performance of any
one of a series of movements depends upon feedback regarding the accomplishment of
a preceding movement. As the terms typically are used, one distinction between preprogramming and open-loop control is that the former applies to nonsequential
dependencies among the elements in a pattern or series; open-loop control usually
does not carry this implication. The difference between chaining and closed-loop
strategies is that in the former case, the stimulus-producing response is a *correct*
(intended) one, but in the latter case it is an *incorrect* one (Greenwald, 1970). That is,
a chaining strategy relies on feedback that confirms the successful realization of a

motor instruction, whereas a closed-loop strategy relies on feedback that constitutes an error signal.

The dichotomy of preprogramming versus chaining is central to the first problem of speech motor control to be considered in this chapter. The problem is that of seriation, or the temporal sequencing of speech.

The Problem of Seriation

Lashley's Classical Hypotheses

In his famous paper on the problem of serial ordering in behavior, Lashley (1951) considered the extent to which various kinds of behavior, but especially speech, could be conceptualized as being under the control of *associative chain* or *hierarchical* mechanisms. The associative chain model (also called *sequential chain* or *chain*) may be given the simple diagrammatic representation that is shown in Figure 3.1(a). In this diagram, the letters *A*, *B*, *C*, and so forth designate control units of some sort— phonemes or syllables, for example. As discussed previously, the chain model proposes that feedback is used to control the sequencing of the successive units in a string; for example, the initiation of the movements for unit B depends upon feedback concerning the movements associated with unit A. This diagram emphasizes that the control strategy requires the transmission of signals from the executive (control center) to the periphery and back again. The letters in the figure correspond to salient events in the control pattern. The hierarchical model (also called a *preplanning* model) is identical to the notion of preprogramming discussed in the preceding section; that is, this model proposes that the ordering of units is prepared in advance as a motor

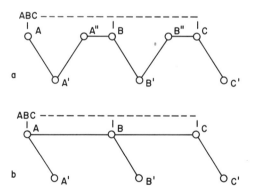

Figure 3.1 Diagrams to illustrate two concepts of the control of motor sequencing: (a) the chaining or feedback strategy, and (b) the hierarchical or preprogramming strategy. The letters in the figure correspond to the following events in the regulation of a response sequence ABC. A, B, C = activation of a command unit at a high level in the central nervous system, the muscle system control center; A', B', C' = beginning of the movement that corresponds to a command unit A, B, or C; A'', B'' = arrival of an afferent impulse (feedback) at the muscle system control center to confirm that movement for a given command unit A or B has been initiated or completed. [After Kozhevnikov and Chistovich, 1965].

program, and that the motor instructions are issued by the executive without reliance on feedback from the effectors. A diagram of this model is presented in Figure 3.1(b), which shows that preorganization, rather than feedback, is the critical feature in such a control strategy.

Objections to Chain Strategies

TRANSPORT DELAY IN FEEDBACK CONTROL

Lashley (1951) and others after him (Kozhevnikov and Chistovich, 1965; Lenneberg, 1967; Ohala, 1970) have assembled a number of arguments against the notion of an associative chain model in the serial ordering of speech. One of the primary objections already has been suggested in the earlier comments on feedback processes: Since feedback control requires both an afferent and an efferent signal for the accomplishment of a skilled movement, the loop delay can be a critical factor in the attainable rate of serial ordering. In a discussion of handwriting, which has interesting similarities to speech in the apparent conversion of discrete linguistic units to continuous motor responses, van der Gon and Wieneke (1969) remarked that feedback strategies are not as capable as preprogramming strategies in the execution of rapid, correct movements because the former necessarily suffer transport delays. These authors observed that delays of up to 200 msec characterize the human neuromuscular system. The importance of this notion to the production of speech was indicated by Kozhevnikov and Chistovich (1965), who cited data indicating that the latencies of motor reactions to auditory and proprioceptive stimuli are on the order of 100—150 msec, a magnitude that comes close to the minimal duration of a syllable. The particular definition given to *syllable* is not crucial to the argument so long as it is recognized that such a unit may consist of one or more phones; the point being made is that the motor reaction time is longer than the intervals that can be assigned to individual speech segments. In short, the associative chain hypothesis does not allow sufficient time for the operation of a feedback loop between serially ordered elements.

THE PERMUTABILITY OF SPEECH UNITS

A second inadequacy of the associative chain hypothesis is that any given unit of speech usually can be followed by a variety of other units: The chain model cannot explain the diversity of contiguities since it predicts that any single unit must perforce be followed by one and the same unit. Lashley (1951) considered the permutability of speech units to be a major obstacle to the possibility of seriation based on associative chaining. His hierarchical solution to the problem was to postulate the operation of at least three interrelated mechanisms in speech behavior: *determining tendency*, *priming of expressive units*, and *schema of order* (the last of which also may be termed the *syntax of the act*). The determining tendency represents the idea or semantic value to be expressed; the priming mechanism arouses and selects the appropriate linguistic units (still cotemporal and hence unordered); and the schema of order, or syntax, performs the actual seriation of the aroused and selected units

ERRORS IN SERIAL ORDERING

Another significant failing of the associative chain hypothesis pertains to the errors that frequently occur in serial ordering, for example, *spoonerisms*. Lashley noted that spoonerisms often take the form of anticipatory errors, and this consideration is one reason for his belief that the units in a phonetic string are *primed* (partially activated) before seriation is imposed. The consensus among writers on speech seems to be that models of speech production should account for the errors in serial ordering——or at least for some of them. Certain errors, such as Fromkin's (1971) report of "a laboratory in our own computer," may be outside the realm of a speech production model if they are thought to be imposed at a higher linguistic (or psychological) level. For that matter, Whitaker (1970) seems to allow (though not necessarily to recommend) that a model of speech production might ignore errors of serial ordering altogether, under the assumption that they occur as the *input* to the speech production mechanism.

The admissability of errors in serial ordering as data for speech production models may be determined partly with reference to the factors that appear to govern the occurrence of such errors. Accounts of reversals and similar errors are available in Boomer and Laver (1968), Fromkin (1971), and MacKay (1970). As a preliminary note to a discussion of tongue slips, the words of Boomer and Laver are used to formulate the following definition: *Tongue slips are transient malfunctions of the sequencing mechanism of speech production.*

From their analyses of tongue slips, Boomer and Laver developed a number of statistical "laws" that govern the occurrence of such errors. Several of the laws relate to the existence of tonic (stressed) words and tone groups (stress groupings or patterns):

1. Slips involve the tonic word in a tone group, such that a stressed word is either the origin or the target of the error.
2. Both the target and the origin are located in the same tone group.
3. In the case of exceptions to Law 2, the target and origin are found in the tonic word of their respective tone groups.
4. Reversals occur for origin and target syllables that are metrically similar, with errors appearing most frequently for elements in a pair of stressed syllables, less frequently for elements in a pair of unstressed syllables, and least frequently for elements in a stressed—unstressed pair.

The factor of stress also is conspicuous in the serial errors reported by MacKay (1970) and Fromkin (1971). Fromkin's data disclose that the overall stress pattern of an utterance may be retained even though entire words are interchanged, as in the case of "a laboratory in our own computer." She took this result to mean that lexical selection is made after decisions regarding syntax and stress pattern. The joint significance of tongue slips and stress patterns to models of speech production was voiced by Boomer and Laver (1968), who concluded that the stressed word "has a phonological, syntactic and semantic predominance *matched* by an analogous neurophysiological prominence, coded in the brain as part of the articulatory programme" (p. 8).

Boomer and Laver continued with two other laws for the phenomena of serial errors:

5. Segmental slips occupy the same syllable position; for example, initial segments of the origin syllable replace initial segments of the target syllable.
6. Segmental slips do not violate the phonological constraints of the speaker's language; they obey "phonologically orthodox sequence rules" (p. 7).

Similar results have been reported by MacKay (1970) and Fromkin (1971). These two laws are compelling statements of the interaction between phonological regularities and motor control in the creation of seriation errors. Of particular interest is Law 6 and Whitaker's (1970) parallel dictum: ". . . regardless of the error or cause of error, the output (at the vocal tract) will be an admissible articulatory sequence in the language" (p. 6). For that matter, studies of aphasic transformations, including neologisms in jargoned speech, reveal that the output sequences are nearly always in accord with the phonological system of the speaker's native language (Lecours and Lhermitte, 1969; Lhermitte, Lecours, and Bertaux, 1969; Buckingham and Kertesz, 1974). In commenting upon their analyses, Lhermitte, Lecours, and Bertaux concluded that "certain of the neurophysiological mechanisms which subtend normal speech production are acting simultaneously on different claviers of linguistic units; i.e., on different stocks of progressively simpler or progressively more complex linguistic units" (pp. 415—416). This summary statement expresses the complexity of the serial ordering problem and reinforces Lashley's rejection of chain mechanisms as the responsible strategy.

It is striking that sequencing errors seem to occur as the result of confusions of words, syllables, phonemes, and features. Apparently, lapses in the control mechanism do not result in a complete disorganization of speech movements but, rather, in a confusion of rather abstract control elements, each of which retains its integrity. Thus, the ultimate motor program of speech is slave to phonetic propriety or, to put it in other words, the motor commands to the articulators are under the direction of units that are highly resistant to corruption or dissolution. The processes of speech production appear to be rather rigidly controlled by these units, with little freedom to fail their implementation, except for misordering.

PATTERNS OF COARTICULATION

Lenneberg (1967) and Ohala (1970) have commented upon a further difficulty of the associative chain concept of serial ordering: Forward (right-to-left) coarticulation is difficult to reconcile with a simple chaining strategy. For example, if the neural instructions for the phone /u/ in the word *stew* cannot be issued until after realization of the /t/, then how is it that anticipatory lip rounding for /u/ may begin during the /s/? Or how is it that anticipatory velopharyngeal opening may be observed during the /aI/ diphthong in the phrase *I intend*? Such coarticulatory patterns have been demonstrated in a number of studies, including Kozhevnikov and Chistovich (1965), Daniloff and Moll (1968), Amerman, Daniloff, and Moll (1970), Moll and Daniloff (1971), Kent, Carney, and Severeid (1974), and Benguerel and Cowan (1974). Figure 3.2 provides several examples of *forward* (or *right-to-left*) coarticulation, in which an articulatory adjustment for one phonetic segment is anticipated during an earlier segment. For example, Part a of the figure is based on Benguerel and Cowan's report that anticipa-

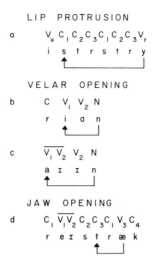

Figure 3.2 Some examples of forward coarticulation. The anticipation of a given articulatory property is shown by the arrow under each phonetic transcription. For example, in (a), the property of lip protrusion associated with vowel /y/ begins to appear with the first consonant in the six-consonant sequence. Similarly, in (b), the velar opening associated with the nasal /n/ begins to appear during the vowel /i/. Phonetic categories are indicated for each sound as follows: V_n ($n = 1, 2, \ldots$), a particular vowel; $V\mu$, an unrounded vowel; Vr, a rounded vowel; C_n, a particular nonnasal consonant; N, a nasal consonant; and $\overline{V_1V_2}$, a diphthong. The illustrations are based on the data of (a) Benguerel and Cowan (1974), (b) Moll and Daniloff (1971), (c) Kent, Carney, and Severeid (1974), and (d) Amerman, Daniloff, and Moll (1970).

tory lip protrusion for a rounded vowel in French may begin during the first consonant in a sequence constituted of an unrounded vowel, six consonants, and a rounded vowel. The other parts of the figure illustrate forward coarticulations occurring for the velum and jaw. Similar effects operate in the opposite direction, so that an articulatory adjustment for one segment may be carried over to a later segment (the phenomenon of *backward*, or *left-to-right*, coarticulation).

Lenneberg (1967) has discussed a related problem that has to do with neural transmission times. Because the peripheral nerves differ in length and diameter, it is conceivable that the order of correlated neuronal events may not be the same as the order of correlated articulatory events. For example, he wrote that "the anatomy of the nerves suggests that innervation time for intrinsic laryngeal muscles may easily be up to 30 msec longer than innervation time for muscles in and around the oral cavity" (p. 96).

SUPRASEGMENTAL ASPECTS OF SPEECH

Ohala (1970) has raised still another objection to the associative chain hypothesis, commenting that using this control strategy, one would have difficulty in accounting for changes in the rate of speaking. In making this complaint, Ohala envisaged the simplest form of the chaining hypothesis, such that delays associated with successive movements are determined completely by neural transit times. The same problem may arise with other voluntary alterations of the timing of speech, including changes in stress patterns and the imitation of dialectal variations.

Chaining and Preprogramming in Some Recent Models

CONTEXT-SENSITIVE ASSOCIATIVE THEORY

Despite Lashley's thoughtful rejection of the associative chain hypothesis, it is not a neglected possibility in recent models for the serial ordering of speech. Wickelgren (1969) questioned Lashley's categorization of diverse behaviors as problems of serial order and argued that *noncreative* behaviors, such as the pronunciation of words, should be treated separately from *creative* behaviors. Wickelgren also disputed one of Lashley's unstated assumptions about the neural coding of noncreative behavior, namely, that behavior sequences are composed of elementary motor responses (emr's) that are context-invariant. Then, maintaining that Lashley had succeeded in rejecting only one particular associative chain theory, Wickelgren proposed an alternative, the *context-sensitive associative theory*. This theory "assumes that serial order is encoded by means of associations between context-sensitive elementary motor responses" (p. 1), with the total set of such emr's constituting "the basic code for speech at the central articulatory level" (p. 2). The individual emr's can be viewed as context-sensitive allophones that serve as the basic units of production.

Wickelgren conceived of these internal representatives of speech in the following way. First, let us assume that the letters x, y, and z designate emr's in a particular phonetic system. Then, context-sensitive emr's can be given a notation such as $_yx_z$, where y and z are the left- and right-hand environments, respectively, of the unit x. This notation is intended to represent the belief that the internal representation for a given x is different with each change in its immediate bilateral context. The various x's, for example, $/_yx_z/$, $/_zx_y/$, $/x_y/$, and $/_zx/$, constitute a finite set of psychological equivalence classes formed from an infinitude of physical response sequences. To demonstrate the applicability of the context-sensitive coding strategy to the problem of serial ordering, Wickelgren took the example of phonemic anagrams, /strʌk/ and /krʌst/, which could not be ordered differentially if priming (partial activation) occurred for all the elements at once and if the elements were not context-sensitive. In Wickelgren's theory, the *word representative* (apparently meaning the lexical selection that corresponds to a given semantic value) effects a partial activation of the unordered set of context-sensitive emr representatives. With the proposed coding system, the unordered set for the word /strʌk/ is not identical to that for the word /krʌst/: the former set is $/_\#s_t, \, _st_r, \, _tr_\Lambda, \, _r\Lambda_k, \, _\Lambda k_\#/$, whereas the latter set is $/_\#k_r, \, _kr_\Lambda, \, _r\Lambda_s, \, _\Lambda s_t, \, _st_\#/$. Hence, the partial activation of the unordered set of context-sensitive emr's is sufficient to achieve a correct ordering of the internal representatives.

Recognizing that his theory suffers from a lack of economy in the internal (neural) representation of speech, Wickelgren sought to show that the number of context-sensitive emr's (estimated to be about 10^6 for English) does not place an excessive demand on cortical functioning. In so doing, he unfortunately implicates that each emr is stored in one neuron, although this tactic of numerical equivalence violates current notions about cortical functioning (Halwes and Jenkins, 1971). One also may criticize Wickelgren's assumption of context-sensitive allophones, for he maintained that *bilateral coarticulation effects* (i.e., the effects of the immediate left- and right-hand phonetic elements) are all that need to be considered. To the contrary, data reveal that coarticulation effects may reach to elements that are three to six positions removed from a given segment (Kozhevnikov and Chistovich, 1965; Daniloff and Moll, 1968; Kent, Carney, and Severeid, 1974; Benguerel and Cowan, 1974). Given this expanded domain of coarticulation, Wickelgren would be forced to increase substantially the minimum number of emr's necessary for the coding of speech, perhaps to the point of creating unsolvable problems in the storage and retrieval of the fundamental speech units.

In a criticism of Wickelgren's theory, Halwes and Jenkins (1971) did not present a formal alternative but they did suggest some directions of thought that may result in a successful model. The authors condemned theories of speech production based on *the associative tradition* in psychology and argued for models in which the responses "are not 'looked up' in a vast rote memory and emitted serially but, rather, are generated by a complex processor operating on abstract entities and emitted by a very complicated series of transformations—transformations that by their very nature cannot even be considered in an associative theory" (p. 128). A glimpse into the nature of the suggested models can be had by noting the two *empirical inadequacies* that Halwes and Jenkins found in Wickelgren's theory. The first of these is the "inability to account for the systematic relationships between events at the phonetic level and events at higher linguistic levels," and the second is the "inability to account for the systematic interactions among events within the phonetic level" (p. 126). The crux of Halwes and Jenkins' complaint is that the context-sensitive associative chain theory ignores important regularities in speech production, among them being the morphological variations in phonology (e.g., plural formation), the acquisition of *pig Latins*, the ability to talk with the teeth clenched, and the ability to talk at different rates and with different degrees of effort.

Halwes and Jenkins' attack on the context-sensitive associative chain theory because of its failure "to account for orderly syntactic relations among phonological events" (p. 126) perhaps reflects too severe a demand on a model of speech production. Whereas a model should account for motor events that *correspond* to phonological regularities, it may be asking too much for the model to *generate* the phonological regularities. At the risk of confusing a grammar (a theory of structure) with a psychological theory, it is reasonable to allow that the input units to a model of speech production have been subjected to allophonic rules contained within the phonology rather than the phonetics (Tatham, 1970). On the other hand, Halwes and Jenkins are justified in criticizing Wickelgren's theory for its inability to explain such speech phenomena as the imitation of other speakers, the manifold variations in speaking rate and vocal effort, and the general problem of *motor equivalence* in which diverse motor responses may achieve the same phonetic consequence.

SPEECH AS A GRAMMATICAL RECODING

Halwes and Jenkins (1971) apparently ally themselves with the position taken by Mattingly and Liberman (1969) and Liberman (1970), who reject the notion that speech is a simple cipher and argue that "the interconversion of phonetic segment and sound is a grammatical recoding, similar in complexity and form to syntax and phonology" (Liberman, 1970, p. 304). In discussing this recoding process, Liberman recognized the interaction of syllables, phones, and features. The features may be called *phonetic* in order to distinguish them from the *distinctive* features of Jakobson, Fant, and Halle (1952), the major difference being that the phonetic features are narrower and more concrete. Each feature is identified with a unitary nervous activity at a relatively high level of control, and several of these features taken together constitute a phone. A feature is thought to have a corresponding characteristic muscle gesture at the articulatory level; these component gestures are largely independent and potentially coincident. A strategy responsible for phone-to-gesture conversion determines the *timing* of the articulatory gestures, apparently operating so as to optimize the patterns of coincidence or mutual overlapping. Syllables are introduced into this schema as follows: "the features that constitute the segments are organized in production into . . . syllabic bundles, each consisting of overlapped and largely independent articulatory components" (Liberman, 1970, p. 313). It appears that the organization of segments into syllables is accomplished at the level of the phone-to-gesture conversion; thus, syllables are entirely a consequence of the organization of speech and have no bearing on the structure of higher-level linguistic operations.

Although Liberman did not provide a definition of the term *syllable*, his use of the word in describing speech production is such as to predict definite constraints on the interval of co-occurrence of features, that is, an upper bound on the range of coarticulatory phenomena. Since each feature has an associated characteristic muscle gesture, and since the component gestures are organized in overlapping fashion *within* syllables, definite points of discontinuity must occur *between* syllables.

It is worth remarking here that syllables are both troublesome and attractive in the development of models of speech production. Whitaker (1970) sums up the current status of the syllable thus: "Syllables have remarkably little usefulness in linguistic models but apparently a great deal of usefulness in speech production models" (p. 9). Tatham (1970) seemed to be in agreement when he commented that "although it is possible to construct a phonological component based on syllable segments (or segments of a similar kind) this is a theoretically clumsy and nonproductive concept in abstract phonological theory" (p. 72). (Fudge (1969), however, has argued to the contrary.) The employment of syllables at the motor level as a means of imposing cohesion for segment groupings (such as a word-initial CV combination) was considered elegant and productive by Tatham. Evidence that syllabic structure is important in speech production has been reported by Kozhevnikov and Chistovich (1965), Lehiste (1972), and MacKay (1974), to mention but a few.

Perhaps then, syllable units operate at the interface between decisions that are properly linguistic and decisions that are properly neuromotor. The problem of serial ordering in speech conceivably could be resolved, at least partly, through the sequential organization of syllabic structures. That is, some seriative decisions may be accomplished by operations performed on units that are larger than phone size, leaving the seriation of intrasyllabic segments as a residual problem. Indeed, two recent models of speech production, to be discussed below, employ jointly the concepts of syllabicity and rhythm to achieve a hierarchical solution to the problem of serial ordering.

SPEECH AS A RHYTHMIC STRUCTURE

Among the many ideas to be found in Lashley's (1951) paper is the concept of rhythmic action. Lashley assigned great importance to this concept and suggested that rhythm is a substratum for virtually all perceptual and motor activities. We may define *rhythm* as *temporal patterning* and note that this definition implies nonsequential dependencies among the elements in a sequence. The resolution of nonsequential dependencies is beyond the capability of simple associative chain mechanisms but within the capability of a hierarchical or preprogramming strategy. Rhythm appears to hold great explanatory power for a number of perceptual and motor skills: Neisser (1967) has speculated upon rhythmic patterning as a factor in echoic memory and speech perception, and Lenneberg (1967) and Allen (1972) have discussed the relevance of this concept to problems in speech production.

Martin (1972) defined rhythm as the "relative timing between adjacent and nonadjacent elements in a behavior sequence," (p.487) and commented as follows on the rhythmic structure of speech.

> "Rhythm" here as in conventional usage refers to the pattern of accents/stresses on a string of syllables. The rhythmic pattern as defined here is assumed ordinarily to consist of up to seven syllables or so. . . In its usage here, the term "accent" is equivalent to linguistic "stress" except that (formally) accent level is applied relationally to *all* syllables in a pattern. [pp. 492—493]

According to Martin, not only is the timing of speech preset by central timing mechanisms, but the temporal organization of an utterance is dominated by accented elements, which are planned before other elements. The conception of accented syllables as the primary targets in the organization of the articulatory program leads to a prediction that decisions concerning *content* words (usually accented syllables) are prior to decisions concerning *function* words (usually unaccented syllables). Martin proposed that the actual rhythmic pattern for an utterance can be determined through the use of either of two obligatory rules which underlie a diversity of surface forms. These rules express the relation between the relative accent levels and the relative timing of the elements in a sequence. Rhythm assignment is supposed to operate on syllable loci (in particular, their vowel onsets), but Martin only hinted as to the structure of the syllable itself; for example, he cited some work by Tatham (1970) to the effect that vowels and their preceding consonants are programmed together.

Martin is not alone in arguing for a syllable-based programming that is matched against a rhythmic structure. Kozhevnikov and Chistovich (1965) elaborated a model of speech production that incorporates syllabic units in a rhythmic sequence called a *syntagma* (which, like Martin's *rhythmic pattern*, has an average length of about seven syllables). The conceptual similarity between the model proposed by Martin and the model of Kozhevnikov and Chistovich is apparent in Kozhevnikov and Christovich's claim that "only sequences of syllable commands are rhythmically organized; individual movements within a syllable which provide for the transition from consonant to vowel adhere to their own intrasyllabic laws" (p. 91). These investigators seem to echo Lashley when they wrote: ". . . the rhythmic figure [pattern] actually exists as some independent sign of a word (phrase) and . . . consequently it is necessary to assume the presence in the nervous system of special setups [groups of interrelated neurons] which provide for the generation of complex rhythmic sequences" (p. 115). Kozhevnikov and Chistovich regarded the basic elements of speech programming to be simple consonant–vowel (CV) combinations and suggested that more complex combinations (e.g., CCV and CCCV) are merely CV groupings assembled so that certain CV units begin before the preceding CV unit is complete. Hence, a CCV combination may be represented as:

$$CCV = CX + CV$$

where X designates a reduced vowel (a vowel that is not physically realized in the speech output). A basic prediction of the Kozhevnikov–Chistovich theory is that the motor programming of speech is discontinuous at certain points, namely, following any vowel segment. This prediction follows from the hypothesis that consonants are programmed with a following vowel. As shown by the coarticulatory patterns in Figure 3.2, this prediction does not agree with results for American English, since forward coarticulation may reach beyond a vowel segment, as in the anticipatory velar opening that may occur during the /aI/ diphthong in the phrase *I intend*.

INTEGRATED MODELS FOR THE DESIGN AND
REGULATION OF MOTOR SEQUENCES IN SPEECH

Possibly, *both* preprogramming and chaining are involved in speech production, so we need not assume that one strategy operates to the exclusion of the other. Schmidt (1971), writing on the general problem of timing of motor responses, has suggested that timing may be governed by programs in some circumstances and by proprioceptive feedback in others. In fact, experimental evidence for both strategies has been observed in the study of speech (Rapp, 1971; Leanderson and Lindblom, 1972; Wright, 1974). Insofar as the employment of programs and feedback is concerned, the motor control of speech may be roughly similar to other motor activities, such as locomotion. If so, Easton's (1972) comment on the latter is of some interest: "The currently accepted notion is that, while peripheral input may regulate motor acts, the essential design of the act is set, or programmed, within the central nervous system" (p. 594). Easton proposed that certain basic reflexes (called *coordinative structures*) may serve as the language for the composition of the motor programs. Similarly, Fitts (1964) has mentioned a hierarchical system of motor control in which higher centers select the correct program and lower centers, which contain the program, execute it upon command.

Such a view of motor control is compatible with much of the existing evidence since it allows for the occurrence of nonsequential dependencies in motor patterns, but also for the disruption of speech by the elimination or alteration of feedback (Yates, 1963; Smith, 1966). The actual degree of dependence on feedback is uncertain, but at the least, peripheral input would provide a *reset* capability to the higher centers that select the motor programs. Preservation of rhythmic sequence may require that such feedback be at least momentarily operational. Continuous disruption of feedback may interfere critically with the reset facility, as perhaps is the case with delayed auditory feedback. In this connection, Chistovich and Kozhevnikov (1969) deliberated the role of feedback in speech and arrived at the conclusion that continuous feedback is not essential to the process of seriation:

> It is not necessary to suppose the obligatory presence of feedback which acts during the fulfillment of the movements. This is especially clear in the case of so-called ballistic movements . . . including rather rapid articulatory movements. The controlling signals, in this case, are preprogrammed for rather long sequences of complex motor acts [p. 314]

Hutchinson and Putnam (1974) concluded from aerodynamic recordings of speech produced under oral anesthetization that peripheral information is important for articulatory positioning but not for the temporal sequencing aspect of speech. Furthermore, Tingley and Allen (1975) found no evidence of peripheral feedback as a means of speech timing control even in children as young as 5 years of age. Perhaps feedback control is important at younger ages, before motor programs have been established. In this connection, DiSimoni's (1974) work indicates that timing control may follow a developmental sequence in which certain durational and timing patterns are acquired before others. For example, 3-year-old children behaved like adults in adjusting phoneme durations to variations in utterance length, but they did not adjust vowel durations to certain contextual influences. Further research on children's timing patterns may tell us not only about the importance of feedback in speech development but also about hierarchies in the acquisition of motor programs.

FEATURE CODING IN MODELS OF SPEECH PRODUCTION

Several models of speech production rely on features as an input to the system of motor control. Although features are not necessarily associated with preprogramming rather than chaining models, most of the work on feature coding speaks to issues in preprogramming. Several approaches have been taken to the use of features (see, for example, Tatham, 1970; Liberman, 1970; Stevens, 1972), but the work of Henke (1966) has been particularly influential in several recent models of speech articulation.

Henke developed a computer simulation of articulation on the idea that segments or portions of the articulatory apparatus continuously are seeking goals, with changes in these goals occurring abruptly in time. Hence, the operation of the model is compatible with a segmental, or unit-by-unit, input. Subtargets for individual segments of the vocal tract are defined by features associated with each input unit. Because the various features are not always specified for any given input unit, the model is equipped with a look-ahead operator that scans the forthcoming units to determine the next specified value of a feature. Thus, forward coarticulation comes about as the result of a forward scan based on compatibility criteria for feature sets. A feature value can be assumed earlier than its required appearance so long as the articulation implied by that value does not contradict current articulatory requirements.

Henke's idea of a look-ahead operator based on feature values has been adopted by several writers to explain the occurrence of forward coarticulation. For example, such a mechanism has been used to explain velar coarticulation (Moll and Daniloff, 1971) and coarticulation of lip protrusion (Benguerel and Cowan, 1974). However, these applications of a feature-coding model are not entirely satisfactory, for reasons discussed by Kent, Carney, and Severeid (1974). A major limitation of this model is its inability to predict the fine aspects of articulatory timing, partly because most feature-coding schemes carry information only about the sequencing of rather abstract entities, usually phonemes. Thus, timing predictions often apply to temporal quanta of phone size, and the timing of submovements within a phonetic interval is not resolved. A second limitation of a feature-coding model is that coarticulation is explained solely on the basis of compatibility criteria for feature sets. But evidence has been reported by Kent and Moll (1972) and by MacNeilage (1972) that anticipatory articulations can occur in the face of apparently contradictory feature values. Hence, simple compatibility criteria may not provide an adequate explanation of the articulatory patterns in speech.

The Problem of Articulatory Representation

The Assumption of a Serial Input

As indicated in the preceding remarks on serial ordering, models of speech production almost invariably assume an input of segmented strings—whether the strings consist of allophones, phonemes, syllables, or whatever. Hence, investigators of speech generally suppose that the process is controlled by discrete units, even though it is recognized that invariant correlates of the control units are very difficult to identify at the peripheral level (MacNeilage, 1970; Harris, 1976). In order to preserve the assumption of a finite set of invariant control units in the face of great peripheral variance, speech investigators usually have attributed the variance to (*1*) mechano-inertial constraints, (*2*) response limitations of the nervous system, and (*3*) temporal overlapping of the vocal tract responses to sequential input units (MacNeilage, 1970). These factors are invoked to explain why a given speech element does not present the same physiological or acoustic appearance when produced in various phonetic environments, with differing degrees of stress, or at altered rates of speaking (Lindblom, 1963; Stevens and House; 1963, Öhman, 1966; MacNeilage and DeClerk, 1969; Kent and Netsell, 1972).

The assignment of the peripheral variability to the listed sources is a step of major consequence. Consider that, for most practical purposes, the student of speech is able to make observations only at the output (response) of the speech production mechanism. Thus, he must infer *both* the system characteristic (the transfer function) and the input (the drive) to that system. Obviously, this inferential problem is insoluble without the imposition of further assumptions to (*1*) constrain the class of transfer functions, or (*2*) constrain the set of admissible inputs. For example, Öhman (1967) made an assumption of the first kind when he considered articulatory behavior to be governed by constant coefficient linear differential equations of second order. Assumptions of the second kind are readily apparent as requirements for, for example, a string of extrinsic allophones (Tatham, 1970), a string of phonemes (Mattingly, 1968; Mac-Neilage, 1970), or a string of syllables (Kozhevnikov and Chistovich, 1965).

Tatham (1970) discussed problems that are inherent in the choice of the input unit and the transfer function in models of speech production. He cautioned that it is not enough that a model be mathematically tractable, for there is "no internal way of evaluating the contending input types" and similarly there is "no way of evaluating the various contending transfer functions" (p. 70). Imagine two hypothetical models, one of which assumes a phonemic input and a particular transfer function *A*, whereas the other operates with a syllabic input and a fundamentally different transfer function *B*. By what criteria should we choose one model over the other? Tatham claimed that there are no internal criteria and concluded: "Accordingly the transfer function must not simply be a mathematical formula which happens to provide the correct output from a particular input: there must be exterior constraints on this function" (p. 70). The candidates that Tatham proposed for such external conditions are mechano-inertial and linguistic constraints.

Control Variables at the Periphery

In his review of speech production models, MacNeilage (1970) discussed two positions concerning the nature of assumed phonemic invariance at the peripheral level. The first maintains that invariance is to be found in the *motor commands* that underlie speech production; the strongest advocates of this view are the scientists of Haskins Laboratories (see, for example, Liberman, Cooper, Harris, and MacNeilage, 1962; Liberman, Cooper, Shankweiler, and Studdert-Kennedy, 1967). The second position is that the invariance exists in the specification of vocal tract configurations (targets or goals) that correspond to the input units (see, for example, Lindblom, 1963; Chistovich and Kozhevnikov, 1969; Stevens, 1972). The two positions are discussed in more detail below.

MOTOR COMMAND MODELS

In order to gather support for the idea that invariance lies in the motor commands of speech production, the Haskins researchers have conducted a number of electro-myographic (EMG) investigations in the hope of identifying consistent EMG correlates of phoneme production. In reviewing the history of this research, MacNeilage (1970) questioned the early claims of success and summarized the investigative effort as follows: "Paradoxically, the main result of the attempt to demonstrate invariance at the EMG level has not been to find such invariance but to demonstrate the ubiquity of variability" (p. 184). The variability arises for several reasons, including the far-reaching effects of contextual variations and the flexibility of the articulatory adjustments for a given sound (as in making the same sound with different positions of the mandible). Cooper (1972), a proponent of the motor theory, acknowledged that muscle contractions (and by implication the concomitant EMG activity) "may be variable in amount due to preplanning at the next higher level or to local adjustment, via gamma-efferent feedback, to produce only so much contraction as is needed to achieve a target length" (p. 33). However, he argued that some constancy can be expected with regard to the muscles that are activated and to the temporal pattern of their activation. Definitive data on this problem await extensive EMG studies of the speech musculature.

MacNeilage (1970) has argued against the motor command model on other grounds: He contrasts the difficulty that a speaker has in performing two production tasks, one of which is to "make a vowel 'half way' between two vowels he habitually uses" (p. 189), and the other of which is to utter any given vowel with his jaws clenched. MacNeilage noted that the latter is much more easily accomplished than the former, and he interpreted the difference in difficulty as evidence for a target model rather than a motor command model since the motor command model predicts about equal difficulty in the two tasks, whereas the target model predicts that production of the alien vowel would be the more difficult (owing to the necessity of formulating a new target). However, it is possible that the difference in difficulty can be explained by other factors, such as the speaker's familiarity or nonfamiliarity with the requisite motor adjustments.

GOAL OR TARGET MODELS

Models of this variety differ from one another in certain respects, but the discussion here is sufficiently general so as to do justice to most of them. These models assume that the system is working to achieve a specified vocal tract configuration that corresponds to a particular input unit or a particular combination of input units. The control at the highest level of the model is exercised through a finite set of static configurations of the vocal tract. One way of viewing the modeling process is to postulate that the specified vocal tract configurations serve as state descriptions for the articulatory apparatus, that is, as overall configurative goals (cf. Henke, 1966). The state description, in turn, may be interpreted as a set of subtargets for the various parts of the vocal apparatus. These subtargets, defined for articulatory segments, can be used to calculate the motor commands that shape the vocal tract as required.

MacNeilage (1970) assumed a *space coordinate system*, much like that proposed by Lashley (1951), to develop a target-based model in which the phonological input is translated into a series of spatial target specifications. The targets, as MacNeilage put it, "would result in a series of demands on a motor system control mechanism to generate movement command patterns which would allow the articulators to reach the specified targets in the required order" (p. 189). MacNeilage considered this process to be a solution to the problem of serial ordering, but it is not clear how the target notion alone obviates the need for the other mechanisms proposed by Lashley. Indeed, the spatial coordinate system, without determining tendency, priming of units, and syntax, would seem capable of only a partial solution to the problem of serial order.

The strongest suggestion that MacNeilage makes in this regard is that the mechanism may generate movement command patterns well in advance of their actual employment as muscle contractions; hence, he seems to argue for preprogramming rather than feedback strategy. On the other hand, MacNeilage's speculations about the role of open-loop and closed-loop control really seem more germane to articulatory positioning than to seriation phenomena.

The model of Chistovich and Kozhevnikov (1969) also predicates goals as the basis for control of the speech mechanism. A goal in their conception is a "description of motor acts abstracted from the concrete executive means" (p. 314) and is considered to be "the basis for choosing or 'calculating' the concrete combination of motor commands to be sent to muscles in accordance with the momentary state of the whole system" (p. 314). Although these authors did not explicitly mention spatial targets, it is clear that they did not expect to find invariant motor commands associated with speech units, since the motor commands must be computed on the basis of an abstract description of the desired articulatory result. (Conceivably, the goal itself may be constrained powerfully by the potential for motor realization, so that *generalized* motor processes might appear as invariant attributes of the control units.)

The MacNeilage and Chistovich–Kozhevnikov models represent attempts to account for the control of speech production at the level of the musculature. In addition, a number of attempts have been made to model speech production at the articulatory or vocal tract level; these endeavors have been prompted largely by the desire to construct articulatory synthesizers (vocal tract analogs).

Henke's (1966) model for the computer simulation of speech articulation realizes the articulatory structures as composites of numerous tiny adjacent segments, each of which continually seeks an absolute position and shape (where shape should be understood as position relative to the adjacent segments). Structural integrity is assured by the action of *physical adjacency constraints* which delimit the shapes for a given articulatory segment. But aside from such restrictions on the structural contour, the individual segments are under separate high-level control so that a large number of control parameters are necessary for implementation of the model.

In another articulatory-analog model of speech production, Coker (1968) attempted to simplify the problem of articulatory control by assigning the control parameters to the position of the tongue body, the lip protrusion, the lip rounding, the place and degree of tongue tip constriction, and the degree of velar coupling. This model has proved useful in the determination of the physiological constraints, movement priorities, and time constants that characterize the major articulators (Coker, 1968; Flanagan, Coker, Rabiner, Schafer, and Umeda, 1970). Mermelstein (1973) introduced a nine-parameter articulatory model that capitalizes upon certain positional dependencies between articulators: in particular, the dependency of tongue and lip positions on the position of the mobile jaw. Using these nine variables, Mermelstein developed a dynamic model for the articulation of VCV utterances. Rather than assign precise targets for all of the control parameters during consonant production, Mermelstein established levels of *pertinence* that distinguish articulators with exact targets, articulators with target regions, and articulators with no targets whatsoever. Hence, the levels of pertinence can account for some of the variations that occur in articulatory positioning. The problem of articulatory variation is challenging for any model of speech production and has particularly compelling implications for certain models of muscular control, which will be discussed later.

THE QUANTAL THEORY OF SPEECH ARTICULATION

Stevens (1968, 1972b) has introduced a *quantal theory* of speech production based on the supposedly nonlinear relationships between articulation and acoustic output. Stevens argued that, for some articulatory configurations, even a slight change in a given articulatory property may have a relatively large acoustic consequence. But for other articulatory configurations, large changes in a given articulatory property may have little effect on the acoustic signal. Hence, the acoustic signal is more sensitive to some articulatory changes than to others, which means that articulatory—acoustic conversions are nonlinear. Given these inherent nonlinearities, a speaker presumably "manipulates his speech generating mechanism to select sounds with well-defined acoustic attributes that are relatively insensitive to small perturbations in articulation" (Stevens, 1972b, p. 65).

This quantal theory has important implications for a variety of problems, ranging from speech development in the infant, to phoneme selection in natural languages, to restrictions on coarticulatory interactions. For example, the quantal theory allows the hypothesis that an infant might be predisposed to the development of certain sounds, namely, those that have a stable articulatory—acoustic conversion. These sounds also would be natural choices for a language's phonetic inventory. In addition, the nonlinearities between articulatory and acoustic variables would place limits on the permissible ranges of articulatory positioning for a given sound. Thus, coarticulatory variations might be determined in part by the tolerance that sounds allow for deviations in articulation. Of course, many coarticulatory patterns do have marked acoustic consequences, so that coarticulation is by no means fully explained by articulatory— acoustic tolerances. But the quantal theory certainly has implications for the precision of articulation that is required for speech, since it states that apparently continuous variations in the place of articulation are not matched by continuous variations in the acoustic signal. Quantal effects may be an important consideration in the specification of targets and goals in the motor control of speech.

Open-Loop versus Closed-Loop Models

One of the earliest closed-loop models of speech production was the servosystem model introduced by Fairbanks (1954), who thought that the process of speech is dependent upon feedback that allows for the generation of an error signal to produce the desired output. More recent work on the notion of closed-loop control has emphasized the contribution of proprioceptive mechanisms (especially muscle spindles) to the regulation of articulatory movements. A large body of literature exists on the topic of closed-loop strategies in motor control, and many of the developments from this active province of research have been discussed with respect to speech production (Öhman, 1967; Tatham, 1969; MacNeilage, 1970; Abbs, 1971; Bowman, 1971;

Sussman, 1972). A block diagram of a closed-loop control system for speech is presented in Figure 3.3, which shows a forward path composed of a muscular control system and articulator positions, and a feedback path composed of muscle spindles.

Some writers have developed Lashley's suggestion that certain aspects of motor control rest on integrative processes that employ systems of space coordinates. Thus, Sussman (1972, p. 262) claims:

> The unique three-dimensional arrangement of the lingual muscle-spindle network is structurally organized to operate as a built-in geometric reference system. This network is capable of signaling higher brain centers as to the changing length, position, and rate of movement of the tongue during the articulatory motions of human speech.

Certainly, the idea of a control loop comprised of muscle spindles and fusimotor fibers is an attractive concept in accounting for the precision of motor performance in speech. Not only could the muscle spindles inform higher centers as to the mechanical state of the muscle, but the fusimotor fibers could afford control of the muscle's mechanical parameters, such as stiffness and damping (Tatham, 1969). The spindles and the fusimotor fibers may constitute a servomechanism (a closed-loop control system that provides for the regulation of position and a power amplification) by which the desired placement of the articulators could be ensured despite variations in phonetic context. But even if the muscle spindle does not function as a *follow-up length servo*, it can provide valuable information to the central nervous system concerning parameters of muscle contraction (Smith, 1973). The real importance of fusimotor contraction may lie in its ability to *bias* the muscle spindle so that the latter can operate over a wide range of muscle lengths. In order for the muscle spindle to furnish continuous information about muscle status, it is imperative that contraction of the muscle does not cause the spindle to become unloaded. Unloading can be prevented if the intrafusal fibers and the extrafusal fibers contract simul-

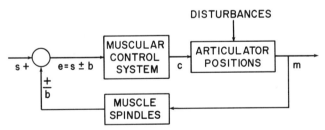

Figure 3.3 Block diagram of a closed-loop control system for speech, incorporating muscle spindles as the feedback elements. The forward path consists of a muscular control system and articulator positions, and the feedback path consists of the muscle spindles. The system has the capability of correcting for disturbances that are applied to it (a general property of closed-loop control systems). The signals or quantities identified by lowercase letters are: s, a reference or command signal from the highest level of motor control; b, a feedback signal which is a function of the controlled movement output m; e, an actuating signal or control action determined by the algebraic sum of the reference signal s plus or minus the feedback signal b; c, a control signal supplied by the muscular control system; and m, a controlled output of articulator movement. An undesired signal or disturbance quantity also may be included at its point of entry into the system (for example, as a perturbation of articulator position).

taneously. For a more thorough discussion of the possible role of muscle spindles in the motor control of speech, see the work of Bowman (1971) and Smith (1973).

The notion of bias in spindle operation has some intriguing implications for the control of articulation. It is conceivable that bias may be part of a system for adjustable feedback as well as being critical for the continuity of spindle feedback. Of note here are Tatham's (1970) attempts to explain the permissible variations in articulatory positioning. In so doing, he rejects simple nonadjustable feedback systems since feedback "cannot control the range of variation unless that feedback has been 'set' with respect to its limits" (p. 75). In making this point, Tatham observed that two languages, one with three palatal consonants and one with five palatal consonants, would share a target value for one consonant; nonetheless, the permissible range of articulator movement for that common sound will be greater for the language with three consonants than for the one with five consonants. He suggested that the best explanation for this situation is that an inertia-derived rule at the muscular level is constrained by a second, linguistically derived rule so that the error in motor control is limited by the phonetic requirements of the language. A biased muscle spindle may be part of the answer to Tatham's demand for an adjustable feedback control.

The role of peripheral feedback in the control of a motor response depends upon the nature of that response. Consider the different types of information required for the control of the following four types of movements: *(1)* static movement in carrying an object, such as a suitcase; *(2)* dynamic movement against resistance, as in pushing an object across a surface; *(3)* movements that involve both an effort exerted upon an object and precision of performance, as in sculpting or watchmaking; and *(4)* movements that are characterized by definite complex patterns but do not involve force directed against an external object, as in the case of speech movements. Konorski (1970) discussed these four types of movement with respect to the effective feedback required for each. The first two, carrying a suitcase and pushing an object, involve primarily joint feedback, with the major difference between them being that pushing an object also requires an estimation of the muscular effort needed. In the third example, that of sculpting or watchmaking, the effective resistance is provided not by an external object but by the contraction of antagonistic muscles. In the performance of these precise movements, joint feedback probably is overshadowed by muscle feedback, because limb position changes only slightly. Finally, in the case of the fourth example, speech movements, the resistance to movement is so slight that the muscular contractions are essentially isotonic, or constant in force. Thus, the feedback suited to the control of speech movements would concern length or position.

Recent experiments involving loading or perturbation have provided much of the evidence on the possibilities of peripheral feedback control for speech (Sears and Newsom-Davis, 1968; Smith and Lee, 1972; Bauer, 1974; Folkins and Abbs, 1975). Generally, these studies reveal that speech muscles are capable of compensating for unexpected loads or perturbations, with the latency of such compensatory response ranging from 15—20 msec for the lip to 33—80 msec for the respiratory system. Whether or not this capability is routinely exploited during speech remains to be determined.

Undoubtedly, the roles of feedforward and feedback systems in speech production will continue to be a lively area of investigation. Questions that bear critically on the controversy of open-loop versus closed-loop control include the following: If feedback is required for the control of speech, is the feedback continuous or noncontinuous? Is the feedback positive or negative? Which levels of the nervous system are involved in the feedback loops? Exactly what kind of information does the feedback convey? Is feedback relatively more important for the acquisition of speech patterns than for their maintenance? If both open-loop and closed-loop control are characteristic of speech production, how are the control systems integrated into a smoothly functioning unit?

Conclusions and Suggestions

This writer is sympathetic with Lashley's contention that the control of skilled behavior is hierarchical, that is, that motor programs are structured in advance for a motor sequence. It may be profitable to conceptualize the control of speech as a tree diagram that incorporates six levels: *(1)* syntagma, *(2)* accents or feet, *(3)* syllables, *(4)* allophones, *(5)* goals, and *(6)* motor commands (see Figure 3.4). This hierarchy is dominated by a rhythmic structure, the syntagma (Kozhevnikov and Chistovich, 1965), which corresponds to an operational memory of approximately seven syllables. Boomer and Laver (1968) have discussed a similar structure under the name of tone group. At the level of the feet (metric units), accents lend neurophysiological prominence to certain syllables and create units such as spondees, trochees, and dactyls. That is, the pattern of accents may be a simple succession or alternation or a complex hierarchy (Allen, 1972; Martin, 1972); in any case, the accents potentiate the motor programming of the syllables so designated. Potentiation of the accented syllables makes them dominant over unaccented syllables, and this hegemony survives to the lowest level of the tree, so that manifestations of accent may be found within motor responses of the vocal tract as well as within motor responses of the respiratory and phonatory systems (Kent and Netsell, 1972). The

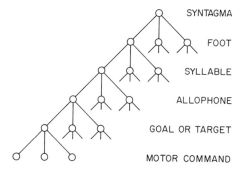

Figure 3.4 Tree diagram to illustrate one conception of the hierarchical organization of speech behavior. The three-way branching at each level is arbitrary and is not meant to suggest that trinary division necessarily occurs at a given node.

patterning of accents serves as a substrate for the neuromotor organization of speech behavior. One line of evidence for such organization is the apparent role of accents in the serial ordering of speech elements (Boomer and Laver, 1968; MacKay, 1970; Martin, 1972). The accent pattern is fundamental to the orchestration of motor responses in connected speech since it provides both organization and continuity to the component muscle activities.

The distribution of accents in the motor program of speech is syllable-bound, but a variety of syllabic forms (V, CV, VC, CCV, VCC, etc.) may be employed. Syllables are units of motor organization that bind allophonic segments by manipulations of goals, or articulatory targets. Although syllables are especially cohesive with respect to the integration of motor activities, they are not discontinuous units of articulation. Indeed, the integration of motor responses during speech need not be interrupted any more than is the integration of motor responses during other rhythmic activities. It is reasonable to expect that a certain degree of motor coherence must result from neural integration and from "the interplay of muscle contractions" (Eccles, 1969, p. 254). Naturally, there is an obvious interruption in motor integration whenever a speaker pauses to think of the proper word or to formulate a new thought.

The goals conceived of here are the fundamental control elements of speech production. A certain combination of goals constitutes a phoneme, but the motor integration within syllables allows goals to be modified both temporally and spatially. For example, the usual goal of the tongue tip for the stop /d/ is an alveolar contact, but this goal is changed to a dental contact whenever the stop is followed closely in time by a dental fricative, as in the word *width*. (It seems likely that dentalization for the stop could occur even if a word boundary intervenes between the stop and the fricative, but only if the rate of utterance is rapid.) The goals are logically prior to motor commands in that goals are articulatory targets that can be used to compute muscle forcing functions in the light of information about the momentary state of the vocal tract. The goals preserve the linguistic distinctions of phonetic features and allow the motor implementation of these distinctions.

Feedback operating at one or more neural levels probably is required to keep the central nervous system informed about the positions of the various structures involved in speech production. As mentioned previously, the exact nature of the feedback is uncertain. However, since the speech control mechanism seems to operate as a ballistic system governed by discrete command units, noncontinuous feedback probably would suffice (Tatham, 1970). A major role of feedback may be to maintain a reset facility that allows a motor program to be executed despite variations in articulatory positions or in the mechanical properties of the speech apparatus. Furthermore, as suggested by Hutchinson and Putnam (1974), peripheral information may contribute to the accuracy of articulatory positioning.

Some sort of space coordinate system (Lashley, 1951; MacNeilage, 1970) is necessary in order that the goals can be interpreted as sets of motor commands. For that matter, a framework for spatial reference would seem to allow a convenient interpretation of feedback for the purposes of deriving motor commands from goal specifications. Peripheral invariance is to be found in spatially defined goals and not in motor commands; this claim implies that goals ensure the best understanding of the process that transforms the phonetic message to a sequence of vocal tract shapes.

Articulatory goals allow for motor equivalence, that is, the accomplishment of a certain phonetic result by two or more motor patterns. Therefore, two speakers may not use exactly the same pattern of muscular activity to produce a given sound, and an individual speaker may adapt his motor patterns to contextual variables. Stevens' quantal theory of speech may help to explain the establishment of articulatory goals, since the presumably nonlinear relationships between articulation and acoustic output would guide a talker in identifying optimal articulatory placements as well as permissible ranges in articulatory positioning.

Of course, these final comments are conjecture. The evidence now at hand is incomplete, so that many hypotheses about the control of speech production await empirical data for their confirmation or dismissal. Judging from recent symposia on motor control, there appears to be a burgeoning interest in motor skills of all types. Accordingly, research on the motor control of speech should have an active milieu in the years ahead.

REFERENCES

Abbs, J. The influence of the gamma motor system on jaw movement during speech. Unpublished doctoral dissertation, University of Wisconsin, 1971.

Allen, G. D. The location of rhythmic stress beats in English: An experimental study. II. *Language and Speech*, 1972, *15*, 179—195.

Amerman, J. D., Daniloff, R. G., and Moll, K. L. Lip and jaw coarticulation for the phoneme /æ/. *Journal of Speech and Hearing Research*, 1970, *13*, 147—161.

Bauer, L. L. Peripheral control and mechanical properties of the lips during speech. Unpublished master's thesis, University of Wisconsin, 1974.

Benguerel, A. -P., and Cowan, H. A. Coarticulation of upper lip protrusion in French. *Phonetica*, 1974, *30*, 41—55.

Boomer, D. S., and Laver, J. D. M. Slips of the tongue. *British Journal of Disorders of Communication*, 1968, *3*, 2—12.

Bowman, J. P. *The muscle spindle and neural control of the tongue.* Springfield, Illinois: Charles C. Thomas, 1971.

Buckingham, H., and Kertesz, A. A linguistic analysis of fluent aphasia. *Brain and Language*, 1974, *1*, 43—62.

Chistovich, L. A., and Kozhevnikov, V. A. Some aspects of the physiological study of speech. In D. Proctor (Ed.), *Biocybernetics of the central nervous system.* Boston: Little, Brown, 1969, 305—321.

Coker, C. H. Speech synthesis with a parametric articulatory model. In *Proceedings of the Kyoto Speech Symposium*, A-4-1A-4-6, Kyoto, Japan, 1968. Also in J. L. Flanagan and L. R. Rabiner (Eds.), *Speech synthesis.* Stroudsburg, Pennsylvania: Dowden, Hutchinson, and Ross, 1973, 135—139.

Cooper, F. S. How is language conveyed by speech? In J. F. Kavanagh and I. G. Mattingly (Eds.), *Language by ear and by eye*: The relationship of speech and reading. Cambridge, Massachusetts: M.I.T. Press, 1972, 22—45.

Daniloff, R. G., and Moll, K. L. Coarticulation of lip rounding. *Journal of Speech and Hearing Research*, 1968, *11*, 707—721.

DiSimoni, F. G. Evidence for a theory of speech production based on observations of the speech of children. *Journal of the Acoustical Society of America*, 1974, *56*, 1919—1921.

Easton, T. A. On the normal use of reflexes. *American Scientist*, 1972, *60*, 591—599.

Eccles, J. C. The dynamic loop hypothesis of movement control. In K. N. Liebovic (Ed.), *Information processing in the nervous system.* New York: Springer-Verlag, 1969, 245—268.

Fairbanks, G. Systematic research in experimental phonetics. I. A theory of the speech mechanism as a servosystem. *Journal of Speech and Hearing Disorders*, 1954, *19*, 133—139.

Fitts, P. M. Perceptual-motor skill learning. In A. W. Melton (Ed.), *Categories of human learning*. New York: Academic Press, 1964, 244—285.

Flanagan, J. L., Coker, C. H., Rabiner, L. R., Schafer, R. W., and Umeda, N. Synthetic voices for computers. *IEEE Spectrum*, 1970, 7, 22—45.

Folkins, J. W., and Abbs, J. H. Lip and jaw motor control during speech: Responses to resistive loading of the jaw. *Journal of Speech and Hearing Research*, 1975, *18*, 207—220.

Fromkin, V. A. The non-anomalous nature of anomalous utterances. *Language*, 1971, *47*, 27—52.

Fudge, E. C. Syllables. *Journal of Linguistics*, 1969, *5*, 253—286.

Greenwald, A. G. Sensory feedback mechanisms in performance control: with special reference to the ideo-motor mechanism. *Psychological Review*, 1970, 77, 73—99.

Halwes, T., and Jenkins, J. J. Problem of serial order in behavior is not resolved by context-sensitive associative memory models. *Psychological Review*, 1971, *78*, 122—129.

Harris, K. S. Physiological aspects of articulatory behavior. In T. A. Sebeok (Ed.), *Current trends in linguistics*. Vol. XII. The Hague: Mouton, 1976.

Henke, W. L. Dynamic articulatory model of speech production using computer simulation. Unpublished doctoral dissertation, Massachusetts Institute of Technology, 1966.

Hutchinson, J. M., and Putnam, A. H. B. Aerodynamic aspect of sensory deprived speech. *Journal of the Acoustical Society of America*, 1974, *56*, 1612—1617.

Jakobson, R., Fant, C. G. M., and Halle, M. *Preliminaries to speech analysis*. Cambridge, Massachusetts: M. I. T. Press, 1952.

Keele, S. W. Movement control in skilled motor performance. *Psychological Bulletin*, 1968, *70*, 387—403.

Kent, R. D., Carney, P. J., and Severeid, L. R. Velar movement and timing: Evaluation of a model for binary control. *Journal of Speech and Hearing Research*, 1974, *17*, 470—488.

Kent, R. D., and Moll, K. L. Tongue body articulation during vowel and diphthong gestures. *Folia Phoniatrica*, 1972, *24*, 286—300.

Kent, R. D., and Netsell, R. Effects of stress contrasts on certain articulatory parameters. *Phonetica*, 1972, *24*, 23—44.

Konorski, J. The problem of the peripheral control of skilled movements. *International Journal of Neuroscience*, 1970, *1*, 39—50.

Kozhevnikov, V. A., and Chistovich, L. A. *Rech' Artikuliatsia i Vospriiatie*, Moscow-Leningrad. Transl. *Speech: Articulation and perception*. Washington, D.C.: Joint Publication Research Service, 1965.

Lashley, K. S. The problem of serial order in behavior. In L. A. Jeffress (Ed.), *Cerebral mechanisms in behavior*. New York: Wiley, 1951, 112—136.

Leanderson, R., and Lindblom, B. E. F. Muscle activation for labial speech gestures. *Acta Otolaryngologica*, 1972, *73*, 362—373.

Lecours, A. -R., and Lhermitte, F. Phonemic paraphasias: Linguistic structures and tentative hypotheses. *Cortex*, 1969, *5*, 193—228.

Lehiste, I. The timing of utterances and linguistic boundaries. *Journal of the Acoustical Society of America*, 1972, *51*, 2018—2024.

Lenneberg, E. H. *Biological foundations of language*. New York: Wiley, 1967.

Lhermitte, F., Lecours, A. -R., and Bertaux, D. Activation and seriation of linguistic units in aphasic transformations. In L. D. Proctor (Ed.), *Biocybernetics of the central nervous system*. Boston: Little, Brown, 1969, 389—417.

Liberman, A. M. The grammars of speech and language. *Cognitive Psychology*, 1970, *1*, 301—323.

Liberman, A. M., Cooper, F. S., Harris, K. S., and MacNeilage, P. F. A motor theory of speech perception. In *Proceedings of the Speech Communication Seminar*. Stockholm, Sweden: Royal Institute of Technology, 1962.

Liberman, A. M., Cooper, F. S., Shankweiler, D. P., and Studdert-Kennedy, M. Perception of the speech code. *Psychological Review*, 1967, *74*, 431—461.

Lindblom, B. E. F. Spectrographic study of vowel reduction. *Journal of the Acoustical Society of America*, 1963, *35*, 1773—1781.

MacKay, D. G., Spoonerisms: The structure of errors in the serial order of speech. *Neuropsychologia*, 1970, *8*, 323—350.

MacKay, D. G. Aspects of the syntax of behavior: Syllable structure and speech rate. *Quarterly Journal of Experimental Psychology*, 1974, *26*, 642—657.

MacNeilage, P. F. Motor control of serial ordering of speech. *Psychological Review*, 1970, *3*, 182—196.

MacNeilage, P. F. Speech physiology. In J. H. Gilbert (Ed.), *Speech and cortical functioning.* New York: Academic Press, 1972, 1—72.

MacNeilage, P. F., and DeClerk, J. L. On the motor control of coarticulation in CVC monosyllables. *Journal of the Acoustical Society of America*, 1969, *45*, 1217—1233.

Martin, J. G. Rhythmic (hierarchical) versus serial structure in speech and other behavior. *Psychological Review*, 1972, *79*, 487—509.

Mattingly, I. G. Synthesis by rule of General American English. Supplement to *Status Report on Speech Research.* New York: Haskins Laboratories, 1968.

Mattingly, I. G., and Liberman, A. M. The speech code and the psychology of language. In K. N. Liebovic (Ed.), *Information processing in the nervous system.* New York: Springer-Verlag, 1969, 97—114.

Mermelstein, P. Articulatory model for the study of speech production. *Journal of the Acoustical Society of America*, 1973, *53*, 1070—1082.

Moll, K. L., and Daniloff, R. G. Investigation of the timing of velar movements during speech. *Journal of the Acoustical Society of America*, 1971, *50*, 678—684.

Neisser, U. *Cognitive psychology.* New York: Appleton, 1967.

Ohala, J. J. Aspects of the control and production of speech. *Working Papers in Phonetics*, *15*, Univ. of California at Los Angeles, 1970.

Öhman, S. E. G., Coarticulation in VCV utterances: Spectrographic measurements. *Journal of the Acoustical Society of America*, 1966, *39*, 151—168.

Öhman, S. E. G. Peripheral motor commands in labial articulation. *Quarterly Progress and Status Report*, *4*, 30—63, Speech Transmission Laboratory, Royal Institute of Technology, Stockholm, Sweden, 1967.

Rapp, K. A study of syllable timing. *Quarterly Progress and Status Report*, *1*, 14—19, Speech Transmission Laboratory, Royal Institute of Technology, Stockholm, Sweden, 1971.

Schmidt, R. A. Proprioception and the timing of motor responses. *Psychological Bulletin*, 1971, *76*, 383—393.

Sears, T. A., and Newsom-Davis, J. The control of respiratory muscles during voluntary breathing. In A. Bouhuys (Ed.), *Sound production in man.* Annals of the New York Academy of Sciences, 1968, *155*, 135—140.

Smith, K. U. Cybernetic theory and analysis of learning. In E. A. Bilodeau (Ed.), *Acquisition of skill.* New York: Academic Press, 1966, 103—139.

Smith, T. S. Review of J. P. Bowman, *The muscle spindle and neural control of the tongue* (Springfield, Illinois: Charles C. Thomas, 1971). *Papers from the Institute of Linguistics*, Publisher 17, 1—16, University of Stockholm, Sweden, 1973.

Smith, T. S., and Lee, C. Y. Peripheral feedback mechanisms in speech production models. In A. Rigoult and R. Charbonneau (Eds.), *Proceedings of the Seventh International Congress of Phonetic Sciences.* The Hague: Mouton, 1972, 1199—1204.

Stevens, K. N. Acoustic correlates of place of production for stop and fricative consonants. *Quarterly Progress Report*, 1968, No. 89, 199—205 (1968). Research Laboratory Electronics, Massachusetts Institute of Technology, Cambridge, Massachusetts.

Stevens, K. N. Segments, features, and analysis by synthesis. In J. F. Kavanagh and I. G. Mattingly (Eds.), *Language by ear and by eye: The relationship between speech and reading.* Cambridge, Massachusetts: M. I. T. Press, 1972, 47—52. (a)

Stevens, K. N. The quantal nature of speech: evidence from articulatory—acoustic data. In P. B. Denes and E. E. David (Eds.), *Human communication: A unified view*, New York: McGraw-Hill, 1972, 51—66 (b).

Stevens, K. N., and House, A. S. Perturbation of vowel articulation by consonantal context: An acoustical study. *Journal of Speech and Hearing Research*, 1963, *6*, 111—128.

Sussman, H. M. What the tongue tells the brain. *Psychological Bulletin*, 1972, *77*, 262—272.

Tatham, M. A. A. The control of muscles in speech. *Language Centre Occasional Paper*, *3*, University of Essex, 1969, 23—40.

Tatham, M. A. A. A speech production model for synthesis-by-rule. *Working Papers in Linguistics,* *6,* Computer and Information Sciences Research Center, Ohio State University, 1970.

Tingley, B. M., and Allen, G. D. Development of speech timing control in children. *Child Development,* 1975, *46,* 186—194.

van der Gon, J. J. D., and Wieneke, G. H. The concept of feedback in motorics against that of pre-programming. In L. D. Proctor (Ed.), *Biocybernetics of the central nervous system.* Boston: Little, Brown, 1969, 287—296.

Whitaker, H. A. Some constraints on speech production models. *Language Centre Occasional Paper,* *9,* University of Essex, 1970, 1—13.

Wickelgren, W. A. Context-sensitive coding, associative memory, and serial order in (speech) behavior. *Psychological Review,* 1969, *76,* 1—15.

Wright, T. W. Temporal interactions within a phrase and sentence context. *Journal of the Acoustical Society of America,* 1974, *56,* 1258—1265.

Yates, A. J. Delayed auditory feedback. *Psychological Bulletin,* 1963, *60,* 213—232.

chapter **4**

Aerodynamics of Speech Production

Donald W. Warren

University of North Carolina, Chapel Hill

The movement of air through the respiratory tract is governed by physical forces and controlled by neural and chemical events. Changes in the shape and size of the airway affect air flow significantly, especially when the system is used for speech purposes. Since the respiratory and speech processes are so interrelated, a description of the mechanical factors involved in breathing should provide an adequate basis for understanding the aerodynamics of sound production.

Generation of Driving Pressures

Air flows from a region of higher pressure to one of lower pressure. For phonation to occur, pressure in the lung must be greater than atmospheric pressure. The movement of air into and out of the lung is controlled by the action of the respiratory muscles, which produce changes in the volume of the chest cage. The muscles have no inherent rhythm and contract only when they receive nerve impulses from the respiratory centers. The increase in lung volume during inspiration occurs in three dimensions: antero-posterior, transverse, and longitudinal, through elevation of the ribs and descent of the diaphragm (Cherniack and Cherniack, 1961). Ordinarily, the muscles used for inspiration include the diaphragm, the external and intercartilaginous segment of the internal intercostals, and the scalene (Campbell, 1968). They are active throughout inspiration as well as during the first part of expiration. During forceful voluntary inspiratory efforts, the sternomastoids, trapezius, and pectorals are used as accessory muscles. The diaphragm is the principal muscle of inspiration, and in quiet breathing may be the only active inspiratory muscle.

While inspiration is an active process, normal expiration is primarily a passive event. The elasticity of stretched tissues and gravitational forces tend to return the thorax to its resting position without any further expenditure of energy. The elastic elements which have been stretched during inspiration have a natural tendency to regain their original positions after relaxation of the inspiratory muscles.

Contraction of the inspiratory muscles enlarges the lung because the outer surface of the lung (visceral pleura) is in intimate contact with the inner surface of the thoracic cavity (parietal pleura). The two pleural layers are in apposition, being separated only by a thin film of fluid. Thus, the lung tends to follow the bony thorax during the expansion which accompanies inspiration. The breathing mechanism can be characterized as a bellows pump having two connective parts: the lung and the chest wall (Agostini and Mead, 1964). The lung is specialized to disperse the gas and the chest wall is specialized to power the pump.

Elastic Resistance

The forces required to overcome elastic resistance are stored during inspiration and, after muscle action is removed, recoil returns the stretched fibers to their resting position. Resting level (Figure 4.1) is actually a balance between elastic forces pulling in opposite directions. That is, the lung would collapse if it were not held in apposition to the thorax and, similarly, the thorax cavity would enlarge if it were not constrained by the elastic properties of the lung.

The elastic behavior of the respiratory system may be described in terms of its pressure—volume relationship. This behavior is exemplified by the relaxation pressure curve [1] illustrated in Figure 4.2. The elastic forces of the lung and chest wall vary with lung volume (Agostini and Mead, 1964). At resting level, pulmonary pressure is atmospheric because the lung and chest wall forces pull in equal but opposite directions.

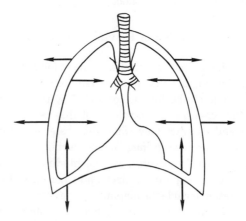

Figure 4.1 At resting level there is a balance of elastic forces from the lung and chest wall pulling in opposite directions.

[1]The relaxation pressure curve is obtained by determining pulmonary pressure at different degrees of lung distension while flow is obstructed at the mouth and all muscles are relaxed. It is a measure of the effort previously exerted in order to overcome elastic resistance of the lung and chest wall. The curve is the result of elastic recoil.

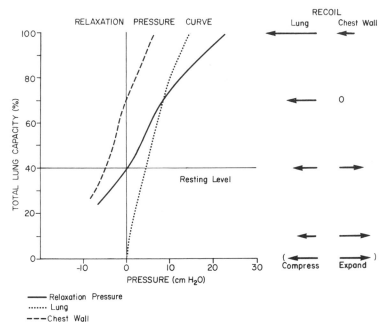

Figure 4.2 The relaxation pressure curve. The pressure at any lung volume is the result of the elastic forces of the lung and chest wall. [Modified from Rahn, Otis, Chadwick, and Fenn, 1946.]

At 60% of total lung capacity, the chest wall is at its natural size; since its elastic fibers are not being stretched, they offer no recoil pressure. On the other hand, the elastic fibers in the lung are being stretched so that, at that volume, lung recoil pressure equals relaxation pressure. As inspiration continues, both the lung and chest wall recoil when the muscles relax and the pressures are additive.

During expiration, when the muscles are relaxed and the lung is deflated below resting level, a negative pressure develops. This negative pressure indicates the effort previously exerted to overcome the elastic resistance of the chest wall and lung. Although the lung would exert a positive pressure until it completely collapsed, the lung's pressure is more than counterbalanced by the chest wall, which exerts a greater negative pressure when it is smaller than its natural size.

Most of the work involved in filling the lung is used to overcome elastic recoil, and the energy required is stored during inspiration and utilized during expiration. The compliance of the respiratory system, or the degree of distensibility which occurs with the application of pressure, is an important factor in determining the amount of energy required to move air into and out of the lung.

Nonelastic Resistances

The respiratory muscles must overcome not only the elastic forces of the lung and chest wall but also certain nonelastic resistances in order to carry out speech or breathing movements. There are essentially two types of nonelastic resistances. The

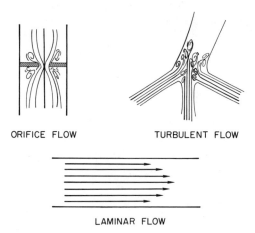

ORIFICE FLOW   TURBULENT FLOW

LAMINAR FLOW

Figure 4.3   Types of air flow in the vocal tract.

first and more important one is airway resistance, and it is produced by the forces of friction (DuBois, 1964). Mechanical energy is dissipated as heat as air moves through the tracheobronchial tree and the upper airway. There are several physical factors which determine the magnitude of resistance encountered in the airway. When air flow is laminar (Figure 4.3), the pressure required to maintain streamline air movement is directly proportional to the viscosity of the fluid, or

$$P = k_1 \hat{V}$$

where P = pressure; k_1 = constant which includes such factors as viscosity, length, and radius; $\hat{V}$ = air flow.

This equation, known as *Poiseuille's law*, can also be written as

$$R = \frac{8\mu l}{\pi r^4}$$

where R = resistance; μ = viscosity; l = length; r = radius; π = 3.1416. Thus, the pressure difference between two points in the airway is proportional to the length of the airway and the coefficient of viscosity and is indirectly proportional to the fourth power of the radius.

Flow is not always laminar, however, because of the branching, irregular shape of the respiratory tract. Eddying occurs at bifurcations and when the surface is rough or constricted. When air flow is turbulent (Figure 4.3), the pressure necessary to produce a given amount of air flow varies with the square of the flow, or

$$P = k_2 \, \mathring{V}^2.$$

Density of the gas, rather than viscosity, becomes important. Turbulence occurs when the relationship of density × velocity × diameter/viscosity exceeds 2000, which is known as *Reynold's number* (Comroe, 1965).

One of the main differences between the air-flow patterns in breathing and those in speech results from an orifice type of air flow which develops as constrictions form within the vocal tract during phonation (Figure 4.3). This type of air flow may occur at the glottis, the velopharyngeal orifice, and at various points along the oral airway. The pressure drop which results is expressed as

$$\Delta P = \frac{d}{2k^2} \left(\frac{\mathring{V}}{A} \right)^2$$

where k is the discharge coefficient which is dependent on the sharpness of the edge of the orifice and on Reynold's number. It has a value of $.6-.7$ in the speech and breathing range of flow. When air flows through a narrow orifice, the gas molecules must be accelerated. The rate of discharge through the orifice is proportionate to the area times the linear velocity of the fluid. A = area; d = air density; ΔP = pressure drop.

In addition to airway resistance, which must be overcome for air flow to occur, there is also tissue viscous resistance (Cherniack and Cherniack, 1961). This resistance is due to friction from the peribronchial tissues, lung parenchyma, and vascular structures sliding over one another during movement of the lung. Tissue viscous resistance is only a small part of the total nonelastic resistance, however, and usually only becomes important in certain disease states.

Surface Forces

Another important factor that must be considered relates to a very special surface film that lines the alveoli of the lung and produces surface tension (Comroe, 1965). Surface tension occurs because of the tendency of a surface to decrease to a minimum area because of an attractive force between molecules.

The molecules present in the surface have an inward component of attraction to adjacent molecules that is not counterbalanced. As a result, the surface shrinks to the smallest possible area. The recoil force of surface tension results in a pressure of about 20 cm H_2O when the lung is fully inflated and about 2 cm H_2O at lower lung volumes. This difference, which occurs at different lung volumes, results from the presence of a surface-active material, surfactant, which changes surface tension when the alveolar lining is compressed or expanded.

Methodological Aspects

Instruments providing precise measurements of the respiratory parameters associated with speech have been used to assess the function of articulatory structures. Aerodynamic techniques are used routinely to estimate the area of constrictions, resistances to air flow, and volume displacements.

Air-Flow Devices

Two types of flowmeters presently are being used to measure air flow rate during speech. The most accepted tool is the heated pneumotachograph, which consists of a flowmeter and a differential pressure transducer (Lubker, 1970) (Figure 4.4). This device utilizes the principle that, as air flows across a resistance, the pressure drop which results is linearly related to the volume rate of air flow. In most cases, the resistance is a wire mesh screen that is heated to prevent condensation. A pressure tap is situated on each side of the screen, and both are connected to a very sensitive differential pressure transducer. The pressure drop is converted to an electrical voltage that is amplified and recorded either on tape or on a direct writing instrument. Pneumotachographs are valid, reliable, and linear devices for measuring ingressive and egressive air-flow rates. In addition, they are inexpensive and easily calibrated with a rotameter.

The other air-flow measuring device in general use is the warm-wire anemometer, which uses a heated wire as the sensing unit (Subtelny, Worth, and Sakuda, 1966) (Figure 4.4). The cooling effect of air flow on a heated wire, through which an electric current flows, alters its resistance. The change in voltage that results is amplified and recorded. There is less restriction on articulatory movements with the warm-wire anemometer since a face mask is unnecessary. However, the anemometer has poor linearity and does not differentiate between ingressive and egressive air flow and, for this reason, is less popular than the heated pneumotachograph.

Air Pressure Devices

The pressure transducers presently in use are either variable resistance, variable capacitance, or variable inductance gauges (Figure 4.5). Resistance wire strain gauges respond to changes in pressure with a change in resistance when the strain-sensitive wire is exposed to stretch. A metal bellows is compressed by pressure within the chamber. This action results in a resistance imbalance in a Wheatstone bridge that is proportional to the applied pressure. The resulting output voltage from the bridge is amplified and recorded.

The electrical capacitance manometer is a condenser formed by an electrode sepa-

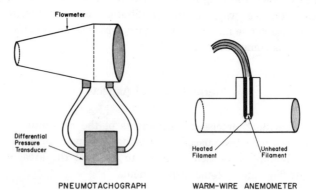

PNEUMOTACHOGRAPH   WARM-WIRE ANEMOMETER

Figure 4.4 (Left) The pneumotachograph consists of a flowmeter and a differential pressure transducer. As air flows across the mesh screen in the flowmeter, a pressure drop results and is recorded by the transducer. The pressure drop is proportional to the rate of air flow. (Right) The warm wire anemometer uses a heated wire as a sensing unit. Air flow across the heated wire cools it and alters its resistance. The change in voltage which results is proportional to the rate of air flow.

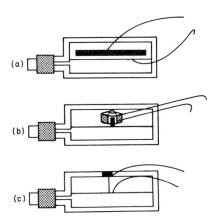

Figure 4.5   Types of transducers used to measure air pressure: (a) Variable capacitance; (b) variable inductance; (c) variable resistance. [Modified from Guyton, 1974.]

rated from a stiff metal membrane by a carefully adjusted air gap. Movements of the membrane in relation to the electrode vary the capacitance, which can be measured by a radio frequency circuit. Membrane displacement is extremely small, and, therefore, the frequency response is excellent. However, this device is more temperature sensitive than the strain gauge manometer.

Variable inductance pressure gauges can be made so small that they can be placed directly on the site to be measured. The transducer utilizes a soft iron slug placed within two coils of wire and fastened to the center of an elastic membrane. Pressure moves the iron slug, and this movement results in a change in magnetic flux. The change in inductance of the coils is then recorded through an appropriate bridge circuit.

It is common practice to amplify the signal from transducers to provide power to drive galvanometers. However, the mechanical inertia of some direct writing galvanometers is so great that the frequency response is limited, and amplification is required to produce any measurable response at all. Usually a carrier wave amplifier is used in combination with a strain gauge transducer. An oscillator supplies an alternating current, and the amplitude is continuously affected by the varying resistance of the Wheatstone bridge. The output of the transducer enters a capacitance-coupled amplifier, which amplifies the modulated carrier wave. Then the signals are rectified and the carrier wave is filtered out, leaving a DC voltage which powers the recording instrument.

Recorders

Five types of recorders are available: (*1*) optical recorders, (*2*) direct writing galvanometers, (*3*) cathode ray oscilloscopes, (*4*) magnetic tape recorders, and (*5*) analog-to-digital recorders. For any particular application, the transducer, amplifier, and recorder must be matched to obtain optimal performance. Usually this process involves a compromise of sensitivity, convenience, stability, and frequency response. Direct writing recorders have the lowest frequency response and are used only for recording low-frequency phenomena. Optical recorders and cathode ray oscilloscopes have an excellent frequency response, and the limiting factor is usually the transducer. Edmonds, Lilly, and Hardy (1971) have studied various pressure measuring systems used in speech research and have reported that the frequency response of most units is, in fact, quite restricted. This is especially so when catheters are attached to the transducers. Needles also dramatically reduce the range of frequency over which flat responses can be obtained. Measurements of air pressure, therefore, are limited by the individual components of the system——in most cases, this is the transducer.

Pressure-Flow Techniques

Pressure- and air-flow devices have been used to estimate the size of the oral port during fricative productions (Hixon, 1966; Klechak, 1971) as well as of the velopharyngeal opening during continuous speech (Warren and DuBois, 1964; Warren, 1964a). Figure 4.6 illustrates the instrumentation used for studying velopharyngeal orifice size. An analog computer, connected to a differential pressure transducer and a heated pneumotachograph, solves an equation based on the theoretical hydraulic principle:

$$A = \frac{\mathring{V}}{k\sqrt{\dfrac{2\Delta P}{d}}}$$

Figure 4.7 shows the placement of catheters above and below the velopharyngeal sphincter to obtain orifice differential pressure. Two stagnant columns of air are created during plosive sound production, one by the closed lips and the other by a cork around the catheter in the nostril. Air flow is recorded by a tube attached to the other nostril.

In a similar way, resistance to air flow can be estimated anywhere in the vocal tract by appropriate placement of catheters on both sides of the resistor. Air flow is

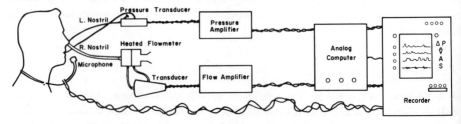

Figure 4.6 Diagrammatic representation of the technique used to measure the area of a constriction in the vocal tract. In this case, the area of the velopharyngeal orifice is computed from the parameters of orifice differential pressure and nasal air flow.

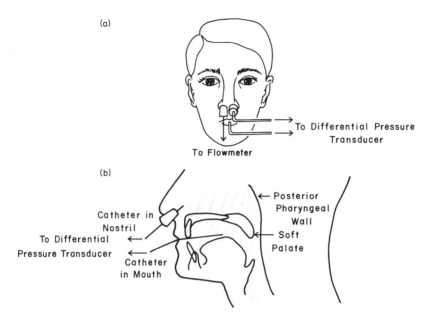

Figure 4.7 Catheters are placed above and below the orifice to measure the differential pressure. The catheter placed in the left nostril is secured by a cork, which plugs the nostril and creates a stagnant air column above the orifice. The second catheter is placed in the mouth. Both catheters are connected to a differential pressure transducer. The pneumotachograph is connected to the right nostril and collects orifice air flow through the nose.

recorded just past the resistance to be measured. The equation

$$R = \frac{\Delta P}{\overset{\circ}{V}}$$

is a modification of *Ohm's law* (Warren, Duany, and Fischer, 1969).

Plethysmographic Techniques

Body plethysmographs are used to study the relationship between pressures, airflow rates, and lung volume during breathing (DuBois, Bothelho, and Comroe, 1956). Recently, the technique has been adapted for use in speech research, and some preliminary data are available (Hixon and Warren, 1971). There are two basic types of plethysmographs: the closed box type and the open box type. In the closed box type, the subject sits and breathes inside the plethysmograph, which is basically an airtight chamber about the size of a telephone booth (Figure 4.8). Its use is based upon the application of Boyle's law relating gas volumes and pressures. When the subject breathes or speaks, lung volume changes, and this change alters box pressure. A very sensitive pressure transducer is attached to the box, and it measures the pressure changes within the box with reference to atmospheric pressure. Since the total amount of gas in the plethysmograph—lung system is constant, any increase in gas pressure inside the lung of the subject—during speech, for example—must cause a decrease in pressure in the gas in the plethysmograph. Therefore, at any instant,

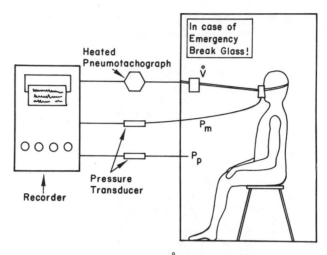

Figure 4.8   The closed box body plethysmograph. $\overset{\circ}{V}$ is volume rate of air flow; P_m is mouth pressure; P_p is plethysmograph pressure.

the resulting pressure change in the box must be opposite in sign to the pressure change in the lung.

There are several factors which, if not carefully controlled, influence box pressure and cause measurement artifacts. There is a uniform and continuous effect on pressure which results from heat production by the subject in the box. This heat produces a baseline drift if it is not compensated by creating a small leak in the chamber, introducing a compensating electronic signal, or air-conditioning the box.

Another problem that must be dealt with is the nonuniform and discontinuous effect of warming and humidifying the inspired air and water vapor condensation of the cooled expired air. This problem can be overcome by electronic compensation, rebreathing in a bag, or keeping the chamber at 100% humidity with a cool air vaporizer. Although there are several other possible sources of error, they are negligible compared to the effects of temperature and humidity if they are not carefully controlled.

The other type of plethysmograph is called the open box; this technique involves displacement of some air during chest movement (Figure 4.9). The displacement is recorded by a pneumotachograph, which provides an indication of the volume change occurring as the subject speaks or breathes. Changes in the lung volume are measured by recording volumes displaced by the body surface. As described by Hixon (1972), the subject is seated in a wooden body chamber and is totally encased except for his head and neck. A collar seals the chamber, and suction is used to make it airtight. As the subject speaks, chamber pressure decreases with chest volume. This change in chamber volume and subsequent lowering of pressure results in air flowing into the chamber through a pneumotachograph screen. The flow measured by the pneumotachograph is then integrated to provide an estimate of volume displaced. The same pressure transducer also provides a measure of the displacement related to gas compression; since the total volume is the sum related to compression and

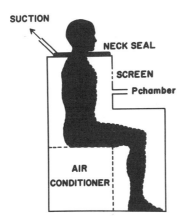

Figure 4.9 The open box body plethysmograph. Changes in lung volume can be measured with the chamber in this configuration. [From Hixon, 1967.]

displacement of gas, true lung volume can be determined by summing the two electronically. Hixon (1972) reports that this technique has the advantage of allowing accurate acoustic recording since there is no interference with articulation as in techniques using a face mask.

With slight modification, the open box plethysmographic technique can be used for measuring subglottal pressures. In this case, a lucite dome is used so that the entire body is encased in the plethysmograph. Subglottal pressure changes are determined from the measurements of compressional volume changes, and the pressure—volume relationships are quantified by using Boyle's law (Figure 4.10). As in the closed box method, the experimenter must be extremely careful to minimize measurement artifacts. Seen in this light, the body plethysmograph offers several real advantages over other techniques for measuring subglottal pressure, airway resistance, and volume displacements.

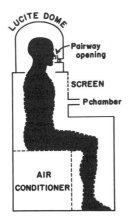

Figure 4.10 Chamber configuration for making plethysmographic measurements of alveolar pressure during speech. [From Hixon, 1967.]

Lower Airway Dynamics

Air flow in the lower airway is influenced by the geometric features of the bronchi (Jaeger and Matthys, 1970). These branch dichotomously, each giving rise to two daughter bronchi. The length and diameter of the bronchi decrease with each generation in a regular fashion. The total cross-sectional area of the bronchi increases with each generation, and the area of the peripheral bronchi is about 1000 times larger than that of the trachea. Since the mean velocity of the air stream varies inversely with cross-sectional area, the velocity of air flow increases as the gas moves from the periphery upward (Figure 4.11). Thus, if the velocity of air flow in the trachea is 100 cm/sec, the velocity in the small bronchi may be less than .1 cm/sec.

The actual generation of pressure in the lower airway and the resulting movement of air appear to be well controlled in spite of the complex interactions of muscular and nonmuscular forces which occur during phonation. There seems to be a need to maintain a constant pressure head or energy source at the level of the lung. Most investigators agree that subglottal pressure does not vary to any great extent during phonation, in spite of the many structural changes which occur in the supraglottal airway (Ladefoged, 1962, 1968; Mead, Bouhuys, and Procter, 1968; Netsell, 1969). This finding suggests that an intricate feedback mechanism may be operating in which pressure is monitored in the lung, information is integrated in the brain, and the respiratory muscles respond as effector organs to maintain a constant subglottal pressure head. At end-inspiration, when lung volume is high, the potential recoil pressure is much greater (possibly 30–40 cm H_2O) and must be balanced by the action of the inspiratory muscles (Figure 4.12). That is, in order to maintain a constant subglottal pressure, the relaxation pressure resulting from the recoil of elastic fibers in the lung and chest wall must be checked by active contraction of the inspiratory muscles (Draper, Ladefoged, and Whitteridge, 1959; Hixon, 1973).

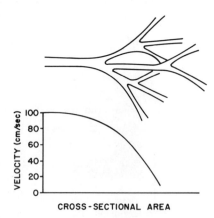

CROSS-SECTIONAL AREA

Figure 4.11   The respiratory tract decreases in cross-sectional area from the alveoli of the lung to the trachea. Velocity of airflow increases as cross-sectional area decreases. The upper figure diagrammatically illustrates this change in size, and the lower illustration demonstrates the relationship between velocity of air movement and cross-sectional area.

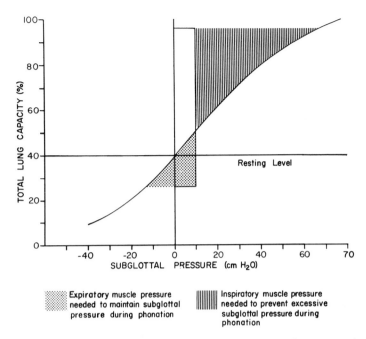

Figure 4.12 Lung volume and pressure relationships during a normal utterance. At high lung volume, inspiratory muscle action is required to check recoil pressure and prevent excessive subglottal pressure. At low lung volumes, expiratory muscle activity is required to maintain subglottal pressure for the utterance. [Modified from Hixon, 1973.]

Similarly, as lung volume decreases, relaxation pressure falls and activation of the expiratory muscles is necessary to maintain the subglottal pressure head. Ladefoged, Draper, and Whitteridge (1958) observed electromyographically that the external intercostals remain in action at the beginning of the utterance to check the descent of the rib cage and to counteract relaxation pressure. As lung volume decreases, external intercostal activity diminishes; it ceases completely when lung volume is slightly less than it is after a normal inspiration. At that point, relaxation pressure seems to be sufficient to provide the pressure head for the utterance. Expiratory muscle activity is then required to maintain pressure, with the internal intercostals gradually increasing activity. Supplemental activity may occur in the latter stage, with the external oblique, rectus abdominis, and latissimus dorsi contracting when lung volume is below resting level.

The increase in subglottal pressure which occurs with increased loudness or stress apparently is due, in large part, to changes in activity of the respiratory muscles. There is less external intercostal muscle suppression of elastic recoil at high lung volumes and greater internal intercostal augmentation at lower lung volumes. The result is a higher subglottal pressure during stressed or loud utterances. Normal conversational speech occurs at the midrange of total lung capacity (Mead, Bouhuys, and Procter, 1968) (Figure 4.13). This occurrence provides a distinct mechanical advantage since

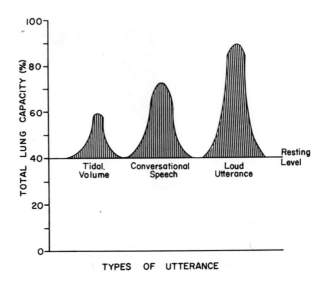

Figure 4.13 Comparison of lung volumes used in breathing, conversational speech, and loud utterance.

less muscle activity is required to check elastic recoil. Greater lung volumes are used when loudness is increased; similarly, respiratory effort is lower when the utterance is softer than normal (Ladefoged and McKinney, 1963; Lieberman, 1967; Hixon, Goldman, and Mead, 1973). There is also evidence indicating that small changes in respiratory muscle activity influence the intensity of the sound produced by the vocal folds. Voice intensity is approximately proportional to the third or fourth power of the subglottal pressure (van den Berg, 1956; Isshiki, 1964; Cavagna and Margaria, 1965). An increase in subglottal pressure also tends to raise the fundamental frequency (Isshiki, 1964). Fundamental frequency is a dominant parameter used to denote stress, although other parameters, such as manner of production and duration, also have an effect (Fry; 1955; Lieberman, 1960; Brown and McGlone, 1974).

Laryngeal Dynamics

Air flow passing through the glottis produces sounds when the vocal folds are properly adducted. During normal phonation the glottis opens and closes, producing quasi-periodic air flow. The vibration-like movement of the folds results from aerodynamic, muscular, and elastic tissue forces which act in a very complex way. The aerodynamic forces which are exerted on the vocal folds include subglottal air pressure, the Bernoulli force produced by negative pressure created transglottally by high-velocity air flow, and supraglottal pressure produced by articulatory constrictions in the upper airway. The Bernoulli equation demonstrates that pressure falls at the site of a constriction when the velocity of the fluid increases. That is,

$$\tfrac{1}{2}\,d\,v^2 + P = \text{constant}$$

where v = air velocity. If velocity increases, pressure must decrease. The pressure at the glottal constriction may fall below atmospheric as the folds come together. Glottal tissue resistance then increases as the area of constriction decreases, thus allowing the Bernoulli force to increase only up to a certain point (van den Berg, Zantema, and Doornenbal, 1957). The vibratory movement of the folds that results from this interaction modulates the airstream and provides the acoustic source for phonation.

Resistance at the vocal folds varies from less than 1.0 cm $H_2O/L/sec$ during quiet breathing to as much as 100 cm $H_2O/L/sec$ during voicing (Rothenberg, 1968). The difference between subglottal and supraglottal pressures during vowel production is approximately 4.0–8.0 cm H_2O, and 1.0–4.0 cm H_2O during voiced consonant productions. These differences are due to lower resistance in the upper airway during vowel productions.

The relationship between glottal opening, transglottal pressure, and air-flow rate is illustrated in Figure 4.14. These data were obtained from unpublished mechanical analog studies of simulated sound productions. Pressure across the glottis decreases very rapidly as glottal area increases. As respiratory effort or air-flow rate is increased, the curve shifts to the right. The relationship between pressure, glottal opening, and air-flow rate can be described by the equation

$$\Delta P = k \left(\frac{\overset{\circ}{V}}{A} \right)^2$$

where k = constant related to the density of air and the discharge coefficient.

Articulatory changes which occur above the glottis affect pressure and air-flow relationships at the vocal folds. Opening the oral port for fricative or vowel productions

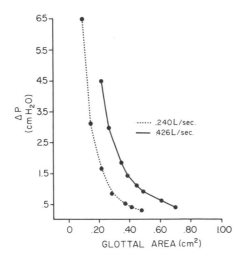

Figure 4.14 The relationship between glottal area and transglottal pressure at different respiratory air-flow rates.

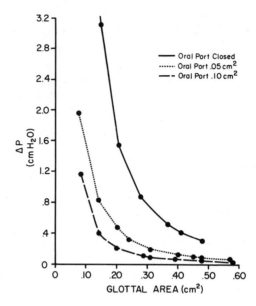

Figure 4.15 The relationship between glottal area and transglottal pressure when the oral port is closed for plosives and open slightly for fricatives (respiratory airflow = .240 L/sec.). Data from mechanical analog studies [Warren, unpublished research].

decreases transglottal pressure amplitude. Figure 4.15 demonstrates the shift that is downward and to the left.

The relationship between glottal opening and glottal resistance is illustrated in Figure 4.16. When the opening is larger than .25 cm², resistance is less than total airway resistance in the entire respiratory tract during normal breathing. As res-

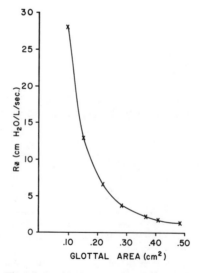

Figure 4.16 The relationship between glottal area and glottal resistance.

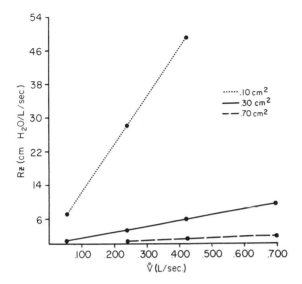

Figure 4.17 The relationship between glottal resistance and respiratory air flow at different degrees of glottal opening.

piratory effort increases, glottal resistance increases; this is demonstrated in Figure 4.17. It is apparent that the effects of vocal fold activity on pressure and air flow depend to a great extent on the activity of the articulators in the upper airway.

GLOTTAL ACTIVITY DURING STOP CONSONANTS

Differences in intraoral pressure among voiced and voiceless consonants have usually been attributed to some feature of glottal activity. Voicing requires air flow across the vocal folds, and to achieve this in the closed system of stop consonants, a differential pressure between the subglottal and supraglottal cavities must occur. Rothenberg (1968) has proposed three mechanisms for producing transglottal air flow during voiced stop productions. These are: *(1)* a passive, pressure-activated expansion of one or more walls of the supraglottal cavity; *(2)* a muscularly activated enlargement of the supraglottal cavity; and *(3)* nasal air flow through a slightly open palatal sphincter. Current thought seems to favor the active-expansion mechanism. Perkell (1969), and Kent and Moll (1969) have demonstrated that voiced stops are produced with larger supraglottal volumes than their voiceless cognates. Further, Kent and Moll's data revealed that pharyngeal expansion occurs simultaneously with the depression of the hyoid bone, which is an active process. They concluded that the increase in supraglottal volume is at least a partial explanation for intraoral pressure differences among cognates.

There is some indirect evidence against passive enlargement of the oropharynx. Rothenberg's (1968) study indicated that, from a consideration of the range of supraglottal cavity compliance, it appears that there are many occurrences of voiced alveolar plosives in which the voiced interval is too long and/or the voicing too strong to be maintained by passive expansion alone.

Similarly, if passive expansion did result from greater thoracic muscle activity during voicing, cognate differences in subglottal pressures should result. Netsell (1969), however, has observed that subglottal pressures generally do not differ among consonants. Lubker (1973) has studied the possibility that velopharyngeal patency may cause transglottal air flow and has concluded that it represents the least likely mechanism, while active cavity enlargement appears to offer the most satisfactory explanation. Bell-Berti (1975) has proposed two modes of expanding the pharynx for voiced stops, each applying to a different group of muscles. She presents evidence of an active mode, requiring increased muscle activity to expand the pharynx, and a passive mode, requiring suppression of muscle activity to expand the pharynx.

GLOTTAL ACTIVITY AND THE PRESSURE PULSE

The effects of glottal activity on the pressure pulse are illustrated in Figures 4.18, 4.19, and 4.20. Figure 4.18 demonstrates the typical pattern of a voiceless stop consonant. The arrow indicates an interval with no glottal activity during the pressure-rise phase of the stop production. The rise in pressure is rapid; then a plateau occurs, followed by a rapid fall in pressure at release as the oral port opens. Figure 4.19 illustrates a voiced stop consonant in which a voice break occurs. A voice break is defined as a silent interval in the sound record during the pressure-rise phase of a voiced stop production. The pressure profile shows that the rate of pressure rise increases when voicing ceases. In this instance, vocal fold resistance decreases

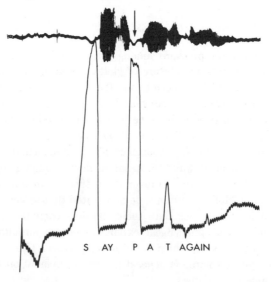

Figure 4.18 Glottal activity influences the intraoral pressure profile. In the case of voiceless stop consonants, there is a rapid rise in pressure, followed by a plateau, and then a rapid fall in pressure when the lips part. The arrow in the sound record identifies the silent interval in which there is no glottal activity.

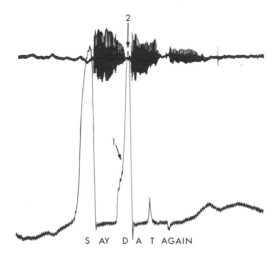

Figure 4.19 Intraoral pressure rises very rapidly when a voice break occurs. Arrow 1 identifies the beginning of the voice break or cessation of glottal activity. Arrow 2 identifies the break in the sound record.

considerably at the voice break, and air-flow rate increases rapidly. If voicing occurs throughout the stop production (Figure 4.20), pressure is considerably lower, and vocal fold resistance limits air flow through the glottis.

The effect of glottal activity on cognate pressure differences is shown in Figure 4.21. When voicing is not present until pressure release, the mean difference in pressure among such consonants as /p/ − /b and /d/ − /t/ is less than .3 cm H_2O.

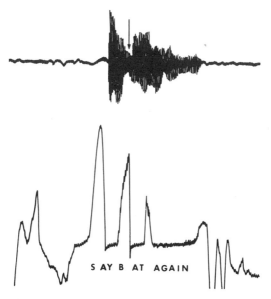

Figure 4.20 Intraoral pressure is of lower magnitude when voicing occurs throughout the consonant production. Arrow notes continuing glottal activity in the sound record.

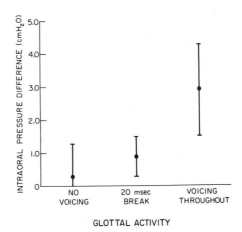

Figure 4.21   Mean intraoral voiced–voiceless pressure differences and standard deviations according to degree of glottal activity.

Where some voicing is evident prior to pressure release, the difference is about 1.0 cm H_2O. A mean pressure difference of 3.0 cm H_2O occurs when there is voicing throughout the interval. The occurrence of voice breaks during this interval may be related to pharyngeal expansion (Warren and Hall, 1973). It is possible that when maximal expansion is reached, voice break results.

GLOTTAL ACTIVITY AND RESPIRATORY VOLUMES

Closure of the vocal folds has a considerable effect on respiratory volume and the volume velocity of air flow (Warren and Wood, 1969). Figures 4.22 and 4.23 illustrate sound, air-flow rate, and volume profiles of typical voiced and voiceless plosive and fricative consonants. Certain differences are readily apparent; namely, air-flow rate is considerably higher and volume slope considerably steeper for the voiceless sounds. This finding indicates greater respiratory effort during voiceless consonant production. A comparison of volumes is made in Figure 4.24. In this instance the values are for the consonant and its associated vowel, which follows. It still has not been determined, however, whether the differences arise simply as a result of vocal fold resistance or whether greater respiratory effort is needed to provide additional acoustic cues in the absence of glottal sound generation.

WHISPER

Glottal resistance during whisper is approximately 4.0–6.0 cm $H_2O/L/sec$ (Warren and Hall, unpublished data). Respiratory effort is greater than in conversational speech, and this fact is reflected by increased air-flow rates, air volumes, and intraoral pressures (Figure 4.25). In spite of the fact that the vocal folds are somewhat apart during whisper, the same voiced–voiceless pressure and air flow differences observed in conversational speech are present. However, the difference in pressure is

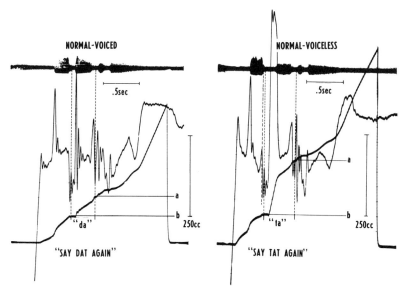

Figure 4.22 Typical sound, volume rate of air flow, and volume patterns for voiced and voiceless plosives. A higher rate of air flow and greater respiratory volume for voiceless sounds is apparent. The distance between a and b represents the volume of air for the consonant—vowel.

much smaller. The time duration of sound production is increased during whisper, and this probably accounts for much of the threefold increase in the respiratory volumes used (Warren and Hall, unpublished data). Perhaps the increased time and effort needed to produce the "sounds" of whispered speech are necessary to generate adequate air flow turbulence.

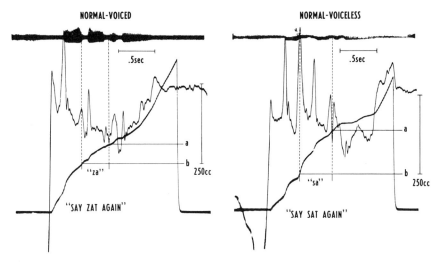

Figure 4.23 Typical patterns for voiced and voiceless fricatives. Voiceless fricatives exhibit higher rates of air flow and greater respiratory volumes than their voiced counterparts.

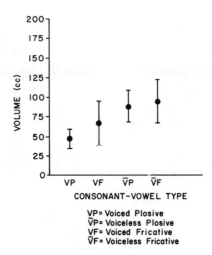

Figure 4.24 Respiratory volume means and standard deviations for voiced plosives, voiceless plosives, voiced fricatives, and voiceless fricatives.

Upper Airway Dynamics

Structures in the upper airway play an essential role in the speech process by modulating the airstream into precise patterns. The direction and velocity of air movement are controlled primarily by changes in airway size. These changes usually result from various constrictions formed by the lips, teeth, tongue, mandible, and

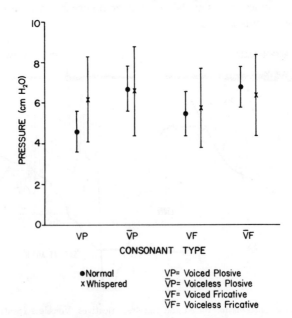

Figure 4.25 Comparison of mean intraoral pressures and standard deviations for conversational speech and whisper.

velum. In addition, the nasal pathway presents a constant resistance of approximately 1.0 cm $H_2O/L/sec$ to 4.0 cm $H_2O/L/sec$ in normal, unobstructed individuals (DuBois, 1964; Warren, Duany, and Fischer, 1969).

During phonation, the oral airway produces resistances of less than 1.0 cm $H_2O/L/sec$ in the case of certain vowels to an infinite resistance or complete obstruction in the case of plosives (Rothenberg, 1968). The effects of continuing changes in shape of the upper airway are illustrated in Figure 4.26. A nearly constant subglottal pressure head is modified into discrete pressure- and air-flow profiles in the upper airway. Intraoral pressure is almost atmospheric for vowel sounds because of the open oral port. On the other hand, intraoral pressure is equal to subglottal pressure for voiceless stop consonants since the vocal tract is closed and the column of air is stagnant. Although the voiceless fricative is produced with a slight oral port opening, resistance is high enough so that intraoral pressure is essentially the same as subglottal pressure. Voiced plosives and fricatives are produced with lower intraoral pressures; as noted previously, the difference appears to be related to changes in intraoral air volume (Warren and Wood, 1969) as well as to glottal resistance during voicing (Isshiki and Ringel, 1964; Arkebauer, Hixon, and Hardy, 1967). In the case of voiced plosives, it is thought that active expansion of the pharyngeal cavity lowers intraoral pressure below subglottal pressure, thus providing the decreased pressure necessary for transglottal air flow. Voiced fricatives may also involve active expansion of the pharyngeal cavity, but, since the oral port is slightly open, transglottal air flow can occur without a change in pharyngeal cavity volume. The difference in subglottal—supraglottal pressures for voiced consonants depends largely on the length of the voicing interval (Warren and Hall, 1973). There is some indirect evidence that the length of the voicing interval for stop consonants may be related to the degree of active expansion of the pharyngeal cavity (Warren and Hall, 1973).

Respiratory effort, in terms of the volume of air released from the lung, the volume rate of air flow, and the length of time devoted to the production of the sound,

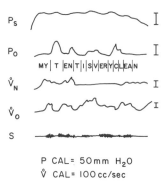

P CAL = 50 mm H_2O
$\mathring{V}$ CAL = 100 cc/sec

Figure 4.26 Comparison of subglottal pressure (P_s), intraoral pressure (P_o), nasal air flow ($\mathring{V}_n$), oral air flow ($\mathring{V}_o$), and sound (S) during phonation of the sentence *My tent is very clean*. A nearly constant subglottal pressure head is modulated into discrete patterns of pressure and air flow.

is much greater for voiceless fricatives than for the other consonant types (Warren and Wood, 1969). Perhaps greater respiratory effort is necessary to produce sufficient acoustic cues in the absence of sound generation at the glottis. Certainly the constant air leak at the oral port during fricative sound production also influences the need for increased effort.

Velopharyngeal Orifice

During the production of non-nasal sounds, the soft palate and pharyngeal walls form a valve that restricts air flow from entering the nasal cavity. Although closure is usually complete, an opening of $2.0-3.0$ mm^2 may occur even during the production of plosive consonant sounds. Figure 4.27 illustrates the variations in velopharyngeal orifice area for the sentence *Are you home, Papa?* Orifice size was computed from an orifice area equation described earlier. Movements associated with different speech sounds apparently overlap in time and thus cannot be considered discrete and independent. As illustrated in Figure 4.27, an interval of preparation for the nasal consonant results in nasalization of the vowel preceding the nasal consonant. The velopharyngeal orifice opens well in advance and, in this instance, began as far back as the voiceless /h/ in preparation for the nasal /m/. For example, the duration of the /m/ segment is 120 msec, compared to an opening interval of 284 msec prior to the initiation of the sound. The orifice, therefore, was open 404 msec, or nearly 3.5 times longer than the actual /m/ segment.

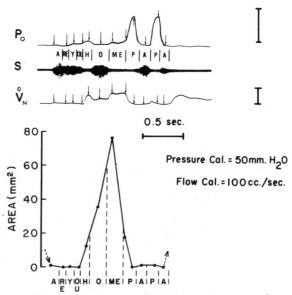

Figure 4.27 A typical intraoral pressure (P$_o$), sound (S), nasal air flow ($\overset{\circ}{V}_n$), and velopharyngeal orifice area record of the sentence *Are you home, Papa?* An interval of preparation for the nasal consonant results in nasal emission during the preceding speech elements.

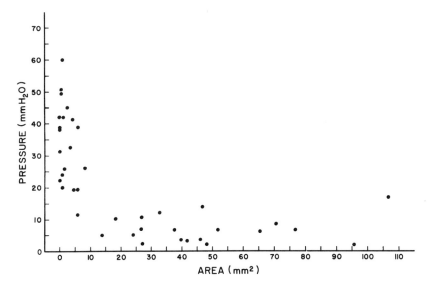

Figure 4.28 The relationship between orifice size and intraoral pressure during consonant productions. The consonants /b/, /t/, and /m/ were studied. A nonlinear pattern is evident, which indicates that adequate intraoral pressure for non-nasal consonants cannot be attained when the orifice is larger than 20 mm².

Although the velopharyngeal orifice is only one of several structures which influence intraoral pressure, its effect can be quite substantial (Warren, 1964a,b). Figure 4.28 demonstrates the relationship between area of the orifice and intraoral pressure. Orifice area was measured during the production of the consonants /b/, /t/, and /m/ produced in sentences. A definite nonlinear pattern is evident which indicates that high intraoral pressure cannot be attained once the opening is larger than 10−20 mm². At approximately this size, nasal airway resistance overshadows the effect of the orifice. Stated in other terms, once the opening is larger than 20 mm², other factors, such as nasal airway resistance, influence intraoral pressure more than palatal valving. Under normal conditions, intraoral pressure for nasal sounds will depend upon respiratory volume as well as nasal cavity resistance.

The relationship between palatal opening and intraoral pressure at different rates of respiratory air flow is shown in Figures 4.29 and 4.30. The data were obtained from mechanical analog studies of the upper speech mechanism under simulated conditions as well as from studies on individuals with cleft palate (Warren and Devereux, 1966). At low rates of air flow, the relationship is described by the equation

$$P = k_1 \left[\frac{\dot{V}}{A} \right]^2 + \tfrac{1}{2} \left[k_3 \dot{V}^2 + k_2 \dot{V} \right]$$

and at higher flow rates by this equation:

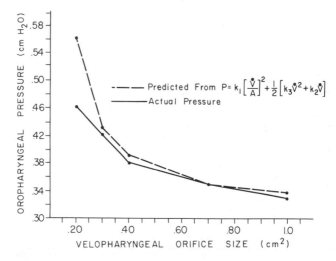

Figure 4.29 The relationship between intraoral pressure and velopharyngeal orifice area during plosive consonant production at a low volume rate of air flow (respiratory air flow = .088 L/sec.).

$$P = k_1 \left[\frac{\mathring{V}}{A} \right]^2 + k_3 \mathring{V}^2.$$

Voice quality is also modified when palatal valving cannot achieve closure below 20 mm^2 (Warren, 1964a). Articulatory errors seem to develop as a result of palatal incompetency. Deficits usually occur as the individual attempts to compensate for the leak with inappropriate movements of other oral structures. Interestingly enough, the palatal mechanism must be open more than 20 mm^2 for nasal sounds, or denasal voice quality results (Warren, 1964a).

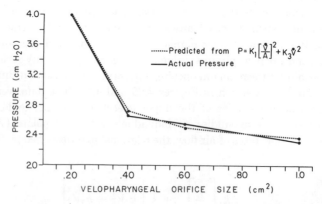

Figure 4.30 The relationship between intraoral pressure and velopharyngeal orifice area during plosive consonant production at an airflow rate of .240 L/sec. At this rate of air flow, turbulence occurs across the velopharyngeal orifice and nose. This occurrence is demonstrated by the quadratic relationship between pressure and air flow.

Oral Cavity

Structures within the oral cavity modulate air flow in several significant ways. The tongue can occlude the airway completely or provide enough resistance to produce turbulence for the generation of fricative sounds. The mandible can constrict the airway and, with labial closure, can create a stagnant column of air as in the prerelease phase of plosive sounds. Generally the lips, tongue, and mandible move in coordinated patterns, and along with the teeth, alveolar ridge, and anterior palate, form variable constrictions which modify the airstream. When the oral airway is open, intraoral pressure is nearly atmospheric. It rises from 3.0 to 8.0 cm H_2O during the production of plosive and fricative sounds (Malecot, 1955; Arkebauer, Hixon, and Hardy, 1967; Warren, 1964a) (Figure 4.31).

Air flows more readily through the oral cavity than it does through the nasal cavity because resistance is approximately half, providing the tongue is not elevated to any great extent (Warren and Ryon, 1967). Figure 4.32 illustrates the effect of oral port opening on velopharyngeal sphincter resistance at different degrees of velopharyngeal opening. It is evident that, in spite of an open velopharyngeal orifice, the nasal chamber, with its smaller cross-sectional area and higher resistance, receives substantial amounts of air flow only when the oral airway is constricted.

The oral port plays a significant role in the production of fricative sounds. A small opening formed by the lips, teeth, tongue, and anterior palate creates the high velocity air flow necessary for generation of turbulence and sound. Hixon (1966) and Klechak (1971) reported that the opening is usually between 3.0 and 10.0 mm². Respiratory effort is usually increased when the oral port is slightly open so that a 4.0—8.0 cm H_2O pressure head can be maintained behind the constriction. The amount of opening may be inversely proportional to consonant sound pressure level (Hixon, 1966). Similarly, as sound levels increase, intraoral pressures and air flow rates also increase (Hixon, 1966).

Adequate oral port closure appears to take priority over other articulatory move-

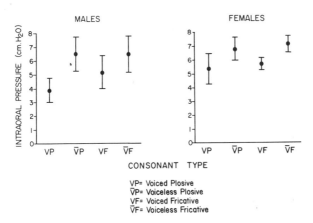

Figure 4.31 Mean intraoral pressures and standard deviations of voiced and voiceless plosives and fricatives in conversational speech.

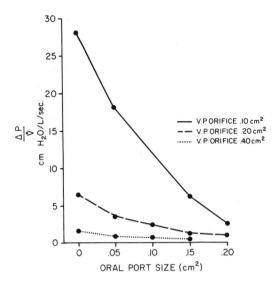

Figure 4.32 The relationship between velopharyngeal orifice resistance and oral port size at varying degrees of velopharyngeal closure (respiratory air flow = .250 L/sec).

ments. Klechak (1971) has shown that individuals with an open-bite malocclusion compensate for the anterior space by lingual and labial adjustments, even at the expense of producing other articulatory distortions. This phenomenon also occurs in cleft palate speakers who exhibit anterior deformities (Claypoole, Warren, and Bradley, 1974).

The duration of oral port constriction, that is, that period in which the oral port is closed for plosives, as in the case of /b/ or /p/ when the lips are together, or when the lips and teeth are in close approximation for fricatives as for /f/ or /v/, varies according to consonant type (Warren and Mackler, 1968). Voiceless fricatives have the longest duration of oral port constriction (Figure 4.33), and it has been suggested that this fact is related to the lack of acoustic reinforcement by the vocal folds. In the absence of voicing, that is, pressure and air flow are sustained over a longer period of time and at higher magnitudes; in this way, acoustic cues sufficient for perception of these sounds are generated.

Research Implications

Although the chemical and neural control of respiration is quite complex, an even more precise and delicate regulatory mechanism is required for speech. The sudden changes in respiratory load that occur when the upper airway closes or opens must be compensated almost instantaneously if subglottal pressure is to be maintained at a near constant level. Otherwise, sound intensity and fundamental frequency would be unstable. This poses a considerable error control problem that is not encountered in breathing.

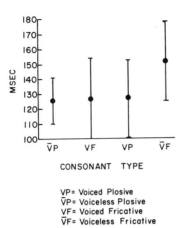

Figure 4.33 Mean durations of oral port constriction and standard deviations for voiced and voiceless plosives and fricatives.

Undoubtedly a complicated feedback system regulating pressure and air flow must be involved. Although there is some general information available, current models are still highly speculative. One possible system is illustrated in Figure 4.34. It consists of a controller unit or computer coordinating center, sensors or receptors to transmit information, and effectors to power the system and produce articulatory movements. The controller most certainly is in the brain, and presumably higher centers as well as the medulla are involved. Sensors may be located in the lung and along the vocal tract. The effectors are the respiratory muscles which power the pump, and the articulatory structures are the variable resistances which modulate the airstream. This hypothetical model is presented only for the purpose of demonstrating how limited our knowledge is. Receptors for sensing such parameters as pressure and air flow have not been identified, yet monitoring is necessary if errors are to be corrected. For example, in breathing, overinflation of the lung is prevented by receptors which transmit information on volume to the respiratory centers. Breathing is a slow process in comparison to speech, however, and regulation of volume can be accomplished to a great extent by the alpha motoneuron system, although the gamma efferent system is available for rapid readjustments when required. More rapid and frequent adjustments of pressure and air flow would be necessary for speech. Gross muscle activity such as checking elastic recoil may be controlled by the alpha system, but changes in respiratory load in response to events in the upper airway require a faster response. The gamma efferent system may provide the rapid, sensitive adjustments necessary to maintain a constant pressure head. In addition, simultaneous preprogramming for the respiratory muscles as well as for the articulators is also a possibility.

There is evidence that the brain prepares the articulators for the production of speech sounds well in advance (Kozhevnikov and Chistovich, 1965; Öhman, 1966, 1967; Daniloff and Moll, 1968; Moll and Daniloff, 1971). As discussed earlier,

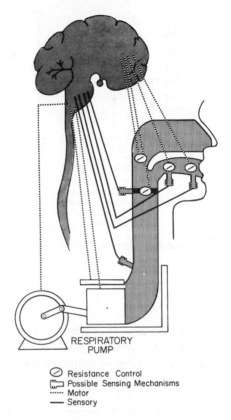

RESPIRATORY
PUMP

⊘ Resistance Control
▭ Possible Sensing Mechanisms
····· Motor
—— Sensory

Figure 4.34 Diagrammatic representation of a possible feedback mechanism controlling the subglottal pressure head.

there is an interval of preparation for consonant sounds, and this interval presumably involves advanced neural input to the articulators. This same advanced programming may provide simultaneous input to the respiratory muscles to prepare for possible events such as transient back pressure. Indeed, coarticulation seems to be a reflection of advanced programming. The gamma loop and the small motor fiber system associated with it would still operate as a servo to drive the main muscle fibers, but their operating range would be smaller with preprogramming of the alpha system.

The point to be made is that our present information is quite limited, especially in terms of the role of the brain as a coordinator and controller of speech aerodynamics. Similarly, the design and function of the transmission system is not well understood. Unfortunately, these are areas that are difficult to study, and progress will be slow. Indirect information can be obtained, however, through aerodynamic techniques. Especially informative are pressure-flow studies combined with electromyography and cineradiography. Although the task is formidable, the answers will come as technology improves.

REFERENCES

Agostini, E., and Mead, J. Statics of the respiratory system. In W. Fenn and H. Rahn (Eds.), *Handbook of physiology, respiration, I.* Washington, D.C.: American Physiological Society, 1964.

Arkebauer, H. J., Hixon, T. J., and Hardy, J. C. Peak intraoral air pressures during speech. *Journal of Speech and Hearing Research*, 1967, *10*, 196—208.

Bell-Berti, F. Control of pharyngeal cavity size for English voiced and voiceless stops. *Journal of the Acoustical Society of America*, 1975, *57*, 456—461.

Brown, W. S., and McGlone, R. E. Aerodynamic and acoustic study of stress in sentence productions. *Journal of the Acoustical Society of America*, 1974, *56*, 971—974.

Campbell, E., J. M. The respiratory muscles. In A. Bouhuys (Ed.), *Sound production in man. Annals of the New York Academy of Science*, 1968, *155*, 135—139.

Cavagna, G. A., and Margaria, R. An analysis of the mechanics of phonation. *Journal of Applied Physiology*, 1965, *20*, 301—307.

Cherniack, R. M., and Cherniack, L. *Respiration in health and disease.* Philadelphia, Pennsylvania: W. B. Saunders, 1961.

Claypoole, W. H., Warren, D. W., and Bradley, D. P. The effect of cleft palate on oral port constriction during fricative productions. *Cleft Palate Journal*, 1974, *11*, 95—104.

Comroe, J. H. *Physiology of respiration.* Chicago, Illinois: Year Book Medical Publishers, 1965.

Daniloff, R. G., and Moll, K. L. Coarticulation of lip rounding. *Journal of Speech and Hearing Research*, 1968, *11*, 707—721.

Draper, M. H. Ladefoged, P., and Whitteridge, D. Respiratory muscles in speech. *Journal of Speech and Hearing Research*, 1959, *2*, 16—27.

DuBois, A. B. Resistance to breathing. In W. Fenn and H. Rahn (Eds.), *Handbook of physiology, respiration, I.* Washington, D.C.: American Physiological Society, 1964, 451—463.

DuBois, A. B., Bothelho, S. Y., and Comroe, J. H. A new method for measuring airway resistance in man using a body plethysmograph: Values in normal subjects and in patients with respiratory disease. *Journal of Clinical Investigation*, 1956, *35*, 327—335.

Edmonds, T. D., Lilly, D. J., and Hardy, J. C. Dynamic characteristics of air-pressure measuring systems used in speech research. *Journal of the Acoustical Society of America*, 1971, *50*, 1051—1057.

Fry, D. B. Duration and intensity as physical correlates of linguistic stress. *Journal of the Acoustical Society of America*, 1955, *27*, 765—768.

Guyton, A. *Function of the human body.* Philadelphia: W. B. Saunders, 1974.

Hixon, T. J. Turbulent noise sources for speech. *Folia Phoniatrica*, 1966, *18*, 168—182.

Hixon, T. J. Some new techniques for measuring the biomechanical events of speech production: One Laboratory's experiences. ASHA Reports, 1972, 7, 68—103.

Hixon, T. J., Respiratory function in speech. In F. Minifie, T. Hixon, and F. Williams (Eds.), *Normal aspects of speech, hearing, and language.* Englewood Cliffs, New Jersey: Prentice-Hall, 1973, 73—125.

Hixon, T. J., Goldman, M. D., and Mead, J. Kinematics of the chest wall during speech production: Volume displacements of the rib cage, abdomen, and lung. Journal of Speech and Hearing Research, 1973, *16*, 78—115.

Hixon, T. J., and Warren, D. W. Use of plethysmographic techniques in speech research: Two laboratories' experiences. Paper presented at the Annual Convention of the American Speech and Hearing Association, November 1971, Chicago, Illinois.

Isshiki, N. Regulatory mechanism of voice intensity variation. *Journal of Speech and Hearing Research*, 1964, 7, 17—29.

Isshiki, N., and Ringel, R. Air flow during the production of selected consonants. *Journal of Speech and Hearing Research*, 1964, 7, 233—244.

Jaeger, M., and Matthys, H. The pressure flow characteristics of the human airways. In A. Bouhuys (Ed.), *Airway dynamics.* Springfield, Illinois: Charles C. Thomas, 1970, 21—32.

Kent, R., D and Moll, K. L. Vocal-tract characteristics of the stop cognates. *Journal of the Acoustical Society of America*, 1969, *46*, 1549—1555.

Klechak, T. L. Anterior open-bite and oral port constriction. Unpublished Masters thesis, University of North Carolina, Chapel Hill, 1971.

Kozhevnikov, V. A., and Chistovich, L. A. *Speech: Articulation and Perception*. Washington, D.C.: U.S. Department of Commerce, Joint Publications Research Service, 1965.

Ladefoged, P. Subglottal activity during speech. *Proceedings of the Fourth International Congress on Phonetic Science*. The Hague: Mouton, 1962, 73—91.

Ladefoged, P. Linguistic aspects of respiratory phenomena. In A. Bouhuys (Ed.), *Sound production in man. Annals of the New York Academy of Science*, 1968, *155*, 141—151.

Ladefoged, P., Draper, M. H., and Whitteridge, D. Syllables and stress. *Miscellania Phonetica*, 1958, *3*, 1—15.

Ladefoged, P., and McKinney, N. P. Loudness, sound pressure and subglottal pressure in speech. *Journal of the Acoustical Society of America*, 1963, *35*, 454—460.

Lieberman, P. Some acoustic correlates of word stress in American English. *Journal of the Acoustical Society of America*, 1960, *32*, 451—454.

Lieberman, P. *Intonation, perception, and language*. Cambridge, Massachusetts: M.I.T. Press, 1967.

Lubker, J. F. Aerodynamic and ultrasonic assessment techniques in speech-dentofacial research. In *Speech and the dentofacial complex: The state of the art. ASHA Reports*, 1970, *5*, 207—223.

Lubker, J. F. A consideration of transglottal airflow during stop consonant production. *Journal of the Acoustical Society of America*, 1973, *53*, 212—215.

Malecot, A. An experimental study of force of articulation. *Studia Linguistica*, 1955, *9*, 35—44.

Mead, J., Bouhuys, A., and Procter, D. F. Mechanisms generating subglottic pressure. In A. Bouhuys (Ed.), *Sound production in man. Annals of the New York Academy of Science*, 1968, *155*, 177—181.

Moll, K. L., and Daniloff, R. G. Investigation of the timing of velar movements during speech. *Journal of the Acoustical Society of America*, 1971, *50*, 678—684.

Netsell, R. Subglottal and intraoral air pressures during the intervocalic /t/ and /d/. *Phonetica*, 1969, *20*, 68—73.

Öhman, S. E. G. Coarticulation in VCV utterances: Spectrographic measurements. *Journal of the Acoustical Society of America*, 1966, *39*, 151—168.

Öhman, S. E. G. Numerical model of coarticulation. *Journal of the Acoustical Society of America*, 1967, *41*, 310—320.

Perkell, J. A. *Physiology of speech production: Results and implications of a quantitative cineradiographic study*. Cambridge, Massachusetts. M.I.T. Press, 1969.

Rahn, H., Otis, A. B., Chadwick, L. E., and Fenn, W. O. *The pressure—volume diagram of the thorax and lung. American Journal of Physiology*, 1946, *146*, 161—178.

Rothenberg, M. The breath-stream dynamics of simple-released-plosive production. *Bibliotheca Phonetica*, 1968, *6*, 1—117.

Subtelny, J. D., Worth, J. H., and Sakuda, M. Intraoral pressure and rate of flow during speech. *Journal of Speech and Hearing Research*, 1966, *9*, 498—518.

van den Berg, J. W. Direct and indirect determination of the mean subglottic pressure *Folia Phoniatrica*, 1956, *8*, 1—24.

van den Berg, J. W., Zantema, J. T., and Doornenbal, P. On the air resistance and the Bernoulli effect of the human larynx. *Journal of the Acoustical Society of America*, 1957, *29*, 626—631.

Warren, D. W. Velopharyngeal orifice size and upper pharyngeal pressure-flow patterns in normal speech. *Plastic and Reconstructive Surgery*, 1964, *33*, 148—162.(a)

Warren, D. W. Velopharyngeal orifice size and upper pharyngeal pressure-flow patterns in cleft palate speech: a preliminary study. *Plastic and Reconstructive Surgery*, 1964, *34*, 15—26.(b)

Warren, D. W., and Devereux, J. L. An analog study of cleft palate speech. *Cleft Palate Journal*, 1966, *3*, 103—114.

Warren, D, W., Duany, L. F., and Fischer, N. D. Nasal pathway resistance in normal and cleft lip and palate subjects. *Cleft Palate Journal*, 1969, *6*, 134—140.

Warren, D. W., and DuBois, A. B. A pressure-flow technique for measuring velopharyngeal orifice area during continuous speech. *Cleft Palate Journal*, 1964, *1*, 52—71.

Warren, D. W., and Hall, D. J. Glottal activity and intraoral pressure during stop consonant productions. *Folia Phoniatrica*, 1973, *25*, 121—129.

Warren, D. W., and Mackler, S. B. Duration of oral port constriction in normal and cleft palate speech. *Journal of Speech and Hearing Research*, 1968, *11*, 391—401.

Warren, D. W., and Ryon, W. E. Oral port constriction, nasal resistance, and respiratory aspects of cleft palate speech: An analog study. *Cleft Palate Journal*, 1967, *4*, 38—46.

Warren, D. W., and Wood, M. T. Respiratory volumes in normal speech: A possible reason for intraoral pressure differences among voiced and voiceless consonants. *Journal of the Acoustical Society of America*, 1969, *45*, 466—469.

chapter **5**

Peripheral Mechanisms of Speech Motor Control

James H. Abbs   Gerald R. Eilenberg

University of Washington, Seattle

The physiological mechanisms underlying the oral communication process represent a scientific challenge of major proportion. It is apparent that these processes are served by some of man's most complex sensorimotor systems. Indeed, the sensorimotor complexity involved in the production and perception of speech is sufficient in itself to serve as a major barrier to serious physiological study. In addition, exploration of animal systems does not provide direct information on the physiological mechanisms underlying human oral communication. This latter difficulty is particularly limiting in relation to the mechanisms underlying the *motor processes* of speech. That is, while it is considered legitimate to investigate the primate nervous system for clues to human speech signal processing, it is considerably more difficult to develop animal models in the study of speech production.[1] In part, these limitations provide the rationale for the focus of the present chapter upon the *peripheral mechanisms of speech production*. Since the investigator with an interest in the motor acts of speech must confine his observations to human subjects, exploration of neuromuscular mechanisms must be limited to what can be inferred from unobtrusive observation of the speech output. Thus, the validity of inferences from the speech output to higher levels of control are dependent upon the degree to which we understand the various levels of the speech motor processes, particularly the peripheral motor systems. The diagram shown in Figure 5.1 should clarify this point. It is a schematic block diagram of the speech motor control system, with specific reference to the accessibility of underlying neuro-

---

[1]In this context, it should be noted that while the development of animal models for the study of speech production is difficult, it certainly is not impossible. Recent research by Sutton and Larson (1974) and Sutton *et al.* (1973) suggests that fundamental neuromuscular mechanisms underlying speech motor control can be studied through the use of nonhuman primate models.

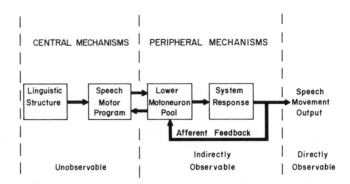

Figure 5.1 A highly schematic diagram of the speech motor control system. The inclusion of central mechanisms is consistent with our systems philosophy, but we do not believe a correspondence to specific physiological processes can be made at this time.

muscular mechanisms. As noted in Figure 5.1, components of the output of the speech control mechanism are, in large part, directly observable. The recent development of speech monitoring capabilities, such as those discussed by Abbs and Watkin (this volume) and Warren (this volume), has greatly facilitated direct observation of speech movements, speech muscle activity, and/or associated aerodynamic events.

The peripheral mechanisms immediately underlying the speech output (Figure 5.1) include (*1*) the mechanical response of the peripheral structures, and (*2*) the contributions of short latency afferent feedback mechanisms. Functionally, these peripheral elements can be approximated through the use of systems analysis techniques and the application of external disturbance paradigms (some of which will be specified in the present chapter). By contrast, however, the central mechanisms are relatively inaccessible, especially in relation to their specific function contributions to speech motor control. The inaccessibility of central mechanisms has led to the development of abstract linguistic or psychological models of higher-level contributions. Unfortunately, these models only indirectly reflect the physiological characteristics of the actual system. The substance of these models is generally a series of consistent but abstract assertions regarding central and/or peripheral contributions to the speech system output. While such models are worthwhile, they are hardly ideal for providing a meaningful description of the actual physical or physiological activity of the speech motor control system. Indeed, it is relatively impossible from observations of system output to make inferences concerning central (or even peripheral) mechanisms of control. That is, it is very difficult to discern, from an observation of speech output activity, which aspects of that output reflect central control or an underlying linguistic code, and which components represent peripheral contributions (afferent feedback mechanisms and/or mechanical properties). One means of beginning to overcome this difficulty is through careful experimental specification of the peripheral mechanisms. That is, if we are able to specify the contributions of the peripheral system, we will be in a more reasonable position to make inferences as to the nature of the central mechanism's contributions.

Based upon the foregoing arguments, the purpose of the present chapter is to (1) synthesize some of the research literature on peripheral speech mechanisms, and (2) further document the necessity of specifically considering these mechanisms in the control of speech production. The data, arguments, and hypotheses presented here are in a preliminary form; the need for continued programs of research is obvious.

As shown in Figure 5.1, we have divided the peripheral speech production mechanisms into two major components: (1) the *peripheral mechanical properties* and (2) the *afferent feedback mechanisms*. A complete quantitative model of the peripheral mechanisms must specify the interdependence of these two components as well as their individual contributions. However, since each of these components has the capability to contribute significantly to speech system output, and their specific contribution is largely unknown, they both represent major deterrents to models that attempt to relate speech system output to higher levels of speech motor control. To specify the nature of these two components, considerable research must be conducted that treats them as elements experimentally isolated from the total mechanism. There are certain dangers as well as advantages in exploring the peripheral speech production system isolated from its actual function for speech. In light of these dangers, it is necessary to confirm hypotheses resulting from these experiments with data that are obtained under conditions which can be related to the speech production function of the system and incorporate the normal contributions of central mechanisms as well.

Peripheral Mechanical Properties

The importance of peripheral mechanical properties has been recognized in most models of speech motor control. However, in large part, these properties have not been measured, simulated, or synthesized into a functional model. Few, if any, studies have evaluated these properties in relation to their actual physical influence upon speech movements, particularly in the articulatory system. Most often, experimenters in speech production have taken the view that mechanical properties limit a speaker's ability to move the speech structures in consistent correspondence with an underlying phonological or phonetic unit. In recent speech literature, the first specific suggestions that mechanical constraints were the basis for interphonemic variation in articulatory movement was made by House (1961) and Stevens and House (1963). They invoked this appealing hypothesis to explain variations in acoustic measures of vowel duration and vowel formant frequency that were observed to relate to changes in phonetic context. A number of more recent authors have implicitly (or explicitly) accepted this explanation as the basis, in part, for the phenomenon of *coarticulation*. In summarizing this argument, Smith (1971, p. 69) stated,

> It would be hypothesized that although the neuronal commands to the muscles are essentially the same in most of the muscles involved in the production of a phoneme, the inertia and damped

response of the articulators themselves could produce different observed gestures depending upon the different positions of the articulators in the immediate phonetic context.

Recent proponents of this view appear to include Cooper (1966), Stevens and Halle (1967), and Daniloff and Moll (1968). Despite these contentions, however, it cannot be assumed that peripheral mechanical influences are *limiting* in their influence upon speech movements. The passive properties of inertia and elasticity most appropriately are considered energy storage mechanisms, and although they may *absorb* energy generated during one interval of time, they have the capability to release that energy for later contributions to the system's output. For example, mechanically stored elastic energy is known to facilitate, not limit, the control of respiratory maneuvers for generation of speech air pressures (Mead, Bouhuys, and Proctor, 1968). Another example more closely related to rapid movement is found in the biomechanics of the frog's jumping capability. The frog's gastrocnemius muscle has a rather long tendon. In this motor phenomenon, as noted by Hill (1950), the energy stored in this tendon elasticity allows the frog to move his hind limb much faster than the gastrocnemius muscle contraction alone can provide. Apparently, mechanical facilitation of this sort is widespread in motor systems; additional examples are provided by Weis-Fogh (1961), Bennet-Clark and Lucey (1967), and Brown (1967). One would expect that in a highly evolved system like the speech production mechanism, similar mechanical facilitation would be operating to assist the generation of speech movements.

One study that apparently supports a mechanical constraint hypothesis was conducted by Lindblom (1967). However, a careful review of Lindblom's findings suggests that he does not actually address the mechanical constraint issue, that the peripheral mechanical properties (and not the forcing function input) were responsible for the observed variations in jaw movement. What Lindblom did accomplish was the selection of an input forcing function to comply with his a priori hypothesis concerning the mechanical influence of the jaw upon acoustic vowel duration. Lindblom was able to demonstrate the feasibility of the mechanical constraint hypothesis but not its actual operation. The only means by which a mechanical influence could be evaluated would involve the observation of relative levels of muscle activity to obtain some indication of system forcing functions. A further limiting factor in the model was that only arbitrary ratios (not measured values) of elasticity, inertia, and viscosity were incorporated; Lindblom assumed the articulators to be critically damped.

While peripheral mechanical properties have been discussed by individuals interested in speech movement control, a review of these properties in the context of what is known concerning motor biomechanics is appropriate. We have found it useful to separate mechanical characteristics into three major categories: (*1*) the active muscle properties, (*2*) variations in the muscle force translation system, and (*3*) passive mechanical contributions. The nature of these properties and their hypothetical interaction are illustrated schematically in Figure 5.2. It should be noted that the interaction of these three factors (as illustrated in Figure 5.2) varies considerably, depending on the speech structure under study and the level of model sophistication that is desired.

Active Muscle Properties

The complex processes involved in the transfer from neural activity to muscle force (i.e., the active properties of muscle) have been the subject of a considerable research effort in physiology and biomechanics. One way to view this transfer is to represent muscle contraction as a biomechanical, rather than a biochemical, process. Such representations, as shown in Figure 5.3, can be made in the context of *second order* mechanical models (with lumped parameters). These models have been shown to simulate a large variety of forces and movements.[2]

Early efforts to model the mechanical properties of muscle (Wilkie, 1956, 1968; Hill, 1953) concentrated on developing precise descriptions of isometric and isotonic contractile states and responses of isolated muscle to twitch and tetanus electrical

---

[2]Articulator properties and movement are measured and modeled utilizing mechanical concepts including applied force, elasticity, viscosity, and inertia. *Elasticity* (K) is a spring-like property which opposes stretch or compression with a force (F) proportional to the displacement (1) from rest length: $F = Kl$. *Viscosity* (B) is a friction-like property which opposes movement with a force proportional to the velocity (v): $F = Bv$. *Inertia* (M) is a weight-like property which opposes changes in motion with a force proportional to the acceleration (a): $F = Ma$. The ideal contractile element (C) generates a force proportional to an input activation signal regardless of movement of position.

It is to be emphasized that the mechanical properties K, B, and M are used to create abstract and exact models. When these models are taken to represent physiological properties, care and ingenuity are required to keep the model within manageable limits and at the same time obtain a useful representation of the actual physiology. In muscle the biomechanical properties are distributed; in the model they are viewed as *lumped parameters*, that is, isolated elements. For a model, mechanical parameters are measured by observing force, displacement, velocity, and/or acceleration of an articulator or muscle due to known external *applied forces*. Hence, the inferred values are viewed as effective values with respect to the applied force and the movement variables l, v, and a. The description of articulator properties obtained in this gross manner may or may not be comparable with muscle fiber properties obtained on a microscopic level (Gordon, Huxley, and Julian, 1966), depending on the method used (Carlson and Wilkie, 1974).

If an articulatory muscle is modeled with its mechanical parameters assembled as in Figure 5.3, the *transfer function* between the input signal (EMG) and the output force (Fm) is the product of the electromechanical transfer function and the transfer function for the mechanical variables Ks, Kp, and B. When a simple linear model (where Ks, Kp, and B have constant values) is assumed, then both transfer functions may be treated as *first order* and the resulting product will form a *second order system* (Gottlieb and Agarwal, 1970). If several second order systems are coupled (several muscle models assembled to form an articulator model), then the order of the resulting system may be higher, depending on the configuration.

Experiments where the displacement is kept constant $(v, a = o)$ are referred to as *isometric*, and the absence of viscous and inertial forces allows the elastic property to be measured. In an isometric experiment at rest length (Figure 5.3, curve b), the contractile force may be calibrated with the input forcing function. In an *isotonic* experiment, a constant applied force creates a constant velocity response which allows the elucidation of viscous properties: $F = C - Bv$ (here, elastic forces are assumed minimal). The initial acceleration due to a known abrupt force (square pulse force) can be used to estimate inertial properties. The *twitch—tension* response to a short electrical stimulus is a basic property which is modeled as the *impulse response* of a constant state system (one activated by an ideal contractile element). The *tetanus* response to a constant stimulus is often made to study the maximally active state.

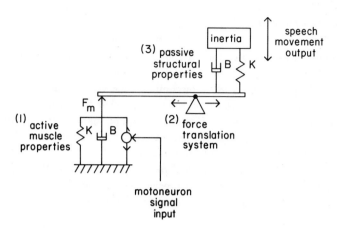

Figure 5.2 A conceptual representation of the three major mechanical elements of the speech motor periphery. F_m, K, and B are the mechanical properties of force, elasticity, and viscosity, respectively. As can be seen in this diagram these elements are thought to mediate between the motoneuron signal input to the peripheral system and the movement output.

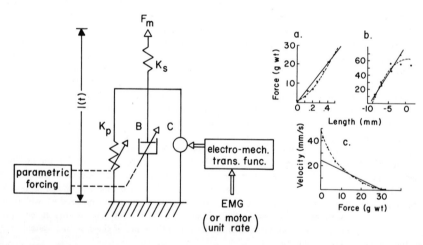

Figure 5.3 A schematic diagram representing the mechanical properties of isolated skeletal muscle and its electrical input. Two competing theories for muscle activation are represented (ideal contractile, C and parametric; refer to text). K_p, K_s, and B are the parallel and series muscle elasticity and apparent viscosity, respectively. The muscle output force, F_m, drives the speech articulator as depicted in Figure 2. The curves shown in the right half of the figure (after Green, 1969) are adaptations of earlier results (Abbott and Wilkie, 1953; Jewell and Wilkie, 1958). They illustrate muscle data that the model attempts to encompass: (a) the load—extension curve of the series elastic element in the frog sartorius muscle, (b) the tension—length curve of contracting frog sartorius muscle, and (c) force—velocity curve of isometrically contracting sartorius muscle. The solid lines are linear approximations to the various corresponding data curves.

stimuli.[3] Wilkie (1956, p. 177) suggests that "resting muscle is soft and freely extensible. On stimulation the muscle passes into a new physical state—it becomes hard, develops tension, resists stretching, lifts loads." This statement illustrates the complexity of the transfer from neural signals to muscle force and the significance of considering the changes in muscle properties that occur as a function of active neural innervation.

More recently, Houk (1963), Milhorn (1966), Milsum (1966), Schwan (1969), and Talbot and Gessner (1973) have discussed muscle models activated by an ideal contractile element (C in Figure 5.3) in parallel or in series with constant viscoelastic elements. These viscoelastic components are linear approximations to empirically derived curves (Figure 5.3, curves a,b,c). The goal of these models was to provide a means of incorporating active muscle properties into larger neural control models, a purpose not inconsistent with the present chapter. Hence, in these models, the muscle output force, F_m, is not a simple function of the level of neural input but depends also on the mechanical parameters associated with the active state. Direct electromyographic (EMG) input can then be employed to give a transfer function between that input and movement. In the model defined here, muscle activity is represented on four different levels: (*1*) bioelectric level (EMG, measured in volts); (*2*) biomechanical contractile force (C, measured in dynes); (*3*) the biomechanical parameters of elasticity (K, measured in dynes/cm) and viscosity (B, measured in dynes/cm/sec); and (*4*) the muscle length (*l*, measured in cm), the associated movement variables (velocity and acceleration measured in cm/sec and cm/sec^2), and the muscle output force F_m (measured in dynes). The relationship among these levels is not simple. However, the observations typically made of EMG or speech movements must take such relations into account for optimal interpretation. For example, the electromechanical transfer function (Figure 5.3) would vary depending on the assumed relationship between EMG and motor unit rate. A model such as that shown in Figure 5.3 offers a quantitative means of comparing human muscle during voluntary contraction (Milner-Brown, Stein, and Yemm, 1973a, b,c) and stimulus-induced contraction of isolated animal muscle (Mannard and Stein, 1973).

Because speech movements involve rapid transitions by the articulatory musculature between the active and passive states, it is apparent that the constant linear models described above (and shown in Figure 5.3) may not provide the best means for simulating speech movements. In a parametrically forced model (Milhorn, 1966), where the state variables (K_p and B in Figure 5.3) are directly influenced by neural input, the change from a compliant to a stiff elastic viscous body (and the implicit dynamics) is accomplished in an explicit manner (unlike a linear model). In an interesting review (Green, 1969), it was shown that a three-element model (K_p, B, and K_s, in Figure 5.3), if parametrically forced, could accurately predict isometric tension as a function of time for twitch and tetanus, and was superior to the ideal contractile model in its prediction of isometric peak tension as a function of stimulus

---

[3]Excellent reviews of this work and related issues may be found in the following books: Wilkie, 1968; Carlson and Wilkie, 1974, Bendall, 1969; and Aidley, 1971.

rate. In a parametrically forced model, the ideal contractile element, C, is no longer required to activate the model, since force is produced by changes in K_p. In a very elaborate, quasi-physiological model (Perkell, 1974)[4] a stepwise, parametrically forced representation already has been successfully utilized to simulate tongue movements.

Based upon the necessity to incorporate mechanical properties that are influenced by the activity level of the neuromuscular system, it is apparent that such properties must be considered in the development of speech models. As noted, one active mechanical property is related to the rate of muscle shortening and is referred to as *apparent viscosity* (B in Figure 5.3) (Fenn and Marsh, 1935; Hill, 1938). The rate at which a muscle can convert chemical energy to mechanical energy is limited. Apparent viscosity is manifest in the observation that the maximum force a muscle can apply is reduced as its rate of shortening increases, as indicated in Figure 5.3, curve C. One would expect this active viscosity to be an important consideration in many of the speech muscles, especially in view of the rather high-velocity, transient movements that are required for speech.

It is possible to document the presence of some of these properties during the motor acts of speech production. In a study conducted by one of the present authors, the muscles that appear to move the lower lip in the inferior—superior dimension were investigated (Abbs, 1973b). The purpose of this study was to specify the relationship between the pattern of EMG activity and the nature of lip movement. The rationale employed was that if the EMG (smoothed and rectified) represents the contractile force, C, applied within a muscle, then the EMG movement relation would have the identity of a *transfer function*. This transfer function would be indicative of the influence of the active (and passive) mechanical forces upon the movement being observed. The data analysis procedure employed in this investigation is illustrated in Figure 5.4.

On the left of the diagram shown in Figure 5.4 is an oscillographic record showing the audio signal, the lower lip movement (independent of jaw movement), and the smoothed and rectified EMG from the orbicularis oris and depressor labii inferior muscles. These EMG and movement signals were recorded during the production of that speech nonsense phrase, *That's a* [hæbæb] *again.* As indicated in the diagram, the lower lip displacement signal was differentiated to provide a continuous velocity signal. Lower lip velocity is shown in the oscillograph record on the right of Figure 5.4. To provide a better basis for comparison of EMG activity and movement,

---

[4]An alternative representation of muscle function has been proposed by Partridge (1967). In his model, the neural input controls a force generator through the muscle's nonlinear, active length—tension properties. Partridge's model incorporates an *internal position feedback mechanism* which is apparently provided by the molecular chemistry of the contractile process. The inclusion by Partridge of a position servo was the result of experiments he conducted on the load-moving characteristics of isolated muscle. In these experiments, he found that variation in inertial load had little influence (in the physiological range) upon the isotonic (position) response of isolated muscle. This experimental preparation is a much better analog to the speech tasks of articulatory muscles than the twitch and tetanic experiments which led to the more traditional models represented in Figure 5.3. Partridge's model has been received favorably by motor control physiologists (Houk, personal communication, 1974) and would appear to have considerable utility in the future modeling of the articulatory system.

bulence, formant frequencies are associated with burst, periodic-like waves, and quasi-random waves respectively, that is, with all types of speech waves other than quiescent. The true vocal tract resonance is specified by the frequency of the damped resonant response when the formant is isolated from other aspects of the behavior of the vocal mechanism, such as the glottal wave and the radiation characteristics of the vocal tract. The formant frequencies are related to the length of the vocal tract; a long tract (as for men) is associated with lower formant frequencies, and a short tract (as for children) is associated with the higher frequencies. Women normally have formant frequencies between those for men and children, since their vocal tracts are usually longer than those of children but shorter than those of men.

FORMANT AMPLITUDE

A *formant amplitude* of a vowel or consonant is the maximum amplitude of its associated formant frequency. That is, each formant frequency will have a maximum amplitude known as the formant amplitude, ordinarily measured in decibels (dB). This amplitude depends upon the force with which the formant is excited. This definition of formant amplitude correlates with, but is distinct from, both the amplitude of the formant peak in the frequency domain and the amplitude of its exponential envelope in the time domain. Although formant frequency is perhaps a more information-bearing parameter than other formant characteristics, amplitude measures provide additional information that should not be overlooked in the acoustical study of speech sounds. Formant amplitudes, as in the case of formant frequencies, are associated with all types of speech waves other than quiescent. It is obvious that in any given study of the acoustical characteristics of speech, the number of relevant formant amplitude measures will be the same as the number of important formant frequency measures.

FORMANT BANDWIDTH

A *formant bandwidth* of a vowel or consonant is the width of the formant 3 dB down from the peak. Thus each formant has associated with it a formant frequency, a formant amplitude, and a formant bandwidth. Since there is a known relation between formant amplitudes and formant bandwidths, many research studies will report only one of the two acoustic phonetic parameters, depending upon the particular subject of interest. Again, only the first several formant bandwidths are normally of interest, and they may be associated with all speech wave types other than quiescent. A classic study of the methods of measuring vowel formant bandwidths was published by Dunn in 1961.

ANTIRESONANCE

An *antiresonance* of a vowel or consonant is the frequency at which a major reduction occurs in the magnitude of the envelope of the speech spectrum. Antiresonances may result from a side branching of the vocal tract, as in nasalization, or from location of sources along the tract, as in constrictions generating turbulence. The frequency of the antiresonance is given in cps or Hz. Although information is gained from the study of three or four formants, it is ordinarily necessary to consider only the first two antiresonances as information-bearing parameters for speech research. Antiresonances are of major importance in studying the properties of nasalization, both for nasalized vowels and for nasal consonants. All speech wave types other than quiescent can have antiresonances associated with them.

Figure 6.2 illustrates the acoustic phonetic parameters of gap in the word *appoints*, broad-band continuous spectrum in the word *shook*, formant frequencies and ampli-

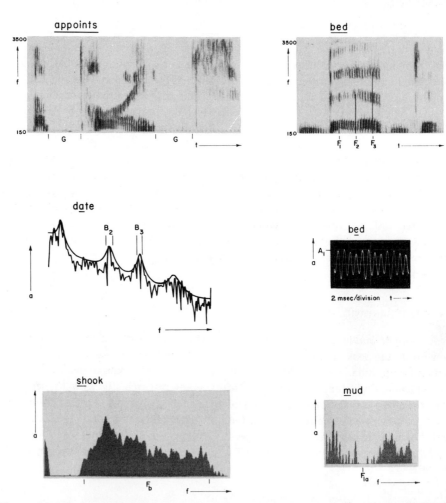

Figure 6.2 Spectrographic and oscilloscopic displays of a selected set of the basic acoustic phonetic parameters: G = gap; F_b = broad-band continuous spectrum; F_1 = frequency of the vowel 1st formant; F_2 = frequency of the vowel 2nd formant; F_3 = frequency of the vowel 3rd formant; A_1 = amplitude of the vowel 1st formant; B_2 and B_3 = bandwidths of the vowel 2nd and 3rd formants; F_{1a} = frequency of the 1st consonant anti-resonance. [From Peterson and Shoup, 1966b.]

control. Observation of speech movements and/or speech EMG without an appreciation of the contribution of active muscle elasticity may well result in conclusions that
are erroneous.

Variations in the Muscle Force Translation System

While the level of muscle force, F_m, can be treated as the result of an electromechanical transfer function from EMG input, as discussed above, the contribution
this force makes to movement in various speech and nonspeech tasks will depend on
its translation to the structure of interest. This kind of variation is especially significant
for researchers who are attempting to relate relative levels of EMG activity to certain
speech production tasks. Most motor acts, including speech, represent the result of many
muscles acting in two or three dimensions to create a net force or torque for the generation
of movement. As structures are changed in their position and a muscle shortens or
lengthens, the *effective muscle force* provided will change, even though the EMG
level recorded from that muscle may not.

One common example of variations in the muscle force translated to a structure is
the lever type of biomechanical mechanism found in skeletal muscle systems. Examination of the motor biomechanics literature reveals that most investigators find it
necessary to take into account changes in effective muscle force that occur as a result
of structure position changes (Penrod *et al.*, 1972).

A hypothetical example of this phenomenon in the orofacial system is the change
in effective muscle force generated by the anterior belly of the digastric (ABD) for
jaw lowering movements. As illustrated in Figure 5.6(a), the ABD has its origin in the
digastric fossa of the mandible and inserts into the hyoid bone via a tendonous loop.
If it can be assumed (for the purpose of this example) that *(1)* the mandible rotates
around an axis at the condyle, and *(2)* during jaw lowering the hyoid bone and skull
remain fixed, the variation in the effective muscle force provided by the ABD as a
function of jaw position can be specified. As illustrated in Figure 5.6(a), of the total
muscle force provided by the ABD (Fm), only that component that is tangent to the
arc of mandibular rotation (Ft) is effective in producing mandibular rotation. It is
also apparent from Figure 5.6(a) that the magnitude of the Ft vector is proportional
to the cosine of the angle θ. Thus, as the jaw is lowered, θ becomes increasingly large,
and the effective force available to rotate the jaw, Ft, is reduced in proportion to the
cosine of this angle. The curve shown in Figure 5.6(b) is an illustration of the hypothetical change in the effective ABD jaw lowering force (Ft) as a function of the
position of the jaw.

The importance of considering peripheral biomechanics in the interpretation of
measures from these systems is apparent from this illustration. Specifically, if one
were to observe EMG levels in the ABD during jaw movement, the relative changes in
those levels for various speech tasks could only be interpreted in relation to the
effective jaw lowering force of that muscle, which appears to be directly dependent
upon jaw position. In other words, the EMG levels would be expected to follow overall
force generated by the ABD (Fm), while the force available to generate movement (Ft)

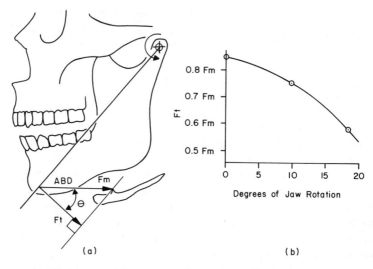

Figure 5.6 An illustration of variation in the effective force generated by the anterior belly of the digastric (ABD) muscle for jaw opening; (a) a schematic representation of the force generated by ABD (Fm) and the vector of that force that is tangent to the arc of rotation of the jaw (Ft), and (b) calculated variation in Ft as a function of degrees of jaw rotation from rest (0 degrees) to approximately 2 cm of inter incisor separation (18.5 degrees).

would be different from these EMG levels. A related, but somewhat more complicated, example of this same phenomenon (with which we have had some experience in our attempts to model the lower lip) is that of the effective lip closing force provided by the orbicularis oris inferior (*OOI*) muscle. When the lower lip is depressed, the muscle force provided by the OOI has a distinct superiorly directed component which acts to raise the lip towards closure. However, when the lip is at rest, the primary vector of muscle force of this OOI is horizontal and would appear to act primarily to draw the corners of the mouth medially. At any position between lip depression and rest, the effective superiorly directed force provided by the OOI would appear to be a function of the sine of the angle between the fibers of this muscle and the horizontal plane. Thus, as with the ABD, it is obvious that EMG from the orbicularis oris can be interpreted only with a knowledge of the position of the lip itself.

While variations in muscle force translation are additional complications in our attempt at understanding the peripheral speech production system, such phenomena in turn highlight the elegance of the neural control mechanisms, which must take into account such variations to generate speech movements. Moreover, there are reasons to expect that there are many other examples of force translation in the speech production system. For example, Hixon, Goldman, and Mead (1973), in their observations of the relative contribution of rib cage and abdominal changes to lung volume variations for speech, found that speech gestures of the respiratory system are produced with the abdomen somewhat reduced in diameter from its rest or relaxed position. One of the ad hoc interpretations offered for this speech production posture was that the respiratory system was positioned so as to give the respiratory muscles optimal mechanical advantage (force translation) in generating large changes in lung volume for small changes in muscle length. Similar *posturing* has been reported for various upper airway structures prior to the beginning of speech production and also may be related to optimizing force translation (Leanderson and Lindblom, 1972; Minifie *et al.*, 1974). Unfortunately, at the present time, findings on upper airway posturing have been confined to EMG activity observations without simultaneous observation of movement.

Passive Mechanical Properties

Often when speech researchers speak of system mechanical properties, they are referring to the passive properties. These components can be thought of as *(1)* the bone, skin, tendons, ligaments, and fatty tissue that do not receive neural input, and *(2)* muscle in the passive state. The forces exerted by passive components are modeled by the same biomechanical parameters described in the section entitled "Active Muscle Properties" (and in footnote 2), that is, inertia, elasticity, and viscosity. Thus, when a mechanical system moves through a certain pattern of motion, these three passive mechanical properties exert their influence, each contributing to the motion in a particular manner and each requiring a special component of the applied force. Components of elasticity and inertia, as noted earlier, are inherent energy storage devices, and hence would tend to redistribute temporally the applied force in relation to the resultant motion. In the respiratory system, as it operates for both speech and life purposes, passive elasticity is an integral component. Moreover, only after the recoil forces were measured and incorporated into models of respiration were physiologists able to evaluate possible neural control of respiration for speech (Mead, Bouhuys, and Proctor, 1968).

An example of the contribution of passive elasticity to the control of upper airway or articulatory systems is observable in the movement of the lips. Our first awareness of these mechanisms came as a function of observing lower lip movements simultaneously with EMG from the orbicularis oris and the depressor labii inferior muscles (Abbs and Netsell, 1973a; Abbs, 1973b). Frequently we observed *(1)* a reduction in depressor muscle activity followed by an elevation movement (without concomitant orbicularis oris or mentalis EMG), and/or *(2)* a sustained contraction of the depressor labii inferior muscle concomitant with a sustained depression of the lower lip. These observations could be explained best as the result of passive elasticity that contributes to lip movement via elastic energy storage and restoration. As a further test of this phenomenon, we asked several subjects in a pilot experiment to perform the following sequence of activities: *(1)* raise the lower lip, *(2)* relax the lip musculature, *(3)* depress the lower lip, and *(4)* relax the lip musculature. Figure 5.7 provides an example of an oscillographic record of the pattern of lower lip movement and orbicularis oris and depressor labii inferior EMG obtained from one repetition of this sequence. As indicated in the figure, one can separate the passive components of lower lip movement from their active counterparts. The schematic representation at the bottom of the diagram is an attempt to represent the condition of the passive elasticity as a function of the displacement of the lip mass from rest. While only inertia and elasticity

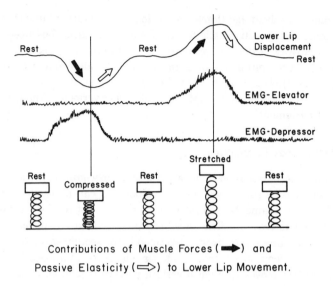

Contributions of Muscle Forces (➡) and
Passive Elasticity (⇨) to Lower Lip Movement.

Figure 5.7 An oscillographic record of lower lip displacement, orbicularis oris, and depressor labii inferior muscle activity. The *spring-mass* system shown in the lower portion of this record is included to provide an indication of the condition of lower lip passive elasticity as a function of various lip positions.

are shown, the EMG movement patterns indicate the presence of viscosity necessary to avoid oscillations.

If one extends the example given here (in relation to passive elasticity) to parallel components of inertia and viscosity, it is apparent that mechanical properties are an integral part of the speech motor control system. Just as the back swing in ball throwing is an attempt to add momentum, it may be that some of the bizarre patterns of movement observed during speech production result from system utilization of inertial or elastic properties. Further, it is possible that some of the movements and muscle activity patterns that have been implicated as evidence of *higher level control* in abstract models (such as *coarticulation*) may represent system activity utilization of mechanical properties. In any case, it is clear that one cannot observe movements and/or EMG patterns and make inferences to underlying neuromuscular mechanisms without an appreciation of these passive properties.

Simulation of Speech System Peripheral Biomechanics

Recently several investigators have reported the development of preliminary quantitative models of the speech production periphery (Eilenberg, 1973; Abbs, 1974; Perkell, 1974). The value of such models is that by simulation one can ascertain whether their conceptual hypotheses of the relationship between applied muscle force and movement are sound; that is, whether their measured values of system biomechanical variables and hypothesized interactions between these variables are reasonable approximations of the actual system. Indeed, quantitative modeling and simulation *require* that one consider (and in many cases measure) all variables that may provide significant contributions to the transfer between muscle forces and the speech movement that results. The biomechanical models generated, to date, admittedly are simplistic and lack the isomorphism required for their optimal use as tools to further explore system function. However, in the future, as these modeling efforts mature, one should be able to *(1)* provide a more meaningful representation of the multiple control signals that must be available to drive articulatory structures during speech production, and *(2)* assess some of the current models of speech motor control.

As noted previously, mechanical properties of the speech mechanism represent only one aspect of the peripheral speech production system. Another important element of the peripheral system involves the afferent feedback mechanisms.

Afferent Feedback Mechanisms

Historically, the role of afferent feedback mechanisms in the control of speech movements has been a controversial issue. In most theoretical discussions of speech motor control, the specific role of these mechanisms has been minimized either implicitly or explicitly (Ohala, 1970; Smith, 1971; Perkell, 1972). In the opinion of the present authors, this theoretical position has resulted from a simple paucity of positive support for the operation of these mechanisms in the control of speech movements. An additional contributing factor relates to the fact that unequivocal support for the contribution of afferent feedback to nonspeech voluntary control also has been lacking.

Since 1969, however, several key studies *(1)* suggest that afferent feedback is an important component of voluntary motor control (for both speech and nonspeech activities), and *(2)* define some basic aspects of its contribution. In keeping with the purposes of the present chapter, the discussion that follows will be an attempt to review these studies and assess the contribution to speech movement that peripheral afferent feedback mechanisms may provide.

The General Nature of Afferent Feedback Contributions

For some time, neurophysiologists have been concerned with the microphysiology of various reflex arcs in the spinal motor system. As a result of this work, we have a very precise understanding of *(1)* the sensorineural information available to the nervous system on the length of a muscle, its tension, and the position of a joint, and *(2)* the influence of this afferent activity on associated efferent fibers. To a large extent, these basic studies have dealt with acute preparations in the spinal motor systems of anesthetized animals. Thus, until recently, it has not been documented (to the satisfaction of most investigators dealing with *voluntary* motor control) that afferent feedback mechanisms are crucial elements in the on-line motor control process. That is, it is conceivable that sensory information, such as that available from spindle, tendon, and joint receptors, is part of a long latency or slow monitoring system employed exclusively *(1)* to control involuntary postural or tonic motor activities, and/or *(2)* to provide peripheral state information as a basis for central nervous system efferent commands.

However, some recent experiments conducted specifically on voluntary movement in human subjects provide evidence that is contrary to this view. In one set of experiments, reported by Smith (1969) and Smith, Roberts, and Atkins (1972), the contribution of a specific afferent mechanism in the control of voluntary movements was investigated directly. These studies involved select anesthetization of the gamma efferent innervation to the muscles that flex the elbow. The special anesthetization procedure employed by Smith (1969) was based upon the relatively high susceptibility of small nerve fibers to local anesthesia. That is, it apparently is possible to block the small gamma efferent fibers of a mixed nerve without influencing the conductive integrity of the larger fibers (viz., the alpha motoneurons and the afferent fibers which innervate spindle, tendon, joint, and tactile receptors), as shown by Matthews and Rushworth (1957, 1958). To verify the selectivity of the anesthesia, Smith monitored the excitability of the stretch reflex, the force of elbow flexor contraction (to assure alpha motoneuron integrity), and sensory responses to light touch, pin prick (pain), and temperature. Sensory fibers innervating the receptors responsible for sensations of pin prick and temperature are as small or smaller than the gamma efferent fibers. Thus, when the stretch reflex, sensation of pin prick, and temperature were hyposensitive or absent, and muscle force and sensations of light touch were normal, it was possible to assume gamma deinnervation. Under these carefully specified nerve block conditions, Smith observed the performance of 20 subjects on a battery of voluntary motor tasks designed to test various aspects of the gamma efferent system's role in control of elbow flexion.

In general, Smith's (1969) results indicated a loss in *fine* motor control. Specifically, she found that subjects demonstrated a loss of normal ability to accelerate the forearm and to stop forearm motion on a finger-to-nose touching task. These results were interpreted to suggest that, in elbow flexion, the gamma loop acts to *(1)* optimize the initiation of movement, via agonist facilitation, and *(2)* damp movement, via antagonist facilitation. It is possible, of course, that reciprocal inhibition of antagonist and agonist, respectively, also may have been involved in these findings. In any case, Smith's very carefully controlled study is evidence for afferent contribution to voluntary movement control, even in systems (unlike speech) where visual feedback information is available.

Studies by Gottlieb, Agarwal, and Stark (1970) and Gottlieb and Agarwal (1972, 1973) further specify the role of afferent feedback in the control of voluntary motor activity. These authors elicited H-reflexes in the popliteal nerve during production of voluntary plantar foot torque. In the H-reflex procedure, electrical stimuli to the popliteal nerve are thought to depolarize the afferent fibers (without influencing the motor fibers, when the stimuli levels are set correctly), resulting in a muscle contraction that is mediated across the spinal cord. The relative level of the EMG responses is taken as an index of the excitability of the spinal afferent-to-efferent pathway. Gottlieb and Agarwal applied their stimuli at a number of time points during the voluntary production of plantar foot torque. Responses were monitored in both antagonistic and agonistic muscles (gastrocnemius and anterior tibial, respectively).

The findings of this study suggested that the afferent activity was facilitory in its influence upon the agonistic motoneurons and inhibitory to the antagonistic muscles. That is, during voluntary plantar contraction, greater increments of EMG were observed in the agonist (gastrocnemius) and reduced increments were observed in the antagonist (anterior tibial). The facilitation and inhibition patterns observed were not static, but displayed transient properties which varied systematically with the time course of foot torque that was produced. More specifically, Gottlieb and Agarwal (1973) suggest that the time sequence of events for a voluntary change in foot torque involved: *(1)* a general stiffening of the motor system (via alpha activation), *(2)* a quickening of the dynamic properties of the agonistic reflex arc by increasing reflex sensitivity, *(3)* muscle activation, and *(4)* inhibition of antagonistic reflex arcs. These authors summarize their experiments by noting, "They [peripheral feedback mechanisms] are not simply convenient devices for regulating a centrally determined muscle length, but rather, are actively recruited into the integrated pattern of dynamic, voluntary motor control" (p. 139).

Employing a paradigm similar to that of Gottlieb and Agarwal, Pierrot-Deseilligny and Lacert (1973) observed both the H-reflex and the tendon reflex in the period immediately prior to the onset of voluntary movement. While the H-reflex reflects the excitability of the afferent-to-efferent pathway, the tendon reflex, elicited mechanically (rather than electrically), is (in addition) indicative of the sensitivity of the spindle receptor. Thus, comparison of the *relative responsiveness* of the reflex arc to these two stimuli provides a basis for assessing the nature of central facilitation of the afferent-to-efferent pathway as well as the spindle receptor sensitivity levels (apparently controlled by gamma efferent drive). The data reported by these authors showed that the H- and tendon reflexes have corresponding transient patterns reflecting facilitation and inhibition for the agonistic and antagonistic muscles, respectively. The findings of Pierrot-Deseilligny and Lacert confirm the reports of Gottlieb and Agarwal. In addition, however, measures of tendon reflex responses suggest that the gamma efferent drive also has transient characteristics that are related to the temporal properties of voluntary movement. Pierrot-Deseilligny and Lacert also found that the pattern of H- and tendon reflex sensitivity varied with different patterns of movement, suggesting that the peripheral feedback loop is adaptable to the demands of the dynamic control process.

Based on these studies and other corroborating data, it appears safe to conclude that afferent feedback (at least that feedback from the spindle receptors) plays an important role in the control of human voluntary movement. Research on nonspeech motor activities also offers some information on the specific influence of these peripheral loops in the control of voluntary movement. Indeed, if we wish to have a meaningful appreciation of the contribution of afferent feedback mechanisms, it is not adequate simply to acknowledge that contribution. We must understand, as much as possible, the exact nature of the peripheral loop contributions in relation to the kind of movement being executed.

Some initial data on the response properties of the peripheral loop are available in the work of Neilson (1972a, 1972b, 1972c, 1973). These studies, although they are not by any means the only ones, appear to provide some fundamental information on variation in peripheral loop responses as a function of *(1)* variation in the muscle contraction being executed and *(2)* peripheral stimuli. Neilson's paradigm involved the voluntary isometric contraction of the biceps brachi against a spring attached to the forearm. The subject, lying supine, was instructed to maintain the forearm in the vertical position. Sinusoidal disturbing forces of varying frequencies were applied to the forearm at several levels of biceps voluntary contraction. The peripheral loop responses to these applied forces, observable as increments of EMG amplitude in the biceps muscle, were then analyzed in relation to the level of voluntary contraction and the frequency of the disturbing forces. As a specific example of Neilson's findings, Figure 5.8 shows peripheral loop gain as a function of the frequency of the disturbing force. We can see from this representation that the peripheral loop, which apparently responds without central influence to stimuli frequencies above 2 Hz (Neilson, 1972a), is not a simple scalar amplifier. Indeed, the afferent—efferent pathway has dynamic response characteristics that vary with the pattern of afferent firing (apparently as elicited by the disturbing forces).

It also can be seen from this diagram that changes in voluntary contraction influence both the gain and tuning characteristics of the peripheral loop. These data would imply that afferent feedback cannot be considered a simple slave execution device for mechanisms of higher control. That is, these peripheral feedback systems (as evidenced by the complexity of the gain curves shown in Figure 5.8) apparently make a contribution to the motor output that is truly supplementary to the driving signals of the central nervous system. It would appear that if afferent feedback is implicated in the control of speech movements, these mechanisms offer yet another limitation (in addition to peripheral mechanical properties) on the validity of inferences one might make from speech output to higher levels of control. Obviously, in light of the data reviewed, the next and most crucial question to be addressed in this discussion concerns the likelihood that afferent feedback is operative in the control of speech movements.

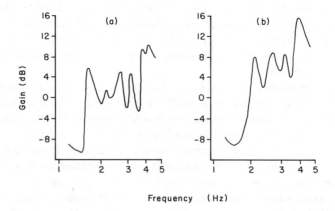

Figure 5.8 Gain of *peripheral feedback loop* plotted as a function of frequency of disturbing force. Curve (a) was obtained with the subject contracting against a load of 4.5 kg, curve (b) against a load of 9.0 kg. Note the differences in overall gain and the actual resonant peaks for these two levels of voluntary contraction. [Adapted from Neilson, 1972c.]

Afferent Feedback Control of Speech

A number of investigators have attempted to outline the role of afferent feedback in the control of speech movements. To the knowledge of the present authors, the first attempt to disrupt nonauditory afferent feedback in the speech system was made by Guttman (1954).[5] Guttman introduced anesthesia bilaterally to "the medial surface of the mandible [resulting in] complete anesthesia to touch and pain of the tongue, lower lip, and superficial tissues of the mandible" (p. 32). Based upon the reports by Guttman of sensory loss, it would appear that he anesthetized the inferior alveolar and lingual branches of the mandibular nerve. Subsequent studies by McCroskey (1958), McCroskey, Corley, and Jackson (1959), Weber (1961), Ringel and Steer (1963), Scott and Ringel (1971a, 1971b), and others involved similar anesthetization procedures, with the addition of local anesthesia to the infraorbital branch of the trigeminal nerve. Other variations in these subsequent studies included the use of intraoral topical anesthesia and/or auditory feedback disruptions.

Unfortunately, due to methodological and conceptual difficulties, these studies have not provided a great deal of specific information concerning the afferent feedback control of speech. One major problem with these investigations was that the techniques employed to assess the speech motor changes resulting from sensory deprivation were either imprecise or inappropriate. For example, in several of these studies, speech errors were counted and categorized as a means of assessing the influence of the neural blockade. If one is attempting to analyze a neuromuscular control system that has muscle tension and/or structural movement as an output, perceptual judgment is inadequate for discerning subtle variations in the nature of that output. Moreover, in many of these oral sensory deprivation studies, although it was generally implied that a *feedback control system* was under investigation, little experimental attention was given to the specific afferent channels that may have been anesthetized. Thus, because of conceptual ambiguity and technical limitations, the specific properties of the speech system's output that might be affected most directly by the anesthetization procedures (i.e., muscle tension, muscle length, joint position and/or movement) were not monitored. As pointed out by one of the present authors, measures such as the acoustic signal, phonetic transcription, and judged *correctness of production* are several transfer functions removed from the specific motor output of the system and are likely to be confounded by physical and perceptual distortion (Abbs, 1973a). Moreover, it is quite likely that the compensatory capabilities of the speech system (as hypothesized by MacNeilage (1970) and documented, in part, by Abbs and Netsell (1973b)) may have resulted in a speech output that was acoustically, perceptually, and phonetically quite acceptable, despite considerable compensatory re-organization in the individual motor activities that generated those productions.

A second major problem with oral sensory deprivation studies in speech has involved imprecision in experimental definition of the sensory (or motor) deprivation that resulted from anesthetization. Typically, measures have not been employed

---

[5]Guttman differentiated between auditory and nonauditory afferent feedback channels. While we recognize the obvious importance of auditory feedback, the present discussion will deal primarily with the nonauditory mechanisms.

to determine *(1)* the exact extent or nature of the sensory deprivation, *(2)* the condition of the mandibular or facial reflexes, and/or *(3)* the postblockade strength of some of the muscles that may have been inadvertently weakened. In essence, the independent variable in these studies has not been manipulated or defined precisely, at least not to the extent that clear cause—effect relations could be established. Some of these difficulties were further discussed in a series of studies by Borden (1972). Borden's studies appeared to suggest that the nerve block procedures employed by Guttman (1954), McCroskey (1958), and others not only resulted in *sensory* deprivation, but also caused *motor* weakness in some of the muscles innervated by the mylohyoid branch of the mandibular nerve. Borden's findings consisted of sizable reductions in the level of EMG recorded from the mylohyoid and digastric muscles following the standard administration of anesthesia. Borden's findings also suggested that some of the speech errors observed in these early studies may have been due, in part, to motor weakness, and could not, as had been previously suggested, be attributed directly to a loss of sensory feedback. Based upon diadochokinetic rate data, Locke (1968) suggested similar limitations to the techniques used for obtaining oral sensory blockade. More recently, based upon a reassessment of the literature in neuroantomy and clinical neurology, Abbs, Folkins, and Sivarajan (1975) reported data that could be interpreted to suggest that some part of the innervation to the facial muscles was provided through trigeminal nerve branches previously thought to contain only sensory fibers. In the first of two studies, they reported evidence that partial motor innervation to the facial muscles was provided through the infraorbital branch of the trigeminal nerve. Analysis of data from the second study (in preparation) which was conducted on the inferior alveolar branch by these same authors suggests similar conclusions. The findings of Abbs, Folkins, and Sivarajan, coupled with the earlier findings of Borden (1972) and Locke (1968), appear to further limit confidence in the interpretation of results from speech studies employing trigeminal nerve anesthesia as a means of eliminating oral sensation.

In the last few years, as a function of a renewed interest in the role of afferent feedback in the control of speech movements, several studies, enjoying the benefit of more refined techniques for the study of speech physiology, have readdressed this issue. These recent studies, in the context of a more clearly designated perspective on feedback control systems, also have provided some specific hypotheses as to the nature of the contribution that afferent feedback might play in the control of speech movements. These recent data have been generated by the use of two experimental paradigms. One series of studies has focused upon articulatory movement coordination, typically involving the observation of movement of one or more articulators. While these movement studies offer only circumstantial evidence for afferent control, they do provide (unlike earlier studies) some substantive hypotheses as to the possible contribution of afferent feedback to particular speech movement patterns. A second group of studies involves experimental disruption of particular aspects of the speech motor control system and analyses of the system's response to these disruptions. The second group of studies provides the most direct evidence for the operation of afferent feedback in speech production.

Afferent Control of Articulatory Coordination

Movement data on articulatory coordination and afferent feedback can be discussed best in relation to a theoretical position taken by MacNeilage (1970). Based upon some earlier suggestions by Lashley (1951), MacNeilage attempted to provide an explanation of the variability of individual speech movements and their common contributory participation in the generation of vocal tract configurations. In essence, MacNeilage suggested that an acoustically or spatially similar output of the speech production system often is achieved with considerable variation in the individual motor behaviors that contribute to that output. This phenomenon was termed *motor equivalence*. Execution of speech movements based upon this abstraction could be achieved most efficiently through the contribution of afferent feedback. That is, if a particular vocal tract configuration is the controlled variable of the speech system, this output could be generally programmed by the central driving mechanisms and specifically executed by peripheral afferent feedback control. Figure 5.9 is an illustration of motor equivalence as observed in a reciprocal compensation pattern of the lower lip and jaw. In this study (Abbs and Netsell, 1973b), inferior displacement of the lower lip (independent of the jaw) and the jaw were observed for the utterance a [hæb bæb] again.

The graph shown in Figure 5.9 displays measures of the extreme position of the

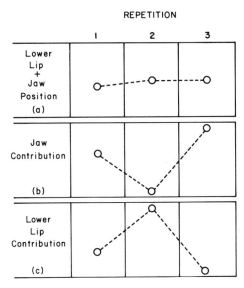

Figure 5.9 Relative contribution of the lower lip (a) and jaw (b) to the absolute height of the lower lip (c) for three productions of the second [æ] in [hæ bæ b]. The measures shown here were obtained at the point of greatest absolute depression of the lower lip for the vowel. Note that the variation in jaw or lower lip from one production to another is quite large, while the acoustically significant output of the system (lower lip + jaw) is relatively constant. [Adapted from Abbs and Netsell, 1973b.]

lower lip (input 1) and the jaw (input 2) for the second [æ] vowel for three repetitions of this utterance. As illustrated in this graph, the jaw and lower lip appear to trade off in their relative contribution to the labial configuration for the vowel production despite a relatively constant lower lip plus jaw position (output). It would seem unlikely that the variability in lower lip or jaw position shown here originated as a part of a central control signal. On the contrary, these compensatory trade-offs would appear to be most efficiently achieved by peripheral mechanisms involving afferent feedback control. Other studies of articulatory coordination appear to suggest comparable patterns of reciprocal compensation between movement of the jaw, lower lip, and upper lip (Hughes, 1975) or the jaw and the tongue (Abbs, Netsell, and Hixon, 1972; Kent, 1970). In particular, the upper and lower lips tend to be inversely complementary in their contribution to the labial closing gesture. In a study by MacNeilage, Krones, and Hanson (1969), it was reported that, although the prespeech position of the jaw varies over a "range of several millimeters," the jaw position adopted for a particular initial utterance shows very little variation. These data were interpreted to suggest that "the production mechanism must take into account the prespeech position of the jaw, and make a speech-initial jaw movement contingent upon the prespeech position" (as cited by MacNeilage, 1970, p. 192).

These findings, showing patterns of speech movement that vary in adaptation to the state of the peripheral system, would tend to support the notion that the central mechanism prepares the system for certain target behaviors and that the peripheral mechanisms are charged with carrying out these general goals employing afferent feedback. Moreover, these observations provide the basis for a more meaningful evaluation of the studies in which the speech motor control system has been experimentally disrupted. In particular, it is of interest to determine if the motor output of the disrupted speech production system displays response patterns that are directly compensatory to the pattern of controlled disruption.

Experimental Disruption of Speech Motor Control

One study, in which a specific feedback system was interrupted for a single articulator, was conducted by one of the present authors (Abbs, 1973a). This study involved application of a differential nerve block technique (as previously employed by Smith, 1969) to the mandibular branch of the trigeminal nerve. This block procedure, involving the innervation to the masticatory muscles, incorporated specific tests of tactile, temperature, and pain sensitivity along with measures of jaw closing force. On the basis of these tests, it was possible to infer, as had been done by Smith (1969) and Smith, Roberts, and Atkins (1972), that gamma efferent innervation to the masticatory system had been interrupted. To provide a meaningful measure of the influence of the blockade on speech control, jaw movement was transduced during productions of a specified speech sample. Analysis of these jaw movements for a number of utterance repetitions revealed that the disrupted jaw control system was unable to apply adequate patterns of jaw opening and closing forces. The other significant finding of this study was that, while the gamma efferent innervation to the jaw musculature was apparently impaired, speech performance was judged to be perceptually normal.

The latter result was surprising inasmuch as the jaw appeared to be limited in its capability to contribute normally to production of the experimental speech sample. In particular, it was observed that the jaw contributed considerably less than normal to bilabial closing gestures under conditions of gamma deinnervation. The reduction in jaw elevation for the bilabial stop (averaging slightly over 3 mm) apparently was compensated by increased depression and elevation movements of the upper and lower lips, respectively. What was particularly intriguing about these compensatory lip movements was that the experimental subjects had no conscious or volitional role in producing them. That is, both of the experimental subjects in this study reported that they employed normal speech control. On the basis of these observations, it would appear that the speech control mechanism is able to institute changes in the motor drive for individual speech articulators without any volitional modification of the overall control program. Pipe smokers, as noted by MacNeilage (1970), have little difficulty in modifying lingual or labial movements to overcome immobility of the jaw.

Based upon observations under these conditions of select anesthesia and the findings discussed earlier concerning the compensatory interaction of individual speech structures, it can be hypothesized that afferent feedback is an on-line compensatory control mechanism which implements (without volitional control or conscious awareness) the fine peripheral details of the speech production process. This hypothesis was tested directly in a recent experiment conducted by Folkins and Abbs (1974). For this study, a custom tooth splint was constructed that permitted the application of loads to the jaw during ongoing speech production. A line illustration of the tooth splint is shown on the left side of Figure 5.10. Attached to the tooth splint were stiff, thin wires which extended through the corners of the mouth (element A). These stiff wires were, in turn, attached to a horizontal bar (element B) which was connected via a hinge joint to a vertical bar (element C). This vertical bar moved in the inferior—superior dimension with the movements of the jaw and provided a means of applying resistive loads. The resistive loads were applied with a device that stopped upward jaw movement in the same manner that a bicycle brake is employed to stop a wheel:

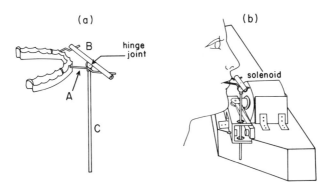

Figure 5.10 (a) Prosthodontic splint and attachments: A = horizontal bar, B = steel wire, C = vertical bar on which resistive loads were applied; (b) Apparatus employed to apply loads to the jaw as it was positioned for the experiment. [Adapted from Folkins and Abbs, 1974.]

via activation of a solenoid (right side of Figure 5.10). To provide a basis for interpreting the responses to these sudden resistive loads, movements of the upper lip, lower lip, and jaw were monitored (Abbs and Gilbert, 1973). Subjects had no prior knowledge of the utterances during which the jaw was to be interrupted. Loads were introduced in such a way that the likelihood of compensation (if compensatory mechanisms were capable of operating) would be very high. In particular, we chose to introduce the load during the jaw closing movement associated with the bilabial closure for the first [p] of the utterance [hæ pæp]. This choice, we felt, would create a situation in which bilabial closure would be disrupted if compensation, either by the upper lip or lower lip, did not occur. For the 3 subjects, a total of 109 loads were introduced. In all cases where a load was introduced, the subjects were able to produce adequate bilabial closure. Observations of lip and jaw activity that accompanied these interrupted productions demonstrated a clear pattern of on-line compensation.

Figure 5.11 shows an oscillographic record of the upper lip, lower lip, and jaw along with speech audio for a normal production of the test phrase and for an interrupted production. From this comparison, compensation is apparent in both the upper and lower lips. The upper lip depresses to a greater extent than normal, and the lower

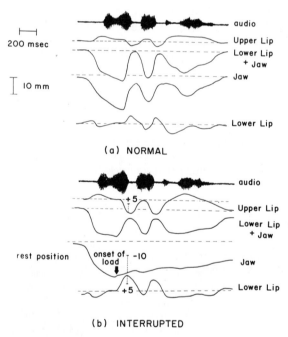

Figure 5.11 Oscillographic records of movement signals recorded during (a) normal repetition *of That's a [hœ pœ p] again,* and (b) the repetition of the same utterance where interruption was introduced. The point of resistive load initiation is indicated by an arrow on the jaw displacement signal. Numbers on record (b) refer to differences in displacement (in mm) of the upper lip, lower lip, and jaw at the point of bilabial closure in comparison with the normal and interrupted utterances. Horizontal dashed lines indicate the *resting positions* assumed by the subject between repetitions of the test utterances. [Adapted from Folkins and Abbs, 1974.]

lip elevates to a considerably higher position than normal. It is also worthwhile to note the relative pattern of compensation demonstrated on these particular records. The jaw was reduced from its normal elevation by approximately 10 mm. In response to that reduction, the upper lip increased its movement by approximately 5 mm and the lower lip did the same, resulting in a net compensatory gesture that was exactly equal to the load-induced change in jaw elevation. This sort of compensatory pattern was observed in almost all of the interruptions.

Figure 5.12 illustrates the mean upper lip displacement for normal productions, and the magnitude of the same movement for the interrupted gestures. As can be seen in the figure, the average upper lip depression movement for bilabial closure was almost twice normal in situations where the jaw was loaded. One might argue that these patterns are the result of two open-loop programs: one for interrupted utterances (in which the lips are activated to maximum activity), and one for normal utterances (in which the jaw provides its normal contribution). This argument appears unlikely since (*1*) all three subjects demonstrated perfect compensations the first time that their jaw motion was interrupted, and (2) each interruption was slightly different, which would make a single preprogram for interrupted utterances unworkable. Indeed, these data suggest that compensatory afferent mechanisms may be a usual form of labial-mandibular intercoordination behavior, as implied by the hypotheses cited previously. This particular study, in conjunction with the observations discussed earlier, provides concrete evidence that the motor control of the lips and jaw is subject to, and depends upon, on-line feedback control for the generation of speech movements, at least for certain movement patterns.[6]

However, one should not make direct inferences from these results to the control processes of other components of the speech production mechanism. The tongue, jaw,

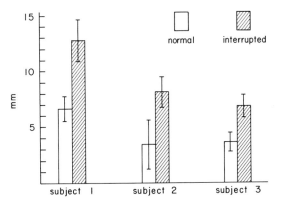

Figure 5.12 Comparison of mean upper lip displacement as a function of normal and interrupted conditions for the three experimental subjects. The length of the brackets indicates the range of variance for each of the means represented (plus and minus one standard deviation).

[6]Recent work by Bauer (1974), where impulsive loads were applied to the lower lip, would appear to corroborate these findings. However, Bauer's findings may be confounded, in part, by the internal (nonafferent feedback) position servo hypothesized by Partridge (1967).

lips, velum, and pharynx vary considerably in their specific movements for speech production and also have different mechanical properties. In addition, these various articulators may not be homogeneously supplied with the sensory receptors most appropriate for feedback control of speech movements. Based upon these inter-articulator differences, each of the motor subsystems of the speech mechanism must be carefully evaluated individually. Sweeping theoretical generalizations concerning open-loop or closed-loop control, or experiments involving massive sensory deprivation, are only appropriate to abstract models of speech production where the specifics of underlying neuromuscular mechanisms are insignificant. By contrast, models which strive for physiological reality must incorporate the heterogeneity of function that is represented in the components of the speech production mechanism.

While the preceding discussion of afferent feedback mechanisms in speech has been quite selective, the implications are clear. First, it appears that the peripheral nervous system for speech production *is capable* of making significant and unique contributions to the speech output. Secondly, the complexity of those contributions (if the data cited earlier on the spinal motor system are representative) requires that we develop a better understanding of these mechanisms before attempting to make major inferences to higher levels of control.

Implications of Peripheral Properties for an Understanding of Speech Production

It is apparent from the preceding discussions that while abstract models of motor control provide a basis for description of speech production as a form of human behavior, they suffer the same difficulties that have always plagued psychological models. That is, although these models provide abstract explanations of speech motor control, in large part they fail to incorporate precise quantitative information on the physical and physiological properties that are hypothesized to be operating. As suggested by Perkell (1972, p. 1), "We have very little knowledge of what these properties actually are." As a consequence, the speech pathologist or neurologist, concerned with the abnormalities of the neuromuscular mechanisms underlying speech, finds little concrete or fundamental information upon which to base programs of diagnosis, rehabilitation, or clinical research.

It would appear that one means to overcome these difficulties is to begin to gather systematic, fundamental data on the peripheral properties of the speech production system. Using such information, perhaps we can anticipate the development of models of speech motor control that are closer to physical and physiological reality and allow for more substantive inferences concerning central nervous system contributions.

It should be emphasized, however, that these complex biomechanical and neuromuscular processes are not especially amenable to modeling efforts where the model itself is only a qualitative interpretation of numerical phenomenology. These processes must be characterized in a framework of quantitative modeling where (*1*) experimenters are required to represent their guesses, premises, assumptions, approximations, and data in a system of universal and defined logic (i.e., mathematics and systems science); and *(2)* the test of these hypotheses is a functional and formal system simulation. From the standpoint of the present authors, this approach, is, as implied by Perkell, the only manner in which we can begin to determine what it is we *know* and *do not know* about the motor control of speech production.

REFERENCES

Abbott, B. C., and Wilkie, D. R. The relation between velocity of shortening and the tension-length curve of skeletal muscle. *Journal of Physiology*, 1953, *120*, 214–223.

Abbs, J. H. The influence of the gamma motor system on jaw movements during speech: a theoretical framework and some preliminary observations. *Journal of Speech and Hearing Research*, 1973, *16*, 175–200. (a)

Abbs, J. H. Some mechanical properties of lower lip movement during speech production. *Phonetica*, 1973, *28*, 65–75. (b)

Abbs, J. H. Peripheral properties of speech motor control. Paper presented at symposium, New Developments in Brain Function for Speech Production and Perception, American Association for the Advancement of Science, February 24–March 1, 1974, San Francisco, California.

Abbs, J. H., Folkins, J. W., and Sivarajan, M. Motor impairment following blockade of the infraorbital nerve: Implications for the use of anesthetization techniques in speech research. *Journal of Speech and Hearing Research*, 1975 (In Press).

Abbs, J. H., andd Gilbert, B. N. A strain gage transduction system for lip and jaw motion in two dimensions: Design criteria and calibration data. *Journal of Speech and Hearing Research*, 1973, *16*, 248–256.

Abbs, J. H., and Netsell, R. A dynamic analysis of two-dimensional muscle force contributions to lower lip movement. *Journal of the Acoustical Society of America*, 1973, *53*, 295 (Abstract). (a)

Abbs, J. H., and Netsell, R. Coordination of the jaw and lower lip during speech production. Paper presented at the Annual Convention of the American Speech and Hearing Association, October, 12–15, 1973, Detroit, Michigan. (b)

Abbs, J. H., Netsell, R., and Hixon, T. J. Variations in mandibular displacement, velocity and acceleration as a function of phonetic context. *Journal of the Acoustical Society of America*, 1972, *51*, 89 (Abstract).

Aidley, D. J. *The physiology of excitable cells*. Cambridge, England: Cambridge University Press, 1971.

Bauer, L. L. Peripheral control and mechanical properties of the lips during speech. Unpublished master's thesis, University of Wisconsin, 1974.

Bendall, J. R. *Muscles, molecules and movement*. New York: American Elsevier, 1969.

Bennet-Clark, H. C., and Lucey, E. C. The jump of the flea: A study of the energetics and a model of the mechanism. *Journal of Experimental Biology*, 1967, *47*, 59–76.

Borden, G. J. Some effects of oral anesthesia on speech: a perceptual and electromyographic analysis. Unpublished doctoral dissertation, City University of New York, 1972.

Brown, R. H. J. Mechanism of locust jumping. *Nature*, 1967, *214*, 939.

Carlson, F. D., and Wilkie, D. R. *Muscle physiology*. Englewood Cliffs, New Jersey: Prentice-Hall, 1974.

Cooper, F. S. Describing the speech process in motor command terms. *Status Reports on Speech Research*, Haskins Laboratories, 1966, SR 5/6, 2.1–2.27.

Daniloff, R., and Moll, K. Coarticulation of lip rounding. *Journal of Speech and Hearing Research*, 1968, *11*, 707–721.

Eilenberg, G. R. Control system models of speech production physiology. Paper presented at Annual Convention of the American Speech and Hearing Association, October 12–15, 1973, Detroit, Michigan.

Fenn, W. O., and Marsh, B. S. Muscular force at different speeds of shortening. *Journal of Physiology*, 1935, *85*, 277–297.

Folkins, J. W., and Abbs, J. H. Lip and jaw motor control during speech: Motor reorganization responses to external interference. *Journal of the Acoustical Society America*, 1974, *55*, 385 (Abstract).

Frankel, V. H., Burstein, A. H., and Brooks, B. D. Biomechanics of internal derangement of the knee. *Journal of Bone and Joint Surgery*, 1971, *53*, 945—962.

Gordon, A. M., Huxley, A. F., and Julian, F. J. The variation in isometric tension with sarcomere length in vertebrate muscle fibres. *Journal of Physiology*, 1966, *184*, 170—192.

Gottlieb, G. L., and Agarwal, G. C. The role of the myotatic reflex in the voluntary control of movements. *Brain Research*, 1972, *40*, 139—143.

Gottlieb, G. L., and Agarwal, G. C. Dynamic relation between isometric muscle tension and the electromyogram in man. *Journal of Applied Physiology*, 1970, *30*, 345—351.

Gottlieb, G. L., and Agarwal, G. C. Coordination of posture and movement. In J. E. Desmedt (Ed.), *New developments in electromyography and clinical neurophysiology*. Basel: S. Karger, 1973, *3*, 418—427.

Gottlieb, G. L., Agarwal, G. C., and Stark, L. Interactions between voluntary and postural mechanisms of the human motor system. *Journal of Neurophysiology*, 1970, *33*, 365—381.

Green, D. G. A note on modelling muscle in physiological regulators. *Medical and Biological Engineering*, 1969, *7*, 41—47.

Guttman, N. Experimental studies of the speech control system. Unpublished doctoral dissertation, University of Illinois, 1954.

Hill, A. V. The heat of shortening and dynamic constant of muscle. *Proceedings of the Royal Society*, 1938, *B126*, 136—195.

Hill, A. V. The series elastic component of muscle. *Proceedings of the Royal Society*, 1950, B *137*, 273—280.

Hill, A. V. The mechanics of active muscle. *Proceedings of the Royal Society*. 1953, *B141*, 104—117.

Hixon, T. J., Goldman, M. D., and Mead, J. Kinematics of the chest wall during speech production: Volume displacements of the rib cage, abdomen, and lung. *Journal of Speech and Hearing Research*, 1973, *16*, 78—115.

Houk, J. C. A mathematical model of the stretch reflex in human muscle systems. Unpublished master's thesis, Massachusetts Institute of Technology, 1963.

House, A. S. On vowel duration in English. *Journal of the Acoustical Society of America*, 1961, *33*, 1174—1178.

Hughes, O. M. An evaluation of speech movement coordination in the labial—mandibular system. Unpublished master's thesis, University of Washington, 1975.

Jewell, B. R., and Wilkie, D. R. An analysis of mechanical components in frog striated muscle. *Journal of Physiology*, 1958, *143*, 515—540.

Kent, R. Investigation of a model of lingual neuro-motor commands. Unpublished doctoral dissertation, University of Iowa, Iowa City, 1970.

Lashley, K. S. The problem of serial order in behavior. In L. A. Jeffress (Ed.), *Cerebral mechanisms in behavior*. New York: Wiley, 1951, 112—136.

Leanderson, R., and Lindblom, E. F. Muscle activation for labial speech gestures. *Acta Otolaryngolica*, 1972, *73*, 362—373.

Lindblom, B. Vowel duration and a model of lip mandible coordination. *Quarterly Progress and Status Report*, Speech Trans. Lab., Royal Institute of Technology, 1967, No. *4*, 1—29.

Locke, J. L. A methodological consideration in kinesthetic feedback research. *Journal of Speech and Hearing Research*, 1968, *11*, 668—669.

MacNeilage, P. F. Motor control of serial ordering of speech. *Psychological Review*, 1970, 77, 182—196.

Mannard, A., and Stein, R. B. Determination of the frequency response of isometric soleus muscle in the cat using random nerve stimulation. *Journal of Physiology*, 1973, *229*, 275—296.

MacNeilage, P. F., Krones, R., and Hanson, R. Closed-loop control of the initiation of jaw movement for speech. Paper presented at the meeting of the Acoustical Society of America, San Diego, California, November, 1969.

McCroskey, R. The relative contributions of auditory and tactile cues to certain aspects of speech. *Southern Speech Journal*, 1958, *24*, 84—90.

McCroskey, R., Corley, N., and Jackson, G. Some effects of disrupted tactile cues upon the production of consonants. *Southern Speech Journal,* 1959, *25,* 55—60.

Matthews, P. B., and Rushworth, G. The relative sensitivity of muscle nerve fibers to procaine. *Journal of Physiology,* 1957, *135,* 263—269.

Matthews, P. B., and Rushworth, G. The discharge from muscle spindle as an indicator of gamma paralysis by procaine. *Journal of Physiology,* 1958, *144,* 421—426.

Mead, J., Bouhuys, A., and Proctor, D. F. Mechanisms generating subglottal pressure. *Annals of the New York Academy Science,* 1968, *155,* 171—181.

Milhorn, H. T. *The application of control theory to physiological systems.* Philadelphia, Pennsylvania: W. B. Saunders, 1966.

Milner-Brown, H. S., Stein, R. B., and Yemm, R. The contractile properties of human motor units during voluntary isometric contractions. *Journal of Physiology,* 1973, *228,* 285—306. (a)

Milner-Brown, H. S., Stein, R. B., and Yemm, R. The orderly recruitment of human motor units during voluntary isometric contractions. *Journal of Physiology,* 1973, *230,* 359—370. (b)

Milner-Brown, H. S., Stein, R. B., and Yemm, R. Changes in firing rate of human motor units during linearly changing voluntary contractions. *Journal of Physiology,* 1973 *230* 371—390. (c)

Milsum, J. H. *Biological Control Systems Analysis.* New York: McGraw-Hill, 1966.

Minifie, F. D., Abbs, J. H., Tarlow, A., and Kwaterski, M. EMG activity within the pharynx during speech production. *Journal of Speech and Hearing Research,* 1974, *17,* 497—504.

Neilson, P. D. Speed of response or bandwidth of voluntary system controlling elbow position in intact man. *Medical and Biological Engineering,* 1972, *10,* 450—459. (a)

Neilson, P. D. Frequency-response characteristics of the tonic stretch reflexes of biceps brachii muscle in intact man. *Medical and Biological Engineering* 1972, *10,* 460—472. (b)

Neilson, P. D. Voluntary and reflex control of biceps brachii muscle in spastic—athetotic patients. *Journal of Neurology, Neurosurgery and Psychiatry,* 1972, *35,* 589—598. (c)

Neilson, P. D. Effect of procaine infiltration into biceps muscle in man on superspinal control of reflex transmission. *Journal of Neurology, Neurosurgery and Psychiatry,* 1973, *36,* 87—93.

Ohala, J. Aspects of the control and production of speech. *UCLA Working Papers in Phonetics,* 1970, No. 15.

Partridge, L. D. Intrinsic feedback factors producing inertial compensation in muscle. *Biophysical Journal,* 1967, *7,* 853—863.

Penrod, D. D., Davy, D. T., and Singh, D. P. An optimization approach to tendon force analysis. Paper presented at the 25th Annual Conference on Engineering in Medicine and Biology, Bal Harbour, California, December, 1972.

Perkell, J. S. Toward a physiological model of speech production. Paper presented at Conference on Mathematical Modeling of Speech Processes, September 29—October 2, 1972, Santa Barbara, California.

Perkell, J. S. Quasiphysiological tongue model. *Journal of the Acoustical Society of America,* 1974, *55,* 578—579 (Supplement-Spring).

Pierrot-Deseilligny, E., and Lacert, P. Amplitude and variability of mono-synaptic reflexes prior to various voluntary movements in normal and spastic man. In J. E. Desmed (Ed.), *New developments in electromyography and clinical neurophysiology.* Basel: S. Karger, 1973, *3,* 538—549.

Ringel, R. L., and Steer, M. D. Some effects of tactile and auditory alterations on speech output. *Journal of Speech and Hearing Research,* 1963, *6,* 369—378.

Schwan, H. P. *Biological Engineering.* New York: McGraw-Hill, 1969.

Scott, C. M., and Ringel. R. L. Articulation without oral sensory control. *Journal of Speech and Hearing Research,* 1971, *14,* 804—818. (a)

Scott, C. M., and Ringel, R. L. The effects of motor and sensory disruptions on speech: A description of articulation. *Journal of Speech and Hearing Research,* 1971, *14,* 819—828. (b)

Smith, J. L. Fusimotor neuron block and voluntary arm movement in man. Unpublished doctoral dissertation, University of Wisconsin, 1969.

Smith T. S. A phonetic study of the function of the extrinsic tongue muscles. *UCLA Working Papers in Phonetics,* 1971, No. 18.

Smith, J. L., Roberts, E. M., and Atkins, E. Fusimotor neuron block and voluntary arm movement in man. *American Journal of Physical Medicine*, 1972, *51*, 225—239.

Stevens, K. N., and Halle, M. Remarks on analysis by synthesis and distinctive features. In W. Wathen-Dunn (Ed.), *Models for the perception of speech and visual form.* Cambridge, Massachusetts: M.I.T. Press, 1967, 88—102.

Stevens, K. N., and House, A. S. Perturbation of vowel articulation by consonantal context: An acoustical study. *Journal of Speech and Hearing Research*, 1963, *6*, 111—128.

Sussman, H. M., MacNeilage, P. F., and Hanson, R. J. Labial and mandibular dynamics during the production of bilabial consonants: Preliminary observations. *Journal of Speech and Hearing Research*, 1973, *16*, 397—420.

Sutton, D., and Larson, C. R. Effects of brain lesions on primate phonation. *Brain Research*, 1974, *71*, 61—75.

Sutton, D., Larson, C. R., Taylor, E. M., and Lindeman, R. C. Vocalization in Rhesus monkeys: Conditionability. *Brain Research*, 1973, *52*, 225—231.

Talbot, S. M., and Gessner, J. *Systems physiology.* New York: John Wiley, 1973.

Weber, B. A. Effect of high level masking and anesthetization of oral structures upon articulatory proficiency and voice characteristics of normal speakers. Unpublished master's thesis, Pennsylvania State University, 1961.

Weis-Fogh, T. Power in flapping flight. In J. A. Ramsey and V. V. Wigglesworth (Ed.), *The cell and the organism.* Cambridge, England: Cambridge University Press, 1961, 120—138.

Wilkie, D. R. The mechanical properties of muscle. *British Medical Bulletin*, 1956, 1200, 177—182.

Wilkie, D. R. *Muscle.* London: Edward Arnold, 1968.

PART III

THE SPEECH SIGNAL

chapter 6

Acoustic Characteristics of Speech Sounds

June E. Shoup   Larry L. Pfeifer

Speech Communications Research Laboratory, Inc., Santa Barbara

The specifications of the acoustic characteristics of speech sounds present problems in all areas of applied speech science: automatic speech recognition, speech understanding systems, speech synthesis, speaker identification, speaker recognition, language identification, and speech aids for the handicapped. The complicated mapping from a continuous acoustic speech signal to a sequence of discrete symbols continues to challenge the speech scientist. Although substantial work has been done in the identification of certain acoustic speech parameters, and much has been learned regarding the acoustic characteristics of speech sounds in isolation and in continuous speech, there remain many unresolved problems for the future.

Relating Speech Physiology and Speech Acoustics

In the preceding chapters it has been evident that there is a direct, but complicated, relationship between the physiological production of speech and the resulting acoustic signal. The classic presentation by Fant (1960) has provided much of the impetus for the study of this complex relationship. It would be a major step forward if a discussion of the acoustic characteristics of speech could include a complete statement of the interrelationship between the two areas of research: the acoustics and the physiology of speech. Such an explanation would provide one of the major fields of research for the future.

A theory specifying the relation between speech physiology and speech acoustics would include a thorough knowledge of respiratory dynamics, laryngeal dynamics, vocal tract response, the generation of turbulence, and the generation of impulses. The studies of van den Berg (1960), Moore and von Leden (1958), Flanagan (1958), Ishizaka and Flanagan (1972), Fant (1960), Mermelstein and Schroeder (1965), Schroeder (1967), Mermelstein (1967), Atal (1970), and Wakita (1972) all have made substantial contributions to the understanding of the relationships between speech physiology and speech acoustics.

Since the theoretical development is still in a relatively embryonic stage, the discussion in the present chapter will include only limited information on physiological explanations for the acoustic characteristics of speech. It is obvious to the authors, however, that in the not-too-distant future a more complete statement of the relationships should be a requirement for any discussion of the acoustics (or of the physiology) of speech sounds. It is hoped that with the increased emphasis on studying the interrelationships, major advances will be forthcoming in this area of research.

The following discussion is divided into two main sections: (*1*) sound units and their properties, and (*2*) practical aspects of the acoustical study of speech sounds.

Sound Units and Their Properties

For years, speech scientists have searched theoretically and experimentally for the characteristics of sounds employed in languages spoken by human beings. It is well known that certain characteristics are more important, or information bearing, than others. The quest for an optimum set of characteristics is a continuing task which may never end but which may be more achievable when the physiological explanations for acoustic speech signals are known. Peterson and Shoup (1966b) suggested two groups of acoustical characteristics of speech: (*1*) speech wave types and (*2*) acoustical speech parameters. Following a brief review of the nature of these acoustical characteristics of speech, the sound units will be treated in terms of their speech wave types and their acoustical speech parameters.

Speech Wave Types

A *speech wave type* is an acoustic speech waveform or combination of waveforms produced by the vocal mechanism in human communication. The speech wave types are described according to the pressure or volume velocity functions of time that are formed during the production of speech. Four basic types are regularly referred to in the literature—namely, quiescent, burst, quasi-random, and quasi-periodic. The last type is sometimes subdivided into three periodic-like types: quasi-periodic, double-periodic, and irregular-periodic. Some of these fundamental wave types can be combined to make an even larger number of speech wave types.

QUIESCENT WAVE

A *quiescent* speech wave might be considered the *null* case since it is a zero-valued sound pressure or volume velocity function of time; that is, all values of the instantaneous amplitude approximate zero. All speech wave types other than the quiescent have an associated sound source, but in the case of the quiescent, there is no sound. The wave is produced during quiet respiration or during certain closures which are formed in the vocal tract in the production of speech. The quiescent speech wave type is associated with speech pauses and with the initial portions of voiceless (unvoiced) plosives, such as /p/, /t/, and /k/.

The importance of relating acoustic and physiological information is illustrated in the analysis of quiescent speech waves. Technically, in analyzing tape recordings, there would be no way to distinguish between silence related to speech pauses or to unvoiced stop sounds and silence not related to speech production at all. Unless there are corroborating physiological records such as X-rays, air pressure measurements, and air flow recordings, initial unvoiced plosives present a problem in acoustic phonetic studies of phone duration. If an utterance begins with $\left[p^h, t^h, k^h\right]$, the first appearance of measurable acoustic data is the burst following the silent portion of the unvoiced plosive. The subinterval of silence associated with the articulatory closure is not measurable unless there are supporting physiological data.

Quite obviously, it is necessary to record speech in a relatively quiet acoustic environment if one is to detect quiescent speech waves. Any background noise will produce an acoustic wave of a quasi-random nature which may be mistaken for a speech signal.

BURST

A speech *burst* is an impulse which is produced by the release of a closure in the vocal tract. The sound source producing a burst is referred to as a *transient source* since it is limited to a short period of time. When the pressure in a vocal cavity is different from the external air pressure, the release of air from, or into, the cavity will result in a burst. The abrupt onset of air flow produces the impulse which characterizes the burst speech wave type. The burst is associated not only with plosives, but also with clicks, ejectives, and implosives (that is, with all stop formations).

QUASI-RANDOM WAVE

A *quasi-random* speech wave is associated with speech sounds for which successive amplitude samples are approximately random in magnitude. A quasi-random speech wave is generated by a frictional sound source. As air passes through the vocal tract egressively or ingressively, the flow will be primarily laminar or primarily turbulent, depending upon the size of the various constrictions and the driving pressure of the air stream. If the constriction is sufficiently narrow and/or if the driving pressure is great enough, the air flow will be turbulent.

Quasi-random speech waves are associated with the unvoiced fricatives and sibilants of speech as well as with all whispered speech. In the case of all sibilants and fricatives other than glottal fricatives, such as $\left[h\right]$, the friction is generated at the place of narrowest constriction in the vocal tract. In whispering and glottal fricatives, the turbulence is generated at the true vocal folds. (In rare instances, the false vocal folds are used in place of the true vocal folds during speech productions, and the resulting sounds are usually considered "defective" or "abnormal" in English.)

QUASI-PERIODIC WAVE

A *quasi-periodic* speech wave is a recurrent sound pressure or volume velocity function of time in which the waveforms for successive periods are approximately the same. The sound source for all periodic-like speech waves is normally the vibration of the true vocal folds, which creates a continuing change in the area of the glottal opening. (Again, the false vocal folds may, on occasion, be used instead of the true ones.) The volume velocity of air flow through the glottal opening varies in a regular manner and results in the quasi-periodic speech wave. Since *quasi-periodic* is the general term for periodic-like speech waves, it is often used in a broader sense to include the double-periodic and irregular-periodic speech waves described below.

A *double-periodic* speech wave has the same properties as the quasi-periodic speech wave except that alternate periods correspond more closely than successive periods. The sound source for double-periodic speech waves is again the vibration of the true vocal folds, but certain physiological conditions, such as growths on the vocal folds, can produce the double-periodicity. Double-periodic waves are produced by normal organs as well, but the laryngeal adjustments involved are not known.

An *irregular-periodic* speech wave also is similar to a quasi-periodic speech wave, but in this case the successive periods vary in an irregular manner. The vibratory motion of the true vocal folds which acts as the sound source is not as regular as that used to produce quasi-periodic speech waves. The irregular vibration is usually heard as *vocal fry*, *creaky voice*, or *laryngealization*, depending upon the terminology.

The three types of quasi-periodic (in the broad sense) speech waves are associated with the voiced sounds, such as most vowels, sonorants, and nasals. Because of the complex nature of the vibration of the vocal folds, emotional cues are also given, as well as modes of verbalization such as speaking, singing, or shouting. The rate of vibration of the vocal folds corresponds to the fundamental frequency of the speech wave. This fundamental frequency is one of the basic prosodic speech parameters associated with voiced sound formations, and it contributes to judgments of pitch and emphasis or stress.

COMBINED WAVES

In speech, it is common to find *combined speech wave types*, for example, quasi-random and quasi-periodic. The combined waves are generated by two sound sources such as a narrow constriction creating friction simultaneously with vibration of the vocal folds. This particular combination is associated with voiced fricatives and sibilants as well as with breathy vowels, sonorants, or nasals. Other combined waves can be formed by multiple generators of sounds, such as simultaneous trills. Quite obviously, it is not possible to combine quiescent speech waves with any other speech wave type.

The various speech wave types described above are illustrated in Figure 6.1. All of the oscilloscope tracings are of an adult male speaker. Since the double-periodic speech wave type was not used in the speech of the subject, a synthesizer was used to generate such a speech wave. The portion of the word shown on each display is indicated by underlining. The capital letters identify the extent of the particular speech wave type illustrated.

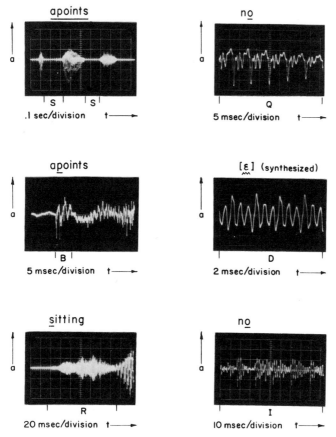

Figure 6.1 Oscilloscope tracings of the basic speech wave types: S = quiescent; B = burst; R = quasi-random; Q = quasi-periodic; D = double-periodic; I = irregular-periodic. [From Peterson and Shoup, 1966b.]

Acoustical Speech Parameters

An *acoustical speech parameter* is a property which may be derived from the speech wave by processing it in some way, such as filtering. The acoustical speech parameter is a transformation of a basic property or combination of properties within the vocal tract and can be related to the physiological production of the speech sound formation in a sometimes complicated manner. As indicated above, there are two fundamental sound sources for speech production: *(1)* friction generation through a narrow constriction or with increased air pressure, and *(2)* vibratory motion of a physio-
logical mechanism (true or false vocal folds, lips, tongue tip, or uvula). From these two sound sources one might expect to find turbulence associated with the friction and frequencies associated with the vibrations. This is indeed the case, and thus the majority of acoustical speech parameters can be specified in reference to these properties.

In speech science it is common to refer to those characteristics associated with individual sounds, or phones, as *phonetic* in nature, and to those which may be thought of as superimposed on the segmental phones as *prosodic* in nature. That is, in physiological terms a sound may be referred to by certain of its physiological phonetic

parameters, such as a bilabial nasal or a high, front vowel, but simultaneous prosodic parameters, such as long duration or high pitch, also may be associated with the sound. This dichotomy between phonetic and prosodic parameters is equally relevant at the acoustic level. The acoustic phonetic parameters include gap, broad-band continuous spectrum, formant frequency, formant amplitude, formant bandwidth, and antiresonance. The acoustic prosodic parameters include acoustic phonetic duration, average fundamental voice frequency, and average speech power.

GAP

A *gap* might be considered to be the *null* set of acoustical phonetic parameters in the same sense that its associated speech wave type, quiescent, might be considered the null speech wave type. Since there is no sound during a quiescent speech wave type, there are no measurable acoustic phonetic parameters. In fact, there is only one acoustic prosodic parameter, that of duration. The term was first used to identify the more or less empty portion of a sound spectrogram evident during the closure of voiceless plosives or during silent pauses in the speech.

BROAD-BAND CONTINUOUS SPECTRUM

A *broad-band continuous spectrum* is a random distribution of pressures over a relatively wide range of frequencies in the speech spectrum. This parameter is associated with quasi-random speech wave types. In the analysis of these quasi-random speech waves, a general frequency region of friction or noise can be determined for the resulting fricative or sibilant formations. The broad-band spectrum is then specified by the upper and lower frequencies of this noise area, in cycles per second (cps), or Hertz (Hz), a term more commonly used today. Since there may be random energy present at a large majority of the frequencies analyzed, the broad-band spectrum is limited to the range of frequencies wherein the amplitudes are relatively high. Although there are severe limitations in considering this acoustic phonetic parameter the most important one for the analysis of quasi-random speech waves, no totally satisfactory set of parameters for such analysis has been found.

FORMANT FREQUENCY

A *formant frequency* of a vowel or consonant is the natural frequency of the decaying sinusoidal response of a resonance of the vocal tract. When the true vocal folds are set into vibration, the air puffs emitted into the vocal tract cause the various cavities (pharyngeal, oral, and nasal) to ring at a set of frequencies referred to as formant frequencies. Each one of the formant frequencies is a separate parameter and usually is specified by number—formant one, two, three, and so on. The numbering begins with the formant of lowest frequency, and the formant frequency is indicated in cps or Hz. Discrimination of most speech sounds is accomplished largely through specification of the first two formant frequencies only, but additional information is provided by the third and possibly by the higher formants. Normally only the first three or four formants are analyzed or synthesized in speech research. Since a formant may be excited by a single impulse, by a series of impulses, or by tur-

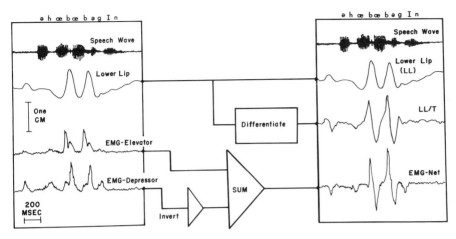

Figure 5.4 Block diagram representation of the analog circuit components employed in the analysis of EMG-to-movement relations for the lower lip. Signals shown here were actually recorded on an optical oscillograph for each step in the analysis.

the smoothed and rectified depressor activity was electronically inverted and added to the elevator activity. The resultant summed EMG signal is shown in the bottom trace of the oscillographic record on the right. Activity below the baseline represents net muscle force directed inferiorly, while activity above the baseline represents net muscle force directed superiorly. The similarity between lower lip velocity and the combined EMG trace is striking. This finding is consistent with data from earlier investigators and tends to suggest that the *apparent viscosity* of active muscle shortening comprises a significant mechanical component of lower lip movement.

In addition to active viscosity, the *inherent parallel elasticity* (K_p in Figure 5.3) of a muscle is known to vary directly with the *level* of active contraction; that is, the greater the contraction, the greater the internal muscle elasticity. This active elastic element again suggests the need for a parametrically forced model. Active elasticity would appear to be a particularly significant element in speech production since many of the moving parts in the speech system, such as the tongue, soft palate, and throat walls, are composed primarily of muscle tissue. It is even conceivable that the mechanical properties of these structures are actively tuned to optimize particular patterns of movement. An active tuning mechanism often has been hypothesized for the vocalis muscle in the control of vocal fold vibration.

In a study that is currently in progress by the present authors, we have been able to observe the functional role of the active elasticity component in the production of bilabial stop consonants. Much of the mass of the lips is muscle tissue; the fibers of the orbicularis oris muscle. As indicated by several EMG studies (Sussman, Mac-Neilage, and Hanson, 1973; Abbs, 1973b), the orbicularis oris muscle acts as a sphincter which closes the oral cavity and provides interlabial contact forces for bilabial occlusion. However, since the orbicularis oris makes up much of the mass of the lips, as the level of contraction increases, the lips appear to become stiffer.

To further document this hypothesis, we conducted a study in our laboratory to determine the elasticity of the lips for two sustained levels of orbicularis oris contraction. In the relaxed state, the lips have an average elasticity of 200 dynes/cm. At a level of contraction *equivalent* to that observed for bilabial closure, this value increased to 2000 dynes/cm. It would appear that without the active muscle stiffening, the lips would not maintain an appropriate seal for the impoundment of intraoral air pressure. Likewise, sudden relaxation of the orbicularis oris would result in reduced elasticity of the lips, thus making them distensible. On the basis of these measures, one might hypothesize that muscle elasticity of the orbicularis oris is related to the mechanism of bilabial stop release.

Figure 5.5 shows an oscillographic record of orbicularis oris EMG, along with the speech acoustic signal, intraoral air pressure, and upper and lower lip movement (inferior—superior dimension only). Just prior to the instant of bilabial release (as indicated on the record), there is a momentary *shutdown* in orbicularis oris EMG activity. This shutdown has been reported consistently in studies where EMG of the orbicularis oris has been observed (Abbs and Netsell, 1973a; Sussman, MacNeilage, and Hanson, 1973; Abbs, 1973b). Based on these observations, it would appear that the release of the bilabial stop is implemented via control of inherent orbicularis oris elasticity. That is, the release event appears to be implemented, at least in part, by a *pulse of inhibition* to the orbicularis oris muscle. Some authors have suggested, however, that labial stop release is generated exclusively by a positive separating force from the depressor labii inferior or levator labii superior muscles. It is obvious from the present example that to generate such interpretations one must appreciate fully peripheral mechanical properties and particularly the central levels of speech motor

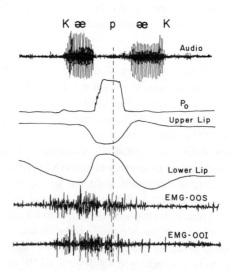

Figure 5.5 An oscillographic record illustrating the momentary *inhibition* of the orbicularis oris muscle (OOI—orbicularis oris inferior, OOS—orbicularis oris superior) in synchrony with the release of the bilabial stop [p]. The time of release is indicated by the vertical dashed lines.

tude in the word *bed*, and antiresonance in the word *mud*. In the broad-band spectrograms at the top, the frequency cutoff is about 3500 Hz, and the baseline is approximately 150 Hz. The amplitude section for the word *shook* extends to approximately 7000 Hz, and that for the word *mud* to 3500 Hz. Formant amplitude in the middle right illustration is shown by means of an oscilloscope tracing. The first formant of the vowel was isolated by means of a bandpass filter and recorded on the oscilloscope. Formant bandwidth is shown in the middle left display. The smooth spectrum envelope in this case was derived by the linear prediction method.

The acoustic phonetic parameters discussed above are not a unique set of phonetic parameters, but they are a set of useful measures for acoustic phonetic research. The reflection coefficients discussed by Wakita in an earlier chapter of this book and other new analysis parameters may serve as better indicators of the acoustical characteristics of speech sounds. The acoustic prosodic parameters and the phonetic ones are of equal importance in understanding the complete acoustical characteristics of speech. As mentioned previously, these prosodic parameters are superimposed on all acoustic phones which have been specified by the acoustic phonetic parameters.

ACOUSTIC PHONETIC DURATION

Acoustic phonetic duration is the time interval of an acoustic phone. Since there is no universally agreed upon definition of an acoustic phone at the present time, it is necessary to determine acoustic phonetic duration by a set of rather arbitrary rules for segmentation in the acoustic domain. Most speech scientists would accept any reasonable method of segmentation to determine acoustic phonetic duration, but the problems in this area are numerous and will be discussed at length in the section of this chapter entitled "Practical Aspects in the Acoustical Study of Speech Sounds." Although certain sounds, such as homorganic stops, can be of an almost instantaneous nature (less than one pitch period of the vocal folds), the average sound formation is between 10 and 100 milliseconds (msec) in duration.

AVERAGE FUNDAMENTAL VOICE FREQUENCY

Average fundamental voice frequency is the frequency of the first harmonic of a periodic-like speech wave which is averaged by a weighting function over an interval of approximately 20 msec. The interval of about 20 msec assures the completion of more than one pitch period of the vocal folds, but it is also short enough that it does not lose rapid changes that may be significant. For this acoustic speech parameter there is a virtual one-to-one correspondence to the related physiological parameter, vibration of the vocal folds. It should perhaps be pointed out that the fundamental voice frequency associated with a speech sound is independent of the formant frequencies of that sound. The former is determined by the rate of vibration of the vocal cords; the higher the rate of vibration, the higher the fundamental frequency, and likewise, the lower the rate, the lower the frequency. The formant frequencies are determined by the configuration of the vocal tract and remain practically constant with a steady-state articulation regardless of a high, low, or changing fundamental frequency.

AVERAGE SPEECH POWER

Average speech power is the product of the pressure and the volume velocity in a
speech wave averaged by a weighting function over an interval of approximately 20
msec. The selection of 20 msec is made on the same basis as it was for determining
average fundamental voice frequency. Average speech power is usually measured in
decibels (dB). There is some rationale for reporting pressure and/or volume velocity
measures, rather than power measures, for certain studies since a measure of zero
for either pressure or velocity will result in a power measure of zero. For example, a
glottal stop may have either a substantial or a minimal subglottal pressure measurement for two given sounds, but both will have zero average speech power due to the
zero measure of volume velocity in the two cases. Although average speech power is
a primary cue in determining shouting from speaking, it is only one of three acoustic
cues for perception of stress or emphasis. Although Fry (1955) reported that fundamental frequency may have the greatest effect on stress judgments, it is possible that
the combination of average speech power and acoustic phonetic duration cues may
override the fundamental frequency influence.

Figure 6.3 illustrates the acoustic prosodic parameters: acoustic phonetic duration,
average fundamental voice frequency, and average speech power. The broad-band
spectrogram at the top shows two sections that cause difficulty in segmentation and
phonetic duration studies. Between the first vowel and the following voiced plosive
there is a section that is simply transitional; it cannot be associated easily with any
acoustic phone. The positing of a new transitional phone would cause substantial
complications, but the criteria for not considering it as part of the vowel or the plosive
are not generally agreed upon. Also, at the end of the word there is a section that clearly
is not a nasal; it appears vowel-like, however, and on the recording is heard to be /u/
in nature. Similar problems will be more fully discussed later in this chapter. The
average fundamental voice frequency plotted at the center of the figure was derived
from the first harmonic on a narrow-band spectrogram for the word *begging*. The tracing of average speech power for the same utterance is shown at the bottom of the figure.
The curve was made by passing the speech wave through a squaring circuit and then a
smoothing filter with a time constant of approximately .02 sec (or 20 msec).

Relation of Wave Types to Parameters

For any given speech sound there is associated one or more speech wave types and
a set of acoustic speech parameters. Thus it is of interest to know the relation that
holds between speech wave types and acoustic speech parameters. This relation is
shown in Table 6.1. The speech wave types are shown in the left column, and the
acoustical speech parameters, both phonetic and prosodic, are indicated above each
of the following columns. In the intersection between each speech wave type and each
acoustic speech parameter, a coded letter indicates particular properties of the parameters; that is, the parameter always or never may be derived from the wave type, or
it may be derived only in certain cases. One of the most interesting relationships
is the duration of the parameter to the speech wave. In certain cases it is normal for
the duration of the parameter to exceed the duration of the speech wave type; for

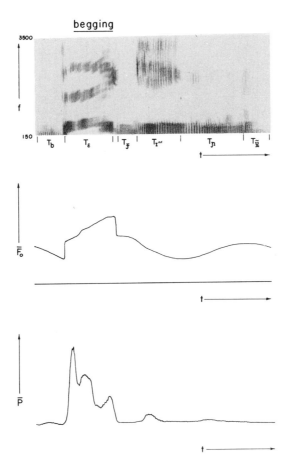

Figure 6.3 The acoustic prosodic parameters: T = acoustic phonetic duration; $\overline{F}_0$ = average fundamental voice frequency; $\overline{P}$ = average speech power. [From Peterson and Shoup, 1966b.]

example, acoustic phonetic duration invariably is longer than the burst speech wave type, which is one of a sequence of wave types for the acoustic phones of a stop manner of articulation. In other cases, the duration of the acoustic phone may be less than the associated speech wave type; for instance, in phrases composed of vowels, sonorants, and nasals it is common to find one speech wave type, quasi-periodic, obtaining for the entire utterance.

Association of Speech Sounds with Acoustic Characteristics of Speech

There are many ways in which speech sounds could be associated with the acoustical characteristics of speech: by manner of articulation, by place of articulation, by laryngeal action, by secondary articulations, and so forth. Two of the most important descriptive phonetic categories are manner of articulation and laryngeal action.

Table 6.1   The Relations of the Acoustical Speech Parameters to the Basic Speech Wave Types[a]

Wave types	Parameters		Phonetic					Prosodic	
	Gap	Broad-band continuous spectrum	Formant frequency	Formant amplitude	Formant band-width	Anti-resonance	Acoustic phonetic duration	Average fundamental voice frequency	Average speech power
Quiescent	c	n	n	n	n	n	g	n	z
Burst	n	c	a	a	a	c	e	n	a
Quasi-random	n	c	a	a	a	c	g	n	a
Quasi-periodic	n	n	a	a	a	c	g	a	a
Double-periodic	n	n	a	a	a	c	g	a	a
Irregular-periodic	n	n	a	a	a	c	g	a	a

[a] From Peterson and Shoup, 1966b.
a —the parameter may always be derived from the speech wave type; c —the parameter may be derived from the speech wave type in certain cases. e — the duration of parameter normally exceeds the duration of the speech wave type; g —the duration of the parameter may be less than, equal to, or greater than the duration of the speech wave type; n —the parameter is never derived from the speech wave type; z —when the parameter value is zero, the parameter may be derived from the speech wave type.

Acoustic Characteristics of Speech Sounds 183

Table 6.2 shows the acoustic characteristics of speech according to these two categories, excepting the stop manners of articulation, which require a special table. The subdivisions suggested for manner of articulation and laryngeal action are those of Peterson and Shoup (1966a). The laryngeal actions are shown as headings for the rows, and the manners of articulation are indicated as headings for the columns. The coding within the cells of intersection is for speech wave types on the upper line of each cell and for acoustic phonetic parameters on the lower line. For convenience in coding, certain symbols indicate groups of wave types or groups of phonetic parameters which are associated with the respective laryngeal actions and manners of articulation. In the case of the trill manner of articulation, it is impossible for a stopped laryngeal action to be associated, thus the cell is marked with an X, indicating that both speech wave types and acoustic phonetic parameters are excluded. In other cases there may be alternates of speech wave types associated with the manners of articulation, and these are shown by a dash between the alternates.

Table 6.3 shows the acoustical characteristics of speech associated with the various laryngeal actions and stop manners of articulation. Since the stops can

Table 6.2 *The Acoustical Characteristics of Speech Associated with the Various Laryngeal Actions and Manners of Articulation, Excepting the Stop Manners of Articulation, for Unit Articulations When the Air Mechanism Is Pulmonic and the Air Pressure Is Normal*[a]

	Nasal	Flap	Trill	Sibilant	Fricative	Sonorant	Vowel
piceless	S	PR	PR	R	R	R	S
	G	F_c	F_c	F_c	F_c	F_f	G
hispered	R	PR	PR	R	R	R	R
	F_f	F_c	F_c	F_c	F_c	F_f	F_nA_n
reathy	PR	PR	P^2R	PR	PR	PR	PR
	F_f	F_c	F_c	F_c	F_c	F_f	F_nA_n
iced	Q	QP	QP	QR	QR	Q	Q
	F_f	F_c	F_c	F_c	F_c	F_f	F_nA_n
aryngealized	D–I	DP–IP	DP–IP	DR–IR	DR–IR	D–I	D–I
	F_f	F_f	F_f	F_c	F_c	F_f	F_nA_n
lsated	P	P^2	P^2	PR	PR	P	P
	F_f	F_f	F_f	F_c	F_c	F_f	F_nA_n
onstricted	R	PR	PR	R	R	R	R
	F_f	F_f	F_f	F_c	F_c	F_f	F_nA_n
ono-nstricted	P	P^2	P^2	PR	PR	P	P
	F_f	F_f	F_f	F_c	F_c	F_f	F_nA_n
pped	S	S	X	S	S	S	S
	G	G		G	G	G	G

[a]From Peterson and Shoup, 1966b.

eech Wave Types—*Basic:* S quiescent; B burst; R quasi-random; Q quasi-periodic; D double-periodic; rregular-periodic; P periodic (Q, D, I); *Combined:* $P^m(QP^{m-1}, DP^{m-1}, IP^{m-1})$; $P^nR(QP^{n-1}R, DP^{n-1}R, ^{n-1}R)$ (m = 1, 2, 3, 4; n = 1, 2, 3). *Acoustic Phonetic Parameters*—*Basic:* G gap; F_b broad-band ntinuous spectrum; F_n frequency of the vowel of consonant nth formant; A_n amplitude of the vowel or nsonant nth formant; B_n bandwidth of the vowel or consonant nth formant; F_{na} frequency of the nth vel or consonant antiresonance; *Combined:* $F_f = F_nA_nF_{na}B_n$; $F_c = F_nA_nF_{na}B_nF_b$. (— = alternates th; X = excluded).

Table 6.3 The Acoustical Characteristics of Speech Associated with the Various Laryngeal Actions, Stop Manners of Articulation, and Air Releases for Unit Articulations[a]

	Plosive				Ejective		Implosive		Click	
	Phonoaspirated	Aspirated	Unaspirated	Unexploded	Unaspirated	Unexploded	Unaspirated	Unexploded	Unaspirated	Unexploded
Voiceless	S/B/PR	S/B/R	S/B	S	X	X	X	X	S/B	S
	$G/F_c/F_c$	$G/F_c/F_c$	G/F_c	G					G/F_c	G
Whispered	S/B/PR	S/B/R	S/B	S	X	X	X	X	S/B	S
	$G/F_c/F_c$	$G/F_c/F_c$	G/F_c	G					G/F_c	G
Breathy	P/B/PR	P/B/R	P/B	P	X	X	X	X	P/B	P
	$V/F_c/F_c$	$V/F_c/F_c$	V/F_c	V					V/F_c	V
Voiced	Q/B/PR	Q/B/R	Q/B	Q	Q/B	Q	Q/B	Q	Q/B	Q
	$V/F_c/F_c$	$V/F_c/F_c$	V/F_c	V	V/F_c	V	V/F_c	V	V/F_c	V
Laryngealized	D-I/B/PR	D-I/B/R	D-I/B	D-I	D-I/B	D-I	D-I/B	D-I	D-I/B	D-I
	$V/F_c/F_c$	$V/F_c/F_c$	V/F_c	V	V/F_c	V	V/F_c	V	V/F_c	V
Pulsated	P/B/PR	P/B/PR	P/B	P	P/B	P	P/B	P	P/B	P
	$V/F_c/F_c$	$V/F_c/F_c$	V/F_c	V	V/F_c	V	V/F_c	V	V/F_c	V
Constricted	S/B/PR	S/B/R	S/B	S	S/B	S	S/B	S	S/B	S
	$G/F_c/F_c$	$G/F_c/F_c$	G/F_c	G	G/F_c	G	G/F_c	G	G/F_c	G
Phonoconstricted	P/B/PR	P/B/R	P/B	P	P/B	P	P/B	P	P/B	P
	$V/F_c/F_c$	$V/F_c/F_c$	V/F_c	V	V/F_c	V	V/F_c	V	V/F_c	V
Stopped	S/B/PR	S/B/R	S/B	S	S/B	S	S/B	S	S/B	S
	$G/F_c/F_c$	$G/F_c/F_c$	G/F_c	G	G/F_c	G	G/F_c	G	G/F_c	G

[a] From Peterson and Shoup, 1966b.

Speech Wave Types—*Basic*: S quiescent; B burst; R quasi-periodic; Q quasi-random; D double-periodic; I irregular-periodic; P periodic (Q, D, I); *Combined*: P^m (QP^{m-1}, DP^{m-1}, IP^{m-1}); P^nR($QP^{n-1}R$, $DP^{n-1}R$, $IP^{n-1}R$); (m = 1, 2, 3, 4; n = 1, 2, 3). *Acoustic Phonetic Parameters*—*Basic*: G gap; F_b broad-band continuous spectrum; F_n frequency of the vowel or consonant nth formant; A_n amplitude of the vowel or consonant nth formant; B_n bandwidth of the vowel or consonant nth formant; X = excluded. *Combined*: $F_f = F_n A_n F_{na} B_n$; $F_c = F_n A_n F_{na} B_n F_b$. (/ = followed by; — = alternates with; X = excluded).

have different air releases (that is, aspirated, unaspirated, phonoaspirated, and unexploded), each stop manner of articulation is divided into the particular air releases which may be associated with that manner. As in Table 6.2, the laryngeal actions are shown as headings for the rows, and the stop manners of articulation, with their various air releases, are indicated as headings for the columns. The coding within the cells is for speech wave types on the upper line and for acoustic phonetic parameters on the lower line. In addition to the coding for combination of speech wave types, combination of phonetic parameters, alternate possibilities, and excluded cases, there is a coding of a slash to indicate *followed by*. This coding applies to most of the speech wave types and acoustic phonetic parameters with reference to stop manners of articulation. As mentioned previously, most stops are initiated with a quiescent or a periodic-like speech wave, depending on their voiceless or voiced laryngeal action. Following the initiation there may be a burst, and, finally, there is the possibility of a quasi-random speech wave type.

Having shown in tabular form the relationships between laryngeal actions and manners of articulation, we will give a fuller description of the particular speech sound classes. Much of the research cited in the following discussion is relatively old, having been done in the 1940s through the 1960s. Lehiste (1967, p. vi) accounts for this fact in her preface to a collection of most relevant articles: "The time appears to be right for a stocktaking in the field of acoustic phonetics. We seem to have reached a plateau, and the focus of research in experimental phonetics seems to have shifted. . . . New and very interesting work in acoustic phonetics continues to be done, but in a very real sense we are witnessing the consolidation of the achievements of a generation of researchers."

Vowels

The acoustical characteristics of vowels have been studied more thoroughly than those of any other class of speech sounds. For over two hundred years vowels have been analyzed according to their resonant frequencies, and distinctions among vowels have been based on these measures. Prior to the development of the sound spectrograph (Koenig, Dunn, and Lacy, 1946), acoustic measures were more laborious to calculate and, consequently, vowel resonance studies were very time consuming. Notable work was done, however, as evidenced in the publications of Lloyd (1890), Helmholtz (1954), Scripture (1973), Stumpf (1926), Miller (1926), Russell (1931), Fletcher (1953), Paget (1930), and Chiba and Kajiyama (1958). Lloyd was one of the first investigators to recognize that absolute frequency measures did not characterize the specific vowels but, rather, that relative measures were needed. The problem of determining the relative measures that will indeed define the vowels distinctively has been elusive throughout the years and still remains to be resolved. This area of future research will be discussed later in this chapter.

With the development of the sound spectrograph, there was a significant increase in the publication of articles and monographs on the acoustic characteristics of speech sounds. Two important contributions to the understanding of acoustic properties of speech sounds, with a concentration of information on the vowels, were those of

Potter, Kopp, and Green (1947) and Joos (1948). From the broad-band spectrograms voluminously shown in *Visible Speech* by Potter, Kopp, and Green, it was easily seen that the formant frequencies were continuously changing as functions of time and that only in steady-state sounds were measurements somewhat independent of time. It was also very obvious that the phonetic context in which a sound was located contributed to the variations of acoustic measures for repetitions of that sound. The problems of time normalization and coarticulation remain today and will be discussed in the following section, "Practical Aspects in the Acoustical Study of Speech Sounds."

One of the most thorough vowel studies using the sound spectrograph, and one which is now considered a classic, is that of Peterson and Barney (1952). In this study, recordings were made of 10 monosyllabic words, *heed, hid, head, had, hod, hawed, hood, who'd, hud,* and *heard,* spoken by 76 speakers (32 men, 28 women, and 15 children). Each speaker recorded these 10 words twice, making a total of 1520 recorded words. The words were randomized and presented to a group of 70 listeners, 32 of whom also had been speakers. The listeners identified certain vowels, such as /i/, /ɜ/, /æ/, and /u/, more easily than others, such as /ɑ/. Those vowels which were not identified were usually judged to be of a quality adjacent to the recorded vowel. *Adjacent to* has reference both to descriptive phonetic vowel charts and to the vowel loop plots presented by Peterson and Barney, as shown in Figure 6.4. This figure plots the first formant frequency against the second formant frequency on a mel scale with the origin at the upper right. The numbers beside each of the vowels are the numbers of sounds, out of the 152, which were unanimously identified as that vowel by the listeners. The small areas shown in the figure are for the vowels repeated by a single speaker on 12 different days. The overlap of vowels when plotted on a first formant versus second formant basis is shown in Figure 6.5 for all 76 speakers. The averages of fundamental frequencies, formant frequencies, and formant amplitudes of vowels

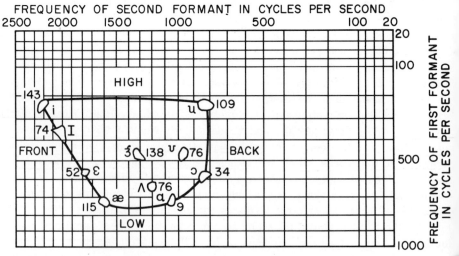

Figure 6.4 Vowel loop with numbers of sounds unanimously classified by listeners; each sound was presented 152 times. [From Peterson and Barney, 1952.]

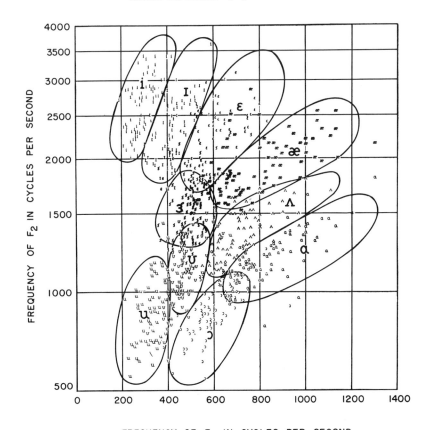

Figure 6.5 Frequency of second formant versus frequency of first formant for 10 vowels spoken by 76 speakers. [From Peterson and Barney, 1952.]

by these speakers are given in Table 6.4. The greatest variations are seen among groups, but within any group (of men, women, or children), there is still overlap and confusion.

Results from many other vowel studies have been compared to the Peterson and Barney results with virtually the same conclusions; namely, that the first two formants give the general discriminations of vowels for a given speaker but that, for many speakers, there is no way to identify all vowels from those measurements alone. Consequently, throughout the years investigators have been seeking a technique for classifying vowels uniquely with these and other acoustic measures.

Although the majority of vowel studies have treated well-articulated, stressed vowels, there has been a recent interest in more casual speech productions. Tiffany (1959) studied the differences between isolated, stressed, and unstressed vowels. He found that the acoustic vowel loop tended to become smaller in those three conditions, respectively. This finding supports many of the linguistic and phonetic studies that have indicated a tendency for American English unstressed vowels to become schwa-

Table 6.4 *Averages of Fundamental and Formant Frequencies and Formant Amplitudes of Vowels by 76 Speakers* [a]

		i	ɪ	ɛ	æ	ɑ	ɔ	ʊ	u	ʌ	ɝ
Fundamental frequencies (cps)	M	136	135	130	127	124	129	137	141	130	133
	W	235	232	223	210	212	216	232	231	221	218
	Ch	272	269	260	251	256	263	276	274	261	261
Formant frequencies (cps)											
F_1	M	270	390	530	660	730	570	440	300	640	490
	W	310	430	610	860	850	590	470	370	760	500
	Ch	370	530	690	1010	1030	680	560	430	850	560
F_2	M	2290	1990	1840	1720	1090	840	1020	870	1190	1350
	W	2790	2480	2330	2050	1220	920	1160	950	1400	1640
	Ch	3200	2730	2610	2320	1370	1060	1410	1170	1590	1820
F_3	M	3010	2550	2480	2410	2440	2410	2240	2240	2390	1690
	W	3310	3070	2990	2850	2810	2710	2680	2670	2780	1960
	Ch	3730	3600	3570	3320	3170	3180	3310	3260	3360	2160
Formant amplitudes (db)	L_1	×4	−3	−2	−1	−1	0	−1	−3	−1	−5
	L_2	−24	−23	−17	−12	−5	−7	−12	−19	−10	−15
	L_3	−28	−27	−24	−22	−28	−34	−34	−43	−27	−20

[a] From Peterson and Barney, 1952.

like and to move to the center of the vowel diagrams. Shearme and Holmes (1962) found a similar phenomenon with British English vowels, but Jassem (1959) did not find this to be true in the Polish language. The explanation may be that greater formant shifts take place in more heavily stressed languages, such as English, than in less-stressed languages, such as Polish.

Joos (1948) noted the acoustical distinction between isolated vowels and those in consonantal contexts to be one of *centralizing*, or becoming schwa-like when in context. Stevens and House (1963) expanded the work of Joos in their study of consonantal context influence on the vowels. Although their study was limited to symmetrical consonantal environments, and not to all possible contexts, it did show a regular influence on the vowels in that there was a shift of formant frequencies from those of isolated vowels. A study which treats both the unstressed or less-stressed conditions of vowels and their consonantal context influence is that of Lindblom (1963). In this article, he defines a *target* as the asymptotic values of the first two formant frequencies of the vowel. Since the target is independent of consonantal context and duration, it is proposed as an invariant attribute of the vowel. The study suggests a simple dynamic model of vowel articulation.

Lindblom's work on the dynamic aspects of vowel production is an important contribution to the field. Earlier work in this area included that of Crandall (1927) at Bell Telephone Laboratories, with more recent studies by Stevens, House, and Paul (1966), Öhman (1966, 1967), and Broad and Fertig (1970). Russell (1970) included in his book, *The Vowel*, three chapters giving a historical summary of vowel theories. More recent treatises on acoustical theories of vowel production depend heavily upon the results of studies using the sound spectrograph. The present theoretical development can be seen in the works of Stevens and House (1955, 1961), Fant (1956, 1960), and House, Stevens, and Paul (1962). The modification and supplementation of acoustical theories of vowel production are most important aspects of work to be researched by future speech scientists. The theories that are developed must explain not only the isolated and consonantal context phenomena, the stressed and unstressed vowel productions, the steady-state and the dynamic properties, but also the secondary articulatory characteristics such as nasalization, rounding, and laryngealization. These acoustic characteristics have not received as much attention in the past as, hopefully, they will receive in the future.

There have not been consistent results from the various studies on nasalized vowels. Hockett (1955) and Delattre (1951) have suggested that nasalization has an associated rise in the third formant of vowels, but the results of House and Stevens (1956) show that the third formant tends to fade. It is their conjecture that studies which propose a rising third formant actually may be confusing the third and fourth formants when the third is weak or missing. Almost all investigators have concluded that during nasalization of vowels extra formant frequencies are introduced. One of the first publications to discuss the extra nasal resonances in vowel productions was that of Potter, Kopp, and Green (1947). Joos (1948) cited extra formants between the first and second formants in nasalized vowels. Although both Heffner (1952) and Smith (1951) reported additional nasal resonances during the production of nasalized vowels, they were not in agreement as to the regions in which the extra resonances were to be found. Another finding which receives general agreement from the researchers is the reduction of overall acoustic energy during nasalization. This finding has been supported by Cotton (1940), Weiss (1954), and House and Stevens (1956). Another generally recognized acoustic characteristic associated with nasalized vowels is a reduction in the amplitude of the first formant for certain vowels accompanied by a simultaneous increase in formant bandwidth and an upward shift in the center frequency of the formant. One of Fant's *Quarterly Status Reports* has an excellent article on nasal formants by Lindquist and Sundberg (1972). They discuss nasalization as a very complicated acoustic phenomenon in that its exact nature depends on such effects as asymmetries in the nasal septum and effects of the frontal and maxillary sinuses. The investigation of *modified* vowels is a challenge for the speech scientists of the future. There are many issues in nasalization, roundedness, laryngealization, and so forth, which are not yet resolved and which should be of interest to the researcher.

The vowels have received considerably more attention than the consonants in the acoustic analysis of speech sounds. There are many reasons for this emphasis, one of which is the development of analysis techniques in the last two centuries. Methods for analyzing quasi-periodic waves and their associated formant frequencies, which provide the most information for vowels, have been better developed than techniques for studying transient bursts and quasi-random speech waves. Although the sound spectrograph was a major advance in acoustic analysis of speech sounds, the computer has helped to bring about even further advances in this field.

Current techniques of extracting information-bearing acoustic parameters and detecting the various speech wave types by computer have accelerated the study of both vowel and consonant sounds. The computer has a speed which allows massive amounts of data to be analyzed in a relatively short period of time. It also permits greater accuracy of measurement for most of the acoustic parameters of interest and an access to parameters that previously were not measurable at all, such as vocal tract reflection coefficients (Wakita, 1973). The sound spectrograph still has an important place in speech research, but computer analysis is beginning to predominate and will continue to provide the more sophisticated and rapid techniques of investigation in the future (Schafer and Rabiner, 1970; Markel, 1972; Atal, 1970; Wakita, this volume). Perhaps the use of computer analysis will bring an upsurge in acoustical study of the consonants.

Sonorants

The term *sonorant* has various meanings associated with it in phonetic writings, but it is used here to specify that group of consonant sounds produced with an airflow that is in an unstable state, neither totally laminar (as associated with vowels) nor totally turbulent (as normally associated with fricatives). The sounds that comprise this group are sometimes referred to as *semivowels*, such as /w/ and /j/, as *laterals*, such as /l/, and as *retroflexed consonants*, such as /r/. Because of the unstable airflow, these sounds have quasi-periodic and/or quasi-random speech waves and the acoustical parameters associated with these wave types.

A classic publication on the sonorants is that of Lehiste (1964). Her study substantiated the phonetic judgments that /w/ is similar to the vowel /u/ and that /j/ is similar to /i/. The distinctions between the respective pairs, however, were clear in that for the sonorants the first two formants were lower in frequency than for the corresponding vowels. Also the third formant for /w/ was occasionally weak and/or missing and for /j/ it was higher in frequency than for /i/. The study of the semivowels is particularly difficult since they are of short duration and their formants are often moving throughout most of the production of the sounds. They never occur in a stressed position as do their similar vowels.

Lehiste corroborated the findings of Tarnóczy (1948) that the formant frequencies for /l/ are dependent upon the vowel context. The second formant in particular tended to follow the second formant of the following vowel; when the /l/ was in final position, the second formant was still somewhat variable. The physiological explanation may be that the speaker may use a slightly different /l/ preceding the various vowels and not one simple *light* /l/ as usually proposed in phonetic charts. The distinctions for *lu*, *la*, and *li* are quite pronounced in Tarnóczy's study, and he indeed suggests this variation in production. In contrast to the variability of /l/ in positions preceding or following vowels, the syllabic /l/ following consonants, such as /k/, /g/, /p/, /b/, and so on, appears more stable. In a comparison of syllabic /l/ with final /l/, Lehiste found that syllabic /l/ has the first formant in approximately the same frequency region as does final /l/, but the second formant is definitely lower, and the third formant usually slightly lower for the syllabic /l/. The highest second formant positions for syllabic /l/ were following /k/ and /g/.

Although it has been shown that /r/ speech sounds are regularly produced in quite distinct physiological formations (Delattre, 1965), Lehiste reports that the various allophones of /r/ have certain common acoustic properties. It has long been known that one acoustic correlate of retroflexion is an exceedingly low third formant with a narrow separation between the second and third formants; indeed, Lehiste found this in her extensive data for all varieties of /r/. The acoustic variations noted in the allophones of /r/ were correlated to position in the sound sequence, such as initial, final, syllabic, rather than to physiological production distinctions. The initial allophones had lower formant frequencies for the first three formants, and thus the low formant frequency was a mark of an initial allophone. Lehiste noted that if formant frequencies alone were considered, only initial allophones of /r/ were clearly distinct from all retroflexed sounds. Although initial allophones of /r/ do not seem to be influenced by the following vowel, the final allophones were quite dependent upon the preceding vowel. Lehiste indicated that the first two formants of the retroflexed vowel /ɜ/ are similar to those of final allophones of /r/ but the third formant for /ɜ/ is considerably higher.

From spectrographic analysis, the acoustic characteristics associated with the sonorants support the rules of synthesis for simulating these speech sounds. The publications of Lisker (1957a) and of O'Connor, Gerstman, Liberman, Delattre, and Cooper (1957) suggest the minimal acoustic cues for the perception of the sonorants; the former study relates to intervocalic position and the latter to initial position. While identification of vowels depends largely on the formant frequencies during the steady-state portion, the sonorants are recognized primarily from transitional cues of the second and third formants. The second formant transition can separate /w/ from /r—l/ from /j/; for /w/ its origin is low, for /r—l/ it is in the middle, and for /j/ it is high. The distinction for /r/ and /l/ is on the third formant transition, which is close to the second formant for /r/, but higher for /l/. The durations of the transitions are also important for identifying the sonorants as a class of sounds. As one might suspect, the transitional durations for sonorant judgments must be longer than those for stops and nasals, but shorter than those for vowels.

The sonorants remain a very interesting group of speech sounds for future investigation not only because of the many allophone types within each phonemic class but also because of the similarity of certain sonorants to vowels or syllable nuclei. The problems relating to syllabicity are perhaps most evident when undertaking a study of the sonorants.

Fricatives and Sibilants

As was stated earlier in this chapter, the voiceless fricatives and sibilants are produced with quasi-random speech waves and their voiced counterparts are produced with combined waves of quasi-random and quasi-periodic types. The speech wave types are rather easily identified in acoustic analysis, but the associated acoustical speech parameters are not so readily obtained and interpreted. The proposed broadband continuous spectrum does not uniquely distinguish all of the friction-like sounds, nor do the resonances and antiresonances. Perception studies by Harris (1954, 1958) indicate that identification of American English fricatives and sibilants is not possible using the noise portion of the speech sounds alone, but requires additional information from the transitions into the vowels. In her study, the sibilants were discriminated primarily from the noise portion but the fricatives depended largely on the transitional cues.

The acoustical analysis of fricatives and sibilants has been, and continues to be, an exceedingly difficult problem. Tarnóczy (1954) gives a summary of the literature through the mid-1950s. In the decade following that publication, several major studies of the fricatives and sibilants were undertaken, the results of which indicate that there is still much to be understood in this area. Hughes and Halle (1956) measured energy density spectra of gated segments of fricative and sibilant consonants. These data were used to develop objective identification criteria. They also were presented to a group of listeners for identification, and the responses of the group were evaluated in terms of the criteria. Two fricatives, /θ/ and /ð/, were not included in the results of the experiment owing to the complex nature of these sounds. As would be expected, there was a clear acoustic cue of voicing to separate the voiced from the unvoiced fricatives and sibilants. This cue was evident in the spectra as a very strong component below 700 Hz. Another separation of the fricatives and sibilants was possible according to place of articulation: labial, alveolar, and palatal. For any single speaker, the spectra of alveolar sibilants have peaks at consistently higher frequencies than do those of palatals. In some labials no high-frequency peak can be observed below 10 kHz. By use of a set of fixed filters, three measurements were made which discriminated these three groups of sounds. Using the results of this discrimination with the voicing detection technique, Hughes and Halle were able to obtain approximately 90 percent correction identification of the American English fricatives and sibilants /f, v, s, z, ʃ, ʒ/.

Strevens (1960) studied a larger group of fricatives and sibilants by means of a spectrographic analysis. He analyzed only the voiceless counterparts since voicing is rather easily discriminated and the greatest difficulty lies in determining the place of articulation. He described the sounds in terms of the frequencies of the upper and lower limits of energy present, the presence or absence of formants, and the overall relative intensity of the sounds. Strevens first discriminated by general groups. The front group, /ɸ, f, θ/, had the lowest relative intensity and the longest spectrum length, between 5000 and 6000 Hz. The mid group, /s, ʃ, ç/, had the highest relative intensity and the shortest spectrum length, between 3000 and 4000 Hz. The back group, /x, χ, h/, had the medium relative intensity and the medium spectrum length, between 4000 and 5500 Hz. Within each group he discriminated primarily according to the top and bottom limits of frequency.

Heinz and Stevens (1961) describe the properties of voiceless fricative consonants in terms of an acoustic theory of speech production. The spectra of these fricatives are characterized by *poles* (approximately equivalent to the term *formants* as it is used in this chapter) and *zeros* (antiresonances) the frequency locations of which are dependent upon the vocal tract shape and the location of the generation of the friction or noise. The locations of the poles and zeros are determined by a matching process whereby comparison spectra synthesized by electric circuits are matched against the spectra under analysis. By this method the frequencies and bandwidths of the important poles and zeros for /f/, /s/, and /ʃ/ are determined. Based on these findings, voiceless fricatives are generated both in isolation and in syllables and are presented to listeners for identification. The results of the listening tests are consistent with the data from the acoustic analyses.

Jassem (1965) presents a study of American English, Swedish, and Polish fricatives and sibilants. He classifies the various sounds by using spectral analysis, according to the relations between their formant frequencies and formant levels. He suggests three binary distinctive features at the acoustic level: spread—compressed formants, higher—lower formants, and higher formant—lower formant emphasis. The *spread—compressed* dichotomy is determined by the distance between the fourth formant and the second formant frequency—whether it is greater or less than 1800 Hz. The term *higher formants* refers to the frequencies of the second, third, and fourth formants being greater than 8000 Hz, and the term *lower* refers to their being less than 8000 Hz. The higher and lower formant emphasis is in reference to the groups determined by the spread—compressed feature: For the spread group of sounds, the higher—lower level refers to the relations between the level of the fourth formant and the level of the second; for the compressed group, it refers to the relation between the level of the third formant and the level of the second.

Throughout the history of the study of fricative and sibilant speech sounds, there is an open admission of the difficulty of the studies and the recognition of the caution with which one must treat the results. Thus it would seem imperative that future speech scientists address the many problems inherent in the investigation of this group of sounds. The acoustic speech parameters which have been extracted and examined may not be complete; perhaps they do not represent even the most information-bearing parameters to be studied. It is the task of the researcher to determine the best set of acoustical characteristics for distinguishing among the fricatives and sibilants.

Trills and Flaps

There is at the present time a minimum of information on the acoustic characteristics of *trills* and *flaps*. This may be in part because of the infrequent occurrence of these speech sounds within any given language. Quite obviously, in all languages the vowels are of primary concern because of their functional load; the consonants become of progressively less concern as their functional load decreases. In American English the flap is easily identified because of its unique acoustic properties of reduced overall sound intensity; consequently large-scale studies are not necessary.

According to Tarnóczy (1948), trills and flaps have not been submitted to thorough acoustic investigation because the periodicity of the wave is interrupted continually and therefore difficult to analyze. In his rather limited study of the voiced alveolar trill, he determined that the first three formants were at approximately 550, 1400, and 2000 Hz, thus more closely resembling an /1/ than any vowel, and that the fourth formant was lacking. Malécot and Lloyd (1968) investigated the duration of vowels preceding American English flaps since it had been hypothesized by Hubbell (1950) that the perception of /t/ rather than /d/ for alveolar flaps in word pairs such as *writing—riding* might be owing to the length of the preceding vowel. Malécot made spectrographic measures and found the durations of the vowels to vary randomly, thus contradicting the hypothesis.

Stops

The stop formations have the unusual property of often involving a sequence of speech wave types and a sequence of associated acoustic speech parameters. During the initial closure of a stop, either the vocal folds are vibrating (as in voiced stops) or they are not (as in voiceless stops). In the former case, the stop begins with a quasi-periodic speech wave with associated low first formant as well as possible higher formants; in the latter case, the initiation is with a quiescent speech wave and its associated gap. Following the closure there is the possibility of a burst speech wave with its relevant acoustic speech parameters. If there is a burst, there may be aspiration following it. The aspiration may involve a quasi-random speech wave or a combined quasi-random and quasi-periodic wave; these speech waves have their respective acoustic speech parameters to be measured. Because of the many allophonic variations found in the stop phonemes of any language, the acoustic description of these speech sounds is very complex. The stop formations have been analyzed from many points of view.

Halle, Hughes, and Radley (1957) investigated the two major cues for stop consonants, that is, the burst of the stop release and the formant transitions in the adjacent vowel. They obtained detailed energy density spectra of the bursts which showed that labial stops have a primary concentration of energy in the low frequencies, between 500 and 1500 Hz, that alveolar stops have either a flat spectrum or one in which the higher frequencies above 4000 Hz predominate, and that the palatal and velar stops have strong concentrations of energy in the intermediate frequency regions of 1500 to 4000 Hz. In the last case, the palatal stops showed spectral peaks in the region between 2000 and 4000 Hz, and the velar stops exhibited spectral peaks at much lower frequencies. The spectrographic analysis of the formant transitions in the adjacent vowels introduced many difficulties since the formants of the vowels are not all evident at the same moment in time on the spectrogram. The need for a linguistic definition of *transition* was obvious, and the results were not as conclusive as they might have been with a rigorous concept of *transition* (as is used in acoustic phonetic studies). They found dependencies not only on the steady-state position of the adjacent vowel, but also on the position of the stop with respect to the preceding or following vowel, and of the feature tense—lax in both the consonant and the vowel. The perceptual judgments elicited from this experiment were not as conclusive as those done on synthetic speech at other laboratories because of the inconsistencies found in "real" speech.

Malécot (1975) has studied the acoustic properties of glottal stop in French. Through spectrographic measurements he found that for glottal stops in initial position, the most obvious acoustic characteristic is a rapid risetime of the following vowel's amplitude, particularly in the second and third formants. In final position the principal features are an abrupt cutoff and a shortening of the preceding phoneme. Glottal stops in medial position combine the acoustic features noted for initial and final positions plus a closure duration in the range normally associated with geminate consonants. Malécot also synthesized utterances to see if the analyzed acoustic characteristics were indeed the perceptual cues for identifying glottal stops. The results proved conclusive; they indicated that these acoustic features are the information-bearing characteristics for glottal stops in French. It would be interesting to see if American English glottal stops exhibit the same acoustic properties.

Fischer-Jorgensen (1954) studied the Danish stop consonants /p/, /t/, /k/, /b/, /d/, and /g/. The phonemic symbols used would indicate a possible voiceless—voiced distinction between the first three stops and the second three stops. This is not the case, however, and her study indicated the differences to be in aspiration and duration: /p/, /t/, and /k/ are strongly aspirated, and their closure time is relatively shorter; /b/, /d/, and /g/ are only slightly aspirated, if at all, and their closure time is longer. In order to discriminate among the classes of stops according to place of articulation, she studied the intensity, the duration, and the frequencies of the bursts and of the aspiration, and the influence on vowel formants. Her results tended to agree with those of Fant (1950) for Swedish stops and those of Potter, Kopp, and Green (1947) for American English stops. The results supported some of the work done on synthetic speech at Haskins Laboratories (Cooper *et al.*, 1952) and in other instances varied from their reports. Her conclusions were that the results suggested the need for further experimentation.

From the previously cited references and many others which were published by Haskins Laboratories (Liberman *et al.*, 1954; Delattre, Liberman, and Cooper, 1955; Harris, Hoffman, Liborman, Delattre, and Cooper, 1958; Hoffman, 1958; and Liberman, 1957, which summarizes most of the work), much knowledge was gleaned about the perceptual cues of stop consonants. It was shown that the second formant transition plays an important part in the perception of the voiced stops and that the third formant transition also contributes to the judgments. When the transition of the second formant was rising, the consonant was identified as /b/. When it was either straight or falling slightly, judgments were made for /d/. When the second formant transition fell from higher points, /g/ was recognized. The cues of the third formant appeared to be independent of those of the second formant, for when they were in agreement with second formant transition movements, the judgments were likewise in agreement; when they were not, the recognition was divided between two stops. A third cue of burst frequency was tested and found to be useful in perceptual judgments. High bursts were cues for alveolar stops; those bursts near the second formant of the vowel were cues for palatal and velar stops; the low bursts which were cues for the voiceless labial stop /p/ did not obtain the same responses for the voiced counterpart /b/, which may have resulted from too coarse a sampling of the lower frequencies. All three sets of cues—second formant transition, third formant transition, and burst frequency—were found to be independent. The addition of cues produced effects similar to the addition of vectors.

Early investigations of stop consonants indicated that voicing of /b/, /d/, and /g/ did not occur throughout the entire production of these American English plosives and, indeed, could be perceived as *voiced* when there was no vibration of the vocal folds present during the closure. Lisker (1957b) studied the closure duration of /p/ and /b/ in intervocalic position. He found that the first, second, and third formant transitions following closure begin at lower frequencies and move less abruptly for /b/ than for /p/ and that the closure duration is greater for /p/ than for /b/. Since the primary purpose of the experiment was to determine whether the difference in closure duration could be used as a distinguishing perceptual cue of *voiced—voiceless* decisions, he artificially varied the duration of the closure while holding constant all other features of the recorded speech by a tape-splicing technique. By inserting blank tape of various duration in the middle of recorded samples, he could determine the influence that duration of the closure had upon the judgment of the voiced—voiceless distinction. His experiment indicated that the closure durational differences play an important role in identifying /p/ or /b/. Closure durations of less than 75 msec will be judged as voiced, and those of greater than 130 msec will be perceived as voiceless. Lisker and Abramson (1964) studied voicing in initial stops. The purpose of the study was to see how well voice onset time serves to separate the stop consonants in a number of languages in which both the number and phonetic characteristics of the stops are said to differ. Results of their experiment indicated that voice onset time may serve as a basis for separating the various stops according to both voicing and certain places of articulation. The results suggested that such features as voicing, aspiration, and force of articulation are predictable consequences of differences in the relative timing of events at the glottis and at the place of oral occlusion.

Nasals

The acoustical characteristics of nasals are basically similar to those of oral vowels and sonorants. The speech wave type is ordinarily quasi-periodic, and the primary acoustical speech parameters are the formant frequencies, amplitudes, and bandwidths. The most distinctive property, however, is the presence of antiresonances in the nasals due to the side-branching of the nasal passage from the vocal tract. As discussed earlier, antiresonances are also associated with nasalized vowels; they are due to the opening of the nasal passageway during nasalized vowel formation. Hattori, Yamamoto, and Fujimura (1958) investigated the nasalization of vowels in relation to nasals. They found that the principal characteristic features of vowel nasalization are an extra resonance around 250 Hz, an antiresonance at about 500 Hz, and comparatively weak and diffuse components between the formants of the vowels, particularly in the frequency region from 1000 to 2500 Hz. The first and third features are also found during the period of articulatory closure for the nasal consonants. The comparatively weak and diffuse components between formants are influenced by the antiresonance of the oral cavity and thus carry information about the tongue position during the oral closure. They suggest that the antiresonances play the major role in the identification of the place of articulation of nasal consonants.

Fujimura (1962) studied the nasal consonants by use of an analysis-by-synthesis technique (Bell *et al.*, 1961). He found that all nasal consonants tend to have three properties in common: *(1)* the existence of a very low first formant that is located at about 300 Hz and is well separated from the higher formants; *(2)* relatively high damping factors of the formants; and *(3)* high density of the formants in the frequency domain and the existence of the antiresonances. He suggests that the latter two properties in combination account for the somewhat even distribution of the energy in the middle-frequency range, between 800 and 2300 Hz. Fujimura found that it is possible to separate the nasals according to place of articulation on the basis of the location of the antiresonances but that the formant transitions of the adjacent vowels often are an even better cue to the distinctions of /m/, /n/, and /ŋ/. The importance of the vowel transitions for the perception of place of articulation among the nasals had been demonstrated previously by the work at Haskins Laboratories (Liberman *et al.*, 1954).

There have been numerous studies of the acoustic cues for the perception of nasal sounds. Malécot (1956) conducted a tape-splicing experiment in parallel with the series of experiments on nasal consonants by Haskins Laboratories so that the results of the Haskins Laboratories work could be tested by using a different method. His findings completely supported their conclusions; that is, that place of articulation of /m/, /n/, and /ŋ/ is conveyed primarily by the transitions of the adjacent vowel formant and that nasal resonances which are produced during the oral closure serve principally as indicators of the nasal manner of articulation. He did find that the nasal formants contribute in a limited way to the place of articulation judgments.

Nakata (1959) investigated the perception of nasal consonants both in isolation and in consonant—vowel syllables. A test was performed to determine the extent to which synthetic nasal consonants could be identified in isolation. The generated nasals had a first formant at 200 Hz, with a bandwidth of 300 Hz; a variable second formant of 900, 1100, 1300, 1500, 1700, 1900, 2100 or 2300 Hz, with a bandwidth ranging between 30 and 100 Hz; and a third formant of 2500 Hz. Maximum response percentages were 64, 52, and 41 for /m/, /n/, and /ŋ/ at second formant frequencies of 1100, 1700, and 2300 Hz, respectively. These results were generally not as high as those obtained by Malécot with natural speech stimuli obtained through tape-splicing techniques, though in the case of /ŋ/ the judgments were better with the synthetic speech. Nakata's experiment with consonant—vowel syllables again showed the importance of the second formant transitions as cues for identification of place of articulation within the nasal consonants.

House (1957) simulated the production of nasal consonants by means of electrical analogs of the nasal and vocal tracts. His first experiment tested the perceptual judgments of nasalized vowel versus nasal consonant. When the average area of coupling to the nasal tract was minimal, the subjects heard vowels, oral or nasalized, but as the degree of coupling increased, the listeners judged the output to be nasal consonants. Thus, with an adequate coupling to ensure nasal consonant judgments to be valid, House conducted listening experiments for identifying the individual nasals /m/, /n/, and /ŋ/. As a class, the most distinguishing characteristics of the nasals were their predominantly low-frequency energy, their low overall level compared to a vowel, and a characteristic spectral prominence near 1000 Hz. For separation of the three nasals, he found that the antiresonances were most important. For /m/ the antiresonance was approximately 1000 Hz, for /n/, about 3500 Hz, and for /ŋ/, higher than 5000 Hz.

Hecker (1962) studied the nasal consonants with an articulatory speech synthesizer. Listening tests were conducted to determine the most suitable vocal tract configurations for producing the nasal consonants in consonant—vowel and vowel—consonant syllables. Other listening tests indicated the most suitable patterns of temporal variables for the syllables. It was found that the more natural-sounding syllables were those obtained when the nasal tract coupling varied slowly in time compared to changes in the vocal tract configuration. The three synthetic stimuli which scored highest in the listening tests for /m/, /n/, and /ŋ/ were those with second formant frequencies at approximately 1300 Hz, 1800 Hz, and 2000 Hz, respectively. These results compare favorably with other experiments using synthetic speech and with results of acoustic analysis of nasal consonants.

The preceding discussion of the speech wave types, the acoustical speech parameters, and the acoustical characteristics of speech sounds should indicate that there is tremendous need for further research in all areas. Many of the problems of current interest will be discussed in the following section. Some of these areas of investigation might be pursued better if there were more knowledge of the wave types, parameters, and acoustical characteristics of speech sounds on which the future studies could build.

Practical Aspects in the Acoustical Study of Speech Sounds

The motivation behind the study of speech is to better understand our own speech production and perceptual processes and to apply what has been learned toward some realization of worthwhile tools or aids for mankind. Many of these realizations are, in turn, used in the study of speech itself. For example, speech synthesizers may have practical application in the areas of voice response systems and speech compression, but they are also of value for studies in speech production and perception, giving the researcher control over certain parameters relating to production and allowing the effects of parameter changes to be monitored by listeners.

Applications which deal with the acoustic speech wave as an input must be prepared to process a complex signal with high information content and tremendous variability. There is still a need for research in the direction of the acoustical characterization of speech. In the area of segmentation, there is much to be learned about the dynamic behavior of speech sounds and about the cues which indicate the locations of segmental boundaries. With regard to speech recognition, there are not yet enough data available on intraspeaker and interspeaker variations to discriminate correctly among all the sounds. This also relates to the problem of speaker normalization, in which the goal is to map acoustic features into a common parameter space when the same sound is repeated by different speakers. The remainder of this chapter is devoted to discussions and illustrations of some of the sources of difficulty which can be encountered in the acoustical study of speech sounds.

Segmentation

One of the basic problems in speech processing is the division of the speech wave into sound units with the objective of obtaining a symbolic representation of a sequence of acoustic events. Human beings seem to be very flexible in their ability to perceive various forms of sound units. It has been proposed that perceptual units range from the lowest level of phonetic elements to the highest level of word or even phrase-structured elements (Wickelgren, 1969; Savin and Bever, 1970; Bond, 1971; Lehiste, 1972).

It is desirable to have the acoustic segments correspond to some meaningful linguistic units. The usual form of linguistic reference is a phonemic transcription. This provides the criteria for making judgments regarding the presence of sound segments. However, there may be discrepancies between transcriptions of the same utterance by different listeners. Also, different listeners, when presented with the same acoustic cues, report different sounds on different occasions. These differences can usually be explained by socio-dialectical variations among listeners. It is also possible for a listener, being very familiar with the language and its linguistic rules, to claim the occurrence of nonexistent or modified speech sounds in a sample of natural or continuous speech. This in no way reflects upon the competence of the listener but, instead, magnifies the qualities of the human perceptual mechanism and the ability to transform an imperfect acoustic stream into meaningful linguistic units.

The derivation of segmental units can be accomplished by examining the time-varying acoustic parameters and by making decisions about the locations of significant events. In one case, an event may be indicated by rapidly changing parameters and, in another case, by parameter stabilization. It is, in general, thought to be possible to detect events based upon the dynamics of articulatory motion.

It is also possible to utilize the knowledge of the acoustic characteristics of speech sounds in order to scan the speech stream for the presence of those sounds. A great deal is known about the acoustic characteristics of sounds under certain conditions, but there is still much to be learned about all sounds in all conditions. Both the acoustic characteristics and the articulatory dynamics of a sound are significantly influenced by speaking rate, stress, and the adjacent sounds. Differences among individual speakers also must be considered.

It may be assumed that speech production is a process in which a series of neural commands is converted to articulator movements and acoustic source controls. Internally, a word may be thought of as, for example, four discrete sounds having four discrete articulatory targets, but at the production level, the physiological components of the system (tongue, lips, jaws, etc.) go through nearly continuous motions as they attempt to pass smoothly from one target position to the next. However, the mapping of the resulting acoustic signal into a phonetic representation is most likely not a procedure of finding and identifying the target articulatory configurations of all the sounds in the utterance. Target positions are considered the ideals and are actually achieved only in simple cases. Instead, target configurations are approached, and this is reflected in the acoustic parameters as *undershoot*.

The acoustic signal does not consist of discrete temporal segments with absolute boundaries between successive phonetic elements. Since the articulators are somewhat independent, a significant amount of parallelism exists such that the acoustic features often simultaneously carry information about two or more phones. This is demonstrated in the case of second-formant transitions indicating the place of the adjacent vowel. Thus, it seems that the important cues for segmentation, and for recognition as well, will come from articulatory dynamics and the temporal behavior of acoustic features.

SEGMENT BOUNDARY CUES

Because of the complex behavior of the acoustic speech signal and the variability in the speech production process, there is no complete set of criteria or procedures for separating speech into discrete units based upon acoustic characteristics. If such information existed, it would be possible to implement algorithms which would perform segmentation automatically. Researchers have commonly relied upon the visual examination of spectrograms as a reference for locating sounds or their boundaries (Öhman, 1966; Stevens, House, and Paul, 1966; Menon, Rao, and Thosar, 1974). There are many instances in which the beginnings and ends of sounds are signaled by relatively unambiguous cues, but there are also many instances where it is difficult to specify a segment boundary. As a result, it is often necessary to use more than one representation of the acoustic behavior in order to make reasonable judgments regarding points of segmentation.

One of the more unambiguous cases of segmentation is a vowel in the context of two voiceless fricatives. Figure 6.6 illustrates both a spectrographic and an oscillographic representation of the word *chess*. In the spectrographic form, the beginning of the vowel is signaled by a rather obvious change from the high-frequency energy concentration of the /tʃ/ to the multiresonant pattern of the /ɛ/. Likewise, the vowel termination is marked by the initiation of another high-frequency energy concentration going into the /s/. The vertical striations throughout the vowel indicate that it is voiced, unlike the two surrounding sounds. In simple cases such as this, the initiation and termination of voicing is a sufficient boundary clue. Voicing is preferred as a segmentation criterion because of its lack of ambiguity; the onset or offset of noise on a spectrogram can vary with the output level. The oscillographic display also contains unambiguous cues for locating the boundaries between the sounds. The high-frequency oscillations of the /tʃ/ give way to the higher-intensity sound of the vowel, which has a periodicity corresponding to the vocal fold oscillations. The intensity of the vowel decreases as the articulators move toward the structure for the /s/, with vowel termination signaled by the end of periodic activity and the beginning of high-frequency, low-intensity, quasi-random oscillations.

The word *well* shown in Figure 6.7, illustrates how ambiguities can arise when the environments of the vowel have the manner of a sonorant. The periodicity of the voiced sounds remains throughout the entire utterance. On the spectrogram, the primary cue of segment boundaries is formant motion. The transitional nature of /w/ itself makes it difficult to specify exactly where the /w/ ends and the vowel begins. A similar problem holds for the boundary between the vowel and /l/. The transition between these two sounds is rather smooth, so the specification of an absolute boundary point could be somewhat arbitrary. The display of the acoustic wave further exemplifies the difficulty of boundary location. There may be an intensity difference between

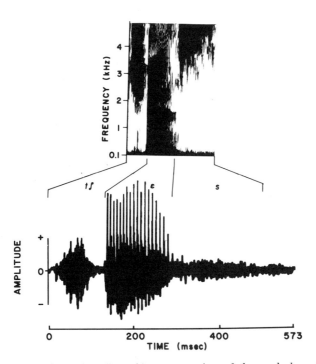

Figure 6.6 Spectrographic and oscillographic representations of the word *chess*. In either form, segment boundaries are relatively unambiguous.

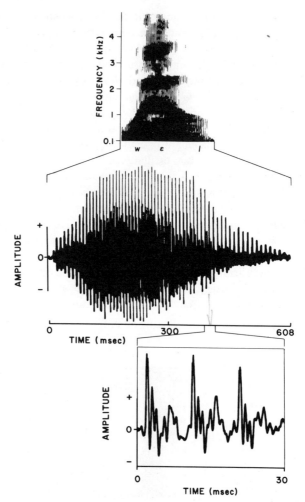

Figure 6.7 Broad-band spectrogram of the CVC sequence /wɛl/ and the corresponding acoustic wave plot. Segment boundaries become more ambiguous when all three sounds have similar properties.

the initial consonant and the vowel, or between the vowel and the final consonant, but these are gross judgments which indicate the possibility of occurrence of three sound units. It might be argued that detection of the presence of three sounds is itself a form of segmentation. This is probably true, but it is possible that knowledge of the steady states or boundaries between steady states also will be desired if discrimination is to be attempted at a later time. Changes in the wave pattern from pitch period to pitch period can be observed on the expanded acoustic wave plot of Figure 6.7, but again the transition is too slow to pinpoint absolute boundaries.

In a study of the duration of syllable nuclei, Peterson and Lehiste (1960) relied primarily upon both broad-band and narrow-band spectrograms in determining segmental boundaries. However, in difficult cases, reference was also made to intensity curves. They described the major cues observed as boundary indicators between vowels and adjacent consonants in CVC syllables, and these are summarized here:

1. *Initial and final plosives.*

   a. *Voiceless initial plosives:* Plosive release appeared as a spike on the spectrogram, but the beginning of the vowel was estimated to occur at the onset of voicing after aspiration. The first formant served as the voice onset indicator by changing from a weak energy concentration during aspiration to a strong resonance with periodic striations at the initiation of the vowel.

   b. *Voiced initial plosives:* There was an absence of aspiration following the voiced plosive release; therefore the segmentation point was located at the center of the plosive spike on the spectrogram.

   c. *Final voiceless plosives:* Beginning of the plosive was determined by the abrupt cessation of all formants. How about the end?

   d. *Final voiced plosives:* The boundary point between a vowel and a final voiced plosive required the comparison of broad-band and narrow-band spectrograms to determine when the energy in the higher harmonics diminished suddenly.

2. *Initial and final nasals.*

   a. *Initial nasals:* The segmentation of an initial nasal was accomplished by identifying the location where the steady nasal formant pattern changed into the on-glide movement of the initiation of the vowel.

   b. *Final nasals:* The boundary between a vowel and the final nasal was sometimes obscured when the vowel itself was nasalized. In such cases, sudden changes in the harmonic structure, as illustrated on a narrow-band spectrogram, were used to determine the beginning of the nasal.

3. *Initial and final fricatives.*

   a. *Initial voiceless fricatives:* The onset of voicing in the region of the first formant was used to determine the beginning of a vowel. An intensity curve was necessary in the segmentation of an /h/ and occasionally with other unvoiced fricatives.

   b. *Initial voiced fricatives:* The termination of these sounds was usually signified by an end to the noise characteristics of the fricatives.

   c. *Final voiceless fricatives:* The initiation of noise, as observed on the broad-band spectrograms, was specified as the beginning of an unvoiced fricative in the final position. How about the end?

   d. *Final voiced fricatives:* The gradual transition between vowel and voiced fricative required the supplementary use of an intensity curve, which showed a rapid decrease in energy at the onset of the consonant.

4. *Initial /w/ and /y/.*

   a. *Initial /w/:* The boundary between a /w/ and the vowel was usually selected as the region in which the slope of the second formant acquired a positive value. The initiation of the vowel also often was accompanied by a sharp increase in energy.

5. *Initial and final /l/ and /r/.*

   a. *Initial /l/ and /r/:* Information from both broad-band and narrow-band spectrograms was used in the segmentation of these sounds, as indicated by changes in the harmonics and frequency movements of the third formant.

b. *Final /l/ and /r/:* Because of the smooth transitions from the vowel to the consonant, it was difficult to determine the beginnings of these sounds. Boundary cues were provided by a combination of spectrographic displays, intensity curves, and a fundamental voice-frequency curve. In some of the syllables, the segmentation criterion was based upon a dip or rapid rise in the third formant. In others, there was a significant change in energy from the vowel to the consonant. Fundamental frequency had the characteristic of reaching a minimum at the end of the vowel and remaining relatively constant throughout the consonant.

Peterson and Lehiste reported that, in general, they believed their measurements of segmental points were accurate to within one or two centiseconds, that is, typically, one or two pitch periods. It was also stated that meaningful boundary points could not be specified when there were overlapping segmentation clues. This is the case especially for sound sequences other than CVC, for example, vowel clusters or consonant clusters. It could therefore be argued that there is no boundary point between adjacent sounds, but rather a boundary region in which the transition from one sound to the next takes place. This region can have the characteristics of one or both of the sounds it separates, and it may carry information regarding the identity of neighboring sounds (Menon, Rao, and Thosar, 1974; Broad and Fertig, 1970; Öhman, 1966; Lehiste and Peterson, 1961). Such a transition region is specifically defined in the physiological domain by Peterson and Shoup (1966a, Definition 57, p. 39).

COMPLEX SOUND CLUSTERS

It is possible to have utterances which are more complex than CVC sequences but in which the existence of individual sound units and their boundaries is still apparent. The word *segmentation* is made up of the sequence of sounds /sɛgmɛnteʃən/ or CVCCVCCVCVC. A broad-band spectrogram and acoustic-wave plot of the word *segmentation* are shown in Figure 6.8. In spite of the word's slightly complicated structure, the boundary regions between sounds are evident from either representation.[1] The contrasts between adjacent sounds are distinct enough that the spectral patterns give a rather clear picture of a sequence of 11 sound units. Intensity differences in the acoustic wave and significant changes in its structure also give evidence of a sequence of 11 sound units. The vowel sounds are often of higher intensity than surrounding consonants, with semi-vowels, glides, and nasals usually having the next highest relative intensity, followed by fricatives and stops. These are not absolute intensity relationships, for the relative intensity levels are also dependent upon context and stress.

[1] It is intended that the reader interpret such statements as an endorsement of both the time-domain representation and the frequency-domain representation of speech. The two forms are complementary and are therefore presented in parallel so that the reader may become familiar with both.

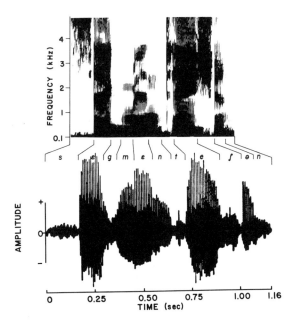

Figure 6.8 The individual sound units of the word *segmentation* are visible on both a spectral representation and a display of the acoustic wave. Boundary points between sounds are not necessarily absolute.

SPEECH STYLE

The acoustic characteristics of speech sounds are greatly affected by the style of spoken utterances; styles range from the phonation of isolated sounds to the natural speech of a person in conversation with another. As the style becomes more natural, the tasks of segmentation and discrimination become more difficult, primarily owing to the increased complexity of sound combinations, the variations in stress, and the increase in speech rate. The isolated sound is the most idealized case of a target position in that the articulators remain relatively static. In monosyllabic or CVC utterances, there is articulator movement, but the tendency is to speak slowly and enunciate carefully. These tendencies are reduced considerably by placing the desired sound sequence in a carrier sentence, for example, "say _____ again." Isolated words can generate complex sound sequences, but the speech rate is usually slower than normal unless the words are embedded within carrier sentences. Citation or read speech results in coarticulations at word boundaries which do not occur in isolated words, and it also results in additional degrees of stress due to intonation patterns within phrases and sentences. However, speech rate and enunciation in read speech are usually considered to be somewhat different from normal. Extemporaneous or conversational speech is considered to be the most natural; it is thought of as slightly less natural if the speaker is aware that he is being recorded.

In the more natural styles of speech production, errors become more likely. Sounds are deleted, inserted, and modified. Coarticulations become increasingly complex, and formant movements become less precise; thus segmentation and recognition tasks based upon acoustic information can achieve only limited results without the aid of higher-level linguistic processing. The acoustic analysis can reflect only the state of the actual acoustic signal, not the intended speech or ideal signal. Thus, in many cases, even a perfect acoustic analysis, followed by a perfect segmentation, followed by a perfect *phonetic* recognition, will not yield a perfect string of sound units that correspond to an ideal *phonemic* transcription of what was spoken. Thus we need to know more about which allophones are used in natural conversational speech.

WORD BOUNDARIES

Unless words are separated by pauses, the boundaries between words can become as obscure as the boundaries between sounds. In natural speech, there is usually a continuous flow from one word to the next, so the final sound of one word becomes fused with the initial sound of the following word. There is usually little acoustic evidence as to the location of word boundaries. Fundamental frequency and energy contours may be useful in locating units of phrase or syllable size (Lea, 1972; Mermelstein, 1974), but syntactic or linguistic rules may be required to find word boundaries when segmentation is done on the basis of elementary sound units. A good example of word boundary fusion is the phrase *my name is*. Both spectrographic and acoustic wave displays of the sound sequence /mɑɪnemɪz/ taken from a sample of extemporaneous speech are shown in Figure 6.9. While there may be sufficient acous-

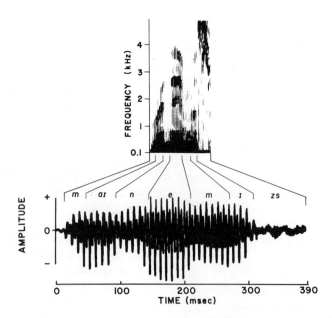

Figure 6.9 Spectrographic and acoustic wave displays of the phrase *my name is*. While there may be acoustic evidence indicating the presence of several sound units, there is no obvious indication of the location of word boundaries.

tic evidence of the occurrence of several sound units, the location of the word boundary is less concise, thus making it possible to claim that the phrase might really be *mine aim is*. Such ambiguities may be more appropriately resolved at some level above the acoustic.

Another condition which complicates word boundaries is that in which the final sound of one word is the same as the first sound of the following word. This common sound unit will probably have the characteristics of a single element, except that the duration *may* be longer than normal. In the words *six seconds*, the medial /s/ seems to have increased duration if the words are spoken so as to retain their meaning; otherwise, if spoken too rapidly, the phrase begins to sound more like *sick seconds*. Figure 6.10 illustrates some of the characteristics of the common /r/ between the two words *year right*. The acoustic wave has an intensity dip in the /r/ region, and an obvious downward shift in the second, third, and fourth formants can be seen on the broad-band spectrogram. However, it is difficult to judge whether there is a single /r/ with a slow initial transition, or a double occurrence of /r/.

PRONUNCIATION VARIATIONS

There are many anomalies related to the segmentation of sound units in natural speech. One of these occurs when the expected sound units are omitted from the speech stream. This can happen when each sound of a particular sequence of sound

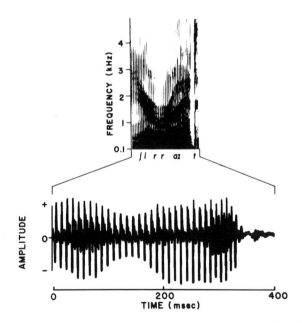

Figure 6.10 The words *year right* share the same sound at the word boundary. There is no strong acoustic evidence in either a spectrographic or acoustic wave display to indicate the location of a word boundary.

units has an articulatory configuration very similar to its preceding or following neighbor. When this occurs, there is a tendency to skip over one or more sounds. For example, in the utterance, *My name is* _____ *and the date is*, the two words *and the* normally would be thought of as having the form /ænd$\eth$ə/. Figure 6.11 (a) illustrates the acoustic behavior of the words *and the* as they might appear when spoken slowly and carefully. Figure 6.11 (b) represents the same two words taken from an extemporaneous speech sample. Based upon perception, the utterance of Figure 6.11 (b) is transcribed as /ænə/; the acoustic data support such a transcription. Thus, it may be that because the tongue position for the ideal /nd $\eth$/ sequence is nearly constant, anticipation of the /ə/ causes the consonants /d$\eth$/ to be omitted. This, of course, results in a string of segmental units that is shorter than expected.

Pronunciation variations include not only sound deletion but insertion and replacement as well. A word such as *warmth* may be pronounced as /wɔrmpθ/ rather than /wɔrmθ/, becoming a longer string of sound units with the insertion of the /p/. Substitution or replacement could cover one or more sound units, thus involving a form of deletion as well. The classic example of this form of modification is the pair of words *did you* pronounced as /dɪdʒə/ rather than /dɪdju/. It may be that pronounciation variations are systematic, that they can occur under certain known conditions, and that therefore phonological rules which account for such modifications can be formulated (Oshika *et al.*, 1975). An acoustic segmentation can reflect only what is actually spoken, so rules of this type could provide a link between the acoustic segment pattern and a lexicon of ideal reference patterns.

Difficulties may arise when attempting to locate segmental boundaries between elements of a long cluster of coupled sounds. In such cases, the acoustic wave may not have the traditional intensity peaks and dips which support segmentation hypotheses. A spectrographic representation gives more definitive indications of articulator movement, and it seems more appropriate to give an acoustic description of the utterance in terms of a series of alternative steady states and transitions. Figure

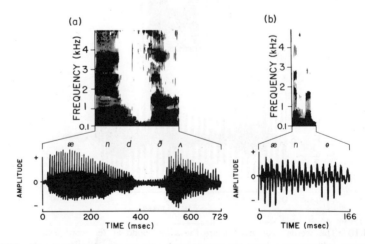

Figure 6.11 Spectrographic and acoustic wave displays of the two-word utterance *and the*: (a) spoken slowly, with all sounds present; (b) from an extemporaneous speech sample, with two sounds missing.

6.12 depicts both the spectrographic and the acoustic wave displays of the word
January as taken from an extemporaneous speech sample. From the acoustic wave, it is
evident that there is a very long sequence of voicing after the initial /dʒ/. Such a long
interval of voicing is itself a clue that more than one sound is present. There are two
significant intensity dips, but there are no apparent segmental boundaries from this
representation. On the other hand, the broad-band spectrogram shows several points
in time where the articulators seem to be passing through target positions, as indicated
by dips or peaks in formant motion. If these locations are treated as steady states,
there is no real need to specify segment boundary points. The one unknown with such
an approach, however, is the remaining question of whether the regions between
steady states are sound transitions or transitional sounds. It would seem, therefore,
that both articulatory motion and stability must be taken into account when attempting to segment sound units.

By first finding the so-called *steady states*, the transition regions can be studied
more carefully for the characteristics of transitional sounds; possibly, the duration
between steady states may provide the cue that further investigation is necessary.
If it is found to be a transition region only, a segment boundary could be placed
at the midpoint between the two steady states. Alternatively, a boundary point could
be placed at the location of maximum formant slope or maximum intensity (or energy)
slope. The primary objective should be some consistent criteria for boundary specification.

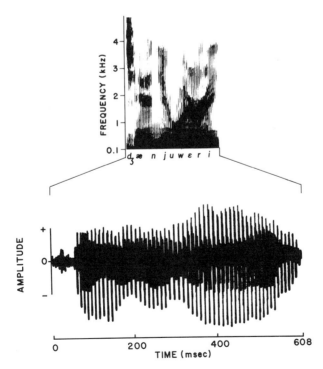

Figure 6.12 Spectrographic and acoustic wave displays of the word *January*. Formant movements
in the spectrographic representation indicate where possible steady states may exist.

Whatever the approach to segmentation, there should be enough flexibility to account for surprising amounts of variation in pronunciation and, therefore, in the acoustic signal. Even the same word repeated by a single speaker can have significantly different forms, especially in natural speech. Figure 6.13 illustrates some of the alterations which the word *photography* has undergone when spoken three times within a 30-second interval during an extemporaneous interview. First of all, each utterance is a different length. This means that each sound unit can have a different duration each time it occurs in speech. As a result, segmentation schemes must be independent of durational variations, although relative durations may be useful. Vowel reduction also has a significant effect on the duration of a vowel. As can be seen, the first /ə/ of Figure 6.13 (b) is reduced to about one pitch cycle, which would probably pose problems to schemes for pitch detection or voiced—unvoiced decisions. In the second utterance, the /ə/ after /r/ is deleted, and in the third utterance, both of the sounds /rə/ essentially are replaced by phonoaspiration.

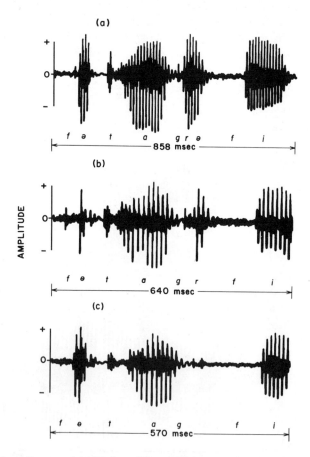

Figure 6.13 Acoustic wave plots for three different instances of the word *photography* spoken by the same speaker during an extemporaneous interview. All three utterances were spoken within a 30-second time span.

Figure 6.13 also illustrates the usefulness of time normalization in acoustical studies. Often it is much simpler to interpret the dynamic behavior of the acoustic parameters if they are examined using the same time scale as is used with other comparative samples (Flanagan, 1971). When a matching procedure is employed, improper time normalization can give erroneous results or false conclusions about the similarity between two samples. In studies of formant trajectories, for example, one way of achieving normalization is to sample the formant frequencies a fixed number of times independent of segment duration. Thus, by varying the interval between formant samples, the number of samples within the segment remains constant. Schemes for word recognition, speaker identification, and speaker verification often involve the matching of formant, pitch, or energy contours from the analysis of words, phrases, or sentences (Lummis, 1973; Atal, 1972). In a speaker verification task, it cannot be expected that a speaker be able to repeat an utterance with the very same timing each time it is spoken. In such cases, sophisticated time-warping functions are utilized to normalize the acoustic parameters in such a way that significant events are aligned in time. Another important application is in situations where the display of acoustic parameters is used as a visual aid in speech training for the handicapped. A person with a hearing defect, attempting to learn intonation patterns by observing pitch contours, probably would find it beneficial for the contour from the input utterance to be aligned temporally with a reference pattern. This alignment would eliminate the confusion of a mismatch if the intonation were correct but the speech rate different.

In spite of the acoustical variations in speech, sounds are understood when heard in context. It may be possible to account for many of the variational phenomena through the application of acoustic phonetic or phonological rules, but as yet not enough data are available on natural speech to formulate any general conclusions.

Discrimination

ACOUSTIC FEATURES

Even given that the speech stream can be segmented into a sequence of units that have some correspondence to speech sounds, the task of determining to which sound each segment corresponds, remains. This task calls for examination of the acoustic characteristics of the speech wave, generally with the objective of extracting from within each segment invariant features which will ultimately allow the classification of the segment as one of the eligible sound units. Unfortunately, the search for the so-called *invariant features* of speech sounds is still continuing, and they remain as elusive as ever.

The same speech conditions which complicated the segmentation process have a strong influence on sound discrimination. When many samples are taken of the same sound unit, rapid articulator movement during connected or natural speech accounts for much of the variation in the acoustic parameters. The lack of stress plays an important part in the shifting of acoustic features away from their ideal or target values. Context also has a significant effect on the position of speech parameters in acoustic feature space. In general, the speech stream is very often *corrupted* by unintended sounds, missing or inserted sounds, or sounds which have deviated from their ideal state.

The formant parameters seem to be the basic acoustic features for discriminating among voiced sounds. There are direct relationships between the formant frequencies and the physiological formations established during speech production. Fant (1960) showed that measurements of the articulatory configuration, taken from X-ray films, could be used to predict accurately formant frequencies. It has since been demonstrated (Schroeder, 1967; Wakita, 1973) that the reverse transformation is possible, that is, that vocal tract shapes can be estimated on the basis of acoustic measurements.

Nearly all forms of analysis can be related in some manner to the formant parameters. Spectral analysis by means of a bank of bandpass filters can be performed in real time, and formant information is available using various interpretations of the filter outputs (Stevens and Klatt, 1968; Klein, Plomp, and Pols, 1970). Fourier analysis, utilizing digital signal processing techniques, has been shown to be an appropriate method for extracting formant parameters (Schafer and Rabiner, 1970). It is also possible to relate zero crossings to formant frequencies. If the acoustic signal is filtered into frequency bands which span the range of each of the formants, then the number of zero crossings, or intervals between zero crossings, in each band is related to the formant frequency occurring on each band (Bezdel and Chandler, 1965; Reddy, 1967; Neiderjon and Thomas, 1973). Allowances must be made, however, for the possibility that there is more than one formant in a filter band or that there are no formants at all. Less conventional analysis schemes, such as the wavefunction representation of filtered speech (Markel, 1970; Carey, 1971; Pfeifer, 1972), can be used to make relatively accurate estimates for formant parameters, but, as with zero crossing analysis, problems exist when there is less than one or more than one formant in a filter band. The linear prediction forms of analysis (Atal and Hanauer, 1971; Markel, 1972) have been demonstrated to be very effective in applications such as formant tracking, speech synthesis, and estimating vocal tract characteristics.

SOURCES OF VARIATION

The vowel sounds have been the subject of a considerable amount of study because they usually form the nucleus of the syllabic unit, because their acoustic characteristics are so accessible, and because they can be synthesized with acceptable quality. However, even under the near ideal conditions of a CVC environment, the vowels exhibit a considerable amount of overlap in an acoustic parameter space.

There are many sources of variation in the acoustic quality of vowel sounds. When the same vowel is generated by different speakers, there is a natural difference in spectral characteristics and in formant frequencies. On the average, the formant frequencies for a male speaker tend to be lower than those for a female speaker. Speakers of the same sex have vocal tract differences sufficient to result in significant variation in formant parameters. Figure 6.14 represents data from the vowel /ɪ/ spoken in the same context by ten different male speakers. Three pitch periods of the acoustic wave from the steady state of the vowel are plotted in part (a), and their corresponding smoothed frequency spectra are plotted in part (b), where the location of the resonant peaks can be observed. The acoustic wave has a structure that is very similar from speaker to speaker since the data represent the same vowel; the samples are not identical, however, owing to the individualities of the speakers. While the acoustic wave samples have been normalized to the same length on the display, the pitch periods are not identical across speakers. Each frequency spectrum in Figure 6.14(b) has the approximate resonant structure of the vowel /ɪ/, but there are variations in the locations of the resonant peaks; these variations further illustrate the nonuniqueness of speech sounds.

Repetitions of a vowel in various contexts by the same speaker give a relatively tight parameter cluster in acoustic space (Broad and Fertig, 1970) when compared with the variations between speakers. When a vowel is repeated in the same context by a single speaker, the resulting parameter variations may be of an essentially random nature. Figure 6.15 demonstrates both intraspeaker and interspeaker differences for smoothed spectral samples of the vowel /ɔ/ spoken twice by each of ten male talkers. The vowel has the same consonantal environment in all cases. These data exemplify the problem of repeatability; that is, each utterance of the sound is unique. A speaker cannot exactly duplicate a sound, and the variation in the acoustic characteristics is partly a function of the time span between utterances (Endres, Bambach, and Flosser, 1971).

Since the formant frequencies are continually changing with time, it may be difficult to get consistent acoustic parameter measurements. The vowels are generally referred to as being steady-state sounds; however, formant motion is seldom steady, or unchanging, throughout the vowel. As a result, the location at which an acoustic sample is taken can have a significant impact on the stability of parameter measurements. There are times when the formant trajectories may pass through peaks or valleys as the articulators approach various target positions. Sampling from the center of a peak or valley decreases parameter variation and the probability of overlap between sounds. There are also times when formant trajectories pass through a vowel in a transitional fashion, passing from low to high frequency, or vice versa. It becomes difficult in such cases to estimate the location of the vowel *steady state* or its target

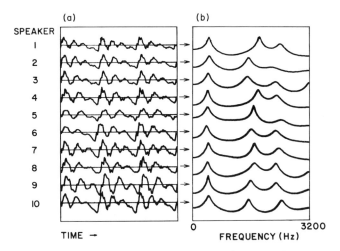

Figure 6.14 (a) Three pitch periods of the acoustic wave of the vowel /ɪ/ from ten male speakers; (b) corresponding smoothed frequency spectra.

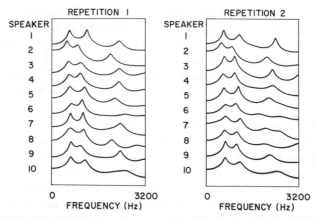

Figure 6.15 Smooth frequency spectra from two different samples of the vowel /ɔ/, all in the same consonantal environments, spoken by ten male talkers.

approximation. Figure 6.16 demonstrates three different states of the vowel /u/ from an extemporaneous interview of a male speaker. Part (a) shows a good example of a steady state /u/ from the words *seems to have*, where the formants are nearly constant across the vowel. In part (b) it can be seen that the /u/ of *January* has in the second formant a valley indicating the vowel target. A transitional form of the vowel /u/ is shown in part (c), taken from the utterance *two weeks*. In the transitional vowel, the second formant is continually moving downward and then arcing upward for the /w/, leaving some question as to the location of the /u/ steady state.

The secondary acoustic characteristics of the vowels also vary significantly in response to changes in consonantal environment (House and Fairbanks, 1953). The duration of vowels in a voiced context is somewhat longer than in an unvoiced context. Actually, this length provides more information about the voicing character of the consonants than it does about the identity of the vowel. The presence or absence of vocal fold vibration during consonants effects the fundamental frequency of adjacent vowels; there is a general tendency for vowels in an unvoiced environment to have a

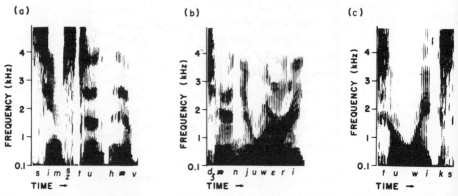

Figure 6.16 Broad-band spectrograms of three samples of the vowel /u/ in natural speech: (a) steady-state form, (b) formant peak—valley form, (c) transitional form.

higher fundamental frequency than those in a voiced context. In addition, the relative power of the vowels is influenced by the surrounding consonants in such a manner that the vowel intensity is lower with unvoiced than with voiced consonants.

Another factor which has significant influence on the acoustic parameters, and therefore on discrimination, is stress. The vowel sounds often are categorized as being stressed, unstressed, or reduced. Energy, fundamental frequency, and duration serve as acoustic correlates of stress, stressed vowels tending to have higher energy, higher fundamental frequency, and longer duration than corresponding unstressed or reduced vowels (Fry, 1955; Lieberman, 1960). These measures can be used only in relative terms, however, for energy is also a measure of speech loudness, duration is also an indicator of speech rate, and the average fundamental frequency is also a function of the physiological or emotional state of the talker.

Vowel reduction is characteristic of languages with heavy stress such as English and Swedish. In these languages, vowel reduction is associated with weakly stressed syllables, increased speech rate, and contextual influence. Formant shifting due to vowel reduction results in a formant pattern approaching that of schwa (Joos, 1948; Tiffany, 1959; Stevens and House, 1963; and Lindblom, 1963).

There is a high incidence of vowel reduction in continuous or natural speech. Words such as *you* and *believe* get transformed from the ideal pronunciation of /ju/ and /biliv/ to alternate forms such as /jə/ and /bəliv/. The acoustic parameters for reduced vowels often possess the qualities of schwa, thereby making it necessary to include such a vowel in any sort of discrimination scheme.

COARTICULATION

Phonetic context is one of the major causes of overlap in the distributions of formant frequencies (Tiffany, 1959; Stevens and House, 1963). The consonantal environment of a vowel causes systematic shifts in the vowel formant frequencies; these shifts depend upon the place of articulation of the consonant, its manner of articulation, and its voicing characteristics. In addition, each vowel is affected differently when placed in the same consonantal context. For example, front vowels with a high second formant may have the formant shifted downward, while the low second formant of a back vowel may be shifted upward.

The overlapping effect of two adjacent sounds is referred to as *coarticulation*. If a vowel is placed in a consonantal environment, measurement of the formant frequencies at its initial, middle, and final locations provides an indication as to the makeup of the entire CVC sequence. The initial and final second formant frequency values, especially, reflect the articulatory configuration of initiation and termination of the vowel. The formant frequencies in the middle of the vowel are determined by the vowel articulation. Stevens, House, and Paul (1966) approximated the motion of formants in symmetric CVC syllables with parabolic curves which provided a means of indirectly measuring *articulatory displacement* between vowel and consonant. Vowels in isolation and in /h-d/ context were considered as being in a null environment, and formant frequencies from these vowels were treated as target frequencies. The difference between the formant frequencies of vowels in the null environment and vowels in a symmetrical environment was computed in order to measure the amount of frequency shift due to consonantal influence. The results illustrated an apparent undershoot in second-formant frequency relative to target values.

The undershoot phenomenon at the midpoint of the vowel depends upon the distance in frequency the formant must traverse between the initiation of the vowel and its midpoint, and upon the distance between the midpoint and the vowel termination. Typically, the displacement of the second formant frequency is downward when the second formant frequency at the initiation and termination of the vowel begins below the target frequency. There is an upward shift if the second formant at the initiation and termination of the vowel is higher than the target frequency.

Broad and Fertig (1970) demonstrated that the influences of both initial and final consonants in a CVC syllable are highly significant throughout the vowel. Formant trajectories for the vowel /ɪ/ were measured when the vowel occurred in the environments of all combinations of 24 consonantal sound elements (including silence). Plots of the final consonant-transition functions showed that, except for three of the consonants and silence, the second-formant transition function was concave toward the abscissa when the final consonant was a fricative or sibilant. It was also noted that the final-consonant transition functions were not mirror images of the corresponding initial-transition functions. Such asymmetries are also described by Stevens, House, and Paul (1966). Broad and Fertig suggest that the lack of symmetry may be due to differences between memory effects of the initial consonant and anticipation effects of the final consonant.

Öhman's (1966) data illustrate that coarticulation effects are not restricted to neighboring sounds only. Spectrographic studies of VCV utterances in both Swedish and American English show that the formant transitions at the termination of the initial vowel are influenced not only by the consonant but also by the final vowel. Likewise, the formant transitions at the initiation of the final vowel are influenced by the initial vowel as well as by the consonant. (Although there are many additional studies on coarticulation, only a few of those which relate to acoustic measurements have been cited here for discussion.)

VOICING CONTRASTS

A decision that often is made early in a discrimination task is that of whether a sound is voiced or unvoiced. As discussed in the previous section of this chapter, the acoustic wave of a voiced sound is described as quasi-periodic, double-periodic, or irregular-periodic. Irregular-periodic waves are probably the most difficult type to handle when a voiced—unvoiced decision is attempted by algorithmic techniques. As a result, the irregular region may be classified as unvoiced, thereby putting the segment in the wrong discrimination category.

There are cases in natural speech where a sound is produced with the wrong voicing quality. This kind of contrast typically results in the production of a voiced sound in an unvoiced manner. One of the more frequent instances is the devoicing of a voiced fricative. Figure 6.17 shows a spectrographic and acoustic wave display of the word *seems*. There is some low amplitude periodicity visible on the acoustic wave just after the nasal, but the fricative sound has the characteristics of an /s/ rather than of a /z/. As a result, based upon acoustic evidence, the classification of the fricative as an

/s/ would not be in error; therefore, the problem would have to be resolved at some other level. The schwa vowel is normally thought of as a voiced sound, but when it occurs in a reduced form, there is a likelihood that it will be produced without voicing, giving it the qualities of an /h/, or aspiration. An example of an unvoiced schwa is given in Figure 6.18, which illustrates both spectrographic and acoustic wave displays of the word *commercial*. The /k/ sound appears to be unusually long because of the unvoiced quality of the /ə/.

schwa

SPEAKER NORMALIZATION

The definition of the invariant properties of speech sounds is only one aspect of the discrimination problem. It is essential not only to distinguish between different sounds from the same speaker, but also to distinguish between the same sounds from different speakers. The Peterson and Barney (1952) data clearly illustrate the overlap in vowel quality for repetitions of the vowels in a single /h—d/ environment when spoken by male, female, and child subjects. Stevens and House (1963) also report significant differences in the formant frequencies of the vowels from one speaker to another when the vowels are in 14 different consonantal environments. Using X-ray measurements, they give supplementary data which confirm that formant frequencies, on the average, tend to be higher for speakers with shorter vocal tracts.

When the first two formant frequencies for the vowels are plotted in the traditional F_1 versus F_2 plane, the vowel clusters tend to fall into a pattern referred to as the *vowel loop*. Since the formants shift as a function of vocal tract length, the position of the vowel loop in F_1 versus F_2 space is dependent upon the speaker. Knowledge of a

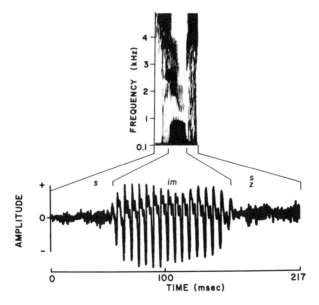

Figure 6.17 Spectrographic and acoustic wave representations of the word *seems*, illustrating the modification of the final /z/ to the unvoiced fricative /s/.

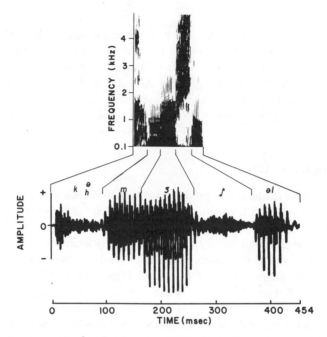

Figure 6.18 Spectrographic and acoustic wave representations of the word *commercial*, illustrating the devoicing of the reduced vowel /ə/ after the /k/.

speaker's vowel loop provides a useful reference for discriminating among the vowel sounds. Setup of the vowel loop is performed by obtaining formant samples from a set of training data.

Gerstman (1968) used the Peterson and Barney data to evaluate a normalized form for the vowels in F_1 versus F_2 space. The normalization was performed by finding the lowest and highest formant frequency for each vowel and then setting them equal to zero and 999, respectively. The remaining formant frequencies were then scaled proportionately. One important observation from the normalized data was that when separate averages were taken for the male, female, and child speakers, no significant F_1 or F_2 differences were found. It was suggested that a reasonably good specification of a vowel loop might be obtained by training on only those vowels which are located on the outermost points of the loop, namely /i/, /a/, and /u/, and that the remaining vowels could be scaled appropriately.

Foulkes (1961) used mathematical transformations to simplify the vowel regions obtained from the Peterson and Barney data. It was found that the original complex boundaries, with some overlap among vowel clusters, could be transformed into rectangular boundaries with significantly less overlap. The improved separability between the vowels was achieved by applying fundamental frequency as a normalizing factor. Nine different vowel classes fell within their own boundaries 76% to 97% of the time, depending upon the vowel, using transformations of F_1 and F_2 with corrections made for a standardized fundamental frequency of 200 Hz.

It would seem that the proper directions for speaker normalization are the application of fundamental frequency and vocal tract length. Female speakers tend to have a smaller vocal tract structure than males; they therefore have higher fundamental frequencies and higher frequency formants. While fundamental frequency can be measured directly from the acoustic wave, the vocal tract length is not available in a similar fashion. The development of techniques for the extraction of vocal tract length from the acoustic data may be an important step toward speaker normalization.

Summary

Two major areas of interest are discussed in this chapter. The first section incorporates a thorough description of the speech wave types, the acoustical speech parameters, and the acoustical characterization of speech sounds. The second section of the chapter describes many of the problems of current interest in the acoustical study of speech sounds.

Sounds are described first at a very basic level as being made up of various wave types; each wave type is defined in terms of the physiological manifestations which generate it. The basic wave type categories are: quiescent, burst, quasi-random, and quasi-periodic. Each sound unit is composed of a combination of one or more of the various wave types.

Acoustical speech parameters are properties derived from the speech wave which can be related to the physiological production of sounds. Those parameters which relate to phonetic characteristics, such as place and manner of articulation, are referred to as *acoustic phonetic parameters*, whereas those parameters which refer to global characteristics, such as duration and fundamental frequency, are referred to as *acoustic prosodic parameters*. The acoustic phonetic parameters discussed include gap, broad-band continuous spectrum, formant frequency, formant bandwidth, formant amplitude, and antiresonance. A description of the acoustic prosodic parameters is also given.

A discussion of the acoustical characteristics of speech sounds begins with the vowels. This class of sounds has been studied more thoroughly than any other. The vowels are traditionally characterized by their resonant frequencies; however, these frequencies are not absolute for each vowel sound. As a result there is overlap among the vowels, with the amount of overlap a function of stress, context, number of speakers, and so on. A set of sounds referred to as sonorants, namely /j, l, r, w/, also are characterized chiefly by their resonant frequencies. These sounds are more transitional in nature than vowels; therefore formant motion is important in distinguishing among them. The fricatives and sibilants are easily identified by their speech wave types, but their associated acoustical parameters are not as readily interpreted. Once separated into their voiced and unvoiced categories, they are usually specified in terms of relative energy and the frequency location of significant spectral peaks. However, there are still many questions about the adequacy of such acoustical specifications for these sounds. Trills and flaps have received little attention due to their relative infrequency of occurrence. Stops, on the other hand, have been the subject of much study, probably due to their interesting allophonic variations and complex acoustical descriptions. Acoustic characteristics such as closure duration, voice onset time, burst frequency, and formant transitions of an adjacent vowel are useful in distinguishing among the stops, but none of these parameters seems to be an absolute cue. Finally, the class of nasal sounds has acoustical characteristics similar to those of vowels and sonorants. While they are made up of quasi-periodic wave types, their most distinctive feature is the presence of antiresonances due to the side branching of the nasal cavity from the vocal tract.

In the study of the acoustical characteristics of speech sounds, problems are encountered in the areas of segmentation and discrimination. For segmentation, there is often difficulty in determining the boundary between two sounds. The derivation of segmental units is usually accomplished by examining the time-varying acoustic parameters of speech. In some cases, segmentation cues are indicated by rapidly changing acoustic parameters, and in other cases cues are derived from parameter stabilization. Segmentation guidelines have been documented for CVC utterances, but they are not sufficient to account for the varied boundary conditions which occur in more complicated utterances.

There are many factors which influence the acoustic characteristics of speech sounds. Acoustic parameters tend to deviate from their ideal (or target) values as the style of speech goes from the more simple form of sustained phonation to the more complex mode of natural conversational speech. In the more natural styles of speech, the boundaries between sounds become more complicated, as do the boundaries between words, the last sound of one word becoming fused with the first sound of the following word. Pronunciation variations become more frequent in natural speech. These variations include such anomalies as sound deletion, sound insertion, and sound replacement, any of which result in a nonideal string of segmental units. It is the task of higher level theories of phonology, such as phonemics or generative phonology, to account for these variations, while it is the task of acoustic phonetics to specify the acoustical properties of each phonetic type that actually occurs.

Additional sources of variation in the acoustic parameters are speaker differences, context, and stress. Speakers have sufficient vocal tract differences to result in significant variation in the acoustic parameters from speaker to speaker. The acoustic parameters relating to a particular sound also are influenced by the adjacent sounds. Thus context and coarticulation affect parameter behavior as a function of time and position in acoustic parameter space. The effect of stress is such that formant shifting due to vowel reduction results in a formant pattern approaching that of schwa.

In general, in spite of the acoustical variations, humans are able to carry on voice communications under a wide variety of conditions. Continued research in the speech sciences will lead to a better understanding of the speech processes and improved simulations of the production and perceptual functions.

ACKNOWLEDGMENTS

The preparation of this chapter was supported in part by the Air Force Office of Scientific Research under Contract F44620-74-C-0034.

REFERENCES

Atal, B. S. Determination of the vocal tract shape directly from the speech wave. *Journal of the Acoustical Society of America*, 1970, *47*, 65(A).

Atal, B. S. Automatic speaker recognition based on pitch contours. *Journal of the Acoustical Society of America*, 1972, *52*, 1687−1697.

Atal, B. S., and Hanauer, S. L. Speech analysis and synthesis by linear prediction of the speech wave. *Journal of the Acoustical Society of America*, 1971, *50*, 637−655.

Bell, C. G., Fujisaki, H., Heinz, J. M., Stevens, K. N., and House, A. S. Reduction of speech spectra by analysis-by-synthesis techniques. *Journal of the Acoustical Society of America*, 1961, *33*, 1725−1736.

Bezdel, W., and Chandler, H. J. Results of an analysis and recognition of vowels by computer using zero crossing data. *Proceedings of IEEE*, 1965, *112*, 2060−2066.

Bond, Z. S. Units in speech perception. *Working Papers in Linguistics*. Columbus, Ohio: Computer and Information Science Research Center, Ohio State University, 1971, *9*, viii−112.

Broad, D. J., and Fertig, R. Formant-frequency trajectories in selected CVC-syllable nuclei. *Journal of the Acoustical Society of America*, 1970, *47*, 1572−1582.

Carey, B. J. A method for automatic time domain analysis of human speech. *Report CRL−19*. Santa Barbara, California: Computer Research Laboratory, University of California at Santa Barbara, 1971.

Chiba, T., and Kajiyama, M. *The vowel—its nature and structure*. Tokyo, Japan: Phonetic Society of Japan, 1958.

Cooper, F. S., Delattre, P. C., Liberman, A. M., Borst, J. M., and Gerstman, L. J. Some experiments on the perception of synthetic speech sounds. *Journal of the Acoustical Society of America*, 1952, *24*, 597−606.

Cotton, J. C. A study of certain phoniatric resonance phenomena. *Journal of Speech Disorders*, 1940, *5*, 289−293.

Crandall, I. B. Dynamical study of the vowel sounds—II. *Bell System Technical Journal*, 1927, *6*, 100−116.

Delattre, P. The physiological interpretation of sound spectrograms. *Publications of the Modern Language Association of America*, 1951, *66*, 864−875.

Delattre, P. *Comparing the phonetic features of English, German, Spanish and French: An interim report*. Heidelberg, Germany: Julius Groos Verlag, 1965.

Delattre, P. C., Liberman, A. M., and Cooper, F. S. Acoustic loci and transitional cues for consonants. *Journal of the Acoustical Society of America*, 1955, *27*, 769−773.

Dunn, H. K. Methods of measuring vowel formant bandwidths. *Journal of the Acoustical Society of America*, 1961, *33*, 1737−1746.

Endres, W., Bambach, W., and Flosser, G. Voice spectrograms as a function of age, voice disguise, and voice imitation. *Journal of the Acoustical Society of America*, 1971, *49*, 1842−1848.

Fant, C. G. M. Transmission properties of the vocal tract, Part II. *MIT Quarterly Progress Report*. Cambridge, Massachusetts: Acoustics Laboratory, MIT, 1950.

Fant, C. G. M. On the predictability of formant levels and spectrum envelopes from formant frequencies. In M. Halle (Ed.), *For Roman Jakobson*. The Hague: Mouton, 1956, 109−120.

Fant, G. *Acoustic theory of speech production*. The Hague: Mouton, 1960.

Fischer-Jorgensen, E. Acoustic analysis of stop consonants. *Miscellanea Phonetica*, 1954, *2*, 42−59.

Flanagan, J. L. Some properties of the glottal sound source. *Journal of Speech and Hearing Research*, 1958, *1*, 99−116.

Flanagan, J. L. Focal points on speech communication research. *IEEE Transactions in Communication Technology*, 1971, COM−19, 1006−1015.

Fletcher, H. *Speech and hearing in communication*. New York: Van Nostrand, 1953.

Foulkes, J. D. Computer identification of vowel types. *Journal of the Acoustical Society of America*, 1961, *33*, 7−11.

Fry, D. B. Duration and intensity as physical correlates of linguistic stress. *Journal of the Acoustical Society of America*, 1955, *27*, 765−768.

Fujimura, O. Analysis of nasal consonants. *Journal of the Acoustical Society of America*, 1962, *34*, 1865−1875.

Gerstman, L. J. Classification of self-normalized vowels. *IEEE Transactions on Audio and Electroacoustics*, 1968, AU−16, 78−80.

Halle, M., Hughes, G. W., and Radley, J.-P.A. Acoustic properties of stop consonants. *Journal of the Acoustical Society of America*, 1957, *29*, 107−116.

Harris, K. S. Cues for the identification of the fricatives of American English. *Journal of the Acoustical Society of America*, 1954, *26*, 952(A).

Harris, K. S. Cues for the discrimination of American English fricatives in spoken syllables. *Language and Speech*, 1958, *1*, 1—7.

Harris, K. S., Hoffman, H. S., Liberman, A. M., Delattre, P. C., and Cooper, F. S. Effect of third-formant transitions on the perception of the voiced stop consonants. *Journal of the Acoustical Society of America*, 1958, *30*, 122—126.

Hattori, S., Yamamoto, K., and Fujimura, O. Nasalization of vowels in relation to nasals. *Journal of the Acoustical Society of America*, 1958, *30*, 267—274.

Hecker, M. H. L. Studies of nasal consonants with an articulatory speech synthesizer. *Journal of the Acoustical Society of America*, 1962, *34*, 179—188.

Heffner, R-M. S. *General phonetics*. Madison, Wisconsin: University of Wisconsin Press, 1952.

Heinz, J. M., and Stevens, K. N. On the properties of voiceless fricative consonants. *Journal of the Acoustical Society of America*, 1961, *33*, 589—596.

Helmholtz, H. L. F. *On the sensations of tone* (2nd English ed.; translated, thoroughly revised and corrected by Alexander, J. E.). New York: Dover Publications, 1954.

Hockett, C. F. A manual of phonology. *International Journal of American Linguistics*, 1955, *21*, 1—246.

Hoffman, H. S. Study of some cues in the perception of the voiced stop consonants. *Journal of the Acoustical Society of America*, 1958, *30*, 1035—1041.

House, A. S. Analog studies of nasal consonants. *Journal of the Speech and Hearing Disorders*, 1957, *22*, 190—204.

House, A. S. and Fairbanks, G. The influence of consonant environment upon the secondary acoustical characteristics of vowels. *Journal of the Acoustical Society of America*, 1953, *25*, 105—113.

House, A. S., and Stevens, K. N. Analog studies of the nasalization of vowels. *Journal of Speech and Hearing Disorders*, 1956, *21*, 218—232.

House, A. S., Stevens, K. N., and Paul, A. P. Acoustic description of syllabic nuclei: an interpretation in terms of a dynamic model of articulation. Paper G-23 in *Proceedings of the Fourth International Congress on Acoustics*. Copenhagen, Denmark: The Acoustical Laboratory, 1962.

Hubbell, A. *The pronunciation of English in New York City: Consonants and vowels*. New York: Octagon Books, 1972. (Earlier edition in 1950).

Hughes, G. W., and Halle, M. Spectral properties of fricative consonants. *Journal of the Acoustical Society of America*, 1956, *28*, 303—310.

Ishizaka, K., and Flanagan, J. L. Synthesis of voiced sounds from a two-mass model of the vocal cords. *Bell System Technical Journal*, 1972, *51*, 1233—1268.

Jassem, W. The phonology of Polish stress. *Word*, 1959, *15*, 252—269.

Jassem, W. The formants of fricative consonants. *Language and Speech*, 1965, *8*, 1—16.

Joos, M. Acoustic phonetics. *Language Monograph No. 23*. Baltimore, Maryland: Waverly Press, 1948.

Klein, W., Plomp, R., and Pols, L. C. W. Vowel spectra, vowel spaces, and vowel identification. *Journal of the Acoustical Society of America*, 1970, *48*, 999—1009.

Koenig, W., Dunn, H. K., and Lacy, L. Y. The sound spectrograph. *Journal of the Acoustical Society of America*, 1946, *18*, 19—49.

Lea, W. A. An approach to syntactic recognition without phonemics. *1972 Conference on Speech Communication and Processing*. New York: Institute of Electrical and Electronic Engineers, 1972, 198—201.

Lehiste, I Acoustical characteristics of selected English consonants. *International Journal of American Linguistics*, 1964, *30*, 1—197.

Lehiste, I. (Ed.). *Readings in acoustic phonetics*. Cambridge, Massachusetts: M.I.T. Press, 1967.

Lehiste, I. The units of speech perception. *Working Papers in Linguistics*. Columbus, Ohio: Computer and Information Science Research Center, Ohio State University, 1972, *12*, 1—32.

Lehiste, I., and Peterson, G. E. Transitions, glides, and diphthongs. *Journal of the Acoustical Society of America.*, 1961, *33*, 268—277.

Liberman, A. M. Some results of research on speech perception. *Journal of the Acoustical Society of America*, 1957, *29*, 117—123.

Liberman, A. M., Delattre, P. C., Cooper, F. S., and Gerstman, L. J. The role of consonant—vowel transitions in the perception of the stop and nasal consonants. *Psychological Monographs General and Applied.* Washington, D.C.: Herbert S. Conrad, 1954, 1—13.

Lieberman, P. Some acoustic correlates of word stress in American English. *Journal of the Acoustical Society of America,* 1960, *32,* 451—454.

Lindblom, B. Spectrographic study of vowel reduction. *Journal of the Acoustical Society of America,* 1963, *35,* 1773—1781.

Lindquist, J., and Sundberg, J. Acoustic properties of the nasal tract. *Speech Transmission Laboratory Quarterly Progress and Status Report.* Stockholm, Sweden: Royal Institute of Technology, 1972, *1,* 13—17.

Lisker, L. Minimal cues for separating /w, r, l, y/ in intervocalic position. *Word,* 1957, *13,* 256—267.(a)

Lisker, L. Closure duration and the intervocalic voiced—voiceless distinction in English. *Language,* 1957, *33,* 42—49.(b)

Lisker, L., and Abramson, A. S. A cross-language study of voicing in initial stops: Acoustical measurements. *Word,* 1964, *20,* 383—422.

Lloyd, R. *Vowel-sound.* London: Turner and Dunnett, 1890.

Lummis, R. C. Speaker verification by computer using speech intensity for temporal registration. *IEEE Transactions on Audio Electroacoustics,* 1973, AU—21, 80—89.

Malécot, A. Acoustic cues for nasal consonants: An experimental study involving a tape-splicing technique. *Language,* 1956, *32,* 274—284.

Malécot, A. The glottal stop in French. *Phonetica,* 1975, *31,* 51—63.

Malécot, A. and Lloyd, P. The /t/: /d/ distinction in American alveolar flaps. *Lingua,* 1968, *19,* 264—272.

Markel, J. D. On the interrelationships between a wave function representation and a formant model of speech. *SCRL Monograph No. 5.* Santa Barbara, California: Speech Communications Research Laboratory, 1970.

Markel, J. D., Digital inverse filtering—a new tool for formant trajectory estimation. *IEEE Transactions on Audio and Electroacoustics,* 1972, AU—20, 129—137.

· Menon, K. M. N., Rao, P. V. S., and Thosar, R. B. Formant transitions and stop consonant perception in syllables. *Language and Speech,* 1974, *17,* 27—46.

Mermelstein, P. Determination of the vocal-tract shape from measured formant frequencies. *Journal of the Acoustical Society of America,* 1967, *41,* 1283—1294.

Mermelstein, P. A phonetic-context controlled strategy for segmentation and phonetic labeling of speech. *Status Report on Speech Research.* New Haven, Connecticut: Haskins Laboratories, 1974, SR—37/38, 191—197.

Mermelstein, P., and Schroeder, M. R. Determination of smoothed cross-sectional area functions of the vocal tract from formant frequencies. Paper A24 presented at the 5th International Congress on Acoustics, Liege, Belgium, September 7—14, 1965.

Miller, D. C. *The science of musical sounds.* New York: Macmillan, 1926.

Moore, P., and Von Leden, H. Dynamic variations of the vibratory pattern in the normal larynx. *Folia Phoniatrica.,* 1958, *10,* 205—238.

Nakata, K. Synthesis and perception of nasal consonants. *Journal of the Acoustical Society of America,* 1959, *31,* 661—666.

Neiderjon, R. J., and Thomas, I. B. Computer recognition of the continuant phonemes in connected English speech. *IEEE Transactions on Audio and Electroacoustics,* 1973, AU—21, 526—535.

O'Connor, J. D., Gerstman, L. J., Liberman, A. M., Delattre, P. C., and Cooper, F. S. Acoustic cues for the perception of initial /w, j, r, l/ in English. *Word,* 1957, *13,* 24—43.

Öhman, S. E. G. Coarticulation in VCV utterances: Spectrographic measurements. *Journal of the Acoustical Society of America,* 1966, *39,* 151—168.

Öhman, S. E. G. Studies of articulatory coordination. *Speech Transmission Laboratory Quarterly Progress and Status Report.* Stockholm, Sweden: Royal Institute of Technology, 1967, *1,* 15—20.

Oshika, B. T., Zue, V. W., Weeks, R. V., Neu, H., and Aurbach, J. The role of phonological rules in speech understanding research. *IEEE Transactions on Acoustics, Speech, and Signal Processing,* 1975, AASP—23, 104—112.

Paget, R. *Human speech.* New York: Harcourt Brace, 1930.

Peterson, G. E., and Barney, H. L. Control methods used in a study of vowels. *Journal of the Acoustical Society of America*, 1952, *24*, 175—184.

Peterson, G. E., and Lehiste, I. Duration of syllable nuclei in English. *Journal of the Acoustical Society America*, 1960, *32*, 693—703.

Peterson, G. E., and Shoup, J. E. A physiological theory of phonetics. *Journal of Speech and Hearing Research*, 1966, *19*, 5—67. (a)

Peterson, G. E., and Shoup, J. E. The elements of an acoustic phonetic theory. *Journal of Speech and Hearing Research*, 1966, *9*, 68—99. (b)

Pfeifer, L. L. The application of wavefunction analysis to single-speaker phoneme recognition. *Report CRL—18*. Santa Barbara, California: Computer Research Laboratory, Inc., University of California at Santa Barbara, 1972.

Potter, R. K., Kopp, G. A., and Green, H. *Visible speech*. New York: Van Nostrand, 1947.

Reddy, D. R. Computer recognition of connected speech. *Journal of the Acoustical Society of America*, 1967, *42*, 329—347.

Russell, G. O. *The vowel*. College Park, Maryland: McGrath Publishing, 1970.

Russell, G. O. *Speech and voice*. New York: Macmillan, 1931.

Savin, H. B., and Bever, T. G. The nonperceptual reality of the phoneme. *Journal of Verbal Learning and Verbal Behavior*, 1970, *9*, 295—302.

Schafer, R. W., and Rabiner, L. R. System for automatic formant analysis of voiced speech. *Journal of the Acoustical Society of America*, 1970, *47*, 634—648.

Schroeder, M. R. Determination of the geometry of the human vocal tract by acoustic measurements. *Journal of the Acoustical Society of America*, 1967, *41*, 1002—1010.

Scripture, E. *The elements of experimental phonetics*. New York: AMS Press, 1973.

Shearme, J. N., and Holmes, J. N. An experimental study of the classification of sounds in continuous speech according to their distribution in the formant 1—formant 2 plane. *Proceedings of the 4th International Congress of Phonetic Science*, The Hague: Mouton, 1962, 234—240.

Smith, S. Vocalization and added nasal resonance. *Folia Phoniatrica*, 1951, *3*, 165—169.

Stevens, K. N., and House, A. S. Development of a quantitative description of vowel articulation. *Journal of the Acoustical Society of America*, 1955, *27*, 484—493.

Stevens, K. N., and House, A. S. An acoustical theory of vowel production and some of its implications. *Journal of Speech and Hearing Research*, 1961, *4*, 303—320.

Stevens, K. N., and House, A. S. Perturbation of vowel articulations by consonantal context: An acoustical study. *Journal of Speech and Hearing Research*, 1963, *6*, 111—128.

Stevens, K. N., House, A. S., and Paul, A. Acoustical description of syllabic nuclei: An interpretation in terms of a dynamic model of articulation. *Journal of the Acoustical Society of America*, 1966, *40*, 123—132.

Stevens, K., and Klatt, M. Study of acoustic properties of speech sounds. *Report No. 1669*. Cambridge, Massachusetts: Bolt Beranek and Newman, 1968.

Strevens, P. Spectra of fricative noise in human speech. *Language and Speech*, 1960, *3*, 32—49.

Stumpf, C. *Die Sprachlaute*. Berlin: J. Springer, 1926.

Tarnóczy, T. Resonance data concerning nasals, laterals, and trills. *Word*, 1948, *4*, 71—77.

Tarnóczy, T. Die akustische struktur der stimmlosen engelaute. *Acta Linguistica*, 1954, *4*, 313—349.

Tiffany, W. R. Nonrandom sources of variation in vowel quality. *Journal of Speech and Hearing Research*, 1959, *2*, 305—317.

van den Berg, Jw. An electrical analogue of the trachea, lungs, and tissues. *Acta Physiological et Pharmacologica, Neerlandica*, 1960, *9*, 361—385.

Wakita, H., Estimation of the vocal tract shape by optimal inverse filtering and acoustic/articulatory conversion methods. *SCRL Monograph No. 9*. Santa Barbara, California: Speech Communications Research Laboratory, 1972.

Wakita, H. Direct estimation of the vocal tract shape by inverse filtering of acoustic speech waveforms. *IEEE Transactions on Audio and Electroacoustics*, 1973, AU—21, 417—427.

Weiss, A. Oral and nasal sound pressure levels as related to judged severity of nasality. Unpublished doctoral dissertation, Purdue University, Lafayette, Indiana, 1954.

Wickelgren, W. A. Context-sensitive coding, associative memory, and serial order in (speech) behavior. *Psychological Review*, 1969, *76*, 1—15.

chapter 7

Suprasegmental Features of Speech

Ilse Lehiste

The Ohio State University, Columbus

Introduction

Suprasegmental features usually are listed either as the set of features consisting of pitch, stress, and quantity, or defined as features whose domain extends over more than one segment. Neither definition is completely adequate. If suprasegmentals are to be defined with reference to their domain, then pitch, stress, and quantity would not qualify as suprasegmentals when they happen to be manifested over a single segment. On the other hand, there are other features whose domain is larger than a single segment, that do not function in the same way as do the suprasegmentals (cf., for example, the palatalization of a consonant cluster in such a manner that the palatalization extends over all segments constituting the cluster). If it is true that stress, pitch, and quantity behave in a way that sets them apart from features determining segmental phonetic quality, the definition should be revised.

It appears that suprasegmental features relate to segmental features by constituting an overlaid function of the inherent features. *Inherent features* can be defined with reference to a segment itself. The fundamental frequency of an inherently voiced segment, besides characterizing the segment as voiced, also may serve to signal a tonal or intonational pattern. To be recognizable as a segment, every segment has a certain duration in the time domain; at the same time, that duration may be contrastive (e.g., characterize the segment as being distinctively short rather than long). Every segment also has a certain amount of intensity; whatever the acoustic and physiological correlates of stress, they consist in intensifying phonetic factors already present in a lesser degree.

Furthermore, suprasegmental features differ from segmental features by the fact that suprasegmental features are established by a comparison of items in sequence, whereas segmental features are identifiable by inspection of the segment itself. For example, the rounding of a vowel in a sequence of rounded vowels can be established for each vowel without comparing that vowel with preceding or following vowels; the stressedness of a vowel cannot be established without reference to other vowels that carry relatively weaker stress. Thus the differences between suprasegmental features and segmental features are simultaneously differences of kind and differences in degree.

Duration and Quantity

The first of the suprasegmental features considered in this chapter is the feature of *quantity*, a linguistic term referring to the contrastive function of duration within a phonological system. Control over the feature of quantity presupposes control over the duration of articulatory gestures. Currently, two models are proposed for explaining the ways in which this control is achieved (Ohala, 1973). According to the first hypothesis, the units of speech are executed according to some underlying pre-programmed time schedule. According to the second hypothesis, there is no underlying time program or rhythm; a given speech gesture simply is executed after the preceding gestures have been completed successfully. The first model has been called the *comb* model, the second the *chain* model (Bernstein, 1967). After considering available evidence, Ohala suggests a compromise: the chain model for long-term timing, the comb model for short-term timing. A model describing the accuracy with which the durations of individual segments are controlled in speech production is offered by Allen (1973).

There is abundant experimental evidence that speakers can articulate repetitions of the same words with extremely small temporal variations. In a study involving Dutch subjects, Nooteboom (1972) found that standard deviations of 5–10 milliseconds were normal within one session, falling in some cases below 5 msec. There is likewise evidence that small, short-term variations in the timing of speech intervals have perceptual value (Lehiste, 1970; Huggins, 1972a,b; Nooteboom, 1973).

Just-noticeable differences in duration have been studied extensively over a number of years (Woodrow, 1951). While the human auditory system is capable of very fine distinctions under favorable experimental conditions, it appears that in the range of the durations of speech sounds—usually from 30 to about 300 msec—the just-noticeable differences in duration are between 10 and 40 msec.

Given that the duration of both segments and sequences of segments can be controlled with considerable precision, it appears natural that languages should make use of temporal distinctions within their phonological systems. For a feature to serve as an element in a phonological system, it must be independently controllable. To establish whether this is so, it is necessary to describe (and thus eliminate from consideration) all conditioned variation in the duration of segments and sequences of segments. These conditioning factors include the phonetic nature of the segment itself (intrinsic, duration), preceding and following sounds, other suprasegmental features, and position of the segment within a higher-level phonological unit.

The duration of vowels appears to be correlated with tongue height: Other factors being equal, a high vowel is shorter than a low vowel. Evidence for this has emerged from experimental studies of many and diverse languages, including English, German, Danish, Swedish, Thai, Lapp, and Spanish. The influence of preceding consonants on the duration of vowels following them appears to be negligible; however, the phonetic nature of a following consonant may exert considerable influence on the duration of a preceding vowel. This influence is perhaps greatest in English: the duration of a vowel preceding a voiced consonant is approximately 1.5 times greater than that of the same vowel preceding a voiceless consonant. In a study by Peterson and Lehiste (1960), it was found that in 118 minimal pairs such as *beat—bead, sight—side,* and so forth, the average duration of the syllable nucleus before the voiceless member of the consonant pair was 197 msec, while the duration before the voiced member was 297 msec, yielding an approximate ratio of 2:3. The effect of voicing is much smaller in other languages, although it may be present.

The point of articulation of a following consonant may likewise influence the duration of a preceding vowel: vowel duration tends to increase as the point of articulation of the postvocalic consonant shifts farther back in the mouth. However, this is dependent largely on the language, as is the influence of the manner of articulation of a consonant upon the duration of a preceding vowel. In English, vowels are shortest before voiceless stops, and their duration increases when the postvocalic consonants belong to the classes of voiceless fricatives, nasals, voiced stops, and voiced fricatives. In the study by Peterson and Lehiste (1960) referred to above, the average duration of short vowels was found to be 147 msec before /t/, 199 msec before /s/, 216 msec before /n/, 206 msec before /d/, and 262 msec before /z/.

The intrinsic duration of consonants is influenced both by their point of articulation and by the manner of articulation. There seems to be general agreement that labials are longer than alveolars and velars, other factors being kept constant. Taps and flaps are shortest; unvoiced fricatives tend to be longer than any other consonants.

It is frequently the case that differences in vowel length are accompanied by equally noticeable quality differences. There is a tendency in many languages for long vowels to be articulated with a more extreme articulatory position; short vowels, on the other hand, tend to be articulated closer to the center of the articulatory vowel space. However, languages differ with respect to the extent and kind of influence the length of a vowel has on its quality, and the given generalization should not be considered a universal property of vowel systems.

One of the problems in the study of suprasegmentals is their tendency to co-occur, so that it is difficult to decide which is the independent variable. In many languages, stress is one of the factors that conditions the duration of a sound or a sequence of sounds. Correspondingly, duration may be considered as one of the phonetic manifestations of stress. There are languages (English being one of them) in which a stressed syllable is regularly longer than an unstressed syllable, other factors being constant. There are other languages (as, for example, Czech) in which stress seems to be manifested to a greater extent by other phonetic features and increase in duration is minimal.

The last of the factors influencing the duration of a sound to be considered here is its position within a higher-level phonological unit, such as a word or an utterance. This phenomenon has been observed in many languages, including English. In a recent study (Lehiste, 1972), I established that the duration of the syllable nucleus of a stem decreases as the duration of the word is increased by the addition of derivative suffixes. Representative average values for one subject and one set of test words were as follows: duration of /i/ in *speed*—266.0 msec; *speedy*—150.5 msec; *speeder*—141.5 msec; *speeding* — 136.0 msec; *speedily* — 120.0 msec; *speediness* — 115.5 msec.

Assuming that all conditioned variation has been identified and accounted for, one may consider further durational features found in a language as independent variables. The term *quantity* is applied to duration when it functions as an independent variable in the phonological system of a language. At sentence level, differences in duration may arise as a result of differences in *tempo*.

The domain of quantity patterns may be a single segment or a higher-level phonological unit: a syllable, a disyllabic sequence, or a word. There are languages in which short and long sounds are opposed to each other; oppositions of long and short vowels seem to be more common than oppositions of long and short consonants. The domain of quantity in these cases appears to be the segment. Quantity manifested over a single segment may be analyzed linguistically in diverse ways. Quantity can be treated as a prosodic distinctive feature, [+long] being included in the list of features characterizing a distinctively long segment. This would seem to be especially appropriate for some languages in which quantity oppositions are restricted to a small subset of speech sounds. Another way to handle the fact that there are long and short sounds in a language is to list long and short vowels and/or consonants in the phonemic inventory of the language. This, however, doubles the number of units in the inventory. If the system is symmetrical, it would be more economical to extract length from the system and treat it as a prosodeme of length.

In many languages it is appropriate to treat long sounds as clusters of two identical sounds. This would seem to be particularly natural if, for example, the language contains diphthongs and if long vowels and diphthongs occupy similar positions within the phonology. With long consonants, a complicating factor enters the discussion: the possible phonetic realization of long consonants as geminates (Lehiste, Morton, and Tatham, 1973). If a language has consonant clusters that function in the same manner as long consonants, it may be useful to analyze these long consonants as clusters of identical consonants, regardless of whether it is possible to demonstrate, phonetically, their geminate nature.

There exist languages in which the quantity of a given segment must be related to the quantity of other segments in the sequence. For example, in Icelandic, Norwegian, and Swedish, there exists an inverse relationship between the quantity of a vowel and that of the following consonant, so that a short vowel is followed by a long consonant, and a long vowel by a short consonant. The domain of the placement of quantity patterns here appears to be a syllable.

In still other languages, quantity patterns have domains that are larger than a single syllable. In Slovak, the unit that is taken into consideration in the assignment of quantity is a disyllabic sequence, since in this language two long syllables may not follow each other. In Estonian, and probably in a number of other languages, the domain of the quantity patterns is the word. In Estonian, the occurrence of contrastively long or short sounds depends on their position within odd- or even-numbered syllables (counted from the beginning of the word) as well as on the quantitative structure of syllables immediately preceding those in which the contrastive sounds occur.

The function of quantity on the sentence level is quite different from its function at the word level. Changes of the relative durations of linguistic units within a sentence do not change the meanings of individual words, as they may do when quantity functions at the word level. However, durational differences at the sentence level convey something about the mood of the speaker or about the circumstances under which the utterance is made.

A considerable amount of information exists regarding the average rates of speech which may be considered "neutral" or unmarked. Significant changes from the unmarked rates constitute use of the feature of quantity at sentence level, manifested as changes in tempo.

In a series of studies (reviewed by Lehiste, 1970), Goldman-Eisler established the average rates of speech for English and some of the factors that condition them. She found that the speed of the actual articulatory movements producing speech sounds occupied a very small range of variation: 4.4 to 5.9 syllables per second. The range of pause time in relation to speech time was five times that of the rate of articulation. Factors influencing the rate of speech included differences in cognitive processes such as selection, abstraction, or planning in speech, as well as emotional attitudes. In a recent study of speech produced at different rates and in different styles, Shockey (1973) has surveyed the phonological processes that apply in so-called *rapid speech* and has related the application of these phonological processes to rate of articulation.

Tone and Intonation

The suprasegmental feature considered in this section is commonly referred to by such terms as *pitch, tone,* and *intonation.* I shall use the term *pitch* to refer to the perceptual correlate of frequency, *tone* to refer to the feature when it functions distinctively at word level, and *intonation* to refer to the feature when it functions at sentence level.

The physiological correlate of the features of tone and intonation is the vibration of the vocal folds in phonation. Phonation is treated elsewhere in this book and will not be considered in detail here. It is, however, necessary to note that there are two basic mechanisms available for producing changes in the rate of vibration of the vocal folds. The rate of vibration may be increased as a result of an increase in the rate of airflow through the glottis (caused by increased activity of the respiratory muscles producing increased subglottal pressure), and as a result of an increase in the tension of the laryngeal musculature itself, especially the vocalis muscle. Decreases in the rate of vibration of the vocal folds may be brought about by decreasing the rate of airflow and/or by relaxing the laryngeal musculature. There is some evidence that some external laryngeal muscles may be involved actively in lowering the rate of vibration of the vocal folds.

The acoustic correlate of vocal fold vibration is the fundamental frequency of the sound wave generated at the glottis. The perceptual correlate of fundamental frequency is pitch. The nonlinear nature of pitch perception is well known; it acquires linguistic importance due to the fact that the normal speaking frequencies of individuals may vary a great deal, ranging from very high frequencies used by children and some women to very low frequencies used by some men. Pitch perception operates by intervals rather than by absolute frequencies, in the sense that a difference between 200 and 100 Hz is considered perceptually equivalent to a difference between 300 and 150 Hz, or to other differences in which the ratio is likewise 2:1. Tonal and intonational signals used by different speakers may differ in absolute frequencies but customarily involve similar ratios.

The absolute differential threshold for fundamental frequency varies with frequency. Subjective pitch increases less and less rapidly as the stimulus frequency is increased linearly, and more and more rapidly as the stimulus frequency is increased logarithmically. The just-noticeable differences in pitch depend on a number of factors and may fluctuate for the same subjects. In the linguistic study of features of tone and intonation, it should be considered necessary and adequate to quantize fundamental frequency in steps of about ± 1 Hz in the octave range 80 to 160 Hz, which is the range usually employed by adult male speakers.

Phonetic conditioning factors of the fundamental frequency at which a syllable nucleus is realized include intrinsic pitch, preceding and following sounds, and other suprasegmental features, especially stress. The term *intrinsic pitch* is used to refer to the pitch determined by the phonetic quality of a vowel. There is a connection between vowel quality and the relative height of the average fundamental frequency associated with it: Other factors being kept constant, higher vowels have higher fundamental frequency. In an investigation by Lehiste and Peterson (1961), the following average fundamental frequencies were found in a total of 1263 syllable nuclei occurring at the peak of the intonation contour produced by one informant: /i/ — 183 Hz; /I/ — 173 Hz; /e^1/ — 169 Hz; /ɛ/ — 166 Hz; /æ/ — 162 Hz; /ə/ — 164 Hz; /a/ — 163 Hz; /ɔ/ — 165 Hz; /o/ — 170 Hz; /U/ — 171 Hz; /u/ — 182 Hz. Similar results have been obtained for various other languages, as, for example, Serbo-Croatian and Itsekiri, a West African tone language.

While preceding consonants seemed to have little influence on the duration of following vowels, there can be no doubt that they exert an influence on the fundamental frequency with which following syllable nuclei are realized. Higher fundamental frequencies are associated with voiceless consonants. The influence of an initial consonant may counterbalance the influence of intrinsic pitch. In the study by Lehiste and Peterson referred to above (1961), it was found that the average for /kæ/ sequences was 171 Hz, while that of /gi/ sequences amounted to 170 Hz. The difference in average peak values due to the voicelessness or voicing of an initial consonant usually is accompanied by a different distribution of the fundamental frequency movement over the studied word. After a voiceless consonant, and especially after a voiceless fricative, the highest peak will occur immediately after the consonant. However, after a voiced consonant, especially a voiced resonant, the fundamental frequency will tend to rise slowly and the peak may be expected to occur approximately in the middle of the test word.

Final consonants appear to have no systematic influence on the fundamental frequency of syllable nuclei except for the fact that a tonal movement may continue during a following voiced resonant. In that respect, sequences consisting of vowels and postvocalic resonants may function as complex syllable nuclei, with a tonal contour distributed over the complete sequence.

Fundamental frequency also may be influenced by other suprasegmental features, especially stress. Quantity appears to have no influence on fundamental frequency, except insofar as long vowels may be articulated with more extreme targets, and long high vowels may thus have higher intrinsic pitch. Stress, however, is frequently associated with higher fundamental frequency. As was discussed above, one of the factors causing the rate of vocal fold vibration to increase is increased rate of airflow. Since stress has been shown to be associated with increased subglottal pressure, the increase in vocal fold vibration may be considered automatic. If no increase is registered, it must be assumed that other adjustments are made (for example, in the tension of the vocal folds) to counteract the influence of the airflow. This matter will be discussed below in more detail.

There are two ways in which tonal features may constitute conditioning factors for other tonal features. Either the occurrence of tone on a syllable (or word) or its phonetic realization may be influenced by the presence or type of tone on an adjacent syllable (or word). This phenomenon is referred to in linguistic literature under the name *tone sandhi*. The other phenomenon involves fundamental frequency functioning at two levels, word level and sentence level, and consists of the fact that the realization of tones in a tone language may be influenced by intonation applied to the sentence as a whole. The latter case is analogous to the influence of tempo on quantity.

Contrastive fundamental frequency at word level is called *tone*; the term *intonation* refers to the linguistically significant functioning of fundamental frequency at the sentence level. There are languages in which contrastive tone is associated with differences in the meanings of roots and stems; this is called *lexical tone*. Chinese constitutes an example of languages of this kind. In other languages, differences in tone may signal different case forms of nouns or different forms within the verbal paradigm.

The smallest possible domain of tone is a single syllabic sound; however, it has been argued persuasively that the proper domain of tones is a syllable (Wang, 1967; Howie, 1974). There are also languages in which a tonal pattern may be realized over a sequence of two or more syllables. Among such languages are Swedish, Norwegian, and Serbo-Croatian. Languages with syllabic tone may be divided into *register tone* languages and *contour tone* languages (Pike, 1948; Maddieson, 1974). The first type includes systems that are comprised largely of level tones: tones that are realized in such a manner that, within the limits of perception, the pitch of a syllable does not rise or fall during its production. The contrastive levels are called *registers*. The second type contains gliding tones. There exist languages that combine elements of both systems.

The use of tonal features to carry linguistic information at the sentence level is one of the meanings of the term *intonation*. Intonation also carries nonlinguistic meanings; in this respect it is analogous to tempo, that is, the use of features of duration at the sentence level to reflect the attitudes of the speaker and the relative urgency of the message. Attempts to separate the linguistic and attitudinal aspects of intonation have not always been successful, and there exists no effective and universally applicable methodology for achieving this separation.

Intonation does not change the meaning of lexical items but constitutes part of the meaning of the whole utterance. Certain changes in intonation may be accompanied by changes in the function of the utterance—signaling, for example, a difference between a statement and a question. There is some difference of opinion regarding the manner in which intonation features are used to achieve this result. In the analysis of English intonation, there have been two schools of thought: those proposing that intonations should be specified in terms of a number of pitch levels, and those suggesting a number of significant contours or pitch configurations. (For a more detailed survey, see Lehiste, 1970.) In spite of the apparent mutual exclusiveness of the two points of view, it nevertheless appears that both levels and configurations have to be specified for certain purposes.

In tone languages, intonation applied to the utterance as a whole may interact with lexical tones in various ways. In one Chinese dialect, for example, intonation affects the pitch level at which the sentence is spoken and the range of pitch the sentence covers, but does not affect the realization of the tonemes except on the final syllable; the tonemes, however, are subject to regular tone sandhi rules everywhere in the sentence (Chang, 1958). In Serbo-Croatian, the realization of word accents is strongly influenced by the intonation applied to the sentence as a whole. In addition, degrees of stress and emphasis play a part in the realization of the accents. Emphasis in statements tends to bring out an optimal (i.e., most clearly contrastive) realization of the accent; in yes—no questions, emphasis makes the appearance of a special *reverse* accent obligatory rather than optional. Without emphasis, words are closest to optimal accentual realization in the middle of the utterance, at the peak of a neutral intonation contour, which normally rises in the beginning of the utterance and falls gradually at the end of the utterance.

Interaction between word tone and sentence intonation has been studied in a fairly large number of languages. Bolinger (1964), in his study of the universality of intonation, was able to find only one language (Amahuaca) in which no system of intonation had been found, although fluctuations of pitch or overall level of the utterance due to emotion were present.

Stress and Emphasis

Of the three suprasegmental features considered in this chapter, stress for a long time has been the most elusive one. There is no single mechanism to which the production of stress can be attributed in the same manner as the generation of fundamental frequency can be attributed to the vibration of the vocal folds. Further, the points of view of the speaker and the hearer have often been confused in defining stress. When the speaker's activity in producing stressed syllables is in focus, stress may be defined in terms of greater effort that enters into the production of a stressed syllable as compared to an unstressed syllable. When stress is defined from a listener's standpoint, the claim is often made that stressed syllables are louder than unstressed syllables. Loudness at least can be tested through psychoacoustic techniques; but until recently, it has been practically impossible to measure *effort*. Experimental techniques developed during the last twenty years have nevertheless made it possible to establish some of the physiological correlates of linguistic stress.

Ultimately, differences in stress are due to differences in physical effort (but cf. van Katwijk, 1974). The effort is reflected directly in the activity of the muscles involved in respiration, and indirectly in subglottal pressure. Electromyographic studies of the activity of the internal intercostal muscles show that bursts of intercostal activity correlate fairly well with occurrences of the principal stresses of the utterances. Measurements of subglottal pressure have shown peaks in the subglottal pressure function when a speaker wishes to emphasize part of an utterance. It is not yet clear, however, whether subglottal activity differentiates between stress and emphasis.

There is no one-to-one correspondence between stress and any single acoustic parameter. Thus, there is also no automatic way to identify stressed syllables. Even though subglottal pressure peaks could be associated with sentence stress and with emphasis, neither electromyography nor measurements of subglottal pressure yield unambiguous evidence for the location of stress within word-level units (unless the word receives sentence stress or emphasis).

There is nevertheless some evidence that stress is judged in terms of effort. If all other factors are kept constant, greater effort will produce a higher degree of stress. The force exerted by respiratory muscles is directly transmitted to the air inside the lungs, and this effort is reflected in subglottal pressure. The subglottal pressure in the lungs produces an airstream that passes through the glottis with a volume velocity that is proportional to the subglottal pressure. In the production of voiced sounds, the airstream sets the vocal folds into vibration, and the kinetic energy of the airflow is transduced into acoustic energy. Acoustic energy is related to effective sound pressure. As a first approximation, peak subglottal pressure is proportional to the .6 power of the peak effective sound pressure. Sound intensity is proportional to the square of the pressure variations of the sound wave.

The smallest amount of pressure that produces an audible sound is approximately .0002 dynes/cm^2. The threshold of audibility varies a great deal from individual to individual and may vary for the same person under different conditions. Moreover, the sensitivity of the ear differs a great deal in the different frequency regions. The ear is most sensitive to frequencies between 1000 and 6000 Hz. If the sensitivity of the ear at the frequency at which hearing is most acute is taken as reference (and the intensity of the just-noticeable sound is assigned a value of 0 dB at that frequency), then a just-audible tone at a frequency of 100 Hz must have an intensity that is 40 dB higher. At a frequency of 10,000 Hz, a tone must be about 10 dB more intense than the reference intensity to be just audible. According to Riesz (1928), the minimum intensity change normal listeners can detect for 1000 Hz at 30 dB sensation level of the reference tone is approximately 1 dB.

Intensity is a physical characteristic of sound. Loudness is the subjective property of a sound that is most directly related to intensity. Sounds with greater intensity are perceived as being louder, other factors being kept constant. Loudness also depends upon the fundamental frequency and the spectral characteristics of the sound as well as on its duration. All of these relationships have been studied extensively. As in most psychophysical studies, the stimuli used in these experiments have been primarily pure tones and noises. The results of such studies usually reveal more about the capacities of the organs of perception than about the function of the perceived differences in speech. In the perception of loudness, it becomes especially clear that when loudness judgments are made with reference to real speech, the results differ a great deal from judgments made with reference to psychoacoustic stimuli.

Stress perception, furthermore, seems to be quite different from the perception of loudness. It presupposes a speech setting and also a certain amount of learning. Daniel Jones (1940) stated explicitly that stress perception also involves knowledge of the language in which the utterance is spoken. Jones distinguishes between *stress* and *prominence*. According to Jones, the *prominence* of a syllable is its general degree of distinctness, this being the combined effect of the timbre, length, stress, and (if voiced) intonation of the syllabic sound. The term *stress* refers only to the degree of force of utterance; it is independent of length and intonation, although it may be combined with these. Prominence is a perceptual quantity that may be decreased or increased by means of any of the sound attributes, such as length, stress, pitch, or timbre; stress is an articulatory gesture. Jones seems to anticipate the motor theory of speech perception (Liberman, Cooper, Harris, and MacNeilage, 1963) when he suggests that a person familiar with a language does not perceive the sounds from the physical stimulus objectively, but perceives them in a subjective way: the sounds he hears call to his mind the manner of making them, and, by means of immediate *inner speech*, he knows where the stress is. Although Jones distinguishes between stress and prominence, he does not make clear which of them has linguistic function or whether or not they may have different linguistic functions. Perhaps it would be advisable to use the term *stress* to refer to prominence produced by means of respiratory effort, and to employ the term *accent* when prominence is achieved by other phonetic means in place of, or in addition to, respiratory effort.

The problem of the phonetic correlates of stress is an intricate one. The intensity of a sound depends to a great extent on its manner of articulation; different configurations of the vocal tract give rise to sounds of differing intensity, even if the input intensity (the effort employed in the production of the sounds) is the same. The intrinsic intensity of a sound is its intensity considered in relation to its phonetic quality. In American English, vowels may differ in intrinsic intensity by 4—5 dB; high vowels tend to have less intensity than low vowels. If the intensity of /i/ is taken as reference level, the intensity of /a/ is approximately 5 dB greater. Intrinsic intensities have been established for a number of other languages; for example, in Hungarian, a range of

12 dB was found between the intensities of long /a/ and long /u/. Hierarchies of intrinsic intensity also have been established for consonants.

Thus, the intrinsic intensity of speech sounds due to their phonetic quality is one factor that must be taken into consideration in the interpretation of intensity data. Another factor is the interaction between fundamental frequency and formant frequency. The spacing of the harmonics generated at the glottis is independent of the center frequencies of the resonances of the vocal tract. If the articulatory configuration of the vocal tract remains fixed and the fundamental frequency of the voice is changed, extensive changes in overall level will occur: The amplitude will increase if a harmonic coincides with the frequency of one of the lower formants, especially the first formant (since most of the energy of the vowel is contained in the first formant). These differences may be of the order of several decibels. Although both the differences in intensity due to intrinsic intensity and the differences due to interaction between fundamental frequency and formant frequency may have magnitudes that would be above the perceptual threshold if the experiment were conducted with pure tones, it appears that listeners discount such differences when listening in a speech mode and making judgments about stress.

One of the main problems in the interpretation of the physiological and acoustic correlates of stress is, indeed, the ambiguous role of intensity in the perception of stress. While there is a direct link between increases in respiratory effort, subglottal pressure, and the amplitude of the sound wave, intensity seems to provide a rather weak cue for the perception of stress. One reason for this lack of a more direct relationship between intensity and stress is the fact, discussed above, that output intensity changes with the articulatory configuration of the vocal tract. Another reason is the fact that subglottal pressure is also one of the physiological factors that control the rate of vocal fold vibration. Thus stress is connected intimately with frequency. Unless an adjustment in the tension of the vocal folds is provided, increased subglottal pressure results automatically in an increased rate of vocal fold vibration. Therefore, in many languages, higher fundamental frequency provides a strong cue for the presence of stress.

While increase in respiratory effort provides an obvious physiological cause for increases in intensity and increases in the rate of vocal fold vibration, no such reason is apparent for a frequent third phonetic correlate of stressedness: greater duration. There are many languages in which a stressed syllable is longer than an unstressed one. However, this is by no means a universal correlate of stress.

The relative importance of intensity, fundamental frequency, and duration in the perception of stress has been studied experimentally in several languages, including English. For English, the order of importance appears to be the following: Duration is more important than intensity, and sentence intonation is an overriding factor in determining the perception of stress; in this sense the fundamental frequency cue may outweigh the duration cue. The order of importance of the various parameters may differ for languages with a different phonological structure.

In considering the linguistic function of stress, it is useful to treat separately the questions of stress type and stress position. In traditional phonetics, stress frequently has been divided into the so-called *dynamic* or *expiratory* stress and the *musical* or *melodic* stress. Other phoneticians have maintained that, in word stress, both dynamic and musical factors are always present but that one may predominate. This view appears satisfactory for treating languages in which there are no independent tonal contrasts, that is, languages in which pitch contrasts are always associated with a stressed syllable. Insistence on the independence of stress and pitch became strong among American linguists who had worked with tone languages in which every syllable could carry contrastive tone, regardless of stress. It is indeed true that there is no automatic positive correlation between increases and decreases of intensity and fundamental frequency; thus one has to assume the possibility of independent control of the two mechanisms. There is valid evidence, however, that various dependence relationships exist between them at the same time. As was mentioned already, increases in subglottal pressure produce an increase in the rate of vibration of the vocal folds unless there is some compensatory adjustment in their tension. Increases in subglottal pressure also result in greater amplitude of the sound wave even if fundamental frequency is kept constant (by the just-postulated compensatory adjustment of the vocal folds). This means that each individual pulse produced by the vocal folds contains a greater amount of acoustic energy. Increases in the amplitude of the sound wave normally result in an impression of greater loudness, since a greater amount of energy reaches the ear in a given unit of time. However, from what is known about the integrating time-constant of the ear, it seems that the same effect should be achieved by a greater number of pulses reaching the ear per unit of time. Higher frequency thus should result not only in an impression of higher pitch but also in an impression of greater loudness. At the frequencies of the human vocal range, the ear is also increasingly sensitive to higher frequences. An increase of perceived loudness thus can be caused both by greater amplitude of the individual pulses (produced by increased subglottal pressure) and by a greater number of these pulses reaching the ear per unit of time (as a secondary result of higher subglottal pressure or as a primary result of increased tension of the vocal folds). It is not surprising, then, that the listener may attribute both types of increase to the same underlying cause and call them by a common name, such as *stress*.

There is no evidence that the listener can distinguish between increases of fundamental frequency that are caused by the two possible physiological mechanisms. However, it is probable that the *speaker* can distinguish between them, since the two mechanisms involve different—and widely separated—organs. The speaker *knows* which syllable he has stressed; the listener uses his knowledge of the language in addition to the phonetic cues present in the sound wave to determine which syllable was stressed. This analysis-by-synthesis approach to stress was anticipated by Daniel Jones (1940), who also discussed the problems involved in identifying the location of stress of unknown languages, and the pitfalls of interpreting prominence achieved by other means as being due to stress.

Stress may function linguistically at word level and at sentence level. The minimum size of the unit of stress placement is the syllable; however, stressed and unstressed monosyllabic words can be distinguished only within a larger utterance. Thus the minimal unit of contrastive stress placement is a sequence of two syllables.

If the placement of stress on one of the syllables of the utterance is not predictable by morphological, lexical, or syntactic criteria, it is said that stress occupies an independent position within the phonology of the language; the term *phonemic stress,* or *free stress* is applied to this kind of linguistically significant stress. Languages in which stress functions to distinguish between otherwise identical words include Russian and English. The functional yield of stress in English is much smaller than in Russian: in English, there are very few pairs of words that are distinguished by nothing except the place of stress. On the other hand, the place of stress is fairly firmly fixed, and placement of stress on a different syllable changes the word into a nonword.

In a number of languages, the placement of stress on a certain syllable is determined with reference to the word; conversely, the position of stress identifies the word as a phonological unit. In languages with such *bound stress,* there is no opposition between stressed and unstressed syllables within word-level phonology. Bound stress may occur on the first syllable of a word, as in Czech or Hungarian; on the last syllable, as in French; or on the penultimate syllable, as in Polish. The placement of bound stress also may follow more complicated rules, as in Latin, where stress is placed on the penultimate syllable, if long, and on the third syllable from the end if the penultimate syllable is short.

Another problem to be considered within word-level phonology is the question of degrees of stress. It has been believed widely that there are four distinctive degrees of stress in English; however, the phonetic reality behind these four degrees of stress has been widely questioned also. There exists no phonetic evidence for differences in degree of expiratory stress. Many linguists nevertheless claim that between strong and weak stress, there are several intermediate degrees of stress that have a certain kind of subjective reality.

It is probable that word-level stress is, in a very real sense, an abstract quality: a potential for being stressed. Word-level stress is the capacity of a syllable within a word to receive sentence stress when the word is realized as part of the sentence. The degrees of stress of other syllables within the word are usually predictable by rules and are therefore noncontrastive. The fact that not all syllables that are perceived as stressed are associated with peaks of subglottal pressure supports the idea that what is realized phonetically is sentence-level stress rather than word-level stress. In other words, our knowledge of the structure of the language informs us which syllables have the potential of being stressed; we "hear" the underlying phonological form.

When stress functions at the sentence level, it does not change the meaning of any lexical item, but it increases the relative prominence of one of the lexical items. Each sentence has, automatically, a *primary stress* (nonemphatic sentence stress). *Contrastive stress* occurs in sequences of sentences with parallel constituents that are filled with different morphemes. In other words, contrastive stress is used to distinguish a particular morpheme from other morphemes that may occur in the same position. *Emphatic stress* is used to distinguish a sentence from its negation. Occasionally, it may be phonetically indistinguishable from contrastive stress, but there are instances (and languages) in which the two are different.

There exists phonetic evidence that emphasized words are associated with sub-glottal pressure peaks; emphasis thus has a first-order phonetic correlate which word stress does not seem to have. As is the case with stress in general, emphasis may be reflected in phonetic parameters other than, or in addition to, increased intensity.

Summary and Outlook

To return to more general questions concerning suprasegmentals, I view supra-segmentals as being connected intimately with phonological units. Suprasegmental features characteristically constitute patterns in time; the domains over which these patterns are manifested are phonological units of varying size (i.e., varying temporal extent). The suprasegmental patterns define the phonological units, and, conversely, phonological units are characterized by suprasegmental patterns. The boundaries between the phonological units, on the other hand, are signaled by segmental modifications, which have been treated in linguistic literature under the term *junctural phenomena*. Consideration of such segmental boundary signals is essential for a complete description of phonological units, but it should be kept in mind that the units themselves constitute the domain of suprasegmental patterns and cannot be defined by reference to their boundaries alone.

As must have become obvious from the foregoing discussion, there are some areas in the study of suprasegmentals in which a relatively great amount of information is available, and there are other areas in which much remains to be done. I hope that one of the directions future research will take is further study of the neural control of the production of suprasegmental patterns. Other areas in which further research is indicated include studies of coordination of segmental and suprasegmental features. Basic research is needed to provide more knowledge about how articulatory movements are coordinated with each other and with processes such as phonation and respiration. Linguistic information must be brought to bear in attempts to explain phonetic observations. For example, the phonetic correlates of stress in English include not only greater respiratory effort (resulting in greater amplitude of the sound wave), but also selection of appropriate allophones of segmental sounds (such as aspirated plosives and vowels of unreduced quality). There is very little information available concerning the level at which this kind of coordination takes place, and what mechanisms are employed to achieve coordination. Phonetic studies, in turn, may be expected to elucidate the constraints within which phonological systems must operate. If carried on within this broad context, studies of suprasegmental features may be expected to lead to further advances in our understanding of the production and perception of spoken language.

REFERENCES

Allen, G. D. Segmental timing control in speech production. *Journal of Phonetics*, 1973, *1*, 219–237.
Bernstein, N. A. *The coordination and regulation of movements*. Oxford: Pergamon Press, 1967.
Bolinger, D. L. Intonation as a universal. *Proceedings of the 9th International Congress of Linguists.* The Hague: Mouton, 1964. Pp. 833–848.

Chang, C. T. Tones and intonation in the Chengtu dialect. *Phonetica*, 1958, *2*, 59—85.

Howie, J. M. On the domain of tone in Mandarin. *Phonetica*, 1974, *30*, 129—148.

Huggins, A. W. F. Just noticeable differences for segment duration in natural speech. *Journal of the Acoustical Society of America*, 1972, *51*, 1270—1278. (a)

Huggins, A. W. F. On the perception of temporal phenomena in speech. *Journal of the Acoustical Society of America*, 1972, *51*, 1279—1290. (b)

Jones, D. *An outline of English phonetics* (6th ed.) New York: Dutton, 1940.

Van Katwijk, A. *Accentuation in Dutch*. Unpublished doctoral dissertation, University of Utrecht, 1974.

Lehiste, I. *Suprasegmentals*. Cambridge, Massachusetts: M.I.T. Press, 1970.

Lehiste, I. The timing of utterances and linguistic boundaries. *Journal of the Acoustical Society of America*, 1972, *51*, 2018—2024.

Lehiste, I., Morton, K., and Tatham, M.A.A. An instrumental study of consonant gemination. *Journal of Phonetics*, 1973, *1*, 131—148.

Lehiste, I., and Peterson, G. E. Some basic considerations in the analysis of intonation. *Journal of the Acoustical Society of America*, 1961, *33*, 419—425.

Liberman, A. M., Cooper, F. S., Harris, K. S., MacNeilage, P. F. Motor theory of speech perception. Paper D 3 in *Stockholm Speech Communication Seminar*, Vol. II. Stockholm: Speech Transmission Laboratory, Royal Institute of Technology, 1963.

Maddieson, I. (ed.). *An annotated bibliography on tone*. UCLA Working Papers in Phonetics, November 1974, No. 28, 1—78.

Nooteboom, S. G. Production and perception of vowel duration: A study of durational properties of vowels in Dutch. Unpublished doctoral dissertation, University of Utrecht, 1972.

Nooteboom, S. G. The perceptual reality of some prosodic durations. *Journal of Phonetics*, 1973, *1*, 25—45.

Ohala, J. J., The temporal regulation of speech. Paper presented at the Symposium on Auditory Analysis and Perception of Speech, Leningrad, U.S.S.R., August 21—24, 1973. Published in *Project on Linguistic Analysis*, Second Series, No. 17, June 1973, 1—22. Berkeley: University of California.

Peterson, G. E., and Lehiste, I. Duration of syllable nuclei in English. *Journal of the Acoustical Society of America*, 1960, *32*, 693—703.

Pike, K. L., *Tone languages*. Ann Arbor: Univ. of Michigan Press, 1948.

Riesz, R. R. Differential intensity of the ear for pure tones. *Physical Review*, 1928, *31*, 867—875.

Shockey, L., Some phonetic and phonological properties of connected speech. Unpublished doctoral dissertation, Ohio State University, 1973.

Woodrow, H. Time perception. In S. S. Stevens (Ed.), *Handbook of experimental psychology*. New York: Wiley, 1951. Pp. 1224—1236.

Wang, W. S-Y. Phonological features of tone. *International Journal of American Linguistics*, 1967, *33*, 93—105.

PART IV

SPEECH PERCEPTION

chapter **8**

Speech Perception

Michael Studdert-Kennedy

Queens College of the
City University of New York,
Flushing
and
Haskins Laboratories
New Haven, Connecticut

> The understanding of speech involves essentially the same
> problems as the production of speech . . . The processes . . .
> have too much in common to depend on wholly different
> mechanisms. [Lashley, 1951, p. 120]

Introduction

We can listen to speech at many levels. We can listen selectively for meaning, sentence structure, words, phones, intonation, chatter, or even, at a distance, Auden's "high, thin, rare, continuous hum of the self-absorbed." The present chapter is concerned solely with phonetic perception, the transformation of a more-or-less continuous acoustic signal into what may be transcribed as a sequence of discrete phonetic symbols. The study of speech perception, in this sense, in recent years has begun to adopt the aims, and often the methods, of the information-processing models of cognitive psychology that have proved fruitful in the study of vision (Haber, 1969; Neisser, 1967; Reed, 1973). The underlying assumption is that perception has a time course during which information in the sensory array is "transformed, reduced, elaborated" (Neisser, 1967, p. 4), and brought into contact with long-term memory (i.e., is recognized). The experimental aim is to intervene in this process (either directly or by inference) at various points between sensory input and final percept, in order to discover what transformations the original information has undergone. The ultimate objective is to describe the process in terms specific enough for neurophysiologists to search for neural correlates.

Let us begin by considering how speech perception differs from general auditory perception. It does so in both stimulus and percept. First, the sounds of speech constitute a distinctive class drawn from the set of sounds that can be produced by the human vocal mechanism. They can be described approximately as the output of a filter excited by an independent source. The source is the flow of air from the lungs, modulated at the glottis to produce a quasi-periodic sound, or above the glottis to produce a noisy turbulence. The filter is the supralaryngeal vocal tract, varying configurations of which give rise to varying resonances (formants). The resulting sound wave may be displayed as an oscillogram or, after spectral analysis, as a spectrogram. It is important to bear in mind that the spectrogram does not display the sensory input, but a transformation of that input, often presumed to represent the output at an early stage of auditory analysis. (For accounts of the speech signal and its mechanisms of production, see Fant, 1960; Stevens and House, 1972; Kent, this volume; Shoup and Pfeifer, this volume.)

Here our main concern is to stress functional differences between speech and nonspeech acoustic structure in perception. Speech does not lie at one end of an auditory (psychological) continuum which we can approach by closer and closer acoustic (physical) approximation. The sounds of speech are distinctive. They form a set of *natural categories* similar to those described by Rosch (1973). She studied form and color perception among the Dani, a Stone Age people of New Guinea, whose language contains "only two color terms which divide the color space on the basis of brightness rather than hue" (p. 331), and no words for the Gestalt *good forms* of square, circle, and equilateral triangle. She found that her subjects were significantly faster in learning arbitrary names for the four primary hue points than for other hues, and for the three *good forms* of Gestalt psychology than for others. She points to the possible physiological underpinnings of these *natural prototypes*. Her work is reminiscent of a study by House, Stevens, Sandel, and Arnold (1962) who constructed several ensembles of sounds along an acoustic continuum from clearly nonspeech to speech. The time taken by subjects to learn associations between sounds and buttons on a box was least for the speech ensemble and did not decrease with the acoustic approximation of the ensembles to speech. In short, a signal is heard as either speech or nonspeech, and, once heard as speech, elicits characteristic perceptual functions that we shall discuss below.

The second peculiarity of speech perception, as we are viewing it, is in perceptual response. The final percept is a phonetic name, and the name (unlike those for *natural categories* of form and color) bears a necessary, rather than an arbitrary, relation to the signal. In other words, speech sounds *name themselves*. Notice that this is not true of the visual counterparts of phonetic entities: the forms of the alphabet are arbitrary, and we are not concerned that, for example, the same visual symbol, *P*, stands for /p/ in the Roman alphabet, for /r/ in the Cyrillic. Nothing comparable occurs in the speech system: the acoustic correlates of [p] or [r] can be perceived as nothing other than [p] or [r]. A central problem for the student of speech perception is to define the nature of this inevitable percept.

Levels of Processing

Implicit in the foregoing is a distinction between auditory and phonetic perception. As a basis for future discussion, we will lay out a rough conceptual model of the perceptual process (cf. Studdert-Kennedy, 1974; also Day, 1968, 1970a). We can conceive of the signals of running speech as climbing a hierarchy through at least these successive transformations: *(1)* auditory, *(2)* phonetic, *(3)* phonological, *(4)* lexical, syntactic, and semantic. The levels must be at least partially successive to preserve aspects of temporal order in the signal. They must also be at least partially parallel, to permit higher decisions to guide and correct lower decisions. See Turvey's (1973) discussion of peripheral and central processes in vision.

The auditory level is itself a series of processes (Fourçin, 1972). Early work (Licklider and Miller, 1951) showed that the speech waveform could be distorted vastly without serious loss of intelligibility. Spectrographic analysis (Joos, 1948; Potter, Kopp, and Green, 1947) and speech synthesis (Liberman, 1957) showed that patterns of speech important to its perception lay not in its waveform but in its time-varying spectrum as revealed by the spectrogram. We may imagine, therefore, an early stage of the auditory display, soon after cochlear analysis, as the neural correlate of a spectrogram. Notice in Figure 8.1: regions of high energy concentration (*formants*, usually labeled from bottom to top as F1, F2, F3); different formant patterns associated with the vowels of *read* and *book*, for example; intervals of silence during stop consonant closure; a sharp scatter of energy (*noise burst*) upon release of the voiceless stop in *to*, and fainter bursts following release of the voiced stops in *began*; rapid formant movements (*transitions*) as articulators move into and out of vowels; a nasal formant (between F1 and F2) at the end of *began*; a broad band of noise associated with the fricative of *she*; and finally, regular vertical striations, reflecting a series of glottal pulses, from which fundamental frequency can be derived. A later, perhaps cortical, stage of auditory analysis may entail detection of just such features in the spectrographic display. Whether there are acoustic feature analyzers specially tuned to speech is an open question that we consider later. In any case, the signal has not been transformed yet into the message, and, indeed, may have passed through the same processes as any other auditory input.

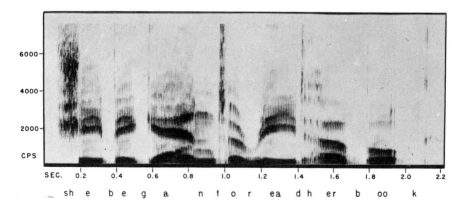

Figure 8.1 Spectrogram of a natural utterance: *She began to read her book.* Frequency is plotted against time, with relative intensity represented by degree of blackness.

The phonetic level is abstract in the sense that its output is a set of properties not inherent in the signal. They derive from the auditory display by processes that must be peculiar to human beings, since they can be defined only by reference to the human vocal mechanism. These properties correspond to the linguistic entities of distinctive feature (Jakobson, Fant, and Halle, 1963) and phoneme. For the psychological reality of these units, there is ample evidence, discussed later. There is also evidence that extraction of these units from the auditory display calls upon specialized decoding mechanisms (Studdert-Kennedy and Shankweiler, 1970; Wood, 1975). In any event, the output from this level is now speech, although much variability remains to be resolved.

Resolution is accomplished at the phonological level at which processes peculiar to the listener's language are engaged. Here, the listener merges phonetic variations that have no function in his language, treating, for example, both the initial segment of $[p^h It]$ and the second segment of $[spIt]$ as instances of /p/. Here, too, the listener may shift distinctions across segments, interpreting English vowel length before a final stop, for example, as a phonetic cue to the voicing value of the stop. In short, this is the level at which phonetic variability is transformed into phonological system. Of course, for untrained listeners all of the time, and for phoneticians most of the time, the distinction between phonetic and phonological levels has little import. Listeners usually hear speech in terms of the categories of their native language (e.g., Day, 1968, 1970a; Lotz, Abramson, Gerstman, Ingemann, and Nemser, 1960; Scholes, 1968). However, since they may learn (at some pain) to make phonetic distinctions, we must assume that phonetic information is available in the system, though not attended to in normal listening. Most of the research to be discussed has concerned itself with a single language and has not distinguished between phonetic and phonological levels. (For an extended discussion of experimental paradigms that serve to reflect several levels of processing from auditory to phonological, see Cutting, 1975.)

The upper levels of lexical, syntactic, and semantic processing complete the normal process of speech perception. There is good evidence that outputs from these levels can affect phonological and phonetic perception. Miller, Heise, and Lichten (1951), for example, showed that words are more intelligible in a sentence than in a list. Pollack and Pickett (1963) and Lieberman (1963) found that words excised from sentences presented to listeners without syntactic and semantic context often are not recognized. Several writers (e.g., Chomsky and Halle, 1968; Chomsky and Miller, 1963; Jones, 1948), in their accounts of speech perception, have placed a heavy load on the syntactic structure and semantic content of an utterance. However, while these higher levels may serve to "clean" the message when phonetic lapse is slight (cf. Cole, 1973a; Warren, 1970; Warren and Obusek, 1971), and even may be brought to bear deliberately while conversing with a foreigner in a railway tunnel, their control is not sufficient to disguise all slips of the tongue (cf. Fromkin, 1971). Unambiguous perception is possible in spite of context, and, as will be seen, presents sufficient theoretical problems. Bearing in mind our primary distinction between auditory and phonetic levels, we turn now to a brief review of acoustic cues and of the problems that emerge for perceptual theory.

The Acoustic Cues

Many of the acoustic cues to the phonetic message have been uncovered over the past 20 years by the complementary processes of analysis and synthesis. Spectrographic analysis of natural speech suggests likely candidates, such as formant frequency, formant movement, silent interval, or burst of noise. Synthesis then permits these *minimal cues* (Liberman, 1957) to be checked for perceptual validity. Results of this work are described elsewhere (Fant, 1960, 1968; Flanagan, 1972; Liberman, 1957; Mattingly, 1968, 1974; Stevens and House, 1972). Here, we do no more than summarize its outcome and frame the problems it raises for speech perception.

The problems are those of invariance and segmentation. The speech signal carries neither invariant acoustic cues nor isolable segments that reliably correspond to the invariant segments of linguistic analysis and perception. The speech signal certainly can be segmented. Fant (1968) and his colleagues have outlined a procedure for dividing the signal in both frequency and time, and have developed a terminology to describe its segments. But these segments do not correspond to the phonetic segments of distinctive feature or phoneme. There are exceptions: fricatives and stressed vowels, for example, may present stable and more-or-less isolable patterns. But, in general, as Fant (1962) has remarked, a single segment of sound contains information concerning several neighboring segments of the message, and a single segment of the message may draw upon several neighboring segments of sound. In short, the sounds of speech are not physically discrete, like letters of the alphabet, but rather are shingled into an intricate, continuously changing pattern (Liberman, Cooper, Shankweiler and Studdert-Kennedy, 1967).

Whether the source of this shingled pattern is to be found in mechanical constraints, in neuromuscular inertia and temporal overlap of successive commands to the articulators (Öhman, 1967), or in elegantly controlled, yet variable, responses to fixed articulatory instructions (MacNeilage, 1970), the result is not only a loss of segmentation but also a loss of acoustic invariance. The cues to a given phonetic segment display enormous variability as a function of phonetic context, stress, and speaking rate (e.g., Kozhevnikov and Chistovich, 1965; Stevens, House, and Paul, 1966).

As a simple instance, consider the acoustic structure of a mirror image CVC such as [bæb]. Experiments with synthetic speech have demonstrated the importance of second and third formant transitions as cues for distinguishing among labial, alveolar, and velar stops (Liberman, Delattre, Cooper, and Gerstman, 1954). Here, the two formants rise rapidly over the first 40 msec or so into the vowel and then, after a relatively sustained formant pattern for, say, 200 msec, drop rapidly back to their starting points. The acoustic cues to initial and final allophones of [b] are mirror images and, separated from the syllable, are heard as distinct nonspeech sounds. Experiments with tone glissandi matching such patterns in duration and frequency range reveal no psychoacoustic basis for the perceived phonetic identity (Klatt and Shattuck, 1973).

Similar discrepancies occur as a function of vowel context. Initial formant transitions in a CV syllable reflect the changing resonances of the vocal tract as the articulators move from consonant closure or constriction into a more open position for the following vowel. Since vowels are distinguished by the positions of their first two or three formant centers on the frequency scale (Delattre, Liberman, Cooper, and Gerstman, 1952; Peterson and Barney, 1952), consonantal approach varies with vowel: for example, both second and third formants fall in the syllable [dæ]; the second rises and the third falls in the syllable [de]. Yet listeners fail to detect these acoustic differences, and phonetic identity of the initial segments is preserved.

As a final example, let us consider vowels. Each stressed vowel, spoken in isolation, has its characteristic set of formant frequencies. However, in running speech, these values are seldom reached, particularly if speech is rapid and vowels unstressed (Lindblom, 1963). If vowel portions are excised from running speech and presented without their surrounding formant transitions, identifications shift (Fujimura and Ochiai, 1963). This suggests (as do the consonantal examples given above) that listeners track formants over at least a syllable in order to make their phonetic decisions. (For other examples of phonetic identity in the face of acoustic variance, see Shearme and Holmes, 1962; Lindblom, 1963; Öhman, 1966; Liberman *et al.*, 1967; and Stevens and House, 1972.)

A different class of acoustic variability is instanced by interspeaker variations. In this case, differences in acoustic quality can be heard clearly, but are disregarded in phonetic perception. Center frequencies of vowel formants of men, women, and children vary widely (Peterson and Barney, 1952), with the result that acoustically identical patterns may be judged phonetically distinct, while acoustically distinct patterns may be judged phonetically identical. *Normalization* probably cannot be accomplished by application of a simple scale factor (Peterson, 1961) because male—female formant ratios are not constant across the vowel quadrilateral (Fant, 1966).

A favored belief is that listeners judge vowels by reference to other vowels uttered by the same speaker. This notion originated with Joos (1948) and was tested by Ladefoged and Broadbent (1957). They demonstrated that the same synthetic vowel pattern could be judged differently depending on the formant pattern of a precursor phrase. Gerstman (1968) developed an algorithm, derived from the formant frequencies of [i, a, u] for each speaker, that correctly identifies 97.5% of the Peterson and Barney (1952) vowels. And Lieberman (1973) claims that unless a listener has heard *calibrating signals*, such as the vowels [i, a, u] or the glides [y] and [w], from which to assess the size of a particular speaker's vocal tract, "it is impossible to assign a particular acoustic signal into the correct class" (p. 91).

However, an algorithm is not a perceptual model, and remarkably little actually is known in this area: there is a dearth of data on how listeners judge the varied vowel patterns of different speakers. Furthermore, the phenomenon of *normalization* is not confined to vowels. Fourçin (1968) demonstrated that a synthetic *whispered* syllable with a constant formant pattern could be heard as a token of [d] if preceded by a man's "Hallo," of [b] if preceded by a child's. Rand (1971) showed a similar systematic shift, without benefit of precursor, when formant frequencies of synthetic CV syllables were increased by 20% above the "male" base. Evidently, normalization can be accomplished within a syllable, presumably from information provided by formant structure and fundamental frequency (cf. Fujisaki and Nakamura, 1969). This is precisely what is suggested by recent work of Strange, Verbrugge, and Shankweiler (1974) and Verbrugge, Strange, and Shankweiler (1974). They found that a speaker's precursor vowels, whether $[i, a, u]$ or $[I, æ, \Lambda]$, do little to reduce listener error in judging following vowels spoken by a panel of men, women, and children. Far more effective in reducing error is presentation of the vowel within a consonantal frame. Of course, formant reference clearly is involved in studies in which consonantal context is held constant (Summerfield and Haggard, 1973). However, the results again suggest perceptual tracking of an entire syllable and emphasize that invariant acoustic segments matching the invariants of perception are not found readily. (For a recent review of the normalization problem, see Shankweiler, Strange, and Verbrugge, in press.)

Nonetheless, the search for acoustic invariance has not been abandoned. A main reason for this is the obvious worth of some form of feature theory in linguistic description and in the description of listener behavior (see next section). Distinctive-feature theorists have always maintained that correlates of the features are to be found at every level of the speech process: articulatory, acoustic, auditory (Jakobson and Halle, 1956; Jakobson *et al.*, 1963; Chomsky and Halle, 1968), and a good deal of current research is directed toward grounding features in acoustics and physiology (cf. Ladefoged, 1971a, b; Lindblom, 1972).

Before giving examples, we should emphasize the redundancy of the speech signal. A given feature may be signaled by several different cues. Studies of synthetic speech have tended to emphasize *sufficient* cues and to disregard their interaction. Harris (1958) provides an exception in her study of noise bands and formant transitions as cues to English fricatives. So, too, do Harris, Hoffman, Liberman, Delattre, and Cooper (1958), and Hoffman (1958), who examined the relative weights of second and third formant transitions in perception of English voiced stops.

Other exceptions include Lisker and Abramson (1964, 1967, 1970, 1971), Abramson and Lisker, (1965, 1970), and Zlatin, (1974) in their extensive series of studies of voicing in many languages. Noting that voicing in initial stops may be cued by explosion energy, degree of aspiration, and first formant intensity, they sought a cover variable that would encompass all these cues. They found it in voice onset time (*VOT*), the interval between release of stop closure and the onset of laryngeal vibration. Figure 8.2 displays spectrograms of synthetic stops in which VOT is a sufficient cue for the distinction between $[ba]$ and $[pa]$. Notice that VOT is not a simple variable either articulatorily or acoustically: It refers to a temporal relation between two distinct events. In production, it calls for precise timing of a laryngeal gesture (approximation of the vocal cords) in relation to supralaryngeal release; in perception, it calls for judgment of a complex acoustic pattern arrayed in time. Nonetheless, within these limits, VOT offers a relatively invariant physical display and a relatively invariant sequence of coordinated articulatory gestures that might serve to define a feature, albeit not a feature within the generally accepted system (Chomsky and Halle, 1968). (For a full account of the underlying rationale, the reader is referred to the publications cited above and, for criticisms of the approach, to Stevens and Klatt, 1974, and Summerfield and Haggard, 1972.)

A second example of the search for feature invariants is provided by the work of

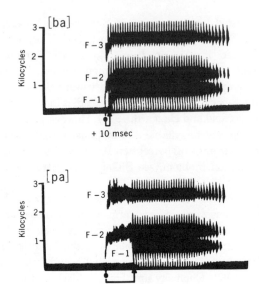

Figure 8.2 Spectrograms of synthetic syllables, [ba] and [pa]. The interval between release and voicing (vertical striations) (VOT) is 10 msec for [ba], 100 msec for [pa]. During this interval, F1 is absent and the regions of F2 and F3 are occupied by *aspirated* noise. [After Lisker and Abramson.]

Stevens (1967, 1968a, b, 1972a,b, 1973). In a recent paper (Stevens, 1973, p. 157), for example, he approaches an acoustic definition of [+ *Consonantal*], describing consonants as displaying "a rapid change in the acoustic spectrum" in the region of F2, following release (cf. Fant, 1962). Emphasizing the entire spectrum rather than individual formants, he develops this description into an acoustic account of place features [+ *Coronal*], [+ *Labial*] and [+ *Velar*], for which he posits *property detectors*. The acoustic description is based on spectrographic analysis and computations from an idealized vocal tract model. The model reveals certain "quantal places of articulation which are optimal from the point of view of sound generation" (Stevens, 1968a, p. 200) since they permit relatively imprecise articulation without serious perturbation of the signal. Obviously, these tract shapes can be correlated with articulatory gestures to provide the needed feature correlates.

Finally, less ambitious attempts to discover feature invariants are instanced by tape-cutting experiments with natural speech, in which consonantal portions of a syllable are removed and presented for identification alone or with vowels other than the original (Cole and Scott, 1974; Fischer-Jørgensen, 1972). If this approach leads to precise definition of acoustic invariants, it will have proved valuable. However, if experiments merely demonstrate that transposing initial portions of two CV syllables, for example, yields no change in perception of initial consonant, we have not advanced.

The transposed patterns remain different both acoustically and, if removed from the speech stream, psychoacoustically, and the demonstrated source of invariance is still the listener. The ultimate test of all these attempts will be in control of a speech synthesizer from a set of invariant articulatory or acoustic feature specifications (Mattingly, 1971).

The Phonetic Percept

Up to this point we simply have assumed the units of speech perception. However, research has puzzled over their definition sporadically for the past 25 years. The puzzle arises, as we have seen, from the mismatch between the acoustic signal and the abstract entities of linguistic analysis, distinctive features, and phonemes. Nonetheless, each of these units has been shown to have psychological reality. Perhaps the most direct evidence comes from studies of speaking errors. Fromkin (1971) has analyzed a large corpus of utterances for errors of metathesis (spoonerism). She finds that speakers may metathesize not only words and phrases, but syllables (*clarinet* and *viola* → *clarinola*), phonemes (*far more* → *mar fore*), and features (*clear blue* → *glear plue*) (cf. Boomer and Laver, 1968; MacKay, 1970; Cairns, Cairns, and Williams, 1974). Of particular interest is her observation that speakers may exchange consonant for consonant, and vowel for vowel, but never consonant for vowel. This suggests that there is in production a distinction between phonetic elements of the syllable that are distinguished in perception, as we shall see. In any case, errors of metathesis logically require that the speaker have independent control over the unit of error, and if these units are independently produced, it is not unreasonable to believe that they are perceived independently.

Evidence from perceptual studies is not lacking. Errors while listening to speech through noise (Miller and Nicely, 1955; Mitchell, 1973) or dichotically (Studdert-Kennedy and Shankweiler, 1970; Studdert-Kennedy, Shankweiler, and Pisoni, 1972; Blumstein, 1974) are patterned according to some form of feature system. Scaling studies, in which the experimenter attempts to determine the psychological space occupied by a set of consonants or vowels, repeatedly reveal a structure parsimoniously described by feature theory (Greenberg and Jenkins, 1964; Hanson, 1967; Shepard, 1972; Singh, 1966; Singh and Woods, 1970). A new paradigm recently has provided further evidence. Goldstein and Lackner (1973), adapting a technique devised by Warren and Gregory (1958) (see also Clegg, 1971; Tekieli and Lass, 1972; Lass and Gasperini, 1973; Lass and Golden, 1971; Lass, West, and Taft, 1973; Obusek and Warren, 1973; Perl, 1970; Warren, 1968, Warren, this volume), played a 200-msec nonsense syllable over and over (200 times per minute), asking listeners to report what they heard. After a few repetitions, listeners began to hear different words (*verbal transformation*). The new words were related systematically to the originals: They entailed changes in value of only one or two distinctive features and reflected phonological constraints of English as described by distinctive feature theory. Finally, errors in short-term memory studies also follow a feature pattern (Sales, Cole, and Haber, 1969;

Wickelgren, 1965, 1966). Several of these studies have used their perceptual data to compare the predictive power (and so validity) of different feature systems. Such work is particularly important if linguistics is to be regarded as a branch of human psychology (Chomsky, 1972), and if the abstract units of phonology are to be grounded in human articulatory and perceptual capacities (Ladefoged, 1971a, b; Liljencrants and Lindblom, 1972; Lindblom, 1972).

The perceptual status of the columns in a feature matrix has proved more controversial. Functionally, the column (phone) represents the grouping of distinctive features within a syllable; it specifies the domain within which a particular feature is to apply. We recognize this perceptually in alliteration (*big boy*) and in rhyme (*bee* and *see*), situations in which two syllables are perceived as identical at their beginning, but not at their end, or vice versa. Listeners reveal this function when asked to judge similarities among words. Vitz and Winkler (1973) found, in fact, that the number of phones shared by a pair of words was a more satisfactory predictor of their judged similarity than the number of shared features. In the *verbal transformation* study described above (Goldstein and Lackner, 1973), transformations were described best in terms of phones and features rather than syllables and features: Consonant transforms and vowel transforms, for example, were independent, reflecting feature shifts within, but not across, phones. Finally, several studies (Day and Wood, 1972; Kozhevnikov and Chistovich, 1965; Savin and Bever, 1970), have shown reaction time differences in identification of consonants and vowels within the same syllables. These differences would not occur if the syllable were an unanalyzed perceptual entity.

Despite such evidence, and despite their clear role in speaking and in writing systems, there has been a temptation for students to regard phoneme-size phonetic segments as "nonperceptual" (Savin and Bever, 1970) or as "fictitious units" based on the historical accident of alphabet invention (Warren, this volume). Among the arguments for this type of conclusion seem to be three solid facts, two (or more) pieces of ambiguous evidence, and one false belief. The facts are: first, that no phoneme-size segment can be isolated in the acoustic signal; second, that some phonemes (stop consonants) cannot be spoken in isolation; third, that we do speak in syllables and that syllables are the carriers of stress and speech rhythm. The ambiguous evidence comes from reaction time studies suggesting that syllables, and even higher order units, may be identified before the elements of which they are composed. Savin and Bever (1970) and Warren (1971) showed that the reaction time of listeners monitoring a monosyllabic list for syllables is faster than their reaction time when monitoring the same list for the initial phoneme of the syllable. Subsequently, Foss and Swinney (1973) showed that, under similar conditions, listeners responded more rapidly to words than to their component syllables, while Bever (1970) revealed that listeners responded more rapidly to three-word sentences than to their component words. It was left to McNeill and Lindig (1973) to release us from this Looking-Glass world in which the trial precedes the crime by demonstrating that reaction time was always fastest to the largest elements of which a list was composed. In other words, listeners' response is most rapid at the level of linguistic analysis to which context has directed their attention.

Finally, the false belief is that invariance and segmentation problems would disappear if the syllable were an unanalyzed unit of perception. This belief is no better founded than Wickelgren's (1969) attempt to solve the invariance problem by positing context-sensitive allophones, and is open to many of the same objections. These objections have been summarized well by Halwes and Jenkins (1971), and we will not review them here. However, it is worth adding that the syllable has resisted acoustic definition only somewhat less than the phoneme-size phonetic segment. Its nucleus may be detected by amplitude and fundamental frequency peak picking (Lea, 1974), and Malmberg (1955) drew attention to the possible role of formant transitions in defining syllable boundaries, but no fully satisfactory definition has emerged yet. Furthermore, coarticulation and perceptual context effects across syllables, though less marked than across phones, still occur. Öhman (1966), for example, found drastic variations in vowel formant transitions on either side of stop closure as a function of the vowel on the opposite side of the closure. And Treon (1970) has demonstrated contextual effects in perception extending across two to three syllables. In fact, as Fodor, Bever, and Garrett (1974) hint, an account of syllable perception may require the same theoretical apparatus as required by an account of phone perception.

Much of the confusion over units of speech perception might be resolved if the distinctions between signal and message and among acoustic, phonetic, and higher levels were maintained strictly. There is wide agreement among writers, whose views may otherwise diverge, that the basic *acoustic* unit of speech perception (and production) is of roughly syllabic length (e.g., Cole and Scott, 1974; Kirman, 1973; Kozhevnikov and Chistovich, 1965; Ladefoged, 1967; Liberman, Delattre, and Cooper, 1952; Liberman *et al.*, 1967; Liberman, 1957; Massaro, 1972; McNeill and Repp, 1973; Öhman, 1966; Savin and Bever, 1970; Stevens and House, 1972; Studdert-Kennedy, 1975; Warren, this volume). This is not to deny that there are longer stretches of the signal over which the perceptual apparatus must compute relations, but simply to say that the smallest stretch of signal on which it works is produced by the articulatory syllabic gesture (Stetson, 1952). This does not mean (as Massaro, 1972, for example, seems to suppose) that the syllable is the basic linguistic and perceptual unit.

To clarify, we may conceptualize the process of constructing an utterance from a lexicon of morphemes. The abstract entity of the morpheme is the fundamental unit in which semantics, syntax, and phonology converge. Each morpheme is constructed from phonemes and distinctive features. At this level, the syllable does not exist. But morphemic structure is matched to (and ultimately must derive from) the articulatory capacities of the speaker. Both universal and language-specific, phonotactic constraints ensure that a morpheme will result in pronounceable sequences of consonants and vowels. Under the control of a syntactic system governing their order and prosody, the morphemes pass through the phonetic transform into a sequence of coarticulated gestures. These gestures give rise to a sequence of *acoustic* syllables, into which the acoustic correlates of phoneme and distinctive feature are woven. The listener's task is to recover the features and their phonemic alignment, and so the morpheme and meaning. In short, perception entails the analysis of the acoustic syllable, by means of its acoustic features, into the abstract perceptual structure of features and phonemes that characterize the morpheme. To some theoretical accounts of how this might proceed we now turn.

Models of Phonetic Perception

We have no models specified in enough detail for serious test, but a brief account of two approaches that have influenced recent research may serve to summarize the discussion up to this point. The two approaches are those of the Haskins Laboratories investigators and of Stevens and his colleagues at the Massachusetts Institute of Technology. Both groups are impressed, in varying degrees, by the invariance and segmentation problem. Both therefore have rejected a passive template- or pattern-matching model in favor of an active or generative model. (For a review see Cooper, 1972.)

Liberman *et al.* (1967), reformulating a theme that had appeared in many earlier papers from the Haskins group, proposed a *motor theory of speech perception*. The crux of their argument was that an articulatory description of speech is not merely the simpler, but the only description that can rationalize the temporally scattered and contextually variable patterns of speech. They argue that phonetic segments undergo, in their passage through the articulatory system, a process of *encoding*. They are restructured acoustically in the syllabic merger so that cues to phonetic identity lose their alignment and are distributed over the entire syllable (Liberman, 1970). Not all phonetic segments undergo the same degree of restructuring: There is a hierarchy of *encodedness* from the highly encoded stop consonants through nasals, fricatives, glides, and semivowels, to the relatively unencoded vowels. Nonetheless, recovery of phonetic segments from the syllable calls for parallel processing of both consonant and vowel; neither can be decoded without the other. This processing demands a specialized decoding mechanism, in which reference is made somehow to the articulatory gestures that gave rise to the encoded syllables.

Liberman *et al.* (1967) assume, reasonably enough, that "at some level . . . of the production system there exist neural signals standing in one-to-one correspondence with the various segments of the language," and that for the phoneme "the invariant is found far down in the neuromotor system, at the level of the commands to the muscles" (p. 454). It is important to note that actual motor engagement is not envisaged. Liberman (1957) has written: "We must assume that the process is somehow short-circuited—that is, that the reference to articulatory movements and their sensory consequences must somehow occur in the brain without getting out into the periphery" (p. 122).

A virtue of the model is that it accounts for a fair amount of data and has generated a steady stream of research. Also, the concept of *encoding*, though descriptive rather than explanatory, draws attention to a process at the base of language analogous to syntactic processes suggested by generative grammar, and hints at formal similarities in their underlying physiological processes (Mattingly and Liberman, 1969; Liberman, 1970; Mattingly, 1973, 1974). Conspicuously absent is any account of first-language acquisition. The child may be presumed to be born with some "knowledge" of vocal tract physiology and an incipient capacity to interpret the output of an adult tract in relation to that of its own (Mattingly, 1973), but a detailed account of the process is lacking.

Stevens (1973) has concerned himself with this problem and addresses it in the most recent version of his analysis-by-synthesis model (Stevens, 1972a; cf. Stevens, 1960; Stevens and Halle, 1967). The model is far more explicit than that of the Haskins group. The perceptual process is conceived of as beginning with some form of peripheral spectral analysis, and acoustic feature and pitch extraction. Pitch and spectral information, obtained over a stretch of several syllables, is placed in auditory store. Acoustic feature information undergoes preliminary analysis by which a rough matrix of phonetic segments and features is extracted and passed to a control system. On occasion, this matrix may provide sufficient information for the control (which knows the possible sequences of phonetic segments and has access to the phonetic structure of earlier sections of the utterance) to pass on the description to higher levels. If this is not possible, the control, on the basis of its inadequate information, "guesses" at a phonetic description and sends it to a generative rule system, the same that in speaking directs the articulatory mechanism. The rule system generates a version of the utterance and passes it to a comparator for comparison with the spectral description in temporary auditory store. The comparator computes a difference measure and feeds it back to the control. If the "error" is small enough, the control system accepts its original phonetic description as correct. If not, it makes a second guess and the cycle repeats until an adequate match is reached.

This rough account does no justice to the model's elegance and subtlety, but it may serve to focus attention on several points. First, the solution to the invariance problem is a more abstract and more carefully specified version of a motor theory. Second, the model emphasizes the necessity of at least a preliminary feature analysis to ensure that the system is not doomed to an infinity of bad guesses, and that the child, given a set of innate *property detectors*, can latch onto the utterance. At the same time, no account is offered of how the invariant acoustic properties are transformed into phonetic segments and features (the process simply is consigned to a *preliminary analysis*), nor of the precise form that the phonetic description takes. Finally, the model emphasizes the need for a short-term auditory store. As we shall see, the form and duration of such a store is currently the focus of a great deal of research.

The Processing of Consonants and Vowels

Preliminary

To brace ourselves for a fairly prolonged discussion of consonants and vowels, let us consider why they are interesting. For theory, the answer is that they lie at the base of all phonological systems. All languages are syllabic, and all languages constrain syllabic structure in terms of consonants and vowels. If we are to ground phonological theory in human physiology, we must understand why this occurred. Lieberman (1970) has argued that phonological features may have been selected through a combination of articulatory constraints and *best matches* to perceptual capacity. One purpose of current research is to understand the nature and basis of the best match between syllables, constructed from consonants and vowels, and perceptual capacity.

For experiment, the interest of consonants and vowels is that they are different. If all speech sounds were perceived in the same way, we would have no means of studying their underlying relations. Just as the biologist could not study the genetics of eye color in *Drosophila melanogaster* until he had found two flies with different eyes, so the student of speech had no means of analyzing syllable perception until he found portions of the syllable that reflected different perceptual processes (cf. Stetson, 1952, *passim*). Fortunately, the interests of theory and research converge.

Categorical Perception

Study of sound spectrograms reveals that portions of the acoustic patterns for related phonetic segments (segments distinguished from one another by a single feature) often lie along an apparent acoustic continuum. For example, center frequencies of the first two or three formants of the front vowels, /i, I, ɛ, æ/, form a monotonic series; syllable-initial voice—voiceless pairs /b, p/, /d, t/, /k, g/, differ systematically in voice onset time; voiced stops, /b, d, g/, before a particular vowel, differ primarily in the extent and direction of their formant transitions.

To establish the perceptual function of such variations speech synthesis is used. Figure 8.3 sketches a schematic spectrogram of a synthetic series in which changes of slope in F2 transition affect perceptual changes from /b/ through /d/ to /g/. Asked to identify the dozen or so sounds along such a continuum, listeners divide it into distinct categories. For example, a listener might consistently identify stimuli −6 through −3 of Figure 8.3 as /b/, stimuli −1 through +3 as /d/, and stimuli +5 through +9 as /g/. In other words, he does not hear, as might be expected on psychophysical grounds, a series of stimuli gradually changing from one phonetic class to another, but rather a series of stimuli, each of which (with the exception of one or two boundary stimuli) belongs unambiguously in a single class. The important point to note is that, although steps along the continuum are well above nonspeech auditory discrimination threshold, listeners disregard acoustic differences within a phonetic category, but clearly hear equal acoustic differences between categories.

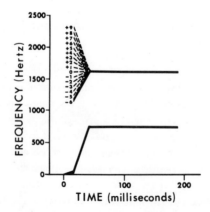

Figure 8.3 Schematic spectrogram for a series of synthetic stop-vowel syllables varying only in F2 transition. F2 steady state, F1 transition and steady state remain constant. As F2 transition changes from −6 to +9, perception of initial consonant shifts from [b] through [d] to [g].

To determine whether listeners can, in fact, hear the acoustic differences belied by their identifications, discrimination tests are carried out, usually in ABX format. Here, on a given trial, the listener hears three stimuli, separated by a second or so of silence: The first (A) is drawn from a point on the continuum two or three steps removed from the second (B), and the third (X) is a repetition of either A or B. The listener's task is to say whether the third stimulus is the same as the first or the second. The typical outcome for a stop consonant continuum is that listeners hear few more auditory differences than phonetic categories: They discriminate very well between stimuli drawn from different phonetic categories, very poorly (somewhat better than chance) between stimuli drawn from the same category. The resulting function displays peaks at phonetic boundaries, troughs within phonetic categories. In fact, discriminative performance can be predicted with fair accuracy from identifications: The probability that acoustically different syllables are discriminated correctly is a positive function of the probability that they are identified differently (Liberman, Harris, Kinney, and Lane, 1961). This close relation between identification and discrimination has been termed *categorical perception*, that is to say, perception by assignment to category. Figure 8.4 (left side) illustrates the phenomenon. Note that, although prediction from identification to discrimination is good, it is not perfect: Listeners sometimes can discriminate between different acoustic tokens of the same phonetic type. Note, further, that neither identification nor discrimination functions display quantal leaps across category boundaries. This is not a result of data averaging, since the effect is given by individual subjects. Evidently, auditory information about consonants is slight but it is not entirely lacking.

We may now contrast categorical perception of stop consonants with *continuous perception* of vowels. Figure 8.4 (right side) illustrates the effect. There are two points to note. First, the vowel identification function is not as clear-cut as the consonant identification function. Vowels, particularly those close to a phonetic boundary, are subject to context effects: For example, a token close to the /i-I/ boundary will tend to be heard as /i/ if preceded by a clear /I/, and as /I/ if preceded by a clear /i/. The second point to note is that vowel discrimination is high across the entire continuum. Phonetic class is not totally irrelevant (there is a peak in the discrimination function at the category boundary), but both within and between categories, listeners discriminate many more differences than they identify. Their perception is said to be *continuous*. (For fuller discussion, see Studdert-Kennedy, Liberman, Harris, and Cooper, 1970, and Pisoni, 1971.)

Continuous perception is typical not only of vowels but also of many nonspeech psychophysical continua along which we can discriminate more steps than we can identify (Miller, 1956). This fact has been taken as evidence both that categorical perception is peculiar to speech and that stop consonants and vowels engage fundamentally different perceptual processes (Liberman *et al.*, 1967; Studdert-Kennedy *et al.*, 1970a). In fact, an early account of the phenomenon invoked a motor theory of speech perception (Liberman *et al.*, 1967). As we have seen, there are independent grounds for hypothesizing that speech is perceived by reference to its articulatory origin. Here seemed to be additional evidence: The discrete articulatory gestures of stop consonants yielded discrete perceptual categories, and the more variable gestures of vowels, more variable categories. However, this account has several weaknesses, and recent work

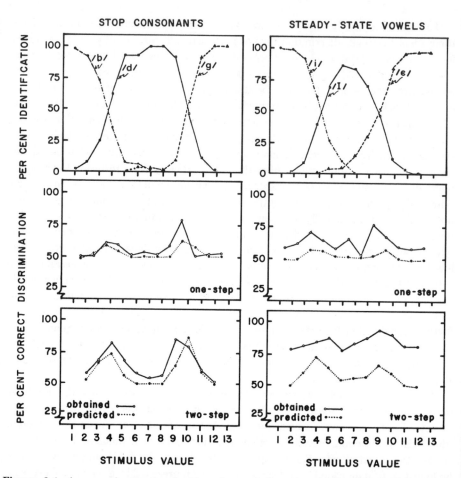

Figure 8.4 Average identification functions for synthetic series of stop consonants and vowels (top). Average one-step (middle) and two-step (bottom) predicted and obtained ABX discrimination functions for the same series. [After Pisoni, 1971.]

has eroded it largely. For one thing, we now know that categorical perception is not confined to speech (Cutting and Rosner, 1974; Locke and Kellar, 1973; Miller, Pastore, Wier, Kelly, and Dooling, 1974).

However, this discovery in no way diminishes the importance of the phenomenon, as will become clear in the following sections. Here, we merely note two facts. First, the acoustic patterns distributed along a speech continuum are not arbitrary. They have been selected from the range of patterns that the articulatory apparatus can produce and that the auditory system can analyze. The categories are therefore *natural*, in the sense that they reflect physiological constraints on both production and perception. As Stevens (1972b) has pointed out, our task is to define the joint auditory and articulatory origin of phonetic categories.

Second, categorical perception reflects a functionally important property of certain speech sounds. The initial sound of /da/, for example, is difficult, if not impossible, to hear: The sound escapes us, and we perceive the event, almost instantly, as phonetic. Rapid sensory decay and transfer into a nonsensory code is probably crucial to an efficient linguistic signaling system. Study of categorical perception has, in fact, revealed functional differences between stop consonants and vowels that are central to the syllabic structure of speech. At the same time it has provided basic evidence for the distinction between auditory and phonetic levels of processing.

In the following sections, we consider two main aspects of categorical perception. First, the division of a physical continuum into sharply defined categories and the assignment of names to the categories; second, listeners' apparent inability to discriminate among members of a category.

The Bases of Phonetic Categories

Phonetic categories do not arise from simple discriminative training, as proposed by Lane (1965). Subjects certainly may learn to divide a sensory continuum into clear-cut categories, with a resultant small peak in the discrimination function at the category boundary. But discrimination within categories remains high (Parks, Wall, and Bastian, 1969; Studdert-Kennedy *et al.*, 1970; Pisoni, 1971); training may increase, but not obliterate, discriminative capacity. Furthermore, the learned boundary is likely to be unstable. The process is familiar to the psychophysicist. For example, if we present a subject with a series of weights and ask him to judge each weight as either heavy or light, he will, with a minimum of practice, divide the range cleanly around its balance point (see Woodworth and Schlosberg, 1954). However, the boundary between *heavy* and *light* can be shifted readily by a change in experimental procedure. If an extreme token is presented for judgment with a probability several times that of other stimuli along the continuum, it comes to serve as an *anchor* with which other stimuli contrast; the result is a shift in category boundary toward the anchoring stimulus. Pisoni and Sawusch (1974) have shown that such shifts occur for a series of tones differing in intensity, and for vowels, but not for stop consonants distributed along a voice onset time continuum. They suggest that response criteria for voicing categories are mediated by internal rather than external references. By thus reframing the observation that stop consonant categories are not subject to context effects, they invite us to consider the nature of the internal reference.

Such a reference must be some distinctive perceptual quality shared by all members, and by no nonmembers, of a category. There is, of course, no reason to suppose that distinctive perceptual qualities are confined to speech continua. They will emerge from any physical continuum for which sensitivity is low within restricted regions and, by corollary, high between these regions. However, while the distinctive perceptual quality of a nonspeech event (such as a click, a musical note, or a flash of light) has the character of its sensory mode, the distinctive perceptual quality of a speech sound is phonetic. It is into a phonetic code that speech sounds are rapidly and automatically transferred for storage and recall.

With this in mind, we turn to several studies of nonspeech continua. We begin with Cutting and Rosner (1974) who determined an auditory boundary between rapid and slow stimulus onsets. Variations in stimulus onset, or rise time, are known to contribute to the affricate—fricative distinction, /tʃa/ vs /ʃa/ (Gerstman, 1957). The authors varied rise time from 0 to 80 msec for sawtooth wave trains generated by a Moog synthesizer and for synthetic affricate—fricatives. The rapid-onset sawtooth waves sounded like a plucked guitar string, the slow-onset waves like a bowed string. Cutting and Rosner presented their two classes of stimuli for identification (*pluck — bow*, /tʃa/ — /ʃa/) and for ABX discrimination. Both speech and nonspeech yielded category boundaries at a 40—50 msec rise time, with appropriate peaks and troughs in the discrimination functions.

A second instance of nonspeech categorical perception is provided by Miller *et al.* (1974). These investigators constructed a rough nonspeech analog of the voice onset time continuum. They varied the relative onset times of bursts of noise and periodic buzz over a range of noise-leads from −10 to +80 msec, and presented them to subjects for labeling and discrimination. Listeners divided the continuum around an average noise-lead of approximately 16 msec, displaying clear discrimination troughs within *no noise-lead* and *noise-lead* categories, and a discrimination peak at the category boundary. The boundary value agrees remarkably well with that reported by Abramson and Lisker (1970) for the English labial VOT continuum, though not with the systematically longer perceptual boundaries associated with English apical and velar VOT continua (Lisker and Abramson, 1970). The authors conclude that the categories of their experiment (and, presumably, of at least the English labial VOT continuum) lies on either side of a *difference limen* for duration of the leading noise. While possibly correct, their conclusion places a misleading emphasis on the boundary between categories rather than on the categories themselves.

The emphasis is reversed in a recent study of Stevens and Klatt (1974). Following Liberman, Delattre, and Cooper (1958), they examined auditory discrimination of two acoustic variables along the stop consonant voice—voiceless continuum: delay in formant onset and presence—absence of F1 transition. For their first experiment, they constructed a nonspeech analog of plosive release and following vowel: a 5 msec burst of noise separated from a vowel-like buzz by between 0 and 40 msec of silence. Listeners' *threshold* for detection of silence between noise and buzz was approximately 20 msec, which closely matched the value for detection of noise-lead found by Miller *et al.* (1974). Stevens and Klatt imply that the unaspirated—aspirated stop consonant perceptual boundary in the 20—40 msec VOT range may represent "a characteristic of the auditory processing of acoustic stimuli independent of whether the stimuli are speech or nonspeech" (p. 654).

We will not pursue the details of their second experiment. However, they were able to confirm the contribution of a detectable F1 transition to the voice—voiceless distinction. Furthermore, by hewing to the articulated speech signal and by focusing on acoustic properties within categories rather than on acoustic differences between them, Stevens and Klatt were able to offer a fully plausible account of systematic increases in the voice —voiceless perceptual boundary that are associated with shifts from labial to apical to velar stop consonants (Lisker and Abramson, 1970; Abramson and Lisker, 1973).

If the argument of the last few pages has given the impression that auditory boundaries between phonetic categories are readily determined, the impression must be dispelled. The criterion for such boundaries is that they be demonstrated in a non-speech analog, a feat that has proved peculiarly difficult for the voiced stop consonants. Usually, when formant patterns controlling consonant assignments are removed from context and presented for discrimination, they are perceived continuously (e.g., Mattingly, Liberman, Syrdal, and Halwes, 1971). A striking instance is provided by the work of Popper (1972). He manipulated F2 transitions within a three-formant pattern (cf. Figure 8.3) to yield a synthetic series from /ab/ to /ad/. He then measured energy passed by a 300 Hz bandwidth filter centered around the F2 steady-state frequency, and noted a sharp drop at the /b-d/ boundary both for isolated F2 and for the full formant pattern. However, subjects only evinced the expected discrimination peak for the full pattern: The isolated F2, despite its acoustic discontinuity, was perceived continuously.

In short, no simple notion of fixed regions of auditory sensitivity serves to account for categorical division even of the /ba, da, ga/ continuum (let alone for perceptual invariance across phonetic contexts), for the normalizing shifts in category boundary associated with speaker variation (cf. Fourçin, 1968; Rand, 1971), or for cross-language differences in boundary placement. The problem is not confined to articulatory place distinctions. Consider, for example, the fact that Spanish speakers typically yield a somewhat shorter labial VOT boundary than do English (Lisker and Abramson, 1964), and that their perceptual boundary shows a corresponding reduction (Lisker and Abramson, 1970). We hardly can account for the perceptual shift by appeal to an inherently sharp threshold. Precise category position along a continuum is clearly a function of linguistic experience (see also Stevens, Liberman, Studdert-Kennedy, and Öhman, 1969). Popper (1972) proposes, in fact, that "people who speak different languages may tune their auditory systems differently" (p. 218). Differential tuning could result from cross-language differences in selective attention to aspects of the signal, and in criterion levels for particular phonetic decisions. Given the close match between perception and production (Stevens *et al.*, 1969; Abramson and Lisker, 1970; Lisker and Abramson, 1970), it seems plausible that such differences arise from complex interplay between speaking and listening during language acquisition (see later section, "From Acoustic Feature to Phonetic Percept").

The notion of *tuning* presupposes the existence of acoustic properties to which the auditory system may be attuned. The first steps toward definition of these properties have been taken by Stevens (see especially 1972b, 1973). As earlier remarked, Stevens has used spectrographic analysis and computations from an idealized vocal tract model to describe possible acoustic correlates of certain phonetic features. He finds, for example, that the spectral patterns associated with a continuously changing place of articulatory constriction along the vocal tract do not themselves change continuously. Rather, there are broad *plateaus*, within which changes in point of constriction have little acoustic effect, bounded by abrupt acoustic discontinuities. These acoustic *plateaus* tend to correlate with places of articulation in many languages. In short, Stevens is developing the preliminaries to a systematic acoustic account of phonetic categories and their boundaries. His work is important for its emphasis on the origin of phonetic categories in the peculiar properties of the human vocal tract. Furthermore, as will be seen below, his approach meshes neatly with recent work on auditory feature analyzing systems as the bases of phonetic categories.

Auditory and Phonetic Processes in Categorical Perception

We turn now to the second main aspect of categorical perception—listeners' failure to discriminate among members of a category—and to the contrast between continuously perceived vowels and categorically perceived stop consonants. A long series of experiments over the past few years has shown that listeners' difficulty in discriminating among members of a category is largely due to the low-energy transience of the acoustic signal on the basis of which phonetic categories are assigned. Lane (1965) pointed to the greater duration and intensity of the vowels and showed that they were perceived more categorically if they were *degraded* by being presentèd in noise. Stevens (1968b) remarked the brief, transient nature of stop consonant acoustic cues and showed, as did Sachs (1969), that vowels are perceived more categorically if their duration and acoustic stability are reduced by placing them in CVC syllables.

The role of auditory memory, implicit in the work just cited, was made explicit by Fujisaki and Kawashima (1969, 1970) in a model of the decision process during the ABX trial. If a listener assigns A and B to different phonetic categories (i.e., if A and B lie on opposite sides of a phonetic boundary), his only task is to determine whether X belongs to the same category as A or as B; his performance in this case is good, and a discrimination peak appears in the function for both consonants and vowels. However, if a listener assigns A and B to the same phonetic category, he is forced to compare X with his auditory memory of A and B; in this case, his performance is reduced slightly for vowels, for which auditory memory is presumed to be relatively strong, but reduced sharply for consonants, for which auditory memory is presumed to be weak. Evidence for the operation of such a two-step process within phonetic categories in man, but not in monkey, recently has been reported by Sinnott (1974).

Before we proceed, let us spell out some distinctions between auditory and phonetic memory stores. The auditory store, or trace, is usually assumed to be rather like an echo: a faint simulacrum, if not of the waveform, at least of its neural correlates at an early stage of processing. Like an echo, the trace is an analog of its original, decays rapidly, and may be displaced if another sound arrives to interfere before decay is complete. The phonetic store, on the other hand, is a set of discrete features, its decay is a good deal slower, and interference can be accomplished only by another phonetic entity with similar phonetic features.

With this in mind, we turn to several experiments by Pisoni (1971, 1973a,b) in which he tested and supported Fujisaki and Kawashima's hypothesis concerning auditory memory for consonants and vowels. In the first (Pisoni, 1973a), he varied A to X delay interval from zero to two seconds in an AX *same—different* task for vowel and stop consonant continua. Between-category performance (presumably based on phonetic store) was high and independent of delay interval for both consonants and vowels; within-category performance (presumably based on auditory store) for consonants was low and independent of delay interval, but for vowels was high and declined systematically as delay interval increased. In subsequent experiments, Pisoni (1973b) demonstrated that the degree of categorical (or continuous) perception of vowels can be manipulated by the memory demands of the discrimination paradigm and by the amount of interference from neighboring stimuli. (See also Glanzman and Pisoni, 1973).

Changing tack, Pisoni and Lazarus (1974) sought methods of increasing apparent auditory memory for stop consonants. This is more difficult, but by a particular combination and sequence of experimental conditions, they were able to demonstrate improved within-category discrimination on a voice—voiceless continuum. The same continuum (/ba-pa/) also elicited reaction time differences in a pair-matching task (Pisoni and Tash, 1974; cf. Posner, Boies, Eichelman, and Taylor, 1969). Here, listeners were asked to respond *same* or *different* to pairs of stimuli drawn from the continuum. *Same* reaction times were faster for identical pairs than for acoustically distinct pairs drawn from the same phonetic category; *different* reaction times decreased as acoustic differences between pairs from different categories increased. This last result recalls Barclay's (1972) finding that listeners can judge correctly and reliably acoustic variants of /d/ drawn from a synthetic continuum, as more similar to /b/ or /g/. If we add these studies to our earlier observation that listeners always display a margin of within-category discrimination for consonants, and that discrimination functions do not display a quantal leap between categories, we must conclude that the auditory system does retain at least some trace of consonantal passage. At the same time, there is little question that this trace is fainter than that for vowels.

The conclusion of all these studies is pointed up by the work of Raphael (1972). He studied voice—voiceless VC continua, manipulating initial vowel duration as acoustic cue to voicing of the final stop. Here, where perceptual object was consonantal but acoustic cue vocalic, perception was continuous. In short, consonants and vowels are distinguished in the experiments we have been considering, not by their phonetic class or the processes of assignment to that class, but by their acoustic characteristics and by the duration of their auditory stores. If the longer store of the vowels is experimentally reduced, their membership in the natural class of segmental phonetic entities is revealed by their categorical perception.

Stages of Auditory Memory

Several independent lines of research, drawing on different experimental paradigms, recently have begun to converge on perceptual and memorial processes below the level of phonetic classification. Experimenters often share neither terminology nor theoretical framework, but we can discern two, not entirely overlapping, lines of division in the perceptual process. The first divides short-term memory into a brief store lasting some hundreds of milliseconds and a longer store lasting several seconds. The second divides peripheral from central processes; this is important, but we will not consider it in detail here, since the cut cannot be made as surely in audition as in vision (owing to incomplete decussation of auditory pathways), and most of the processes to be discussed are certainly central.

SHORT-TERM AUDITORY STORES

Store I. As a step toward further analysis of auditory memory for speech, let us consider the concept of parallel processing. Liberman *et al.* (1967) used this term to describe the decoding of a CV syllable in which acoustic correlates of consonant and vowel are distributed over an entire syllable (see also Liberman, 1970). Obviously, the process requires a store at least as long as the syllable to register auditory information, and presumably somewhat longer to permit transfer into phonetic code.

Direct evidence of this type of parallel processing comes from several sources. Liberman *et al.* (1952) showed that phonetic interpretation of a stop release burst varied with its following vowel, and they concluded that we perceive speech over stretches of roughly syllabic length (cf. Schatz, 1954). Lindblom and Studdert-Kennedy (1967) demonstrated that the phonetic boundary for a series of synthetic vowels shifted as a function of the slope and direction of initial and final formant transitions: listeners judged vowels in relation to their surrounding consonantal frames (cf. Fujimura and Ochiai, 1963; Strange *et al.* 1974). More recently, Pisoni and Tash (1974) have studied reaction time to CV syllables: They called for *same—different* judgments on vowels or consonants of syllable pairs in which nontarget portions of the syllables were also either the same or different. Whether comparing consonants or vowels, listeners consistently were faster when target and nontarget portions of the syllable were redundant (i.e., both *same*, or both *different*). In other words, information from an entire syllable contributed to listeners' decisions concerning *segments* of the syllable. In a related study by Wood and Day (1975), listeners identified either vowel or consonant of synthetic CV syllables, /ba,da bæ,dæ/. If all test items were identical on the nontarget dimension (i.e., if all had the same vowel on a consonant test, or all the same consonant on a vowel test), subjects' reaction times were significantly faster than if both target and nontarget dimensions varied. In the latter case, the *unattended* vowel (or consonant) retarded listeners' decisions on the attended consonant (or vowel). In short, we have a variety of evidence that, for at least some syllables, consonant and vowel recognition are interdependent, parallel processes, requiring a short-term auditory store of at least syllabic duration.

Massaro (1972) made the functional distinction between such a *perceptual auditory image* and a longer, *synthesized* auditory store; he initiated attempts to estimate duration of the *image* by backward masking studies. First discovered in visual experiments (Werner, 1935), the paradigm takes advantage of the fact that perception of a stimulus may be blocked if a second stimulus is presented some hundreds of milliseconds later; it has been used to good effect in vision to separate and describe peripheral and central processes (Turvey, 1973). However, the belief that the critical interstimulus interval (*ISI*), at which the first stimulus is freed from interference by the second, may be taken as an estimate of the duration of primary auditory display (Massaro, 1972) is, as we shall see, difficult to sustain, and application of the technique to the study of speech perception has proved problematic for several reasons.

Auditory information is displayed over time, so that perception of a target CV syllable of natural duration (e.g., 200—300 msec) can be interrupted only by a masking syllable that begins before the first syllable is complete. Temporal relations between syllables must then be expressed in terms of stimulus onset asynchrony (*SOA*) rather than in terms of ISI, and the effectiveness of the mask is reduced, because it is itself masked by the first syllable (forward masking). For example, Studdert-Kennedy, Shankweiler, and Schulman (1970) found that the first syllable was freed completely from masking by the second at an SOA of 50 msec, certainly an underestimate of display time, since it is no more than the duration of the critical consonant information in the formant transitions of the target CV syllable.

There are two solutions to this impasse: to make the syllables unnaturally short, or to present target and mask to opposite ears (dichotically), thus evading peripheral masking of the second syllable. Several investigators (Massaro, 1972; Pisoni, 1972; Dorman, Kewley-Port, Brady-Wood and Turvey, 1973) have attempted the first solution. Results are difficult to interpret because both degree of masking and critical ISI for release from masking vary with target (consonant or vowel); size and range (acoustic or phonetic) of target set; target and mask energy; relations between target and mask structure (acoustic or phonetic); and individual listeners, many of whom show no masking whatsoever even for brief (15.5 msec) vowels (Dorman *et al.*, 1973). Where masking could be obtained, the shortest critical ISI observed in these studies (80 msec) was for 40 msec steady-state vowels, and the longest (250 msec) for 40 msec CV syllables (Pisoni, 1972). Note, incidentally, that complete absence of masking has been observed only with vowels; just as categorical perception of vowels can be induced by degrading them with noise, so too can their masking (Dorman *et al.*, 1974).

In any event, these variable results do not encourage one to believe that critical ISI is measuring the fixed duration of auditory display. The case is no better when we turn to dichotic masking paradigms. Pisoni and McNabb (1974), for example, observed a critical SOA for release from dichotic backward masking of between 20 and 150 msec, depending upon target and mask vowel relations. A somewhat longer estimate of 200—250 msec can be extrapolated from the data of Studdert-Kennedy *et al.* (1970b). A narrower estimate comes from McNeill and Repp (1973). They studied forward masking of dichotically presented CV syllables, determining SOA necessary for features of the leading syllable to have no further effect on errors in the lagging syllable, and so presumably to have passed out of the phonetic processor. Their estimate of 80—120 msec may be more realistic for running speech than others, since their procedure eliminated a component present in all previous studies, namely, time taken to prepare a response, a period during which effective interruption still may occur (Repp, 1973).

However, it is more likely that the entire endeavor is misguided. It seems intuitively plausible that syllable processing time is not constant, but varies, under automatic attentional control, with speaking rate and other factors. The studies reviewed are simply measuring time required for release from masking under a variety of more or less adverse conditions. This is certainly not without interest, particularly if we can show it to be a function of well-specified target—mask relations. However, in that case we shall be turning attention away from the notion of a primary auditory store and toward the more important question of what acoustic dimensions are extracted in the very earliest stage of processing and how they interact to determine the phonetic percept.

Store II. Nonetheless, some form of auditory store is clearly necessary. Otherwise, we would be unable to interpret the prosody of running speech, and there is ample experimental evidence of cross-syllabic auditory interaction (Atkinson, 1973; Hadding-Koch and Studdert-Kennedy, 1964; Studdert-Kennedy and Hadding, 1973).

Detailed analysis of this longer store, which perhaps lasts several seconds, was made possible by the work of Crowder and Morton (1969) (see also Crowder, 1971a,b, 1972, 1973). They were the first experimenters to undertake a systematic account of what they termed *precategorical acoustic storage (PAS)*.

Evidence for the store comes from studies of immediate, ordered recall of span-length digit lists. Typically, error probability increases from beginning to end of list with some slight drop on terminal items *(recency effect)*. The terminal drop is increased significantly if the list is presented by ear rather than by eye *(modality effect)*. Crowder and Morton argue that these two effects reflect the operation of distinct visual and auditory stores for precategorical (prelinguistic) information, and of an auditory store that persists longer than the visual. Support comes from demonstrations that the recency effect is significantly reduced, or abolished, if subjects are required to recall the list by speaking rather than by writing (Crowder, 1971a), or if an auditory list is followed by a redundant spoken suffix (such as the word *zero*), as a signal for the subject to begin recall *(suffix effect)*. That the suffix interferes with auditory, rather than linguistic, store is argued by the facts that the effect *(1)* does not occur if the suffix is a tone or burst of noise; *(2)* is unaffected if the spoken suffix is played backward; *(3)* is unaffected by degree of semantic similarity between suffix and list; *(4)* is reduced if suffix and list are spoken in different voices; *(5)* is reduced if suffix and list are presented to opposite ears.

Of particular interest in the present context is that all three effects (modality, recency, suffix) are observed for CV lists of which members differ in vowel alone, or in both vowel and consonant (spoken letter names), but not for voiced stop consonant CV or VC lists of which members differ only in the consonant (cf. Cole, 1973b). Crowder (1971a, p. 595) concludes that "vowels receive some form of representation in PAS while voiced stop consonants receive none." Liberman, Mattingly, and Turvey (1972, p. 329) argue further that phonetic classification "strips away all auditory information" from stop consonants.

However, this last claim is unlikely to be true. First, there is no good reason why the process of categorization should affect vowels and consonants differently. Second, we have a variety of evidence that listeners retain at least some auditory trace of stop consonants (see previous section). Third, consonant and vowel differences in PAS can be reduced by appropriate manipulation of the signal array (Darwin and Baddeley, 1974). These investigators demonstrated a recency effect for tokens of a stop CV, /ga/, and two highly discriminable CV syllables in which the consonantal portion is of longer duration, /ʃa/, /ma/. They also demonstrated that the recency effect for vowels can be eliminated if the vowels are very short (30 msec of a 60 msec CV syllable) and are close neighbors on an F1—F2 plot. They conclude that "the consonant—vowel distinction is largely irrelevant" (p. 48) and that items in PAS cannot be accessed reliably if, like /ba, da, ga/ or /I, ɛ, æ/, they are acoustically similar. The effect of acoustic similarity is, of course, to confound auditory memory. As we shall see shortly ("The Acoustic Syllable," following) and, as Darwin and Baddeley (1974) themselves argue, it is to the more general concept of auditory memory that we must have recourse if we are to understand the full range of experiments in which consonant—vowel differences have been demonstrated.

We turn now to the duration of PAS and the mechanisms underlying its reflection in behavior. Notice, first, that if an eight-item list is presented at a rate of two per second and is recalled at roughly the same rate, time between presentation and recall will be roughly equal for all items. Therefore, the recency effect cannot be attributed to differential decay across the list, but is due rather to the absence of *overwriting* or interference from succeeding items. Second, since degree of interference (i.e., probability of recall error) decreases as time between items increases, and since the suffix effect virtually disappears if the interval between the last item and suffix is increased to 2 seconds, we are faced with the paradox that performance improves as time allowed for PAS decay increases. Crowder's (1971b) solution is to posit an active *readout* or rehearsal process at the articulatory level. Time for a covert run through the list is "a second or two" (p. 339). If a suffix occurs during this period, PAS for the last couple of items is spoiled before they are reached; if no suffix occurs, the subject has time to check his rehearsal of later items against his auditory store, and so to confirm or correct his preliminary decision. Crowder (1971b) goes on to show that there is, in fact, no evidence for any decay in PAS: In the absence of further input, PAS has an infinite duration. This is intuitively implausible, but we will not pursue the matter here.

Notice, however, that the term *precategorical* refers to the nature of the information stored, not to the period of time during which it is stored. A preliminary (or even final) articulatory, if not phonetic, decision must be made before PAS is lost, if rehearsal is to permit cross-check with the store. We are thus reminded of the temporary auditory store hypothesized in the analysis-by-synthesis model of Stevens (1960, 1972a). Crowder's account, with its preliminary analysis and generative rehearsal loop, is so similar to Stevens' model that we may be tempted to identify the two and to see evidence for PAS function as support for Stevens' hypothesis.

We may remark, however, one important difference. Stevens introduced a synthesis loop to handle the invariance problem, a problem at its most acute for stop consonants. But these are precisely the items excluded from PAS, and all our evidence for consonantal auditory memory suggests a store considerably less than infinite, probably less than a second. We may, of course, assume that a synthesis loop goes into operation very early in the process while consonant auditory information is still available, and that the PAS rehearsal loop is simply a sustention beyond the point at which stop consonantal auditory information can be accessed. We would then be forced to posit decay of consonantal information from auditory store. Continuation of the loop might be automatic during running speech, enabling prosodic pattern to emerge, but under attentional control for special purposes, such as listening to poetry and remembering telephone numbers. However, we have, at present, no direct evidence for the earlier stage of the loop.

Stages of Processing

Nor, as we have seen, do we have direct evidence for the primary auditory store inferred from parallel processing. In fact, we may do well to dismiss division of the process into hypothetical stores and concentrate attention on types of information extracted during early processing, and their interactions. Several experimental paradigms have already been applied.

Day and Wood (1972) and Wood (1974) have reported evidence for parallel extraction of pitch (fundamental frequency) and spectral information bearing on segmental classification. For the first experiment they synthesized two CV syllables, /ba, da/, each at two pitches, and prepared two types of random test order. In one, they varied a single dimension, either fundamental frequency or phonetic class; in the other, they varied both dimensions independently. They then called on subjects to identify, with a reaction time button, either pitch or phonetic class, each in its appropriate one-dimensional test and also in the two-dimensional test. Reaction times were longer for both tasks on the two- than on the one-dimensional test, but the increase was significantly greater on the phonetic than on the pitch task: Unpredictable pitch differences interfered with phonetic decision more than the reverse. The authors took this finding as evidence for separate nonlinguistic and linguistic processes, the first mandatory, the second optional. In a follow-up experiment, Wood (1974) substituted a two-dimensional test in which fundamental frequency and phonetic class variations were correlated rather than independent. Reaction times were now significantly shorter for both tasks on the two-dimensional test: Subjects drew on both pitch and phonetic information for either pitch or phonetic classification. Wood concluded that the two types of information are separately and simultaneously extracted (as required, incidentally, by Stevens' (1960) model).

There is more to these experiments. The phonetic task called for a decision on the consonant (/ba/ versus /da/), but pitch information was primarily carried by the vowel. In fact, had fundamental frequency differences been carried solely by initial formant transitions, it is doubtful whether or not they would have interacted with phonetic decision. Dorman (1974) has shown that listeners are unable to discriminate intensity differences carried by the 50 msec initial transitions of a voiced stop CV syllable, but are well able to discriminate identical differences carried by isolated transitions or by the first 50 msec of a steady-state vowel. While the experiment has not been done, it seems likely that if Dorman had used fundamental frequency instead of intensity, his results would have held. We would then be forced to conclude that, in Wood's (1974) experiment, subjects were using adventitious pitch information carried by the vowel to facilitate judgment of the consonant, and vice versa. The experiments thus reflect parallel processing both of linguistic and nonlinguistic information and of consonant and vowel.

Experimental separation of auditory and phonetic processes also has been attempted in dichotic studies. Consider, for example, the following series. Shankweiler and Studdert-Kennedy (1967; also Studdert-Kennedy and Shankweiler, 1970) found that listeners were significantly better at identifying the consonants of dichotically competing CV or CVC syllables if the consonants shared a phonetic feature than if they did not. Since the effect was present both for pairs sharing vowel (e.g., /bi, di; du, tu/, etc.) and for pairs not sharing vowel (e.g., /bi, du; di, tu/, etc.), and since the latter pairs differ markedly in the auditory patterns by which the shared features are conveyed, Studdert-Kennedy *et al.* (1972) concluded that the effect had a phonetic rather than an auditory basis. In another experimental paradigm, Studdert-Kennedy *et al.* (1970b) presented CV syllables at various values of SOA and demonstrated dichotic backward masking. They attributed the masking to interruption of central processes of speech perception, but left the level at which the interruption occurred uncertain (cf. Kirstein, 1971, 1973; Porter, 1971; Berlin, Lowe-Bell, Cullen, Thompson and Loovis, 1973; Darwin, 1971a).

Recently, Pisoni and McNabb (1974) have combined and elaborated the two paradigms in a dichotic feature-sharing study, varying both masks and SOA. Their targets were: /ba, pa, da, ta/; their masks were: /ga, ka, gæ, kæ, gɛ, kɛ/. If target and mask consonants shared voicing, little or no masking was observed. If they did not share voicing, masking of target consonant increased both as masking syllable vowel approached target syllable vowel from /ɛ/ through /æ/ to /a/, and as mask intensity increased. In other words, identification of target consonant was facilitated by similarity of masking consonant, but, in the absence of facilitation, was impeded by similarity of masking vowel, particularly if the vowel was of relatively high intensity. In a theoretical discussion of these results, Pisoni (1975) concludes that masking and facilitation occur at different stages of the perceptual process: Masking reflects integration (rather than interruption) at the auditory level, while facilitation reflects integration at the phonetic level.

However, these results are also open to a purely auditory interpretation. They seem, in fact, to be consistent with a system that extracts the acoustic correlates of voice onset time separately for each vowel context (cf. Cooper, 1974b). Thus we are led to consider the possible role of discrete acoustic feature analyzing systems which are tuned to speech. This has proved among the most fruitful approaches to analysis of early processing, but we defer discussion to a later section (see subsequent section, "Feature Analyzing Systems").

The Acoustic Syllable

We have touched now on some half dozen paradigms—categorical perception, backward masking, short-term memory, reaction time studies, and others—in which consonant and vowel perception differ. As a final example, we may mention dichotic experiments (Berlin and McNeil, this volume). Shankweiler and Studdert-Kennedy (1967) (also, Studdert-Kennedy and Shankweiler, 1970) showed a significant right-ear advantage for dichotically presented CV or CVC syllables differing in their initial or final consonants, but little for steady-state vowels or CVC syllables differing in their vowels. Day and Vigorito (1973) and Cutting (1974) reported a hierarchy of ear advantages in dichotic listening from a right-ear advantage for stop consonants through liquids, to a null or small left-ear advantage for vowels. Weiss and House (1973) have demonstrated that a right-ear advantage emerges for vowels, if they are presented at suitably unfavorable signal-to-noise ratios, while Godfrey (1974) has shown that the right-ear advantage for vowels may be increased by adding noise, reducing duration, or using a more confusable set of vowels (cf. Darwin and Baddeley, 1974).

The pattern is familiar. In virtually every instance, a consonant—vowel difference can be reduced or eliminated by taxing the listener's auditory access to the vowel, or by sensitizing his auditory access to the consonant. These qualifications only serve to emphasize the contrast between consonants and vowels, and to pinpoint its source in their acoustic structure. The consonant is transient, low in energy, and spectrally diffuse; the vowel is relatively stable, high in energy, and spectrally compact. Together they form the syllable, each fulfilling within it some necessary function.

Consider, first, vowel duration. Long duration is not necessary for recognition. We can identify a vowel quite accurately and very rapidly from little more than one or two glottal pulses, lasting 10 to 20 msec. Yet in running speech, vowels last ten to twenty times as long. The increased length may be segmentally redundant, but it permits the speaker to display other useful information: Variations in fundamental frequency, duration, and intensity within and across vowels offer possible contrasts in stress and intonation, and increase the potential phonetic range (as in tone languages). Of course, these gains also reduce the rate at which segmental information can be transferred, increase the duration of auditory store, and open the vowel to contextual effects; the larger the phonetic repertoire the more these changes occur. A language built on vowels, like a language of cries, would be limited and cumbersome.

Adding consonantal *attack* to the vowel inserts a segment of acoustic contrast between the vowels, reduces vowel context effects, and increases phonetic range. The attack, itself part of the vowel (the two produced by "a single ballistic movement" [Stetson, 1952, p. 4]), is brief, and so increases the rate of information transfer. Despite its brevity, the attack has a pattern arrayed in time, and the full duration of its trajectory into the vowel is required to display the pattern. To compute its phonetic identity, time is needed, and this is provided by the segmentally redundant vowel. Vowels are the rests between consonants.

Finally, rapid consonantal gestures cannot carry the melody and dynamics of the voice. The segmental and suprasegmental loads are therefore divided over consonant and vowel: the first, with its poor auditory store, taking the bulk of the segmental load; the second, the suprasegmental load. There emerges the syllable, a symbiosis of consonant and vowel, a structure shaped by the articulatory and auditory capacities of its user, fitted to, defining, and making possible linguistic and paralinguistic communication.

Specialized Neural Processes

Cerebral Lateralization

That in most persons the left cerebral hemisphere is specialized for language functions is among the most firmly established findings of modern neurology. That one of those functions may be to decode the peculiar acoustic structure of the syllable into its phonetic components was first suggested by the results of dichotic studies (Berlin and McNeil, this volume). Kimura (1961a,b, 1967) discovered that if different digit triads were presented simultaneously to opposite ears, those presented to the right ear were more accurately recalled than those presented to the left. She attributed the effect to functional prepotency of contralateral pathways under dichotic competition and to left hemisphere specialization for language functions. Later experiments have amply supported her interpretation.

Shankweiler and Studdert-Kennedy (1967) applied the technique to analysis of speech perception. They demonstrated a significant right-ear advantage for single pairs of nonsense syllables differing only in initial or final stop consonant, and separable advantages for place of articulation and voicing (see also Studdert-Kennedy and Shankweiler, 1970; cf. Halwes, 1969; Darwin, 1969; Haggard, 1971). Among the questions raised by these studies was whether the left hemisphere was specialized only for phonetic analysis, or also for extraction of speech-related acoustic properties such as voice onset, formant structure, temporal relations among portions of the signal, and so on. We will not rehearse the argument here, but simply state the conclusion that "while the auditory system common to both hemispheres is equipped to extract the auditory parameters of a speech signal, the dominant hemisphere may be specialized for the extraction of linguistic features from those parameters" (Studdert-Kennedy and Shankweiler, 1970, p. 594).

Striking evidence in support of this conclusion recently has been gathered by Wood (1975) and Wood, Goff, and Day (1971). Wood's work deserves careful study as an exemplary instance of the use of electroencephalography (EEG) in the study of language-related neurophysiological processes. Wood synthesized two CV syllables, /ba/ and /ga/, each at two fundamental frequencies, 104 Hz (low) and 140 Hz (high). From these he constructed two types of random test order: In one, items differed only in pitch (e.g., /ba/ [low] versus /ba/ [high]); in the other, they differed only in phonetic class (e.g., /ba/ [low] versus /ga/ [low]). Subjects were asked to identify with reaction time buttons either the pitch or the phonetic class of the test items. While they did so, evoked potentials were recorded from a temporal and a central location over each hemisphere. Records from each location were averaged and compared for the two types of test. Notice that both tests contained an identical item (e.g., /ba/ [low]) identified on the same button by the same finger. Since cross-test comparisons were made only between EEG records for identical items, the only possible source of differences in the records was in the task being performed, auditory (pitch) or phonetic. Results showed highly significant differences between records for the two tasks at both left hemisphere locations, but at neither of the right hemisphere locations. A control experiment, in which the "phonetic" task was to identify isolated initial formant transitions (50 msec), revealed no significant differences at either location over either hemisphere. Since these transitions carry all acoustic information by which the full syllables are phonetically distinguished, and yet are not recognizable as speech, we may conclude that the original left hemisphere differences arose during phonetic, rather than auditory, analysis. We will discuss the adequacy of isolated formant transitions as control patterns in the next section. However, the entire set of experiments strongly suggests that different neural processes go on during phonetic, as opposed to auditory, perception in the left hemisphere, but not in the right (cf. Molfese, 1972).

The distinctive processes of speech perception would seem to lie in linguistic rather than acoustic analysis. Two other types of evidence suggest the same conclusion. First,

visual studies have shown repeatedly a right field (left hemisphere) advantage for tach-
istoscopically presented letters and, by contrast, a left field (right hemisphere) advantage for nonlinguistic geometric forms (for a review, see Kimura and Durnford, 1974).
Second, Papçun, Krashen, Terbeek, Remington, and Harshman (1974) and Krashen
(1972) have shown a right-ear advantage in experienced Morse code operators for
dichotically presented Morse code words and letters. If the arbitrary patterns of both
a visual and an auditory alphabet can engage left hemisphere mechanisms, there
might seem to be little ground for claiming special status for the speech signal.

However, alphabets are secondary, and while their interpretation may engage
specialized linguistic mechanisms, analysis of their arbitrary signal patterns clearly
should not. The speech signal, on the other hand, is primary; its acoustic pattern is
at once the natural realization of phonological system and the necessary source of
phonetic percept. Given its special status and peculiar structure, we would be, perhaps,
less surprised if there were, than if there were not, specialized mechanisms adapted
to its auditory analysis.

Hints of such processes have begun to appear. Halperin, Nachshon, and Carmon
(1973), for example, showed a shift from left-ear advantage to right-ear advantage
for dichotically presented tone sequences as a function of the number of alternations in
the sequence. Their stimuli were patterned permutations of brief (200 msec) tone
bursts, presumably not unlike those of Papçun *et al.* (1974), who showed a right-ear
advantage in naive subjects for Morse code patterns up to seven units in length. Both
studies suggest left hemisphere specialization for assessing the sort of temporal relations important in speech. Both studies suffer from having called upon subjects to label
the patterns, a process that might well invoke left hemisphere mechanisms.

This weakness is avoided in recent work by Cutting (1974). He synthesized two
normal CV syllables, /ba/ and /da/, and two phonetically impossible "syllables"
identical with the former, except that their first formant transitions fell rather than
rose along the frequency scale, so they were not recognized as speech. In a nonlabeling
dichotic task, subjects gave equal right-ear advantages for both types of stimulus.
The outcome suggests a left hemisphere mechanism for extraction of formant transitions and is reminiscent of a study by Darwin (1971b), who found a right-ear
advantage for synthetic fricatives when formant transitions from fricative noise into
vowel were included, but no ear advantage when transitions were excluded.

There are, then, grounds for believing that the left hemisphere is specialized not
only for phonetic interpretation of an auditory input, but also for extraction of auditory information from the acoustic signal. The evidence is tenuous, but systematic
study of feature analyzing systems—whether lateralized or not remains to be seen
(cf. Ades, 1974b)—has opened a new range of possibilities.

Feature Analyzing Systems

Neurophysiological systems of feature detectors, selectively responsive to light
patterns, were first reported by Lettvin, Maturana, McCulloch, and Pitts (1959).
They found receptive fields in the visual ganglion cells of frog that responded, under
specific conditions, to movement. The biological utility of the system to an animal that

preys on flies is obvious. Moving up the nervous system, and the evolutionary scale, Hubel and Wiesel (1962) reported yet more complex detectors: single cells in the visual cortex of cat that responded selectively to the orientation of lines, to edges, and to movement in a certain direction. Since then, work on visual feature detecting systems has proliferated (see Julesz, 1971, pp. 58—68, for a review).

Complex auditory feature detectors in the cortex of cat were reported by Evans and Whitfield (1964): single cells responsive to specific gradients of intensity change, and others (*miaow* cells) to the rate and direction of frequency change (Whitfield and Evans, 1965). Similar cells were reported by Nelson, Erulkar, and Bryan (1966) in the inferior colliculus of cat. Other research has borne directly on acoustic signaling systems. Frishkopf and Goldstein (1963) and Capranica (1965) reported single units in the auditory nerve of bullfrog responsive only to the male bullfrog's mating call. Recently, Wollberg and Newman (1972) have described single cells in the auditory cortex of squirrel monkey that answer to that species' *isolation peep*. Stimulus and response were isomorphic: Presentation of the peep with portions gated out yielded a response in which corresponding portions were absent. Furthermore, the remaining portions were no longer normal: If a central portion of the signal was missing, the response pattern to the final portion changed. Interaction of this kind is particularly interesting in light of the contextually variant cues of speech, for which interpretation may demand details of a complete pattern, such as the syllable.

The relevance of all this to speech has not gone unnoticed. The possible role of feature detecting systems in speech perception was scouted briefly by Liberman *et al.* (1967), by Studdert-Kennedy (1974) and, at considerable length, by Abbs and Sussman (1971). However, advance awaited a telling experimental procedure. This was found in *adaptation* studies, a method with a long history in visual research (Woodworth and Schlosberg, 1954). The paradigm is simple enough. For example, after prolonged fixation of a line curved from the median plane, a vertical line, presented as a test stimulus, appears curved in the opposite direction; there is a *figural aftereffect* in which portions of the image are displaced (Köhler and Wallach, 1944). Related effects in color and tilt also occur. While none of these effects is understood in any detail, they are frequently interpreted in terms of specific receptors or of feature analyzing systems. Prolonged stimulation *adapts* or *fatigues* one system and relatively *sensitizes* a physically adjacent or related (perhaps opponent) system. Based on this interpretation, to demonstrate perceptual shifts upon prolonged exposure to a particular physical (or psychological) *feature* is to demonstrate the presence of analyzing systems for that feature and its relative.

The method was first used by Warren and Gregory (1958; see also Warren, 1968, and this volume), yielding an effect that they termed *verbal transformation*. Subjects listen to a meaningful word played repeatedly once or twice per second for several minutes and are asked to report any changes in the word that they hear. They report a large number of transformations, usually meaningful words and not always closely related phonetically to the original. However, Goldstein and Lackner (1973) refined the method by using nonsense syllables to reduce semantic influence (CV, V, VC) and by presenting them monaurally. They analyzed transforms phonetically and showed that each was confined to a single phone, usually on one or two distinctive features (as defined by Chomsky and Halle, 1968) and that they were independent of their syllabic context. Furthermore, the right ear gave significantly more transforms than the left on consonants but not on vowels, and the transforms followed the phonological constraints of English. These last two points are among the arguments that the authors present for suspecting the effects to result from adaptation of phonetic, rather than auditory, analyzing systems.

In a further refinement, Lackner and Goldstein (1975) used a natural CV syllable, repeated monaurally 36 times in 30 seconds and a final test item, presented to either the same or the opposite ear. Both adapting and test items were drawn from the set of six English stop consonants followed by the same vowel (either /i/ or /e/). Subjects reported the last adapting item and the test item. Transforms in the test item occurred on both cross-ear (30%) and same-ear (40%) trials. They were significantly more likely to occur if the final adapting item also was transformed, and to be on the same feature(s) (place and/or voice) as the adapting item transform, a result that again hints at phonetic feature detecting systems. The authors conclude from the cross-ear trials that adaptation is central rather than peripheral, but since in this study they were unable to distinguish phonetic effects from the acoustic effects that underlie them, they withhold judgment on whether the transforms are auditory or phonetic.

This last is, of course, the crucial question. It can be approached only by use of synthetic speech in which acoustic features can be specified precisely and, within limits, manipulated independently of phonetic category. Eimas, working independently of the previous authors, took this step in a series of experiments growing out of his work on infants (discussed later) and has concluded that the effect is phonetic. We will consider his work in some detail because it introduced a fruitful paradigm that already has been put to good use by others.

In the first experiment (Eimas and Corbit, 1973), the authors used two voice—voiceless series synthesized along the voice onset time continuum, one from /ba/ to /pa/, the other from /da/ to /ta/ (Lisker and Abramson, 1964). On the assumption of two voicing detectors, each differentially sensitive to VOT values that lie clearly within its phonetic category, and both equally sensitive to a VOT value at the phonetic boundary, the authors reasoned that adaptation with an acoustically extreme token of one phonetic type should desensitize its detector and relatively sensitize (a metaphor, not an hypothesis) its opponent detector to boundary values of VOT, with a resulting displacement of the identification function toward the adapting stimulus. They, therefore, collected unadapted and adapted functions for both labial and alveolar series. The adapting stimuli were drawn from the extremes of both series, and their effects were tested within and across series. Figure 8.5 shows the results for one of their three subjects (the experiment is taxing and prohibits large samples, but the other two subjects gave similar functions). The predicted results obtain. Furthermore, the effect is only slightly weaker across series than within. (This result was replicated in an experiment, briefly reported in their next paper, for which they used eight subjects to demonstrate boundary shifts on alveolar and velar stop consonant VOT continua after adaptation with labial stops.) In a supporting experiment, the authors showed that, following adaptation, the peak in an ABX discrimination function is shifted neatly to coincide with the adapted phonetic boundary (cf. Cooper, 1974a).

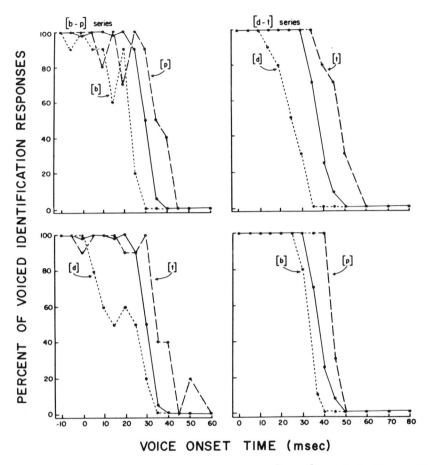

VOICE ONSET TIME (msec)

Figure 8.5 Percentages of voiced identification responses ([b or d]) obtained with and without adaptation, for a single subject. The functions for the [b, p] series are on the left and those for the [d, t] series are on the right. The solid lines indicate the unadapted identification functions and the dotted and dashed lines indicate the identification functions after adaptation. The phonetic symbols indicate the adapting stimulus. [From Eimas and Corbit, 1973.]

In a second study (Eimas, Cooper, and Corbit, 1973), the authors reported three experiments. The first demonstrates that the site of the adaptation effect is probably central rather than peripheral: It obtains as strongly when the adapting stimulus is presented to one ear and the test stimulus to the other, as when both are presented binaurally (cf. Ades, 1974b). The second demonstrates that the effect does not obtain if the adapting stimulus is simply the first 50 msec of the syllable /da/, an acoustic pattern that contains all the voicing information but is not heard as speech. The third experiment assesses the relative strengths of the two hypothesized detectors, finding that, as in the first study (see Figure 8.5), voiced stops tend to be more resistant to adaptation (yield smaller boundary shifts) than voiceless stops. The result encourages the hypothesis of separate detectors for each phonetic value along an acoustic continuum, a notion with obvious relevance to categorical perception.

Additional support comes from the work of Cooper (1974a), who found evidence of three distinct detectors along a /b-d-g/ continuum: adaptation with /b/ shifted only the /b-d/ boundary, with /g/ only the /d-g/ boundary, with /d/ both neighboring boundaries.

Let us remark first the striking achievement of these studies. Whatever the underlying mechanism, Eimas and his colleagues have demonstrated in a novel, direct, and peculiarly convincing manner the operation of some form of feature analyzing system in speech perception. The conclusion was not foregone. There might have been, after all, no adaptation effect at all. Alternatively, the effect might have been on the whole syllable or on the unanalyzed phonemic segment. But these possibilities were ruled out by the cross-series results. The effect proved to be on a feature within the phonemic segment, and so has provided the strongest evidence to date of a physiologically grounded feature system (cf. Cooper and Blumstein, 1974).

What now is the evidence for phonetic rather than auditory adaptation? First, the cross-series effect: Phonetic tokens drawn from labial, alveolar, or velar VOT continua differ acoustically in the extent and direction of their second and third formant transitions, yet they are mutually effective adaptors. If the effect were acoustic, the argument runs, the acoustic differences should eliminate the effect. Note, however, that the differences were in acoustic cues to place of articulation, while the feature being tested was voice onset time. The cues to this feature are complex and, as we have seen, relational. Furthermore, Cooper (1974b) has shown recently that VOT adaptation may be vowel-specific: simultaneous adaptation with $[\text{da}]$ and $[\text{t}^{\text{h}}\text{i}]$ produced opposite shifts on $[\text{ba-p}^{\text{h}}\text{a}]$ and $[\text{bi-p}^{\text{h}}\text{i}]$ series. Nonetheless, if outputs from such detectors were funneled into acoustic analyzers tuned to presence or absence of energy in the region of the first formant at syllable onset, we would expect precisely the results that were obtained (cf. Stevens and Klatt, 1974).

The second piece of evidence is the failure of the truncated /da/, not heard as speech, to *sensitize* the supposed /ta/ detector. Here the main problem is the status of the truncated /da/ as a control (cf. Wood, 1975). There are two possible types of design that may throw light on the auditory—phonetic issue. In one, control and test items are acoustically identical (on dimensions relevant to the phonetic dimension under test), but phonetically distinct; in the other, they are acoustically distinct, but phonetically identical. The first design, chosen by Eimas and his colleagues, may yield ambiguous results. If adaptation with the control item shifts the phonetic boundary, we have evidence for the existence of auditory detectors tuned to acoustic features of speech. Precisely this outcome has, in fact, been reported by Ades (1973), using the first 38 msec of the extreme test stimuli to shift the /bæ/ —/dæ/ boundary. If, on the other hand, the control item does not shift the boundary, the outcome is ambiguous. It may mean, as Eimas and his colleagues concluded, that the hypothetical detector is phonetic. It also may mean, however, that an acoustic detector tuned to features of speech is adapted only if stimulated by a complete (i.e., phonetically identifiable) signal (cf. Wollberg and Newman, 1972). It is not, after all, implausible to suppose that the human cortex contains sets of acoustic detectors tuned to speech and capable of mutual lateral inhibition. Each detector may respond to a particular acoustic property, but, in the absence of a collateral response in other detectors, may be inhibited from output to the phonetic system. The auditory system thus would be immune to adaptation by an incomplete signal.

The second type of design calls for control and test items that are acoustically distinct (on dimensions relevant to the phonetic dimension under study), but phonetically identical. This design rests, of course, on the fact that the speech signal may carry several acoustic cues, each a more or less effective determinant of a particular phonetic percept. The procedure becomes to synthesize two acoustic continua, manipulating in each a different acoustic cue to the same phonetic distinction. If, in this case, the two series are mutually effective in shifting the phonetic boundaries of the other, we have some preliminary support for the hypothetical phonetic detector. This was the outcome of studies by Ades (1974a), Bailey (1973), and Cooper (1974a), all of whom demonstrated cross-series adaptations for /b-d/ continua with different vowels. The use of different vowels meant that formant transitions cuing a given phonetic type could be falling in one token (e.g., /dæ/), and rising in another (e.g., /de/). Thus, adaptation of simple acoustic detectors responsive only to rising or only to falling formants (cf. Whitfield and Evans, 1965) was ruled out. Of course, a more complex *acoustic invariance* derived from some weighted ratio of F2 and F3 transitions might be posited (Cooper, 1974d). But the conclusion that the detectors are phonetic tempted both Ades and Cooper. Ades qualified his conclusion because in a previous experiment (Ades, 1974a) he had found no cross-series adaptation of CV and VC continua (/bæ-dæ/, /æb-æd/): The phonetic detector, unlike phonetic listeners and phonological theory, evidently distinguishes between initial and final allophones. A funnel into a second level of phonetic analysis, possibly the point of contact with an abstract generative system, would be needed to account for the listener's inability to make this distinction.

For Bailey (1973), the phonetic conclusion was less compelling. He pointed to spectral overlap in the transitions of his two series and suggested an acoustic system involving "some generalizing balanced detectors of positive and negative transitions" (p. 31). To test for the effect of spectral overlap, he constructed two /ba-da/ series, one with a fixed F2 and all place cues in F3, the other with no F3 and all place cues in F2. This, by far the most stringent version of the phonetically identical—acoustically distinct design, yielded cross-adaptation from the F2 cues series to the fixed F2, but none from the F3 cues series to the no F3. The outcome argues strongly for auditory adaptation, and Bailey concluded that the system contains "central feature extractors which process the phonetically relevant descriptors of spectral patterns" (p. 34).

Clearly, the issue of auditory versus phonetic detectors is not resolved. But let us consider implications of each possible resolution for speech perception theory and research. First, if discrete auditory detectors are being isolated by the adaptation technique, we may be in a position to begin more precise definition of the acoustic correlates of distinctive feature systems, ultimately essential if phonological theory is to be given a physical and physiological base. To the extent that this proves possible, we may be isolating invariants in the speech signal, thus aligning speech perception with other *natural categories*, such as those of color and form (Rosch, 1973). But it is not inevitable that acoustic features will be invariant correlates of phonetic features; both the work of Ades (1974a) on initial and final stop consonants and the work of Cooper (1974b) on vowel-specific VOT analyzers suggest that invariance may lie at some remove from the signal. In either event, to isolate acoustic features is not to define them phonetically, nor to explain how they are gathered from syllables of the signal into phonemes, each with its peculiar, nonarbitrary name; the auditory-to-phonetic transformation would remain obscure.

If, on the other hand, the adaptation technique isolates discrete phonetic detectors, its unequivocal achievement will have been to undergird the psychological and physiological reality of features in speech perception. Salutary though this may be for those of little faith, the outcome would be disappointing for research, for the process by which these features are drawn from the acoustic display and granted phonetic dimension will remain hidden. A new technique must then be developed to analyze the analyzer.

Finally, we should not discount the possibility that the auditory—phonetic distinction is misleading in this context and that the adapted systems are both auditory and phonetic. If, for example, the output from auditory analyzers tuned to speech funneled directly into phonetic processors so that adaptation of one set entailed adaptation of the other, a convincing separation of the two would be difficult to demonstrate. Precisely this is suggested by recent evidence (Cooper, 1974d) that each system can be adapted selectively, yet is intimately related to the other. The closeness of the relation is revealed by Cooper's (1974c) extension of the adaptation technique to the study of relations between perceptual and motor aspects of speech. He has shown that adaptation on a [bi-pi] continuum yields not only shifts in the perceptual boundary, but also correlated shifts in subjects' characteristic VOT values in production. If his findings are replicable, we have here clear evidence for the frequently hypothesized link between perception and production, and one that may supersede the auditory—phonetic distinctions we have been attempting to establish for these adaptation studies. To the origin of this link in the processes of language acquisition we turn in the final section.

From Acoustic Feature to Phonetic Percept

As we have seen, template-matching models of speech perception are not in good standing. Faced with gross acoustic variations as a function of phonetic context, rate, stress, and individual speaker, theorists have had recourse to motor, or analysis-by-synthesis, accounts of speech perception: They have sought invariance in the articulatory control system. Nonetheless, there are grounds for believing that some form of template-matching may operate in both speaking and listening, and there are more fundamental grounds than lack of acoustic invariance for positing a link between production and perception.

Consider the infant learning to speak. Several writers (e.g., Stevens, 1973; Mattingly, 1973) have pointed out that the infant must be equipped with some mechanism by which it plucks from the stream of speech just those acoustic cues that convey the phonetic distinctions it will eventually learn to perceive and articulate. This fact motivates, in part, Stevens' (1973) pursuit of acoustic invariants and his hypothesized property detectors. Evidence for the existence of such detectors comes from the work of Eimas and his colleagues (Eimas, Siqueland, Jusczyk and Vigorito, 1971; Eimas, 1975; for a review, see Cutting and Eimas, 1975). They have invest-igated the capacity of infants as young as one month to discriminate synthetic speech sounds. We will not describe their method in detail; but broadly, it employs operant conditioning, a synthetic speech continuum, an adapting stimulus, and a test item. The results are reliable and striking: Infants discriminate between pairs of stimuli drawn from different adult phonetic categories, but not between pairs drawn from the same phonetic category. The effect has been repeatedly demonstrated on both voicing and place of articulation continua (cf. Moffitt, 1971; Morse, 1972). Further-more, the effect is absent for truncated control syllables, which are not heard by adults as speech, exactly as in the adult adaptation studies. Eimas and his col-leagues interpret the effect as evidence for the operation of phonetic feature detectors, presumably innate. Unfortunately, the outcome is ambiguous for the same reasons as is the adult outcome: There is no way of assuring that the adapted detectors are phonetic rather than auditory (see Cutting and Eimas, 1975, for further discussion of this point). The more cautious, and perhaps more plausible, view is that they are auditory (cf. Stevens and Klatt, 1974).

We are then faced with two questions. First, do the acoustic features extracted by such detector systems bear an invariant relation to phonetic features? This is an empirical question, and we will say no more here than that; given the inconstancy of the speech signal, it is unlikely that they do. Second, and more importantly, how does the infant "know" that the extracted properties are speech? This, of course, is simply another version of the question: How are we to define the phonetic percept? But, asked in this form, an answer immediately suggests itself: The infant learns that sounds are speech by discovering that it can make them with its own vocal apparatus.

Before elaborating this point, let us consider the work of Marler (1970, 1975). He has proposed a general model of the evolution of vocal learning based on studies of the ontogenesis of male "song" in certain sparrows (see also Marler and Mundinger, 1971). Briefly, the hypothesis is that development of motor song-pattern is guided by sensory feedback matched to modifiable, innate auditory templates (cf. Mattingly, 1972). Marler describes three classes of birds. The first (for example, the dove or the chicken) needs to hear neither an external model nor its own voice for song to emerge: If the birds are reared in isolation, and even if they are deafened shortly after birth, crowing and cooing develop normally. The second (for example, the song sparrow) needs no external model, but does need to hear its own voice: If reared in isolation, song develops normally unless the bird is deafened in early life, in which case song is highly abnormal and insect-like.

An example of the third class of bird is the white-crowned sparrow, which needs both an external model and the sound of its own voice. Reared in isolation, the white-crown develops an abnormal song with "certain natural characteristics, particularly the sustained pure tones which are one basic element in the natural song" (Marler and Mundinger, 1971, p. 429). If the bird is deafened in early life, even this rudi-mentary song does not develop. There emerges instead a highly abnormal song "rather like that of a deafened song sparrow ... perhaps the basic output of the passive syringeal apparatus with a passive flow of air through it" (Marler, 1975, p. 26).

However, reared in isolation, but exposed to recordings of normal male song during a critical period (10—50 days after birth), the male (and the female, if injected with male hormone) develops normal song some 50 or more days after exposure. Exposure to the songs of other species will not serve, and deafening either before or after exposure to conspecific song prevents normal development (Konishi, 1965, cited by Marler, 1975).

Marler (1975, p. 26) proposes that the rudimentary song of the undeafened, isolated white-crown reflects the existence of an auditory template, "lying in the neural pathways for auditory processing embodying information about the structure of vocal sounds." The template matches certain features of normal song and serves to guide development of the rudimentary song, as well as to "focus . . . attention on an appropriate class of external models" (p. 26). Exposure to these models modifies and enriches the template, which then serves to guide normal development, through subsong and plastic song, as the bird gradually discovers the motor controls needed to match its output with the modified template. (Several studies have reported evidence for the *tuning* by experience of visual detecting systems in cat (Hirsch and Spinelli, 1970; Blakemore and Cooper, 1970; Pettigrew and Freeman, 1973) and man (Annis and Frost, 1973), and of auditory detecting systems in rhesus monkey (Miller, Sutton, Pfingst, Ryan, and Beaton, 1972).

Marler (1975) draws the analogy with language learning. He suggests that sensory control of ontogenetic motor development may have been the evolutionary change that made possible an elaborate communicative system as pivot of avian and human social organization. He argues that "new sensory mechanisms for processing speech sounds, applied first, in infancy, to analyzing sounds of others, and somewhat later in life to analysis of the child's own sounds, were a significant evolutionary step toward achieving the strategy of speech development of *Homo sapiens*" (p. 32). On the motor side, he points out, vocal development must have become dependent on auditory feedback, and there must have developed "neural circuitry necessary to modify patterns of motor outflow so that sounds generated can be matched to preestablished auditory templates" (p. 33).

Certainly, human and avian parallels are striking. Deafened at birth, the human infant does not learn to speak: babbling begins normally but dies away around the sixth month (Marvilya, 1972). Whether this is because the infant has been deprived of the sound of its own voice, of an external model, or of both, we do not know. But there does seem to be an (ill-defined) critical period during which exposure to speech is a necessary condition of normal development (Lenneberg, 1967; but see Fromkin, Krashen, Curtis, Rigler, and Rigler, 1974). And the work of Eimas and his colleagues has demonstrated the sensitivity of the infant to functionally important acoustic features of the speech signal. At least one of these features, the short VOT lag associated with stops in many languages (Lisker and Abramson, 1964), is known to be among the first to appear in infant babble (Kewley-Port and Preston, 1974). Finally, Sussman (1971) and his colleagues (Sussman, MacNeilage, and Lumbley, 1974; Sussman and MacNeilage, 1975) have reported evidence for a speech-related auditory sensorimotor mechanism that may serve to modify patterns of motor outflow to match sounds generated by the vocal mechanism against some standard. In short,

Marler's account is consistent with a good deal of our limited knowledge of speech development. Its virtue is to emphasize sensorimotor interaction and to accord the infant a mechanism for discovering auditory—articulatory correspondences.

Paradoxically, if we are to draw on this account of motor development for insight into perceptual development, we must place more emphasis on the relatively rich articulatory patterns revealed in early infant babble. The infant is not born without articulatory potential. In fact, the work of Lieberman and his colleagues would suggest quite specific capacities (Lieberman, 1968, 1972, 1973; Lieberman and Crelin, 1971; Lieberman, Harris, Wolff and Russell, 1971; Lieberman, Crelin, and Klatt, 1972). They have developed systematic evidence for evolution of the human vocal tract from a form with a relatively high larynx, opening almost directly into the oral cavity, capable of producing a limited set of schwa-like vowel sounds, to a form with a lowered larynx, a large pharyngeal cavity, and a right-angle bend in the supralaryngeal vocal tract, capable of producing the full array of human vowels. Lieberman (1973) argues that this development, taken with many other factors, including the capacity to encode and decode syllables, paved the way for the development of language. Associated with changes in morphology must have come neurological changes to permit increasingly fine motor control of breathing and articulation, including, in all likelihood, cerebral lateralization (cf. Geschwind and Levitsky, 1968; Lenneberg, 1967; Nottebohm, 1971, 1972). The outcome of these developments would have been a range of articulatory possibilities as determinate in their form as the patterns of manual praxis that gave rise to toolmaking. The inchoate forms of these patterns might emerge in infant babble under the control of rudimentary articulatory templates.

In short, we hypothesize that the infant is born with both auditory and articulatory templates. Each embodies capacities that may be modified by, and deployed in, the particular language to which the infant is exposed. Presumably, these templates evolved more or less *pari passu* and are matched, in some sense, as key to lock. However, they differ in their degree of specificity. For effective function in language acquisition, the auditory template must be tuned to specific acoustic properties of speech. The articulatory template, on the other hand, is more abstract, a range of gestural control, potentially isomorphic with the segmented feature matrix of the language by which it is modified (cf. Chomsky and Halle, 1968; Mattingly, 1975).

Among the grounds for this statement are the results of several studies of adult speech production. Lindblom and Sundberg (1971), for example, found that, if subjects were thwarted in their habitual articulatory gestures by the presence of a bite block between their front teeth, they were nonetheless able to approximate normal vowel quality, even within the first pitch period of the utterance. Bell-Berti (1975) has shown that the pattern of electromyographic potentials associated with pharyngeal enlargement during medial voiced stop consonant closure varies from individual to individual and from time to time within an individual. Finally, Ladefoged, DeClerk, Lindau and Papçun (1972) have demonstrated that different speakers of the same dialect may use different patterns of tongue height and tongue root advancement to achieve phonetically identical vowels. They do not report formant frequencies for their six speakers, so the degree of acoustic variability associated with the varied vocal tract shapes is not known. But since individuals obviously differ in the precise dimensions of their vocal tracts, it would be surprising if they accomplished a particular gesture and a particular acoustic pattern by precisely the same pattern of muscular action. In short, it seems likely that both infant and adult articulatory templates are control systems for a range of functionally equivalent vocal tract shapes rather than for specific patterns of muscular action. In fact, it is precisely to exploration of its own vocal tract and to discovery of its own patterns of muscular action that the infant's motor learning must be directed.

We should emphasize that neither template can fulfill its communicative function in the absence of the other. Modified and enriched by experience, the auditory template may provide a "description" of the acoustic properties of the signal, but the description can be no different in principle than that provided by any other form of spectral analysis; alone, the output of auditory analysis is void. Similarly, babble without auditory feedback has no meaning. The infant discovers phonetic "meaning" (and linguistic function) by discovering auditory—articulatory correspondences, that is, by discovering the commands required by its own vocal tract to match the output of its auditory template. Since the articulatory template is relatively abstract, the infant will begin to discover these correspondences before it has acquired the detailed motor skills of articulation: perceptual skill will precede motor skill. In rare instances of peripheral articulatory pathology, the infant (like the female white-crowned sparrow, who learns the song without singing) may even discover language without speaking (cf. MacNeilage, Rootes, and Chase, 1967).

We hypothesize, then, that the infant is born with two distinct capacities and that its task is to establish their links. Auditory feedback from its own vocalizations serves to modify the articulatory template, to guide motor development, and to establish the links. The process endows the communicatively empty outputs of auditory analysis and articulatory gesture with communicative significance. In due course, the system serves to segment the acoustic signal and perhaps, as analysis-by-synthesis models propose, to resolve acoustic variability. But its prior and more fundamental function is to establish the *natural categories* of speech. To perceive these categories is to trace the sound patterns of speech to their articulatory source and recover the commands from which they arose. The phonetic percept is then the correlate of these commands.

ACKNOWLEDGMENTS

Preparation of this chapter was supported, in part, by a grant to Haskins Laboratories from the National Institute of Child Health and Human Development, Bethesda, Maryland. I thank Alvin Liberman, Ignatius Mattingly, and Donald Shankweiler for their valuable comments and criticism, and David Pisoni for fruitful conversation and for drawing my attention to the work of Eleanor Rosch.

REFERENCES

Abbs, J. H., and Sussman, H. M. Neurophysiological feature detectors and speech perception: a discussion of theoretical implications. *Journal of Speech and Hearing Research*, 1971, *14*, 23—36.
Abramson, A. S., and Lisker, L. Voice onset time in stop consonants: acoustic analysis and synthesis. In D. E. Commins (Ed.), *Proceedings of the 5th International Congress of Acoustics*. Liege: Imp. G. Thone, A—51, 1965.

Abramson, A. S., and Lisker, L. Discriminability along the voicing continuum: cross-language tests. *Proceedings of the 6th International Congress of Phonetic Sciences* Prague: Academia, 1970. Pp. 569—573.

Abramson, A. S., and Lisker, L. Voice-timing perception in Spanish word-initial stops. *Journal of Phonetics*, 1973, *1*, 1—8.

Ades, A. E. Some effects of adaptation on speech perception. *Quarterly Progress Report*, Research Laboratory of Electronics, M.I.T., 1973, *111*, 121—129.

Ades, A. E. A bilateral component in speech perception. *Journal of the Acoustical Society of America*, 1974a, *56*, 610—616.

Ades, A. E. A study of acoustic invariance by selective adaptation. *Perception and Psychophysics*, 1974b, *16*, 61—66.

Annis, R. C., and Frost, B. Human visual ecology and orientation anisotropies in acuity. *Science*, 1973, *182*, 729—731.

Atkinson, J. E. Aspects of intonation in speech: implications from an experimental study of fundamental frequency. Unpublished Doctoral dissertation, Univ. of Connecticut, 1973.

Bailey, P. Perceptual adaptation for acoustical features in speech. *Speech Perception*, Series 2, 29—34. Department of Psychology, The Queen's Univ. of Belfast, 1973, *2*, 29—34.

Barclay, R., Noncategorical perception of a voiced stop. *Perception and Psychophysics*, 1972, *11*, 269—274.

Bell-Berti, F. Control of pharyngeal cavity size for English voiced and voiceless stops. *Journal of the Acoustical Society of America*, 1975, *57*, 456—461.

Berlin, C. I., Lowe-Bell, S. S., Cullen, J. K., Thompson, C. L., and Loovis, C. F. Dichotic speech perception: an interpretation of right-ear advantage and temporal offset effects. *Journal of the Acoustical Society of America*, 1973, *53*, 699—709.

Bever, T. G. The influence of speech performance on linguistic structure. In Flores D'Arcais, G. B., and Levelt, W. J. M. (Eds.) *Advances in psycholinguistics*. Amsterdam: North-Holland, 1970. Pp. 4—30.

Blakemore, C., and Cooper, G. F. Development of the brain depends on visual environment. *Nature*, 1970, *228*, 477—478.

Blumstein, S. The use and theoretical implications of the dichotic technique for investigating distinctive features. *Brain and Language*, 1974, *4*, 337—350.

Boomer, D. S., and Laver, J. D. M. Slips of the tongue. *British Journal of Disorders of Communication*, 1968, *3*, 1—12.

Cairns, H. S., Cairns, C. E., and Williams, F. Some theoretical considerations of articulation substitution phenomena. *Language and Speech*, 1974, *17*, 160—173.

Capranica, R. R. *The evoked vocal response of the bullfrog*. Cambridge, Massachusetts: M.I.T. Press, 1965.

Chomsky, N. *Language and mind*. New York: Harcourt, 1972 (enlarged edition).

Chomsky, N., and Halle, M. *The Sound Pattern of English*. New York: Harper, 1968.

Chomsky, N., and Miller, G. A. Introduction to the formal analysis of natural languages. In R. D. Luce, R. R. Bush, and E. Galanter (Eds.), *Handbook of mathematical psychology*. New York: Wiley, 1963. Pp. 269—321.

Clegg, J. M. Verbal transformations on repeated listening to some English consonants. *British Journal of Psychology*, 1971, *62*, 303—309.

Cole, R. A. Listening for mispronunciations: A measure of what we hear during speech. *Perception and Psychophysics*, 1973, *13*, 153—156.(a)

Cole, R. A. Different memory functions for consonants and vowels. *Cognitive Psychology*, 1973, *4*, 39—54. (b)

Cole, R. A., and Scott, B. Toward a theory of speech perception. *Psychological Review*, 1974, *81*, 348—374.

Cooper, F. S. How is language conveyed by speech? In J. F. Kavanagh and I. G. Mattingly (Eds.), *Language by ear and by eye: The relationships between speech and reading*. Cambridge, Massachusetts: M.I.T. Press, 1972. Pp. 25—45.

Cooper, W. E. Adaptation of phonetic feature analyzers for place of articulation. *Journal of the Acoustical Society of America*, 1974, *56*, 617—627. (a)

Cooper, W. E. Contingent feature analysis in speech perception. *Perception and Psychophysics*, 1974, *16*, 201—204. (b)

Cooper, W. E. Perceptuo-motor adaptation to a speech feature. *Perception and Psychophysics*, 1974, *16*, 229—234. (c)

Cooper, W. E. Selective adaptation for acoustic cues of voicing in initial stops. *Journal of Phonetics*, 1974, *2*, 255—266. (d)

Cooper, W. E. Selective adaptation to speech. In F. Restle, R. M. Shiffrin, J. N. Castellan, H. Lindman, and D. B. Pisoni (Eds.), *Cognitive theory*. Potomac, Maryland: Erlbaum Press, 1975. Pp. 23—54.

Cooper, W. E., and Blumstein, S. E. A *labial* feature analyzer in speech perception. *Perception and Psychophysics*, 1974, *15*, 591—600.

Crowder, R. G. The sound of vowels and consonants in immediate memory. *Journal of Verbal Learning and Verbal Behavior*, 1971, *10*, 587—659. (a)

Crowder, R. G. Waiting for the stimulus suffix: Decay, delay, rhythm and readout in immediate memory. *Quarterly Journal of Experimental Psychology*, 1971, *23*, 324—340. (b)

Crowder, R. G. Visual and auditory memory. In J. F. Kavanagh and I. G. Mattingly (Eds.), *Language by ear and by eye: The relationships between speech and reading*. Cambridge, Massachusetts: M.I.T. Press, 1972. Pp. 251—275.

Crowder, R. G. Precategorical acoustic storage for vowels of short and long duration. *Perception and Psychophysics*, 1973, *13*, 502—506.

Crowder, R. G., and Morton, J. Precategorical acoustic storage (PAS). *Perception and Psychophysics*, 1969, *5*, 365—373.

Cutting, J. E. Levels of processing in phonological fusion. Unpublished doctoral dissertation, Yale Univ., New Haven, Connecticut, 1973. (a)

Cutting, J. E. A parallel between degree of encodedness and the ear advantage: evidence from an ear-monitoring task. *Journal of the Acoustical Society of America*, 1973, *53*, 358 (Abstract). (b)

Cutting, J. E. Two left-hemisphere mechanisms in speech perception. *Perception and Psychophysics*, 1974, *16*, 601—612.

Cutting, J. E. Aspects of phonological fusion. *Journal of Experimental Psychology: Human Perception and Performance*, 1975, *104*, 105—120.

Cutting, J. E., and Eimas, P. D. Phonetic feature analyzers in the processing of speech by infants. In J. F. Kavanagh and J. E. Cutting (Eds.), *The role of speech in language*. Cambridge, Massachusetts; M.I.T. Press, 1975 Pp. 127—148.

Cutting, J. E., and Rosner, B. S. Categories and boundaries in speech and music. *Perception and Psychophysics*, 1974, *16*, 564—570.

Darwin, C. J. Auditory perception and cerebral dominance. Unpublished doctoral dissertation, Univ. of Cambridge, 1969.

Darwin, C. J. Dichotic backward masking of complex sounds. *Quarterly Journal of Experimental Psychology*, 1971, *23*, 386—392. (a)

Darwin, C. J. Ear differences in the recall of fricatives and vowels. *Quarterly Journal of Experimental Psychology*, 1971, *23*, 46—62. (b)

Darwin, C. J., and Baddeley, A. D. Acoustic memory and the perception of speech. *Cognitive Psychology*, 1974, *6*, 41—60.

Day, R. S. Fusion in dichotic listening. Unpublished doctoral dissertation, Stanford Univ., 1968.

Day, R. S. Temporal order judgements in speech: are individuals language-bound or stimulus-bound? *Status Report on Speech Research*, 1970, SR—21/22, 71—75, Haskins Laboratories. (a)

Day, R. S. Temporal order perception of reversible phoneme cluster. *Journal of the Acoustical Society of America*, 1970, *48*, 95 (Abstract). (b)

Day, R. S., and Vigorito, J. M. A parallel between encodedness and the ear advantage: Evidence from a temporal-order judgment task. *Journal of the Acoustical Society of America*, 1973, *53*, 358 (Abstract).

Day, R. S., and Wood, C. C. Mutual interference between two linguistic dimensions of the same stimuli. Paper presented at the Eighty-Third Meeting of the Acoustical Society of America, April 18—21, 1972, Buffalo, New York.

Delattre, P. C., Liberman, A. M., Cooper, F. S., and Gerstman, L. J. An experimental study of the acoustic determinants of vowel color: Observations on one- and two-formant vowels synthesized from spectrographic patterns. *Word*, 1952, *8*, 195—210.

Dorman, M. Discrimination of intensity differences on formant transitions in and out of syllable context. *Perception and Psychophysics*, 1974, *16*, 84—86.

Dorman, M., Kewley-Port, D., Brady-Wood, S., and Turvey, M. T. Forward and backward masking of brief vowels. *Status Report on Speech Research*, 1973, *SR—33*, 93—100, Haskins Laboratories.

Dorman, M., Kewley-Port, D., Brady-Wood, S., and Turvey, M. T. Two processes in vowel perception: Inferences from studies of backward masking. *Status Report on Speech Research*, 1974, *SR—37/38*, 233—253, Haskins Laboratories.

Eimas, P. D. Speech perception in early infancy. In L. B. Cohen and P. Salapatek (Eds.), *Infant perception*. New York: Academic Press, 1975. Pp. 193—231.

Eimas, P. D., Cooper, W. E., and Corbit, J. D. Some properties of linguistic feature detectors. *Perception and Psychophysics*, 1973, *13*, 247—252.

Eimas, P. D., and Corbit, J. D. Selective adaptation of linguistic feature detectors. *Cognitive Psychology*, 1973, *4*, 99—109.

Eimas, P. D., Siqueland, E. R., Jusczyk, P., and Vigorito, J. M. Speech perception in infants. *Science*, 1971, *171*, 303—306.

Evans, E. F., and Whitfield, I. C. Classification of unit responses in the auditory cortex of the unanaesthetized and unrestrained cat. *Journal of Physiology*, 1964, *17*, 476—493.

Fant, C. G. M. *Acoustic theory of speech production*. The Hague: Mouton, 1960.

Fant, C. G. M. Descriptive analysis of the acoustic aspects of speech. *Logos*, 1962, *5*, 3—17.

Fant, C. G. M. A note on vocal tract size factors and non-uniform F-pattern scalings. Speech Transmission Laboratory, Royal Institute of Technology, Stockholm, Sweden, *QPSR—4*, 1966.

Fant, C. G. M. Analysis and synthesis of speech processes. In B. Malmberg (Ed.), *Manual of phonetics*. Amsterdam: North-Holland, 1968. Pp. 173—277.

Fischer-Jørgensen, E. Perceptual studies of Danish stop consonants. *Annual Report No. 6*, Institute of Phonetics, Univ. of Copenhagen, 1972, 75—176.

Flanagan, J. L. *Speech analysis, synthesis and perception*. (2nd ed.) New York: Academic Press, 1972.

Fodor, J. A., Bever, T. G., and Garrett, M. F. *The psychology of language*. New York: McGraw Hill, 1974.

Foss, D. J., and Swinney, D. A. On the psychological reality of the phoneme: Perception, identification and consciousness. *Journal of Verbal Learning and Verbal Behavior*, 1973, *12*, 246—257.

Fourcin, A. J. Speech source inference. *IEEE Transactions on Audio and Electroacoustics*, 1968, *AU—16*, 65—67.

Fourcin, A. J. Perceptual mechanisms at the first level of speech processing. In Rigaut, A., and Charbonneau, R. (Eds.), *Proceedings of the 7th International Congress of Phonetic Sciences*. The Hague: Mouton, 1972. Pp. 48—62.

Frishkopf, L., and Goldstein, M. Responses to acoustic stimuli in the eight nerve of the bullfrog. *Journal of the Acoustical Society of America*, 1963, *35*, 1219—1228.

Fromkin, V. A. The nonanomalous nature of anomalous utterances. *Language*, 1971, *47*, 27—52.

Fromkin, V. A., Krashen, S., Curtiss, S., Rigler, D., and Rigler, M. The development of language in Genie: a case of language acquisition beyond the *Critical Period*. *Brain and Language*, 1974, *1*, 81—107.

Fujimura, O., and Ochiai, K. Vowel identification and phonetic contexts. *Journal of the Acoustical Society of America*, 1963, *35*, 1889 (Abstract).

Fujisaki, H., and Kawashima, T. On the modes and mechanisms of speech perception. *Annual Report of the Engineering Research Institute*, Univ. of Tokyo, 1969, *28*, 67—73.

Fujisaki, H., and Kawashima, T. Some experiments on speech perception and a model for the perceptual mechanism. *Annual Report of the Engineering Research Institute*, Univ. of Tokyo, 1970, *29*, 207—214.

Fujisaki, H., and Nakamura, N. Normalization and recognition of vowels. *Annual Report*, Division of Electrical Engineering, Engineering Research Institute, Univ. of Tokyo, 1969, No. *1*.

Gerstman, L. J. Perceptual dimensions for the friction portion of certain speech sounds. Unpublished doctoral dissertation, New York Univ., 1957.

Gerstman, L. J. Classification of self-normalized vowels. *I.E.E.E. Transactions on Audio and Electroacoustics*, 1968, *AU—16*, 78—80.

Geschwind, N., and Levitsky, W. Human brain: Left-right asymmetries in temporal speech region. *Science*, 1968, *161*, 186—187.

Glanzman, D. L., and Pisoni, D. B. Decision processes in speech discrimination as revealed by confidence ratings. Paper presented at the Eighty-Fifth meeting of the Acoustical Society of America, April 10—13, 1973, Boston, Massachusetts.

Godfrey, J. J. Perceptual difficulty and the right-ear advantage for vowels. *Brain and Language*, 1974, *4*, 323—336.

Goldstein, L. M., and Lackner, J. R. Alterations of the phonetic coding of speech sounds during repetition. *Cognition*, 1973, *2*, 279—297.

Greenberg, J. J., and Jenkins, J. J. Studies in the psychological correlates of the sound system of American English. *Word*, 1964, *20*, 157—177.

Haber, R. N. (Ed.) *Information-processing approaches to visual perception.* New York: Holt, 1969.

Hadding-Koch, K., and Studdert-Kennedy, M. An experimental study of some intonation contours. *Phonetica*, 1964, *11*, 175—185.

Haggard, M. Encoding and the REA for speech signals. *Quarterly Journal of Experimental Psychology*, 1971, *23*, 34—45.

Haggard, M. P., Ambler, S., and Callow, M. Pitch as a voicing cue. *Journal of the Acoustical Society of America*, 1970, *47*, 613—617.

Halperin, Y., Nachshon, I., and Carmon, A. Shift of ear superiority in dichotic listening to temporally patterned nonverbal stimuli. *Journal of the Acoustical Society of America*, 1973, *53*, 46—50.

Hwales, T. Effects of dichotic fusion on the perception of speech. Unpublished doctoral dissertation, Univ. of Minnesota, 1969.

Halwes, T., and Jenkins, J. J. Problem of serial order in behavior is not resolved by context-sensitive associative memory models. *Psychological Review*, 1971, *78*, 122—129.

Hanson, G. Dimensions in speech sound perception: An experimental study of vowel perception. *Ericsson Technics*, 1967, *23*, 3—175.

Harris, K. S. Cues for the discrimination of American English fricatives in spoken syllables. *Language and Speech*, 1958, *1*, 1—17.

Harris, K. S., Hoffman, H. S., Liberman, A. M., Delattre, P. C., and Cooper, F. S. Effect of third-formant transitions on the perception of the voiced stop consonants. *Journal of the Acoustical Society of America*, 1958, *30*, 122—126.

Hirsch, H. V. B., and Spinelli, D. N. Visual experience modifies distribution of horizontally and vertically oriented receptive fields in cat. *Science*, 1970, *168*, 869—871.

Hoffman, H. S. Study of some cues in the perception of the voiced stop consonants. *Journal of the Acoustical Society of America*, 1958, *30*, 1035—1041.

House, A. S., Stevens, K. N., Sandel, T. T., and Arnold, J. B. On the learning of speech-like vocabularies. *Journal of Verbal Learning and Verbal Behavior*, 1962, *1*, 133—143.

Hubel, D. H., and Wiesel, T. N. Receptive fields, binocular interaction and functional architecture in the cat's visual cortex. *Journal of Physiology*, 1962, *60*, 106—154.

Jakobson, R., Fant, C. G. M., and Halle, M. *Preliminaries to speech analysis.* Cambridge, Massachusetts: M.I.T. Press, 1963.

Jakobson, R., and Halle, M. *Fundamentals of language.* The Hague: Mouton, 1956.

Jones, D. *Differences between spoken and written language.* London: Association Phonétique Internationale, 1948.

Joos, M. A. Acoustic phonetics. *Language,* Suppl., 1948, *24*, 1—136.

Julesz, B. *Foundations of Cyclopean perception.* Chicago: Univ. of Chicago Press, 1971.

Kewley-Port, D., and Preston, M. S. Early apical stop production: A voice onset time analysis. *Journal of Phonetics*, 1974, *3*, 195—210.

Kimura, D. Some effects of temporal lobe damage on auditory perception. *Canadian Journal of Psychology*, 1961, *15*, 156—165. (a)

Kimura, D. Cerebral dominance and the perception of verbal stimuli. *Canadian Journal of Psychology*, 1961, *15*, 166—171. (b)

Kimura, D. Functional asymmetry of the brain in dichotic listening. *Cortex*, 1967, *3*, 163—178.

Kimura, D., and Durnford, M. Normal studies on the function of the right hemisphere in vision. In

S. J. Dimond, and J. G. Beamont (Eds.), *Hemisphere function in the human brain.* London: Paul Elek (Scientific Books), 1974. Pp. 25—47.

Kirman, J. H. Tactile communication of speech: A review and an analysis. *Psychological Bulletin,* 1973, *80,* 54—74.

Kirstein, E. Temporal factors in perception of dichotically presented stop consonants and vowels. Unpublished doctoral dissertation, Univ. of Connecticut, 1971.

Kirstein, E. The lag effect in dichotic speech perception. *Status Report on Speech Research,* 1973, *SR—35/36,* 81—106, Haskins Laboratories.

Klatt, D. H., and Shattuck, S. R. Perception of brief stimuli that resemble formant transitions. Paper presented at the Eighty-Sixth meeting of the Acoustical Society of America, October 30—November 2, 1973, Los Angeles, California.

Köhler, W., and Wallach, H. Figural after-effects: An investigation of visual processes. *Proceedings of the American Philosophical Society,* 1944, *88,* 269—357.

Konishi, M., The role of auditory feedback in the control of vocalization in the white-crowned sparrow. *Zeitschrift für Tierpsychologie,* 1965, *22,* 770—783.

Kozhevnikov, V. A., and Chistovich, L. A. *Rech' Artikuliatsia i vospriiatie.* Moscow-Leningrad. Transl. as *Speech: Articulation and perception.* Washington: Clearinghouse for Federal Scientific and Technical Information, J.P.R.S., 1965, 30.

Krashen, S. Language and the left hemisphere. *Working Papers in Phonetics,* UCLA Phonetics Laboratory, 1972, *24* (whole volume).

Lackner, J. R., and Goldstein, L. M. The psychological representation of speech sounds. *Quarterly Journal of Experimental Psychology,* 1975, *27,* 173—185.

Ladefoged, P. *Three areas of experimental phonetics.* New York: Oxford Univ. Press, 1967.

Ladefoged, P. *Preliminaries to linguistic phonetics.* Chicago: Univ. of Chicago Press, 1971.(a)

Ladefoged, P. Phonological features and their phonetic correlates. *Working Papers in Phonetics,* Univ. of California at Los Angeles, 1971, *21,* 3—12.(b)

Ladefoged, P., and Broadbent, D. E. Information conveyed by vowels. *Journal of the Acoustical Society of America,* 1957, *29,* 98—104.

Ladefoged, P., DeClerk, J., Lindau, M., and Papçun, G. An auditory-motor theory of speech production. *Working Papers in Phonetics,* Univ. of California at Los Angeles, 1972, *22,* 48—75.

Lane, H. L. The motor theory of speech perception: a critical review. *Psychological Review,* 1965, *72,* 275—309.

Lashley, K. S. The problem of serial order in behavior. In L. A. Jeffress, (Ed.), *Cerebral mechanisms in behavior.* New York: Wiley, 1951. Pp. 112—136.

Lass, N. J., and Gasperini, R. M. The verbal transformation effect: A comparative study of the verbal transformations of phonetically trained and nonphonetically trained subjects. *British Journal of Psychology,* 1973, *64,* 183—192.

Lass, N. J., and Golden, S. S. The use of isolated vowels as auditory stimuli in eliciting the verbal transformation effect. *Canadian Journal of Psychology,* 1971, *25,* 349—359.

Lass, N. J., West, L. K., and Taft, D. D. A non-verbal analogue to the verbal transformation effect. *Canadian Journal of Psychology,* 1973, *27,* 272—279.

Lea, W. A. An algorithm for locating stressed syllables in continuous speech. *Journal of the Acoustical Society of America,* 1974, *55,* 411 (Abstract).

Lenneberg, E. H. *The biological foundations of language.* New York: Wiley, 1967.

Lettvin, J. Y., Maturana, H. R., McCulloch, W. S., and Pitts, W. H. What the frog's eye tells the brain. *Proceedings of the Institute of Radio Engineers,* 1959, *47,* 1940—1951.

Liberman, A. M. Some results of research on speech perception. *Journal of the Acoustical Society of America,* 1957, *29,* 117—123.

Liberman, A. M. The grammars of speech and language. *Cognitive Psychology,* 1970, *1,* 301—323.

Liberman, A. M., Cooper, F. S., Shankweiler, D. S., and Studdert-Kennedy, M. Perception of the speech code. *Psychological Review,* 1967, *74,* 431—461.

Liberman, A. M., Delattre, P. C., and Cooper, F. S. The role of selected stimulus variables in the perception of the unvoiced stop consonants. *American Journal of Psychology,* 1952, *65,* 497—516.

Liberman, A. M., Delattre, P. C., and Cooper, F. S. Some cues for the distinction between voiced and voiceless stops. *Language and Speech*, 1958, *1*, 153—167.

Liberman, A. M., Delattre, P. C., Cooper, F. S., and Gerstman, L. H. The role of consonant-vowel transitions in the perception of the stop and nasal consonants. *Psychological Monographs*, 1954, *68*, 1—13.

Liberman, A. M., Harris, K. S., Kinney, J., and Lane, H. The discrimination of relative onset time of the components of certain speech and nonspeech patterns. *Journal of Experimental Psychology*, 1961, *61*, 379—388.

Liberman, A. M., Mattingly, I. G., and Turvey, M. T. Language codes and memory codes. In A. W. Melton, and E. Martin, (Eds.), *Coding processes in human memory*. New York: Wiley, 1972. Pp. 307—334.

Licklider, J. C. R., and Miller, G. A. The perception of speech. In S. S. Stevens (Ed.), *Handbook of experimental psychology*. New York: Wiley, 1951. Pp. 1040—1074.

Lieberman, P. Some effects of semantic and grammatical context on the production and perception of speech. *Language and Speech*, 1963, *6*, 172—179.

Lieberman, P. Primate vocalizations and human linguistic ability. *Journal of the Acoustical Society of America*, 1968, *44*, 1574—1584.

Lieberman, P. Toward a unified phonetic theory. *Linguistic Inquiry*, 1970, *1*, 307—322.

Lieberman, P. *The speech of primates*. The Hague: Mouton, 1972.

Lieberman, P. On the evolution of language: A unified view. *Cognition*, 1973, *2*, 59—94.

Lieberman, P., and Crelin, E. S. On the speech of Neanderthal man. *Linguistic Inquiry*, 1971, *2*, 203—222.

Lieberman, P., Crelin, E. S., and Klatt, D. H. Phonetic ability and related anatomy of the newborn, adult human, Neanderthal man and the chimpanzee. *American Anthropology*, 1972, *74*, 287—307.

Lieberman, P., Harris, K. S., Wolff, P., and Russel, L. H. Newborn infant cry and nonhuman primate vocalizations. *Journal of Speech and Hearing Research*, 1971, *14*, 718—727.

Liljencrants, J., and Lindblom, B., Numerical simulation of vowel quality systems: the role of perceptual contrast. *Language*, 1972, *48*, 839—862.

Lindblom, B. E. F. Spectrographic study of vowel reduction. *Journal of the Acoustical Society of America*, 1963, *35*, 1773—1781.

Lindblom, B. E. F. Phonetics and the description of language. In A. Rigault and R. Charbonneau (Eds.), *Proceedings of the Seventh International Congress of Phonetic Sciences*. The Hague: Mouton, 1972. Pp. 63—97.

Lindblom, B. E. F., and Studdert-Kennedy, M. On the role of formant transitions in vowel recognition. *Journal of the Acoustical Society of America*, 1967, *42*, 830—843.

Lindblom, B. E. F., and Sundberg, J. Neurophysiological representation of speech sounds. Paper presented at the XVth World Congress of Logopedics and Phoniatrics, Buenos Aires, Argentina, August 14th—19th, 1971.

Lisker, L., and Abramson, A. S. A cross-language study of voicing in initial stops: acoustical measurements. *Word*, 1964, *20*, 384—422.

Lisker, L., and Abramson, A. S. Some effects of context on voice onset time in English stops. *Language and Speech*, 1967, *10*, 1—28.

Lisker, L., and Abramson, A. S., The voicing dimension: some experiments in comparative phonetics. In *Proceedings of the Sixth International Congress of Phonetic Sciences*. Prague: Academia, 1970. Pp. 563—567.

Lisker, L., and Abramson, A. S. Distinctive features and laryngeal control. *Language*, 1971, *47*, 767—785.

Locke, S., and Kellar, L. Categorical perception in a nonlinguistic mode. *Cortex*, 1973, *9*, 355—369.

Lotz, J., Abramson, A. S., Gerstman, L. H., Ingemann, F., and Nemser, W. J. The perception of English stops by speakers of English, Spanish, Hungarian and Thai: A tape-cutting experiment. *Language and Speech*, 1960, *3*, 71—77.

MacKay, D. G. Spoonerisms: The anatomy of errors in the serial order of speech. *Neuropsychologia*, 1970, *8*, 323—350.

MacNeilage, P. F. Motor control of serial ordering of speech. *Psychological Review*, 1970, 77, 182—196.

MacNeilage, P. F., Rootes, T. P., and Chase, R. A. Speech production and perception in a patient with severe impairment of somesthetic perception and motor control. *Journal of Speech and Hearing Research*, 1967, 10, 449—467.

Malmberg, B. The phonetic basis for syllable division. *Studia Linguistica*, 1955, 9, 80—87.

Marler, P. Bird song and speech development: Could there be parallels? *American Scientist*, 1970, 58, 669—673.

Marler, P. On the origin of speech from animal sounds. In J. F. Kavanagh, and J. E. Cutting (Eds.), *The role of speech in language*. Cambridge, Massachusetts: M.I.T. Press, 1975. Pp. 12—37.

Marler, P., and Mundinger, P. Vocal learning in birds. In H. Moltz (Ed.), *Ontogeny of vertebrate behavior*. New York: Academic Press, 1971. Pp. 380—450.

Marvilya, M. P. Spontaneous vocalization and babbling in hearing-impaired infants. In C. G. M. Fant (Ed.), *Speech communication ability and profound deafness*. Washington, D.C.: A. G. Bell Association for the Deaf, 1972.

Massaro, D. W. Preperceptual images, processing time, and perceptual units in auditory perception. *Psychological Review*, 1972, 79, 124—145.

Mattingly, I. G. Synthesis by rule of General American English. Supplement to *Status Report on Speech Research*, April, 1968, Haskins Laboratories.

Mattingly, I. G. Synthesis by rule as a tool for phonological research. *Language and Speech*, 1971, 14, 47—56.

Mattingly, I. G., Speech cues and sign stimuli. *American Scientist*, 1972, 60, 327—337.

Mattingly, I. G. Phonetic prerequisites for first-language acquisition. *Status Report on Speech Research*, 1973, SR—34, 65—69, Haskins Laboratories.

Mattingly, I. G. Speech synthesis for phonetic and phonological models. In T. A. Sebeok (Ed.), *Current trends in linguistics*, Vol. 12. The Hague: Mouton, 1974.

Mattingly, I. G. The human aspects of speech. In J. F. Kavanagh, and J. E. Cutting (Eds.), *The role of speech in language*. Cambridge, Massachusetts: M.I.T. Press, 1975. Pp. 63—72.

Mattingly, I. G., and Liberman, A. M. The speech code and the physiology of language. In K. N. Leibovic (Ed.), *Information processing in the nervous system*. New York: Springer Verlag, 1969. Pp. 97—114.

Mattingly, I. G., Liberman, A. M., Syrdal, A. K., and Halwes, T. Discrimination in speech and nonspeech modes. *Cognitive Psychology*, 1971, 2, 131—157.

McNeill, D., and Lindig, L. The perceptual reality of phonemes, syllables, words and sentences. *Journal of Verbal Learning and Verbal Behavior*, 1973, 12, 419—430.

McNeill, D., and Repp, B. Internal processes in speech perception. *Journal of the Acoustical Society of America*, 1973, 53, 1320—1326.

Miller, G. A. The magical number seven plus or minus two, or, some limits on our capacity for processing information. *Psychological Review*, 1956, 63, 81—96.

Miller, G. A., Heise, G. A., and Lichten, W. The intelligibility of speech as a function of the context of the test materials. *Journal of the Acoustical Society of America*, 1951, 41, 329—335.

Miller, G. A., and Nicely, P. An analysis of perceptual confusions among some English consonants. *Journal of the Acoustical Society of America*, 1955, 27, 338—352.

Miller, J. D., Pastore, R. E., Wier, C. C., Kelly, W. J., and Dooling, R. J. Discrimination and labeling of noise-buzz sequences with varying noise-lead times. *Journal of the Acoustical Society of America*, 1974, 55, 390 (Abstract).

Miller, J. N. Sutton, D., Pfingst, B., Ryan, A., and Beaton, R. Single cell activity in the auditory cortex of rhesus monkeys: behavioral dependency. *Science*, 1972, 177, 449—451.

Mitchell, P. D. A test of differentiation of phonemic feature contrasts. Unpublished doctoral dissertation, City Univ. of New York, 1973.

Moffitt, A. R., Consonant cue perception by twenty- to twenty-four-week old infants. *Child Development*, 1971, 42, 717—731.

Molfese, D. L., Cerebral asymmetry in infants, children and adults: Auditory evoked responses to speech and noise stimuli. Unpublished doctoral dissertation, Pennsylvania State Univ., 1972.

Morse, P. A., The discrimination of speech and nonspeech stimuli in early infancy. *Journal of Experimental Child Psychology*, 1972, *14*, 477–492.

Neisser, U. *Cognitive psychology*. New York: Appelton, 1967.

Nelson, P. G., Erulkar, S. D., and Bryan, S. S. Response units of the inferior colliculus to time-varying acoustic stimuli. *Journal of Neurophysiology*, 1966, *29*, 834–860.

Nottebohm, F. Neural lateralization of vocal control in a passerine bird. I. Song. *Journal of Experimental Zoology*, 1971, *177*, 229–262.

Nottebohm, F. Neural lateralization of vocal control in a passerine bird. II. Subsong, calls and theory of vocal learning. *Journal of Experimental Zoology*, 1972, *179*, 35–50.

Obusek, C. J., and Warren, R. M. A comparison of speech perception in senile and well-preserved aged by means of the verbal transformation effect. *Journal of Gerontology*, 1973, *28*, 184–188.

Öhman, S. E. G. Coarticulation in VCV utterances: spectrographic measurements. *Journal of the Acoustical Society of America*, 1966, *39*, 151–168.

Öhman, S. E. G. Numerical model of coarticulation. *Journal of the Acoustical Society of America*, 1967, *41*, 310–320.

Papçun, G., Krashen, S., Terbeek, D., Remington, R., and Harshman, R. Is the left hemisphere specialized for speech, language and/or something else? *Journal of the Acoustical Society of America*, 1974, *55*, 319–327.

Parks, T., Wall, C., and Bastian, J. Intercategory and intracategory discrimination for one visual continuum. *Journal of Experimental Psychology*, 1969, *81*, 241–245.

Perl, N. T. The application of the verbal transformation effect to the study of cerebral dominance. *Neuropsychologia*, 1970, *8*, 259–261.

Peterson, G. E. Parameters of vowel quality. *Journal of Speech and Hearing Research*, 1961, *4*, 10–29.

Peterson, G. E., and Barney, H. L. Control methods used in a study of vowels. *Journal of the Acoustical Society of America*, 1952, 25, 175–184.

Pettigrew, J. D., and Freeman, R. D. Visual experience without lines: effect on development of cortical neurons. *Science*, 1973, *182*, 599–601.

Pisoni, D. B. On the nature of categorical perception of speech sounds. Unpublished doctoral dissertation, Univ. of Michigan, 1971.

Pisoni, D. B. Perceptual processing time for consonants and vowels. *Status Report on Speech Research*, 1972, *SR–31/32*, 83–92, Haskins Laboratories.

Pisoni, D. B. Auditory and phonetic memory codes in the discrimination of consonants and vowels. *Perception and Psychophysics*, 1973, *13*, 253–260.(a)

Pisoni, D. B. The role of auditory short-term memory in vowel perception. *Status Report on Speech Research*, 1973, *SR–34*, 89–118, Haskins Laboratories.(b)

Pisoni, D. B. Dichotic listening and the processing of phonetic features. In F. Restle, R. M. Shiffrin, N. J. Castellan, H. Lindam, and D. B. Pisoni (Eds.), *Cognitive theory*, Vol. I. Potomac, Maryland: Erlbaum Associates, 1975.

Pisoni, D. B., and Lazarus, J. H. Categorical and noncategorical modes of speech perception along the voicing continuum. *Journal of the Acoustical Society of America*, 1974, *55*, 328–333.

Pisoni, D. B., and McNabb, S. D. On dichotic interactions of speech sounds and the processing of phonetic features. *Brain and Language*, 1974, *4*, 351–362.

Pisoni, D. B., and Sawusch, J. R. Category boundaries for speech and non-speech sounds. *Research on Speech Perception, Progress Report No. 1*, Indiana University, Bloomington, Indiana, 1974, 162–173.

Pisoni, D. B., and Tash, J. Reaction times to comparisons within and across phonetic categories. *Perception and Psychophysics*, 1974, *15*, 285–290.

Pollack, I., and Pickett, J. M., The intelligibility of excerpts from conversation. *Language and Speech*, 1963, *6*, 165–172.

Popper, R. D. Pair discrimination for a continuum of synthetic voiced stops with and without first and third formants. *Journal of Psycholinguistic Research*, 1972, *1*, 205–219.

Porter, R. J., The effect of delayed channel on the perception of dichotically presented speech and nonspeech sounds. Unpublished doctoral dissertation, Univ. of Connecticut, 1971.

Posner, M. I., Boies, S. J., Eichelman, W. H., and Taylor, R. L. Retention of visual and name codes of single letters. *Journal of Experimental Psychology Monograph*, 1969, *79*, 1—16.

Potter, R. K., Kopp, G. A., and Green, H. C. *Visible speech*. Princeton, New Jersey: Van Nostrand-Reinhold, 1947.

Rand, T. C. Vocal tract size normalization in the perception of stop consonants. *Status Report on Speech Research*, 1971, *SR—25/26*, 141—146, Haskins Laboratories.

Raphael, L. J. Preceding vowel duration as a cue to the perception of the voicing characteristic of word-final consonants in American English. *Journal of the Acoustical Society of America*, 1972, *51*, 1296—1303.

Reed, S. K. *Psychological processes in pattern recognition*. New York: Academic Press, 1973.

Repp, B. H. Dichotic forward and backward masking of CV syllables. Unpublished doctoral dissertation, Univ. of Chicago, 1973.

Rosch, E. H. Natural categories. *Cognitive Psychology*, 1973, *4*, 328—350.

Sachs, R. M. Vowel identification and discrimination in isolation vs. word context. *Quarterly Progress Report*, Research Laboratory of Electronics, M.I.T., Cambridge, Massachusetts, 1969, No. *93*, 220—229.

Sales, B. D., Cole, R. A., and Haber, R. N. Mechanisms of aural encoding: V. Environmental effects of consonants on vowel encoding. *Perception and Psychophysics*, 1969, *6*, 361—365.

Savin, H. B., and Bever, T. G. The nonperceptual reality of the phoneme. *Journal of Verbal Learning and Verbal Behavior*, 1970, *9*, 295—302.

Schatz, C. The role of context in the perception of stops. *Language*, 1954, *30*, 47—56.

Scholes, R. J. Phonemic interference as a perceptual phenomenon. *Language and Speech*, 1968, *11*, 86—103.

Semmes, J. Hemispheric specialization: A possible clue to mechanism. *Neuropsychologia*, 1968, *5*, 11—26.

Shankweiler, D. P., Strange, W., and Verbrugge, R. Speech and the problem of perceptual constancy. In R. Shaw, and J. Bransford, (Eds.), *Perceiving, acting and comprehending: Toward an ecological psychology*. Potomac, Maryland: Erlbaum Associates, 1976.

Shankweiler, D. P., and Studdert-Kennedy, M. Identification of consonants and vowels presented to left and right ears. *Quarterly Journal of Experimental Psychology*, 1967, *19*, 59—63.

Shearme, J. N., and Holmes, J. N. An experimental study of the classification of sounds in continuous speech according to their distribution in the formant 1-formant 2 plane. In A. Sovijärvi, and P. Aalto, (Eds.), *Proceedings of the Fourth International Congress of Phonetic Sciences*. The Hague Mouton, 1962.

Shepard, R. N. Psychological representation of speech sounds. In E. E. David, and P. B. Denes, (Eds.), *Human communication: A unified view*. New York: McGraw-Hill, 1972. Pp. 67—113.

Singh, S. Cross language study of perceptual confusion of plosive phonemes in two conditions of distortion. *Journal of the Acoustical Society of America*, 1966, *40*, 635—656.

Singh, S., and Woods, D. Multidimensional scaling of 12 American English vowels. *Journal of the Acoustical Society of America*, 1970, *48*, 104 (Abstract).

Sinnott, J. M. A comparison of speech sound discrimination in humans and monkeys. Unpublished doctoral dissertation, Univ. of Michigan, 1974.

Stetson, R. H. *Motor phonetics*. Amsterdam: North-Holland, 1952.

Stevens, K. N. Toward a model for speech recognition. *Journal of the Acoustical Society of America*, 1960, *32*, 47—55.

Stevens, K. N. Acoustic correlates of certain consonantal features. Paper presented at Conference on Speech Communication and Processing, M.I.T., November 6—8, 1967, Cambridge, Massachusetts.

Stevens, K. N. Acoustic correlates of place of articulation for stop and frictive consonants. *Quarterly Progress Report*, Research Laboratory of Electronics, M.I.T., 1968, 199—205. (a)

Stevens, K. N. On the relations between speech movements and speech perception. *Zeitschrift für Phonetik, Sprachwissenschaft und Kommunikations Forschung*, 1968, *213*, 102—106. (b)

Stevens, K. N. Segments, features and analysis by synthesis. In J. F. Kavanagh, and I. G. Mattingly, (Eds.), *Language by ear and by eye: The relationships between speech and reading*. Cambridge, Massachusetts: M.I.T. Press, 1972, 47—52. (a)

Stevens, K. N. The quantal nature of speech: evidence from articulatory-acoustic data. In E. E. David, and P. B. Denes, (Eds.), *Human communication: A unified view*. New York: McGraw Hill, 1972. Pp. 51—66. (b)

Stevens, K. N. Potential role of property detectors in the perception of consonants. *Quarterly Progress Report*, Research Laboratory of Electronics, M.I.T., 1973, No. *110*, 155—168.

Stevens, K. N., and Halle, M. Remarks on analysis by synthesis and distinctive features. In W. Wathen-Dunn, (Ed.), *Models for the perception of speech and visual form*. Cambridge, Massachusetts: M.I.T. Press, 1967. 88—102.

Stevens, K. N., and House, A. S. The perception of speech. In J. Tobias, (Ed.), *Foundations of modern auditory theory*, Vol. 2. New York: Academic Press, 1972. Pp. 3—62.

Stevens, K. N., House, A. S., and Paul, A. P. Acoustical description of syllabic nuclei: An interpretation in terms of a dynamic model of articulation. *Journal of the Acoustical Society of America*, 1966, *4*, 123—132.

Stevens, K. N., and Klatt, D. H. Role of formant transitions in the voiced-voiceless distinction for stops. *Journal of the Acoustical Society of America*, 1974, *55*, 653—659.

Stevens, K. N., Liberman, A. M., Studdert-Kennedy, M., and Öhman, S. E. G. Cross-language study of vowel perception. *Language and Speech*, 1969, *12*, 1—23.

Strange, W., Verbrugge, R., and Shankweiler, D. P. Consonantal environment specifies vowel identity. Paper presented at the Eighty-Seventh Meeting of the Acoustical Society of America, April 23—26, 1974, New York City.

Studdert-Kennedy, M. The perception of speech. In T. A. Sebeok, (Ed.), *Current trends in linguistics* (Vol. XII). The Hauge: Mouton, 1974. Pp. 2349—2385.

Studdert-Kennedy, M. From continuous signal to discrete message: syllable to phoneme. In J. F. Kavanagh, and J. E. Cutting, (Eds.), *The role of speech in language*. Cambridge, Massachusetts: M.I.T. Press, 1975. Pp. 113—125.

Studdert-Kennedy, M., and Hadding, K. Auditory and linguistic processes in the perception of intonation contours. *Language and Speech*, 1973, *16*, 293—313.

Studdert-Kennedy, M., Liberman, A. M., Harris, K. S., and Cooper, F. S. Motor theory of speech perception: A reply to Lane's critical review. *Psychological Review*, 1970, *77*, 234—249. (a)

Studdert-Kennedy, M., and Shankweiler, D. P. Hemispheric specialization for speech perception. *Journal of the Acoustical Society of America*, 1970, *48*, 579—594.

Studdert-Kennedy, M., Shankweiler, D. P., and Pisoni, D. B. Auditory and phonetic processes in speech perception: evidence from a dichotic study. *Cognitive Psychology*, 1972, *2*, 455—466.

Studdert-Kennedy, M., Shankweiler, D. P., and Schulman, S. Opposed effects of a delayed channel on perception of dichotically and monotically presented CV syllables. *Journal of the Acoustical Society of America*, 1970, *48*, 599—602. (b)

Summerfield, A., and Haggard, M. Perception of stop voicing. *Speech Perception*, Department of Psychology, The Queen's Univ. of Belfast, 1972, *2*, 1—14.

Summerfield, A., and Haggard, M. Vocal tract normalization as demonstrated by reaction times. *Speech Perception*, Department of Psychology, The Queen's Univ. of Belfast, 1973, *2*, 1—12.

Sussman, H. The laterality effect in lingual-auditory tracking. *Journal of the Acoustical Society of America*, 1971, *49*, 1874—1880.

Sussman, H. M., and MacNeilage, P. F. Studies of hemispheric specialization for speech production. *Brain and Language*, 1975, *2*, 131—151.

Sussman, H. M., MacNeilage, P. F., and Lumbley, J. Sensorimotor dominance and the right ear advantage in mandibular-auditory tracking. *Journal of the Acoustical Society of America*, 1974, *56*, 214—216.

Tekieli, M. E., and Lass, N. J. The verbal transformation effect: Consistency of subjects' reported verbal transformations. *Journal of General Psychology*, 1972, *86*, 231—245.

Treon, M. A. Fricative and plosive perception-identification as a function of phonetic context in CVCVC utterances. *Language and Speech*, 1970, *13*, 54—64.

Turvey, M. On peripheral and central processes in vision. *Psychological Review*, 1973, *80*, 1—52.

Verbrugge, R., Strange, W., and Shankweiler, D. P. What information enables a listener to map a talker's vowel space? Paper presented at the Eighty-Seventh Meeting of the Acoustical Society of America, April 23—26, 1974, New York City.

Vitz, P. C., and Winkler, B. S. Predicting the judged *similarity of sound* of English words. *Journal of Verbal Learning and Verbal Behavior*, 1973, *12*, 373—388.

Warren, R. M. Verbal transformation effect and auditory perceptual mechanisms. *Psychological Bulletin*, 1968, *70*, 261—270.

Warren, R. M. Perceptual restoration of missing speech sounds. *Science*, 1970, *167*, 392—393.

Warren, R. M. Identification times for phonemic components of graded complexity and for spelling of speech. *Perception and Psychophysics*, 1971, *9*, 345—349.

Warren, R. M., and Gregory, R. L. An auditory analogue of the visual reversible figure. *American Journal of Psychology*, 1958, *71*, 612—613.

Warren, R. M., and Obusek, C. J. Speech perception and phonemic restorations. *Perception and Psychophysics*, 1971, *9*, 358—362.

Weiss, M. S., and House, A. S. Perception of dichotically presented vowels. *Journal of the Acoustical Society of America*, 1973, *53*, 51—58.

Werner, H. Studies on contour: I. Qualitative analyses. *American Journal of Psychology*, 1935, *47*, 40—64.

Whitfield, I. C., and Evans, E. F. Responses of auditory cortical neurons to stimuli of changing frequency. *Journal of Neurophysiology*, 1965, *28*, 655—672.

Wickelgren, W. A. Distinctive features and errors in short-term memory for English vowels. *Journal of the Acoustical Society of America*, 1965, *38*, 583—588.

Wickelgren, W. A. Distinctive features and errors in short-term memory for English consonants. *Journal of the Acoustical Society of America*, 1966, *39*, 388—398.

Wickelgren, W. A. Context-sensitive coding, associative memory and serial order in (speech) behavior. *Psychological Review*, 1969, *76*, 1—15.

Wollberg, Z., and Newman, J. D. Auditory cortex of squirrel monkey: Response patterns of single cells to species-specific vocalizations. *Science*, 1972, *175*, 212—213.

Wood, C. C. Parallel processing of auditory and phonetic information in speech perception. *Perception and Psychophysics*, 1974, *15*, 501—508.

Wood, C. C. Auditory and phonetic levels of processing in speech perception: neurophysiological and information-processing analyses. *Journal of Experimental Psychology: Human Perception and Performance*, 1975, *104*, 1—33.

Wood, C. C., and Day, R. S. Failure of selective attention to phonetic segments in consonant-vowel syllables. *Perception and Psychophysics*, 1975, *17*, 346—350.

Wood, C. C., Goff, W. R., and Day, R. S. Auditory evoked potentials during speech perception. *Science*, 1971, *173*, 1248—1251.

Woodworth, R. S., and Schlosberg, H. *Experimental psychology*. New York: Holt, 1954.

Zlatin, M. A. Development of the voicing contrast: A psychoacoustic study of voice onset time. *Journal of the Acoustical Society of America*, 1974.

chapter 9

Speaker Recognition

Peter D. Bricker   Sandra Pruzansky

Bell Laboratories, Murray Hill, New Jersey

Introduction

The human listener's ability to recognize speakers by voice alone is manifest in a variety of everyday situations. An old friend telephones you unexpectedly and you know who it is before he declares himself. After watching a TV talk show for a few minutes, you know which panel member is speaking before the camera picks her up. You know that the voice behind you in the crowded elevator is unfamiliar, but you develop a clear notion of the age and sex of the speaker and some indication about the region of the country where the speaker was born. Despite some important differences among these situations, in each of them the listener gains from a speech signal some nonlinguistic information that enables him to distinguish the speaker from at least some other potential speakers. In this chapter, we review some research that sheds light on how the listener performs this feat.

Researchers in the field of speaker recognition have been studying the laboratory analogs of the above life situations and related tasks for about 40 years. Much of this work has recently been reviewed by Hecker (1971), who distinguished three methods of recognizing talkers: by listening, by machine, and by visual inspection of spectrograms. Whereas Hecker treated these three methods as coordinate-level topics, we focus our attention on speaker recognition by listening (*SRL*) and subordinate the other two. We are in basic agreement with Hecker's definition of speaker recognition as "any decision-making process that uses the speaker-dependent features of the speech signal" (Hecker, 1971, p. 2). This definition implies a perceptual process of extracting the speaker-dependent information from the speech signal in the case of recognition by listening. It is this process that makes speaker recognition a topic of interest to students of speech perception.

In the remainder of this introductory section, we deal with two background topics. The first is a history of the major sources of support for speaker recognition research. We feel that knowledge of the extrinsic motivations of researchers fosters an understanding of why they pursued some topics and not others. The second topic is a conceptual framework, not elegant enough to be called a model, but general enough to encompass all SRL phenomena. Each element of the framework is identified with the operational feature of SRL experiments to which it corresponds. The balance of this chapter is divided into four sections. In the first section, we discuss how research results are affected by procedural choices with regard to each operational feature. The second section summarizes the experimental findings on the SRL process proper. An attempt is made to sort out those studies more concerned with the nature of speaker-dependent features of the speech signal from those directed toward understanding the perceptual process. The third section deals with speaker recognition by machine and by visual inspection of spectrograms. Finally, we suggest some potentially rewarding research topics and some techniques likely to be useful in pursuing them.

Sources of Support

The history of speaker recognition research and the present state of its achievements may be understood more easily by looking briefly at what has motivated the researchers. While some studies have been undertaken solely to increase our basic knowledge of the process, by far the greater number have been motivated by some practical considerations. One of the earliest published studies (McGehee, 1937) grew out of the introduction of voice identification as evidence in a famous criminal case. Except for another paper by the same author (McGehee, 1944), forensic problems sparked no other research for the next quarter century. During World War II, the United States military became interested in identifying monitored radio voices. This latter problem produced some work with the newly invented sound spectrograph, but the results remained classified for nearly two decades (Gray and Kopp, 1944), until Kersta (1962) introduced voice identification by spectrography to forensic scientists and thus, again, to the courts. The controversy about forensic applications of voice identification has generated within the last decade some comparison of visual and aural methods of voice identification (Stevens, Williams, Carbonell, and Woods, 1968), and some work on issues in spectrographic voice identification (Endres, Bambach, and Flosser, 1971; Hazen, 1973; Tosi, Oyer, Lashbrook, Pedrey, Nicol and Nash, 1972).

Another major motivating factor has been the proliferation of novel speech communication systems, especially of the analysis-synthesis variety, since World War II. Developers of such systems found that intelligible resynthesis of coded speech did not necessarily preserve talker identity, and their customers began to demand evidence of the voice-identification performance of systems. Work prompted by a concern for talker identity fidelity tended to aim for means of comparing systems in this regard. Some of this work went beyond its utilitarian purpose and contributed to our store of basic information.

A third major impetus to speaker recognition research was the need for security in such computer-based schemes as electronic banking and data file access control. The work in this area has been, quite understandably, concerned with verification of cooperative talkers rather than identification of one among many, with the problem of mimicry rather than disguise, and with recognition by machine rather than by human listeners. Nevertheless, this area has made progress in identifying the acoustic parameters of the speech signal that carry speaker information and has produced some SRL data of interest in their own right.

Research supported by these three sources has contributed some solid findings in the areas it has addressed. Predictably, however, many areas have been left unexplored in the course of pursuing questions related to practical applications. For this reason, our present understanding of the perceptual process of speaker recognition is spotty.

Conceptual Framework

We shall now set forth a schematic representation of the process thought to underlie SRL phenomena. Our purpose is to provide a framework for organizing and summarizing the results of diverse experiments. Some sort of process, similar to the one we shall describe, is presumed implicitly by most researchers studying speaker recognition by listening, but is described formally by only a few (Voiers, Cohen, and Mickunas, 1965; Matsumoto, Hiki, Sone, and Nimura, 1973).

We conceive of the speaker recognition process as a sequence of stages leading to a recognition response. Speaker information exists in some form at each stage of the process. By *speaker information* we mean simply those attributes that vary distinctively from speaker to speaker (see Hecker's [1971] discussion of interspeaker and intraspeaker variability). At each stage, the speaker information is transformed before it is passed to the next stage. Specifically, speaker information is latent in the speaker in the form of anatomical features and neurally stored habit patterns (Garvin and Ladefoged, 1963). It is converted to activity of the speaking apparatus, which we shall call *speech gestures*, as the talker forms an utterance. This activity results in an acoustic signal in which speaker information is encoded as an *extra message* (Peters, 1954) that eventually reaches the ear of the listener along with the speech intelligence. The listener's sensory apparatus converts the acoustic signal to neural (eighth nerve) messages which, in turn, serve as input to a perceptual processor. The processor is specialized for converting sensory speaker information into perceptual data for use by a decision-making process. Examples of ways of characterizing these perceptual data are the perceived acoustic traits of Voiers *et al.* (1965) and the coordinates of the psychological auditory space of Matsumoto *et al.* (1973). In this form, speaker information is used by some decision process to arrive at a response for every stimulus.

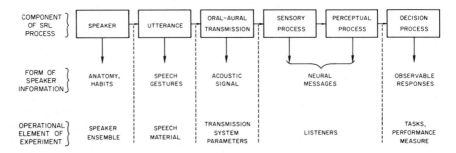

Figure 9.1   Schematic representation of the process of speaker recognition by listening, with related forms of speaker information and experimental operations.

Each component of this simple scheme has an operational counterpart in some element of the procedure on which every SRL experimenter must decide. To make these connections clear, we have arranged the components of the speaker recognition process and the operational elements of the SRL experiment in parallel rows in Figure 9.1. We also show the form of speaker information associated with each stage.

Because this section of the book concerns speech perception, we would like to focus on the perceptual part of the overall process schematized in Figure 9.1. It is immediately apparent, however, that this relatively inaccessible process can be reached only by considerable inference. The speech signal and the responses can be observed and measured directly. In contrast, the perceptual process is preceded by sensory processing and followed by a decision process, each of which performs its own transformation. Very little of the work we shall review has in fact dealt directly with the perceptual process. Most researchers have been concerned with assessing the relative importance to speaker recognition of aspects of speaker information at the stage of speech gestures or acoustic signals. In general, they have proceeded by manipulating parameters at these stages and observing responses that can be scored for accuracy. Some researchers have been concerned more directly with the perceptual process and have employed tasks which they hope will reveal more of its function. Their principal technique has been to correlate measurements made at earlier stages with results of these tasks. A few studies have used elements of both approaches.

Both types of studies have contributed to our understanding of the speaker recognition process in general and the perceptual process in particular. However, the variety of experimental paradigms employed makes it difficult to organize these diverse contributions into a consistent picture. For this reason, we now consider those experimental results that have some general procedural significance.

Speaker Recognition by Listening: Procedural Effects

Our aim in this section is to illustrate how the choices an experimenter makes with regard to each element of the experimental procedure influence the outcome of studies on speaker recognition by listening. Several of the studies cited were originally methodological in nature, having been designed to devise efficient procedures for transmission system evaluation. We shall take up the elements shown in the last row of Figure 9.1 in left-to-right order, looking ahead or back when necessary to point out interactions between elements.

Speaker Ensemble

The term *speaker ensemble* refers to the set of voices that the listener is exposed to during an experiment. The nature of this set is usually specified in terms of the characteristics of the population to which the experimenter wishes to generalize; the most salient characteristics are age, sex, and accent. By far the most studied talker group is adult male speakers of (American) English without pronounced regional accent or speech defect. Populations sampled in studies requiring listeners to recognize talkers seldom cross the adult—child or the male—female barrier. presumably because confusions between such categories are not expected. There is experimental evidence that supports this tacit assumption. When the task required only two-category age classification, Ptacek and Sander (1966) found performance virtually perfect on the basis of complete passages, and still above chance when the utterance was merely a sustained vowel. Both Ryan and Burk (1972) and Shipp and Hollien (1969) found that listeners could make age discriminations which were even finer than the young—old distinction. Identification of sex alone remains robust even when talkers whisper (Schwartz and Rine, 1968), utter only voiceless fricatives (Ingemann, 1968; Schwartz, 1968), use a monotone artificial larynx (Coleman, 1971) or esophageal speech (Weinberg and Bennett, 1971a), or are sampled from among only five- and six-year-olds (Weinberg and Bennett, 1971b).

Large differences in recognition scores can occur between ensembles that are homogeneous with respect to sex and regional accent. For example, Williams (1964) divided 12 adult male speakers into two ensembles of six by random assignment and collected recognition data on each ensemble by identical procedures. The final test scores were 62% correct for one ensemble and 50% correct for the other. Williams (1964, p. 22) observed: "speaker identification depends not only on the individual characteristics of each of the speakers but also on the characteristics of the other speakers with whom he is being compared." Attempts to identify these characteristics and use them to predict confusions among speakers have not met with much success (Carbonell, Grignetti, Stevens, Williams, and Woods, 1965; Clarke and Becker, 1969). We note that discovery of additional characteristics that do predict confusions is a major goal of speaker recognition research. Only after a characteristic becomes identified and quantified can it be used to match speaker ensembles.

The literature affords little information about how large an ensemble must be to represent adequately the subpopulation of interest. Williams' result cited above indicates that six is not enough. In another part of his study, Williams varied ensemble size over the range of four through eight but did not test for reliability. Pollack, Pickett, and Sumby (1954) used ensembles as large as 16 without reaching the limit of information transmitted, suggesting that more speakers could have been identified. We are forced to conclude that there are substantial real differences of undetermined origin in recognition scores among the small, superficially similar ensembles typical in the literature reviewed here.

Speech Material

The second essential of any SRL experiment is that one or more voice samples be presented on every trial. One of the earliest experiments (Pollack *et al.*, 1954) studied the effect of the duration of the sample on performance, where the task was the identification of familiar voices, and the sample was excerpted from connected speech. They found that performance improved rapidly up to approximately one second, and more slowly thereafter. Additional evidence from Pollack *et al.* and later studies (Bricker and Pruzansky, 1966; Murry and Cort, 1971) established that performance depends on the size of the sample of the talker's repertoire rather than on the duration *per se.*

Not only *how much*, but also *what part*, of a talker's repertoire is sampled has an effect on accuracy scores and confusion patterns. Systematic selection of utterances often has been employed in studies of substantive questions, so we shall defer discussion of special samples until later.

It is important to note that specifying the speaker and the text of the utterance does not specify the stimulus, for no one says anything exactly the same way twice. Variation from utterance to utterance by the same talker is a salient aspect of speaker recognition that sets it apart from other perceptual skills of the type studied by psychophysicists. What we wish to stress here is a conceptual point about the role of the stimulus—utterance in speaker recognition: It is used by the listener as a basis for inference about the mechanism that produced it (the speaker). It is this mechanism that is judged to have a certain identity or quality or difference from another, not the stimulus itself.

Transmission System

In her first experiments, McGehee (1937) separated speakers and listeners visually and used the natural air path to convey the acoustic signal from the speaker's mouth to the listener's ears. By the time she began her second series (McGehee, 1944), recording techniques were sufficiently developed to permit electronic reproduction, with its attendant procedural advantages and without significant degradation. Since that time, the transmission system has posed no procedural problem. Since selective degradations of the signal are entirely elective, we shall not treat the subject here. Findings with regard to filtering and other transmission variables are discussed in the next section.

Listeners

Systematic investigations of listener differences are lacking, but a few studies provide an indication of the magnitude of interlistener variability. Stevens *et al.* (1968), whose listeners had free access to utterances of the same test word by each of 8 possible talkers, obtained error rates from 5% to 16% for 6 selected listeners. The 16 listeners who performed *same—different* judgments in Clarke and Becker's (1969) Experiment II ranged from about 8% to 26% error.

The chief practical significance of interlistener differences in ability is that listener groups must be large enough to achieve stable average performance. Williams (1964) reports an experiment that bears on the question of adequate group size in this regard. After being trained to identify 6 speakers, 3 groups of 12 listeners each performed identifications using 3 types of material. No statistically significant differences among groups were found, suggesting that we may regard results based on groups of such a size as typical.

Experience and training, even when not directly related to the recognition task, can effect differences between listener groups. Naive listeners in Clarke and Becker's (1969) Experiment I achieved 58% correct recognition in a 4-alternative forced choice task, whereas 5 speech science students who had worked extensively with the ensemble of 20 speakers scored 67%.

Using the task of identifying familiar voices creates special problems with regard to both the listener and speaker groups. Unless celebrities are used as speakers, the two groups limit each other in size, and one is bound to encounter differential familiarity in any practical situation. Nevertheless, the error rates for Bricker and Pruzansky's (1966) 16 listeners ranged from 2% to 27% for disyllables spoken by 10 speakers. This range overlaps quite closely that found by Clarke and Becker, cited above.

Tasks and Performance Measures

No element of the procedure has as pervasive an effect on what can be learned from an experiment on speaker recognition as does the task chosen by the experimenter. Each type of task represented in the literature has characteristics that must be kept in mind when attempting to construct a picture of the SRL process. The taxonomy of tasks presented here is organized in terms of two of these characteristics: the type of judgment required and the manner of presenting voice samples. In addition, we shall take special note of the range of performance measurement options associated with each type of task.

TAXONOMY OF TASKS

Figure 9.2 depicts a hierarchical scheme for classifying tasks described in the experimental literature. The most fundamental distinction concerns the nature of the response. We classify as an *identification* task any in which some or all of the available responses denote an individual speaker. The term *evaluation* is applied to tasks that require the listener to judge the value of the stimulus—voice on some attribute, dimension, or characteristic. The accuracy criterion intrinsic to identification tasks (i.e., the scorability of identifications as to correctness) generally does not obtain for evaluation tasks.

Identification tasks always involve a test stimulus—the voice sample to be classified—and one or more response categories defined by other voice-sample stimuli.

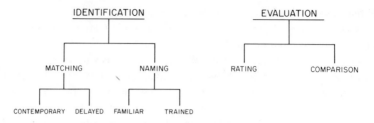

Figure 9.2   A taxonomy of speaker recognition tasks.

The term *matching*, on the second level of the hierarchy in Figure 9.2, refers to tasks in which the comparison stimuli that define the response categories are presented during the trial on which the test stimulus is judged. In the *naming* task, the listener's experience with voice samples corresponding to the response alternatives has been acquired prior to the judgment trial. Matching is considered to entail short-term memory, while naming involves long-term memory.

The term *rating* refers to evaluation tasks involving a single voice sample at a time and one or more attribute scales. The literature contains no examples of comparative evaluations of two or more samples, although such procedures (e.g., pair-wise similarity judgments) have been used in the closely related area of speech transmission system quality (McDermott, 1969).

At the second level, then, all tasks used to date fall into one of three categories: naming, matching, or rating. We next consider variations of each type in turn, discussing salient characteristics and citing examples.

Naming. The speaker-naming task is the laboratory analog of the everyday occurrence of recognizing the voice of an unseen individual. In the variant used by most investigators (Bricker and Pruzansky, 1966; Compton, 1963; Dukiewicz, 1970; Pollack *et al.*, 1954), listeners had become familiar with the voices of the talker set prior to the time of the experiment through normal business and/or social contact. We shall refer to this task as *familiar speaker naming.* In the version of the naming task used by Williams (1964), learning of the talker set was under the control of the experimenter, who used a paired-associate task to train the listeners. Note that familiar speaker naming is the task most appropriate to the evaluation of communication systems when the question is whether familiar voices will be recognizable via the system under evaluation. There are many practical impediments to using that task for systems evaluation, however; these have been discussed by Hecker (1971), Clarke, Becker, and Nixon (1966), Voiers (1965), and others.

The performance measure most commonly used with naming tasks is $P(c)$, the percentage of responses correct. However, Pollack *et al.* (1954) showed quite early that this measure has an undesirable property—namely, it decreases with increasing size of the set of response alternatives, even when the speaker ensemble size remains constant. Pollack *et al.* preferred to estimate the *amount of information transmitted,* designated T, from the square stimulus—response contingency matrices inherent in naming experiments. They were able to show that the *relative information transmitted,* which is defined as T/T_{max}, was independent of response set size, at least over a limited range. Other investigators (Bricker and Pruzansky, 1966) have reported the entire stimulus—response (or *confusion*) matrix. Confusion matrices from naming experiments can be summarized by multidimensional scaling techniques, but no examples are found in the literature.

Matching. Most experimenters who used the matching task have presented the test stimulus at the same session with the comparison(s). The *delayed testing* branch under *matching* in Figure 9.2 is exemplified only in the work of McGehee (1937, 1944), who presented the comparison stimuli after delays ranging from one day to five months. Contemporary matching experiments offer the listener one or more comparison stimuli during the trial on which the test stimulus is presented. When there are two or more alternatives, the listener may be forced to choose among them. In this case, there is a one-to-one stimulus—response correspondence, and the scoring options applicable to the naming task are available. Examples of this format are the ABX and 4AFC (four-alternative forced-choice) formats of Clarke *et al.* (1966) and the eight-alternative closed set experiments of Stevens *et al.* (1968).

When there are two or more comparison utterances, listeners may have difficulty comparing the test utterance equally effectively with each of them. Clarke *et al.* (1966) found, in a four-alternative forced-choice task, that accuracy decreased as the temporal separation between the test utterance and its matching comparison increased. This effect may be presumed to be related to short-term memory rather than to the perceptual process of SRL. To overcome this problem, Stevens *et al.* (1968) made the comparison utterances randomly accessible by the listeners, who matched each test utterance to one of eight alternatives.

When only one comparison stimulus is presented, the listener's task is simply to decide whether the test stimulus was or was not uttered by the same talker. This basic structure is common to procedures called *same—different testing, discrimination,* and *verification.* Since this task allows a no-match response, the question of the listener's criterion for matching must be considered. Clarke and Becker (1969) and Matsumoto *et al.* (1973) required subjects to estimate their confidence in each same—different judgment and used the confidence ratings to construct a receiver operating characteristic, or *ROC.* A criterion-free measure of performance designated $P_o(c)$ is derived from the empirical receiver operating characteristics. The $P_o(c)$ is that point on the ROC at which the probability of a false acceptance (incorrect "same" judgment) is equal to the probability of a false rejection (incorrect "different" judgment). Another measure, called the *similarity index,* can be derived for each pair of speakers in a same—different experiment by finding the mean confidence rating with which two different talkers were judged to be the same. Matsumoto *et al.* (1973) used similarity indexes as input to a multidimensional scaling procedure in order to construct perceptual spaces for their speaker ensembles.

The open set experiments of Stevens *et al.* (1968) are the only published examples of a matching task with a large comparison set ($n=8$) plus a no-match alternative. Although this format may mimic certain practical situations, its utility as a research tool is limited by the complexity of the required performance measure.

Rating. The rating task has been used to study listeners' perceptions of a wide variety of characteristics, from the objectively verifiable through the purely subjective. Among the former are sex (e.g., Schwartz, 1968) and age (e.g., Shipp and Hollien, 1969). Intermediate between objective and subjective characteristics are psychophysical scales, of which Clarke and Becker (1969) selected six for study. Performance in such cases can be expressed in terms of the degree of relationship between the ratings and the objective measures thought to be their chief physical correlates. A subjective procedure, usually called the *semantic differential technique* (Osgood, Suci, and Tanenbaum, 1957), has been used by Voiers (1965), Holmgren (1967), and Clarke and Becker (1969). Listeners are required to rate voice samples on a number of bipolar adjective scales such as beautiful—ugly, sharp—dull. The procedure produces data that can be factor-analyzed in various ways, some of which can be mapped onto a perceptual space. Clarke and Becker (1969) attempted to incorporate accuracy scoring in this procedure by applying a plausible decision rule to the factor scores. Intrinsically, however, subjective ratings are not directly scorable for accuracy.

SUMMARY OF TASK CHARACTERISTICS

In this section, we have tried to indicate what kind of perception, memory, and judgment is tapped by each task, as well as what performance measures each affords. The major purpose of this survey is to form an estimate of how readily results from different tasks can be combined in an attempt to develop an understanding of speaker recognition by listening. We recommend keeping the following points in mind throughout the next section: (1) naming and matching use different memory systems; (2) rating produces an inherently different kind of output from either naming or matching; (3) the most commonly used performance measure for naming and matching is dependent on response set size; and (4) only occasionally has an experimenter converted the results from one type of task into a form comparable with others.

Speaker Recognition by Listening: Experimental Findings

This section summarizes studies of the relations between parameters of the speakers and/or the speech signal and measures of listeners' speaker recognition performance. The first part deals with studies that manipulate variables and measure accuracy of identification. The second part covers studies that determine correlations among variables and seek performance measures that characterize the perceptual process involved in speaker recognition by listening.

In Table 9.1 we summarize procedural features of the experiments in the order they are cited. For reasons outlined in the previous section, these choices may be expected to affect the interpretation, generalizability, and applicability of the results. We suggest that the reader take particular note of the speech material used. It should be remembered that in connected speech each speech sound may be affected by what precedes and follows it; there is a very complex relationship between speech gestures, vocal tract shape, and the speech signal. We caution against generalizing from the findings on talker recognition performance for isolated speech sounds to connected speech.

Manipulation of Parameters

CONTROLLING SPEECH GESTURES

Experimenters have used three techniques for controlling speech gestures: (*1*) requiring speakers to vary their sound source in some way; (*2*) asking some speakers to mimic others; and (*3*) selecting the text to be spoken.

Controlling the Source. Several investigators have studied the importance of voicing by comparing recognition results from whispered speech with results from normal speech. Williams (1964) found that recognition for normally spoken sentences was much better than for whispered speech. Pollack *et al.* (1954) studied the effects of whispered speech as a function of duration of speech sample. They concluded that a whispered speech sample had to be over three times the duration of normal speech for equivalent levels of speaker identification.

Coleman (1973) eliminated possible glottal source variations by the use of an artificial larynx with a fixed frequency of 85 Hz as the sound source. The average accuracy for 28 listeners was 90% correct discrimination, errors being concentrated in relatively few speaker pairs. He concluded that there was a lot of speaker identity information left when source variation was eliminated, and that the fundamental was probably not a good clue for speaker verification.

The importance of pitch has been studied by having talkers alter their *normal* pitch in some manner. McGehee (1937) found that when the target speaker disguised his voice by changing the pitch, identification was reduced by about 13%. Listeners' identification performance for Polish vowels, spoken at normal, higher than normal, and lower than normal pitch was not always best for the *normal* pitch condition (Dukiewicz, 1970). On the other hand, Matsumoto *et al.* (1973) found that a listener's speaker discrimination performance was much better when the pitches of two samples were the same than when they differed by 40 Hz.

Mimicry. The effects of mimicry on speaker recognition are of both practical and theoretical interest. On the practical level, any system that uses the voice as a means of verifying the identity of an individual will have to contend with the problem of mimicry. On a more basic level, results of studies using mimics may reveal some information about the relative importance of organic versus learned factors in listeners' recognition of speakers.

Rosenberg (1973) conducted two speaker verification studies in order to compare listener performance with performance of an automatic speaker verification system.

Table 9.1 *Description of Experimental Procedures For Studies of Speaker Recognition by Listening*

Experiment	Speaker ensemble	Speech materials	Transmission system	Listeners	Task	Performance measure[a]
Controlling speech gestures						
1. Controlling the source						
Williams (1964)	$N_S = 6$ m	Sentences—normal and whispered	—	$N = 36$	Naming (trained)	$P(c)$
Pollack et al. (1954)	16 m	Passage—normal and whispered; var. dur.	—	7	Naming (familiar)	T; T/T_{max}
Coleman (1973)	10 m 10 f	5 Sec. passage; 85 Hz. artif. larynx	—	28	Same—diff. and confid. ratings	$P(c)$
McGehee (1937)	5 m	Passage; normal, altered pitch	—	?	Delayed matching	$P(c)$
Dukiewicz (1970)	5 m	3 Polish vowels; 3 pitch levels	—	10	Naming (familiar)	$P(c)$
Matsumoto et al. (1973)	8 m	Japanese vowel /a/	—	6	Same—Diff. and confid. ratings	$P_0(c)$
2. Mimicry						
Rosenberg (1973)	8 m cust. 33 m cas. imp.	One sentence	—	10	Verification	$P(c)$
Rosenberg (1973)	8 m cust. 4 m mimics	One sentence	—	9	Verification	$P(c)$
3. Speech sound selection						
Ramishvili (1966)	6 m	Isolated Russian phonemes	—	?	Naming (familiar)	$P(c)$
Dukiewicz (1970)	5 m	3 isolated Polish vowels	—	10	Naming (familiar)	$P(c)$
Stevens et al. (1968)	8 m	Spondees	—	6	8-choice matching random access	$P(c)$
Bricker and Pruzansky (1966)	10 m	Excerpted vowels /a/ and /i/	—	16	Naming (familiar)	$P(c)$; Confusion Matrices

	Duration	Material	Manipulation	Subjects	Task	Measure
Compton (1963)	9 m	Sustained /i/	High pass filter	15	Naming (familiar)	P(c)
Dukiewicz (1970)	5 m	3 Polish vowels	Bandpass filter	10	Naming (familiar)	P(c)
Pollack et al. (1954)	16 m	Monosyllables	High and low pass filter	7	Naming (familiar)	P(c)
Clarke et al. (1966)	16 m	Sentences	High and low pass filter	6	ABX	P(c)
				8	Same—diff. and confid. ratings	$P_0(c)$
2. Backward speech						
Clarke et al. (1966)	16 m	Sentences	Reversed with and without filtering	6	ABX	P(c)
Williams (1964)	6 m	Sentences	Reversed and normal	36	Naming (trained)	P(c)
Bricker and Pruzansky (1966)	10 m	Sent., disyl, monosyl; vowels	Reversed and normal	2	Naming (familiar)	P(c)
3. Analysis—synthesis						
Shearme and Holmes (1959)	6 m	Passage	Monotone vocoder freq. shifter	8	Same—diff.	P(c)
Miller (1964)	2 m / 6 m	Nonsense syl. vowel /a/	Source—tract separation	?	Informal	Majority
Matsumoto et al. (1973)	5 m	Japanese /a/	Source—tract separation	6	Same—diff. and confid. ratings	Similarity index
Correlational studies						
Voiers (1965)	24 m	Passage	—	32	Semantic—diff. rating	Factor analysis
Holmgren (1967)	10 m	Passage	—	20	Semantic—diff. rating	Factor analysis
Clarke and Becker (1969)	20 m	Sentences	—	5 sp. sci. students	ABX; Psychophys. scale rating	P(c); Mechanical decision rule
	16 m	Sentences	—	16	Same—diff. and confid. ratings	$P_0(c)$
	8 m	Sentences	—	16	Semantic—diff. ratings	Factor analysis; mechan. decis.

In the first experiment, where *customers* (people who wanted to be verified) were paired only with *casual impostors* (people speaking in their natural voices), both the false acceptance rate and the false rejection rate were about 4%. Most of the errors occurred on only a few pairs. Included in this study was a casual impostor who was the identical twin of a customer. The identical twin impostor was falsely accepted 96% of the time when he was paired with his brother.

The second experiment involved professional mimics. Each mimic could practice imitating a particular customer as many times as he wanted until he felt satisfied that it was the best he could do. The mimics also recorded sentences in their natural voices which served as casual impostor samples for comparison. Subjects were not told, and did not suspect, that mimicry had been attempted. When a customer was compared with an impostor using his natural voice, the false acceptance rate was about 4%, as it had been in the first experiment. When a customer was compared with a mimic impostor, the mean false acceptance rate was about 20%.

Results showed that some mimics were better than others and that some voices were more susceptible to mimicry than others. Some listeners made few errors, while others often accepted the mimic impostors. Implications of these studies will be discussed in the section on comparison of machine and listener recognition.

Differential Effects of Speech Sounds. Variations in the anatomy of the vocal mechanism of different talkers may be reflected in isolated utterances of different speech sounds. Some experimenters have considered the importance of anatomical features and their corresponding speech signal parameters by comparing talker recognition performance for different isolated phonemes.

Ramishvili (1966), studying identification performance based on Russian phonemes in isolation, found that performance was better than chance for all phonemes. Identification was best for vowels, with the exception of the high back vowel /u/; voiced consonants were better than unvoiced consonants. The range of mean identification scores was 90% for /ɛ/ to 30% for /k/. Dukiewicz (1970) also concluded that recognition was poorest for the back vowel /u/, which has a low second formant.

Stevens *et al.* (1968) observed that recognition for words containing a front stressed vowel was slightly better than for words with back stressed vowels. They argued that better recognition for words with front vowels might be due to the higher second formant, and that more speaker identification information is contained in the higher frequencies.

Bricker and Pruzansky (1966), on the other hand, found slightly better familiar speaker naming performance for /a/ than for the high front vowel /i/ excerpted from the stressed vowel of a disyllable. Furthermore, they reported that the patterns of confusions between speakers differed for the two vowels.

CONTROLLING THE ACOUSTIC SIGNAL

One of the difficulties with experiments that manipulate parameters by means of instructions to the speakers is that the experimenter does not have direct control of the speech signal during the experiment. Several studies have been concerned with manipulating the acoustic signal by varying parameters of the transmission system. The speech signal has been altered by: (*1*) selective filtering; (*2*) playing the speech backward; and (*3*) analysis and synthesis techniques.

Filtering. Considerable interest has been shown in determining the parts of the frequency spectrum that contribute the most speaker identification information. Several studies have reported the effects of low-pass, high-pass, and band-pass filtering on talker recognition for isolated vowels, words, and sentences.

Ramishvili (1966) found that there was little loss in recognition when vowels were low passed at 4 kHz with a lower cutoff of 200 Hz, or high passed at 700 Hz with an upper cutoff of 10 kHz. Compton (1963) studied the effects of filtering on the vowel /i/. He concluded that attenuation of frequencies below 1020 Hz does not affect listeners' ability to identify speakers, at least for that vowel. However, another study indicated that other vowels can give different results. Dukiewicz (1970) found that for the two 3-octave bands, 128–1024 Hz and 1024–8192 Hz, speaker identification was indeed better in the higher range for the vowel /i/ but better in the lower band for /u/. Identification was only slightly better in the higher band for /a/. It was concluded that frequency ranges in which a vowel's spectral energy is concentrated carry more speaker information than do ranges of low energy.

Pollack *et al.* (1954) studied the effects of low-pass and high-pass filtering on monosyllables. They found a gradual decrease in speaker identification above 500 Hz high pass and below 2 kHz low pass, but recognition was still better than chance at the extreme filter conditions. They concluded that identification performance was resistant to selective frequency emphasis of the type used over a wide frequency range. Although the material and the task were different from those of Pollack *et al.* (1954), Clarke *et al.* (1966) also found a gradual decrease in discrimination as degradation increased, and better than chance results at the most severe filter condition.

All of the results of filtering support the suggestion by Pollack *et al.* (1954, p. 404) that "identification of a speaker's voice is not critically dependent upon the delicate balance of different frequency components in any single portion of the speech frequency spectrum."

Backward Speech. Playing speech backward does not affect the frequency spectrum of the speech at any one point in time, but it disturbs the temporal patterns of speech, such as directions of formant transitions and patterns of fundamental frequency. Presumably, different temporal patterns of speech reflect learned differences of speakers, while differences in frequency spectrum reflect organic differences.

Several investigators have found that playing speech backward reduces listeners' ability to recognize speakers. Clarke *et al.* (1966) played sentences backward with and without filtering. On the average, performance was slightly better for 250 Hz high-pass backward speech than unfiltered backward speech. Low passing the backward speech at 500 or 1000 Hz showed a slight decrement in performance. Performance of Williams' (1964) subjects was better for backward sentences than for whispered sentences played forward, but poorer than for undistorted sentences. Bricker and Pruzansky (1966) compared results for speech played backward with recognition for undistorted speech. They used speech materials of varying length and composition. Reduction in recognition of the backward material was greatest for monosyllables and least for sentences. There was an approximate 10% reduction in recognition for vowel excerpts played backward. This finding suggests that there is some speaker information in the normal time course of even a 100 msec vowel excerpt, which often is thought of as a quasi-steady state signal.

It appears that temporal cues are important for speaker recognition regardless of speaker ensemble, materials, or task. However, Hecker (1971) points out that it is not clear whether reduction of talker recognition for backward speech is due to the temporal cues per se or to the novel form of speech distortion that can exist only in the laboratory.

Analysis and Synthesis Techniques. The kinds of degradations that have been discussed here can be introduced in the transmission system easily, but they have very complex effects on the speech waveform. In order to determine the effects on speaker recognizing behavior of particular features of the speech signal such as pitch, formant frequencies and bandwidths, or intonation contours, it would be necessary to have independent control over these features. Development of speech processing devices such as vocoders and sophisticated computer techniques has allowed manipulation of parameters of the speech signal never before possible.

An early attempt to manipulate formant frequencies by use of a vocoder is reported by Shearme and Holmes (1959). Several seconds of speech were processed through a channel vocoder that shifted the spectral envelope in the frequency range of the first formant upward by 100 Hz, and the second and third formant regions by 300 Hz. Laryngeal frequency characteristics were eliminated by using a fixed voicing frequency. Results for trials untreated except for the fixed frequency suggest that removal of natural laryngeal cues reduced discrimination. When only one voice of the pair was treated by frequency shifting, the false acceptance rate for different-speaker pairs was only about 7%, but the false rejection rate for same-speaker pairs was about 90%. When both voices were treated, the false acceptances went up to almost 50%; no same-speaker pairs with both samples treated were presented. The nature of the experimental design makes it difficult to determine how much the difference in listeners' responses for the treated and untreated conditions was due to the shift of frequencies and how much to shifts in criterion. Although their speech processing was somewhat crude, Shearme and Holmes (1959) were the first to demonstrate the feasibility of analyzing speech, altering specific features, and then presenting resynthesized speech for listener judgments of speaker identity.

Miller (1964) used a more sophisticated computerized analysis—synthesis technique to study the relative importance of source function versus the vocal tract resonances in speaker identification. Using inverse filtering in synchrony with fundamental frequency (Mathews, Miller, and David, 1961), she analyzed speech samples and, in effect, separated the glottal waveform and the vocal tract transfer function. The speech was recombined in several intriguing ways. Examples include one case in which the tract information for two speakers, who spoke the nonsense word /hod/ at about the same pitch and duration, were interchanged. At an informal session, listeners judged the same-tract samples to sound more like the original utterances than did the same-source samples. To discover the importance of the glottal source, tract data for six speakers were combined with two artificial glottal pulse shapes that were tailored to simulate realistic shapes. Listeners reported that, although the effects of the glottal wave were noticeable, the voices still sounded like those of their tract donors. Two other resynthesis procedures also suggested that the synthesized voice sounded like the speaker whose tract was represented. However, Miller points out several serious technical problems involved in the pitch synchronous technique that may have influenced her results.

Matsumoto *et al.* (1973) also used inverse filtering to estimate glottal waveform and formant frequency pattern from a single pitch period of the vowel /a/. They formed monotone synthetic vowels for hybrid voices by repeating the glottal waveform and recombining tract and source information from different speakers. All possible pairs of eight of these hybrid voices and sustained vowel utterances of the five original voices were presented to listeners for same—different judgments. Their results also indicate that the hybrid voices were more similar to those of the tract donors than to those of the source donors.

Limitations of each of these three studies still leave the source—tract issue some-what in doubt. However, use of new speech analysis—synthesis techniques, such as predictive coding (Atal and Hanauer, 1971), which allows estimation of vocal tract parameters independent of pitch, along with formal procedures for collecting data from listeners, should contribute substantially to our understanding of speaker information.

Correlational Studies

Observing the correlations among two or more variables is a widely used experimental technique in many fields. In principle, the correlational approach could be applied to observations made at the output of any two components of the talker recognition process, as described in Figure 9.1. In practice, only some relations between measures of the acoustic signal and performance on matching or rating tasks have been studied.

Two studies (Holmgren, 1967; Voiers, 1965) that investigated the relation between physical measures and rating performance used identical methods. Ratings of several voices were obtained on a variety of semantic differential scales, and various physical measures were taken on the same samples. All measures were intercorrelated, and the matrix of correlations subjected to factor analyses. Varimax rotations of the factor solutions were interpreted in terms of the loadings of both physical and perceptual scales.

Similar difficulties of interpretation were encountered in the two studies: (*1*) in both cases, two out of five factors loaded only on physical measures; (*2*) unexpected relations emerged, such as, in Voiers' (1965) study, a high loading for *duration* on a factor that otherwise seemed to reflect pitch; (*3*) expected relations, such as a *rate* factor with high duration loading, failed to emerge; (*4*) factor definitions were not stable across studies; and (*5*) some factors were not readily interpretable. Nevertheless, both studies revealed some evidence for the perceptual significance of glottal fundamental frequency, or pitch, as well as a perceptual factor related to speech intensity or effort.

Clarke and Becker (1969) used various correlation techniques to study the relations between physical measures and three kinds of data taken from human listeners: ratings of selected attributes, ratings on semantic differential scales, and performance on a matching task. Their principal interest was in determining how well matching performance could be predicted from perceptual data or physical measurements.

Clarke and Becker's basic physical measures were mean glottal period, period variability, long-term power spectrum, and utterance duration. Five graduate students in speech science selected six attributes, called *psychophysical scales*, that they deemed useful in characterizing speaker individuality. They were pitch, pitch variability, sibilant intensity, click-like elements, breathiness, and rate. Only two of these, however, were reported to have substantial correlations with physical measures. Judgments of *pitch* correlated $r = -.80$ with mean period, and judgments of *rate* correlated $r = -.90$ with duration. This last finding differs from the results of Voiers (1965) and Holmgren (1967), neither of whom found a strong relation between the semantic differential factor related to rate and a physical measure of duration.

Clarke and Becker (1969) report a multiple correlation between physical measures and the similarity indexes obtained from a same—different task of $R = .75$. They also reported a multiple correlation of $R = .65$ between semantic differential factors and the similarity indexes. Both physical measurements and semantic differential data, then, predict matching task performance to a statistically significant but practically unimpressive degree.

Clarke and Becker applied a decision rule to each form of measurement—physical, psychophysical, and semantic differential—in order to obtain accuracy scores for comparison with matching performance. The psychophysical measures were compared only to 4AFC performance. While subjects performing the 4AFC task achieved 67% correct matches, all six psychophysical scales combined yielded only 51% correct. Applying the decision rule to the semantic differential factor scores for the median subject yielded an accuracy score of 68% correct. For the same set of stimuli and the same listeners, direct same—different judgments for the median listener were 90% correct, while power spectrum data produced 83%, and pitch alone 66%. Information on the qualitative similarities among the three kinds of information contained in the confusion matrices is reported only informally. The authors find "very poor predictability from one method to another" (Clarke and Becker, 1969, p. 760). We are left with the conclusion that the physical and perceptual correlates of speaker recognition by listening remain obscure after this most comprehensive study, to date, of the problem.

A study of the relation between acoustical parameters derived from analysis-by-synthesis and same—different performance recently has been reported by Matsumoto *et al.* (1973). Their method involved constructing a psychological auditory space (*PAS*) by applying multidimensional scaling to similarity indexes derived from the matching task. Rather than rotate the solution to satisfy some abstract structural criterion, Matsumoto *et al.* (1973) achieved an *interpretable* rotation by orienting the axes along directions taken by certain physical parameters of the speech samples.

Three experiments using this technique were conducted to assess the relative contribution of tract and source parameters to the individuality of voices. The glottal source measures were glottal fundamental mean frequency, variance of the same, and slope of the glottal spectrum. The vocal tract parameters were the first three formant center frequencies. Matsumoto *et al.* (1973) interpret their findings to be in support of several conclusions:

1. Mean glottal fundamental frequency makes a greater contribution to perceived voice individuality than any other parameter.
2. The other source parameters (spectral slope and pitch period variability) make a contribution, regardless of the vowel spoken and independent of tract characteristics.
3. Formant frequencies make a contribution that varies in magnitude depending on the vowel spoken.

These results are more provocative than conclusive for a number of reasons. Only the five Japanese vowels, uttered in isolation at a pitch dictated by the experimenter, were used. The conclusion about mean fundamental, while consistent with that of other experimenters, is based on an experiment in which the parameter was manipulated deliberately over a range of 40 Hz. Nevertheless, these experiments make at least two valuable contributions: (*1*) they illustrate a way of representing matching performance results—spatially—that renders them comparable to representations of results from rating tasks, such as semantic differential or similarity judgments, that are not inherently scorable for accuracy; and (*2*) they suggest a technique for relating any number of physical measures to performance in a way that may suggest testable hypotheses about physical correlates of speaker information.

Other Speaker Recognition Methods

Speaker Recognition by Machine

The major impetus for research on speaker recognition by machine (*SRM*) has been interest in the development of a computer-based speaker recognition procedure to be used for security purposes. The practical considerations of developing such a system appear to contribute little to understanding how listeners recognize speakers. However, SRM experiments can be useful for identifying acoustic parameters that carry speaker information and for developing and testing models of the human perceptual and decision processes. We shall, therefore, describe briefly the research problems that have been considered in SRM studies and discuss what we consider to be some of the major contributions to the field.

A typical SRM study involves having speakers read some selected speech materials and transmitting the speech wave or speech spectrum to an analog-to-digital converter which transforms the speech to numbers usable by a computer. The major effort of SRM research has been aimed at developing computer procedures for (*1*) defining and extracting a set of acoustic parameters that might carry speaker information; (*2*) reducing these parameters to a set of features used in the decision process of recognizing speakers; and (3) developing a decision rule that is tailored to the set of features and the task being studied.

Machine recognition tasks can be divided into two types: speaker verification and speaker identification. For both tasks the machine has stored reference features of many speakers. In the speaker verification task, a cooperative speaker saying a test utterance claims to be Person X. The machine's decision is either to accept or reject that speaker as Person X. In a speaker identification task, the speaker of the test sample does not claim an identity. The machine must decide the identity of the speaker from the ensemble of possible speakers. One study (Hair and Rekieta, 1972) has allowed the possibility that the test speaker is not from the reference ensemble. Most of the recent SRM studies have been interested in speaker verification because of its potential commercial value. The identification task has been used chiefly as a research tool for comparing recognition results using different parameter sets.

First in the remainder of this section we shall discuss some of the data collection considerations prior to digitalization. Then we shall describe the computer procedures themselves. Finally, we wish to compare the process of speaker recognition by listening with speaker recognition by machine.

DATA COLLECTION

Speaker Ensemble. Although most SRM experiments selected speaker ensembles to be of the same sex, similar age, and regional dialect, several studies contained both males and females. In these studies, identification was based on spectral data with no pitch information, and confusions did cross sex boundaries (Bricker, Gnanadesikan, Mathews, Pruzansky, Tukey, Wachter, and Warner, 1971; Pruzansky, 1963; Pruzansky and Mathews, 1964).

The speaker ensemble in verification experiments is divided into two groups: the known speakers or customers, for whom the correct response is positive, and the unknowns or impostors, for whom the response should be negative. Some verification studies have selected impostors that are similar to customers, using an identical twin or professional mimics to imitate some customers (Doddington, Hydrick, and Beek, 1973; Lummis, 1973).

Most SRM experiments have involved small populations of 10 to 30 speakers. However, one identification study reported high recognition using 172 speakers (Bricker *et al.*, 1971), and a recent verification study containing 118 voices, 50 knowns and 68 impostors, showed promising results (Das and Mohn, 1971).

Speech Material. Most SRM experiments have required that the text of the reference and test utterances be the same so that corresponding speech events can be compared. Speech sounds, whole words, phrases, and sentences have been used. A few studies have used context-free measures with some success (Atal, 1972a; Furui, Itakura, and Saito, 1972; Hargreaves and Starkweather, 1963; Smith, 1962).

Furui *et al.* (1972) were concerned about the length of speech required to keep the phonetic sequence from influencing the long-term average spectrum. They concluded that the sample length necessary for determining average spectrum patterns is of the order of 10 seconds. Atal (1972a) recently described a procedure that resulted in high identification accuracy for speech of two seconds in duration, even though the texts of the test and reference samples were different.

Reference Patterns. Speaker recognition by machine requires establishing a reference pattern for each member of the known speaker ensemble. A *reference pattern* is a set of averaged or weighted features that are determined from several reference samples of a given speaker. Researchers have been concerned about the amount of time over which the reference samples are collected, the time elapsed between the last reference sample and the test sample, and the minimum number of samples needed to form a representative reference pattern. Several studies have shown that utterances spoken during one recording session tend to be similar and do not represent variations of speech patterns that may be expected over a period of time (Das and Mohn, 1971; Furui *et al.*, 1972; Hargreaves and Starkweather, 1963; Luck, 1969; Sambur, 1975). The amount of time over which speech samples have been collected has ranged from several days to $3\frac{1}{2}$ years. Furui *et al.* (1972) determined that if the reference samples are collected over a long enough time, for example, 3 months, and a suitable distance measure is used, it is possible to recognize a speaker even after intervals of from 3 to 12 months.

Fewer utterances (generally five or six) have been used in reference patterns for speaker identification experiments than for speaker verification studies, one of which used as many as 125 utterances collected over 8 days (Luck, 1969). However, very high verification has been achieved using only 10 reference utterances collected over a 2-month period (Doddington, 1970; Lummis, 1973).

COMPUTER PROCEDURES

Defining and Extracting Acoustic Parameters. Acoustic parameters that have been considered in SRM studies can be divided into three groups: (*1*) time-varying measures made on prescribed text material; (*2*) parameters measured from specific speech events; and (*3*) measures of long-time average spectra.

The simplest measures of the first type that have been investigated are time-by-frequency matrices of spectral energies for words and phrases (Li, Dammann, and Chapman, 1966; Pruzansky, 1963; Pruzansky and Mathews, 1964). Several investigators, arguing that spectral measures are sensitive to degradation of the transmission medium, have studied recognition performance using parameters such as pitch, formant, and intensity contours for sentences (Atal, 1972b; Doddington, 1970; Lummis, 1973; Rosenberg and Sambur, 1975).

Since different utterances of the same text are not identical, measures requiring pattern matching need some procedure for properly aligning the reference and test patterns. Some studies have applied linear time normalization procedures or have aligned with respect to particular time intervals. These procedures still do not assure that similar phonetic elements will be aligned throughout the whole word or sentence.

A promising time normalization procedure, developed by Doddington (1970), time-registers the test sentence with the reference sentence by nonlinear warping of the time axis of the test utterance.

Several studies have avoided the alignment problem by selecting acoustic para-meters measured at specific speech events in an utterance (Das and Mohn, 1971; Glenn and Kleiner, 1968; Hair and Rekieta, 1972; Luck, 1969; Sambur, 1975; Su, Li, and Fu, 1974; Wolf, 1971). However, this procedure requires some prior segmenta-tion and recognition of the linguistic component of the speech signal. Only one study, whose goal was a completely automated speaker verification system, segmented auto-matically (Das and Mohn, 1971). The system was unable to make a verification decision for about 10% of the utterances tested because the utterances could not be properly segmented.

Some researchers have studied the effectiveness of measures that do not require temporal alignment or segmentation. These have included various measures of the long-time average spectra of prescribed words and sentences and of extemporaneous speech (Hargreaves and Starkweather, 1963; Pruzansky, 1963; Bricker *et al.*, 1971; Furui *et al.*, 1972; Li and Hughes, 1972). This is a promising approach to speaker recognition by machine but may require too much speech to be practical (Furui *et al.*, 1972; Li and Hughes, 1972).

Some parameters used in SRM studies have been considered primarily because of the ease and accuracy with which they could be obtained. Spectral and pitch measures were used in the early SRM experiments partly because the analysis could be done with hardware in real time. Recently developed speech analysis techniques, such as linear prediction (Atal and Hanauer, 1971), allow convenient automatic extraction of a large number of acoustic parameters for further evaluation of their effectiveness as speaker-characterizing features.

Data Reduction and Feature Evaluation. SRM experiments have used dimensionality reduction techniques for two reasons. The first is simply to make the recognition system computationally more efficient by reducing the number of measures represent-ing a single speech sample. The second, and more intrinsically interesting reason, is to identify a set of acoustic attributes that carry sufficient speaker information to allow recognition of a speaker.

The original set of acoustic parameters from a particular utterance can be thought of as a set of coordinates in multidimensional space. Mohn (1971) distinguished two ways of reducing the dimensionality of this space: subsetting and transformation. *Subsetting* involves selecting a smaller number of measures from the original set without changing them. *Transformation* involves selecting a new set of coordinates in the space such that the new coordinates are a linear combination of the original ones.

Two different subsetting procedures have been used in SRM experiments: analysis of variance (Das and Mohn, 1971; Pruzansky and Mathews, 1964; Wolf, 1971) and probability-of-error criterion (Rosenberg and Sambur, 1975; Sambur, 1975). Both allow a ranking of the original set of measures according to their ability to discriminate speakers. Wolf (1971), using analysis of variance, found that some useful parameters were various measures of fundamental frequency, glottal source spectrum shape, and features of vowel and nasal consonant spectra. His speech samples were all collected on a single day. Sambur (1975), using the probability-of-error criterion he developed, was able to evaluate parameters, taking into consideration intersession variability. Speech samples were collected over a $3\frac{1}{2}$-year period. His results showed that average fundamental frequency of a speaker remains relatively stable in a particular recording session, but shifts significantly from one session to another. Some features that had high intersession stability and low intraspeaker variability were certain parameters measured during nasals, and the second, third, and fourth formants of selected vowels.

Discriminant analysis, a transformation method, also has been used in SRM experiments as a dimensionality reduction technique (Bricker *et al.*, 1971; Mohn, 1971; Smith, 1962). It has been shown to produce efficient dimensionality reduction, but little attempt has been made to interpret the discriminant coordinates. In one study, the first coordinate effectively separated male and female speakers, but further coordinates, although useful statistically, could not be interpreted in terms of meaningful characteristics of speakers (Bricker *et al.*, 1971).

Decision Rules. As we have just mentioned, it is convenient to think of the features selected by one of the aforementioned procedures as coordinates of a multidimensional space. Speech samples of different speakers may be represented as points in this space. The choice of decision rule depends, in part, on the distribution of speech samples in this space. For identification tasks, the distance is computed between the test sample and each of the reference patterns. The speaker associated with the smallest distance is chosen as the speaker of the test utterance. Generally, some Euclidean distance measure has been used; various distance measures have been investigated (Atal, 1972b; Bricker *et al.*, 1971; Furui *et al.*, 1972). One study, involving a large number of talkers, used a two-stage decision process. First, a subset of features was used to restrict the set of speakers with whom an unknown was compared. The final identification of a speaker, selected from this restricted speaker set, was based on a larger number of features (Bricker *et al.*, 1971).

For speaker verification, only the distance between the test sample and the reference pattern of the claimed speaker need be computed. If the distance is less than some threshold value, the speaker is accepted; otherwise, he is rejected. The selection of threshold is part of the design of the verification scheme, and, in an experimental system, actually is determined after distances are computed. There are two kinds of errors possible in verification: A customer can be falsely rejected, or an impostor can be falsely accepted. The *equal error threshold*, the most commonly used threshold determination, is the distance at which the two types of errors are equal.

Lummis (1973) computed five different distance measures for each of six different features and for all possible combinations of features. In this manner, he was able to evaluate the effectiveness of his features for speaker verification. He obtained very low error rates when using only pitch and gain contours of a sentence. Including formant information did not improve his results except when the impostor set included professional mimics. It appeared that, overall, formants were more difficult to mimic than pitch, gain, and timing. However, false acceptance rates showed that gain and pitch functions of some speakers were more difficult to imitate than their formants (Lummis and Rosenberg, 1971). In an extension of this study, Rosenberg and Sambur (1975) tailored their decision rules (choice of distance measures and set of features) to each customer in their experimental system. They were able to reduce the false acceptance rate for professional mimics from over 20% to an acceptable 4%.

COMPARISON WITH SPEAKER RECOGNITION BY LISTENING

Researchers conducting SRL studies can only infer from the listeners' responses the nature of the human perceptual and decision processes, while in machine recognition experiments, the features of the speech signal and the decision rule are specified precisely. By comparing results achieved by human beings and machines, we may gain some insight into the less understood listener processes.

Rosenberg (1973) compared speaker verification performance of listeners with machine verification results based on the same speech material. He found that false acceptance error rate for machines was significantly lower than the average performance of listeners for both casual and mimic impostors. However, the performance of the best listeners compared favorably with, or even exceeded, the performance of the automatic system. Unfortunately, no comparisons of individual test items were reported, so we do not know if listener and machine errors were made on the same samples. This information might contribute to our knowledge about the perceptual data used by listeners.

Lummis (1973) reported interesting results for a small set of utterances of an identical twin impostor. All of the utterances were rejected correctly by the machine using only pitch and gain as a function of time. The same twin utterances were almost always accepted by listeners. It appears that organic cues were more salient to the listeners than the timing and intensity cues, which differed substantially between the identical twins as evidenced by the machine results.

Lummis' (1973) results show that speakers can be distinguished, at least statistically, using only speaker information in pitch and intensity contours. However, other recent SRM results demonstrate that these features of the signal are not essential for recognizing speakers. In an identification study using ten speakers with utterances collected over a month, Atal (1974) achieved 98% correct identification for .5 sec of speech. Recognition was based only on spectral envelope measures; there were no pitch or intensity parameters used. These two results illustrate dramatically that potentially useful speaker information is distributed over different aspects of the speech signal. However, it is still not at all clear that listeners can, or do, use the same information in the same manner as the machine.

Speaker Recognition by Visual Inspection of Spectrograms

Speaker recognition by spectrography (*SRS*) has been the subject of controversy concerning its forensic application (Bolt, Cooper, David, Denes, Pickett, and Stevens, 1970, 1973; Black, Lashbrook, Nash, Oyer, Pedrey, Tosi, and Truby, 1973); also, it has been the focus of several research papers since Kersta (1962) introduced the possibility more than a decade ago. Fundamentals of the technique are similar to those of other methods: Samples of speech are recorded, converted to graphic (time—frequency—energy) patterns by use of a sound spectrograph, arranged in various ways for visual inspection, and judged by human observers. Hecker (1971) has reviewed the effects of many variables on SRS results and has also summarized the extensive comparisons of SRS and SRL carried out by Stevens *et al.* (1968). In this section, we touch briefly on three more recent studies, two of which employed a matching task, while the other more closely resembled the evaluation format.

MATCHING EXPERIMENTS

The chief conditions of both the Tosi *et al.* (1972) and the Hazen (1973) experiments are listed in Table 9.2. In both cases, both the test (unknown) and reference (known) speakers were represented by spectrograms of one or more utterances of several common words assembled on one card per speaker. Subjects were required to identify the test speaker as one of the N_s reference speakers in closed-set tasks, or make either an identification or a no-match response in open-set tasks. Major results were as follows:

Ensemble Size. Tosi *et al.* (1972) found a significant increase in errors with speaker ensemble (and response set) size, as have SRL investigators.

Context. Both studies agree with Young and Campbell (1967) that contextual differences between test and reference patterns yield higher errors, but the studies differ as to the absolute size of the effect. The figures in Table 9.3 illustrate the difference between same and random context for comparable conditions in the two studies.

Manner of Speaking. Although Hazen's (1973) and Tosi *et al.*'s (1972) observers were performing comparably at the end of training, their test results, of which Table 9.3 is typical, were very different. While it is impossible to assign this difference to any single cause, Hazen's use of spontaneous speech is very likely a major factor. Hazen (1973) concluded that further study was needed to determine the extent to which reading from text reduces the amount of intraspeaker variability encountered in spontaneous speech.

Time Lapse. Tosi *et al.*'s (1972) finding that test patterns recorded at different sessions from reference patterns produce more than twice the error rate of contemporary patterns (12% versus 5% overall) is consistent with findings on machine recognition.

Transmission System. The absence of a transmission system effect in Tosi *et al.*'s (1972) study at first seems curious. The report indicates, however, that under a given condition of the transmission-system variable, both test and reference patterns were recorded over the same system. These experiments, then, do not test the effect of a difference in transmission conditions between test and reference patterns.

Table 9.2 Experimental Variables for Two Studies of Speaker Recognition by Visual Inspection of Spectrograms

Study	Speaker ensemble	Speech materials					Transmission system	Observers		Tasks (N_R = Number of response alternatives)
		Number of different cue words	Number of utterances of each	Contexts	Manner of speaking	Time lapse between test and reference recording		Number	Training	
Tosi et al. (1972)	$N_S = 10, 20$ or 40	6 or 9	1, 2, or 3	1. Isolated 2. Fixed or 3. Random	Reading from text	1. Same session 2. One month separation	1. Hi-Fi 2. Telephone (quiet) 3. Telephone (noisy environment)	$N = 29$ in groups of 1, 2, or 3	One month (achieved less than 4% error on standard task)[a]	Matching 1. closed set: $N_R = N_S$ 2. open set: $N_R = N_S + 1$
Hazen (1973)	$N_S = 50$	5	2	1. Isolated (for training only) 2. Fixed or 3. Random	Reading (for training only) Extemporaneous conversation	Same session	Hi-Fi	$N = 14$ in groups of 2	8 Sessions (achieved 2–3% error on standard task)[a]	Matching 1. closed set: $N_R = N_S = 50$ 2. open set: $N_R = N_S + 1 = 51$

[a]Standard Task: Closed set matching; words in isolation; test and reference—same session; number of reference speakers = 10 for TOSI et al., 50 for HAZEN.

Table 9.3 *Percentage Error for Comparable Conditions of Two Studies of Speaker Recognition by Visual Inspection of Spectrograms*

	Same context	Random context
Tosi *et al.*		
(Contemporary, Closed Set, Six Cue Words)	1%	6%
Hazen		
(Contemporary, Closed Set, Five Cue Words)	20%	74%

Task. Both experimenters found more errors with open than with closed sets. These experiments contribute little to our understanding of the nature of speaker information because they do not communicate publicly how the observers performed their identifications. However, they do call attention to two variables that generally have been neglected by SRL researchers, namely, differences in speech samples between recording sessions and differences between spontaneous speaking and reading from text. Any demonstration of effects of either of these variables on speaker recognition by listening would have both theoretical and practical implications.

EVALUATION

A study by Endress *et al.* (1971) examined the effects of aging, mimicry, and disguise on measurements made from spectrograms. They recorded voices of actors and politicians over periods of up to 29 years, recorded mimics in natural and imitating modes, and measured *pitch melodies* and formant frequencies. They found that aging produces changes with plausible physiological and anatomical correlates. Disguise can effect substantial changes in formant and pitch patterns, but mimicry does not produce accurate imitations of these parameters. This latter finding is consistent with machine verification results using mimicry (Rosenberg and Sambur, 1975; Doddington *et al.*, 1973). A practical implication of these results is that voice identification systems for security purposes look more promising than those for criminal identification.

Outlook

Speaker recognition research has produced considerable knowledge about the nature of speaker information at various stages of the recognition process. In this section, we shall evaluate this knowledge, indicate gaps in our understanding, and note some techniques likely to be useful in filling those gaps.

Studies of machine recognition have identified a number of attributes on which speakers vary distinctively. Although these studies have dealt exclusively with the acoustic signal, they have used knowledge of the acoustics of speech production to interpret acoustic measurements in terms of the anatomy and habits of speakers and the gestures of speech. Features that carry speaker information include the spectra of nasals and vowels, the spectral envelope of longer segments, glottal frequency and spectrum, and the time contours of pitch, intensity, and formants. Careful measurement has shown that speakers produce specific speech events in characteristic ways, and that some events carry more speaker information than others. No source of speaker information is infallible, and many are intercorrelated. Yet, the power of a sufficient number of partially independent cues to differentiate or identify speakers solely on the basis of physical measurement is impressive.

The distinctiveness of a cue depends in part on its variability within speakers. There is evidence that many of the above characteristics are much more variable in spontaneous speech than in the readings from text, which have provided the bulk of the data for research to date. Difficult though it may be to work with, spontaneous speech deserves more attention than it has received from both listener and machine recognition researchers.

Little progress has been made in characterizing how listeners perceive and distinguish among voices. Studies that manipulated speech gestures and signal parameters have identified several parameters that are related to speaker recognition performance, but have not shown *how* these parameters are related to distinctive attributes of the voices as perceived by listeners. Manipulative studies are more likely to contribute to an understanding of the perceptual process if they are designed to test predictions derived from a model of that process. For example, the notion that there is a finite number of attributes on which speakers differ implies that the perceptual process has a limited capacity to transmit speaker information. The truth of this prediction can be tested experimentally by varying ensemble size and using the information measure. An even stronger form of the speaker-attributes model suggests that the perceptual form of speaker information is independent of the task. Testing this prediction requires collecting data with different tasks on the same speaker ensemble and comparing results in various ways.

Correlational studies, which have addressed the perceptual problem more directly, have lacked adequate techniques for data collection, perceptual measurement, physical measurement, and relating perceptual and physical measurements. Developments in other fields provide tools that should help solve each of these technical problems. Researchers collecting identification data often have used severely restricted speech samples in order to produce sufficient errors for study. Choice reaction time techniques, used in other fields of perception and information processing research (e.g., Sternberg, 1969), might offer more sensitive means of measuring recognition performance on long samples of speech. For deriving perceptual dimensions, multidimensional scaling should be useful. New techniques that take advantage of individual differences among listeners to define perceptually significant dimensions (Carroll, 1972) are especially appropriate. Recently developed computer techniques for speech analysis can provide a variety of physical measures, and linear or nonlinear regression techniques can be used to relate the physical measures to the perceptual dimensions.

The human decision process, the last element in the overall process of speaker recognition by listening, has received very little attention. Speaker recognition by machine, on the other hand, requires that decision rules be made explicit. It is likely that the techniques developed for SRM could be used to explore models of the human decision process. Proposed decision rules could be simulated on a computer and adjusted to produce a pattern of response similar to that of the human listeners. Some features of the models themselves might be patterned after procedures that have been successful in SRM work. Examples of such procedures are the two-stage decision rule that first selected a subset of speakers on which to make a subsequent identification, and the verification procedure that tailored decision rules to individual speakers. It might be instructive to determine to what extent human listeners perform analogous functions.

To sum up, there are opportunities for students of speech perception to increase our basic knowledge of speaker recognition by listening and thus improve the scientific basis for practical applications. Chances of success in this research, we feel, will be enhanced by close cooperation with colleagues in speech analysis and perceptual measurement.

REFERENCES

Atal, B. S. Text-independent speaker recognition. Paper presented at the Eighty-Third Meeting of the Acoustical Society of America, April 18—21, 1972, Buffalo, New York. (a)

Atal, B. S. Automatic speaker recognition based on pitch contours. *Journal of the Acoustical Society of America*, 1972, *52*, 1687—1697. (b)

Atal, B. S. Effectiveness of linear prediction characteristics of the speech wave for automatic speaker identification and verification. *Journal of the Acoustical Society of America*, 1974, *55*, 1304—1312.

Atal, B. S., and Hanauer, S. L. Speech analysis and synthesis by linear prediction of the speech wave. *Journal of the Acoustical Society of America*, 1971, *50*, 637—655.

Black, J. W., Lashbrook, W., Nash, E., Oyer, H. J., Pedrey, C., Tosi, O. I., and Truby, H. Reply to "Speaker identification by speech spectrograms: Some further observations." *Journal of the Acoustical Society of America*, 1973, *54*, 535—537.

Bolt, R. H., Cooper, F. S., David, E. E., Denes, P. B., Pickett, J. M., and Stevens, K. N. Speaker identification by speech spectrograms: A scientists' view of its reliability for legal purposes. *Journal of the Acoustical Society of America*, 1970, *47*, 597—612.

Bolt, R. H., Cooper, F. S., David, E. E., Denes, P. B., Pickett, J. M., and Stevens, K. N. Speaker identification by speech spectrograms: some further observations. *Journal of the Acoustical Society of America*, 1973, *54*, 531—534.

Bricker, P. D., Gnanadesikan, R., Mathews, M. V., Pruzansky, S., Tukey, P. A., Wachter, K. W., and Warner, J. L. Statistical techniques for talker identification. *Bell System Technical Journal*, 1971, *50*, 1427—1454.

Bricker, P. D., and Pruzansky, S. Effects of stimulus content and duration on talker identification. *Journal of the Acoustical Society of America*, 1966, *40*, 1441—1449.

Carbonell, J. R., Grignetti, M. C., Stevens, K. N., Williams, C. E., and Woods, B. Speaker authentication techniques. Report 1296 prepared under Contract No. DA-28-043-AMC-00116(E) by Bolt Beranek and Newman Inc., Cambridge, Mass., 1965.

Carroll, J. D. Individual differences and multidimensional scaling. In R. N. Shepard, A. K. Romney, and S. Nerlove (Eds.), *Multidimensional scaling: Theory and applications in the behavioral sciences*. Vol. 1: *Theory*. New York: Seminar Press, 1972. Pp. 105—155.

Clarke, F. R., and Becker, R. W. Comparison of techniques for discriminating among talkers. *Journal of Speech and Hearing Research*, 1969, *12*, 747—761.

Clarke, F. R., Becker, R. W., and Nixon, J. C. Characteristics that determine speaker recognition. Report ESD-TR-66-636, Electronic Systems Division, Air Force Systems Command, Hanscom Field, December, 1966.

Coleman, R. O. Male and female voice quality and its relationship to vowel formant frequencies. *Journal of Speech and Hearing Research*, 1971, *14*, 565—577.

Coleman, R. O. Speaker identification in the absence of inter-subject differences in glottal source characteristics. *Journal of the Acoustical Society of America*, 1973, *53*, 1741—1743.

Compton, A. J. Effects of filtering and vocal duration upon the identification of speakers, aurally. *Journal of the Acoustical Society of America*, 1963, *35*, 1748—1752.

Das, S. K., and Mohn, W. S. A scheme for speech processing in automatic speaker verification. *I.E.E.E. Transactions on Audio and Electroacoustics*, 1971, *AU—19*, 32—43.

Doddington, G. R. A method of speaker verification. Paper presented at the Eightieth Meeting of the Acoustical Society of America, November 3—8, 1970, Houston, Texas.

Doddington, G., Hydrick, B., and Beek, B. Some results on speaker verification using amplitude spectra. Paper presented at the Eighty-Sixth Meeting of the Acoustical Society of America, October 30—November 2, 1973, Los Angeles, California.

Dukiewicz, L. Frequency-band dependence of speaker identification. In W. Jassem (Ed.), *Speech analysis and synthesis*, Vol. II. Warsaw, Poland: Institute of Fundamental Technical Research, Polish Academy of Sciences, 1970.

Endres, W., Bambach, W., and Flosser, G. Voice spectrograms as a function of age, voice disguise, and voice imitation. *Journal of the Acoustical Society of America*, 1971, *49*, 1842—1848.

Furui, S., Itakura, F., and Saito, S. Talker recognition by longtime averaged speech spectrum. *Electronics and Communications in Japan*, 1972, *55—A*, 54—61.

Garvin, P. L., and Ladefoged, P. Speaker identification and message identification in speech recognition. *Phonetica*, 1963, *9*, 193—199.

Glenn, J. W., and Kleiner, N. Speaker identification based on nasal phonation. *Journal of the Acoustical Society of America*, 1968, *43*, 368—372.

Gray, C. H. G., and Kopp, G. A. Voice print identification. Unpublished report, Bell Laboratories, 1944.

Hair, G. D., and Rekieta, T. W. Techniques for objective speaker identification. Paper presented at the Eighty-Fourth meeting of the Acoustical Society of America, November 28—December 1, 1972, Miami Beach, Florida.

Hargreaves, W. A., and Starkweather, J. A. Recognition of speaker identity. *Language and Speech*, 1963, *6*, 63—67.

Hazen, B. Effects of differing phonetic contexts on spectrographic speaker identification. *Journal of the Acoustical Society of America*, 1973, *54*, 650—660.

Hecker, M. H. L. Speaker recognition: An interpretive survey of the literature. *ASHA Monographs*, No. *16*, 1971.

Holmgren, G. L. Physical and psychological correlates of speaker recognition. *Journal of Speech and Hearing Research*, 1967, *10*, 57—66.

Ingemann, F. Identification of the speaker's sex from voiceless fricatives. *Journal of the Acoustical Society of America*, 1968, *44*, 1142—1144.

Kersta, L. Voiceprint identification. *Nature*, 1962, *196*, 1253—1257.

Li, K. P., Dammann, J. E., and Chapman, W. D. Experimental studies in speaker verification, using an adaptive system. *Journal of the Acoustical Society of America*, 1966, *40*, 966—978.

Li, K. P., and Hughes, G. W. Talker differences as they appear in correlation matrices from spectra of continuous speech. Paper presented at the Eighty-Fourth Meeting of the Acoustical Society of America, November 28—December 1, 1972, Miami Beach, Florida.

Luck, J. E. Automatic speaker verification using cepstral measurements. *Journal of the Acoustical Society of America*, 1969, *46*, 1026—1032.

Lummis, R. C. Speaker verification by computer using speech intensity for temporal registration. *I.E.E.E. Transactions on Audio and Electroacoustics*, 1973, *AU—21*, 80—89.

Lummis, R. C., and Rosenberg, A. E. Test of an automatic speaker verification method with intensively trained professional mimics. Paper presented at the Eighty-Second Meeting of the Acoustical Society of America, October 19—22, 1971, Denver, Colorado.

Mathews, M. V., Miller, J. E., and David, E. E. Pitch synehronous analysis of voiced sounds. *Journal of the Acoustical Society of America*, 1961, *33*, 179—186.

Matsumoto, H., Hiki, S., Sone, T., and Nimura, T. Multidlmensional representation of personal quality and its acoustical correlates. *I.E.E.E. Transactions on Audio and Electroacoustics*, 1973, *AU—21*, 428—436.

McDermott, B. J. Multidimensional analyses of circuit quality judgments. *Journal of the Acoustical Society of America*, 1969, *45*, 774—781.

McGehee, F. The reliability of the identification of the human voice. *Journal of General Psychology*, 1937, *17*, 249—271.

McGehee, F. An experimental study in voice recognition. *Journal of General Psychology*, 1944, *31*, 53—65.

Miller, J. E. Decapitation and recapitation, a study of voice quality. Paper presented at the Sixty-Eighth Meeting of the Acoustical Society of America, October 21—24, 1964, Austin, Texas.

Mohn, W. S. Two statistical feature evaluation techniques applied to speaker identification. *I.E.E.E. Transactions on Computers*, 1971, *C—20*, 979—987.

Murry, T., and Cort, S. Aural identification of children's voices. *Journal of Auditory Research*, 1971, *11*, 260—262.

Osgood, C. E., Suci, G. J., and Tanenbaum, P. H. *The measurement of meaning*. Urbana: Univ. of Illinois Press, 1957.

Peters, R. W. Studies in extra messages: Listener identification of speakers' voices under conditions of certain restrictions imposed upon the voice signal. U.S. Naval School of Aviation Medicine, Joint Project NM 001-064-01, Report 30, Pensacola, Florida, 1954.

Pollack, I., Pickett, J. M., and Sumby, W. H. On the identification of speakers by voice. *Journal of the Acoustical Society of America*, 1954, *26*, 403—406.

Pruzansky, S. Pattern-matching procedure for automatic talker recognition. *Journal of the Acoustical Society of America*, 1963, *35*, 354—358.

Pruzansky, S., and Mathews, M. V. Talker-recognition procedure based on analysis of variance. *Journal of the Acoustical Society of America*, 1964, *36*, 2041—2047.

Ptacek, P. H., and Sander, E. K. Age recognition from voice. *Journal of Speech and Hearing Research*, 1966, *9*, 273—277.

Ramishvili, G. S. Automatic voice recognition. *Engineering Cybernetics*, 1966, *5*, 84—90.

Rosenberg, A. E. Listener performance in speaker verification tasks. *I.E.E.E. Transactions on Audio and Electroacoustics*, 1973, *AU—21*, 221—225.

Rosenberg, A. E., and Sambur, M. New techniques for automatic speaker verification. *I.E.E.E. Transactions on Acoustics, Speech, and Signal Processing*, 1975, *ASSP—23*, 169—176.

Ryan, W. J., and Burk, K. W. Predictors of age in the male voice. Paper presented at the Eighty-Fourth Meeting of the Acoustical Society of America, November 28—December 1, 1972, Miami Beach, Florida.

Sambur, M. R. Selection of acoustic features for speaker identification. *I.E.E.E. Transactions on Acoustics, Speech, and Signal Processing*, 1975, *ASSP—23*, 176—182.

Schwartz, M. F. Identification of speaker sex from isolated, voiceless fricatives. *Journal of the Acoustical Society of America*, 1968, *43*, 1178—1179.

Schwartz, M. F., and Rine, H. E. Identification of speaker sex from isolated, whispered vowels. *Journal of the Acoustical Society of America*, 1968, *44*, 1736—1737.

Shearme, J. N., and Holmes, J. N. An experiment concerning the recognition of voices. *Language and Speech*, 1959, *2*, 123—131.

Shipp, T., and Hollien, H. Perception of the aging male voice. *Journal of Speech and Hearing Research*, 1969, *12*, 703—710.

Smith, J. E. K. Decision-theoretic speaker recognizer. Paper presented at the Sixty-Fourth Meeting of the Acoustical Society of America, November 7—10, 1962, Seattle, Washington.

Sternberg, S. Memory-scanning: Mental processes revealed by reaction-time experiments. *American Scientist*, 1969, *57*, 421—457.

Stevens, K. N., Williams, C. E., Carbonell, J. R., and Woods, B. Speaker authentication and identification: A comparison of spectrographic and auditory presentations of speech material. *Journal of the Acoustical Society of America*, 1968, *44*, 1596—1607.

Su, L.-S, Li, K.-P, and Fu, K. S. Identification of speakers by use of nasal coarticulation. *Journal of the Acoustical Society of America*, 1974, *56*, 1876—1882.

Tosi, O., Oyer, H., Lashbrook, W., Pedrey, C., Nicol, J., and Nash, E. Experiment on voice identification. *Journal of the Acoustical Society of America*, 1972, *51*, 2030—2043.

Voiers, W. D. Performance evaluation of speech processing devices II. The role of individual differences. Report AFCRL-66-24, Air Force Cambridge Research Laboratories, Office of Aerospace Research, Bedford, Massachusetts, December 1965.

Voiers, W. D., Cohen, M. F., and Mickunas, J. Evaluation of speech processing devices I. Intelligibility, quality, speaker recognizability. Report AFCRL-65-826, Air Force Cambridge Research Laboratories, Office of Aerospace Research, Bedford, Massachusetts, July 1965.

Weinberg, B., and Bennett, S. A study of talker sex recognition of esophageal voices. *Journal of Speech and Hearing Research*, 1971, *14*, 391—395. (a)

Weinberg, B., and Bennett, S. Speaker sex recognition of 5- and 6-year-old children's voices. *Journal of the Acoustical Society of America*, 1971, *50*, 1210—1213. (b)

Williams, C. E. The effects of selected factors on the aural identification of speakers. Sect. III of Report ESD-TDR-65-153, Electronics Systems Division, Air Force Systems Command, Hanscom Field, 1964.

Wolf, J. J. Efficient acoustic parameters for speaker recognition. *Journal of the Acoustical Society of America*, 1971, *51*, 2044—2055.

Young, M. A., and Campbell, R. A. Effects of context on talker identification. *Journal of the Acoustical Society of America*, 1967, *42*, 1250—1254.

chapter 10

Dichotic Listening

Charles I. Berlin

Louisiana State University
Medical Center, New Orleans

Malcolm R. McNeil

Veterans Administration Hospital,
Denver, Colorado

Introduction and Orientation

When two different words are presented simultaneously, one to each ear, most listeners perceive more of the right ear messages accurately. This effect was reported first by Broadbent (1954), but Kimura (1961a) was the first to ascribe this right ear advantage (*REA*) to the dominance of the left hemisphere for speech. She reasoned that, since crossed pathways are prepotent in the auditory system, and since the left hemisphere was believed to be dominant for speech functions, the right ear advantage was related to the crossed nature of the pathways. Since 1954, over 300 papers pertaining directly or indirectly to dichotic listening and hemispheric asymmetry have been published (Thompson and Thompson, 1975). Reviews of theoretical issues related to dichotic listening (Studdert-Kennedy and Shankweiler, 1970; Berlin, 1971, 1972; Berlin and Lowe, 1972) are now available.

In this chapter we plan to outline six theories on the nature of the dichotic right ear advantage; this will be followed by a tabular analysis of over 300 articles and papers pertaining to dichotic speech perception. Finally, we will present data from the Kresge Hearing Research Laboratory on acoustic and phonetic considerations important to incorporate in a working theory of dichotic speech perception.

Why Is There a Dichotic Right Ear Advantage?

Morphologic and Functional Asymmetry

One of the important assumptions underlying the study of left—right brain asymmetries in human beings is that most normal listeners are left-brained for speech and language. Strong anatomic support for this position comes from the brief note published by Geschwind and Levitsky in 1968. They performed post-mortem examinations on 100 adult human brains, exposing the upper surface of the temporal lobe on each side by a cut made in the plane of the Sylvian fissure. Geschwind and Levitsky then showed conclusively that the area behind Heschl's gyrus was larger on the left side in 65% of the brains, and larger on the right side in only 11%. The planum temporale was, on the average, one-third longer on the left side than it was on the right. The area in question involves the auditory association areas classically called *Wernicke's area*, in the temporal convolution, known to be of major importance in language function. Witelson and Pallie (1973) have shown a comparable asymmetry in newborns. Since this area makes up a large part of the temporal speech cortex, Geschwind and Levitsky have confirmed anatomic asymmetries that correlate with the dominance of the left hemisphere for speech and language function. One weakness of their report is that language, speech, hearing, and handedness data were not available on these subjects. Of course, both authors are quite aware of this weakness in their study; they argue that, since about 93% of the adult population are right-handed and 96% are left-brained for speech, it would be reasonable to assume that their 100 subjects must have consisted primarily of those who were left-brain dominant for speech.

A physiologic sign of left hemisphere dominance for speech becomes evident following an intracarotid amytal injection (Penfield and Roberts, 1959). As the amytal disables portions of the cortex, *speech loss* is usually seen in conjunction with right hemiparesis. Additional studies have reported a high correlation between dichotic listening and intracarotid amytal results (Wada and Rasmussen, 1960). Milner, Taylor, and Sperry (1968) highlighted the nature of functional brain asymmetry in human beings with a convincing report on seven patients with presumed complete midline section of the cerebral commissures including the corpus callosum. By using competing number tasks, these researchers observed that the patients with midline section of the corpus callosum had virtually no perception of speech in the left ear in the dichotic mode, but they showed 100% perception in both ears when the ears were tested individually. With this rather simple technique, Milner's team has shown that while the right and left hemispheres have some similarity in function, speech perception or expression, or both, are related predominantly to the left hemisphere.

Selective Attention

Broadbent (1954), in his original description of dichotic listening performance, felt that his subjects were unable to process two incoming stimuli simultaneously, and that they were alternating their attention from one channel to another at extremely fast rates. He noted that information fed to the right ear often elicited the first response; his conclusion, then, was that the normal listener could well have a response bias toward speech signals sent to the right ear.

Cherry (1953), Broadbent (1954), Moray (1959), Deutsch and Deutsch (1963),

Triesman (1964a,b,c,d), Deutsch, Deutsch, and Lindsay (1967), Triesman and Geffen (1968), Wilson, Dirks, and Carterette (1968), Triesman (1969), Triesman and Riley (1969), and Gerber and Goldman (1971) are among those who have studied the effect of selective listening and report strategies on dichotic right ear advantages. They found that asking subjects to listen selectively to one channel altered (within certain limits) both the size and direction of the right ear advantage.

This apparent supremacy of the right ear over the left ear in dichotic listening cannot be ascribed solely to superior selective attention to one channel over another; we need additional information on *why* one channel seems to be able to "attend more closely" to speech information while the other channel seems to "attend more naturally" to nonspeech acoustic information.

A Memory or Storage Model

Kimura (1961b) and Milner (1962), among others, have shown that patients with left temporal lobe lesions seem to have poorer *verbal* recall, while patients with right temporal lobe lesions have poorer *musical* pattern recall; as the dichotic messages are lengthened (e.g., as the subject is asked to recall three or four strings of digit pairs in each ear, thus putting greater stress on memory function than does asking him to recall a simple pair of CVs), the right ear advantages appear to increase. Bakker (1970) has shown that superior right ear performance can be demonstrated in monaural listening simply by making the recall task long enough or complex enough.

In all probability, it would be safe to conclude that such factors as acoustic perception, memory (Yeni-Komshian, Gordon, and Sherman, 1972), selective attention, and functional asymmetry of the hemispheres probably all interact in some way, as yet unclear, to generate a right ear advantage in dichotic speech perception tasks. However, the above variables do not lend themselves to systematic manipulation without possible contamination of findings. For example, asking the patient to selectively attend to one channel must, of necessity, affect his memory functions for material to which he does not attend closely. The question of functional asymmetry in favor of the left hemisphere for speech raises this key question: Why does this asymmetry of brain function resulting in different ear advantages seem to occur, at least on the surface, only with speech tasks? The next section offers a possible explanation.

Vocal Tract Gesture Coding

Berlin, Lowe-Bell, Cullen, Thompson, and Loovis (1973a) suggested that the right ear advantages in speech-like tasks may be related to the use of *any* acoustic event which is perceptually linkable to rapid gliding motions of the vocal tract. The evidence for this working hypothesis is, at best, tenuous; we first cite the work of Sussman (1971) who shows that, in a *tone*-tracking task, if the right ear and tongue are used interactively to track the target tone, fewer errors are made than if the tongue and left ear are used interactively. Sussman, MacNeilage, and Lumbley (1973, 1974, 1975) find a similar effect using the jaw as a tracker for these tones.

There are other special conditions, related to vocal tract motions, for which the right ear advantage can be demonstrated without placing the ears in a competitive situation. For example, Abbs and Smith (1970) have shown that when delayed auditory feedback is generated to the right ear, there are more articulatory types of errors than when delayed feedback is generated to the left ear. We have shown also that the left ear will be suppressed in a dichotic listening task even if there is an unintelligible signal in the right ear, so long as that unintelligible signal in the right ear has been derived from what sounds like a rapid vocal tract transition (Berlin, Porter, Lowe-Bell, Berlin, Thompson, and Hughes, 1973b).

It is important to note here that Kimura (1964), among others, reports a *left* ear advantage for dichotic melodies; this left ear advantage was ascribed to the dominance of the right hemisphere for nonverbal acoustic processing.[1] However, much of the relevant literature suggests that, for a right ear advantage to be seen, dichotic *speech* rather than musical stimuli should be presented. Noise alone presented to the right ear will not suppress perception of CVs in the left ear, but even dichotic Morse code signals can generate a right ear advantage if the signals are meaningful to the listeners (Papçun, Krashen, and Terbeek, 1972). Since, reportedly, dichotically presented melodies generate a *left* ear advantage, the arguments over why tones and Morse code sometimes can generate a *right* ear advantage (instead of the predicted left ear advantage) are exceedingly important. One hypothesis that we suggested (Berlin *et al.*, 1973b) to explain the right ear advantage with Morse code was that the operators might have used a vocal-tract-related type of encoding of the Morse code (with *da-da-dit-dit-dit*, or a subvocalized verbal encoding) to generate the paradoxical right ear advantage for these nonverbal stimuli.

It is possible, in fact it is quite likely, that both the dichotic right ear advantage for speech and the dichotic right ear advantage seen for tongue-tracked tones and Morse stimuli may be related to separate functions of the left hemisphere. However, the notion that "any acoustic signal may become lateralized to the left hemisphere, if a difficult enough auditory task can be related to a complex vocal tract movement" (Berlin *et al.*, 1973a, p. 705) is an intriguing working hypothesis; it will constitute a rationale of a plan of action for subsequent experiments.

---

[1]Most research suggests a right hemisphere—left ear dichotic advantage for melodies and chords. My (CIB) intuitive experience as a professional musician suggests to me that the *left* hemisphere and the right ear may be more active in musicians than nonmusicians. Most pianists of my acquaintance are unable to play interpretive melodies and carry on meaningful discourse simultaneously, and I find this to be true from my own experience. The phenomenon occurs also when pianists play only left-handed or only right-handed passages. This interference of function has never been tested systematically, to my knowledge, but it is a provocative thought when one considers music as a special form of communication for certain groups of people. Bever and Chiarello (1974) suggest that this *reversal* may be seen in selected musicians.

Is the Right Ear Advantage Related to the Perceived Source of Auditory Space?

Fodor and Bever (1965) asked subjects to locate the position of a click with respect to an ongoing sentence. The click was presented to one ear and the sentence to the other. While not a dichotic task in the sense that competing speech messages are commonly called *dichotic*, it is nevertheless an intriguing task with respect to possible evidence for the routing of speech signals to the left hemisphere and nonspeech signals to the right. Fodor and Bever reported that subjects tended to perceive clicks presented to the left ear as coming earlier than those presented to the right ear.

Superficially, one might predict such an effect by reasoning that processing nonverbal signals via the left-ear-to-right-hemisphere route is simply more efficient (but should it be necessarily faster?). However, the relative accuracy of the click placements was the same for both right click and left click conditions; it was the tendency of the left click condition to generate a perception of location *earlier* in the sentence than the right click, which led Bertelson and Tisseyre (1972) to an unusual but important set of experiments on the nature of this asymmetry. Four experiments were reported, each one contingent, to some extent, on the results of the previous experiment. In their first experiment, they replicated the Fodor and Bever findings closely but not exactly.

Bertelson and Tisseyre reasoned, however, that the effect might be related to where in space either the click or the speech seemed to originate. They therefore designed an experiment in which the speech or the clicks were sometimes given *to the midline* (that is, binaurally at equal sensation levels), while the other stimulus was given either to the left, to the right, or to the midline. They reported that when the click seemed to come from a position to the left of the speech, it also tended to cause the subject to locate the click earlier in the sentence than he would if presented to the right. Note again that *earlier* did not mean *more accurately*. Note also that the *relative*, not *absolute*, position of the click to the speech was important; thus when the speech was presented to the right ear and the click to the midline (i.e., the click still seemed to be coming from a position in space relatively to the left of the speech), the *early perception* was still noted.

This finding led them to a third experiment in which they created listening conditions which they called *full-head* and *half-head* separations. In a full-head separation, the speech is clearly in one ear, while the click is perceived clearly in the other. The half-head conditions had the speech or click in the midline, while the other stimulus was given to one ear alone. They found that in the conditions with full-head separations there was a larger asymmetry than in those with half-head separations. The larger asymmetry seen in the full-head separation, however, was due entirely to the conditions where the click was perceived to the left of the speech. This finding led them to their fourth experiment, which added a condition in which speech and click both were presented to the midline, a *double monotic* condition, according to the literature coding system. Again, conditions under which the click was perceived as coming to the left of the speech generated more *early perceptions* than those under which the click was either to the right or seemed to come from the same source as the speech.

Some subtle underlying questions are implicit in this recurrent finding that the earlier processing of a click relates to its apparent position in space.

1. Has man's survival with respect to predators on the left or right built in an earlier or more efficient response, or spatial distribution of attention (Kinsbourne, 1970) to environmental noise on the left versus speech on the right? If this were the case, reaction time studies and temporal order judgment tasks for speech should show lateral asymmetries, and they do (e.g., Day and Vigorito, 1972; Springer, 1972). But why then did not the left click condition simply generate more *accuracy* rather than shifted perception?

2. Is the dichotic right ear advantage for speech related to apparent localization in space? If this were the case, MLD studies might show some asymmetries for speech versus tones and clicks, but they do not (Cullen and Thompson, 1972). Furthermore, it is clear that the localization rules that give precedence to the stimulus that arrives earlier are not in effect in dichotic listening; it is the *second* signal rather than the first signal presented that is better perceived in the range of 30 to 60 msec (to be discussed later). Here we have to separate *detection* tasks from *recognition* tasks. The click location task requires little labeling and virtually no competitive phonetic processing per se. The dichotic speech task requires accurate recognition of two competing acoustic and phonetic elements.

Bertelson and Tisseyre (1972) quite correctly point out that there are not enough data to relate the perceptual click asymmetry effect to the dichotic right ear advantage for speech; they suggest that it is doubtful that a single mechanism might explain both the REA for speech and the phenomenon they studied. Nevertheless, it is a provocative notion that the perceived temporal position of a stimulus is related to the position in space from which one believes the signal is coming. Such an observation needs more attention vis-a-vis dichotic listening. For this reason, it has been included in this discussion of important theoretical positions.

Temporal Sequencing Is a Left Hemisphere Function and Speech Is a Special Case of a Temporal Sequence

Papçun *et al.* (1972) have shown that dichotically presented Morse code can generate unusually large right ear advantages when experienced Morse operators are used as subjects. The researchers relate this observation to a general superiority of the left temporal lobe in handling temporal sequences.

Efron (1963a,b) believed that the left temporal lobe was active in processing all temporal sequences. Jerger, Weikers, Sharbrough, and Jerger (1969) showed that, in a patient with bilateral temporal lobe involvement, ear asymmetries were seen in most auditory tasks; in temporal sequence judgments, however, both ears performed poorly.

This position has been supported recently by Halperin, Nachsohn, and Carmon (1973). They presented dichotic nonverbal stimuli with either two, one, or no frequency transitions between the stimuli. The subjects were asked to identify the stimuli according to a code. As the number of transitions increased, the ear advantage shifted from the left (at zero transitions) to the right (at two transitions). This finding supports the temporal sequence hypothesis but questions the vocal tract sequencing phenomenon postulated previously in this chapter.

The left hemisphere may be active in organizing additional temporal order tasks. Temporal lobe patients and aphasics have had reported difficulty with two-click localization and lateralization tasks, filtered speech tasks, and tasks that generally reflect a problem in managing temporal sequences (Berlin and Lowe, 1972).

Benton (1970, pp. 302—303), in his lecture to the Israeli Medical Society, well summarized the problem of clarifying left hemisphere function when he said,

> the investigative work of the past decade has led to radical revision of the theory of hemispheric cerebral dominance. Perhaps the single most important feature of this revision is that we can no longer think in terms of a major or dominant hemisphere and a minor or subordinate hemisphere. Instead, as earlier work suggested, each hemisphere appears to have its own distinctive functions and these are reflected in a remarkably broad spectrum of activities.
>
> It is obvious that the left hemisphere is involved in language activities but its role appears to be much broader, encompassing conceptual thinking, the perceptual integration of events in time and certain aspects of awareness of one's body. It may or may not prove possible to explain all these performances on the basis of the established language functions of the left hemisphere; further study is required to resolve this issue. Similarly, an impressive body of empirical findings indicate [sic] that the right hemisphere possesses at least a relative dominance for a number of perceptual and motor activities which appear on the surface to be of a rather diverse character. It is reasonable to assume that there are not more than two or three basic functions underlying performance in these diverse activities. But these basic functions remain to be identified.

Tabular Literature Summary

Over 300 articles on dichotic listening have been analyzed and codified in the appendix of this chapter according to the following system:

I. Type of Presentation.
   A. *Dichotic*: two different messages presented to two different ears in some form of competition.
   B. *Monaural*: one message presented to one ear at a time.
   C. *Monotic*: two different messages presented to one ear in some form of competition.
II. Linguistic Status of the Stimuli.
   A. *Verbal*: those stimuli using language-coded symbols such as:
      1. *Semantic Value*: This category refers to the control in stimulus selection, accounting for the relative semantic meaning or emotional impact of the stimuli. Also included in this category are approxima-

tions of English, meaningfulness in terms of language, and syntax of the stimuli.

2. *Sentences* (phrases): strings of words put together often in varying grammatical and syntactical approximations to English.

3. *Words*: either meaningful words (i.e., animal names, verbs, proper nouns, etc.) or CVCs or VCVs.

4. *Digits*: numbers, usually the whole numbers from 1 to 10, excepting 7.

5. *Nonsense CVs*: most often the six English stops with the vowel /a/ (/pa/, ba/, /ka/, /ga/, /ta/, /da/); sometimes VCs.

6. *Letters or Vowels*

7. *Natural Speech*: produced and recorded from a human vocal tract.

8. *Synthetic Speech*: generated digitally or by terminal analog synthesizers.

B. *Nonverbal*: music, clicks, tones, environmental noises, formant, glides, or transitions, etc.

III. Subject Variables.

A. *Age*: Age was either controlled in subject selection or accounted for in the results of the report. *A*—adults; *C*—children; *O*—the old or aging population; and 3—all three age groups.

B. *Sex*: Sex of the subjects was either critical in subject selection or accounted for in the results of the report. *M*—males; *F*—females; and *B*—both males and females.

C. *Handedness*: Handedness of the subjects was either controlled in subject selection or accounted for in the results of the report.

D. *Brain Damage*: Subjects had confirmed cerebral damage and the results of this damage were evaluated or used in the report.

E. *Intelligence*: Intelligence of the subjects was critical in subject selection and accounted for in the results of the report.

F. *Stuttering*: Verbal fluency of the subjects was critical in subject selection and accounted for in the results of the report.

G. *Peripheral Hearing*: Hearing sensitivity of the subjects was abnormal, a critical factor in subject selection; the abnormality was accounted for in the results of the report.

H. *Learning Disability*: Subjects were confirmed to have a learning disability such as dyslexia, which was important in subject selection and was accounted for in the results of the report.

I. *Socioeconomic Status*: Socioeconomic status of the subjects was either important in subject selection or accounted for in the results of the report.

IV. Administration and Stimuli Variables.

A. *Report Bias*: Instruction given pre- or postpresentation to report one message before reporting the other, or to report one ear before the other.

B. *Intensity Bias*: Stimuli deliberately presented at different intensities, or a difference between presentation levels occurring between tasks.

C. *Memory (M) or Recognition (R)*: Method of reporting the stimuli; *recogni-*

tion refers to the reporting after *each* pair of stimuli is presented, whereas *memory* refers to the reporting after a *series* of two or more pairs have been presented, thus requiring a storage or memory component. When both *memory* and *recognition* are used in the same report, the code letter *B* (for both) is used.

D. *Temporal Order*: Time of onset or of offset between the two stimuli as critical to the experiment.

E. *Rate Bias*: Number of individual stimuli presented in a given sequence or amount of time. Time-compressed speech also is included in this category. *R.T.* denotes those few studies using reaction time in dichotic tasks.

F. *Length of Stimulus*: Studies which manipulated the length of stimuli and/ or the number of stimuli in a series as critical variables.

G. *Frequency Range*: Filtering of certain frequencies in the presentation of the message or messages. Also included under this frequency range heading is the variable of male—female voice, when critical to the design and accounted for in the results.

H. *Masking*: Interference of a speech signal by noise or other unrelated competition.

I. *Response Modality*: How the subject responds. *G*——gestural; *V*——verbal; *Gr*——graphic or written; *3*——all three modalities.

V. Theory. Summaries of new or controversial theories.

Regardless of why we think there is a right ear advantage in speech perception, there are basic acoustic and phonetic dichotic data that recently have been documented and are worthy of note. Restricting ourselves generally to the framework of the single syllable pair (e.g., /pa/ to one ear, /da/ to the other; /ka/ to one ear, /ta/ to the other, etc.), now we will present much of our laboratory's data on how the right ear advantage varies with changes in intensity of signals, frequency bandwidth, onset time, retest, age, and a number of other parameters.

Our Basic Dichotic Paradigm

The Stimuli

In most of our experiments, the CV stimuli were six English stops, both voiced and voiceless, each followed by the vowel /a/. In some of these experiments, stimuli were aligned by a specially constructed two-channel delay line (Lowe, Cullen, Berlin, Thompson, and Willet, 1970), while in others, onset alignment was done by computer (Berlin *et al.*, 1973a); however, in all cases, onset alignment was accurate within at least $\pm 2\frac{1}{2}$ msec, and amplitudes of the vowel segments of the CV were within at least $2\frac{1}{2}$ dB of one another. Since we used only /pa/, /ta/, /ka/, /ba/, /da/, and /ga/, we were able to study the types of substitutions which were generated by each pair. To obtain consistent data, we asked subjects in most of our experiments to give two responses to each pair as submitted. Most of our results were obtained with natural rather than synthetic speech samples; but, in order to assure ourselves that our results were not related to sample specificity, we duplicated our preliminary experiments with synthetic CVs (Lowe *et al.*, 1970). The synthetic CVs were taken from the Abramson and Lisker (1967) continuum; these synthetic CVs generated dichotic right ear advantages and phonetic patterns of error that were virtually identical with those obtained with our natural speech CVs.

Subjects

Unless otherwise stated, our subjects were normal hearing, right-handed, adult females from 18 to 40 years of age.[2] The subjects also showed virtually 100% discrimination on monaural presentations of each of the syllables without contralateral competition.

Method of Presentation

Carefully calibrated earphones were used with a two-channel half-track playback unit. Often two to four subjects were studied simultaneously, with half of the subjects receiving Channel I to the left ear and the other half receiving Channel I to the right. Periodically throughout the experiments, those subjects receiving Channel I information to one ear would then reverse the phones and receive Channel I information to the other ear. This arrangement permitted each syllable to compete with each other syllable an equal number of times, and from each ear an equal number of times.

Simple Dichotic Listening to Words and Syllables with Intensity and Time of Onset Held Constant

Ear Advantage

The expected right ear advantage in these experiments has been observed repeatedly in this laboratory. Natural or synthetic syllables and rhyming CVC words presented to the right ear usually generated between 70% and 80% accuracy, while syllables presented to the left ear usually generated between 58% and 70% accuracy (Berlin, Lowe-Bell, Cullen, Thompson, and Stafford, 1972a, Berlin *et al.*, 1973a; Cullen, Thompson, Samson, and Hughes, 1973; Hannah, 1971; Lowe, 1970; Thompson, Stafford, Cullen, Hughes, Lowe-Bell, and Berlin, 1972).

Not all of our right-handed normal subjects, however, generated right ear advantages; perhaps one subject in six showed either no right ear advantage, or a distinct left

---

[2]We did not note consistent sex differences in our dichotic listening experiments in which such data could be extracted.

ear advantage. Attention is called to the fact that both ears were suppressed from the 96%—100% monaural intelligibility level, but that left ears generally performed more poorly than right ears. It also should be noted that the sum of the information correctly identified from both ears of normal subjects usually came to about 130% out of a possible 200%. (We shall return to this apparent *information ceiling* later.)

Both the envelope and the microstructure of a pair of CVs (one voiced, the other unvoiced), aligned on *onsets*, can be seen in Figure 10.1. This was our most common alignment. However, instead of aligning the CVs by their onsets, Hannah (1971) studied the effect on the REA of aligning synthetic CVs at various points on their envelopes. For example: He aligned the two vocalic peaks, or the two transitions, or combinations of transition, onset, and vocalic burst, and so on. He thus used a total of nine possible alignments; the largest right ear advantages were seen when the onsets of the syllables themselves were simultaneous. While the other alignment criteria seemed to change phonetic error patterns to some extent, they did not generate right ear advantages larger than the simultaneous onset alignments (Hannah, Thompson, Cullen, Hughes, and Berlin, 1971).

Phonetic Effects

In all the experiments we performed with syllables aligned at their onset, the voiceless stop consonants were more intelligible than the voiced consonants (e.g., Berlin *et al.*, 1973a; Hannah, 1971; Lowe *et al.*, 1970; Stafford, 1971; Thompson *et al.*, 1972). This effect was confirmed by Roeser, Johns, and Price (1972b); it is so robust that, if one were to systematically present *voiceless* consonants to the *left* ear and *voiced* consonants to the *right* ear during a dichotic listening task, the results would show a *left* ear advantage. Often we would note a pattern as follows: If /pa/ were presented to the right ear and /da/ to the left ear, there would be a great likelihood that only the right

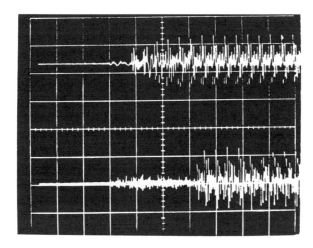

Figure 10.1 Oscillographic tracing of dichotic CV pair; top trace voiced, bottom trace voiceless.

ear syllable (voiceless) would be correctly reported. However, if /pa/ were presented to the left ear and /ba/ to the right, then both syllables would often be reported accurately. In addition, when *both* consonants were unvoiced, we were likely to have more accurate subject responses than when both competing consonants were voiced. The above observations were generally true as long as the syllables were presented symmetrically with respect to onset time, intensity, signal-to-noise ratio, or frequency bandwidth. Aligning the syllables on different points in the microstructure or envelope tended to reduce the voiceless-over-voiced preponderance as well as the size of the right ear advantage.

Many of the new dichotic effects we have to report involve changes in this basic voiceless-over-voiced pattern in dichotic presentations.

Test—Retest Reliability of the Right Ear Advantage

Ear Advantage

If the right ear advantage does, in fact, reflect hemispheric dominance, the advantage should be relatively immutable with repeated trials.

We tested this hypothesis by presenting 60-item dichotic tapes to the same subjects over an eight-week period (Troendle, Porter, and Berlin, 1973); results are shown in Figure 10.2. In essence, the *total number of correct responses* apparently improved slightly for the first five weeks only, reaching an asymptote at that point. It should be noted, however, that the relative size of the right ear advantage for the group

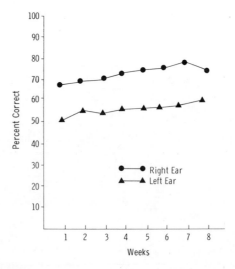

Figure 10.2   Percent correct of right and left ear dichotic messages over eight weeks. [From Troendle *et al.*, 1973.]

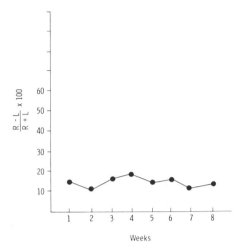

Figure 10.3 Relative change of the right ear advantage over eight weeks. [From Troendle *et al.*, 1973.]

of subjects did *not* change. Figure 10.3 shows the relative size of the right ear advantage as a function of the successive weeks. The y-axis shows the REA as $R - L/R + L \times 100$. These results were confirmed by Ryan and McNeil (1974).

Phonetic Effects

In all of our earlier studies on dichotic listening, we noted a substantially better recognition of voiceless syllables over their voiced cognates. This test—retest study (Troendle *et al.*, 1973) showed essentially the same results. The velar syllables were reported correctly more often than were the alveolar syllables, and the latter, in turn, were reported more accurately than were the labial syllables. Furthermore, these same effects were observed consistently from the beginning to the end of our eight-week project.

Variations with Age

Children

It would be valid at this point to ask whether this presumed asymmetry of the human brain, as revealed by studies on dichotic listening, is present at birth or develops with age. Eimas, Siqueland, Jusczyk, and Vigorito (1971) and Entus (1975) suggest that perceptual asymmetries can be seen in infants as young as 3 months of age. Their findings, however, await corroboration since their high-amplitude, nonnutritive sucking technique has some methodological problems attached to it. Asymmetries need not be indices of language skills.

Language skills undoubtedly improve as children develop from age 5 to age 13; however, we do not believe these changes are reflected in the relative *size* of the right ear advantage to nonsense CVs. Figure 10.4 shows that, of 150 children, 75 of each sex with an age range of 5 to 13, the group right ear advantage was virtually identical at each age.[3] This observation holds if we analyze only the single correct items in a pair (Berlin, Hughes, Lowe-Bell, and Berlin, 1973c). If we were also to include the *double corrects*, we noted an increase in the total syllable accuracy with the increase in age from 5 to 13.[4] This result is consistent with the notion that increased language skills might be correlated with total number of correct responses in a dichotic listening task. However, it would be unwise to assume that the magnitude of a right ear advantage for nonsense syllables necessarily should be related directly to overall language skills (Porter and Berlin, 1975). Satz, Bakker, Goebel, and Van der Vlugt (1975) feel that the REA does develop with age, and this development reflects maturity in the cortical structures pertinent to language.

Phonetic Effects

One of the unexpected observations we made while studying these young children was a reversal of our earlier results on phonetic effects in dichotic listening. The unvoiced consonants continued to be more intelligible than the voiced consonants in the single correct modes (Figure 10.5); however, an analysis of the double correct responses showed that the 5- and 7-year-olds behaved significantly differently from the 9-, 11-, and 13-year-olds. Figure 10.6 shows that the younger children perceived voiced con-

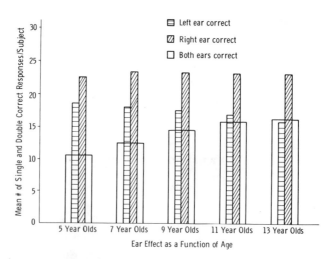

Figure 10.4   Dichotic performance of 150 children (30 in each age group) with single correct and double correct items listed separately. [From Berlin *et al.*, 1973c.]

[3]No sex differences were seen.

[4]Horning (1972, see later) has shown that the total syllable accuracy seems to decrease with advancing age.

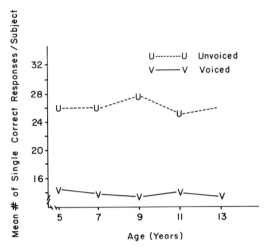

Figure 10.5 Phonetic analysis of single correct items in dichotic listening by 150 children. [From Berlin *et al.*, 1973c.]

sonants somewhat better than they perceived voiceless consonants. At present we have no rationale for this observation.

Elderly Subjects

In a study of elderly patients, Horning (1972) showed that, on our nonsense-syllable tapes, the right ear advantages for young subjects were virtually identical with those for the older subjects only as long as single correct data were analyzed. However, when she included the double correct data, the results showed that the elderly patients did not process as well, nor did they get as much left ear information, as did the younger

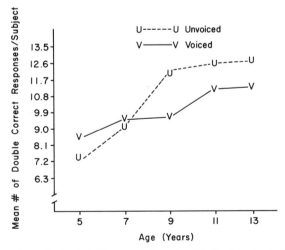

Figure 10.6 Phonetic analysis of double correct items in dichotic listening by 150 children. [From Berlin *et al.*, 1973c.]

subjects. Here we see how dichotic CV tests can, at one moment, shed light on a number of essential hearing processes: the right versus left ear difference, the voiceless versus voiced differences, and the total amount of information processed from both channels.

Effects of Varying Intensity

Varying the Intensity to One Ear While Syllables to the Other Ear Were Held at a Constant Intensity

Figure 10.7 shows that the right ear advantage in dichotic listening was evident even when the CVs in the right ear were 10 dB less intense than those in the left ear (Berlin *et al.*, 1972a). This asymmetry in favor of the right ear as a function of intensity has been confirmed recently by Brady-Wood and Shankweiler (1973). One should note that, as the intensity of the CVs in the left ear decreased, the syllables presented to the right ear were more accurately reported.

Figure 10.8 shows the effect of keeping one syllable at 50 dB SPL while the intensity of the other syllable was varied in 5 dB steps above and below the 50 dB reference. Note also the top line in Figure 10.8 which shows the sum of both ears as a function of intensity. The *asymmetry* in favor of the right ear was 5 dB in this experiment, which presented syllables at 50 dB to the reference ear; when the syllables were presented at 80 dB in the first experiment, the asymmetry appeared to be 10 dB in favor of the right ear.

Varying Intensity of Both Ears Simultaneously

Figure 10.9 shows that the right ear advantage in dichotic listening was maintained despite systematic reduction of the intensity in both channels from 80 dB SPL down to

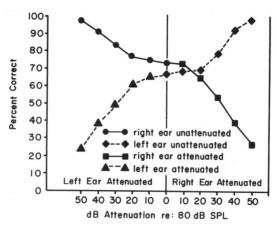

Figure 10.7   Percentage of correct responses to dichotic syllables with right ear attenuated. [From Berlin *et al.*, 1972a.]

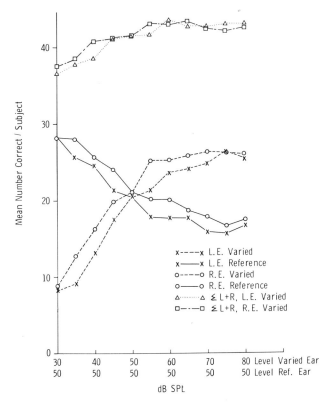

Figure 10.8 Mean left, right, and sum-of-left-and-right scores for dichotic syllables with right or left ear attenuated. [From Cullen *et al.*, 1974.]

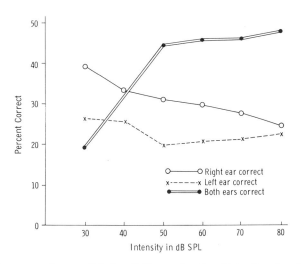

Figure 10.9 Percentage of correct dichotic syllables as a function of intensity, where both channels were always at equal intensity. [From Cullen *et al.*, 1974.]

30 dB SPL (Thompson and Hughes, 1972). These data show that the right ear advantage is not relatable to any occult asymmetry of middle ear muscle reflexes, since such reflexes were not elicited at any of the intensities used. Furthermore, these data confirm that the right ear advantage as seen at 60 dB SPL is not contaminated by any mixing of signals due to poor interaural attenuation, since the REA held relatively constant as intensity decreased below that level.

Phonetic Effects

Figure 10.10 shows the expected voiceless-over-voiced preponderance at the high intensities; it should be noted, however, that as intensity dropped, the voiced consonants became more intelligible (see later "Phonetic Effects" under filtered conditions section).

Effects of Varying Signal-to-Noise Ratio

Ear Advantage

It is often proper to view intensity-with-respect-to-a-reference as a special case of signal-to-noise ratio. In addition to our intensity work, our group has also studied dichotic right ear advantages as a function of varying signal-to-noise ratio in one or both channels (Cullen *et al.*, 1973).

Figure 10.11 shows the effects of varying the signal-to-noise ratio in one ear while keeping the other ear under *no-noise* conditions. Note that the expected right ear advantage still is maintained; almost surprisingly, a monotically benign 18 dB signal-

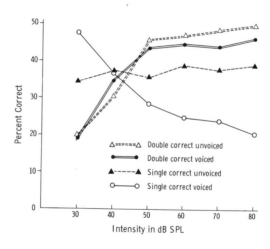

Figure 10.10   Percentage of correct dichotic syllables for voiced and unvoiced items in single and double correct responses, where both channels were always at equal intensity. [From Cullen *et al.*, 1974.]

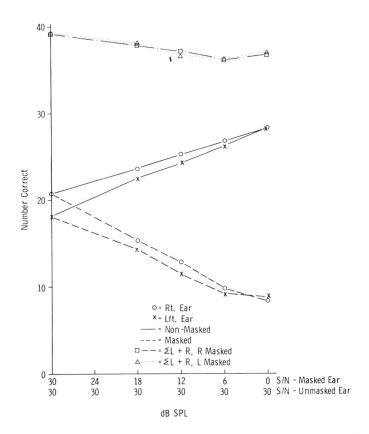

Figure 10.11 Number correct for right, left, and right-plus-left when one ear received messages at a 30dB signal-to-noise ratio, while the other ear had less favorable listening conditions. [From Cullen *et al.*, 1974.]

to-noise ratio in the right ear is sufficient to reduce its usual and expected advantage over the left ear. Note also in Figure 10.10 the *reciprocal effect* seen first in the intensity experiments. As information was lost to the masked ear, unmasked ear performance rose. The top lines show that, if we were to add the total number of items correct for both ears, we appear to have an almost constant information throughput for this system (Cullen, Thompson, Hughes, Berlin, and Samson, 1974).

Figure 10.12 shows the effect of changing the signal-to-noise ratio from 30 dB down to 0 dB in both ears simultaneously. Here we see that the right ear advantage is maintained until intelligibility of both syllables is so seriously impaired that no difference between ears can be observed.

Phonetic Effects

Phonetic effects were the same for both masked and filtered conditions. (See next section for more detailed analysis.)

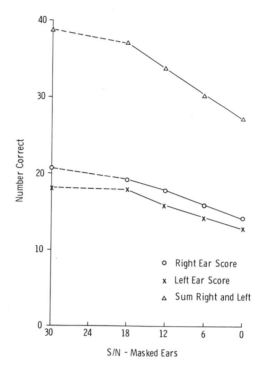

Figure 10.12 Dichotic performance for both ears as the signal-to-noise ratio was changed for both ears simultaneously. [From Cullen *et al.*, 1974.]

The Effects of Varying Frequency Bandwidth

Ear Advantages

With systematic reduction of frequency bandwidth in one channel, we again find the reciprocation of the two ears: As the intelligibility of one channel decreases, the information transmitted through the other channel increases. The sum of that information tends to be almost constant (see top line, Figure 10.13), with expected right ear superiority. When the high-frequency cutoff is set at 4000 Hz, right ears outperform left ears; however, when the high-frequency cutoff to the right ear syllables starts at 3000 Hz, both left and right ears perform equally well. When the cutoff starts at 2000 Hz, the right ear begins to perform more poorly than the left. At a 1500 Hz cutoff, the difference between the two channels begins to be most marked (Thompson, Samson, Cullen, and Hughes, 1973). Students of monaural speech perception are aware that a 24 dB/octave filter beginning at 3000 Hz has little effect on nonsense syllable intelligibility. The obliteration of the right ear advantage with a 3000 Hz right ear filter cannot be explained by a loss of phonetic intelligibility in one channel alone.

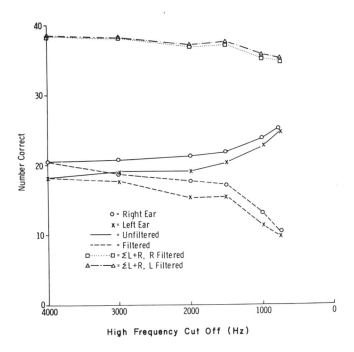

Figure 10.13   Mean left, right, and sum-of-left-plus-right scores for dichotic CV syllables with one ear receiving a filtered CV while the CV to the other ear was unfiltered. [From Cullen *et al.*, 1974.]

Phonetic Effects

For comparable conditions of noise and filtering, phonetic effects were similar: Voiceless consonants were more intelligible than voiced consonants at the favorable signal-to-noise, intensity, or filter conditions. When the listening conditions were degraded (e.g., at approximately 40 dB SPL, a 1.5 kHz low-pass filter, or a 6 dB signal-to-noise ratio), voiced items were more intelligible.

Under favorable listening conditions, velar items were more intelligible than alveolar syllables. The alveolar syllables were only slightly more intelligible than the labial syllables. However, under the less favorable conditions, the intelligibility of the velar syllables dropped, while the intelligibility of the alveolar and labial syllables actually improved slightly over the scores generated in the more favorable listening conditions. This enhancement of the front and middle syllables came as a result of the marked loss in intelligibility suffered by the back syllables, coupled with a corresponding response bias in favor of front or middle syllables. Actually, the most common response to the pairs in the degraded listening condition was /p/ or /b/, thus creating errors with respect to the /k/ and /g/ presentations and increasing the apparent performance accuracy of the labials.

Under all conditions, information about the voicing of the syllables was most often preserved. If one item in a competing pair (e.g., /ka/) were correct, then the incorrect item in the pair (e.g., /ba/) might be missed with a /ga/ substituted for it. The voicing information in the /ba/ would have been retained, with some tendency for the error to include the place information from the /ka/.

Effects of Varying Onset Time

Ear Advantages

In auditory theory, it is generally expected that the first signal presented in a pair of overlapping speech signals will be better perceived (e.g., Haas, 1951). This first-signal superiority is, in fact, observed when both messages are presented monotically (Berlin and Lowe, 1972; Berlin *et al.*, 1973a). However, in dichotic speech presentation, when two different syllables are delivered in a time-staggered fashion, one notes that the *trailing* syllable is recovered better than is the *leading* syllable (Kirstein, 1970; Studdert-Kennedy, Shankweiler, and Schulman, 1970; Berlin *et al.*, 1973a). Our data in Figure 10.14 show that when syllables are separated by a time span of between 30 and 60 msec, it is the second syllable which tends to be perceived better than the first (Berlin, Lowe-Bell, Jannetta, and Kline, 1972b; Berlin *et al.*, 1973a). The dotted lines in Figure 10.14 show the results of retest of 5 of the original 12 subjects a year later. Olsen, Noffsinger, and Kurdziel (1973) recently have confirmed these data. We suggested at the time that the lag effect in this figure might be related to a finite pro-

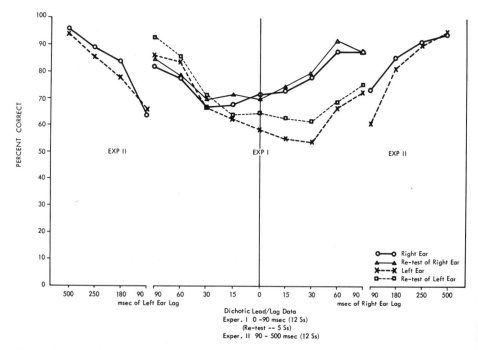

Figure 10.14 The *lag effect*: the second message received was better perceived than the first message between 30 and 90 msec of time separation. [From Berlin *et al.*, 1973a.]

cessing time for CV syllables; that is, while the first syllable was being processed, the second syllable had interrupted that processing and attenuated the likelihood that the first syllable would have enough time for an acceptable analysis. This model presupposes a single speech processor with relatively independent input from two separate channels.

Phonetic Effects

As voiced consonants entered the trailing mode, their intelligibility in dichotic listening improved. Figure 10.15 shows that the voiceless consonants retained their intelligibility, while the voiced consonants gained comparable intelligibility as a result of their being second in the pair (Berlin *et al.*, 1973b). We (Berlin and Lowe, 1972) suggested then that this voiceless—voiced effect might be a special case of the *lag effect*, wherein the vocalic burst of the voiceless CV occurs roughly 30 to 60 msec *after* the release of the voiced CV in the simultaneous alignment condition. To test this notion, we aligned the syllables at the vocalic burst and observed a marked attenuation of the voiced—voiceless differences (Berlin *et al.*, 1973b; Hannah, 1971).

Pathological Cases

Dyslexic Children

In light of the preceding sections, one well might speculate on the effects of dyslexia on dichotic test performance. Using the same tapes which we presented to our 5- through 13-year-old children, Sobotka (1973) studied 24 dyslexic children aged 7 through 13. She showed essentially normal right ear advantages for both her normal and dyslexic group. It was interesting to us to note that she also used tapes with

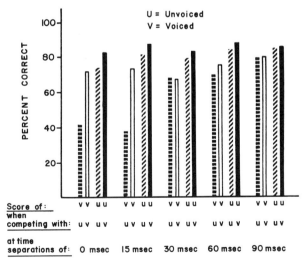

Figure 10.15 Syllable intelligibility as a function of manner of the competing CV; V = voiced syllables, U = unvoiced syllables. [From Berlin *et al.*, 1973a.]

multiple strings of digits tied together as in the work of Satz (Satz *et al.*, 1975). The correlation between Satz's digit tests and our syllable tests was astoundingly poor for some subjects, yet quite good for some others. While differences in results between CV and digit tasks do not lend themselves to easy interpretation, they do suggest that dichotic CV syllable tests and dichotic digit tests tap different modalities, at least with respect to recall, familiarity, and acoustic content (Porter and Berlin, 1975).

Temporal Lobectomees

Loss of the anterior temporal lobe generally leads to a decrease in the dichotic score for the ear contralateral to the lesion. If the corpus callosum is sectioned in an adult patient who has had normal corpus callosum function during life, a dramatic left ear suppression is seen (Milner *et al.*, 1968), suggesting that there is a one-way path to the left hemisphere for signals identified by the auditory nervous system as *speech*. We have also shown that there is no *lag effect* after temporal lobectomy and hemispherectomy, and that the ear contralateral to the lesion performs poorly throughout most of

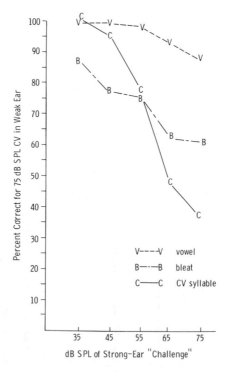

Figure 10.16   The effect of three *challenges* in the right ear on the perception of CVs in the left ear in normal subjects. *Percent correct* is corrected for guessing in this figure and in Figures 10.17 and 10.18 as follows:

$$\text{Corrected Score} = K - E\left[\frac{P_c}{1 - P_c}\right]$$

Where K = Percent correct; E = Percent errors; P_c = Probability of being correct by chance. [From Berlin *et al.*, 1973b.]

the time-staggering range (Berlin *et al.*, 1972b). Olsen *et al.* (1973), using our tapes, obtained virtually identical findings.

We have found also that dichotic competition with identifiable syllables is not necessary to generate contralateral ear suppression (Berlin *et al.*, 1973b). In that particular study we generated vowels, bleats, noise, and CVs as *challenges* to the stronger ear of temporal lobectomees, hemispherectomees, and normal subjects whose stronger ear was the right ear. In each of the above cases, the weak ear always received a CV at a constant intensity. We then noted that, as we increased the intensity of the *challenge* in the stronger ear, the perception of the CV in the weaker ear generally was reduced. This reduction of weak ear performance did not occur to the same extent when the challenging competition was noise. Figures 10.16, 10.17, and 10.18 summarize those data. We therefore concluded that *before* final linguistic or phonetic processing, interference was taking place at the acoustic level of analysis; the presence of an un-intelligible acoustic bleat in the stronger ear was enough to suppress CV perception in the weak ear.

Patient versus Normal Data

The dichotic right ear advantage seen in most normal subjects is different in both quality and nature from the contralateral ear suppression seen in temporal lobecto-mees. Results in four patients who have undergone hemispherectomy (Berlin, Cullen, Hughes, Berlin, Lowe-Bell, and Thompson, 1975) show that the lesion-ipsilateral ear

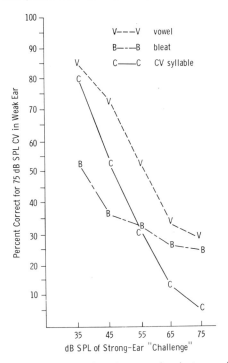

Figure 10.17 Weak ear (contralateral ear) performance for six temporal lobectomees in response to the three *challenges*. [From Berlin *et al.*, 1973b.]

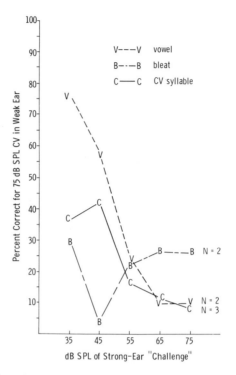

Figure 10.18 Weak ear (contralateral ear) performance for patients with total hemispherectomy in response to the three *challenges*. [From Berlin *et al.*, 1973b.]

performs at or near 100% throughout the time-staggers of dichotic listening, while the contralateral ear performs at or near chance. In a patient with agenesis of the corpus callosum, we found poor performance in both ears with no large right ear advantage. This finding suggested to us some form of subcortical interference with equally prepotent hemispheres for speech processing (Berlin *et al.*, 1972b). Performing near 100% in a dichotic listening task implies that the ear in question is getting *complete* access to the speech analyzer with no competition from any other channel. Total disconnection of the contralateral ear from the speech analyzer in hemispherectomees or surgically separated corpus callosi would lead to such a finding if our model on *information maximum* has merit. It is also clear that the contralateral ear suppression in such patients is unrelated to any vocal tract gesture coding because such signals coming into the ear do not relate to vocal tract gestures until they are coded into phonetic or linguistic homologues.

Comparing Dichotic Studies

The data discussed in the initial portions of this chapter show that the right ear advantage is far more vulnerable to acoustic variables than hitherto suspected. This vulnerability makes interpretation of the literature and reconciliation of findings between studies difficult since many researchers failed to describe the acoustic sub-strata of their tapes; comparing results of studies given at different intensities, and possibly with different bandpass between channels, would put each at different points of the curves and the graphs which are reported earlier in this chapter. Another difficulty in the interpretation of dichotic results arises with respect to the nature of the stimuli as presented to the different subjects (e.g., syllables versus digits versus sentences, etc.).

Is the lag effect unique to speech? Bever (1971) and Massaro (1972) remind us that there are lag effects in modalities other than the auditory—speech modality. Whenever signals have to be coded and labeled, there is a high likelihood that the second signal to reach a processor will interfere with the first, rather than vice versa.

It is also important for the serious student of speech perception to recognize that, while we may be predisposed to manage speech signals by certain anatomic and physiologic constraints, speech signals are primarily acoustic signals and must follow physical acoustic laws as well as more abstract phonetic and linguistic amendments.

Discussion

Does a Dichotic Right Ear Advantage Reflect that the Left Hemisphere Is Specialized for Language?

Linguistic stimuli are not always necessary, nor are they always sufficient, to gene-rate a right ear advantage. The right ear advantage is, as we have said, different from the lesion-contralateral ear suppression seen in patients with anterior temporal lobec-tomies. In the latter case, there is strong evidence that the contralateral ear suppres-sion is not related to syntactic and phonetic levels of language. If dichotic ear differences reflected the language-dominant hemisphere, it would be unreasonable to assume, following a left anterior temporal lobectomy and concomitant right ear suppression,[5] that the dominant hemisphere for language suddenly moved to the opposite side. We already have discussed that almost any signal that resembles speech, even though it has no phonetic or semantic value, can cause tremendous suppression in patients' lesion-contralateral ears when delivered as a competing stimulus to the lesion-ipsilateral ear (Berlin *et al.*, 1973b).

Van Lancker and Fromkin (1973) have raised a strong argument that the right ear advantage is language-related. They found that in Thai languages, where tonal dif-ferences between the same phonetic utterances generate different meanings, the tone differences in fact did generate *right* ear advantages; *hums* of the same pitch contours, without the necessary linguistic translations, did not generate right ear advantages. Haggard and Parkinson (1971) showed that verbal material need not generate a right ear advantage if the subjects were asked to listen to nonlinguistic attributes of the speech stimuli (i.e., their emotional tone). However, Haggard and Parkinson were

---

[5]This phenomenon, incidentally, is not always seen if the left temporal lobe lesion is deep enough to interrupt transmission from the right hemisphere (Sparks, Goodglass, and Nickel, 1970).

unable to show a right ear advantage for the sentences they used as targets in their experiment. Quite properly, they say, "The LEA for emotions must be interpreted cautiously in view of the failure to obtain any REA for the sentences" (p. 175). However, as a competing dichotic stimulus, Haggard and Parkinson used a "babble consisting of many people talking at once . . . recorded on a typical Friday night in a college bar" (p. 173). Thus, it is fair to say that the acoustic simultaneity of syllable pulses in one ear versus the other was only roughly approximate, and certainly not controlled, in the part of their experiment in which sentences competed against babble. We have discussed the fact that the acoustic and temporal concomitance of portions of the competing syllables are important in controlling the size of the right ear advantage (Hannah, 1971), and that the acoustic content of the target and the challenge should be similar in order for one to interfere with the other in a dichotic listening task (Berlin *et al.*, 1973b).

If the right ear advantage is, in fact, solely related to language dominance, nonlinguistic or nonphonemic stimuli should not generate right ear advantages. However, we know that speech played backward can generate a right ear advantage (Kimura and Folb, 1968), as can unintelligible bleats (Berlin *et al.*, 1973b). We know also that tones sometimes can generate a right ear advantage (Sussman, 1971; Sussman *et al.*, 1973), and Morse code also can generate a right ear advantage (Papçun *et al.*, 1972). The right ear advantage for nonspeech shown by Sussman *et al.* (1973) and Papçun *et al.* (1972) may be related to entirely different processes than the dichotic right ear advantage for speech. It is clear, however, that *acoustic* competition can generate a right ear advantage; dichotic competition of linguistically lawful material is not *always* necessary (Berlin *et al.*, 1973b). Thus, we conclude that probably all three levels of acoustic, phonetic, and linguistic processing contribute to the right ear advantage when speech is presented dichotically. However, acoustic and phonetic competition heighten the likelihood of observing the right ear advantage.

What Are the Differences between Dichotic CV Tasks and Other Dichotic Tasks?

Aligning digits so that their onsets are simultaneous leaves a considerable amount of acoustic and phonetic differentiation between the digits during the rest of the utterances. Thus, if the syllable *three* competes against the syllable *five*, we are faced with two different vowels, a CVC competing against a CCV, and possible duration differences depending upon speaker characteristics. Now if we further visualize that the digit pairs *three* and *five* appear along with two other pairs in a string, it is clear that arranging these strings of digits to be *truly simultaneous* is a task requiring compromise somewhere in choosing the landmarks for the alignment. The same holds for more complex competitive messages. In the CV tasks, it is a relatively simple matter to choose arbitrarily the first oscillographic waves in a digitized display and align CV syllables within a millisecond of their first energy bursts. Since the consonants in the CVs we used were all plosives, and the vowels were all the same, phonetic and acoustic competition were maximized. In this way we might say that the broader linguistic value of the CV dichotic task is reduced to a minimum, and the acoustic and phonetic competition are heightened. Compared to other, more complex, tasks, does this arrangement tap more or less of the *language system* sampled by dichotic listening, or does it simply tap different processes inherent in speech perception?

Dichotic Listening: What Can It Tell Us?

The why's and wherefore's of the dichotic right ear advantage are intriguing. However, we find it useful to use the presence of the dichotic right ear advantage as a biological index of the overloading of a speech processor. By manipulating the nature of the competing signals in dichotic listening, we hope to study not so much why there is a right ear advantage, as what elements of the signal, if removed, will switch the listener out of the *speech mode.* Thus, in addition to tapping the vocal tract gesture notion in our further experiments, we plan also to remove what we feel may be critical speech elements from one channel while watching for a corresponding improvement in score from the other channel. This improvement will indicate that a critical element has been removed from the other channel.

Future Research Directions

Is the right ear advantage morphologically predetermined in the fetus as a function of hemispheric asymmetry? Informal scanning of brain sections suggests this might be true. Does it develop with age, or atrophy with disuse? Is the left hemisphere morphologically as asymmetrical in the congenitally deaf as it appears to be in normal subjects? Is the effect of a right ear hearing loss in childhood more or less devastating than a left ear hearing loss? Does binaural amplification in some patients who do not have equally sensitive ears help or hurt processing of speech material? What relationship does the right ear advantage have to the nature of a person's speech and language abilities? What relationships exist between the right ear advantage, the lag effect, and stuttering, functional articulation defects, congential speech apraxias, other language and phonologic systems, life styles, and talents? For example, do musicians use music as a special form of language? Will they show right ear advantages for music the way nonmusicians show right ear advantages for speech? Bever and Chiarello (1974) have suggested that they do.

If the dichotic right ear advantage is generated by competing speech signals, and a left ear advantage is generated by competing musical signals, what will happen to competing messages which are sung? There is some evidence to suggest that for most people singing is not mediated by the left hemisphere; but if our vocal tract hypothesis is correct, singing should generate a right ear advantage if the discrimination between the sung messages in some way hinges on the vocal tract gesture and not on the melodic intonation.

To even mention a majority of the important questions raised by dichotic listening studies would be a formidable epistemological task. The tools developed in dichotic listening, however, promise to elicit new insights into the phenomena surrounding the coding and extraction of information from the speech stream.

Appendix to Chapter 10

		Type of presentation			Linguistic status Verbal								
Author(s)	Date	Dichotic	Monaural	Monotic	Semantic value	Sentences	Words or CVC or VCV	Digits	Nonsense CVs or VCs	Letters	Natural speech	Synthetic speech	Nonverbal
		1	2	3	4	5	6	7	8	9	10	11	12
Achenbach	1967	X						X			X		
Axelrod, Guzy, & Diamond	1968	X	X										X
Babkoff & Sutton	1966	X	X										X
Bakker	1967		X					X			X		X
Bakker	1968		X					X			X		X
Bakker	1969		X							X	X		
Bakker	1970		X					X			X		X
Bakker & Boeijenga	1970		X					X			X		X
Bakker, Smink, & Reitsma	1973	X	X					X					
Barr & Carmel	1970		X				X				X		X
Bartholomeus	1974	X								X			X
Bartz	1968a	X				X	X				X		
Bartz	1968b	X						X			X		
Bartz, Satz, & Fennel	1966	X					X	X			X		
Bartz, Satz, & Fennel	1967	X					X	X			X		
Bartz, Satz, Fennel, & Lally	1967	X			X		X	X			X		
Berlin	1971												
Berlin	1972												
Berlin et al.	1973c	X							X		X		
Berlin & Lowe	1972	X		X					X		X		
Berlin et al.	1973a	X		X					X		X		
Berlin et al.	1972a	X							X		X		X
Berlin et al.	1972b	X							X		X		
Berlin et al.	1973b	X							X		X	X	X
Bertelson & Tisseyre	1972	X	X	Bin		X							X
Blumstein	1974												
Blumstein & Cooper	1972	X							X		X		
Blumstein & Cooper	1974	X				X			X		X		X
Borkowski, Spreen, & Stutz,	1965	X			X		X				X		
Bradshaw, Nettleton, & Geffen	1971	X			X	X	X						X

	Subject variables								Administration and stimuli variables									
Sex	Handedness	Brain damage	Intelligence	Stuttering	Peripheral hearing	Learning disability	Socioeconomic status	Report bias	Intensity bias	Memory or recognition	Temporal order	Rate bias	Length of stimulus	Frequency range	Masking	Response modality	Theory
14	15	16	17	18	19	20	21	22	23	24	25	26	27	28	29	30	31
	X								X		M							
										X		X						
										X		X			X	X	V	
B											M						G/V	
M	X				X				X		M			X			G/V	
F	X				X				X		M			X			V	
B	X				X						M						G/V	
											M						G/V	
B	X				X						M			X				
		X							X						X	X	V	
B	X										B						GR	
	X								X		M						V	
									X		M							
	X								X		M							
	X								X		M	X						
	X										M						V	
																		X
																		X
B	X										R						G/V	
B		X									R	X					Gr	X
F	X										R	X					Gr	
		X								X	R						Gr	
B		X									R	X					Gr	
B	X	X								X	R						Gr	
	X																	X
																		X
B	X										R						Gr	
	X										R					X	V–Gr	
											M							
B	X										R	X	X	X		X	V	

Author(s)	Date	Dichotic	Monaural	Monotic	Semantic value	Sentences	Words or CVC or VCV	Digits	Nonsense CVs or VCs	Letters	Natural speech	Synthetic speech	Nonverbal
		1	2	3	4	5	6	7	8	9	10	11	12
Brady, Sommers, & Moore	1973	X					X	X			X		
Brady-Wood & Shankweiler	1973	X		X					X				
Broadbent	1954	X	X					X			X		
Broadbent	1956a												
Broadbent	1956b	X	X					X			X		
Broadbent	1957	X						X			X		
Broadbent	1958												
Broadbent	1962												
Broadbent	1967												
Broadbent & Gregory	1963	X						X			X		
Broadbent & Gregory	1964a	X						X			X		
Broadbent & Gregory	1964b	X	X				X	X		X	X		
Broadbent & Ladefoged	1957												
Brown & Jaffe	1975												
Brunt & Goetzinger	1968	X	X				X	X			X		
Bryden	1962	X						X			X		
Bryden	1963	X						X			X		
Bryden	1964	X			X		X	X			X		
Bryden	1965							X			X		
Bryden	1966	X						X			X		
Bryden	1967										X		
Bryden	1969	X	X	X			X	X			X		
Bryden	1970	X						X					
Bryden & Zurif	1970	X						X			X		
Caird	1965	X					X				X		
Caird & Inglis	1961	X						X			X		
Carr	1969	X						X			X		
Chaney & Webster	1966	X								X	X		X
Cherry	1953	X	X	X	X	X					X		
Cherry & Sayers	1956												
Cherry & Taylor	1954	X				X	X				X		
Clark, Knowles, & MacLean	1970	X						X			X		
Clifton & Bogartz	1968	X					X				X		

	Subject variables								Administration and stimuli variables									
Age	Sex	Handedness	Brain damage	Intelligence	Stuttering	Peripheral hearing	Learning disability	Socioeconomic status	Report bias	Intensity bias	Memory or recognition	Temporal order	Rate bias	Length of stimulus	Frequency range	Masking	Response modality	Theory
13	14	15	16	17	18	19	20	21	22	23	24	25	26	27	28	29	30	31
C/A		X			X				X		R							
										X	M							
	M										R		X				Gr	
																		X
											M		X		X		Gr	
									X		M		X				Gr	
																		X
																		X
																		X
		X									M				X		Gr	
		X									M						Gr	
									X			X					V	
																		X
																		X
	B										B		X	X	X			
											M		X	X			V	
									X		M							
											M			X			V	
	B	X							X		M							
											M			X			V	
																		X
		X							X		B			X		X	V	
	B	X		X			X				M			X			V	
	M	X	X						X		M		X	X				
	B										B			X				
	B			X							B			X			V	
	B	X									M							
									X					X	X		G	
									X		B	X			X		Gr/V	
																		X
											R	X	X					
	B								X		M						Gr/V	
									X		R						G	

Author(s)	Date	Dichotic	Monaural	Monotic	Semantic value	Sentences	Words or CVC or VCV	Digits	Nonsense CVs or VCs	Letters	Natural speech	Synthetic speech	Nonverbal
		1	2	3	4	5	6	7	8	9	10	11	12
Conners, Kramer, & Guerr	1969	X						X			X		
Cooper, Achenbach, Satz & Levy	1967	X						X			X		
Craik	1965	X						X			X		X
Cullen & Thompson	1972		X				X						
Cullen & Thompson	1974	X					X						
Cullen et al.	1974	X	X						X		X		
Cullen et al.	1973	X	X						X		X		
Curry	1967	X					X				X		
Curry	1968	X					X				X		X
Curry & Gregory	1969	X	X				X				X		X
Curry & Rutherford	1967	X			X		X				X		
Cutting	1974	X							X			X	
Darwin	1971a	X							X	X	X		X
Darwin	1971b	X					X		X	X	X	X	
Day & Vigorito	1972	X							X	X			
Dee	1971	X					X				X		X
Deutsch & Deutsch	1963												
Deutsch, Deutsch, & Lindsay	1967												
Dirks	1964	X	X				X	X			X		
Dirks & Bower	1969	X				X					X		
Dobie & Simmons	1971	X							X		X		
Dodwell	1964	X			X		X				X		
Doehring	1972		X										X
Doehring & Bartholomeus	1971	X							X	X			
Dorman & Geffner	1974	X							X				
Efron & Yund	1975	X											X
Egan, Carterette, & Thwing	1954	X	X			X					X		
Elfner & Tomsic	1968	X											X
Elliott	1962	X		X									X
Emmerich	1965	X					X				X		

	Subject variables								Administration and stimuli variables									
Sex	Handedness	Brain damage	Intelligence	Stuttering	Peripheral hearing	Learning disability	Socioeconomic status	Report bias	Intensity bias	Memory or recognition	Temporal order	Rate bias	Length of stimulus	Frequency range	Masking	Response modality	Theory
14	15	16	17	18	19	20	21	22	23	24	25	26	27	28	29	30	31
B						X				B			X				
	X							X		M							
B								X			X						
			X												X		X
			X												X		
F	X								X					X	X	Gr	
F	X								X	R				X	X	Gr	X
	X									B							
	X	X								B							
B	X			X						B							
B	X									M						V	
	X							X		R				X		Gr	
	X							X			X			X			
	X									R						Gr	
											X						
	X									M							
																	X
																	X
B	X							X		M		X		X			
B								X		R			X			G	
	X	X						X	X	R	X					Gr	
B										M						V	
	X								X	R					X	G	
B	X									R			X			G–V	
	X					X										V	
	X								X	M				X		V	
								X	X	R				X	X	Gr	
									X		X						
								X	X			X		X	X	G	
								X		M				X		Gr	

Charles I. Berlin and Malcolm R. McNeil

		Type of presentation			Linguistic status								
					Verbal								
Author(s)	Date	Dichotic	Monaural	Monotic	Semantic value	Sentences	Words or CVC or VCV	Digits	Nonsense CVs or VCs	Letters	Natural speech	Synthetic speech	Nonverbal
		1	2	3	4	5	6	7	8	9	10	11	12
Fodor & Bever	1965	X				X					X		X
Folsom	1969	X						X			X		
Geffner & Hochberg	1971	X						X			X		
Gerber	1968	X		X			X				X		
Gerber & Goldman	1971	X							X			X	
Gilliom & Sorkin	1974												
Gilroy & Lynn	1971	X		X		X	X				X		
Gilroy & Lynn	1974	X		X		X	X				X		
Godfrey	1974	X								X	X		
Goodglass	1967	X						X			X		
Goodglass	1973	X					X				X		
Goodglass & Peck	1972	X			X		X						
Gordon	1970	X						X			X		X
Gordon	1975		X				X						
Gray & Wedderburn	1960	X				X	X	X			X		
Haaland	1974	X	X				X						
Haggard	1971	X					X			X		X	
Haggard & Parkinson	1971	X			X	X			X		X	X	
Halperin, Nachsohn, & Carmon	1973	X	X										X
Hedrick	1966	X					X				X		
Higenbottam & Spreen	1970	X				X					X		X
Horning	1972	X	X						X		X		
Howarth & Ellis	1962		X		X		X	X			X		
Hutchinson	1973	X					X				X		
Inglis	1960	X						X			X		
Inglis	1962a												
Inglis	1962b												
Inglis	1964	X						X			X		
Inglis	1965a												
Inglis	1965b												
Inglis & Ankus	1965	X						X			X		
Inglis & Caird	1963	X						X			X		
Inglis & Sanderson	1961	X						X			X		
Inglis & Sanderson	1962												

				Subject variables						Administration and stimuli variables									
Age	Sex	Handedness	Brain damage	Intelligence	Stuttering	Peripheral hearing	Learning disability	Socioeconomic status	Report bias	Intensity bias	Memory or recognition	Temporal order	Rate bias	Length of stimulus	Frequency range	Masking	Response modality	Theory
13	14	15	16	17	18	19	20	21	22	23	24	25	26	27	28	29	30	31
									X		R						Gr	
	F	X							X		M						V	
	B	X						X			M						V	
											M		X					
		X							X									
																		X
	B		X						X	X	R				X			
	B		X						X	X	R				X			
	M	X									X			X			Gr	
			X								B			X				
	R			X														
		X	X						X									
	M	X									B						Gr	
		X	X						X		R		X				V–G	
	B								X		M						Gr	
	M	X															Gr	
		X		i					X		R			X	X		Gr	
		X							X		R					X	Gr	
	F	X							X		M			X				
	B								X	X							G	
	B	X							X		R						Gr	
	B	X									R						Gr	X
									X	X	R					X	Gr	
			X														V	
											B		X					
																		X
																		X
	B								X		M							
																		X
																		X
	B								X		B			X			V	
	B										B			X			V	
	B										M						V	
																		X

Author(s)	Date	Type of presentation			Linguistic status / Verbal								
		Dichotic	Monaural	Monotic	Semantic value	Sentences	Words or CVC or VCV	Digits	Nonsense CVs or VCs	Letters	Natural speech	Synthetic speech	Nonverbal
		1	2	3	4	5	6	7	8	9	10	11	12
Inglis & Sykes	1967	X						X			X		
Inglis & Tansey	1967a	X					X	X			X		
Inglis & Tansey	1967b	X						X			X		
Ingram	1975	X					X						
Jerger	1960	X	X				X				X		X
Jones & Spreen	1967a	X			X		X				X		
Jones & Spreen	1967b			X	X		X				X		
Karp & Birch	1969		X				X						X
Katz	1962	X	X				X				X		
Katz	1968	X	X				X				X		
Katz, Basil, & Smith	1963	X	X				X				X		
Kimura	1961a	X						X			X		
Kimura	1961b	X	X					X			X		
Kimura	1962										X		
Kimura	1963a										X		
Kimura	1963b	X						X			X		
Kimura	1964	X						X			X		X
Kimura	1967										X		
Kimura	1973												
Kimura & Folb	1968	X			X		X				X		
King & Kimura	1972	X											X
Klisz & Parsons	1975		X										X
Knox & Boone	1970	X		X			X	X			X		
Knox & Kimura	1970	X					X	X			X		X
Konecni & Slamecka	1972	X			X		X						
Krashen	1973												
Krashen et al.	1972	X					X				X		X
Kuhn	1973												
Lawson	1966	X				X					X		X
Levy & Bowers	1974	X						X			X		
Lewis	1970	X			X		X				X		
Liberman et al.	1967												

			Subject variables								Administration and stimuli variables									
Age	Sex	Handedness	Brain damage	Intelligence	Stuttering	Peripheral hearing	Learning disability	Socioeconomic status	Report bias	Intensity bias	Memory or recognition	Temporal order	Rate bias	Length of stimulus	Frequency range	Masking	Response modality	Theory
13	14	15	16	17	18	19	20	21	22	23	24	25	26	27	28	29	30	31
	B	X									B			X			V	
	B								X		B			X				
	B								X		M				X			
	B																G	
	B	X													X			
	B			X							M						V	
	B			X							R					X	V	
		X									R				X		G	
	B	X			X						R						V	
											R						V	
				X	X						R						V	
		X	X								M							
			X								M							
																		X
																		X
	B	X									B			X			V	
	F	X									M						V	
																		X
																		X
	B	X									R							
	B	X									R							
	B	X							X						X		G	
		X									B					X	V	
	B	X						X			B			X			G/V	
	B								X								V	
																		X
	F						X				R							
																		X
									X		R				X		G/V	
	F	X									M						G	
	B								X		R						V	
																		X

Author(s)	Date	Type of presentation Dichotic	Monaural	Monotic	Linguistic status Verbal Semantic value	Sentences	Words or CVC or VCV	Digits	Nonsense CVs or VCs	Letters	Natural speech	Synthetic speech	Nonverbal
		1	2	3	4	5	6	7	8	9	10	11	12
Lindsay	1967												
Ling	1971	X	X					X			X		
Lowe et al.	1970	X		X			X		X		X	X	
Lynn et al.	1972	X	X			X	X				X		
Lynn & Gilroy	1972	X	X			X	X				X		
Lynn & Gilroy	1973	X	X			X	X				X		
Maccoby & Konrad	1966	X		X			X				X		
MacKay & Inglis	1963	X						X			X		
Mangrum	1968	X						X			X		
Manning	1964	X					X				X		
Marshall, Capian, & Holmes	1975												
Marston & Goetzinger	1972	X	X			X	X						
McClellan, Wertz, & Collins	1973	X	X				X				X		
McCormick & Porter	1973	X	X						X			X	
McGlone & Davidson	1973	X					X				X		
Mewhort	1973	X						X		X	X		
Mewhort, Thio, & Birkenmayer	1971	X			X			X		X	X		
Milner	1962												
Milner	1971												
Milner, Taylor, & Sperry	1968	X	X			X		X			X		
Morais & Darwin	1974		X						X			X	
Moray	1958	X			X	X					X		
Moray	1959	X				X	X	X			X		
Moray	1960	X						X			X		
Moray & Jordan	1966	X						X			X		
Moray & O'Brien	1967	X	X					X		X	X		
Moray & Taylor	1958	X			X	X					X		
Murdock	1965	X					X				X		
Murphy & Venables	1971		X										X
Myers	1970	X							X				X
Nachsohn & Carmon	1975	X			X				X		X		
Nagafuchi	1970	X		X			X				X		
Netley	1972	X						X					
Neufeldt	1966	X						X		X	X		
Ohta, Hayashi, & Morimoto	1967	X	X				X	X			X		

		Subject variables								Administration and stimuli variables									
	Sex	Handedness	Brain damage	Intelligence	Stuttering	Peripheral hearing	Learning disability	Socioeconomic status	Report bias	Intensity bias	Memory or recognition	Temporal order	Rate bias	Length of stimulus	Frequency range	Masking	Response modality	Theory
3	14	15	16	17	18	19	20	21	22	23	24	25	26	27	28	29	30	31
																		X
		X				X					B						V	
	M	X															Gr	
	B		X						X	X	R				X			
	B		X						X	X	R				X			
		X	X						X	X	R				X			
	B							X	X		R				X		V	
	B										B		X				V	
							X										V	
									X	X								
																		X
											R				X	X	V	
			X								R							
	B	X											X					X
	B	X									M							
											M		X				G/V	
									X		M		X			X	Gr/V	
																		X
																		X
			X								B		X				G/V	
	B	X																
									X	X	R						V	
	B								X	X							V	
									X		M	X	X				V	
									X		M						V/G	
									X		R						G	
									X								V	
	B								X		B						Gr/V	
	B	X											X			X		
		X							X				X			X	G	
		X															G	
	B									X				X			V	
			X	X							M							
	B		X	X					X		M	X	X				V	
			X							X				X				

		Type of presentation			Linguistic status								
					Verbal								
Author(s)	Date	Dichotic	Monaural	Monotic	Semantic value	Sentences	Words or CVC or VCV	Digits	Nonsense CVs or VCs	Letters	Natural speech	Synthetic speech	Nonverbal
		1	2	3	4	5	6	7	8	9	10	11	12
Olsen, Noffsinger, & Kurdziel	1973	X					X		X		X		
Oscar-Berman, Goodglass, & Donnefeld	1974	X											X
Oscar-Berman, Zurif, & Blumstein	1975	X							X			X	
Oxbury & Oxbury	1969	X						X			X		
Oxbury, Oxbury, & Gardiner	1967	X						X			X		
Palmer	1964		X				X						
Papçun, Krashen, & Terbeek	1972	X	X										X
Papçun et al.	1974	X											X
Perl	1968												
Perl	1970	X						X			X		X
Perl & Haggard	1975	X								X		X	
Peterson & Kroener	1964	X			X		X	X		X	X		
Pettit	1969	X					X	X			X		X
Pinheiro & Tobin	1969	X											X
Pinheiro & Tobin	1971												
Pisoni & McNabb	1974	X							X			X	
Pizzamiglio, DePascali & Vignati	1974	X						X			X		
Porter	1971	X		X					X			X	
Porter	1973a	X							X			X	X
Porter	1973b	X							X			X	
Porter & Berlin	1975												
Porter, Shankweiler, & Liberman	1969	X							X	X		X	
Provins & Jeeves	1975		X										X
Rand	1974	X							X			X	
Repp	1975a	X		X					X				
Repp	1975b	X							X	X			
Roeser & Daly	1974	X						X			X		

			Subject variables								Administration and stimuli variables								
Age	Sex	Handedness	Brain damage	Intelligence	Stuttering	Peripheral hearing	Learning disability	Socioeconomic status	Report bias	Intensity bias	Memory or recognition	Temporal order	Rate bias	Length of stimulus	Frequency range	Masking	Response modality	Theory
13	14	15	16	17	18	19	20	21	22	23	24	25	26	27	28	29	30	31
			X								R	X			X	X	Gr	
		X							X		R				X		G	
			X								R							X
			X								M							
		X							X		M		X				V	
	M									X	R						V	
	M	X									R	X	X	X				X
		X							X		R			X			G/Gr	
																		X
	B								X		R					X	Gr	
	F	X							X								V	
			X						X		B			X	X		V	
	B										B						3	
			X		X					X				X	X	X	G	
																		X
		X							X	X	R	X						
	M	X									M							
		X									R	X		X			Gr	
		X									R	X					Gr	
		X									R	X					Gr	
																		X
		X									R	X					Gr	
	M	X									R						G	
										X					X		Gr	
	B	X							X	X	R	X					Gr	
	B	X							X	X	R	X					Gr	
	F	X	X						X	X	B						Gr	

		Type of presentation			Linguistic status							
					Verbal							
Author(s)	Date	Dichotic	Monaural	Monotic	Semantic value	Sentences	Words or CVC or VCV	Digits	Nonsense CVs or VCs	Letters	Natural speech	Synthetic speech	Nonverbal
		1	2	3	4	5	6	7	8	9	10	11	12
Roeser, Johns, & Price	1972a	X						X			X		
Roeser, Johns, & Price	1972b	X						X	X		X		
Rosenzweig	1951												
Rubino	1972												
Ryan & McNeil	1974	X							X		X		
Satz	1968												
Satz, Achenbach, & Fennel	1967	X						X			X		
Satz et al.	1965	X						X			X		
Satz et al.	1975	X						X			X		
Satz, Fennel, & Jones	1969												
Satz, Levy, & Tyson	1970	X						X			X		
Schulhoff & Goodglass	1969	X						X			X		X
Shanks	1973	X	X				X		X		X		
Shankweiler	1966	X						X			X		X
Shankweiler	1971												
Shankweiler & Studdert-Kennedy	1967	X							X	X		X	
Shanon	1974	X				X					X		
Simon	1967		X										X
Sobotka	1973	X						X	X		X		
Sommers et al.	1972	X					X	X			X		
Sommers & Taylor	1972							X	X		X		
Sparks & Geschwind	1968	X	X				X	X	X		X		
Sparks, Goodglass, & Nickel	1970	X						X	X		X		
Speaks et al.	1975	X		X					X		X		
Spellacy	1970	X											X
Spellacy & Blumstein	1970a	X					X		X	X	X		X
Spellacy & Blumstein	1970b	X					X			X	X		X
Spieth, Curtis, & Webster	1954												
Spieth & Webster	1955	X			X	X					X		X
Spreen & Boucher	1970	X					X				X		
Spreen, Spellacy, & Reid	1970	X											X

Subject variables (columns 13–21) · Administration and stimuli variables (columns 22–31)

Age	Sex	Handedness	Brain damage	Intelligence	Stuttering	Peripheral hearing	Learning disability	Socioeconomic status	Report bias	Intensity bias	Memory or recognition	Temporal order	Rate bias	Length of stimulus	Frequency range	Masking	Response modality	Theory
13	14	15	16	17	18	19	20	21	22	23	24	25	26	27	28	29	30	31
A	B	X								X								Gr
		X			X					X	B	X						
																		X
																		X
A	B	X																Gr
																		X
A	B	X									M						V	
A	F	X							X		M				X		V	
	B	X									M						V	X
																		X
		X									M	X						
	M	X	X						X		M				X		G/V	
	B	X	X								R						3	
		X									M						V	
																		X
	B	X									R						Gr	
		X									R						G	
	B	X							X	X	R			X			G	
	B	X			X						B							
	B	X	X		X						R						V	
	B					X	X				B			X				
	M		X								B				X	X		
		X	X								R						V	
			X							X	R						V	
	B	X									R			X			G/V	
	B	X									R			X			Gr	
	B	X									R						Gr	
																		X
									X		R				X		Gr	
		X									M				X			
		X								X			X					

Author(s)	Date	Type of presentation			Linguistic status								
					Verbal								
		Dichotic	Monaural	Monotic	Semantic value	Sentences	Words or CVC or VCV	Digits	Nonsense CVs or VCs	Letters	Natural speech	Synthetic speech	Nonverbal
		1	2	3	4	5	6	7	8	9	10	11	12
Springer	1971	X							X				
Springer	1972	X							X				
Springer	1973	X							X		X		X
Springer & Gazzaniga	1975	X	X						X		X		
Studdert-Kennedy & Shankweiler	1970	X							X		X		
Studdert-Kennedy, Shankweiler, & Pisoni	1972	X							X			X	
Studdert-Kennedy, Shankweiler, & Schulman	1970	X		X					X	X	X		
Sullivan	1975												
Sussman	1971	X											X
Sussman & MacNeilage	1975	X							X		X		X
Sussman, MacNeilage, & Lumbley	1973	X							X		X		X
Sussman, MacNeilage, & Lumbley	1975	X											X
Thies & Thies	1972	X				X					X		
Thompson & Hughes	1972	X	X						X		X		
Thompson et al.	1972	X	X						X		X		
Triesman	1960	X				X					X		
Triesman	1964a	X			X	X	X	X			X		
Triesman	1964b												
Triesman	1964c	X		X		X	X	X		X	X		
Triesman	1964d	X			X	X					X		
Triesman	1969												
Triesman	1971	X						X			X		
Triesman & Geffen	1968	X			X	X	X				X		
Triesman & Riley	1969	X			X			X		X	X		
Troendle, Porter, & Berlin	1973	X							X		X		
Tsunoda	1969	X											X
Tsunoda & Oka	1971	X						X			X		X
Van Duyne & Scanlan	1974		X		X						X		
VanLancker	1972	X			X	X	X				X		

				Subject variables						Administration and stimuli variables								
Age	Sex	Handedness	Brain damage	Intelligence	Stuttering	Peripheral hearing	Learning disability	Socioeconomic status	Report bias	Intensity bias	Memory or recognition	Temporal order	Rate bias	Length of stimulus	Frequency range	Masking	Response modality	Theory
13	14	15	16	17	18	19	20	21	22	23	24	25	26	27	28	29	30	31
A	B	X							X		R						G	
												X						
A	B											X				X	G	
A	M	X	X						X		R						Gr	
A	B	X									R						Gr	
		X															Gr	
	F	X									R	X					Gr	
																		X
	M	X							X		R				X		G	
	B	X		X							R				X		G	
		X		X					X		R				X		G	
	B	X								X	R						G	
					X										X			
	F	X								X	R						Gr	X
	F	X								X	R						Gr	
									X		R						V	
									X		R	X	X				V	
																		X
									X	X	R			X	X		V	
									X		R						V	
																		X
		X									M		X	X	X			X
		X							X		R						G/V	
		X							X		R				X		V	
	B	X									R						Gr	X
									X	X		X					G	
			X							X	B						G/Gr	
	B	X															G	
		X									R						V	

Author(s)	Date	Type of presentation			Linguistic status								
					Verbal								
		Dichotic	Monaural	Monotic	Semantic value	Sentences	Words or CVC or VCV	Digits	Nonsense CVs or VCs	Letters	Natural speech	Synthetic speech	Nonverbal
		1	2	3	4	5	6	7	8	9	10	11	12
VanLancker & Fromkin	1973	X					X					X	X
Webster & Thompson	1954	X	X	X		X					X		
Weiss & House	1973	X					X			X	X		
Whitmore	1972	X			X		X				X		
Wilson, Dirks, & Carterette	1968	X						X	X				
Witelson & Rabinovitch	1971	X						X					
Witelson & Rabinovitch	1972	X						X			X		
Yates, Martin, & DiLollo	1970	X			X	X		X			X		
Yates et al.	1968–1969												
Yeni-Komshian & Gordon	1974	X					X				X		X
Yeni-Komshian, Gordon, & Sherman	1972	X					X						
Yntema & Trask	1963	X					X	X			X		
Yund & Efron	1975	X											X
Zurif	1974												
Zurif & Bryden	1969	X						X			X		
Zurif & Carson	1970	X						X			X		
Zurif & Mendelson	1972	X			X	X			X		X		
Zurif & Ramier	1972	X						X	X		X	X	
Zurif & Sait	1970	X			X	X					X		

ACKNOWLEDGMENTS

We thank the National Institutes of Health for support through USPHS Grant Nos. NS—07005 and Program Project NS 11647—01. Necessary laboratory facilities were provided through a grant from The Kresge Foundation. Our colleagues, Jack Cullen, Larry Hughes, Bob Porter, Gae Decker, Martha Hahn, Katherine McNeil, Yvonne Beck, Penny Bernard, Angele Jackson, and Harriet Berlin contributed to the completion of this work.

REFERENCES

Abbs, J. H., and Smith, K. U. Laterality differences in the auditory feedback control of speech. *Journal of Speech and Hearing Research*, 1970, *13*, 298–303.

Abramson, A. S., and Lisker, L. Discriminability along the voicing continuum: Cross-language tests. *Proceeding of the 6th International Congress on Phonemic Science*, Prague: Academia, 1967. Pp. 569–573.

	Subject variables								Administration and stimuli variables									
Age	Sex	Handedness	Brain damage	Intelligence	Stuttering	Peripheral hearing	Learning disability	Socioeconomic status	Report bias	Intensity bias	Memory or recognition	Temporal order	Rate bias	Length of stimulus	Frequency range	Masking	Response modality	Theory
13	14	15	16	17	18	19	20	21	22	23	24	25	26	27	28	29	30	31
A	X																	X
										X				X	X			
										X	M				X			
	F								X		M						V	
A	X								X							X	V/Gr	
C	B			X							M		X	X			V	
C	B	X					X				M		X	X			V	
A	B										M		X				V	
																		X
		X									B				X			
											M						G/Gr	X
									X		M						V	
		X								X	R				X		V	
																		X
	M	X							X		M							
	M	X					X				M							
	M	X																
	X	X									B						G/V	
	M	X									R						V	

Achenbach, K. The effect of repetition on short term storage in dichotic listening. *Dissertation Abstracts*, 1967, *27*, 2883-B.

Axelrod, S., Guzy, L. T., and Diamond, I. T. Perceived rate of monotic and dichotically alternating clicks. *Journal of the Acoustical Society of America*, 1968, *43*, 51–55.

Babkoff, H., and Sutton, S. End point of lateralization for dichotic clicks. *Journal of the Acoustical Society of America*, 1966, *39*, 87–102.

Bakker, D. J. Left–right differences in auditory perception of verbal and non-verbal material by children. *Quarterly Journal of Experimental Psychology*, 1967, *17*, 334–336.

Bakker, D. J. Ear asymmetry with monaural stimulation. *Psychonomic Science*, 1968, *12*, 62.

Bakker, D. J. Ear-asymmetry with monaural stimulation: Task influences. *Cortex*, 1969, *5*, 36–42.

Bakker, D. J. Ear asymmetry with monaural stimulation: Relations to lateral dominance and lateral awareness. *Neuropsychologia*, 1970, *8*, 103–117.

Bakker, D. J., and Boeijenga, J. A. Ear-order effects on ear asymmetry with monaural stimulation. *Neuropsychologia*, 1970, *8*, 385–386.

Bakker, D. J., Smink, T., and Reitsma, P. Ear dominance and reading ability. *Cortex*, 1973, *9*, 301–312.

Barr, D. F., and Carmel N. R. Stuttering inhibition with live voice interventions and masking noise. *Journal of Auditory Research*, 1970, *10*, 59—61.

Bartholomeus, B. Effects of task requirements on ear superiority for sung speech. *Cortex*, 1974, *10*, 215—223.

Bartz, W. H. Dichotic listening and paired-associate recall. *Psychological Reports*, 1968, *23*, 436—438. (a)

Bartz, W. H. Serial position effects in dichotic listening. *Perceptual and Motor Skills*, 1968, *27*, 1014. (b)

Bartz, W. H., Satz, P., and Fennel, E. Recall strategies in dichotic listening. *Proceedings of the American Psychological Association*, 1966, *2*, 17—18.

Bartz, W. H., Satz, P., and Fennel, E. Grouping strategies in dichotic listening: The effects of instruction, rate and ear asymmetry. *Journal of Experimental Psychology*, 1967, *74*, 132—136.

Bartz, W. H., Satz, P., Fennel, E., and Lally, J. R. Meaningfulness and laterality in dichotic listening. *Journal of Experimental Psychology*, 1967, *73*, 204—210.

Benton, A. L. Hemispheric cerebral dominance. *Israel Journal of Medical Science*, 1970, *6*, 294—303.

Berlin, C. I. Review of binaural effects — 1969. *American Academy of Ophthalmology and Otolaryngology Monograph. 1970 Reviews of the Literature*, 1971, 7—28.

Berlin, C. I. Critical review of the literature on dichotic effects — 1970. *American Academy of Ophthalmology and Otolaryngology Monograph, 1971 Reviews of Scientific Literature on Hearing*, 1972, 80—90.

Berlin, C. I., Cullen, J. K., Jr., Hughes, L. F., Berlin, H. L., Lowe-Bell, S.S., and Thompson, C. L. Acoustic variables in dichotic listening. *Proceedings of a Symposium on Central Auditory Processing Disorders*, 1975. Pp. 36—46.

Berlin, C. I., Hughes, L. F., Lowe-Bell, S. S., and Berlin, H. L. Dichotic right ear advantage in children 5 to 13. *Cortex*, 1973, *9*, 394—401. (c)

Berlin, C. I., and Lowe, S. S. Temporal and dichotic factors in central auditory testing. In Katz, J. (Ed.), *Handbook of clinical audiology*. Baltimore: Williams & Wilkins, 1972. Pp. 280—312.

Berlin, C. I., Lowe-Bell, S. S., Cullen, J. K., Jr., Thompson, C. L., and Loovis, C. F. Dichotic speech perception: An interpretation of right-ear advantage and temporal offset effects. *Journal of the Acoustical Society of America*, 1973, *53*, 699—709. (a)

Berlin, C. I., Lowe-Bell, S. S., Cullen, J. K., Jr., Thompson, C. L., and Stafford, M. R. Is speech *special*? Perhaps the temporal lobectomy patient can tell us. *Journal of the Acoustical Society of America*, 1972, *52*, 702—705. (a)

Berlin, C. I., Lowe-Bell, S. S., Jannetta, P. J., and Kline, D. G. Central auditory deficits after temporal lobectomy. *Archives of Otolaryngology*, 1972, *96*, 4—10. (b)

Berlin, C. I., Porter, R. J., Jr., Lowe-Bell, S. S., Berlin, H. L., Thompson, C. L., and Hughes, L. F. Dichotic signs of the recognition of speech elements in normals, temporal lobectomees, and hemispherectomees. *I.E.E.E. Transactions and Audio Electroacoustics*, 1973, *AU-21*, 189—195. (b)

Bertelson, P., and Tisseyre, F. Lateral asymmetry in the perceived sequence of speech and nonspeech stimuli. *Perception and Psychophysics*, 1972, *11*, 356—362.

Bever, T. G. The nature of cerebral dominance in speech behaviour of the child and adult. In Huxley, R., and Ingram, E. (Eds.), *Language acquisition: Models and methods*. London: Academic Press, 1971, 231—254.

Bever, T. G., and Chiarello, R. J. Cerebral dominance in musicians and nonmusicians. *Science*, 1974, *185*, 537—539.

Blumstein, S. E. The use of theoretical implications of the dichotic technique for investigating distinctive features. *Brain and Language*, 1974, *1*, 337—350.

Blumstein, S., and Cooper, W. Identification versus discrimination of distinctive features in speech perception. *Quarterly Journal of Experimental Psychology*, 1972, *24*, 207—214.

Blumstein, S., and Cooper, W. E. Hemispheric processing of intonation contours. *Cortex*, 1974, *10*, 146—157.

Borkowski, J. G., Spreen, O., and Stutz, J. Z. Ear preference and abstractness in dichotic listening. *Psychonomic Science*, 1965, *3*, 547—548.

Bradshaw, J. L., Nettleton, N. C., and Geffen, G. Ear differences and delayed auditory feedback: Effects on a speech and music task. *Journal of Experimental Psychology*, 1971, *91*, 85—92.

Brady, W. A., Sommers, R. K., and Moore, W. H. Cerebral speech processing in stuttering children and adults. Paper presented at the American Speech and Hearing Association Convention, October 12–15, 1973, Detroit, Michigan.

Brady-Wood, S., and Shankweiler, D. Effects of one of the two channels on perception of opposing pairs of nonsense syllables when monotically and dichotically presented. Paper presented at the Eighty-Fifth Meeting of the Acoustical Society of America, April 10–13, 1973, Boston, Mass.

Broadbent, D. E. The role of auditory localization in attention and memory span. *Journal of Experimental Psychology*, 1954, *47*, 191–196.

Broadbent, D. E. Growing points in multichannel communication. *Journal of the Acoustical Society of America*, 1956, *28*, 533–535. (a)

Broadbent, D. E. Successive responses to simultaneous stimuli. *Quarterly Journal of Experimental Psychology*, 1956, *8*, 145–152. (b)

Broadbent, D. E. Immediate memory and simultaneous stimuli. *Quarterly Journal of Experimental Psychology*, 1957, *9*, 1–11.

Broadbent, D. E. *Perception and communication.* London: Pergamon Press, 1958.

Broadbent, D. E. Attention and the perception of speech. *Scientific American*, April 1962, *206*, 143–151.

Broadbent, D. E. Word-frequency effect and response bias. *Psychological Review*, 1967, *74*, 1–15.

Broadbent, D. E., and Gregory, M. Division of attention and the decision theory of signal detection. *Proceedings of the Royal Society (London)*, 1963, Series B, *158*, 222–231.

Broadbent, D. E., and Gregory, M. Accuracy of recognition for speech presented to the right and left ears. *Quarterly Journal of Experimental Psychology*, 1964, *16*, 359–360. (a)

Broadbent, D. E., and Gregory, M. Stimulus set and response set: The alternation of attention. *Quarterly Journal of Experimental Psychology*, 1964, *16*, 309–317. (b)

Broadbent, D. E., and Ladefoged, P. On the fusion of sounds reaching different sense organs. *Journal of the Acoustical Society of America*, 1957, *29*, 708–710.

Brown, J. W., and Jaffe, J. Hypothesis on cerebral dominance. *Neuropsychologia*, 1975, *13*, 107–110.

Brunt, M., and Goetzinger, C. P. A study of three tests of central function with normal hearing subjects. *Cortex*, 1968, *4*, 288–297.

Bryden, M. P. Order of report in dichotic listening. *Canadian Journal of Psychology*, 1962, *16*, 291–299.

Bryden, M. P. Ear preference in auditory perception. *Journal of Experimental Psychology*, 1963, *65*, 103–105.

Bryden, M. P. The manipulation of strategies of report in dichotic listening. *Canadian Journal of Psychology*, 1964, *18*, 126–138.

Byrden, M. P. Tachistoscopic recognition, handedness and cerebral dominance. *Neuropsychologia*, 1965, *3*, 1–8.

Bryden, M. P. Short-term memory for unbalanced dichotic lists. *Psychonomic Science*, 1966, *6*, 379–380.

Bryden, M. P. An evaluation of some models of laterality effects in dichotic listening. *Acta Otolaryngologica*, 1967, *63*, 595–604.

Bryden, M. P. Binaural competition and division of attention as determinants of the laterality effects in dichotic listening. *Canadian Journal of Psychology*, 1969, *23*, 101–113.

Bryden, M. P. Laterality effects in dichotic listening: Relations with handedness and reading ability in children. *Neuropsychologia*, 1970, *8*, 443–450.

Bryden, M. P., and Zurif, E. B. Dichotic listening performance in a case of agenesis of the corpus callosum. *Neuropsychologia*, 1970, *8*, 371–377.

Caird, W. K. Effects of age on the recall of dichotic words. *Nature*, 1965, *207*, 109.

Caird, W. K., and Inglis, J. The short term storage of auditory and visual two-channel digits by elderly patients with memory disorders. *Journal of Mental Science*, 1961, *107*, 1062–1069.

Carr, B. M. Ear effect variables and order of report in dichotic listening. *Cortex*, 1969, *5*, 63–68.

Chaney, R. B., and Webster, J. C. Information in certain multidimensional sounds. *Journal of the Acoustical Society of America*, 1966, *40*, 447–455.

Cherry, C. E. Some experiments on the recognition of speech, with one and with two ears. *Journal of the Acoustical Society of America*, 1953, *25*, 975–979.

Cherry, C. E., and Sayers, B. M. Human *cross-correlator*—a technique for measuring certain parameters of speech perception. *Journal of the Acoustical Society of America*, 1956, *28*, 889—895.

Cherry, C. E., and Taylor, W. K. Some further experiments upon the recognition of speech, with one and two ears. *Journal of the Acoustical Society of America*, 1954, *26*, 554—559.

Clark, L., Knowles, J. B., and Maclean, A. The effects of method of recall on performance in the dichotic listening task. *Canadian Journal of Psychology*, 1970, *24*, 194—198.

Clifton, C., and Bogartz, R. S. Selective attention during dichotic listening by preschool children. *Journal of Experimental Psychology*, 1968, *6*, 483—491.

Conners, C. K., Kramer, K., and Guerr, F. Auditory synthesis and dichotic listening in children with learning disabilities. *Journal of Special Education*, 1969, *3*, 163—170.

Cooper, A., Achenbach, K. E., Satz, P., and Levy, C. M. Order of report and ear asymmetry in dichotic listening. *Psychonomic Science*, 1967, *9*, 97—98.

Craik, F. I. M. The nature of the age decrement in performance on dichotic listening tasks. *Quarterly Journal of Experimental Psychology*, 1965, *12*, 227—240.

Cullen, J. K., Jr., and Thompson, C. L. Release from masking in subjects with temporal lobe resections. Paper presented at the American Speech and Hearing Association Convention, November 18—21, 1972, San Francisco, California.

Cullen, J. K., Jr., and Thompson, C. L. Masking release for speech in subjects with temporal lobe resections. *Archives of Otolaryngology*, 1974, *100*, 113—116.

Cullen, J. K., Jr., Thompson, C. L., Hughes, L. F., Berlin, C. I., and Samson, D. S. The effects of varied acoustic parameters on performance in dichotic speech perception tasks. *Brain and Language*, 1974, *1*, 307—322.

Cullen, J. K., Jr., Thompson, C. L., Samson, D. S., and Hughes, L. F. The effects of monaural and bi-aural masking on a dichotic speech task. Paper presented at the American Speech and Hearing Association Convention, October 12—15, 1973, Detroit, Michigan.

Curry, F. K. W. A comparison of left-handed and right-handed subjects on verbal and non-verbal dichotic listening tasks. *Cortex*, 1967, *3*, 343—352.

Curry, F. K. W. A comparison of the performances of a right-hemispherectomized subject and twenty-five normals on four dichotic listening tasks. *Cortex*, 1968, *4*, 144—153.

Curry, F. K. W., and Gregory, H. H. The performance of stutterers on dichotic listening tasks thought to reflect cerebral dominance. *Journal of Speech and Hearing Research*, 1969, *12*, 73—82.

Curry, F. K. W., and Rutherford, D. R. Recognition and recall of dichotically presented verbal stimuli by right- and left-handed persons. *Neuropsychologia*, 1967, *5*, 119—126.

Cutting, J. E. Different speech-processing mechanisms can be reflected in the results of discrimination and dichotic listening tasks. *Brain and Language*, 1974, *1*, 363—374.

Darwin, C. J. Dichotic backward masking of complex sounds. *Quarterly Journal of Experimental Psychology*, 1971, *23*, 386—392. (a)

Darwin, C. J. Ear differences in the recall of fricatives and vowels. *Quarterly Journal of Experimental Psychology*, 1971, *23*, 46—62. (b)

Day, R., and Vigorito, J. A parallel between degree of encodedness and the ear advantage: Evidence from a temporal order judgment task. Paper presented at the Eighty-Fourth Meeting of the Acoustical Society of America, November 28—December 1, 1972, Miami, Florida.

Dee, H. L. Auditory asymmetry and strength of manual preference. *Cortex*, 1971, *7*, 298—303.

Deutsch, J. A., and Deutsch, D. Attention: Some theoretical considerations. *Psychological Review*, 1963, *70*, 80—90.

Deutsch, J. A., Deutsch D., and Lindsay, P. H. Comments on selective attention: Perception or response? and Triesman, A. M., *Reply*. *Quarterly Journal of Experimental Psychology*, 1967, *19*, 362—367.

Dirks, D. D. Perception of dichotic and monaural verbal material and cerebral dominance for speech. *Acta Oto-laryngologica*, 1964, *58*, 73—80.

Dirks, D. D., and Bower, D. R. Masking effects of speech competing messages. *Journal of Speech and Hearing Research*, 1969, *12*, 229—245.

Dobie, R. A., and Simmons, F. B. A dichotic threshold test: Normal and brain damaged subjects. *Journal of Speech and Hearing Research* 1971, *14*, 71—81.

Dodwell, P. C. Some factors affecting the hearing of words presented dichotically. *Canadian Journal of Psychology*, 1964, *18*, 72—91.

Doehring, D. G., Ear asymmetry in the discrimination of monaural tonal sequences. *Canadian Journal of Psychology*, 1972, *26*, 106—110.

Doehring, D. G., and Bartholomeus, B. N. Laterality effects in voice recognition. *Neuropsychologia*, 1971, *9*, 425—430.

Dorman, M. F., and Geffner, D. S. Hemispheric specialization for speech perception in six-year-old black and white children from low and middle socioeconomic classes. *Cortex*, 1974, *10*, 171—176.

Efron, R. Temporal perception, aphasia and Déjà vu. *Brain*, 1963, *86*, 403—424. (a)

Efron, R. The effect of handedness on the perception of simultaneity and temporal order. *Brain*, 1963, *86*, 261—284. (b)

Efron, R., and Yund, E. W. Dichotic competition of simultaneous tone bursts of different frequency. III. The effect of stimulus parameters on suppression and ear dominance functions. *Neuropsychologia*, 1975, *13*, 151—161.

Egan, J. P., Carterette, E. C., and Thwing, E. J. Some factors affecting multi-channel listening. *Journal of the Acoustical Society of America*, 1954, *26*, 774—782.

Eimas, P. D., Siqueland, E. R., Jusczyk, P., and Vigorito, J. Speech perception in infants. *Science*, 1971, *171*, 303—306.

Elfner, L. F., and Tomsic, R. T. Temporal and intensive factors in binaural lateralization of auditory transients. *Journal of the Acoustical Society of America*, 1968, *43*, 746—751.

Elliott, L. L. Backward masking: Monotic and dichotic. *Journal of the Acoustical Society of America*, 1962, *34*, 1108—1115.

Emmerich, D. S., Goldenbaum, D. M., Hayden, D. L., Hoffman, L. S., and Treffts, J. L. Meaningfulness as a variable in dichotic hearing. *Journal of Experimental Psychology*, 1965, *69*, 433—436.

Entus, A. K. Hemispheric asymmetry in processing of dichotically presented speech and nonspeech stimuli by infants. Paper presented at Conference on Language Development and Neurological Theory, May 9—10, 1975.

Fodor, J. A., and Bever, T. G. The psychological reality of linguistic segments. *Journal of Verbal Learning and Verbal Behavior*, 1965, *4*, 414—420.

Folsom, L. C. Left—right differences in the auditory perception of verbal material by children, ages eight and fourteen. Unpublished Master's thesis, University of Montana, 1969.

Geffner, D. S., and Hochberg, I. Ear laterality performance of children from low and middle socioeconomic levels on a verbal dichotic listening task. *Cortex*, 1971, *8*, 193—203.

Gerber, S. E. Dichotic and diotic presentation of speeded speech. *Journal of Communication*, 1968, *18*, 272—282.

Gerber, S. E., and Goldman, P. Ear preference for dichotically presented verbal stimuli as a function of report strategies. *Journal of the Acoustical Society of America*, 1971, *49*, 1163—1168.

Geschwind, N., and Levitsky, W. Human brain: Left—right asymmetries in temporal speech region. *Science*, 1968, *161*, 186—187.

Gilliom, J. D., and Sorkin, R. D. Sequential vs. simultaneous two-channel signal detection: More evidence for a high-level interrupt theory. *Journal of the Acoustical Society of America*, 1974, *56*, 157—164.

Gilroy, J., and Lynn, G. E. Significance of reversible central auditory test findings in patients with cerebral hemisphere lesions. Paper presented at the American Speech and Hearing Association Convention, November 17—20, 1971, Chicago, Illinois.

Gilroy, J., and Lynn, G. E. Reversibility of abnormal auditory findings in cerebral hemisphere lesions. *Journal of Neurological Science*, 1974, *21*, 117—131.

Godfrey, J. J. Perceptual difficulty and the right ear advantage for vowels. *Brain and Language*, 1974, *1*, 323—336.

Goodglass, H. Binaural digit presentation and early lateral brain damage. *Cortex*, 1967, *3*, 295—306.

Goodglass, H. Developmental comparison of vowels and consonants in dichotic listening. *Journal of Speech and Hearing Research*, 1973, *16*, 744—752.

Goodglass, H., and Peck, E. A. Dichotic ear order effects in Korsakoff and normal subjects. *Neuropsychologia*, 1972, *10*, 211—217.

Gordon, H. W. Hemispheric asymmetries in the perception of musical chords. *Cortex*, 1970, *6*, 387—398.
Gordon, H. W. Comparison of ipsilateral and contralateral auditory pathways in callosum-sectioned patients by use of a response-time technique. *Neuropsychologia*, 1975, *13*, 9—18.
Gray, J. A., and Wedderburn, A. A. I. Grouping strategies with simultaneous stimuli. *Quarterly Journal of Experimental Psychology*, 1960, *12*, 180—184.
Haaland, K. Y. The effect of dichotic monaural, and diotic verbal stimuli on auditory evoked potentials. *Neuropsychologia*, 1974, *12*, 339—345.
Haas, H. Über den einfluss eines einfachechos auf die Hörsamkeit von sprache. *Acustica*, 1951, *1*, 49—58.
Haggard, M. P. Encoding and the REA for speech signals. *Quarterly Journal of Experimental Psychology*, 1971, *23*, 34—45.
Haggard, M. P., and Parkinson, A. M. Stimulus and task factors as determinants of ear advantages. *Quarterly Journal of Experimental Psychology*, 1971, *23*, 168—177.
Halperin, Y., Nachsohn, I., and Carmon, A. Shift of ear superiority in dichotic listening to temporally patterned nonverbal stimuli. *Journal of the Acoustical Society of America*, 1973, *53*, 46—50.
Hannah, J. E. Phonetic and temporal titration of the dichotic right ear effect. Unpublished doctoral dissertation, Louisiana State University, 1971.
Hannah, J. E., Thompson, C. L., Cullen, J. K., Jr., Hughes, L. F., and Berlin, C. I. Size of the dichotic right-ear effect as a function of alignment criteria. Paper presented at the Eighty-First Meeting of the Acoustical Society of America, April 20—23, 1971, Washington, D.C.
Hedrick, D. An investigation of children's abilities to respond to competing messages varied in intensity and content: A developmental study. Unpublished doctoral dissertation, University of Washington, 1966.
Higenbottam, J., and Spreen, O. Perceptual asymmetry with dichotically presented click-sentence stimuli. *Journal of Auditory Research*, 1970, *10*, 164—175.
Horning, J. K. The effects of age on dichotic listening. Unpublished Master's thesis, San Diego State College, 1972.
Howarth, C. I., and Ellis, K. The relative intelligibility threshold for one's own name compared with other names. *Quarterly Journal of Experimental Psychology*, 1962, *14*, 236—239.
Hutchinson, B. B. Performance of aphasics on a dichotic listening task. *Journal of Auditory Research*, 1973, *13*, 64—70.
Inglis, J. Dichotic stimulation and memory disorder. *Nature*, 1960, *186*, 181—182.
Inglis, J. Dichotic stimulation, temporal lobe damage, and the perception and storage of auditory stimuli—a note on Kimura's findings. *Canadian Journal of Psychology*, 1962, *16*, 11—17. (a)
Inglis, J. Effect of age on responses to dichotic stimulation. *Nature*, 1962, *194*, 1101. (b)
Inglis, J. Influence of motivation, perception and attention on age-related changes in short-term memory. *Nature*, 1964, *204*, 103—104.
Inglis, J. Dichotic listening and cerebral dominance. *Acta Oto-laryngologica*, 1965, *60*, 231—238. (a)
Inglis, J. Immediate memory, age and brain function. In Welford, A. T., and Birren, J. E. (Eds.), *Behavior, aging and the nervous system*. Springfield, Illinois: Charles C. Thomas, 1965. Pp. 88—113. (b)
Inglis, J., and Ankus, M. L. Effect of age on short-term storage and serial rote learning. *British Journal of Psychology*, 1965, *56*, 183—195.
Inglis, J., and Caird, W. K. Age differences in successive responses to simultaneous stimulation. *Canadian Journal of Psychology*, 1963, *17*, 98—105.
Inglis, J., and Sanderson, R. E. Successive responses to simultaneous stimulation in elderly patients with memory disorders. *Journal of Abnormal Social Psychology*, 1961, *62*, 709—712.
Inglis, J., and Sanderson, R. E. Immediate memory and memory disorders. In Tibbits, C., and Donahue, W. (Eds.), *Social and psychological aspects of aging*. New York: Columbia University Press, 1962. Pp. 182—188.
Inglis, J., and Sykes, D. H. Some sources of variation in dichotic listening performance in children. *Journal of Experimental Child Psychology*, 1967, *5*, 480—488.
Inglis, J., and Tansey, C. L. Age differences and scoring differences in dichotic listening performance. *Journal of Psychology*, 1967, *66*, 325—332. (a)

Inglis, J., and Tansey, C. L. Perception and short-term storage in dichotic listening. *Psychonomic Science*, 1967, 7, 273—274. (b)

Ingram, D. Cerebral speech lateralization in young children. *Neuropsychologia*, 1975, 13, 103—105.

Jerger, J. F. Observations on auditory behavior in lesions of the central auditory pathways. *Archives of Otolaryngology*, 1960, 71, 797—806.

Jerger, J., Weikers, N. J., Sharbrough, F. W., and Jerger, S. Bilateral lesions of the temporal lobe. *Acta Oto-laryngologica*, 1969, Suppl. 258, Uppsala, Sweden.

Jones, D., and Spreen, O. Dichotic listening by retarded children: The effect of ear order and abstractness. *Child Development*, 1967, 38, 101—105. (a)

Jones, D., and Spreen, O. The effects of meaningfulness and abstractness on word recognition in educable retarded children. *American Journal of Mental Deficiency*, 1967, 71, 987—989. (b)

Karp, E., and Birch, H. G. Hemispheric differences in reaction time to verbal and non-verbal stimuli. *Perceptual and Motor Skills*, 1969, 29, 475—480.

Katz, J. The use of staggered spondaic words for assessing the integrity of the central auditory system. *Journal of Auditory Research*, 1962, 2, 327—337.

Katz, J. The SSW test: An interim report. *Journal of Speech and Hearing Disorders*, 1968, 33, 132—146.

Katz, J., Basil, R. A., and Smith, J. M. A staggered spondaic word test for detecting central auditory lesions. *Annals of Otology, Rhinology and Laryngology*, 1963, 72, 908—917.

Kimura, D. Cerebral dominance and the perception of verbal stimuli. *Canadian Journal of Psychology*, 1961, 15, 166—171. (a)

Kimura, D. Some effects of temporal-lobe damage on auditory perception. *Canadian Journal of Psychology*, 1961, 15, 156—165. (b)

Kimura, D. Perceptual and memory functions of the temporal lobe: A reply to Dr. Inglis. *Canadian Journal of Psychology*, 1962, 16, 18—22.

Kimura, D. Right temporal-lobe damage. *Archives of Neurology*, 1963, 8, 264—271. (a)

Kimura, D. Speech lateralization in young children as determined by an auditory test. *Journal of Comparative Physiology and Psychology*, 1963, 56, 899—902. (b)

Kimura, D. Left—right differences in the perception of melodies. *Quarterly Journal of Experimental Psychology*, 1964, 16, 355—358.

Kimura, D. Functional asymmetry of the brain in dichotic listening. *Cortex*, 1967, 3, 163—178.

Kimura, D. The asymmetry of the human brain. *Scientific American*, 1973, 227, 70—78.

Kimura, D., and Folb, S. Neural-processing of backwards speech sounds. *Science*, 1968, 161, 395—396.

King, L. F., and Kimura, D. Left ear superiority in dichotic perception of vocal non-verbal sounds. *Canadian Journal of Psychology*, 1972, 26, 111—116.

Kinsbourne, M. The cerebral basis of lateral asymmetries in attention. In Sanders, A. F. (Ed.), *Attention and performance, III*. Amsterdam: North-Holland, 1970. Pp. 192—201.

Kirstein, E. F. Selective listening for temporally staggered dichotic CV syllables. Paper presented at the Seventy-Ninth Meeting of the Acoustical Society of America, April 21—24, 1970, Atlantic City, New Jersey.

Klisz, D. K., and Parsons, O. A. Ear asymmetry in reaction time tasks as a function of handedness. *Neuropsychologia*, 1975, 13, 323—330.

Knox, A. W., and Boone, D. R. Auditory laterality and tested handedness. *Cortex*, 1970, 6, 164—173.

Knox, C., and Kimura, D. Cerebral processing of nonverbal sounds in boys and girls. *Neuropsychologia*, 1970, 8, 227—237.

Konecni, V. J., and Slamecka, N. J. Awareness in verbal nonoperant conditioning: An approach through dichotic listening. *Journal of Experimental Psychology*, 1972, 94, 248—254.

Krashen, S. D. Lateralization, language, learning and the critical period: Some new evidence. *Language and Learning*, 1973, 23, 63—74.

Krashen, S., Fromkin, V., Curtiss, S., Rigler, D., and Spitz, S. Language lateralization in a case of extreme psychosocial deprivation. Paper presented at the Eighty-Fourth Meeting of the Acoustical Society of America, November 28—December 1, 1972, Miami, Florida.

Kuhn, G. M. The phi coefficient as an index of ear differences in dichotic listening. *Cortex*, 1973, 9, 447—457.

Lawson, E. A. Decisions concerning the rejected channel. *Quarterly Journal of Experimental Psychology*, 1966, *18*, 260—265.

Levy, C. M., and Bowers, D. Hemispheric asymmetry of reaction time in a dichotic discrimination task. *Cortex*, 1974, *10*, 18—25.

Lewis, J. L. Semantic processing of unattended messages using dichotic listening. *Journal of Experimental Psychology*, 1970, *85*, 225—228.

Liberman, A. M., Cooper, F. S., Shankweiler, D. P., and Studdert-Kennedy, M. Perception of the speech code. *Psychological Review*, 1967, *74*, 431—461.

Lindsay, P. H. Comments on selective attention: Perception or response? *Quarterly Journal of Experimental Psychology*, 1967, *19*, 363—364.

Ling, A. H. Dichotic listening in hearing-impaired children. *Journal of Speech and Hearing Research*, 1971, *14*, 793—803.

Lowe, S. S. Perception of dichotic and monotic simultaneous and time-staggered syllables. Unpublished doctoral dissertation, Louisiana State University, 1970.

Lowe, S. S., Cullen, J. K., Jr., Berlin, C. I., Thompson, C. L., and Willett, M. E. Perception of simultaneous dichotic and monotic monosyllables. *Journal of Speech and Hearing Research*, 1970, *13*, 812—822.

Lynn, G. E., Benitez, J. T., Eisenbrey, A. B., Gilroy, J., and Wilner, H. I. Neuroaudiological correlates in cerebral hemisphere lesions: Temporal and parietal lobe tumors. *Audiology*, 1972, *11*, 115—134.

Lynn, G. E., and Gilroy, J. Neuroaudiological abnormalities in patients with temporal lobe tumors. *Journal of Neurological Science*, 1972, *17*, 167—184.

Lynn, G. E., and Gilroy, J. Auditory disorders and the parietal lobe. Paper presented at the American Speech and Hearing Association Convention, October 12—15, 1973, Detroit, Michigan.

Maccoby, E. E., and Konrad, K. W. Age trends in selective listening. *Journal of Exceptional Child Psychology*, 1966, *3*, 113—122.

MacKay, H. R., and Inglis, J. The effect of age on a short-term auditory storage process. *Gerontology*, 1963, *8*, 193—200.

Mangrum, C. T. A comparison of the performance of normal and dyslexic readers on the auditory test of dichotic stimuli and the visual test of dichotic stimuli. Unpublished doctoral dissertation, Indiana University, 1968.

Manning, C. C. A study of the intelligibility of competing messages as a function of relative intensity and message similarity. Unpublished doctoral dissertation, University of Washington, 1964.

Marshall, J. C., Capian, D., and Holmes, J. M. The measure of laterality. *Neuropsychologia*, 1975, *13*, 315—321.

Marston, L. E., and Goetzinger, C. P. A comparison of sensitized words and sentences for distinguishing nonperipheral auditory changes as a function of aging. *Cortex*, 1972, *8*, 213—223.

Massaro, D. Pre-perceptual images, processing time, and perceptual units in auditory perception. *Psychological Review*, 1972, *79*, 124—145.

McClellan, M. E., Wertz, R. T., and Collins, M. J. The effects of interhemispheric lesions on central auditory behavior. Paper presented at the American Speech and Hearing Association Convention, October 12—15, 1973, Detroit, Michigan.

McCormick, C., and Porter, R. J., Jr. The effect of delayed channel on the perception of dichotically presented VC syllables. Paper presented at the Eighty-Sixth Meeting of the Acoustical Society of America, October 29—November 2, 1973, Los Angeles, California.

McGlone, J., and Davidson, W. The relation between cerebral speech laterality and spatial ability with special reference to sex and handedness. *Neuropsychologia*, 1973, *11*, 105—113.

Mewhort, D. J. K. Retrieval tags and order of report in dichotic listening. *Canadian Journal of Psychology*, 1973, *27*, 219—226.

Mewhort, D. J. K., Thio, H., and Birkenmayer, A. C. Processing capacity and switching attention in dichotic listening. *Canadian Journal of Psychology*, 1971, *25*, 111—129.

Milner, B. Laterality effects in audition. In Mountcastle, V. B. (Ed.), *Interhemispheric relations and cerebral dominance*. Baltimore: Johns Hopkins Press, 1962, Pp. 177—195.

Milner, B. Interhemispheric differences in the localization of psychological processes in man. *British Medical Bulletin*, 1971, *27*, 272—277.

Milner, B., Taylor, S., and Sperry, R. W. Lateralized suppression of dichotically presented digits after commissural section in man. *Science*, 1968, *161*, 184—185.

Morais, J., and Darwin, C. J. Ear differences for same—different reaction times to monaurally presented speech. *Brain and Language*, 1974, *1*, 383—390.

Moray, N. The effect of the relative intensities of dichotic messages in speech and shadowing. *Language and Speech*, 1958, *1*, 110—113.

Moray, N. Attention in dichotic listening: Affective cues and the influence of instructions. *Quarterly Journal of Experimental Psychology*, 1959, *11*, 56—60.

Moray, N. Broadbent's filter theory: Postulate H and the problem of switching time. *Quarterly Journal of Experimental Psychology*, 1960, *12*, 214—220.

Moray, N., and Jordan, A. Practice and compatibility in two channel short term memory. *Psychonomic Science*, 1966, *4*, 427—428.

Moray, N., and O'Brien, T. Signal detection theory applied to selective listening. *Journal of the Acoustical Society of America*, 1967, *42*, 765—772.

Moray, N., and Taylor, A. The effect of redundancy in shadowing one of two dichotic messages. *Language and Speech*, 1958, *1*, 102—109.

Murdock, B. B. Associative symmetry and dichotic presentation. *Journal of Verbal Learning and Verbal Behavior*, 1965, *4*, 222—226.

Murphy, E. H., and Venables, P. H. The effects of caffeine citrate and white noise on ear asymmetry in the detection of two clicks. *Neuropsychologia*, 1971, *9*, 27—32.

Myers, T. F. Asymmetry and attention in phonic decoding. *Acta Psychologica*, 1970, *33*, 158—177.

Nachsohn, I., and Carmon, A. Stimulus familiarity and ear superiority in dichotic listening. *Journal of the Acoustical Society of America*, 1975, *57*, 223—227.

Nagafuchi, M. Development of dichotic and monaural hearing abilities in young children. *Acta Oto-laryngologica*, 1970, *69*, 409—414.

Netley, C. Dichotic listening performance of hemispherectomized patients. *Neuropsychologia*, 1972, *10*, 233—240.

Neufeldt, A. H. Short-term memory in the mentally retarded: An application of the dichotic listening technique. *Psychological Monographs*, 1966, *80*, 1—31.

Ohta, F., Hayashi, R., and Morimoto, M. Differential diagnosis of retrocochlear deafness: Binaural fusion test and binaural separation test. *International Audiology*, 1967, *6*, 58—62.

Olsen, W. O., Noffsinger, D., and Kurdziel, S. Masking level differences and dichotic speech perception by cortical lesion patients. Paper presented at the American Speech and Hearing Association Convention, October 12—15, 1973, Detroit, Michigan.

Oscar-Berman, M., Goodglass, H., and Donnefeld, M. Dichotic ear-order effects with nonverbal stimuli. *Cortex*, 1974, *10*, 270—277.

Oscar-Berman, M., Zurif, E. B., and Blumstein, S. Effects of unilateral brain damage on the processing of speech sounds in two languages. *Brain and Language*, 1975, *2*, 345—355.

Oxbury, J. M., and Oxbury, S. M. Effect of temporal lobectomy on the report of dichotically presented digits. *Cortex*, 1969, *5*, 3—14.

Oxbury, S. M., Oxbury, J., and Gardiner, J. Laterality effects in dichotic listening. *Nature*, 1967, *214*, 742—743.

Palmer, R. D. Cerebral dominance and auditory asymmetry. *Journal of Psychology*, 1964, *58*, 157—167.

Papçun, G., Krashen, S., and Terbeek, D. The left hemisphere is specialized for speech, language, and something else. *U.C.L.A. Working Papers in Phonetics*, 1972, *22*, 118—119.

Papçun, G., Krashen, S., Terbeek, D., Remington, R., and Harshman, R. Is the left hemisphere specialized for speech, language and/or something else? *Journal of the Acoustical Society of America*, 1974, *55*, 319—327.

Penfield, W., and Roberts, L. *Speech and brain mechanisms*. Princeton, N.J.: Princeton University Press, 1959.

Perl, N. T. The recall of dichotic stimuli: Is order or laterality more important? *Papers in Psychology*, 1968, *2*, 25—27.

Perl, N. T. The application of the verbal transformation effect to the study of cerebral dominance. *Neuropsychologia*, 1970, *8*, 259—261.

Perl, N., and Haggard, M. Practice and strategy in a measure of cerebral dominance. *Neuropsychologia*, 1975, *13*, 347—352.

Peterson, L. R., and Kroener, S. Dichotic stimulation and retention. *Journal of Experimental Psychology*, 1964, *68*, 125—130.

Pettit, J. M. Cerebral dominance and the process of language recovery in aphasia. Unpublished doctoral dissertation, Purdue University, 1969.

Pinheiro, M. L., and Tobin, H. Interaural intensity differences for intracranial lateralization. *Journal of the Acoustical Society of America*, 1969, *46*, 1482—1487.

Pinheiro, M. L., and Tobin, H. The interaural intensity difference as a diagnostic indicator. *Acta Otolaryngologica*, 1971, *71*, 326—328.

Pisoni, D. B., and McNabb, S. D. Dichotic interaction and phonetic feature processing. *Brain and Language*, 1974, *1*, 351—362.

Pizzamiglio, L., DePascalis, C., and Vignati, A. Stability of dichotic listening test. *Cortex*, 1974, *10*, 203—205.

Porter, R. J., Jr. The effect of temporal overlap on the perception of dichotically and monotically presented CV syllables. Paper presented at the Eighty-First Meeting of the Acoustical Society of America, April 20—23, 1971, Washington, D.C.

Porter, R. J., Jr. Effects of asynchrony on the preception of dichotically presented speech and non-speech. Paper presented at the Eighty-Fifth Meeting of the Acoustical Society of America, April 10—13, 1973, Boston, Mass. (a)

Porter, R. J., Jr. Differences in the dichotic *lag effect* as a function of the type of CV syllables presented. Paper presented at the Eighty-Sixth Meeting of the Acoustical Society of America, October 29—November 2, 1973, Los Angeles, California. (b)

Porter, R. J., Jr. and Berlin, C. I. On interpreting developmental changes in the dichotic right-ear advantage. *Brain and Language*, 1975, *2*, 186—200.

Porter, R. J., Jr., Shankweiler, D., and Liberman, A. Differential effects of binaural time differences on the perception of stop consonants and vowels. *Proceedings of the 77th Annual Convention A.P.A.*, 1969. Pp.15—16.

Provins, K. A., and Jeeves, M. A. Hemisphere differences in response time to simple auditory stimuli. *Neuropsycholgia*, 1975, *13*, 207—211.

Rand, T. C. Dichotic release from masking for speech. *Journal of the Acoustical Society of America*, 1974, *55*, 678—680.

Repp, B. H. Dichotic forward and backward "masking" between CV syllables. *Journal of the Acoustical Society of America*, 1975, *57*, 483—496. (a)

Repp, B. H. Dichotic masking of consonants by vowels. *Journal of the Acoustical Society of America*, 1975, *57*, 724—735. (b)

Roeser, R. J., and Daly, D. D. Auditory cortex disconnection associated with thalamic tumor: A case report. *Neurology*, 1974, *24*, 555—559.

Roeser, R. J., Johns, D. F., and Price. L. L. Effects of intensity on dichotically presented digits. *Journal of Auditory Research*, 1972, *12*, 184—186. (a)

Roeser, R. J., Johns, D. F., and Price, L. L. Effects of sensorineural hearing loss on two dichotic listening tasks. Paper presented at the American Speech and Hearing Association Convention, November 18—21, 1972, San Francisco, California. (b)

Rosenzweig, M. R. Representation of the two ears at the auditory cortex. *American Journal of Physiology*, 1951, *167*, 147—158.

Rubino, C. A. A simple procedure for constructing dichotic listening tapes. *Cortex*, 1972, *8*, 335—338.

Ryan, W., and McNeil, M. Listener reliability for a dichotic listening task. *Journal of the Acoustical Society of America*, 1974, *56*, 1922—1923.

Satz, P. Laterality effects in dichotic listening. *Nature*, 1968, *218*, 277—278.

Satz, P., Achenbach, K., and Fennel, E. Correlations between assessed manual laterality and predicted speech laterality in a normal population. *Neuropsychologia*, 1967, *5*, 295—310.

Satz, P., Achenbach, K., Pattishall, E., and Fennel, E. Order of report, ear asymmetry and handedness in dichotic listening. *Cortex*, 1965, *1*, 377—396.

Satz, P., Bakker, D. J., Goebel, R., and Van der Vlugt, H. Developmental parameters of the ear asymmetry: A multivariate approach. *Brain and Language*, 1975, *2*, 171—185.

Satz, P., Fennel, E., and Jones, M. B. Comments on: A model of the inheritance of handedness and cerebral dominance. *Neuropsychologia*, 1969, *7*, 101—103.

Satz, P., Levy, C. M., and Tyson, M. Effects of temporal delays on the ear asymmetry in dichotic listening. *Journal of Experimental Psychology*, 1970, *84*, 372—374.

Schulhoff, C., and Goodglass, H. Dichotic listening, side of brain injury and cerebral dominance. *Neuropsychologia*, 1969, *7*, 149—160.

Shanks, J. A comparison of aphasic and non-brain injured adults on a dichotic CV-syllable listening task. Unpublished Master's thesis, University of New Mexico, 1973.

Shankweiler, D. Effects of temporal lobe damage on perception of dichotically presented melodies. *Journal of Comparative Physiology and Psychology*, 1966, *62*, 115—119.

Shankweiler, D. An analysis of laterality effects in speech perception. In Horton, D. L., and Jenkins, J. J. (Eds.), *The perception of language*. Columbus, Ohio: Merrill, 1971. Pp. 185—200.

Shankweiler, D., and Studdert-Kennedy, M. Identification of consonants and vowels presented to left and right ears. *Quarterly Journal of Experimental Psychology*, 1967, *19*, 59—63.

Shanon, B. Lateralization effects in reaction time to simple sentences. *Cortex*, 1974, *10*, 360—365.

Simon, J. R. Ear preference in a simple reaction time task. *Journal of Experimental Psychology*, 1967, *75*, 49—55.

Sobotka, K. Neuropsychological and neurophysiological correlates of reading disability. Unpublished Master's thesis, Louisiana State University, New Orleans, 1973.

Sommers, R. K., Moore, W., Brady, W., and Jackson, P. Cerebral speech dominance, laterality and fine motor skills of articulatory defective children. Paper presented at the American Speech and Hearing Association Convention, November 18—21, 1972, San Francisco, California.

Sommers, R. K., and Taylor, M. L. Cerebral speech dominance in language-disordered and normal children. *Cortex*, 1972, *8*, 224—232.

Sparks, R., and Geschwind, N. Dichotic listening in man after section of neocortical commissures. *Cortex*, 1968, *4*, 3—16.

Sparks, R., Goodglass, H., and Nickel, B. Ipsilateral versus contralateral extinction in dichotic listening resulting from hemisphere lesions. *Cortex*, 1970, *6*, 249—260.

Speaks, C., Gray, T., Miller, J., and Rubens, A. B. Central auditory deficits and temporal-lobe lesions. *Journal of Speech and Hearing Disorders*, 1975, *40*, 192—205.

Spellacy, F. Lateral preferences in the identification of patterned stimuli. *Journal of the Acoustical Society of America*, 1970, *47*, 574—578.

Spellacy, F., and Blumstein, S. Ear preferences for language and non-language sounds: A unilateral brain function. *Journal of Auditory Research*, 1970, *10*, 349—355. (a)

Spellacy, F., and Blumstein, S. The influence of language set on ear preference in phoneme recognition. *Cortex*, 1970, *6*, 430—439. (b)

Spieth, W., Curtis, J. F., and Webster, J. C. Responding to one of two simultaneous messages. *Journal of the Acoustical Society of America*, 1954, *26*, 391—396.

Spieth, W., and Webster, J. C. Listening to differentially filtered competing voice messages. *Journal of the Acoustical Society of America*, 1955, *27*, 866—871.

Spreen, O., and Boucher, A. R. Effects of low pass filtering on ear asymmetry in dichotic listening and some uncontrolled error sources. *Journal of Auditory Research*, 1970, *10*, 45—51.

Spreen, O., Spellacy, F. J., and Reid, J. R. The effect of interstimulus interval and intensity on ear asymmetry for nonverbal stimuli in dichotic listening. *Neuropsychologia*, 1970, *8*, 245—250.

Springer, S. P. Ear asymmetry in a dichotic detection task. *Perception and Psychophysics*, 1971, *10*, 239—241.

Springer, S. A reaction time investigation into the nature and extent of hemispheric specialization for speech. Paper presented at the American Speech and Hearing Association Convention, November 18—21, 1972, San Francisco, California.

Springer, S. Hemispheric specialization for speech opposed by contralateral noise. *Perception and Psychophysics*, 1973, *13*, 391—393.

Springer, S. P., and Gazzaniga, M. S. Dichotic testing of partial and complete split brain subjects. *Neuropsychologia*, 1975, *13*, 341—346.

Stafford, M. R. Dichotic speech perception with interaural intensity differences. Unpublished Master's thesis, Tulane University, 1971.

Studdert-Kennedy, M., and Shankweiler, D. Hemispheric specialization for speech perception. *Journal of the Acoustical Society of America*, 1970, *48*, 579—594.

Studdert-Kennedy, M., Shankweiler, D., and Pisoni, D. Auditory and phonetic processing in speech perception: Evidence from a dichotic study. *Cognitive Psychology*, 1972, *3*, 455—466.

Studdert-Kennedy, M., Shankweiler, D., and Schulman, S. Opposed effects of a delayed channel on perception of dichotically and monotically presented CV syllables. *Journal of the Acoustical Society of America*, 1970, *48*, 599—602.

Sullivan, M. D. (Ed.) *Central auditory processing disorders.* Proceedings of a Conference held at the Universtiy of Nebraska Medical Center, 1975.

Sussman, H. M. The laterality effect in lingual—auditory tracking. *Journal of the Acoustical Society of America*, 1971, *49*, 1874—1880.

Sussman, H. M., and MacNeilage, P. F. Hemispheric specialization for speech production and perception in stutterers. *Neuropsychologia*, 1975, *13*, 19—26.

Sussman, H. M., MacNeilage, P. F., and Lumbley, J. Speech-related sensorimotor laterality in mandibular auditory tracking. Paper presented at the American Speech and Hearing Association Convention, October 12—15, 1973, Detroit, Michigan.

Sussman, H. M., MacNeilage, P. F., and Lumbley, J. Sensorimotor dominance and the right-ear advantage in mandibular-auditory tracking. *Journal of the Acoustical Society of America*, 1974, *56*, 214—216.

Sussman, H. M., MacNeilage, P. F., and Lumbley, J. L. Pursuit auditory tracking of dichotically presented tonal amplitudes. *Journal of Speech and Hearing Research*, 1975, *18*, 74—81.

Thies, T. L., and Thies, H. H. Responses to distorted speech and competing messages of children with severe language disorders. Paper presented at the American Speech and Hearing Association Convention, November 18—21, 1972, San Francisco, California.

Thompson, C. L., and Hughes, L. F. Effects of stimulus intensity in competing message tasks: I. Equal intensity dichotic stimuli. Paper presented at the American Speech and Hearing Association Convention, November 18—21, 1972, San Francisco, California.

Thompson, C. L., Samson, D. S. Cullen, J. K., Jr., and Hughes, L. F. The effect of varied bandwidth, signal-to-noise ratio, and intensity on the perception of consonant—vowels in a dichotic context: Additivity of central processing. Paper presented at the Eighty-Sixth Meeting of the Acoustical Society of America, October 29—November 2, 1973, Los Angeles, California.

Thompson, C. L., Stafford, M., Cullen, J. K., Jr., Hughes, L., Lowe-Bell, S. S., and Berlin, C. I. Interaural intensity differences in dichotic speech perception. Paper presented at the Eighty-Third Meeting of the Acoustical Society of America, April 18—21, 1972, Buffalo, New York.

Triesman, A. M. Contextual cues in selective listening. *Quarterly Journal of Experimental Psychology*, 1960, *12*, 242—248.

Triesman, A. M. Monitoring and storing of irrelevant messages in selective attention. *Journal of Verbal Learning and Verbal Behavior*, 1964, *3*, 449—459. (a)

Triesman, A. M. Selective attention in man. *British Medical Journal*, 1964, *20*, 12—16. (b)

Triesman, A. M. The effect of irrelevant material on the efficiency of selective listening. *American Journal of Psychology*, 1964, *77*, 533—546. (c)

Triesman, A. M. Verbal cues, language and meaning in selective attention. *American Journal of Psychology*, 1964, *77*, 206—219. (d)

Triesman, A. M. Strategies and models of selective attention. *Psychological Review*, 1969, *26*, 282—299.

Triesman, A. M. Shifting attention between the ears. *Quarterly Journal of Experimental Psychology*, 1971, *23*, 157—167.

Triesman, A. M., and Geffen. G. Selective attention and cerebral dominance in perceiving and responding to speech messages. *Quarterly Journal of Experimental Psychology*, 1968, *20*, 139—150.

Triesman, A. M., and Riley, J. G. A. Is selective attention selective perception or selective response? A further test. *Journal of Experimental Psychology*, 1969, *79*, 27—34.

Troendle, R., Porter, R. J., Jr., and Berlin, C. I. The effects of practice on the presentation of dichotically presented stop—consonant—vowel syllables. Paper presented at the Eighty-Sixth Meeting of the Acoustical Society of America, October 29—November 2, 1973, Los Angeles, California.

Tsunoda, T. Contralateral shift of cerebral dominance for nonverbal sounds during speech perception. *Journal of Auditory Research*, 1969, *9*, 221—229.

Tsunoda, T., and Oka, M. Cerebral hemisphere dominance test and localization of speech. *Journal of Auditory Research*, 1971, *11*, 177—189.

Van Duyne, H. J., and Scanlan, D. Left—right ear differences in auditory perception of verbal instruction for nonverbal behavior: A preliminary report. *Neuropsychologia*, 1974, *12*, 545—548.

Van Lancker, D. Language processing in the brain. Paper presented at the American Speech and Hearing Association Convention, November 18—21, 1972, San Francisco, California.

Van Lancker, D., and Fromkin, V. A. Hemispheric specialization for pitch and *tone*. Evidence from Thai. *Journal of Phonetics*, 1973, *1*, 101—109.

Wada, J., and Rasmussen, T. Intracarotid injection of sodium amytal for the lateralization of cerebral speech dominance, *Journal of Neurosurgery*, 1960, *17*, 266—282.

Webster, J. C., and Thompson, P. O. Responding to both of two overlapping messages. *Journal of the Acoustical Society of America*, 1954, *26*, 396—402.

Weiss, M. S., and House, A. S. Perception of dichotically presented vowels. *Journal of the Acoustical Society of America*, 1973, *53*, 51—58.

Whitmore, M. G. Stimulus meaning as a variable in dichotic listening. *Psychonomic Science*, 1972, *26*, 207—209.

Wilson, R. H., Dirks, D. D., and Carterette, E. C. Effects of ear preference and order bias on the perception of verbal materials. *Journal of Speech and Hearing Research*, 1968, *11*, 509—522.

Witelson, S. F., and Pallie, W. Left hemisphere specialization for language in the newborn: Neuroanatomical evidence of asymmetry. *Brain*, 1973, *96*, 641—646.

Witelson, S. F., and Rabinovitch, M. S. Children's recall of strategies in dichotic listening. *Journal of Experimental Child Psychology*, 1971, *12*, 106—113.

Witelson, S. F., and Rabinovitch, M. S. Hemispheric speech lateralization in children with auditory—linguistic deficits. *Cortex*, 1972, *8*, 412—426.

Yates, A. J., Martin, M., and DiLollo, V. Retrieval strategy in dichotic listening as a function of presentation rate and structure of material. *Journal of Experimental Psychology*, 1970, *86*, 26—31.

Yates, A. J., Smith, P. J., Burke, B. D., and Keane, M. A. A technique for the construction of discrete dichotic stimulation material. *Behavior Research Methods and Instrumentation*, 1968—1969, *1*, 257—258.

Yeni-Komshian, G. H., and Gordon, J. F. The effect of memory load on the right ear advantage in dichotic listening. *Brain and Language*, 1974, *1*, 375—382.

Yeni-Komshian, G., Gordon, J., and Sherman, P. The effect of memory load on the right ear advantage in dichotic listening. Paper presented at the Eighty-Fourth Meeting of the Acoustical Society of America, November 28—December 1, 1972, Miami, Florida.

Yntema, D. B., and Trask, F. P. Recall as a search process. *Journal of Verbal Learning and Verbal Behavior*, 1963, *2*, 65—74.

Yund, E. W., and Efron, R. Dichotic competition of simultaneous tone bursts of different frequency. II. Suppression and ear dominance functions. *Neuropsychologia*, 1975, *13*, 137—150.

Zurif, E. B. Auditory lateralization: Prosodic and syntactic factors. *Brain and Language*, 1974, *1*, 391—404.

Zurif, E. B., and Bryden, M. P. Familial handedness and left—right differences in auditory and visual perception. *Neuropsychologia*, 1969, *7*, 179—187.

Zurif, E. B., and Carson, G. Dyslexia in relation to cerebral dominance and temporal analysis. *Neuropsychologia*, 1970, *8*, 351—361.

Zurif, E. B., and Mendelson, M. Hemispheric specialization for the perception of speech sounds: The influence of intonation and structure. *Perception and Psychophysics*, 1972, *11*, 329—332.

Zurif, E. B., and Ramier, A. M. Some effects of unilateral brain damage on the perception of dichotically presented phoneme sequences and digits. *Neuropsychologia*, 1972, *10*, 103—110.

Zurif, E. B., and Sait, P. E. The role of syntax in dichotic listening. *Neuropsychologia*, 1970, *8*, 239—244.

chapter 11

Auditory Illusions and Perceptual Processes

Richard M. Warren

University of Wisconsin — Milwaukee

Perceptual processes usually remain hidden and inaccessible in normal, veridical functioning. Illusions represent a breakdown in veridical perception. As in an old medical maxim, disorders can present normal functions laid bare. This paper uses errors in auditory perception in an attempt to uncover and study normal perceptual mechanisms, with special emphasis given to the relation of verbal and nonverbal processes. Three interconnected topics will be explored: (*1*) illusory changes in repeated auditory patterns; (*2*) perceptual cancellation of masking, with illusory presence of obliterated sounds; and (*3*) perception and confusions of temporal orders within sequences of sounds. In addition, there will be some brief excursions into related areas.

Illusory Changes in Repeated Auditory Patterns

In the seventeenth century, John Locke noted that *"the mind cannot fix long on one invariable idea"* (Locke, 1894, p. 244). He concluded that any attempt by an individual to restrict his thoughts to any one concept would fail, and new concepts or modifications of the old "will constantly succeed one another in his thoughts, let him be as wary as he can" (p. 245). Locke's principle has been well verified for perception: It seems that continued stimulation with an unchanging pattern can lead to illusory changes or, under some conditions, to perceptual fading and disappearance.

Perceptually unstable figures have had a long history as designs. A mosaic floor depicting stacked cubes which reverse in apparent perspective has been uncovered at the Temple of Apollo at Pompeii. This design, as well as more intricate and ingenious reversible figures, can be seen in medieval and renaissance Italian churches.

Perhaps the richest collection is on the floor of Saint Mark's in Venice, providing a dynamic counterpoint for the nonreversible devotional figures found in the ceiling mosaics. The illusory changes seen in these churches, unlike the swinging chandelier in Pisa, do not seem to have invoked any scientific interest. But, in the early nineteenth century, Necker (1832) observed the illusory changes in apparent perspective of an outline drawing of a rhomboid, and tried to explain the inversions in terms of perceptual processes. Many reversible figures have been constructed and studied since.

All of the visual reversible figures are actually ambiguous; that is, they have plausible alternative interpretations. These interpretations employ the same contours as part of separate perceptual organizations, so that at any given time, one interpretation precludes the other. While three or more interpretations may be possible (especially with the classical mosaics), most figures have only two. A consideration of these facts led me to look for an auditory analogue of the visual reversible figures.

If a person repeats a word over and over, he generally will experience a lapse of meaning called *semantic* or *verbal satiation* (see Titchener, 1915; Amster, 1964). It seemed that it should be possible to create an ambiguous verbal stimulus by repeating aloud a word such as *ace* over and over without pauses—the stimulus should be acoustically equivalent to *say* repeated. Would perceptual alternation occur between these two plausible interpretations of the stimulus, and so prevent lapse of meaning? When I tried this for myself (as you can for yourself), such alternations seemed to occur. This observation suggested the desirability of further work. In a preliminary study, Richard Gregory and I prepared short, endless loops of recorded tapes. When we played these tapes to ourselves and others in the laboratory, we found that changes of the sort anticipated seemed to occur. But surprisingly, compelling illusory changes in phonetic structure were observed as well, even though the words were played clearly and listeners knew each iteration was identical. Our bias was such that the note describing our observations was entitled "An auditory analogue of the visual reversible figure" (Warren and Gregory, 1958). However, after subsequent work, I concluded that passive listening to repeated words produces both phonetic and semantic lability (repeating words to one's self produces only semantic effects without illusory change to other phonemes). I came to believe that the auditory illusion based on listening to recorded repetitions, which I named the *verbal transformation* (*VT*) effect, was not closely analogous to visual reversals (Warren, 1961a).

To illustrate the sorts of changes observed for VTs in this first detailed study, let me give a few examples obtained from subjects listening to a loop of tape containing a clear statement of a single word or phrase repeated over and over, without pauses between repetitions, for three minutes. Subjects were instructed to call out what they heard initially and then to call out each change as it occurred, whether the change was to something new or to a form reported previously. The changes generally seemed quite real, and listeners believed that they were simply reporting what the voice was saying. The first example of illusory changes given below is based upon the stimulus *seashore* (since British naval ratings were used as subjects, a voice with standard English pronunciation was employed, and the terminal /r/ was not pronounced). The intial perceptual organization and all of the illusory changes reported by one subject during three minutes are listed in order of occurrence: seashore, sea-shove, seashore, she-saw, seesaw, sea-shove, seashore, she-saw-seesaw, seashore, she-saw-seesaw, seashore, she-sawve, seashore-seesaw, she-saw, seashore, seesaw-saw, seashell. Another subject listening to *ripe* reported: ripe, right, white, white-light, right, right-light, ripe, right, ripe, bright-light, right, ripe, bright-light, right, bright-light. As a final example, a third subject listening to *fill-up* experienced somewhat fewer changes and greater phonetic distortion than most: fill-up, clock, fill-up, build-up, true love, build, broad, lunch, fill-up. It should be noted that changes which occur in going from one perceptual form to the next are frequently quite complex phonetically and sometimes suggest semantic linkages.

The main distinctions between VTs and visual reversible figures revealed by this study seem to be: *(1)* visual reversible figures correspond to relatively few special configurations—VTs occur with all syllables, words, and phrases; *(2)* reversible figures generally involve reinterpretation without appreciable distortion of the stimulus configuration—VTs usually involve considerable distortion of clear auditory stimuli; *(3)* each of the reversible figures generally involves the same perceptual forms for different people—VTs vary greatly with individuals; *(4)* reversible figures generally invoke changes between two (occasionally three or four) forms—VTs usually involve more than four (sometimes more than a dozen) different forms during a period of two or three minutes. Yet, there is some relation between these two types of illusions. In broad terms, both seem to reflect Locke's principle that any particular "thought" or perceptual organization cannot be maintained without change for any length of time. A visual effect seeming to resemble verbal transformations more closely than reversible figures is observed when the effects of normally continuous small eye movements are cancelled to produce a fixed retinal image. As Wheatstone (1835) concluded (after considering the rapid fading of images when shadows of retinal blood vessels became stationary), such an unchanging pattern of retinal stimulation leads to perceptual disappearance; but, in addition, more recent studies have shown that the perceptual images, especially regular or meaningful ones, also fragment and reappear in parts (Riggs *et al.*, 1953; Pritchard, Heron, and Hebb, 1960) in a dynamic display of illusory changes. While the selective suppression of portions of a pattern is found for verbal transformations as well, the auditory illusion produces a greater distortion and synthesis of physically absent elements than do fixed retinal images.

Subsequent studies in our laboratory have indicated that this illusion may be of value as a tool for studying speech perception (Warren, 1961b, 1962, 1968a, 1968b; Warren and Warren, 1966, 1970, 1971; Obusek, 1971; Obusek and Warren, 1973a, 1973b; Warren and Ackroff, 1974).

A number of investigators in other laboratories have taken up work in verbal transformations and have studied aspects related to the phonetics, cognitive factors, and neurophysiology of this illusion (Axelrod and Thompson, 1962; Taylor and Henning, 1963; Barnett, 1964; Paul, 1964; Natsoulas, 1965; Jain, 1967; Evans *et al.*, 1967; Evans and Kitson, 1967; Evans and Wilson, 1968; Fenelon and Blayden, 1968; Kish and Ball, 1969; Naeser and Lilly, 1970; Perl, 1970; Lass and Golden, 1971, Clegg, 1971; Scott and Cole, 1972; Harper, 1972; Tekieli and Lass, 1972; Ben-Zeev,

1972; Naeser, 1972; Lass, West, and Taft, 1973; Wolin and Mello, 1973; Lass and Gasperini, 1973; Goldstein and Lackner, 1974; Lass, Silvis, and Settle, 1974; Lackner, 1974; Lackner and Goldstein, 1975).

No attempt will be made to cover all aspects of VTs which have been reported. The discussion below will deal briefly with acoustic and phonetic factors involved in VTs, and (in somewhat more detail) implications concerning the mechanisms employed normally for perceptual processing of speech sounds. In addition, the connection of VTs with other research on speech perception will be described.

The first detailed phonetic analysis of the verbal transformation effect was that of Barnett (1964). After using a variety of words as stimuli, she concluded that the articulatory positions of both vowels and consonants were relatively labile and subject to frequent illusory changes. Stability was noted for the voiced—voiceless property of consonants and for the type of movement characteristic of individual consonants and vowels. Intervowel glides were, in general, stable both in position and type of movement.

A detailed study of the nature of phone-type substitutions by linguists and non-linguists (each group consisting of native and nonnative speakers of English) listening to the repeated word *cogitate* was reported at a meeting of the Acoustical Society of America (Naeser and Lilly, 1970). In an unpublished manuscript based upon this paper, they reported that the linguists and nonlinguists gave similar reponses. It was stated that consonants generally were substituted by the manner of articulation (not place) so that, for example, stops most often were substituted by other stops. On the other hand, vowels most often were substituted on the basis of similarity of place of articulation. A resemblance was noted to the articulatory feature-type substitution described by Wickelgren (1965, 1966) in his work involving errors in short-term memory. More recently, Lass and Gasperini (1973) reported a study comparing verbal transformations for a number of stimulus words presented to phonetically trained and phonetically untrained subjects. They noted some quantitative differences between the two groups, but emphasized that responses were qualitatively similar. The phonetically trained group reported more forms and transitions, and required fewer repetitions of the stimuli to induce the first illusory change.

Clegg (1971) used 18 separate repeating syllables, each consisting of a different consonant followed by the vowel /i/. He ignored the illusory changes of the vowel, which he stated were minimal, and analyzed the transformations of the consonants. His analysis was in rough agreement with Naeser and Lilly's (1970) but considerably more detailed. He concluded that a consonant and its transform tended to share the features of voicing, nasality, and affrication, but not of duration and place of articulation.

Evans and Wilson (1968) used a variety of consonants followed by the same vowel as stimuli for VTs. They analyzed responses only for changes in the initial consonant and reported a surprisingly high frequency of responses involving the aspirated phoneme /h/. Goldstein and Lackner (1974), in a more comprehensive phonetic study, used a variety of nonsense syllables as stimuli and also found a large number of responses involving illusory /h/ as well as /j/ in both the initial and final positions of the syllables reported. However, they were not interested in these intrusions and constructed matrices for illusory transformation of consonants and vowel for which /h/ and /j/ were excluded. Analyses of these matrices in terms of distinctive features revealed a number of "very systematic" types of changes governing vowels and consonants which were summarized by Goldstein and Lackner.

Lass and Golden (1971) employed repeating stimuli consisting of short segments of tape excised from recordings of steady-state vowels. Onset and decay characteristics of single utterances of the vowels were lacking so that the stimuli differed from normal speech productions. A high proportion of nonphonetic alternatives were reported (such as a telephone busy signal), perhaps reflecting the difference of the stimulus from normal speech productions. Changes usually involved illusory consonants, generally plosives, possibly due to the rapid onset and termination of the vowels. No analysis in terms of distinctive features was offered.

In a published abstract of a paper delivered at a meeting, Scott and Cole (1972) reported that VTs with consonant—vowel syllables involve "embedded" sounds which are masked by other sounds. Thus, they claimed that *dah* is embedded in *sah*, and verbal transformations permit the perceptual peeling away of a portion of one sound to reveal another (most of the /s/, in this case, leading to perception of the plosive). Not enough details of their experimental work are available at this time for proper evaluation of their findings. But superficially, the verbal transformations they report seem more restricted than those obtained with similar stimuli in other laboratories.

The effect of noise upon VTs is curious. The rate of VTs does not depend upon the signal-to-noise ratio, for decreasing the intensity of the voice does not change the rate of illusory changes until the voice starts to become unintelligible (Warren, 1961a; verified in unpublished study by Warren and Ackroff, 1974). The first observations on the effect of repetition upon unintelligible verbal stimuli were reported by B. F. Skinner (1936). In the days before he became a *Skinnerian*, he was interested in developing a projective test—as he put it, "a sort of verbal ink-blot" (p. 71). He used a phonograph recording of a series of indistinct vowels without consonants played over and over. After several repetitions, the listener perceived illusory words and phrases. Since Skinner considered that repetition caused meaning to summate, he called the device *the verbal summator*. He turned the device off after the first response (as did later investigators using this technique). Had the stimulus been left on by Skinner, VTs would have been discovered some 20 years earlier. When we allowed the repeated indistinct speech to remain on, it was observed that the initial perceptual organization was unstable and VTs took place (Warren, 1961a). Common sense indicates that a word which is heard less clearly should change more readily, but such was not the case. Masked speech had a considerably lower rate of VTs than clear speech. Some theoretical implications of the effect of noise on VTs have been described elsewhere (Warren, 1968a) and will not be repeated here, except for their relevance to age differences to be discussed below.

Is it possible to observe any illusory changes while listening to repeated nonverbal stimuli? A number of experimenters have reported such illusory changes, but they seem rather different in important respects from VTs. Repetitions of white noise bursts were used by Lass, West, and Taft (1973); tone bursts by Fenelon and Blayden (1968), Perl (1970), and Lass, West, and Taft (1973); and melodic phrases by Guilford and Nelson (1936), Obusek (1971), and Lass, West, and Taft (1973). The changes reported in these studies generally were slight alterations in loudness, pitch, and tempo, with the rate of such changes sometimes similar to and sometimes slower than the rates corresponding to VTs. However, experimenters generally have ignored the fact that tape recorders do produce variations in intensity (loudness) and speed (pitch and tempo). Even high quality professional recorders can have a moment-to-moment variability of about 1 dB in intensity and .3% in speed, which correspond to changes at or above the just-noticeable differences for "unchanging" stimuli. Anyone who has tried using a tape recording of an extended tone (e.g., 1000 Hz) rather than on-line output from an oscillator probably has encountered this stimulus instability. This real change should be kept in mind when evaluating the fact that reported changes with nonverbal stimuli all seem to involve relatively subtle changes along the perceptual continua of loudness, pitch, and tempo, rather than the characteristically gross and categorical suppression, synthesis, and transformation of individual sounds observed with VTs.

Of course, it may be that illusory variations are introduced with repetition of nonverbal stimuli which go beyond those corresponding to recorded stimulus instability, and that a general lability of unchanging patterns has been specially modified for speech. The verbal lability seems related to processes normally leading to an improved intelligibility. Studies of age differences in VTs have suggested that this illusion is based upon mechanisms employed for comprehension of speech which change systematically from childhood through old age.

The same set of stimulus tapes was used throughout cross-sectional age studies of VTs in our laboratory. Experiments with children (Warren and Warren, 1966) showed that virtually no illusory changes were experienced at 5 years of age. At 6 years, almost half the subjects tested heard illusory changes, and those who did, experienced them at the high rate found for older children. At age 8, all subjects heard illusory changes (average rate for all subjects with all words was 34 changes for 3 minutes). This rate remained about the same (32 in 3 minutes) at 10 years. In an earlier study (Warren, 1961b), it was found that the average rate of changes for young adults (18–25 years) was equivalent to that of older children (31 in 3 minutes). However, this study also revealed that the rate for aged adults (62–86 years) was very much lower (5.6 in 3 minutes). Using subjects with a median age of 35 years and different stimulus words, Taylor and Henning (1963) reported a rate of illusory changes intermediate between that for young and aged adults reported earlier. This suggested that the decrease in susceptibility during adulthood occurs gradually. The decrease in VTs with older adults does not seem to reflect a decrease in auditory acuity with age, since the aged are not only stable but they are accurate, generally reporting the correct word and staying with it. Continuing to look for an explanation for the reduced rate of VTs, one might think that an increase in so-called "neural noise" associated with aging would reduce the effective signal-to-noise ratio for a given sound pressure level, and that this reduced ratio is responsible for the difference between young and old adults listening to a stimulus delivered at the same intensity. However, as noted earlier, the same VT rate has been observed for different signal-to-noise ratios as long as the signal remains intelligible for young adults. A suggestion concerning the basis for the decrease with aging will be offered after we have considered some additional factors.

In addition to counting the numbers of illusory changes, the groupings of speech sounds were examined to determine the functional groupings for reorganization at different ages. Children respond in terms of the sounds of English but may group these sounds in ways not permitted in the language. For example, with the repeated word *tress*, a child might report *sreb*, although the initial /sr/ sequence is not found in English words. Young adults seem to group speech sounds only in clusters permitted in English, but they do report nonsense syllables: Given the stimulus *tress*, they might report *tresh* as one of the forms they hear. However, older people tend to report only meaningful words. Presented with *tress*, they will typically hear *tress* continuously, and when infrequent changes do occur, they usually are to such closely related forms as *dress*. Even when presented with a nonsense syllable such as *flime*, the aged usually did not report this stimulus but distorted it into a meaningful word such as *flying*, frequently hearing the distorted word throughout the 3 minute test. An interesting exception is the incorrect past participle *flyed*, reported more frequently than the actual stimulus by the aged.

When the extent of phonemic differences between successive forms reported by individual subjects was analyzed, a regular change with age was found. For the five age groups (subjects ranging from 6 through 86 years of age), the number of phonemic changes decreased with increasing age. Thus, perceptual reorganization involved finer and finer distinctions with advancing age. Such changes seem to be associated with normal, healthy aging; the extent of phonemic changes observed for a senile group of subjects approximated that of 10-year-old children (Obusek and Warren, 1973a).

These observations on the effect of aging upon VTs, together with other considerations to be dealt with shortly, suggest that: *(1)* this illusion reflects reorganizational processes normally leading to the correction of errors in speech perception; and *(2)* the age differences observed for VTs mirror changes in processing strategies over our life span in keeping with changes in functional capacity. Since performance as measured by comprehension may be similar at different ages, it is all too easy to assume that the same perceptual processes are used. However, it may well be that it is necessary to change processing to maintain performance over one's life span. In other words, adaptive changes in perceptual processing may be requisite for healthy maturing and aging.

Before dealing further with age differences in processing mechanisms, let us first consider the evidence that reorganizational processes are necessary to correct errors made while listening to speech. Bryan and Harter (1897, 1899) claimed that for skilled telegraphers a telegraphic language existed similar to other languages. Mastery required several years of continual application, perhaps 10 years for the speed and accuracy required for a press dispatcher. When this peak was attained, the receiver could work effortlessly and automatically, often transcribing complex messages while thinking about something quite different. The expert usually delayed 6 to 12 words before transcribing the ongoing text in normal messages. If redundancy and linkages between elements were reduced by transmitting in cipher, or by sending stock quotations, the task became much harder for experts. Sending was slowed down, and the number of words held in storage was reduced by decreasing the delay between receiving and transcribing. It seems as if long storage was used only when context permitted useful interactions between information received at different times, allowing the correction of errors and the resolution of ambiguities. Skilled storage similar to that observed for telegraphy has been observed for typewriting (Book, 1925), for reading aloud (Huey, 1968), and for tactile reading by the blind (Moore and Bliss, 1975). It seems probable that storage with continuing processing and revision is important for a listener's comprehension of speech as well, and the need for such mechanisms has been noted in the past (although the literature has been rather silent on how to study these covert processes). Brain (1962, p. 209) has pointed out that "the meaning of a word which appears earlier in a sentence may depend upon the words which follow it. In such a case, the meaning of the earlier word is held in suspense, as it were, until the later words have made their appearance." Lashley (1951, p. 120) has given a classic example of this process. He spoke of *rapid writing* to an audience, and after creating a set for the word *writing*, several sentences later stated: "Rapid righting with his uninjured hand saved from loss the contents of the capsized canoe." He pointed out that the context required for the proper attribution of meaning to the sounds corresponding to *righting* were not activated for 3 to 5 seconds after hearing the word.

It is not only meaning that can depend upon future context. Chistovich (1962) has noted that subjects, who repeated speech heard through headphones as quickly as possible, made many phonemic errors. She suggested that these mistakes reflect the temporal course of speech identification, with an appreciable delay necessary for the correction of such errors. Miller (1962) and Lieberman (1963) have emphasized that skilled speech perception cannot be a simple Markovian process, with perception occurring first on phonemic and then on higher levels. Such a process does not take advantage of the redundancy of the message and does not allow for the correction of mistakes. Without such correction, an error would continue to provide incorrect context, producing other errors until perception became disrupted.

Returning to VTs, I am suggesting that these illusory changes reflect reorganizations which occur normally when part of a continued message is not confirmed by context. With repeated words there can be no stabilizing grammatical and semantic environment provided by surrounding words. Hence, the repeated word is subject to successive reorganizations, none of which can receive contextual confirmation. It is important to note that the processes involved are quite automatic and under little cognitive control. They are not accessible through introspective search but only through their perceptual effects.

The age differences observed for VTs are consistent with the explanation just offered. If VTs reflect skilled reorganizational processes, they could not appear until language skills had attained a certain level in children. The requisite level seems to be reached normally by the age of 6 or 7. Certainly, the healthy aged (over 60 years of age) have mastery of language, so why then do they exhibit a reduced susceptibility to VTs? The answer may be that they lack the requisite capacity for short-term storage of verbal information. It is well established that special difficulty is encountered by the aged for complex storage tasks involving intervening activity (Welford, 1958). Concurrent processes of coding, storing, comparing, and reorganizing may not be possible, so the optimal strategy for the aged is to employ only the past context of the message as an aid to the organization of the current input, and to abandon reorganization contingent upon subsequent context. The fact that more meaningful words are reported by the aged (Warren, 1961b) is consistent with the fact that they could not afford to be perceptually locked to a meaningless word. VTs, when they do occur with the healthy aged, usually involve changes of a single phoneme to form another meaningful word. Such a change applied to discourse would involve less complex processing than the typical changes of the young. The extensive phonetic changes observed for senile aged in their (infrequent) VTs do not represent a strategy capable of optimizing their capabilities; and while it might lead to meaningful organization when applied to discourse, the meaning might not be the speaker's (Obusek and Warren, 1973a).

Recent work on VTs in my laboratory has indicated that illusory changes can be heard independently in the two ears. If one repeated syllable (such as *flime*) is delivered to one ear, and another repeated syllable (such as *tress*) is delivered to the other, changes in each ear can be monitored readily. The two stimuli seem to change independently, with no intrusions of forms heard in one ear upon the other. This observation suggested a more interesting condition. What if the dichotic stimulus consisted of the same word delivered to each ear? By delaying the input to one ear by a digital delay line for exactly half the duration of the word, fusion into a single auditory image can be prevented, and a temporally dichotic, but otherwise identical, stimulus would be heard in each ear. Neither ear would lead and acoustic symmetry of the simultaneous contralateral input would be present. Would independent VTs occur for each side? The answer, whether "yes" or "no," would have some theoretical interest. If changes occurred synchronously in each ear, it would indicate that a single set of analyzers is employed for dichotic input, either through successive processing or through some type of time sharing. But if it is found that VTs occur independently for each ear, it can be concluded that two sets of functionally separate speech analyzers are used for processing dichotic stimuli.

We found that with temporally dichotic presentation of a single repeated stimulus (*tress*), VTs occurred independently on each side (Warren and Ackroff, 1976). Each of our 20 subjects heard different words in different ears at the same time so that the input on the one side might be identified as *tress*, while the illusory word *transit* might be heard clearly on the other side. These results indicate the use of separate analyzers for identical stimuli.

There was no significant difference between scores for numbers of changes heard on the two sides when listeners reported all changes and identified them as occurring on the left or right. But an interesting difference was found when the complexity of changes going from one perceptual form to the next was measured for individuals. Changes involving only one phoneme (such as *tress* to *dress*) were scored as simple, and changes involving two or more phonemes as complex. The proportion of complex changes was significantly greater for the right than for the left side, as if the analyzers used for right side input were more "adventurous."

Further work has demonstrated that independent changes are not limited to two competing versions of the same word. In an unpublished study with James Bashford, headphones were used to deliver three asynchronous versions of the same repeated word; two were monaural with one on the right and one on the left, and one was diotic with localization in the medial plane. Each version was separated from the other two by exactly one-third the duration of the word. We found that all of our five listeners heard the three versions change independently, and hence were using three sets of verbal analyzers.

These observations indicate that there may be a degree of equipotentiality within cortical areas employed for speech analysis. If one set of analyzers is occupied with a particular task, others can be assembled for related analyses, at least for processing up to the level of words. It is suggested that the *right ear advantage* reported frequently in the literature for competing dichotic speech might reflect functional differences in sets of analyzers rather than, as sometimes hypothesized, superiority of contralateral over ipsilateral pathways to a common set of speech analyzers in the left hemisphere (for discussion, see Studdert-Kennedy and Shankweiler, 1970; Berlin *et al.*, 1973); Berlin and McNeil, this volume).

Illusory Continuity of Interrupted Auditory Patterns: Phonemic Restorations and Auditory Induction

With verbal transformation, the stimulus is clear, but context is absent. Another illusion, *phonemic restoration*, is found if the context is clear, but a portion of the verbal stimulus is absent.

While experiments on speech in the laboratory usually isolate subjects from intrusive intermittent noises, we frequently encounter such interfering sounds when listening to speech in everyday life. I thought it might be of interest to look for perceptual mechanisms for restoration of masked portions of speech. Such mechanisms should minimize errors in perceptual organization and reduce the need for the reorganizational correction of errors discussed earlier in the section on verbal transformations.

In the first experiments with phonemic restorations (Warren, 1970; Warren and Obusek, 1971), college students heard the sentence, *The state governors met with their respective legislatures convening in the capital city*, in which the /s/ in *legislatures* was deleted and replaced with a variety of sounds (cough, tones, buzzes). In order to minimize transitional cues to the identity of the missing sound, portions of the preceding and following phonemes were also deleted. Removal of this much of the sentence would not be expected to influence intelligibility since the identity of the /s/ is completely determined by context prior to the deletion, and also confirmed by the subsequent context. Yet, it seems reasonable to expect that listeners, if they tried, could tell readily which of the speech sounds was missing. However, it was not possible to identify the absent sound even when told that a speech sound was missing: The /s/ was "heard" as clearly as the phonemes physically present, and was perceptually indistinguishable from them. Attempts to identify the missing sound through localization of the extraneous sound were unsuccessful since this sound (whether a cough, tone, or buzz) was mislocalized; it seemed to coexist with other phonemes without interfering with their intelligibility. The position of the intrusive sound seemed indefinite to listeners: they were uncertain as to its location and made errors when required to identify where it occurred in the sentence.

The mislocalization of extraneous sounds in sentences had been reported by Ladefoged (1959) and later described in more detail by Ladefoged and Broadbent (1960). They had employed brief sounds (clicks and short hisses) and took care not to obliterate any phoneme, and hence phonemic restorations could not arise. A number of investigators have used this mislocalization phenomenon as an indirect way of measuring verbal organizational processes, and several studies have reported that systematic errors in locating the clicks are caused by various deep and surface features of sentence structure (see, for example, Garrett, 1965; Garrett, Bever, and Fodor, 1966; Fodor and Bever, 1965; Reber, 1973). Warren and Obusek (1971) compared mislocalization of a short click within a phoneme with mislocalization of noises completely replacing the same phoneme in a rerecording of the same sentence. We found that the direction of localization errors was rather different: The longer sounds associated with phonemic restorations were judged to be earlier in the sentence than the click. It appears that the delay in perceptual organization accompanying phonemic restoration causes an earlier portion of the sentence to appear as simultaneous with the marker furnished by the extraneous sound. This delay in processing associated with phonemic restoration should be reduced by familiarity; and, as would be anticipated, it was found that replaying the stimulus to the listener resulted in a pronounced shift toward later localization of the long extraneous sound, and judgments of location more nearly symmetrically distributed about the true position. Phonemic restoration itself was not reduced by replaying, and the listener's certainty that all speech sounds were present was unchanged after four successive presentations.

If the extraneous sounds replacing the missing phoneme are eliminated, and a silent gap is used in place of the phoneme, phonemic restorations are inhibited, and the listeners can localize the gap and recognize which speech sound is missing. A recent experiment has shown that the context identifying the phoneme replaced by an extraneous sound need not precede the missing speech sound (Warren and Sherman, 1974). This study employed a variety of sentences all having some of the information required for identification of the deleted segments following their occurrence. Also, in order to eliminate the possibility that cues to the missing sounds were furnished by articulatory characteristics of the neighboring phonemes, the deleted phonemes were deliberately mispronounced in each of the seven stimulus sentences are recorded initially prior to deletion. Care was taken that the mispronounced deleted phonemes matched the durations of the contextually correct items. Under these conditions, the contextually appropriate phoneme was restored according to the rules and restrictions of English.

Phonemic restorations under noisy conditions encountered outside the laboratory may be aided by several types of cues to the identification of the masked sound: not only context and temporal matching, but transitional probabilities, coarticulation with neighboring phonemes, and possibly even visual observation of the articulatory positions of the speaker's lips and jaw. Also, rather than restriction to a single extraneous sound in an otherwise clear sentence, phonemic restorations probably occur in nature along with multiple interruptions. It is pertinent that when Miller and Licklider (1950) interrupted the reading of *PB* (phonetically balanced) word lists 10 to 15 times per second with a louder noise, they found that "the listener feels that the speech is certainly more natural and probably more intelligible" (p. 173) than when the interruptions were left silent. However, they found that no actual improvement in intelligibility occurred. Now, if the intermittent noise tended to invoke phonemic restorations, the lack of supplementary cues to the identities of the missing phonemes would halt the process with the PB lists short of perceptual synthesis. But, if similar interruptions by noise occurred with normal discourse, then contextual cues should permit phonemic restorations and result in a higher intelligibility than if the interruptions consisted of silent gaps. There have been experiments reported which indicate that such multiple phonemic restorations do occur. Cherry and Wiley (1967) and Holloway (1970) described experiments in which the strongly voiced components in discourse were removed and either filled with noise or left as silent gaps separating the other components in the sentences. Intelligibility was found to be considerably greater when the noise was present. In an interesting unpublished study, Wiley (1968) reported an experiment resembling that of Miller and Licklider with regularly interrupted PB word lists, except that Wiley used regularly interrupted discourse. Wiley found that addition of noise to the periodic gaps improved intelligibility, indicating that the effect of noise described by Cherry and Wiley and by Holloway was not restricted to replacement of the strongly voiced components of speech. Powers (1973) has also reported that addition of noise to silent gaps in regularly interrupted speech increases intelligibility. This curious effect of increasing the clarity of speech by the addition of noise indicates that silence functions as a masking agent for the comprehension of interrupted speech and that, somewhat paradoxically, noise furnishes a release from this masking of intelligibility by silence.

It seems likely that the processes underlying verbal transformations and phonemic restorations are related and supplementary. Phonemic restorations correspond to a highly skilled mechanism permitting perceptually restored segments of masked speech to be incorporated within verbal organizations. Verbal transformations seem to represent a mechanism employed normally for correcting errors in initial perceptual organization (and also for resolving ambiguities). The two illusions may be combined by presenting a repeating word which has a portion deleted and replaced by a noise. It would be anticipated that the perceptually restored speech sound would be the weakest link in the phonemic chain and that changes would be focused upon the perceptually synthesized phoneme. Obusek and Warren (1973b) used the repeated word *magistrate* in an experiment testing this hypothesis. The /s/ was removed and replaced by a louder noise. It was found that 42% of the illusory changes involved the position corresponding to the deleted /s/, compared to 5% when a different group of subjects heard the intact word as the repeated stimulus. When the /s/ was deleted and replaced by silence rather than noise (so that phonemic restorations were inhibited), the lability of phonemes heard in this position was more than with the intact word but considerably less than that associated with the noise-filled gap: Only 18% of the changes involved this position. When the noise was present, it was not possible for the listener to detect which phoneme corresponded to the noise bursts any more than with phonemic restorations involving nonrecycled sentences. Yet, at some level of processing, the distinction between phoneme-based and noise-based organization was maintained, leading to the predicted increase in lability of the restored phoneme.

Illusory perception of obliterated sounds is found not only for speech, but for non-verbal stimuli as well. The generic term *auditory induction* has been suggested for processes common to phonemic restoration and nonverbal perceptual synthesis (Warren, Obusek, and Ackroff, 1972). There seem to be two classes of auditory induction, *homophonic* and *heterophonic*. Homophonic induction (sounds having identical spectral characteristics and differing only in intensity) was encountered by chance when I was preparing a stimulus for an experiment in perception of temporal order. A 2000 Hz octave band of noise was presented through headphones at three successive intensity levels (60, 70, and 80 dB SPL); each level lasted for 300 msec, and the sequence recycled without pause. Subjects could not tell the order in which the intensity levels were presented for an unexpected reason. The faintest sound seemed to be on all the time, coexisting at a fixed level with each of the two louder noise bursts. Of course, if the faintest sound were on constantly, it would fuse acoustically with the louder sounds of the same spectral characteristics and could not even produce a noticeable change in the intensity of the loudest sound. Nevertheless, it seemed quite clear to the listeners, whether psychoacoustically sophisticated or naive, that the softest sound continued along with the louder ones. However, silent gaps of 50 msec separating each sound destroyed auditory induction, and three sounds were heard as separate bursts.

Homophonic auditory induction did not require that the repeated sequence consist of three intensities; alternating 300 msec noise bursts at 70 and 80 dB SPL produced apparent continuity of the fainter. The durations, absolute intensity levels, and extent of discriminable differences between louder and softer sounds were not critical variables. Any band of noise or any tone alternating between two intensity levels seemed to produce homophonic auditory induction. These observations suggested that it would be interesting to determine how apparent continuity was influenced by the extent of spectral difference between a pair of sounds, such as tones of two frequencies or a tone and a noise band. Such a heterophonic auditory induction (sounds differing in both spectrum and intensity) has been reported independently by several investigators for nonverbal sounds.

Miller and Licklider (1950) seemed to be the first to report this type of illusory continuity. They found that if tone and noise bursts each lasting 50 msec were alternated, the tone appeared to be on all the time. They called this *the picket fence effect*. Vicario (1960) described what he called *acoustic tunneling* of a fainter sound through a louder one. Others (see Thurlow, 1957; Elfner, 1971), working with sounds lasting 5 to 90 msec, explored illusory continuity of the fainter of two alternating sounds. Houtgast (1972, 1973), with the aid of some assumptions, employed this illusion to investigate cochlear lateral inhibition.

In our investigation of heterophonic auditory induction with nonverbal stimuli, we worked with conditions producing illusory continuity with sounds lasting from a few hundred milliseconds to some tens of seconds (Warren and Obusek, 1972b; Warren, Obusek, and Ackroff, 1972). Our examination of the intensities and spectral characteristics necessary for auditory induction revealed a resemblance to masking functions. Thus, auditory induction produced by a narrow-band noise was greatest for those tones having frequencies falling within the noise band. Broad-band noise with a narrow-band reject produced effective auditory induction for all tonal frequencies except those corresponding to the rejected band. The illusory continuity induced by a louder tone alternated with a fainter tone of different frequency had a general resemblance to, but differed from a masking function in interesting ways, as shown in Figure 11.1. The inducing tone in this study was always a 1000 Hz tone at a sound pressure level of 80 dB above 20 μN/m^2 alternating with a fainter tone having the frequencies indicated in Figure 11.1 and presented at adjustable intensities. The alternating tone bursts each lasted 300 msec. The curve for auditory induction (based on means from six subjects) corresponds to the highest intensities at which the fainter tones seemed to be on all the time. The ordinate values correspond to *Sensation Level* (dB above detection threshold for the fainter sound when alternated with the louder one). It can be seen from the figure that virtually no auditory induction occurred until the frequency of the fainter tone was above 700 Hz, so for these lower frequencies, when the tone was loud enough to be heard clearly, it was perceived as pulsating. Auditory induction increased rapidly for frequencies from 800 to 1000 Hz, and then declined slowly, reaching threshold at about 8000 Hz. Simultaneous masking was measured for the same six subjects by determining the threshold for detection of the tones, keeping the 1000 Hz tone on continuously at 80 dB SPL, and determining the threshold for detection of pulsed superimposed tones (on for 300 msec and off for 300 msec). The thresholds for simultaneous masking are shown in Figure 11.1 as Sensation Levels (dB above threshold for the fainter sound when alternated with the louder one, as in the procedure

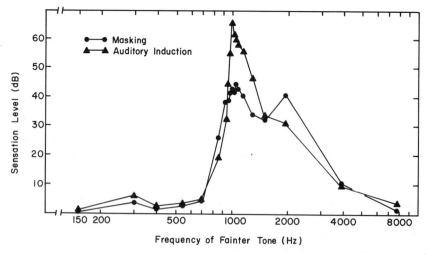

Figure 11.1   Auditory induction and masking for tones in the presence of a louder 1000 Hz tone presented at a sound pressure level of 80 dB. Values are means for six subjects. [From R. M. Warren, C. J. Obusek, and J. M. Ackroff, "Auditory induction: Perceptual synthesis of absent sounds," *Science*, 1972, *176*, 1149−1151, Fig. 1. Copyright 1972 by the American Association for the Advancement of Science.]

described for auditory induction). It can be seen that the induction and masking curves are quite close at frequencies of 975 Hz and below. At higher frequencies, two major differences in the functions appear: At frequencies near that of the louder tone (1000 Hz), the auditory induction curve rises well above the function for simultaneous masking, and at frequencies one octave higher (2000 Hz) masking rises above auditory induction. The increase in masking at frequencies one octave above the masker has been known for some time (see Wegel and Lane, 1924), and the lack of a corresponding change in the auditory induction function indicates some fundamental difference in the processes underlying these two phenomena. When the inducer and inducee are both 1000 Hz (stimuli from the same tone generator to eliminate phase differences), the homophonic auditory induction discussed earlier is produced, and it can be seen that homophonic and heterophonic induction have quite different relations to the masking function.

These experiments with tones and noises demonstrate that auditory induction for nonverbal stimuli requires detailed comparison of the spectral intensities of successive sounds. It might be thought that storage of some *echoic* or *tape recorder* neural trace is necessary for such comparisons. However, there is a relatively simple process involving analysis of cochlear response that could serve as the basis for invoking both homophonic and heterophonic auditory induction. If the peripheral neural units stimulated by louder sounds include those which had been stimulated by fainter sounds, auditory induction may occur. When this illusion takes place, the neural discharges corresponding to the fainter sound are subtracted from the overall pattern of the louder sound and perceived as a separate component. This neural basis is supported by both the general resemblance of heterophonic induction to masking functions and the special increase relative to masking for homophonic induction. Phonemic restoration can be considered as a verbal form of heterophonic auditory induction, and if the neural units stimulated by the extraneous sound include those which would be stimulated by the missing phoneme (as identified through contextual cues), then perceptual synthesis of this phoneme may occur.

Phonemic restoration seems to be a highly specialized verbal adaptation of a general auditory effect. The inability to locate the extraneous sound causing induction of the phoneme also appears to reflect general auditory rules: in this case, those governing detection of simultaneity and succession. Similar temporal confusions have been observed within tonal sequences and for sequences of unrelated sounds such as hisses, tones, and buzzes. This topic is discussed in some detail in the next section.

Perception and Confusions of Temporal Order

Phonemic restorations, verbal transformations, and indeed much of verbal and nonverbal auditory perception in general require the ability to distinguish between different temporal arrangements of the same sounds.

Up to a few years ago, the literature on temporal order seemed to be in fairly tidy shape. Auditory temporal acuity appeared analogous in some respects to visual spatial acuity: Resolving power could be measured in milliseconds with one, and seconds of arc with the other. It was shown by Hirsh (1959) and Hirsh and Sherrick (1961) that detection of order within a pair of sounds such as a tone and a hiss was possible down to 15 or 20 msec. These studies were confirmed by other workers, although thresholds from other laboratories were generally somewhat higher (see Fay, 1966 for review). The experimental values seemed quite adequate to permit the correct ordering of items in speech and music.

There were a few curious observations which did not fit with a general threshold for the perception of order. One of these—the inability to localize extraneous sounds in sentences—has been described already in the section dealing with the phonemic restoration effect. A similar phenomenon has been reported for tonal sequences: If all but one of the tones have frequencies close to some central value, then the odd tone seems to "pop out" of the group (Heise and Miller, 1951), and this tone alone cannot be localized relative to its neighbors. However, these difficulties in perception of temporal order usually have been considered to reflect special attentional and information processing mechanisms associated with speech and music.

Another more recent finding was quite difficult to reconcile with the concept of a general threshold for perception of temporal order and suggested a new look and interpretation of the literature. This finding, first reported at a conference on pattern recognition (Warren, 1968b), was based on a procedure for recycling sequences resembling that employed in studies on verbal transformations. A loop of tape was constructed consisting of spliced 200 msec segments of recorded steady statements of a tone, a hiss, a buzz, and a vowel. When the loop was played back, the four items were heard in a fixed order which was repeated over and over. Subjects could listen for as long as they wished and could name the order starting with whichever sound they chose (there were factorial three or six possible arrangements of the four items). Even when each of the sounds could be identified clearly, the order could not be detected. It was not that a wrong order was perceived by the listener, but rather that a decision could not be reached with confidence, even though the duration of each sound was considerably greater than the classical values for durations permitting detection of temporal order.

Yet a repeated sequence of four successive stimuli could be ordered correctly when each stimulus was a 200 msec word. As part of the initial study, a tape was prepared consisting of four spoken digits repeated over and over, each complete statement of the four items taking 800 msec. In order to avoid any transitional cues to order, each digit was recorded separately and the sequence spliced together. Despite the fact that each of the digits was itself complex, so individual phonemic orders were established within digits, correct identification was accomplished readily by all listeners.

The last part of the initial study dealt with identification of temporal order for vowels. Sequences of four vowels were prepared by cutting 200 msec segments from longer steady statements of each vowel and splicing the segments into a loop which repeated them without pauses. Though it was fairly difficult to judge the order, performance of a group of 30 subjects was significantly above chance. It was easier when each vowel was reduced to 150 msec with 50 msec of silence between items, and it was easiest of all with single statements of each vowel with natural onset and decay characteristics for each statement, each vowel again lasting about 150 msec with 50 msec silences (Warren, 1968b). Subsequent work by Thomas *et al.* (1970) with recycled synthesized vowels led them to conclude that the ease of identifying temporal order was a possible way of measuring the speechlike quality of synthetic speech sounds. Dorman, Cutting, and Raphael (1975) also used recycled synthetic vowels and introduced formant transitions resembling coarticulation between adjacent vowels for some sequences, and formant transitions resembling stop consonants separating successive vowels for other sequences. They concluded that the more their stimuli resembled sequences which could be produced by a speaker, the easier it was to identify temporal order.

The initial observations concerning recycled sequences of three or four unrelated sounds (hisses, tones, buzzes) were extended in a series of experiments which explored the influence of details of experimental procedure on performance (Warren *et al.*, 1969; Warren and Warren, 1970; Warren and Obusek, 1972a). Without the introduction of silent pauses (the role of silence will be discussed subsequently), the threshold for identification of order remained above 200 msec for such sequences with untrained subjects. Practice without furnishing information concerning the accuracy of responses did not help much; thresholds generally remained close to 200 msec.

It should not be thought that lower limits for the identification of order correspond to thresholds for temporal discrimination. Subjects can distinguish among patterns with permuted orders much more readily than they can name the order of items within these patterns. Wilcox, Neisser, and Roberts (1972) and Warren (1972a, 1973b, 1974b) found that subjects could tell whether two sequences presented successively had their component items in the same or different order when the items in each sequence lasted between 100 and 200 msec.

Other experiments have shown that thresholds for same—different judgments with permuted orders consisting of three recycled items, or consisting of two or three sounds each presented once, could be accomplished for item durations as low as 5 or 10 msec (Warren, 1972a, 1973a, 1974a). At durations below 5 or 10 msec, the individual items are too brief to have separate identities, and discrimination between temporal arrangements can be considered as a task involving pitch or phase perception. Thus, Green (1971) has used sounds having a constant energy spectrum but varying in phase spectrum (*Huffman sequences*) and has shown that differences in phase with these special stimuli can be discriminated down to 1 or 2 msec by trained listeners.

The studies dealing with recognition of permuted orders of nonrelated sounds lasting between 5 and 200 msec seem to have implications applicable to speech perception, and have suggested some common mechanisms for verbal and nonverbal pattern recognition. Recent work in my laboratory has explored perception of such sequences with brief components.

In a study of same—different judgments with recycled sequences, it was found that accurate discrimination was not possible if the sequences to be compared differed somewhat in duration of items (Warren, 1972a, 1974b). Thus, same—different judgments could be made by untrained subjects at levels significantly better than chance when the recycled sequences to be compared both had items lasting 200 msec, or if the duration of one of the sequences was increased up to 315 msec. However, when one sequence had items kept at 200 msec, and the other had durations decreased to 160 msec or increased to 415 msec, accurate same—different judgments could not be made. The temporal specificity observed raises an interesting consideration which will become clearer if we turn for a moment to vision. One can recognize a face despite changes in the visual angle subtended. It is not required that the pattern of stimulation evoked by a retinal image match a stored template as a casting matches its mold. A smaller portrait may be placed alongside an enlargement of the same negative, and recognition of identity or difference is easy despite disparity in sizes. Since the temporal dimension in hearing is often considered as analogous to the spatial dimension in vision, we might expect that same—different judgments could be made over a wide range of temporal differences. However, the observed limits for temporal disparities permitting matching suggest that *temporal templates* play a role in auditory pattern recognition. Of course, with speech and music, some degree of temporal flexibility is tolerated in pattern recognition. But the allowable temporal variability may be quite small compared with the spatial variability allowing object recognition at various distances in vision.

A recent series of experiments was designed using a tentative hierarchical scheme for classifying discrimination of temporal order (Warren, 1972a, 1974a). The four ranks in this scheme are presented in order of increasing levels, with mastery at one task level considered to permit performance at all lower levels: *(1)* same—different judgments with sequences to be compared separated by a period of less than one second (so that the requisite time for information storage is well within the accepted limits for raw acoustic storage or *echoic* memory); *(2)* same—different judgments with sequences to be compared separated by intervals up to several seconds; *(3)* absolute judgments or identification using separate verbal labels for each of the sequential permutations (this level requires that a distinctive verbal label be attached to each sequence); and *(4)* naming of order of component items within each of the sequential permutations (the naming of order can be considered a special type of absolute judgment in which the verbal label consists of ordered terms for each of the component items). Using recycled and nonrecycled sequences consisting of 2500 Hz tone, 1000 Hz square wave, and white noise all passed through a 500 to 4000 Hz bandpass filter, it was found that subjects could be trained readily to achieve excellent performance at levels *(1)*, *(2)*, and *(3)* with item durations from either 5 or 10 msec through 200 msec. (At item durations above approximately 200 msec, level *(4)* can be reached directly without special training.)

It is of interest that listeners could be taught readily to perform at level *(3)* (absolute judgments involving the use of learned verbal labels distinguishing between permuted orders of items). While any verbal labels could have been supplied by the experimenter, those actually provided were the names of the component sounds in their proper order. Hence, operationally, subjects were performing at level *(4)* with item durations as low as 5 msec (even though they could not name the order without special training and were responding correctly only by rote when they recognized the overall pattern). There is reason to believe that many experiments in the literature designed to measure thresholds for naming of order (see Fay, 1966, for review) provided opportunities for some degree of unintended training so that subjects were performing by rote at the reported thresholds. This suggestion is similar to that of Broadbent and Ladefoged (1959) when they reported that detection of order within sequences at brief item durations seemed to be accomplished through *quality* differences which emerged only after practice with the sequences, rather than through order perception per se. I wish to go just a bit beyond Broadbent and Ladefoged and suggest how this identification of *quality* and proper order can be accomplished without the experimenter training the subject directly. A special kind of self-training occurs when subjects, presented first with long item durations for which unaided naming of order is possible, are then presented with the same sequences having decreasing item durations. We have seen that permuted arrangements of sounds within sequences can be distinguished at durations too brief for naming of order, and since same—different order judgments are possible with sequences having slightly different item durations, a verbal label describing the order within a slower sequence may be identified with, and transferred to, a faster one. By a series of successive generalizations to ever shorter items, a level can be reached which is well below the threshold possible without training. Using this procedure for threshold training in an unpublished study, I found it possible to obtain correct identification of order in recycled three-item sequences down to 10 msec item durations without communicating information concerning the order directly to the subject. For optimal training with this procedure, the steps employed for successive threshold mastery should be quite small. (Successive steps decreasing between 10% and 25% seem to be within the temporal template permitting direct comparison of patterns by experienced listeners.) As will be discussed shortly, there is reason to believe that identification of phonemic components of speech in their proper order also is accomplished indirectly through prior identification of familiar complex patterns.

The stored templates used for comparing patterns heard at different times may be considered as *temporal compounds*; that is, an aggregation of auditory items into groupings having special holistic characteristics. Temporal compound formation in some ways is analogous to compound formation in chemistry. When elements are combined in certain lawful manners, a compound is formed having specific non-colligative properties (that is, properties which do not reflect in an additive fashion those of the constituent elements). A particular compound may be distinguished from others, but it may not be possible for an observer to analyze these compounds into their elements directly. However, if the components and their arrangements have been learned earlier, then a two-stage process is possible: first, identification of the compound; second, production of a remembered analytical description in terms of components and their internal arrangement. While temporal compounds can be formed readily in the laboratory using arbitrarily selected groups of sounds, outside the laboratory we find temporal compounds for both speech and music.

Temporal compounds in speech perception function in some ways as the perceptual units for speech. There is evidence from experiments with identification times that the size of these units can be considered, for some purposes, as syllabic or larger. Savin and Bever (1970) reported that identification time for phonemes is longer than for the entire syllables containing the phonemes. (The term *identification time* seems preferable to *reaction time* since it appears that subjects do not react directly to phonetic components.) Warren (1971) confirmed these findings in an independent study and also varied levels of stimulus organization, going from nonsense syllable list to word list to sentence. Organization level of the searched stimulus had surprisingly little effect on identification times for target words and phonemes within these words. However, when prior contexts of meaningful sentences were manipulated to facilitate or inhibit target word recognition, identification times for phonemes within these words were changed correspondingly, indicating that phoneme identification was derived from word identification. This study also measured identification time for letter targets in the spelling of auditory stimuli, and provided evidence that letter identification and phoneme identification represented functionally separate processes, each derived from prior word identification.

McNeill and Lindig (1973) measured auditory identification times using targets of phonemes, syllables, words, and sentences, and search lists consisting of phonemes (actually consonant—vowel syllables with a common vowel), syllables, words, and sentences. They reported that, in general, identification time was shortest when the levels of target and search list coincided, and suggested that the conclusions of Savin and Bever (1970) concerning the nonperceptual reality of phonemes were not justified. However, McNeill and Lindig seemed unaware of the identification time study by Warren (1971) which, like theirs, varied both levels of search lists and targets, but which produced results conflicting with theirs and supporting the position of Savin and Bever.

The phonemic restoration effect provides additional evidence that phonemes are not perceived directly. As discussed previously, the perceptually restored speech sound could not be distinguished by our listeners from those speech sounds physically present, so both types of phonemes (actual and restored) were perceptually equivalent. This equivalence is consistent with the hypothesis that all phonemes are in a sense synthetic, being inferred following recognition and identification of the larger pattern. Since this model does not consider speech perception to proceed sound by sound, it might be anticipated that noises within sentences could not be localized accurately relative to phonemes. Accurate temporal ordering of brief sounds would be expected only for those sounds forming part of the same temporal compound. Typically, listeners do not perceive the extraneous sound to be clearly at any particular location, but rather located within a sort of *temporal smear* coexisting with a portion of the sentence. Experiments have not yet tried to measure the extent and gradient of this localization smear for individual subjects, but by requiring them to guess one particular position for the exact location, quantitative data based upon maximum probability estimates have been obtained for individuals, and localization uncertainties have been derived for groups (Warren and Obusek, 1971; Warren and Sherman, 1974). Since extraneous noises in sentences are not anchored, the apparent positions can be induced to drift in one direction or the other. Some of the factors reported to control this perceptual drift are: deep structure of sentential material (Bever, Lackner, and Kirk, 1969); surface structure of the sentence (Chapin, Smith, and Abrahamson, 1972); attentional factors related to Titchenerian *prior entry* (Ladefoged and Broadbent, 1960); and duration of the noise and familiarity with the sentence (Warren and

Obusek, 1971). It should be noted that these factors deal primarily with the extent and direction of drift, not with the reason for the lability of localization.

What is the perceptual status of the phoneme, if it is not perceived as such during speech and is derived following recognition of syllables and words? It would seem that, while phonemes are constructs useful for transcribing and analyzing, they are without direct perceptual basis. Perhaps, as suggested by some linguists (see Lüdtke, 1969), phonemes are fictitious units needed originally for alphabetic writing (which, in turn, is derived largely from historical contingencies). It is practical to base alphabets on the relatively small number of discrete articulatory positions that a speaker can recognize when slowly and thoughtfully producing fragments of speech. However, once established, alphabetic spelling and phonetics can develop separately, as we see in English. Both graphemes and phonemes are inventions useful for transcription and analysis of speech, but neither seem to have direct relevance to perceptual processes leading to comprehension of speech.

Temporal compounds in music seem to consist of melodic groupings of tones. In order to form such compounds, component notes all must lie within a limited frequency range. A tone differing greatly from the frequencies of others in a sequence functions as an extraneous sound, and, as described earlier, it appears to "pop out" of the tonal sequence. The requirement of pitch contiguity for perceptual inclusion within a temporally ordered sequence has been reported by a number of other investigators (Ortmann, 1926; Kinney, 1961; Norman, 1967; Bregman and Campbell, 1971; Thomas and Fitzgibbons, 1971). This basic principle is illustrated by a classic illusion in music. Baroque composers such as J. S. Bach have used a single instrument to produce two simultaneous melodies by interleaving notes in two separate frequency ranges or registers (see discussion of *implied polyphony* by Bukofzer, 1947). Norman (1967) has listed available recordings of Baroque compositions illustrating this illusion.

However, the limits of frequency separation employed for melodic sequences do not represent the limits for tonal temporal compound formation. With no special training, sequences of tones separated widely in frequency readily form recognizable temporal compounds, much as do the unrelated sequences of hisses, tones, and buzzes already described. In a study by Warren and Byrnes (1975), it was found that permuted orders of recycled sequences of four 200-msec tones having frequency separations greater (9 semitone steps) and smaller (.3 semitone steps) than used in music of our culture could be matched through same—different judgments as accurately as sequences having frequency separations within the range used in melodies. Only a few minutes practice (with no knowledge of results) was required to make these matches by our subjects, who had no special musical training. But when the listeners heard sequences with component frequencies higher than the pitches used in music (4500 Hz and above), pitch did not seem to change appreciably with frequency, and differences between permuted orders of tones could not be distinguished. It is interesting that even when listeners could make accurate same—different judgments with tonal sequences, they could not name the order of items correctly within a high—low continuum (except for the sequences containing the holistically identifiable glissandi or regularly increasing or decreasing pitches).

Let us return to speech. Considering that syllables and words behave like perceptual units or temporal compounds, it is clear that there must be further linkage of these units into higher-order groupings of phrases, sentences, and passages. As an almost unlimited number of proteins can be formed through the bonding in sequential arrangements of a limited number of organic units (amino acids), so an almost limitless number of sentences can be formed by the sequential bonding of a limited number of lexical units (words). The linkage of verbal units, of course, follows syntactic and semantic rules. In order to perceptually resynthesize and comprehend the utterance of the speaker, the listener uses familiarity with the rules employed by the speaker to cancel interference by extraneous sounds. Some extraneous sounds encountered are intermittent nonverbal noises, such as those used in studying the phonemic restoration effect, but frequently interference by other voices must be excluded, as in the *cocktail party problem* (Cherry, 1957). Broadbent (1958) noted the need to keep competing messages in separate *channels*. Some other terms used to describe the segregation of linked items within the same verbal or musical passages are: *parallel auditory continua* (Warren, 1968b); *rhythmic fission* (Dowling, 1968); *implied polyphony* (Bukofzer, 1947); *compound melodic line* (Piston, 1947); and *primary auditory stream segregation* (Bregman and Campbell, 1971). This important topic is somewhat beyond the scope of this paper, although the effects of this phenomenon impinge upon some of the observations described here, especially in connection with contextual determinants of perception.

If sounds in a sequence do not form temporal compounds, but rather unfamiliar strings of nonrelated sounds, it is possible to name the order of items if their durations are sufficiently long. If a recycled sequence of hisses, tones, and buzzes is heard with each sound lasting three seconds, virtually everyone can name the order correctly. This achievement hardly seems surprising. Listeners can, of course, name each sound aloud as it occurs and then repeat this order, if required, after the sequence terminates. But why do listeners fail to make this identification at roughly 200 msec per item (Warren and Obusek, 1972a)? A clue to a possible answer is furnished in an experiment by Garner (1951).

Garner found that accurate counting of the number of identical tone bursts in an extended series was not possible when the rate was 6 per second or more, corresponding to 167 msec per item or less. Both counting and the naming of order of items consist of the attaching of distinctive verbal labels to successive events. I am suggesting that it is the time required for verbal labeling of an ongoing stimulus which determines the limiting rate of item presentation both for counting and for naming of order within unfamiliar sequences. Successful performance of these tasks would require that verbal encoding of one item be completed before the onset of the next.

Short sequences may not require labeling of each item as it occurs. Garner (1951) found that low numbers (up to about four to six) could be counted with accuracy at twice the presentation rate required for higher numbers, and Warren (1972b) reported that the introduction of three seconds of silence between repetitions of sequences containing three or four unrelated sounds, each lasting 200 msec, made it possible for subjects to name the order of the items accurately. Perhaps both counting and ordering can be accomplished after termination of a short sequence if verbal labeling of the successive items can be completed before an echoic memory trace fades. Assuming that readout speed from storage corresponds to the speed of verbal labeling observed with extended sequences (roughly 170 msec per item for numbering or counting and 250 msec per item for naming nonrelated sounds), the storage time between termination of a sound and completion of its verbal encoding need be no more than about one second in the four- to six-item sequences used by Garner (1951) and the three- or four-item sequences used by Warren (1972b). This time limit for perceptual readout of stored auditory waveforms is within the limits of one or two seconds observed with other tasks (see Neisser, 1967; Norman, 1972). Additional help in naming order with short sequences is given by the special ease with which initial and terminal items can be identified (Warren, 1972b).

Returning to extended sequences, the durations required for naming of order while a sequence is continuing vary somewhat with practice, response procedure, and stimuli employed. For untrained subjects listening to recycled four-item sequences containing hisses, tones, and buzzes, thresholds were between 200 and 300 msec per item when the verbal descriptions for the sounds were on separate cards which subjects tried to arrange in order of occurrence. However, when vocal responses were used by subjects, thresholds for the same stimuli were considerably higher: between 450 and 670 msec (Warren and Obusek, 1972a). The use of card ordering permits subjects to deal with the sequences in parts, allowing them to make judgments involving only two of the names at a time. The vocal responses require description of the entire sequence at one time; further, the possibility that the vocal description of one sound might coincide with the occurrence of another would be an additional source of difficulty.

Especially interesting recycled sequences are formed by vowels. Rapid verbal encoding would be anticipated since subjects are very familiar with the sounds, and perhaps more importantly, the names used are acoustic copies of the stimuli. As noted earlier, recycled sequences consisting of steady-state segments of four vowels can be ordered by unpracticed subjects using vocal responses at durations of 200 msec per item, and the proportion of correct responses at this duration became higher as the vowel segments approximated normal utterances (and vocal labels) more closely. Using practiced listeners, and avoiding concatenated steady-state segments, Thomas, Cetti, and Chase (1971) and Dorman, Cutting, and Raphael (1975) found it possible for sequences of four recycled vowels to have the order of components named at presentation rates of about 100 msec per item. Dorman and his associates noted that this limiting rate is still well above the average of 30 or 40 msec per phoneme permitting comprehension of accelerated speech.

Thus, there seem to be two distinct categories of auditory temporal discrimination (Warren, 1974a). One category involves direct naming of successive items in order of occurrence. It requires completion of verbal encoding of one sound before the onset of the next in extended sequences. Successful naming of order for such sequences depends upon the nature of the sounds and the response procedure, and generally requires items considerably longer than 150 msec. The other category involves holistic recognition of temporal patterns, and permits both same—different judgments and (following appropriate training) absolute identification of overall patterns. This holistic discrimination does not require verbal processing and is probably, in an evolutionary sense, the more primitive category. It requires item durations of only a few milliseconds for formation of recognizable patterns that have been called *temporal compounds*. New temporal compounds have been formed quite readily in the laboratory through training with a variety of arbitrarily chosen sounds such as square waves, tones, and noise bands. Such recognizable groupings can consist of much briefer sounds than those used in speech and music (which have special restrictive rules governing their temporal compounds).

If the speech sounds used in discourse are generally well above the limit for recognizing and distinguishing between permuted orders of sounds, why have we not developed faster speech? One factor might be the time required for muscles to produce the movements responsible for articulatory and acoustic changes. But, perhaps most importantly, what may at first appear to be a wasteful redundancy may be necessary to ensure comprehension under normal listening conditions.

Summary

It appears that some general auditory mechanisms have been modified in special ways for comprehension of speech. Temporal auditory induction permits listeners to restore verbal and nonverbal sounds masked by intermittent louder sounds through detailed spectral and intensive comparison of masker and maskee. A common neural basis for this comparison has been proposed for all types of auditory induction. Verbal auditory induction (phonemic restoration) employs contextual information of speech in determining the identity of the missing sound. The restored phoneme is indistinguishable to the listener from those physically present, and while the induced sound is placed in its proper position in the verbal sequence, the inducing sound seems to float alongside the sentence without being in temporal contact at any point. The apparent position of the extraneous sound can be made to drift forward or backward in the sentence, although its exact location remains unclear. The inability to detect simultaneity or succession of brief sounds which do not enter into larger recognizable patterns has been appreciated for a long time in music, and seems to represent a general characteristic of temporal resolution in hearing.

Verbal transformations represent a special form of the general perceptual instability found with unchanging patterns of stimulation. Evidence is presented indicating that verbal transformations reflect mechanisms employed for correction of errors when listening to discourse. This illusion involves selective disruption of discrete steps in verbal processing and provides an access for study of organizational mechanisms. It appears that age differences in frequency and types of transformations represent adaptive changes in perceptual processing, enabling listeners to compensate for changes in functional capacity accompanying normal aging. The complementary nature of mechanisms underlying phonemic restorations and verbal transformations in young adults is supported by experimental evidence.

Experiments with speech and with sequences of nonspeech sounds such as hisses, tones, and buzzes have indicated that much of what passes for direct identification of temporal order is actually based on prior identification of a larger pattern. Two principal mechanisms seem to mediate discrimination of temporal order, whether the sequences are phonetic groupings, tonal groupings, or groupings of arbitrarily selected sounds: (*1*) recognition of overall patterns capable of operating down to item durations of a few milliseconds; and (*2*) naming of items in order of occurrence, allowing direct naming of order within extended sequences and having a lower limit of resolution generally of about 150 to 250 msec per item.

Studies of auditory illusions and confusions have provided clues to general mechanisms underlying auditory perception. It is suggested that it is heuristic to continue to consider that these effects reflect processes normally enhancing accurate perception.

ACKNOWLEDGMENTS

Preparation of this chapter, and part of the research described, was supported by the National Science Foundation (Grant BMS73-06787), the National Institutes of Health (Grant HDO7855), and the University of Wisconsin-Milwaukee Graduate School.

REFERENCES

Amster, H. Semantic satiation and generation: Learning? Adaptation? *Psychological Bulletin*, 1964, *62*, 273—286.

Axelrod, S., and Thompson, L. On visual changes of reversible figures and auditory changes in meaning. *American Journal of Psychology*, 1962, *75*, 673—674.

Barnett, M. R., Perceived phonetic changes in verbal transformation effect. Unpublished doctoral dissertation, Ohio University, 1964.

Ben-Zeev, S., The influence of bilingualism on cognitive development and cognitive strategy. Unpublished doctoral dissertation, University of Chicago, 1972.

Berlin, C. I., Lowe-Bell, S. S., Cullen, J. K. Thompson, C. L., and Loovis, C. F. Dichotic speech perception: An interpretation of right-ear advantage and temporal offset effects. *Journal of the Acoustical Society of America*, 1973, *53*, 699—709.

Bever, T. G., Lackner, J. R., and Kirk, R. The underlying structures of sentences are the primary units of immediate speech processing. *Perception & Psychophysics*, 1969, *5*, 225—234.

Book, W. F. *The psychology of skill with special reference to its acquisition in typewriting.* New York: Gregg, 1925.

Brain, W. R. Recent work on the physiological basis of speech. *Advancement of Science*, 1962, *19*, 207—212.

Bregman, A. S., and Campbell, J. Primary auditory stream segregation and perception of order in rapid sequences of tones. *Journal of Experimental Psychology*, 1971, *89*, 244—249.

Broadbent, D. E. *Perception and communication.* London: Pergamon, 1958.

Broadbent, D. E., and Ladefoged, P. Auditory perception of temporal order. *Journal of the Acoustical Society of America*, 1959, *31*, 1539.

Bryan, W. L., and Harter, N. Studies in the physiology and psychology of the telegraphic language. *Psychological Review*, 1897, *4*, 27—53.

Bryan, W. L., and Harter, N. Studies on the telegraphic language: The acquisition of a hierarchy of habits. *Psychological Review*, 1899, *6*, 345—375.

Bukofzer, M. F. *Music in the Baroque Era.* New York: Norton, 1947.

Chapin, P. G., Smith, T. S., and Abrahamson, A. A. Two factors in perceptual segmentation of speech. *Journal of Verbal Learning and Verbal Behavior*, 1972, *11*, 164—173.

Cherry, C. *On human communication.* Cambridge, Massachusetts: M.I.T. Press, 1957.

Cherry, C., and Wiley, R. Speech communication in very noisy environments. *Nature*, 1967, *214*, 1164.

Chistovich, L. A. Temporal course of speech sound perception. In *Proceedings of the 4th International Commission on Acoustics.* (Article H 18) Copenhagen: 1962.

Clegg, J. M. Verbal transformations on repeated listening to some English consonants. *British Journal of Psychology*, 1971, *62*, 303—309.

Dorman, M. F., Cutting, J. E., and Raphael, L. J. Perception of temporal order in vowel sequences with and without formant transitions. *Journal of Experimental Psychology*, 1975, *104*, 121—129.

Dowling, W. J. Rhythmic fission and perceptual organization. *Journal of the Acoustical Society of America*, 1968, *44*, 269 (Abstract).

Elfner, L. F. Continuity in alternately sounded tonal signals in a free field. *Journal of the Acoustical Society of America*, 1971, *49*, 447—449.

Evans, C. R., and Kitson, A. An experimental investigation of the relation between the familiarity of a word and the number of changes which occur with repeated presentation as a "stabilized auditory image." *National Physical Laboratory* (England), *Autonomics Division Publication* No. 36, Sept. 1967.

Evans, C. R., Longden, M., Newman, E. A., and Pay, B. E. Auditory "stabilized images," fragmentation and distortion of words with repeated presentation. *National Physical Laboratory* (England), *Autonomics Division Publication* No. 30, June 1967.

Evans, C. R., and Wilson, J. Subjective changes in the perception of consonants when presented as "stabilized auditory images." *National Physical Laboratory* (England), *Division of Computer Science Publication* No. 41, Nov. 1968.

Fay, W. H., *Temporal sequence in the perception of speech*. The Hague: Mouton, 1966.

Fenelon, B., and Blayden, J. A. Stability of auditory perception of words and pure tones under repetitive stimulation in neutral and suggestibility conditions. *Psychonomic Science*, 1968, *13*, 285—286.

Fodor, J. A., and Bever, T. G. The psychological reality of linguistic segments. *Journal of Verbal Learning and Verbal Behavior*, 1965, *4*, 414—420.

Garner, W. R. The accuracy of counting repeated short tones. *Journal of Experimental Psychology*, 1951, *41*, 310—316.

Garrett, M. F. Syntactic structures and judgments of auditory events: A study of the perception of extraneous noise in sentences. Unpublished doctoral dissertation, University of Illinois, 1965.

Garrett, M., Bever, T., and Fodor, J. The active use of grammar in speech perception. *Perception & Psychophysics*, 1966, *1*, 30—32.

Goldstein, L. M., and Lackner, J. R. Alterations in the phonetic coding of speech sounds during repetition. *Cognition*, 1974, *2*, 279—297.

Green, D. M. Temporal auditory acuity. *Psychological Review*, 1971, *78*, 540—551.

Guilford, J. P., and Nelson, H. M. Changes in the pitch of tones when melodies are repeated. *Journal of Experimental Psychology*, 1936, *19*, 193—202.

Harper, M. J. Distributional effects on verbal transformations of two-word strings. Unpublished master's thesis, San Diego State College, 1972.

Heise, G. A., and Miller, G. A. An experimental study of auditory patterns. *American Journal of Psychology*, 1951, *64*, 68—77.

Hirsh, I. J. Auditory perception of temporal order. *Journal of the Acoustical Society of America*, 1959, *31*, 759—767.

Hirsh, I. J., and Sherrick, C. E. Perceived order in different sense modalities. *Journal of Experimental Psychology*, 1961, *62*, 423—432.

Holloway, C. M. Passing the strongly voiced components of noisy speech. *Nature*, 1970, *226*, 178—179.

Houtgast, T. Psychophysical evidence for lateral inhibition in hearing. *Journal of the Acoustical Society of America*, 1972, *51*, 1885—1894.

Houtgast, T. Psychophysical experiments on "Tuning Curves" and "Two-Tone Inhibition" *Acoustica*, 1973, *29*, 168—179.

Huey, E. B. *The psychology and pedagogy of reading*. Cambridge, Massachusetts: M.I.T. Press, 1968.

Jain, S. Personality and drug effects on illusory changes in speech upon repetition. *Indian Journal of Experimental Psychology*, 1967, *1*, 11—16.

Kinney, J. A. S. Discrimination in auditory and visual patterns. *American Journal of Psychology*, 1961, *74*, 529—541.

Kish, G. B., and Ball, M. E. Some properties of the verbal transformation (VT) effect. *Psychonomic Science*, 1969, *15*, 211—212.

Lackner, J. R. Speech production: Evidence for corollary-discharge stabilization of perceptual mechanisms. *Perceptual and Motor Skills*, 1974, *39*, 899—902.

Lackner, J. R., and Goldstein, L. M. The psychological representation of speech sounds. *Quarterly Journal of Experimental Psychology*, 1975, *27*, 128—140.

Ladefoged, P. The perception of speech. In NPL Symposium No. 10, *Mechanisation of Thought Processes*, (Vol. 1). London: Her Majesty's Stationery Office, 1959.

Ladefoged, P., and Broadbent, D. E. Perception of sequence in auditory events. *Quarterly Journal of Experimental Psychology*, 1960, *12*, 162—170.

Lashley, K. S. The problem of serial order in behavior. In Jeffress, L. A. (Ed.), *Cerebral mechanisms in behavior: The Hixon Symposium*. New York: Wiley, 1951.

Lass, N. J., and Gasperini, R. M. The verbal transformation effect: A comparative study of the verbal transformations of phonetically trained and non-phonetically trained listeners. *British Journal of Psychology*, 1973, *64*, 183—192.

Lass, N. J., and Golden, S. S. The use of isolated vowels as auditory stimuli in eliciting the verbal transformation effect. *Canadian Journal of Psychology*, 1971, *25*, 349—359.

Lass, N. J., Silvis, K. J., and Settle, S. A. Verbal transformation effect: Effect of context on subjects' reported verbal transformations. *Journal of Auditory Research*, 1974, *14*, 157—161.

Lass, N. J., West, L. K., and Taft, D. D. A non-verbal analogue to the verbal transformation effect. *Canadian Journal of Psychology*, 1973, *27*, 272—279.

Lieberman, P. Some effects of semantic and grammatical context on the production and perception of speech. *Language and Speech*, 1963, *6*, 172—187.

Locke, J. *Concerning human understanding*. London: Holt, 1690. Book 2, Chapter 14, Section 13. (Reprinted Oxford: Clarendon, 1894.)

Lüdtke, H. Die Alphabetschrift und das Problem der Lautsegmentierung. *Phonetica*, 1969, *20*, 147—176.

McNeill, D., and Lindig, K. The perceptual reality of phonemes, syllables, words, and sentences. *Journal of Verbal Learning and Verbal Behavior*, 1973, *12*, 419—430.

Miller, G. A. Decision units in the perception of speech. *IRE Transactions on Information Theory*, 1962, *IT-8*, 81—83.

Miller, G. A., and Licklider, J. C. R. The intelligibility of speech. *Journal of the Acoustical Society of America*, 1950, *22*, 167—173.

Moore, M. W., and Bliss, J. C. The Optacon reading system. *Education of the Visually Handicapped*, 1975, *7*, 15—21.

Naeser, M. A. The repeating word effect: Analysis of alternates reported by aphasics and normals. Paper delivered at 10th Meeting, Academy of Aphasia, Rochester, New York, October, 1972.

Naeser, M. A., and Lilly, J. C. Preliminary evidence for a universal detector system—perception of the repeating word. *Journal of the Acoustical Society of America*, 1970, *48*, 85 (Abstract).

Natsoulas, T. A study of the verbal-transformation effect. *American Journal of Psychology*, 1965, *78*, 257—263.

Necker, L. A. Observations on some remarkable optical phaenomena seen in Switzerland; and on an optical phaenomenon which occurs on viewing a figure of a crystal or geometrical solid. *London & Edinburgh Philosophical Magazine & Journal of Science*, 1832, *1* (3rd Series), 329—337.

Neisser, U. *Cognitive psychology*. New York: Appleton, 1967.

Norman, D. A. Temporal confusions and limited capacity processors. *Acta Psychologica*, 1967, *27*, 293—297.

Norman, D. A. The role of memory in the understanding of language. In Kavanagh, J. F., and Mattingly, I. G. (Eds.), *Language by ear and by eye: The relationships between speech and reading*. Cambridge, Massachusetts: M.I.T. Press, 1972. Pp. 277—288.

Obusek, C. J. An experimental investigation of some hypotheses concerning the verbal transformation effect. Unpublished doctoral dissertation, University of Wisconsin, Milwaukee, 1971.

Obusek, C. J., and Warren, R. M. A comparison of speech perception in senile and well-preserved aged by means of the verbal transformation effect. *Journal of Gerontology*, 1973, *28*, 184—188. (a)

Obusek, C. J., and Warren, R. M. Relation of the verbal transformation and the phonemic restoration effects. *Cognitive Psychology*, 1973, *5*, 97—107. (b)

Ortmann, O. On the melodic relativity of tones. *Psychological Monographs*, 1926, *35* (1) (Whole Number 162), 1–47.

Paul, S. K. Level of cortical inhibition and illusory changes of distinct speech upon repetition. *Psychological Studies*, 1964, *9*, 58–65.

Perl, N. T. The application of the verbal transformation effect to the study of cerebral dominance. *Neuropsychologia*, 1970, *8*, 259–261.

Piston, W. *Counterpoint*. New York: Norton, 1947.

Powers, G. L. Intelligibility of temporally interrupted speech with and without intervening noise. *Journal of the Acoustical Society of America*, 1973, *54*, 300 (Abstract).

Pritchard, R. M., Heron, W., and Hebb, D. O. Visual perception approached by the method of stabilized images. *Canadian Journal of Psychology*, 1960, *14*, 67–77.

Reber, A. S. Locating clicks in sentences: Left, center, and right. *Perception & Psychophysics*, 1973, *13*, 133–138.

Riggs, L. A., Ratliff, F., Cornsweet, J. C., and Cornsweet, T. N. The disappearance of steadily fixated visual test objects. *Journal of the Optical Society of America*, 1953, *43*, 495–501.

Savin, H. B., and Bever, T. G. The nonperceptual reality of the phoneme. *Journal of Verbal Learning and Verbal Behavior*, 1970, *9*, 295–302.

Scott, B. L., and Cole, R. A. Auditory illusions as caused by embedded sounds. *Journal of the Acoustical Society of America*, 1972, *51*, 112 (Abstract).

Skinner, B. F. The verbal summator and a method for the study of latent speech. *Journal of Psychology*, 1936, *2*, 71–107.

Studdert-Kennedy, M., and Shankweiler, D. Hemispheric specialization for speech perception. *Journal of the Acoustical Society of America*, 1970, *48*, 579–594.

Taylor, M. M., and Henning, G. B. Verbal transformations and an effect of instructional bias on perception. *Canadian Journal of Psychology*, 1963, *17*, 210–223.

Tekieli, M. E., and Lass, N. J. The verbal transformation effect: Consistency of subjects' reported verbal transformations. *Journal of General Psychology*, 1972, *86*, 231–245.

Thomas, I. B., Cetti, R. P., and Chase, P. W. Effect of silent intervals on the perception of temporal order for vowels. *Journal of the Acoustical Society of America*, 1971, *49*, 84 (Abstract).

Thomas, I. B., and Fitzgibbons, P. J. Temporal order and perceptual classes. *Journal of the Acoustical Society of America*, 1971, *50*, 86–87 (Abstract).

Thomas, I. B., Hill, P. B., Carroll, F. S., and Garcia, B. Temporal order in the perception of vowels. *Journal of the Acoustical Society of America*, 1970, *48*, 1010–1013.

Thurlow, W. An auditory figure–ground effect. *American Journal of Psychology*, 1957, *70*, 653–654.

Titchener, E. B. *A beginner's psychology*. New York: Macmillan, 1915.

Vicario, G. L'effetto tunnel acustico. *Revista di Psicologia*, 1960, *54*, 41–52.

Warren, R. M. Illusory changes of distinct speech upon repetition—the verbal transformation effect. *British Journal of Psychology*, 1961, *52*, 249–258. (a)

Warren, R. M. Illusory changes in repeated words: Differences between young adults and the aged. *American Journal of Psychology*, 1961, *74*, 506–516. (b)

Warren, R. M. An example of more accurate auditory perception in the aged. In Tibbitts, C., and Donahue, W. (Eds.), *Social and psychological aspects of aging*. New York: Columbia University Press, 1962. Pp. 789–794.

Warren, R. M. Verbal transformation effect and auditory perceptual mechanisms. *Psychological Bulletin*, 1968, *70*, 261–270. (a)

Warren, R. M. Relation of verbal transformations to other perceptual phenomena. In *Conference Publication No. 42, I.E.E./N.P.L. Conference on Pattern Recognition*. Teddington, England: Institution of Electrical Engineers, 1968. (b)

Warren, R. M. Perceptual restoration of missing speech sounds. *Science*, 1970, *167*, 392–393.

Warren, R. M. Identification times for phonemic components of graded complexity and for spelling of speech. *Perception & Psychophysics*, 1971, *9*, 345–349.

Warren, R. M. Temporal resolution of auditory events. Paper presented at the American Psychological Association, Honolulu, Hawaii, September, 1972. (a)

Warren, R. M. Perception of temporal order: Special rules for the initial and terminal sounds of sequences. *Journal of the Acoustical Society of America*, 1972, *52*, 167 (Abstract). (b)

Warren, R. M. Temporal order discrimination: Identification and recognition by trained listeners. *Journal of the Acoustical Society of America*, 1973, *53*, 316 (Abstract). (a)

Warren, R. M. Temporal order discrimination: Recognition without identification by untrained subjects. *Journal of the Acoustical Society of America*, 1973, *53*, 316 (Abstract). (b)

Warren, R. M. Auditory temporal discrimination by trained listeners. *Cognitive Psychology*, 1974, *6*, 237—256. (a)

Warren, R. M. Auditory pattern recognition by untrained listeners. *Perception & Psychophysics*, 1974, *15*, 495—500. (b)

Warren, R. M., and Ackroff, J. M. Dichotic verbal transformations and evidence of separate processors for identical stimuli. *Nature*, 1976, *259*, 475—477.

Warren, R. M., and Byrnes, D. L. Temporal discrimination of recycled tonal sequences: Pattern matching and naming of order by untrained listeners. *Perception & Psychophysics*, 1975, 18, 273—280.

Warren, R. M., and Gregory, R. L. An auditory analogue of the visual reversible figure. *American Journal of Psychology*, 1958, *71*, 612—613.

Warren, R. M., and Obusek, C. J. Speech perception and phonemic restorations. *Perception & Psychophysics*, 1971, *9*, 358—362.

Warren, R. M., and Obusek, C. J. Identification of temporal order within auditory sequences. *Perception & Psychophysics*, 1972, *12*, 86—90. (a)

Warren, R. M., and Obusek, C. J. Auditory induction: Illusory continuity of the fainter of two alternating sounds. *Journal of the Acoustical Society of America*, 1972, *51*, 114 (Abstract). (b)

Warren, R. M., Obusek, C. J., and Ackroff, J. M. Auditory induction: Perceptual synthesis of absent sounds. *Science*, 1972, *176*, 1149—1151.

Warren, R. M., Obusek, C. J., Farmer, R. M., and Warren, R. P. Auditory sequence: Confusion of patterns other than speech and music. *Science*, 1969, *164*, 586—587.

Warren, R. M., and Sherman, G. L. Phonemic restorations based on subsequent context. *Perception & Psychophysics*, 1974, *16*, 150—156.

Warren, R. M., and Warren, R. P. A comparison of speech perception in childhood, maturity, and old age by means of the verbal transformation effect. *Journal of Verbal Learning and Verbal Behavior*, 1966, *5*, 142—146.

Warren, R. M., and Warren, R. P. Auditory illusions and confusions. *Scientific American*, December 1970, *223*, 30—36.

Warren, R. M., and Warren, R. P. Some age differences in auditory perception. *Bulletin of the New York Academy of Medicine*, 1971, *47*, 1365—1377.

Wegel, R. L., and Lane, C. E. The auditory masking of one pure tone by another and its probable relation to the dynamics of the inner ear. *Physical Review*, 1924, *23*, 266—285.

Welford, A. T. *Ageing and human skill*. London: Oxford University Press, 1958.

Wheatstone, C. Remarks on Purkinje's experiments. *Report of the British Association*, 1835, 551—553.

Wickelgren, W. A. Distinctive features and errors in short-term memory for English vowels. *Journal of the Acoustical Society of America*, 1965, *38*, 583—588.

Wickelgren, W. A. Distinctive features and errors in short-term memory for English consonants. *Journal of the Acoustical Society of America*, 1966, *39*, 388—398.

Wilcox, G. W., Neisser, U., and Roberts, J. Recognition of auditory temporal order. Paper presented at the Eastern Psychological Association, Boston, Spring, 1972.

Wiley, R. L. Speech communication using the strongly voiced components only. Unpublished doctoral dissertation, Imperial College, University of London, 1968.

Wolin, S. J., and Mello, N. K. The effects of alcohol on dreams and hallucinations in alcohol addicts. *Annals New York Academy of Sciences*, 1973, *215*, 266—302.

chapter 12

Time- and Frequency-Altered Speech

Daniel S. Beasley

Jean E. Maki

Michigan State University, East Lansing

Rochester Institute of Technology

Time-Altered Speech

In recent years there has been increasing interest in the temporal aspects of speech perception. That the time domain is important to the perception and production of speech and language is indisputable. The exact nature of the temporal processing of speech and language, however, is as yet unclear. Indeed, only in recent years have procedures been developed which allow for experimentally adequate manipulation of the temporal characteristics associated with speech and language perception and production. Prior to these developments, investigators were confined, in a sense, to psychophysical measurements of stimuli that were limited in linguistic characteristics. (A comprehensive review of the psychophysical studies of the temporal sequencing of physical stimuli, including phonemes, can be found in the monograph by Fay, 1966.)

The purpose of the first section of this chapter is to discuss the evaluation of temporal processing in speech perception, including brief descriptions of procedures for making such measurements and the results of studies which have employed these procedures. The theoretical interpretations of data obtained via these procedures will also be discussed.

Methods of Investigation

Temporal manipulation of speech and language has taken several forms. To describe all of them in detail would be beyond the scope of the present discussion. However, it would be useful for the reader to have at least a cursory awareness of these methods in order to understand the limitations of the research findings to date.

SPEAKING RAPIDLY

One procedure for temporally modifying a speech signal is simply to manipulate the rate of speech. This procedure, while having the distinct advantage of requiring no special apparatus beyond that of the human vocal mechanism, has the disadvantage of introducing undesirable alterations in the spectral and temporal qualities of the verbal output. By attempting to talk fast (or slow), the speaker unintentionally changes the normal relative attributes of vocal inflections, consonant—vowel durations, and pause durations, and alters the coarticulatory interactions between adjacent speech units (Daniloff and Hammarberg, 1974). In addition, such a procedure has a relatively low physiological upper limit; that is, the speaker can shift his rate of speaking only by approximately 30% from normal when attempting to talk faster. Further, the temporal variability inherent in the articulatory mechanism reduces the reliability and validity of data acquired through the use of this procedure. In general, this technique is not sufficiently exact as a research tool for the study of temporal processing in speech and language. The problems associated with this procedure have been discussed in greater detail by Calearo and Lazzaroni (1957), deQuiros (1964), Enc and Stolurow (1960), Fergen (1955), Goldstein (1940), Harwood (1955), Nelson (1948), and Kozhevnikov and Chistovich (1965).

SPEED-CHANGING METHOD

Another method of modifying speech rate is by simply reproducing a recorded signal at a speed different from the recorded speed. Thus, the resultant playback signal is compressed or expanded in time relative to the original recording. The major advantage of this procedure is that it is simple to perform and requires no special apparatus beyond a common two-speed tape recorder. Furthermore, the recorder can be rather easily modified to allow the speed of reproduction to be continuously variable. However, this procedure produces a frequency shift in the resultant signal which is proportional to the change in playback speed. Such frequency shifting confounds the temporal alteration of the signal and introduces artifacts into the data acquired through the use of this method. For further discussion of problems with the speed changing method, the reader is referred to Fletcher (1965), Foulke (1966b), Garvey (1953a,b), Klumpp and Webster (1961), and Kurtzrock (1957).

SAMPLING PROCEDURES

A more precise means of modifying the speech signal involves the use of various sampling procedures, whereby *samples* of the speech signal are alternately discarded and retained and the retained portions are abutted in time. Such procedures minimize frequency distortion during the change in rate of the reproduced speech signal.

The most cumbersome of these procedures involves a manual sampling technique, wherein portions of the signal are manually excised (with scissors or other such unsophisticated tools). The manual sampling technique has the advantage of allowing for rather precise specification of that aspect of the signal to be modified. That is, within limits, the experimenter can discard any segment, syllable, word, or other linguistic unit he wishes to eliminate or modify, while leaving neighboring units of the speech signal relatively intact. Furthermore specific elements of the signal can be retained differentially (or discarded) without abutting the retained portions (Shriner and Daniloff, 1970; Beasley and Beasley, 1973; Beasley and Shriner, 1973; Beasley *et al.*, 1974; Schuckers, Shriner, and Daniloff, 1973). However, Garvey (1953a,b) noted that the manual chop—splice procedure was extremely tedious and cumbersome, and generally required spectrographic verification of the success or failure of segmentation.

A more efficient sampling procedure for time compression—expansion was developed by Fairbanks, Everitt, and Jaeger (1954) (Figure 12.1). This electromechanical compressor—expander made use of a tape loop which received the signal to be compressed on a continuous basis from an original tape recording. The tape loop passed over a rotating head assembly comprised of four record heads. As the head assembly rotated in the same direction as the tape loop, one of the four heads would periodically touch the recorded portion of the tape loop and transfer the information at that point in time to a variable speed storage tape recorder. The information retained was known as the *sampled interval.* If a single head was fixed in position (0% time compression), all the information from the tape loop was sampled. However, if the head assembly rotated, then portions of the information on the tape loop periodically were not recorded (that is, this information passed

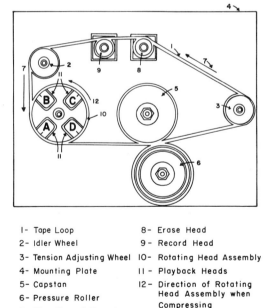

1- Tape Loop	8- Erase Head
2- Idler Wheel	9- Record Head
3- Tension Adjusting Wheel	10- Rotating Head Assembly
4- Mounting Plate	11- Playback Heads
5- Capstan	12- Direction of Rotating
6- Pressure Roller	Head Assembly when
	Compressing
7- Direction of Tape Loop	
Travel	

Figure 12.1 Schematic representation of the compressor unit devised by Fairbanks, Everitt, and Jaeger (1954). [Adapted from Cramer, 1967.]

between record heads), and this was known as the *discard interval*. The degree of
time compression was determined by varying the relative velocity between the tape
loop and head assembly. The tape loop subsequently passed over an erase head prior
to recording information from the source tape recorder. The end product was a time-
compressed speech signal which maintained generally high quality up to, and including, 80% time compression (that is, 80% less time to play back than the original
recording).

The Fairbanks procedure had the distinct advantages of minimizing the frequency
distortion associated with temporal alteration while eliminating the tedious necessity
of manually cutting and splicing the recording. In addition, this procedure had inherent
potential to allow for any percentage of temporal modification of the original recording
by simply varying the relative velocities of the rotating head assembly and tape loop.
The major disadvantages of this procedure were two-fold: (*1*) the special apparatus
necessary for electromechanical time compression—expansion was expensive and
bulky, and (2) the discarded and retained elements of the speech signal were non-
selective. That is, although the head assembly and tape loop velocities could be held
constant, thereby fixing the size of the intervals of the discarded and retained portions
of the signal, the specific content of what was discarded and retained from the
speech sample could vary, depending upon speaker characteristics, the linguistic
context, and so on. Thus, the sampling could occur anywhere within or between any
linguistic segment, and, in this sense, the portion discarded (or retained) was *random*.
The same disadvantage applies to the electromechanical device developed by Springer
(the *Information Rate Changer*) (Foulke, 1971) and the electronic time compressor—
expander developed by Lee (1972) (the *Varispeech I*). The Fairbanks procedure had
an advantage over the smaller and simpler Springer device, however, in that the size
of the interval discarded in the Fairbanks device could be varied over a wide range,
whereas in the Springer device the discard interval was fixed at approximately 35 to
40 msec. This is an important point in that Kurtzrock (1957) has shown that for
maximum efficiency and intelligibility the discarded interval should lie between
18 and 25 msec.

Of the methods discussed so far, the Varispeech I device is probably the most
useful in that it is the size of a portable tape recorder, making it convenient for field
work. In addition, it is simple to use and is relatively inexpensive to purchase and
operate. It operates on the same principles as the Fairbanks compressor, with a
minicomputer replacing the bulky mechanical aspects of the Fairbanks compressor.

The most sophisticated methods for temporally modifying speech signals involve
the use of digital computers and speech synthesizers. They not only have the several
advantages of the techniques discussed thus far, but they also allow for linguistic
selectivity in processing the signal. These methods, however, are currently in the developmental stage and are extremely expensive compared to other techniques. Thus, there
is a paucity of research data using computer time-compression—expansion, although
the increased use of computers in the near future is inevitable (Campanella, 1967;
Huggins, 1972).

Thus, there are several means to temporally alter the speech signal, each with
certain advantages and disadvantages. The choice of method must lie, at least in part,

with the questions under investigation. For example, even today there are certain investigators who find the manual chop—splice procedure the most effective simply because of the nature of the questions under investigation. The remainder of this chapter will center on results of research findings associated with various aspects of temporal processing in the perception of speech and language.

Effects of Time Alteration on Perception

Since it would be beyond the scope of this chapter to discuss all the relevant studies in this area, only a few studies will be discussed which represent several theoretical viewpoints and investigatory techniques. Such an approach should give the reader an adequate introduction to the various facets of the study of temporal alteration, and should provide the reader with the necessary detail pertaining to various points of view in order to allow him to pursue his interest in this area.

There are three listener task behaviors commonly elicited as perceptual reaction to any temporally altered signal. They are the intelligibility of the stimuli, the comprehensibility of the stimuli, and, of course, the subjective preference which the listener has for the stimuli. That is, before a stimulus can be comprehended, it must be intelligible. And further, if the stimulus is comprehensible, the listener must not find it particularly aversive if he is expected to listen to it over a period of time. Of further interest is the nature of the verbal stimuli that are studied; for example, are the stimulus items digits, word lists, or other more linguistically sophisticated sequences? This section, then, will deal with the results and theoretical interpretations of the intelligibility, comprehension, and preference for time-altered speech as reflected in studies using several methods of temporal alteration and several types of stimuli.

STUDIES OF TEMPORAL MODIFICATION OF WORD DURATION

A number of investigators have concurred that speech which has been temporally altered using the speed-changing method results in significantly poorer intelligibility when compared to the manual sampling and electromechanical procedures (Fletcher, 1965; Foulke, 1966b; Garvey, 1953a,b; Klumpp and Webster, 1961; and McLain, 1962), (Figure 12.2). Generally, the intelligibility for words using the speed-changing method declines dramatically when approximately 33% of the original duration is discarded, whereas with the other two methods intelligibility remains above approximately 85% up to a signal duration of about 40% of normal (that is, 60% time compression). This typically has been attributed to the difficulty in perceptually processing a signal with distorted spectral characteristics.

Using the Fairbanks electromechanical sampling technique, Fairbanks and Kodman (1957) investigated word intelligibility as a function of time compression. Using a phonetically balanced monosyllabic word list, they found that intelligibility in terms of accuracy of word recall remained above 85% when the signal duration was shortened by as much as 80% of the original length. They also found, however, that this high degree of intelligibility was dependent upon the size of the discard and sampling intervals. Thus, in Table 12.1, it can be observed that as the sampling and discard

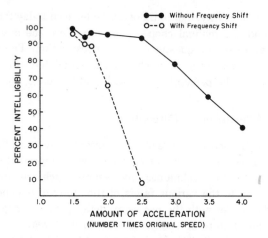

Figure 12.2 Intelligibility score differences of time-compressed speech with frequency shifting and without frequency shifting (i.e., manually sampling and discarding segments of the signal). [Adapted from W. D. Garvey, "The intelligibility of speeded speech," *Journal of Experimental Psychology*, 1953, *45*, 104. Copyright 1953 by the American Psychological Association. Reprinted by permission.]

intervals increased, the intelligibility decreased for the several levels of time compression. They attributed this effect to the fact that as the duration of the discard intervals increased in size, they approached the duration of phonemes, syllables, or words. Hence, an entire linguistic unit could be eliminated and the resultant item intelligibility would, of course, have approached zero.

Using a fast-playback procedure, Klumpp and Webster (1961) found that intelligibility scores were higher under time compression for linguistically simpler messages. Thus, digits yielded scores which were superior to those for phrases and the scores for phrases, in turn, were superior to scores for phonetically balanced word lists. Further, they concluded that the decrease in intelligibility was related more to the

Table 12.1 *Mean percentage of Word Intelligibility at Various Combinations of Time Compression Ratio and Discard Interval*[a]

Time compression ratio	Discard interval (sec)				
	.01	.04	.08	.16	.24
.40				86	
.50	100			85	
.60	100			87	72
.65	100	99	99	86	71
.70	99	98	98	84	68
.75	99	98	98	76	61
.80	90	94	95	74	55
.85	72	73	88	56	42
.90	15	56	47	38	21

[a]8 observers, 50 words. (Adapted from Fairbanks and Kodman, 1957.)

inability of the ear to process the distortion of the frequency spectrum than to the reduction in the message playback time.

Daniloff, Shriner, and Zemlin (1968) investigated the effect of the intelligibility of vowels altered in duration and frequency. They presented adult listeners with electromechanically time-compressed (from 20% to 80% in 10% steps) vowels embedded in an /h V d/ context as spoken by a male and female speaker. In addition to time compression, they also presented the stimuli under frequency-shifted (essentially slow-play) and frequency-shifted—time-restored conditions.

The results of the Daniloff, Shriner, and Zemlin study are presented in Figure 12.3. Note that the female talker was generally more intelligible than the male talker under the several conditions of frequency and time distortion. Further, they found that there was a major decrease in vowel intelligibility at 70% time compression. The time compression-only condition generally was more intelligible than the two conditions involving frequency distortion. These results supported the earlier conclusion by Klumpp and Webster (1961) that the distortion of the frequency spectrum, and not the duration of the signal, was a major factor limiting the intelligibility of compressed speech. That is, the duration of vowels could be drastically manipulated and intelligibility would remain high as long as the spectral distortion of frequency was minimized. Daniloff, Shriner, and Zemlin pointed out that under moderate frequency shifting, the formants associated with the vowels were only moderately shifted from their original position in phonetic space. Under these conditions intelligibility remained high up to a frequency shift of about 40%, as would be expected if the listener performed a perceptual normalization of vowel space (Peterson and Barney, 1952; Gerstman, 1968). However, beyond this point, phonemic quality was altered such that phonetic labeling errors occurred. Finally, Daniloff, Shriner, and Zemlin speculated that consonants would prove to be less resistant to time compression than the longer and more intense vowels. They based this suggestion upon the earlier work of

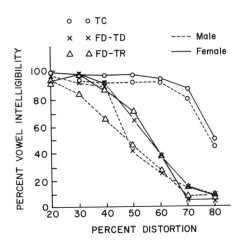

Figure 12.3 Percentage vowel intelligibility for a male and female speaker for various degrees of time compression (*TC*), frequency-division—time-distortion (*FD*−*TD*), and frequency-division—time-restored to normal (*FD*−*TR*). [Adapted from Daniloff, Shriner and Zemlin, 1968.]

Kurtzrock (1957), who found that such was the case for his male talker using the Fairbanks sampling procedure. However, since Kurtzrock did not use a female talker, whether such a finding would hold for the more intelligible female speaker is still open for investigation.

Several investigators have studied the effects of temporal alteration upon intelligibility using stimuli and populations which ordinarily are found in clinical settings. Sticht and Gray (1969) and Luterman, Welsh, and Melrose (1966) studied the effects of age and sensorineural hearing impairment upon the intelligibility of electromechanically time-compressed speech. Luterman, Welsh, and Melrose presented the CID W-22 test of auditory discrimination, compressed to 10% and 20% of normal duration, to a group of normal listeners, a group of young adult listeners with high-frequency hearing losses, and a group of aged listeners with high-frequency hearing losses. As shown in Figure 12.4, they found that the modification of the temporal duration of the words via compression (and expansion) yielded a slight decrease in intelligibility. The normal listeners performed somewhat better than the young sensorineural group, which, in turn, performed better than the older sensorineural group. Luterman, Welsh, and Melrose suggested that the performance of the aged population was not significantly different in function over the two levels of compression and expansion from that of the other two groups. Unfortunately, in this study, the sensorineural groups performed more poorly than the normal group at 0% compression, suggesting that the three groups were not adequately matched on speech reception thresholds under normal conditions.

Sticht and Gray (1969) presented the CID W-22 word lists, electromechanically time-compressed by 36%, 46% and 59%, to a group of seven young normal-hearing adults (under 60 years of age), seven older normal-hearing adults (over 60 years of age), seven young sensorineural hearing-impaired listeners, and seven older sensorineural hearing-impaired listeners. They reasoned, in line with Bocca and Calearo

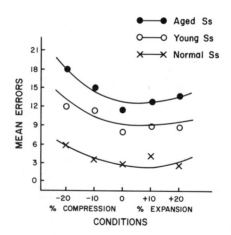

Figure 12.4   The effect of time compression and time expansion upon intelligibility scores for normal-hearing adults, and for young and aged subjects with high-frequency hearing losses. [Adapted from Luterman, Welsh, and Melrose, 1966.]

(1963) and deQuiros (1964), that listeners with pathologies of the central auditory system should have difficulty with temporally modified speech stimuli. In addition, they predicted that elderly patients with normal hearing would perform poorly on an intelligibility task comprised of temporally modified stimulus items. Their results (Figure 12.5) demonstrated that as age increased, the effect of time compression upon intelligibility increased. This effect held for both the younger and older normal-hearing groups. Thus, sensorineural hearing impairment appeared not to be a necessary and sufficient cause of the decrement in the intelligibility of temporally altered speech for the aged. Because the normal and sensorineural groups showed similar response functions across comprehension levels, they suggested that time-compressed speech signals did not effectively differentiate normal and abnormal aged populations. According to Sticht and Gray, the fact that the aged populations performed more poorly than the normal populations was probably due to the fact that the channel capacity (Miller, 1956) for information transfer in the neurological system of the elderly simply was exceeded, even at lower compression ratios, when compared to the younger subjects. This hypothesis was supported in a study by Konkle, Beasley, and Bess (1974) who found that aged subjects with normal pure-tone hearing thresholds peformed significantly more poorly than younger subjects, even for minimal time compression conditions (Figure 12.6).

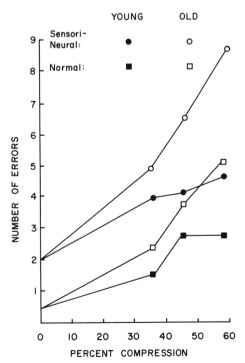

Figure 12.5   Effect of time compression on intelligibility scores of normal and sensorineural hearing-impaired young and elderly listeners. [Adapted from Sticht and Gray, 1969.]

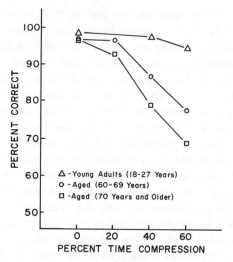

Figure 12.6 Comparison of the effect of time compression on intelligibility scores for the young adults of the Beasley, Schwimmer, and Rintelmann (1972b) study to the results of intelligibility scores of an aging population. [Adapted from Konkle, Beasley, and Bess, 1974.]

The findings of Luterman *et al.* (1966) and Sticht and Gray (1969) were limited in that they were based upon small samples, limited compression levels, and auditory discrimination measures which have been criticized as being too easy. In order to overcome these problems, Beasley, Schwimmer, and Rintelmann (1972) presented the Northwestern University Auditory Test No. 6 (NU-6) (Tillman and Carhart, 1966), under electromechanically time-compressed conditions of 0% and 30% to 70% in 10% steps, to 96 normal-hearing young adults. The stimuli were presented at four sensation levels (8, 16, 24, and 32 dB), and the subjects were divided into left ear and right ear groups. They found that as time compression increased, intelligibility decreased. In turn, as sensation level increased, intelligibility increased (Figure 12.7). The results of this study also suggested that a gradual decrement in intelligibility occurred at approximately 40% time compression, with a pronounced decrease in intelligibility at 70% time compression. However, for each level of compression, the slopes of the articulation curves across sensation levels were approximately the same, (i.e., 2% to 3.5%/dB) as those found for the undistorted NU-6 lists (Rintelmann and Jetty, 1968). There were no differential effects between the left and right ears. A further study (Beasley, Forman, and Rintelmann, 1972), in which the stimuli were presented at 40 dB SL, showed that there was some improvement in the intelligibility scores at the higher sensation level, but the improvement was not significant (Figure 12.8).

The results of the Beasley *et al.* (1972b) and Beasley *et al.* (1972a) investigations, while in agreement with the Daniloff *et al.* (1968) vowel study, conflict with the findings of Fairbanks and Kodman (1957), whose results, using phonetically balanced words, showed no dramatic decrease in intelligibility until approximately 80% time compression. However, Fairbanks and Kodman used a 10 msec discard interval rather than the 20 msec discard interval used in the Daniloff *et al.* (1968) and Beasley *et al.*

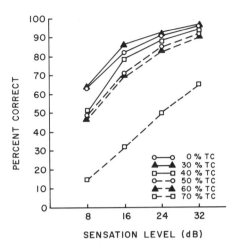

Figure 12.7 Effects of time compression (*TC*) of varying percentages of time as a function of sensation level (in dB) on intelligibility scores for normal-hearing young adults. [Adapted from Beasley, Schwimmer, and Rintelmann, 1972b.]

(1972a) studies. Smaller time samples were discarded in the Fairbanks and Kodman study, thereby potentially enhancing intelligibility. Furthermore, Fairbanks and Kodman used sophisticated listeners as compared to naive listeners in the Daniloff, Shriner, and Zemlin, and the Beasley, Forman, and Rintelmann studies. Finally, Fairbanks and Kodman presented their stimuli at a higher intensity level (re: SL) than that used in the other two studies. The fact that increasing sensation level has been shown to offset partially the effect of temporal distortion suggests that the Fairbanks and Kodman experimental task was essentially easier than the task in the other two studies.

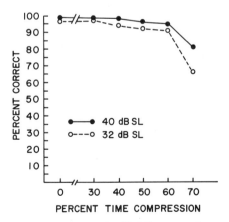

Figure 12.8 Effects of time compression on intelligibility scores for normal-hearing young adults using the N.U. Auditory Test No. 6, presented at 40 dB SL compared to 32 dB SL (Beasley, Schwimmer, and Rintelmann, 1972). [Adapted from Beasley, Forman, and Rintelmann, 1972.]

Maki, Beasley, and Orchik (1975) carried out one of the few studies to date that has dealt with the effect of time compression on children's auditory perception. They presented the Word Intelligibility by Picture Identification (WIPI) test (Ross and Lerman, 1970) and the Phonetically Balanced Kindergarten (PBK-50) test (Haskins, 1949) to 60 normal hearing children at age levels of 4, 6, and 8 years. Each test list was time compressed at 0%, 30%, and 60% and presented at sensation levels of 16 dB and 32 dB. They found that intelligibility increased as age increased, as sensation level increased, and as percentage of time compression decreased (Figure 12.9). The WIPI was found to be more difficult than the PBK-50 even under the most extreme time compression conditions. Further, the PBK-50 was more adversely affected by time compression. Of interest was the fact that at 32 dB SL, the 8-year-olds performed nearly as well at 30% time compression as they did at 0% time compression; and, at 60% time compression, they performed only 10% below their scores on the 0% condition. This finding was true for both the WIPI and PBK-50, although the WIPI showed the least change from normal. In addition, on the WIPI, the 6-year-olds performed nearly as well as the 8-year-olds at all compression levels. In fact, on the WIPI, the children performed nearly as well as the adults in the Beasley *et al.* study (1972b). Thus, it appears safe to assume that temporal manipulation of the speech signal, which has heretofore been used as a research tool with adults, very well may provide a unique method for studying the language processing systems of children, without undue concern regarding whether or not children can adequately process such stimuli under normal conditions.

The studies cited so far have dealt primarily with modifications of the word and segment durations of the stimulus items. In general, these studies support the *subtlety principle* put forth by Jerger (1960). Jerger hypothesized that as the auditory path-

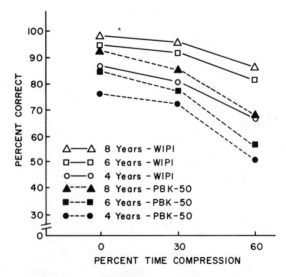

Figure 12.9 Percentage correct scores for children (ages 4, 6, and 8 years) on time-compressed versions of the WIPI and PBK-50 discrimination measures. [Adapted from Maki, Beasley, and Orchik, 1975.]

ways of the nervous system increased in complexity, the stimuli needed to study adequately the function of these pathways also must increase in complexity. One method of placing stress upon the central auditory pathways and central auditory perceptual processing system is to decrease the extrinsic redundancy of the auditory signal via time compression (Calearo and Lazzaroni, 1957). This is predicated, of course, on the assumption that the time domain is crucial to auditory perception. While such an assumption appears to be valid in intelligibility testing, whereby only the word duration is modified, the question arises as to whether manipulation of the stimulus temporal patterns other than word duration would also affect signal intelligibility.

TEMPORAL MODIFICATION OF INTERSTIMULUS INTERVALS

Aaronson and her colleagues have examined the perceptual effects associated with covarying the word duration and interstimulus intervals of time-compressed digits. In essence, she has suggested that in the early sensory stages of auditory perceptual processing, the word duration plays an important role, but in the later stages of processing, the interval between stimulus items becomes significant. Thus, increasing the silent interval between time-compressed stimulus items should provide the necessary means to allow scores on a recall task to equal or better the recall scores for normal stimulus sequences with relatively shorter interstimulus intervals.

Aaronson, Markowitz, and Shapiro (1971), using the chop—splice method to temporally vary their stimuli, studied the effect of covarying word duration and interstimulus intervals upon accuracy of recall of digit sequences. In the first experiment, they presented normally spoken seven-digit sequences and similar sequences compressed by removing 33% of the word duration, to normal listeners in a recall task. The presentation rate was fixed at 3 digits/sec; thus, the normal digits had a shorter interstimulus interval than the compressed digits. The results revealed that the compressed digit sequences were associated with better recall accuracy than the normal digit sequences. Furthermore, while there were no overall differences in item errors between the normal and compressed conditions, there were significant differences in order errors between the two conditions, whereby the normal condition resulted in more order errors during recall than the compressed condition. The authors postulated that, in both the normal and compressed conditions, the word duration was adequate to allow accurate early processing of the stimulus item per se. However, in the process of ordering the stimuli, which theoretically occurs at higher perceptual levels, the normal sequences were perceived inaccurately simply because the interstimulus intervals, during which time the stimuli were ordered, were too short.

In a second experiment, Aaronson et al. (1971) studied the reaction time of subjects' perceptions of a critical pair of digits embedded in a sequence of digits. The word durations and interstimulus intervals were similar to the stimuli used in the first study. The results showed that the reaction times and item and order errors were greater for the normal than for the compressed sequences. The reaction time results were attributed to the fact that subjects experienced a perceptual delay in the processing of the normal sequences due to the decreased interstimulus interval.

Aaronson, Markowitz, and Shapiro then argued that perceptual accuracy would improve under time compression if the duration of the words was shortened, while maintaining the duration of the interstimulus intervals. This suggestion was predicated on Broadbent's (1956, 1958) theory of perceptual processing, which characterized the short-term memory perceptual processor as a two-stage hierarchy (Aaronson, 1967) (Figure 12.10). Stage 1 is characterized as a large capacity, rapid decay *sensing* system which operates directly upon the immediate sensory representations of the input stimulus. The psychophysical representations in Stage 1 are relatively unstable and therefore can be interfered with easily. Further, the storage system of Stage 1 can receive and process stimulus items in parallel, thereby permitting several items to enter the system simultaneously. Stage 2, the higher-level storage system, is characterized as having a smaller capacity but longer decay time and more stability than Stage 1. Items enter Stage 2 in serial order. It is in Stage 2 that linguistic search strategies are applied to the auditory signal; that is, identification processes begin in Stage 2. Based on this description, item errors would be expected to occur during processing in Stage 1 whereas order errors (that is, errors associated with serial processing) would be associated with Stage 2. Thus, temporal modifications of word duration would have their greatest effect at Stage 1, whereas modifications of the interstimulus intervals would probably be most detrimental to the processing in Stage 2. Aaronson (1967) and Aaronson *et al.* (1971) have provided empirical support for these contentions.

Miscik, Smith, Hamm, Deffenbacher, and Brown (1972) studied the covaried effects of electromechanically compressed word durations and interstimulus intervals. They found that recall accuracy (as defined by correct serial position) improved when either the word duration or the interstimulus interval differentially increased. In a second experiment, they found improved recall could be induced by having subjects *chunk* the stimuli in units of two or three elements. Further, when the retention interval (that is, time immediately following the stimulus presentation) was increased, recall accuracy increased. They attributed this effect to the fact that larger retention intervals permitted increased time for the subject to rehearse his response. However, this interpretation is equivocal in that the authors attempted to minimize rehearsal by having the subject repeat letters aloud during the retention intervals.

Kuhl and Speaks (1972) presented time-compressed sentential material to normal listeners. In one condition, the words in the time-altered stimuli were abutted in time; in the other conditions, the compressed words were separated by silent intervals ranging from 50 to 200 msec in duration. They found that the compression condition

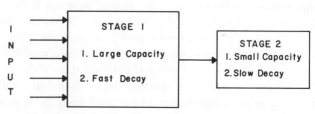

Figure 12.10 Schematic representation of Broadbent's model as described by Aaronson (1967).

resulted in poorer intelligibility scores than any of the silent interval conditions. They also found that the size of the silent interval had no major effect on the scores. All that seemed necessary was that the silent interval be used between words. They suggested that, indeed, the silent interval, as Aaronson (1967) argues, may have permitted the listener a moderate degree of processing time. It would seem, however, that if this were true, then as the silent interval increased in duration, the intelligibility score would have improved; this was not the case. Kuhl and Speaks offered two other explanations for their findings. First, they noted that possibly the word segments need only be recognized as separate, not continuous, events in order for accurate perception to occur. Even a short silent interval would have served this purpose. They also suggested that the silent interval may have served as a deletion marker cue for the listener. These findings and interpretations by Kuhl and Speaks provide alternative speculations for the Aaronson *et al.* (1971) and Miscik *et al.* (1972) studies.

Another approach to the study of interstimulus intervals has been the insertion of silent intervals between phonemic elements of words (i.e., *interphonemic intervals*). Shriner and Daniloff (1970) and Beasley and Beasley (1973) investigated the auditory reassembly abilities of normal first- and third-grade children. They used 10 meaningful and 10 nonmeaningful CVC units and manually inserted silent interphonemic intervals of 50, 100, 200, 300, and 400 msec between the phonemes of the CVC syllables. The results of these two studies (Figure 12.11) showed that the meaningful stimuli were significantly easier for the children to reassemble and repeat than the nonmeaningful stimuli. Furthermore, the older children were superior to the younger children in their auditory reassembly abilities. Finally, reassembly ability decreased markedly when the interphonemic interval was increased beyond 100 msec. The investigators in these studies suggested that the large differences associated with the semantic factor were

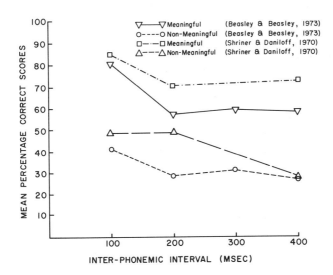

Figure 12.11   Percentage correct scores on meaningful and nonmeaningful CVC monosyllables as a function of variable interphonemic intervals. [Adapted from Beasley and Beasley, 1973.]

related to the child's ability to process the incoming stimuli, including his ability to apply subsequently the necessary linguistic rules to permit accurate encoding of the signal. Thus, according to the paradigm presented by Osgood (1957), the meaningful *and* nonmeaningful stimuli can be processed adequately in the lower level automatic processor (perhaps this would be analogous to Aaronson's concept of Broadbent's *Stage 2*). At the higher representational level, however, only the meaningful stimuli would be further processed because, unlike the nonmeaningful stimuli, they involve the use of linguistic rules (learned or otherwise).

In an extension of this line of reasoning, Beasley *et al.* (1974) suggested that children who exhibit severe articulation problems should be able to reassemble the meaningless stimuli with about the same accuracy as normal children. However, on the meaningful stimuli, assuming that stored rules of language play a role in the perceptual process, the normal children should perform significantly better than the children with misarticulations. And this, in fact, is exactly what Beasley *et al.* (1974) found. In addition, they found that, as in the two preceding studies, the resynthesis (or reassembly) abilities of the children broke down dramatically under the 200 msec interphonemic interval condition. Of interest, however, is the fact that in all of these studies, when the interphonemic interval reached 400 msec, there was a trend for the reassembly abilities to show a slight improvement. This effect was particularly evident for younger children and for meaningful stimuli. It may be reasoned that stimuli which were modified temporally with interphonemic intervals at less than 200 msec were processed as single "chunked" units (CVC). However, stimuli which included inter-phonemic intervals of 400 msec were processed as three units (C−V−C). In addition, stimuli with intervals greater than 100 msec but less than 400 msec were difficult to process simply because the child was unable to determine effectively the size of the chunk to process, thereby burdening the child's perceptual processing abilities.

More research, however, is needed before this hypothesis is acceptable. For example, would such findings hold for linguistic units other than the CVC type? Would the trend for improved scores hold for interphonemic intervals beyond 400 msec? The answers to these and other questions are needed, particularly if reassembly tasks are to be applied for remediation purposes. For example, Katz and Burge (1971) have suggested that such tasks are useful with learning-disordered children. However, they do not indicate that they adequately have controlled the stimulus parameters associated with the material to be resynthesized. Thus, if the interphonemic intervals are too long, the child, in effect, may not resynthesize but rather simply echo a series of meaningless phonemes (or words). Indeed, to make the most use of such techniques in educational settings, controlled manipulation of the several stimulus parameters may be necessary.

In this section, an attempt has been made to describe results of serveral studies and their interpretations associated with the effect of temporally modifying the pause times or intervals between stimuli. It is apparent that the interstimulus interval plays a prominent role in the accurate perception of auditory stimuli. However, up to this point the discussion has been limited to studies involving comparatively low-level linguistic phenomena. It is now appropriate to turn our attention to studies which have extended the investigation of temporal processing in auditory perception to include more complex or, at least, more sophisticated linguistic stimuli.

TIME-ALTERED PHRASES AND SENTENCES

Gerver (1969) investigated the effects of grammaticalness, presentation rate, and message length on auditory short-term memory. Using Coleman's (1965) system for ranking the complexity of grammatical constructions, Gerver presented adult listeners seven- and nine-word sentences which varied over four levels of grammatical sophistication. In addition, the sentences were electromechanically time-compressed and time-expanded by 50%. His results revealed that recall accuracy was better for the expanded signals and that sentences judged as more grammatically complex yielded higher recall scores. Further, the larger word sets yielded poorer scores than the shorter word sets. The length effect, however, interacted with only the lowest grammatical level. In an analysis of order errors, he found that most order errors occurred with the larger, slower word sets of lower grammatical levels. Gerver interpreted his data to mean that the more linguistic constraints placed upon the language stimuli, the easier it is to encode and recall, thereby concluding that syntactic structure indeed facilitates the retention and recall of language. He also noted that apparently longer messages were easier to encode when adequate linguistic structure was available (that is, higher levels of grammaticalness) and, under such conditions, message rate was relatively significant. However, in the linguistically unstructured conditions, message rate played an important role in that more processing time was required for perceptual accuracy. In line with Aaronson's (1967) view, Gerver suggested that the long, fast, unstructured input to the Stage 1 perceptual storage system would be likely to decay before being processed by Stage 2 since Stage 1 had a fast decay time.

Thompson (1973) presented 40 sentences, divided into two grammatically based difficulty levels, to children ranging in age from 5.6 to 9.6 years. The sentences were electromechanically time-compressed and time-expanded. She found that recall accuracy (termed *comprehension*) improved as a function of increasing age, decreasing sentence complexity, and decreasing rate of presentation. However, as shown in Figure 12.12, the effect of speaking rate and sentence complexity became less

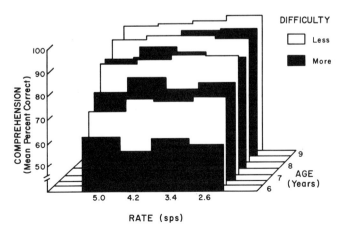

Figure 12.12 Percentage correct scores by children for comprehension of sentences varying in difficulty and presented at several rates (syllables per second). [Adapted from Thompson, 1973.]

significant with increasing age. Furthermore, her data suggested that while the slower rates assisted the perceptual processing of the stimuli by the younger children, the reverse was true for the older children; that is, the older children tended to perform better under the more rapid speech condition than under the slower condition. It is interesting to note here that Gerver (1969) found that increased sentence complexity assisted the recall accuracy of time-compressed speech by adults, whereas Thompson did not find this to be true with children, particularly younger children. Investigators may find that the perception of time-compressed speech reflects potently upon the stages of language acquisition and development. If so, then temporal distortion may prove to be a unique instrument for the study of language development.

King and Weston (1974) studied the ability of children to recall electromechanically time-compressed three-, five-, and seven-word sentences. They found that younger children had significantly more difficulty recalling sentences time-compressed by 50% of the original time than older children (age range: 4 to 8 years). Furthermore, there was not a strong age-by-sentence length interaction at the 0% time-compressed condition. However, in the 50% compressed condition, the younger children performed significantly more poorly than the older children, particularly on the longer sentences. They suggested that younger children, unlike older children, have not fully developed all the necessary strategies used in the perceptual processing of language, and consequently they need the normal word durations and interstimulus intervals for accurate perceptual processing.

Beasley and Shriner (1973), using a chop—splice procedure, investigated auditory perceptual analysis of sentential approximations which were characterized by covaried word durations and interstimulus intervals. Ten first-order and ten second-order seven-word sentential approximations were constructed in a manner described by Speaks and Jerger (1965). The 20 sentential sequences were then used in 12 experimental conditions, which were characterized by word duration (in msec)—interstimulus interval (in msec) ratios of 400:100, 400:200, 400:300, 400:400; 300:100, 300:200, 300:300, 300:400; 200:100, 200:200, 200:300, 200:400. The stimulus sequences were presented to normal hearing young adult subjects. Beasley and Shriner found that as word duration increased, recall accuracy increased for both orders of sentential approximations (Figure 12.13). However, this effect was most prevalent for the second-order sequences at the word duration of 300 msec. They also found that, while recall accuracy was improved with increasing interstimulus intervals, this effect was not as dramatic as the increase in accuracy associated with increasing word durations. Finally, a significant interaction between word duration and interstimulus interval revealed that the 200 msec word durations were most affected by modification of the interstimulus intervals. The authors concluded that it is imperative that time-altered word durations and interstimulus intervals not be studied independently.

In essence, they supported the notions of Aaronson (1967) in that the interstimulus interval is an important ingredient for accurate perceptual processing of auditory stimuli. Beasley and Shriner noted, however, that as the stimuli become more like natural language (particularly when compared to the digit stimuli used by Aaronson), modified word durations will have a greater effect on perceptual accuracy than will the modified interstimulus intervals. This finding is reasonable in that the multiple

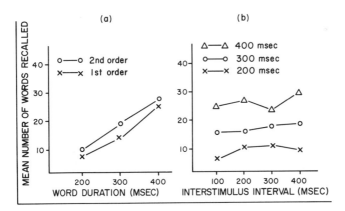

Figure 12.13 Recall accuracy as a function of covaried word durations, interstimulus intervals, and order of sentential approximation. [Adapted from Beasley and Shriner, 1973.]

cues of language (Harris, 1960) are associated basically with the stimulus word per se. That is, the subjects accurately perceived natural utterances with temporally modified interstimulus intervals because of the redundancy (multiple cues) inherent in the language. However, when the stimulus redundancy was reduced (for example, with shortened word durations), then the difficulty in perceptually processing the stimuli was increased. This difficulty, in turn, could be offset only by increasing the interstimulus interval to the point at which the stimulus itself was too distorted to be processed accurately at Stage 1, regardless of how long the interstimulus interval might be.

Schuckers *et al.* (1973), using a chop—splice procedure, studied children's auditory reassembly abilities for sentences. They inserted silent interstimulus intervals of 125, 250, 500, and 750 msec between the words of simple sentences ranging from four to nine words in length. Generally, as sentence length increased, the accuracy of word recall decreased. In addition, as the interstimulus interval increased, the accuracy of recall decreased. They also found that the nouns were most accurately recalled, followed by verbs and modifiers, respectively. Further, they noted that, in line with the findings of other studies (Aaronson *et al.*, 1971; King and Weston, 1974), it was the terminal half of the sentences which was associated with the greatest number of errors. They concluded that when perceptually processing auditory stimuli, children rely in part on the normal prosodic patterning of language. Such prosody, of course, was interfered with when silent interstimulus intervals were inserted between words. They further concluded that the short-term store for children was exceeded when more than eight words were used in a sentential sequence. However, they, like Beasley and Shriner, pointed out that the use of sequences that approach normal language allows the subject to apply stored linguistic rules to the stimulus input, and that such rule application in fact enhances the perceptual processing and subsequent encoding of this input.

Thus, the Stage 1 processor may store physical representations of words, as described by Aaronson (1967). In Stage 2, language processing can occur if either the interstimulus interval is increased and/or the stimuli are such that they permit the perceiver readily to apply his linguistic competence. In support of this contention, Pantalos, Schuckers, and Hipskind (1975) found that when silent interstimulus intervals of 200 msec and 1000 msec were inserted between the words of sentences, children performed approximately the same when required to recall normal sentential sequences when compared to 30% time-compressed sentential sequences. Schill and Schuckers (1973) found that children repeated temporally segmented sentences with greater accuracy when the normal prosodic characteristics of the sentences were retained. Furthermore, even with sentences which did not have normal prosodic cues, the children tended to repeat the sentences using prosodic patterns typically associated with normal articulatory performance.

STUDIES OF TEMPORAL INTERRUPTION

Several investigators have studied the perceptual effects of temporally *interrupted* speech. Using a shadowing task (whereby subjects had to repeat a message simultaneously with the presentation of the message), Huggins (1964) investigated the intelligibility of speech alternately switched between the left and right ear. Intelligibility was most affected when the alternations occurred from one ear to the other at least once during a syllable. Intelligibility was less affected, however, if the alternations occurred between syllables. He suggested that these results pointed to some sort of *syllable unit* as a basic unit of perception rather than some unit of smaller segments such as phonemes.

As noted earlier, Beasley and Shriner (1973) found that word duration was a more potent factor in recall accuracy than were interstimulus intervals, although Aaronson, Markowitz, and Shapiro (1971) had shown that the interstimulus interval was also an important perceptual processing variable. Huggins (1972, p. 139) investigated the covariation of word durations and interstimulus intervals in word sequences. He suggested that intelligibility was dependent upon two factors:

1. the probability that a speech interval will be recognized *in isolation* decreases as its duration decreases, and
2. the probability that signal parameters can be followed from one speech interval to the next increases as the duration of the intervening silent interval increases.

Using a shadowing paradigm, he found that both the word duration and interstimulus intervals affected intelligibility. More specifically, he showed that if the interstimulus interval was greater than 120 msec, intelligibility was not strongly affected, suggesting that a listener can extract no more information from words in a speech sequence than is possible by simply combining words in isolation. As he pointed out, his experimental procedures and data very well may prove to be a unique means to predict the intelligibility of various time-altered stimuli, particularly when the effect of the discard interval is under study. In fact, the earlier work by Fairbanks and his colleagues (Fairbanks and Kodman, 1957) indirectly supported the Huggins hypothesis in that they found that as the discard interval of the electromechanical time compressor was increased beyond approximately 30 msec, intelligibility decreased.

Speaks and Trooien (1974) studied the effects of interaural alternation of speech (that is, switching back and forth between ears) upon shadowing scores. They found that such alternations ranging from 2 to 10 per second had a minimal effect upon the shadowing scores unless the original speech signal was presented at a very rapid rate (194 words per minute as opposed to 135 words per minute) (Figure 12.14). Furthermore, they found that listener judgments of intelligibility after shadowing were somewhat higher than the actual shadowing score, and intelligibility judgments were even higher when subjects were required only to listen to, and not to shadow, the interrupted speech. This finding suggested to the authors that the shadowing task, and not the alternation of stimuli, had the major effect upon intelligibility. Wingfield and Wheale (1975) suggested that stimulus alternation would affect intelligibility if the appropriate linguistic complexity characterized the stimulus items. However, Speaks (1975, personal communication) has noted that such a contention is unacceptable in toto based upon the limited amount of data available to date.

Miller and Licklider (1950), by switching monosyllabic speech signals on and off, found that very slow and very fast switching rates yielded higher intelligibility scores than intermediate switching rates. They contended that the slow rates permitted the on-time to be long enough to allow a large portion of the stimuli to be perceived at any one time, and the fast rates permitted the listener to receive several chunks of the stimulus without long interfering off-time pauses.

However, whereas Miller and Licklider suggested that the amount of on-time was the prime determiner of intelligibility, Powers and Speaks (1973) pointed out that the amount of off-time very well may be the major determiner of intelligibility. In order to answer this question, Powers and Speaks studied the effects of varying the speech-time fractions (proportion of time the speech was on) of .33, .50, and .67 at a

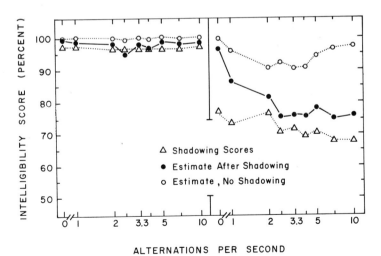

Figure 12.14 Effect of shadowing alternately presented signals to the left and right ears upon intelligibility. [Adapted from Speaks and Trooien, 1974.]

slow (186 wpm) rate of speaking, at interruption rates of .42/sec through 20/sec. Subjects were simply required to estimate the intelligibility of a passage presented under the several combinations of conditions. They found that under both the slow and fast speaking rates, estimated intelligibility was greater as the interruption rate decreased or increased from the midrange. However, they also found that this effect was strongest for the speech-time fraction of .33. As the speech-time fraction increased, intelligibility increased at all interruption rates, although this increase in intelligibility was most observable *between* interruption rates rather than *within* interruption rates. Powers and Speaks concluded that indeed the speech-time fraction had a major effect on estimates of intelligibility. As the speech-time fraction decreased, the decrease in intelligibility was partially offset by decreasing the interruption rate. However, decreasing the interruption rate had a negligible effect when the speech-time fraction was large. Thus, the major contributor to intelligibility was the on-time of the signal (relative to the off-time). That is, decreasing the on-time relative to off-time will have a more detrimental effect upon intelligibility than will decreasing the off-time relative to on-time. This finding supports the results of Beasley and Shriner (1973), who also found that stimulus duration time appeared to play a more significant role in recall accuracy than did the silent interstimulus interval.

Huggins (1972) studied the effects of varying the temporal characteristics of the prosodic aspects of spoken sentences. He pointed out that prosodic features of speech are extremely important in speech intelligibility and comprehension, as evidenced by their resistance to natural distortion, listeners' ability to determine syntactic breaks on the basis of prosody, the apparent storage of prosodic features in memory, and the apparent increase in the perceived intelligibility of deaf speakers who are trained to use normal prosodic patterns. In his study, Huggins found that perceptual accuracy appeared to be related to a syllabic unit rather than to segmental units. He suggested that distorting the temporal factors associated with the prosodic characteristics of language had a detrimental effect on the syllable unit that was processed for speech perception. In a related study, Berry, Daniloff, and Holstead (1972) found that a CCV syllabic unit, suggested by Kozhevnikov and Chistovich (1965) as a basic unit of perception, was more resistant to distortion from interaural switching than a VCC-type syllable. They suggested that these results were tentative support for Kozhevnikov and Chistovich's hypothesis. (See chapters by Kent and Studdert-Kennedy in this volume.)

Obviously, there are many varieties of experimentation associated with the study of the temporal aspects of speech perception. Up to this point, several of these experiments have been discussed. However, it is sometimes difficult to determine if the investigator(s) have actually been studying intelligibility of speech signals or the comprehension of such signals. This problem now will be briefly discussed.

COMPREHENSION OF TIME-ALTERED SPEECH

It is often difficult to determine whether the data from a specific study reflect upon intelligibility or comprehension, or both, because the distinction between these two concepts is often tenuous. Operationally, *intelligibility*, or the recognition of signal components, is a necessary prerequisite to *comprehension*, or the cognitive processing of the signal. In the extreme, word lists ordinarily provide information pertaining to intelligibility, whereas comprehension may be measured by asking subjects to respond to questions pertaining to a recently heard passage of material.

Sticht (1969) found that electromechanical time compression of speech more adversely affected listening comprehension scores of subjects with high mental aptitude than subjects of low mental aptitude. He also demonstrated that repetition of time-compressed messages did not provide improvement in comprehension scores, contrary to the findings of Fairbanks, Guttman, and Miron (1957). Sticht noted that persons of low mental aptitude did more poorly on a simple discrimination task, suggesting that this may have contributed to their overall poorer comprehension scores. Finally, his data revealed that the addition of normal linguistic cues, such as prosodic characteristics, resulted in improved comprehension scores on time-compressed stimuli. Sticht (1969, 1971) went on to suggest that the loss of comprehension was due not to the time compression per se, but rather to the limitations of the human storage and retrieval system used for language comprehension.

Foulke (1971) discussed several studies, the results of which indicated that comprehension decreased dramatically when listening material was compressed beyond approximately 50% of the original time. Further, while the comprehension of passages compressed via the sampling procedure may have had a slight advantage over the fast-playback method (Foulke, 1962; McLain, 1962), under certain circumstances, in other situations such an advantage was nonexistent (Foulke, 1966b). If future investigations uphold these findings, then the major detrimental effects of time compression may be considered to be associated with the intelligibility of the signal and not necessarily with an individual's ability to comprehensively process that signal. However, poor comprehension, if related to poor intelligibility, may be enhanced by increasing the linguistic constraints upon the message, that is, by retaining normal prosodic patterning, by increasing linguistic redundancy, and so on.

While Foulke (1971, p. 98) argued that "comprehension does not appear to depend heavily upon the intelligibility of single words," what in fact is more likely is that comprehension *is* heavily dependent upon intelligibility, but that perceived intelligibility (and, ipso facto, comprehension) can be enhanced by expanded use of other linguistic characteristics associated with the compressed message. (This suggestion is supported by the findings of Huggins, as discussed earlier.) Thus, the listener very well may encounter processing problems in comprehension when the input word rate to the neurological system exceeds the processing time of the system. This would be apparent particularly if, as Foulke suggested, a person cannot chunk linguistic stimuli aurally as well as he can visually. However, if chunking can be used with aurally presented material, then perhaps comprehension of compressed speech or language can be improved. The nature of such chunking, however, is as yet unclear. Speculatively, perhaps it is possible to allow a sequence of aurally presented material to enter short-term memory (using the Aaronson concept presented earlier) in some linguistically intact manner (for example, NP_1—pause—VP—pause—NP_2) such that comprehension actually could be enhanced. The listener could then process a *chunk of language* (so to speak) and thus eliminate the necessity of word-by-word processing for comprehension. Such a concept, of course, is contingent upon the findings of future investigations, but preliminary findings (Gerver, 1969; King and Westen, 1974) support the feasibility of this suggestion.

The importance of intelligibility and comprehension relative to the use of time-altered speech is clear. However, listener preference also plays a role when the use of such stimuli is to be considered. That is, regardless of how intelligible or comprehensible speech signals may be, if, for whatever reason, a listener does not like to listen to such signals, then the use of time-altered speech is limited. This problem as related to time-altered speech will be discussed in the next section.

LISTENING RATE PREFERENCE

Several investigators have attempted to relate oral reading rate to preferred listening rates. Foulke (1966a) found that blind subjects most preferred a listening rate that was almost double the average rate of speech. Lass and Cain (1972) and Cain and Lass (1974), on the other hand, found that sighted adults preferred a listening rate which was approximately the same as the subjects' oral reading rates. Furthermore, Lass and Prater (1973) found that normal subjects preferred to listen to about the same speech rates in an impromptu speaking task as in an oral reading task. Thus, persons whose major avenue of information reception is the auditory channel (that is, blind subjects) are able to tolerate faster rates of speech than normal-sighted subjects. However, such conclusions are tentative, awaiting the results of further research. For example, as noted earlier, female speakers have been shown to be more intelligible under temporal alteration conditions than male speakers, at least for monosyllabic stimuli (Daniloff et al. 1968). In addition, male speakers have been shown to be preferred and to be rated more intelligible than female speakers under both time-compressed and frequency-shifted—time-restored speech conditions (Beasley, Zemlin, and Silverman, 1972; Zemlin, Daniloff, and Shriner, 1968). Thus, the studies by Lass and his colleagues, for example, may very well have yielded different results if a female rather than a male speaker had been used.

Age is another important variable to consider when using time-compressed speech. As noted earlier, there have been very few investigations of children's perception of temporally altered speech signals. The only study to date of children's preference for such signals was carried out by Lass and Fultz (1976). They found that children between the ages of 11 and 13 years rank-ordered a passage that had been time compressed to various degrees in nearly the same order as the adults in the Lass and Cain (1972) study. This finding is not entirely unexpected, however, since the children used by Lass and Fultz were beyond the 7-year age limit, which often has been noted as the point in language development when certain characteristics of children's language behavior mature. It would be interesting to extend this study to younger children in order to determine if there is a developmental sequence that could be detected in the preference for temporally altered speech.

Another factor which may be of considerable significance to preference studies of time-compressed speech is that of experience. That is, as listeners have more exposure to time-altered speech, their tolerance or preference for it may increase. On an informal basis, we have found that, following a 30-minute or so exposure to time-compressed speech, listeners become uncomfortable if they are forced to return to the normal rate of presentation. An investigation of this effect was recently completed by Lass *et al.* (1976), in which they exposed their experimental group of subjects to progressively increasing rates of time compression (from 225 to 350 wpm) over a six-week period and compared their listening rate preferences before and after such exposure. They found that the subjects' listening rate preference shifted to faster rates after the exposure period. Further investigations of this nature are necessary, however if we are to appropriately determine the effect that exposure to time-altered speech has upon the listener.

Without belaboring the issue, it is important to recognize that if time-compressed speech is to be used, it will be necessary to determine what factors play a role in the listener tolerance level for such signals.

Summary

An attempt has been made to describe several aspects of time-altered speech. The presentation of the methods available for time compression and the results of several investigations which have dealt with various factors that play a role in the temporal processing associated with the perception of speech and language have been presented. In addition, an attempt has been made to provide some of the theoretical interpretations associated with these investigations.

This chapter is not intended to be an exhaustive review of the literature. For example, studies by Foulke concerning application of time-compressed speech to the blind were discussed only briefly. Other studies concerned with the application of time-altered speech were also minimized. For example, a time-altered speech discrimination test for use in audiological diagnoses has been developed (Rintelmann and Beasley, 1974), and this measure has been found to be useful in the diagnosis of auditory disorders (Rintelmann, Beasley, Linn, Forman, and Ciliax, 1974; Kurdziel and Noffsinger, 1973; Kurdziel, Rintelmann, and Beasley, 1975). Few studies on time-altered speech have been conducted using children who exhibit speech and language problems; application to this population may have far-reaching implications. For example, Orchik and Oeschlager (1974) found that children who exhibited severe articulation disorders also tended to perform significantly more poorly on 60% time-compressed speech than normal children or children who exhibited mild articulation disorders. In another vein, Johnston and Manning (personal communication) are investigating the processing abilities of children with auditory perceptual problems and other learning disabilities using time-altered speech. However, the purpose of this chapter was to simply provide the reader with an introduction to this area of study. It is hoped that this brief introduction has increased the reader's awareness of the verified and potential effects of the time alteration of speech, and that the reader has been provided with an adequate base from which to pursue the study of temporal processing in speech perception.

Frequency-Altered Speech

Introduction

Within the realm of auditory perception, two major parameters under continual investigation are the temporal and frequency (spectral) characteristics of the auditory signal. As can be seen from the preceding section on temporal alteration, investigators who are collectively considering diverse practical applications have in common the one primary purpose of gathering information concerning the auditory stimuli and/or the processing organism. This is also true for the frequency domain, for which advancements have resulted in such concepts and technological advancements as filtering, vocoding systems, frequency transportation, and disproportionate and proportionate frequency shifting. Use of such systems has added to the existing knowledge concerning the frequency spectrum and its contributions to auditory perception.

This section, then, is intended to parallel the preceding section by introducing various methods of frequency manipulation and by reviewing some of the related research in which frequency-altered speech has been employed. It is hoped that, in this way, sufficient information will be presented to provide understanding of conceptual and methodological developments in both areas. And further, by exploring the thinking of previous investigators, it is hoped that a background will be provided against which investigators can adequately assess future needs.

Filtering Systems

While filtering in itself is a means of altering the frequency spectrum of a speech signal, filters also are used commonly as components in other systems of frequency manipulation. Therefore, an understanding of filtering is requisite to understanding more sophisticated means of frequency manipulation, such as vocoders and frequency transposers.

There are four major types of filters used extensively in frequency manipulation, each used for removing different regions of the frequency spectrum. These include the low-pass, high-pass, bandpass, and rejection filters.

A low-pass filter is pictured in Figure 12.15a; all frequencies below 1000 Hz are allowed to pass through the filter at peak intensity. Above 1000 Hz, energy in the frequency spectrum is differently rejected by the filter. The effect that the filter has on frequencies above 1000 Hz is determined by the rejection rate of the filter, i.e., the degree of attenuation.

Whereas the low-pass filter rejects higher frequencies while passing lower frequencies, the high-pass filter operates in the reverse manner. Figure 12.15 shows that part of the frequency range which is preserved and which is rejected by the high-pass filter. In this case, the frequencies below 2000 Hz are differentially transmitted according to the rejection rate of the filter, commonly reported in dB/octave.

Rejection rate is one of several filter specifications which should be noted in research reports where filters are used. The major characteristics include the half-

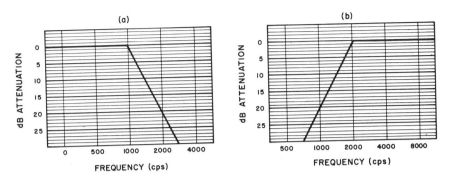

Figure 12.15 (a) Low–pass filter showing 1000 Hz cutoff frequency and 20 dB per octave rejection rate; (b) high-pass filter showing 2000 Hz cutoff frequency and 20 dB per octave rejection rate.

power points, the rejection rate, the center frequency, and the bandwidth. The *cutoff frequency* (or *half-power point*) is that frequency at which the filter has attenuated the signal to half the peak intensity within the pass band. The rejection rate is the difference in the number of decibels between the decibel level at the cutoff frequency (or the center frequency for band-pass filters) and the decibel level at the frequency marking the next octave, thus resulting in the dB/octave specification.

A third specification is the bandwidth, which applies to another type of filter, the bandpass filter. This filter type may be viewed as the combination of low-pass and high-pass filters. For the bandpass filter shown in Figure 12.16, the crosshatching represents that frequency range passed by both filters. The slashes under *a* represent the area passed by the low-pass filter but rejected by the high-pass filter. The slashed section under *c* represents the frequency range passed by the high-pass filter and rejected by the low-pass filter. Thus, through the bandpass filter, sections *a* and *c* are rejected and only a specific area, *b*, is passed by both filters.

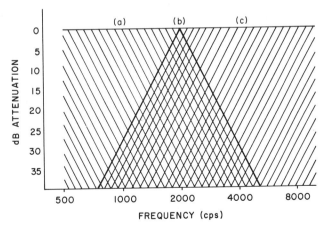

Figure 12.16 Combined low–pass (a) and high-pass (c) filters resulting in bandpass filter with center frequency of 2000 Hz (b) and rejection rate of approximately 30 dB per octave.

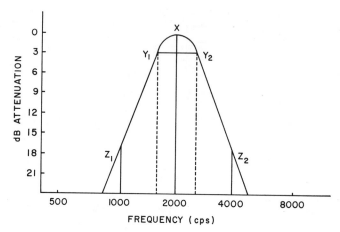

Figure 12.17   Bandpass filter showing filter characteristics of center frequency (X), half-power points (Y_1 and Y_2), bandwidth (Y_2-Y_1), and 18 dB/octave rejection rate (Z_1 and Z_2).

In Figure 12.17, Section b from Figure 12.15 has been extracted and the bandwidth increased; thus, several other filter specifications can be identified. For the filter shown in Figure 12.16, the center frequency is 2000 Hz and is that frequency at the midpoint of the frequency band and for which the filter responds most efficiently, i.e., passes energy with the least amount of interference. The half-power points, Y_1 and Y_2, are the frequencies on either side of the center frequency which are down 3 dB relative to the power measured in dB at the center frequency. These are points which commonly are used for filter description and for determining the bandwidth of the bandpass filter. As mentioned previously, the rejection rate of the filter is an important characteristic. In Figure 12.17, points Z_1 and Z_2 represent octave differences from the center frequency and show an 18dB per octave rejection rate for this filter.

The final major specification is the bandwidth, determined by calculating the difference (in cycles per second) between the two half-power points. It can be seen that the bandwidth is directly related to the rejection rate of the filter, since a filter with a gradual rejection rate would have half-power points located farther from the center frequency than a filter with a rapid rejection rate. Since the distance, in cycles per second, between the half-power points is the bandwidth, the farther apart the half-power points, the wider the bandwidth. Subsequently, with a wider bandwidth, more frequency information will be available. In the area of speech perception, the high-pass, low-pass and bandpass filters are used often in determining which frequency ranges are essential to intelligibility of different speech stimuli.

The fourth filter type, the rejection filter, is similar to the bandpass filter in that it is a combination of a high-pass and low-pass filtering. It operates in essentially the same manner as the bandpass filter but with a different result. Figure 12.18 shows a rejection filter where the low-pass filter (*a*) and the high-pass filter (*b*) are combined in such a way that only one band of frequencies is rejected from the signal, the bandwidth of which is governed by the specific filter characteristics. And again, when studying speech perception, such instrumentation has been valuable in determining

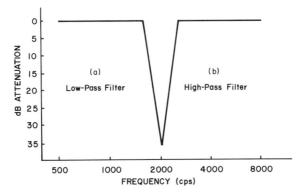

Figure 12.18 Combination of low-pass (a) and high-pass (b) filters resulting in rejection filter at 2000 Hz.

the effect on speech intelligibility when eliminating certain frequency information, other than either a high or low frequency region, which would require a low- or high-pass filter, respectively. Thus, the filtering technique has been, and continues to be, highly valuable in alteration of the frequency domain used both alone and in conjunction with other components in systems such as vocoders, frequency transposers, and some systems of frequency shifting.

Vocoding Systems

Of the methods included in this section, the vocoders are probably the most electronically complex of the systems used for frequency manipulation of the auditory signal. Vocoders have numerous disadvantages and, when compared to other methods, relatively little intelligibility and comprehension data are available. On the other hand, the vocoder can alter the signal in ways unique to that system, and this fact alone warrants its inclusion in this discussion. For an in-depth explanation of the different types of vocoders and their operation, the reader is referred to Flanagan (1972). In addition to the extensive coverage by Flanagan, other investigators have discussed various types of vocoders, including the channel vocoder (Dudley, 1939), the formant vocoder (Vilbig and Haase, 1956), the voice-excited vocoder (Golden, 1963), the phase vocoder (Flanagan and Golden, 1966), and the combined channel and formant vocoder (Gold, 1965).

Basically, the vocoder is constructed using a series of bandpass filters. During operation of this system, portions of the speech signal are filtered, altered in some manner, and then resynthesized with a second series of filters. Those vocoders listed above comprise only a partial list of the many types available, the specific type determining which portion of the signal is filtered. Often the vocoder name gives an indication of which portion of the speech signal is filtered and used for resynthesis. The formant vocoder, for example, has filters at formant regions, those areas of high energy concentration. As Vilbig and Haase (1956) described it, the frequency regions of major concern are the first three formant regions. Through one of three methods of formant extraction, a representative frequency for each formant region is determined, and the three representative frequencies combined provide the envelope from which a synthesizer, the second component of the vocoder, reconstructs the original input signal. This component is similar to the first in that it is a series of bandpass filters, the synthesizer having 20 filters, each with a bandwidth of 150 cycles per second. Whereas formant vocoders operate only at formant regions, the channel vocoders are constructed with adjacent bandpass filters and are thus responsive to energy in adjacent channels of frequency bands. As Gold (1965) reported, it is also possible to combine the characteristics of two types of vocoders to benefit from the best of each system. In all cases, the energy transmitted is determined by the filter characteristics of the center frequency and bandwidth.

The intent of researchers dealing with vocoders is essentially to analyze and extract from the signal those characteristics which are necessary for synthesis or, more accurately, resynthesis, of intelligible and perceptually acceptable speech. The practical value of such a system is seen when one considers the use which industry, government, advertising, and other communication-dependent units could make of systems which significantly reduce the channel requirements necessary for signal transmission. At present, however, the systems are costly, take too long for analysis in some cases, and have not been perfected to reconstruct a perceptually acceptable synthesized output.

Although some research has been conducted solely for the purpose of comparing different vocoding systems (Schroeder, 1966; Voiers, 1968) and using different speech stimuli (Williams and Hecker, 1968), the vocoders have not been used a great deal in comparison to other methods of frequency manipulation, possibly because of any or all of the existing disadvantages of the system. The exceptions to this will be discussed in subsequent sections in which specific vocoder types are used to process stimuli which are either frequency shifted or frequency transposed.

Frequency Transposition

Vocoders used for the purpose of frequency transposition have been described by several investigators, including Pimonow (1963), Johansson (1966), and Ling and Druz (1967).

Johansson (1966) reported positive results from frequency transposition through a two-channel system. On one channel, the range of speech frequencies was amplified, and through the second channel, high-frequency information from voiceless consonants was transposed to a lower frequency range. Six hearing-impaired children with low-frequency residual hearing received 10 days of training, 20 minutes per day, on stimuli consisting of bisyllabic rhyming word pairs. Prior to training, the children received the stimuli using direct channel presentation of the signal (amplification only) as well as pretesting using the transposed signal. Posttests were administered using direct channel presentation following the training with the transposed stimuli. The author reported that all subjects showed increased scores as a result of training with the transposed signal and that the children subjectively preferred the transposed signal.

The results from a series of three experiments conducted by Ling (1968) were not as encouraging as the results of Johansson, which favored use of frequency-transposed speech signals with hearing-impaired children. The first of the three experiments by Ling included eight children as subjects, each displaying low-frequency residual hearing. Five discrimination tests were vocoded using the Ling—Druz Vocoder (Ling and Druz, 1967), which amplified the frequency range from 70 to 700 Hz and simultaneously transposed a higher frequency range, 2000 to 3000 Hz, down to the lower range of 750 to 1000 Hz. Two subgroups of four subjects each received 7 hours of training, one group using the vocoder and the other using a speech training aid providing conventional amplification. Posttests were administered and both groups showed essentially equivalent progress, indicating no additional advantage to using the vocoder.

The second experiment was performed to compare performances when varying training conditions, that is, using two types of transposers and adding the conditions of plus and minus frequency-transposed signals. The transposers were the Johannson—Wedenberg Transposer (Johansson and Wedenberg, 1960) and the Ling—Druz Vocoder (Ling and Druz, 1967). In this study, eight hearing-impaired children were placed in two groups, one group training with each instrument. Two training periods were conducted, with groups switching instruments for the second training period. Each training period lasted 10 days with one 40-minute training session per day. The authors reported no significant differences related to the type of transposer used or the presence or absence of transposed speech. The third experiment simply added 12 hours of additional training with both instruments and still no significant differences were found.

Further studies with hearing-impaired children as subjects showed no significant differences using frequency transposition during either auditory training (Guttman and Nelson, 1968; Ling and Doehring, 1969) or articulation training (Ling and Maretic, 1971). There may no longer be such a strong need for further experimentation with frequency transposition since further investigation is beginning to show success with other methods of frequency alteration in areas where frequency transposition has been ineffective (Guttman and Nelson, 1968; Ling, 1968; Ling and Doehring, 1969).

Another area which has only recently received empirical attention is that of disproportionate and proportionate frequency-shifting techniques. The exact boundaries of definitions become somewhat obscure at this point. For example, frequency transposition can be considered to be a form of frequency shifting and could be considered further in a discussion of vocoding systems. With the profusion of terms occurring in the literature—such as *spectral compression, frequency compression, bandwidth compressed, frequency-altered, frequency-distorted, frequency divided—time restored, frequency divided—time distorted, slow-played, frequency transposed,* and *proportionate and disproportionate frequency shifting*—it is highly recommended that the reader determine specifically how the investigator processed his stimuli.

Frequency Shifting: Disproportionate versus Proportionate Techniques

For the purposes of this discussion, *frequency shifting* will be defined as moving the entire frequency spectrum up or down, thus affecting the entire spectrum proportionately, as opposed to disproportionately shifting single-frequency bands (as is typically done with frequency transposition). And again, be reminded that in some literature, frequency shifting well may include frequency transposition as well as other concepts, depending upon how the individual authors wish to view the techniques they are using.

Numerous investigators have considered speech perception through study of acoustic characteristics of the signal, frequency being one of the parameters studied. A great number of researchers, including Peterson and Barney (1952), Fairbanks and Grubb (1961), Slawson (1968), and Daniloff, Shriner, and Zemlin (1968), have studied the role of vocalic formants in speech perception. Some of the data are contradictory relative to how freely the listener may manipulate phonetic space. Supporters of the absolute vowel theory contend that vowel space is relatively invariant and non-transposable, whereas supporters of the relative vowel theory disagree. The first position is predicated upon the assumption that fixed formant frequency regions are necessary for identification of vowels, particularly F_1 and F_2; the second position is predicated upon the assumption that a constant ratio for F_2 and F_1 is necessary to account for accurate vowel perception. Regardless of which theory better reflects reality, the two theories offer a basis for distinguishing between disproportionate and proportionate frequency shifting. The differential effect of each system can be seen in the resulting formant regions and relative ratios.

Information concerning intelligibility has been of primary concern with this as well as other methods of frequency distortion. It has been shown that intelligibility of frequency-altered speech decreases with increasing percentages of distortion (Takefuta and Swigart, 1968; Daniloff et al., 1968) (see Table 12.2), but that intelligibility scores can improve with training (Raymond and Proud, 1962; Zemlin, 1967).

Raymond and Proud (1962) used a frequency converter to shift the frequency spectrum by a specified amount. Training was provided and lists of the CID W-22 (Hirsh, Davis, Silverman, Reynolds, Eldert, and Bensen, 1952) words were used for posttesting hard-of-hearing children under normal undistorted and two distorted conditions of 400 and 750 Hz frequency shifted. Results revealed that the highest scores were obtained on the undistorted PB lists, and improvement in scores was observed as a result of training.

Table 12.2   *The Effect of Proportionate and Disproportionate Frequency Shifting on the First Three Formant Frequencies*

Undistorted				Distorted	
Formants	Ratio		Distortion	Formants	Ratio
Disproportionate frequency shifting					
F_1 300	1 →		Frequency	→ 150	1
F_2 600	2 →		Shifted by	→ 450	3
F_3 1200	4 →		150 Hz	→ 1050	7
Proportionate frequency shifting					
F_1 300	1 →		Frequency	→ 150	1
F_2 600	2 →		Shifted by 50%	→ 300	2
F_3 1200	4 →		or by a factor of 2	→ 600	4

Zemlin (1967), using a modified version of the Fairbanks compressor, processed tapes consisting of vowels in an /h V d/ context under both normal and frequency-shifted—time-restored conditions. The mean percentage of correct scores of hearing-impaired children was 55% for the undistorted stimuli and 16% for the distorted stimuli on the first trial. On the fourth trial, the percentage of correct score for distorted vowels increased to 38%, showing substantial improvement with relatively little training.

With some systems, the entire frequency spectrum is shifted by a fixed Δf, e.g., 400 Hz. For other systems, such as slow-play techniques, each frequency is shifted by a constant proportion of the base frequency (Kf). Thus, both techniques affect the acoustic energy of the entire frequency spectrum but differentially shift the formant regions. Table 12.2 shows the effect each system has on the first three formant regions, the frequencies of which have been contrived for ease of demonstration. The studies by Raymond and Proud (1962) and Zemlin (1967) are examples of each frequency shifting type; that is, Raymond and Proud used a disproportionate method by shifting frequency bands an equal amount, and Zemlin used the Fairbanks compressor (Fairbanks *et al.*, 1954), which is a proportionate-shifting method requiring that the signal be slow-played by a specified amount and then time compressed by a like amount.

Kurtzrock (1957), using the Fairbanks compressor, found that consonants were more intelligible than vowels during frequency shifting, although the intelligibility of initial consonants did not differ from final consonants in his study. Picard and Bode (1973) replicated the results of Kurtzrock, but they found that final consonants were more intelligible than vowels and initial consonants for 50% frequency shifting. Daniloff *et al.* (1968) had posited that consonants were more intelligible than vowels during frequency shifting simply because the chopping effect of the time compressor was more detrimental to consonants than to vowels. Picard and Bode (1973), however, disagreed with this interpretation. Rather, they explained the vowel—consonant differences according to an hypothesis which they termed *perceptual incongruity*. That is, during the first two phonemes of a C_1VC_2 sequence, the listener was in the process of perceptually adapting to unusual (that is, incongruent) stimuli, but by the time C_2 arrived, the listener overcame the incongruity and was able to process more accurately C_2 as compared to C_1 and V. A third possibility, of course, is that C_2 was shorter than C_1 and V in the normal condition, and when the speech was processed, it simply approached maximum permissible duration during time expansion. During the frequency-shifted—time-compression condition, however, the Daniloff, Shriner, and Zemlin hypothesis could be applied. Future investigations are needed to clarify this issue, that is, to determine if the misperception of consonants that have been frequency shifted is psychologically (see Picard and Bode) and/or physically (see Daniloff, Shriner, and Zemlin) based. Clarification of this issue, of course, has implications for the application of frequency-shifted speech.

Bennett and Byers (1967) found that, with adults displaying high-frequency sensorineural hearing losses, intelligibility improved as the speech signal was frequency shifted up to 20%, but beyond the 20% point, intelligibility decreased. The systematic error in such a system is that in using slow-played speech without temporal restoration, two factors are modified: the altered time factor in addition to the downward shift of the frequency spectrum.

Shriner, Beasley, and Zemlin (1969) investigated the effect upon intelligibility of 35% frequency shifting of the words on the *Picture Identification for Children—A standardized Index* (PICSI) (Seidel, 1963) using normal children in kindergarten through third grade. They found that frequency shifting (*TD*) alone (essentially slow-played speech) resulted in a 12% decrease in intelligibility compared to the normal signal (Figure 12.19). Although restoring the time to the frequency-shifted signal (*TR*) resulted in a further decrease in intelligibility, the difference between the TD condition and the TR condition was not significant. Finally, time compressing the TR signal by 35% beyond the original time resulted in a further, although nonsignificant, decrease in intelligibility. Shriner, Beasley, and Zemlin also included measures of reaction time in their study. The reaction times for the three experimental conditions differed significantly from normal, but there were no significant differences between experimental conditions. The reaction time results supported the findings of Shriner and Sprague (1969). Furthermore, they suggested that their results supported the contention of Tiffany and Bennett (1961); that is, that frequency-shifted signals may have potential application to hearing-impaired populations.

Although it has been shown that intelligibility is affected by frequency shifting the signal (Daniloff *et al.*, 1968; Shriner *et al.*, 1969; Zemlin, 1967), it could be concluded that the use of this procedure is well worth a certain degree of loss of intelligibility if it can be found that more information is available to the hearing-impaired through shifting of the frequency spectrum, particularly if auditory training is enhanced. This was the question investigated by Beasley and Mosher (1975), who provided auditory training to hearing-impaired children using frequency-shifted—time-restored (*FS—TR*) speech. Eighteen hearing-impaired children demonstrating low-frequency residual hearing served as subjects. Pre- and posttests were given under 0% FS—TR and 35% FS—TR conditions. During the interim, 15 days of intensive auditory training were provided for each of the two groups. One group received training using the 35% FS—TR stimuli and the other, the control group, received the 0% FS—TR stimuli. Posttests showed that both training conditions resulted in improved scores; however,

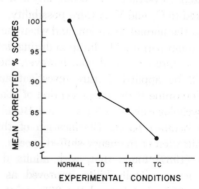

Figure 12.19 Percentage correct scores for children presented normal, 35% frequency shifted only (*TD*), frequency-shifted—time-restored (*TR*), and frequency-shifted—time-compressed (*TC*) words. [Adapted from Shriner, Beasley, and Zemlin, 1969.]

improvement was substantially greater for the 35% trained group on both posttests. Table 12.3 shows the mean percentage of correct scores for each group under both distortion conditions for both the pre- and posttests.

When comparing types of training, it is interesting to note that the 35% training condition, in addition to showing greater differences between pre- and posttesting periods on the 35% FS—TR testing condition, also showed improved scores for the 0% FS—TR from pre- to posttests. These results suggest the strong possibility that frequency shifting may be within the usable reach of hearing-impaired persons, at a fairly reasonable cost and with comparative ease of operation, in the near future. At any rate, this area of study is ripe for further investigation.

Implications for Future Research

When considering the area of auditory training using frequency-shifted stimuli, the research needed in this area alone approaches staggering proportions. For example, Beasley and Mosher (1975) found differing responses from individual subjects. That is, some children obtained optimal scores after 5 days of training; some showed continual progress throughout the 15-day training period; and some showed a decrease in scores with continued auditory training (possibly attributable to boredom with the stimulus materials). The ultimate goal of research in this area would be to ascertain not only the causes of such differences (if that is possible) but, more importantly, to determine and develop auditory training programs suitable for children displaying different performance behaviors. Since Beasley and Mosher used stimulus items from the Word Intelligibility by Picture Identification discrimination measure (Ross and Lerman, 1970), only discrimination of monosyllables was required. Use of other stimuli which provide more language cues, such as phrases and sentential stimuli, may result in better scores and simultaneously provide training with stimuli presenting more complex language structures. After determination of how hearing-impaired children perform with each stimulus type alone, data should be collected using various

Table 12.3 *Percentage Correct Scores for Experimental and Control Groups of Hearing-Impaired Children under 0% and 35% Frequency-Shifted—Time-Restored Training and Testing Conditions*[a]

Experimental training		Testing conditions	
		0% FS—TR	35% FS—TR
35% FS—TR	Pretest	22.2	20.8
	Posttest	34.7	35.1
	Difference	*12.5*	*14.3*
0% FS—TR	Pretest	29.6	19.4
	Posttest	31.0	24.0
	Difference	*1.3*	*4.6*

[a] Adapted from Beasley and Mosher, 1973.

stimulus types in different combinations to investigate interactive effects. Studies to determine carryover are needed, as are longitudinal studies to investigate the effect of various types of auditory training programs over an extended period of time.

In summary, the research into frequency-altered speech and language systems is indeed in its infancy. While a great deal of research has been performed using filters alone, the use of more sophisticated techniques is only beginning. It is important that future investigators attempt to answer the myriad of questions in this area of study.

REFERENCES

Aaronson, D. Temporal factors in perception and short-term memory. *Psychological Bulletin*, 1967, *67*, 130–144.

Aaronson, D., Markowitz, N., and Shapiro, H. Perception and immediate recall of normal and compressed auditory sequences. *Perception and Psychophysics*, 1971, *9*, 338–344.

Beasley, D. S., and Beasley, D. C. Auditory reassembly abilities of black and white first- and third-grade children. *Journal of Speech and Hearing Research*, 1973, *16*, 213–221.

Beasley, D. S., Forman, B. S., and Rintelmann, W. F. Perception of time-compressed CNC monosyllables. *Journal of Auditory Research*, 1972, *12*, 71–75. (a)

Beasley, D. S., and Mosher, N. L. The use of frequency shifted and time restored speech with hearing impaired children. *Audiology: Journal of Auditory Communication*, 1975, in press.

Beasley, D. S., Schwimmer, S., and Rintelmann, W. F. Intelligibility of time-compressed CNC monosyllables. *Journal of Speech and Hearing Research*, 1972, *15*, 340–350. (b)

Beasley, D. S., and Shriner, T. H. Auditory analysis of temporally distorted sentential approximations. *Audiology: Journal of Auditory Communication*, 1973, *12*, 262–271.

Beasley, D. S., Shriner, T. H., Manning, W. H., and Beasley, D. S. Auditory assembly of CVC's by children with normal and defective articulation. *Journal of Communication Disorders*, 1974, *7*, 127–133.

Beasley, D. S., Zemlin, W. R., and Silverman, F. H. Listeners' judgments of sex, intelligibility, and preference for frequency-shifted speech. *Perceptual and Motor Skills*, 1972, *34*, 782. (c)

Bennett, D. N., and Byers, V. W. Increased intelligibility in the hypacusic by slow-play frequency transposition. *Journal of Auditory Research*, 1967, *7*, 107–119.

Berry, R. C., Daniloff, R. G., and Holstead, L. Perception of interaurally segmented syllables. *Perceptual and Motor Skills*, 1972, *35*, 383–386.

Bocca, E., and Calearo, C. Central hearing processes. In J. Jerger (Ed.), *Modern developments in audiology*. New York: Academic Press, 1963. Pp. 339–370.

Broadbent, D. E. Growing points in multi-channel communication. *Journal of the Acoustical Society of America*, 1956, *28*, 533–535.

Broadbent, D. E. *Perception and communication*. New York: Pergamon Press, 1958.

Cain, C. J., and Lass, N. J. Listening rate preferences of adults. In S. Duker (Ed.), *Time-compressed speech*. Metuchen, New Jersey: Scarecrow Press, 1974. Pp. 674–678.

Calearo, C., and Lazzaroni, A. Speech intelligibility in relation to the speed of the message. *Laryngoscope*, 1957, *67*, 410–419.

Campanella, S. J. Signal analysis of speech time-compression techniques. In E. Foulke (Ed.), *Proceedings of Louisville Conference on Time-Compressed Speech*. Louisville: University of Louisville, 1967.

Coleman, E. Responses to a scale of grammaticalness. *Journal of Verbal Learning and Verbal Behavior*, 1965, *4*, 521–527.

Cramer, H. L. The intelligibility of time-compressed speech. In E. Foulke (Ed.), *Proceedings of Louisville Conference Time-Compressed Speech*. Louisville: Univ. of Louisville, 1967.

Daniloff, R. G., and Hammarberg, R. On defining coarticulation. *Journal of Phonetics*, 1974, *1*, 185–194.

Daniloff, R. G., Shriner, T. H., and Zemlin, W. R. Intelligibility of vowels altered in duration and frequency. *Journal of the Acoustical Society of America*, 1968, *44*, 700–707.

deQuiros, J. Accelerated speech audiometry, an examination of test results. (Trans. by J. Tonndorf). *Transactions of The Beltone Institute of Hearing Research, No. 17.* Chicago: Beltone Institute of Hearing Research, 1964.

Dudley, H. Remaking speech. *Journal of The Acoustical Society of America*, 1939, *11*, 169—177.

Enc, M. E., and Stolurow, L. M. A comparison of the effects of two recording speeds on learning and retention. *New Outlook for the Blind*, 1960, *54*, 39—48.

Fairbanks, G., Everitt, W. L., and Jaeger, R. P. Methods for time or frequency compression-expansion of speech. *Transactions of I.R.E.—P.G.A. AU—2*, 1954, 7—12.

Fairbanks, G., and Grubb, P. A psychophysical investigation of vowel formants. *Journal of Speech and Hearing Research*, 1961, *4*, 203—219.

Fairbanks, G., Guttman, N., and Miron, M. S. Auditory comprehension of repeated high-speed messages. *Journal of Speech and Hearing Disorders*, 1957, *22*, 10—19.

Fairbanks, G., and Kodman, F. Word intelligibility as a function of time compression. *Journal of Acoustical Society of America*, 1957, *29*, 636—641.

Fay, W. H. *Temporal sequence in the perception of speech.* The Hague: Mouton, 1966.

Fergen, G. Listening comprehension at controlled rates for children in grades IV, V, and VI. Unpublished doctoral dissertation, Univ. of Missouri, 1955.

Flanagan, J. L. *Speech analysis synthesis and perception.* New York: Springer-Verlag, 1972.

Flanagan, J. L., and Golden, R. M. Phase vocoder. *Bell System Technical Journal*, 1966, *45*, 1493—1509.

Fletcher, H. *Speech and hearing in communications.* New York: Van Nostrand, 1965.

Foulke, E. A comparison of two methods of compressing speech. Paper presented at Southeastern Psychological Association, Louisville, March 1962.

Foulke, E. A survey of the acceptability of rapid speech. *New Outlook for the Blind*, 1966, *60*, 261—265. (a)

Foulke, E. Comparison of comprehension of two forms of compressed speech. *Journal of Exceptional Children*, 1966, *33*, 169—173. (b)

Foulke, E. The perception of time compressed speech. In D. Horton and J. Jenkins (Eds.), *The perception of language.* Columbus, Ohio: Charles E. Merrill, 1971. Pp. 79—107.

Garvey, W. D. The intelligibility of abbreviated speech patterns. *Quarterly Journal of Speech*, 1953, *39*, 296—306. (a)

Garvey, W. D. The intelligibility of speeded speech. *Journal of Experimental Psychology*, 1953, *45*, 102—108. (b)

Gerstman, L. J. Classification of self-normalized vowels. IEEE *Transactions on Audio and Electroacoustics*, 1968, *AU—16*, 78—80.

Gerver, D., Effects of grammaticalness, presentation rate, and message length on auditory short-term memory. *Quarterly Journal of Experimental Psychology*, 1969, *21*, 203—208.

Gold, B. Techniques for speech bandwidth compression using combinations of channel vocoders and formant vocoders. *Journal of the Acoustical Society of America*, 1965, 38, 2—10.

Golden, R. M. Digital computer simulation of a sampled-data voice excited vocoder. *Journal of Acoustical Society of America*, 1963, *35*, 1358—1367.

Goldstein, H. Reading and listening comprehension at various controlled rates. *Contributions to Education No. 821, Teachers College, Columbia University.* New York: Bureau of Publications, Teachers College, 1940.

Guttman, N., and Nelson, J. An instrument that creates some artificial speech spectra for the severely hard of hearing. *American Annals of the Deaf*, 1968, *113*, 295—302.

Harris, J. D. Combinations of distortion in speech: The twenty-five percent safety factor by multiple-cueing. *Archives of Otolaryngology*, 1960, *72*, 227—232.

Harwood, D. Listenability and rate of presentation. *Speech Monographs*, 1955, *22*, 57—59.

Haskins, H. A phonetically balanced test of speech discrimination for children. Unpublished Master's thesis, Northwestern Univ. Evanston, Illinois, 1949.

Hirsh, I. J., Davis, H., Silverman, S. R., Reynolds, E. G., Eldert, E., and Bensen, R. W. Development of materials for speech audiometry. *Journal of Speech and Hearing Disorders*, 1952, *17*, 321—337.

Huggins, A. W. F. Distortion of the temporal pattern of speech: Interruption and alternation. *Journal of the Acoustical Society of America*, 1964, *36*, 1055—1064.

Huggins, A. W. F. Second experiment in temporally segmented speech. *Quarterly Progress Report,* M.I.T. 1972, *106,* 137—141.

Jerger, J. Observations on auditory lesions in the central auditory pathways. *Archives of Otolaryngology,* 1960, *71,* 797—806.

Johansson, B. The use of the transposer for the management of the deaf child. *International Audiology,* 1966, *5,* 363—372.

Johansson, B., and Wedenberg, E., Speech compression techniques applied to aids for the hard of hearing. (1) Hearing aids. *Quartery Progress Speech Research* (Speech Transmission Lab.), 1960, *1,* 25—26.

Katz, J., and Burge, C. Auditory perception training for children with learning disabilities. *Menorah Medical Journal,* 1971, *2,* 18—29.

King, K. M., and Weston, P. L. The effect of the percentage of time compression, sentence length, and age on children's recall performance of well-formed sentences. Paper presented at Annual Convention of the American Speech and Hearing Association, Las Vegas, Nevada, November 5—8, 1974.

Klumpp, R. G., and Webster, J. C. Intelligibility of time compressed speech. *Journal of the Acoustical Society of America,* 1961, *33,* 265—267.

Konkle, D. F., Beasley, D. S., and Bess, F. H. A study of time-compressed speech with an elderly population. Paper presented at the Annual Convention of the American Speech and Hearing Association, Las Vegas, Nevada, November 5—8, 1974.

Kozhevnikov, V. A., and Chistovich, L. A. *Speech: Articulation and perception.* Joint Publications Research Services—30543, Clearing House for Federal Scientific Technical Information, U.S. Dept. of Commerce, National Bureau of Standards, Washington, D.C., 1965.

Kuhl, P., and Speaks, C. Temporal processing of speech. Paper presented at the Meeting of the Acoustical Society of America, Buffalo, New York, April 18—21, 1972.

Kurdziel, S., and Noffsinger, D. Performance of cortical lesion patients on 40% and 60% time compressed speech materials. Paper presented at the Annual Convention of the American Speech and Hearing Association, Detroit, Michigan, October 12—15, 1973.

Kurdziel, S., Rintelmann, W. F., and Beasley, D. S. Performance of noise-induced hearing-impaired persons on time-compressed CNC monosyllables. *Journal of the American Audiology Society,* 1975, in press.

Kurtzrock, G. H. The effects of time and frequency distortion upon word intelligibility. Unpublished doctoral dissertation, Univ. of Illinois, 1957.

Lass, N. J., and Cain, C. J. A correlational study of listening rate preferences and listeners' oral reading rates. *Journal of Auditory Research,* 1972, *12,* 308—312.

Lass, N. J., Foulke, E., Nester, A. A., and Comerci, J. The effect of exposure to time-compressed speech on subjects' listening rate preferences and listening comprehension skills. *Journal of Auditory Research,* 1976, in press.

Lass, N. J., and Fultz, V. A. A normative study of children's listening rate preferences. *Language and Speech,* 1976, in press.

Lass, N. J. and Prater, C. E. A comparative study of listening rate preferences for oral reading and impromptu speaking tasks. *Journal of Communication,* 1973, *23,* 95—102.

Lee, F. F. Time compression and expansion of speech by the sampling method. *Journal of Audio Engineering Society,* 1972, *20,* 738—742.

Ling, D. Three experiments on frequency transposition. *American Annals of the Deaf,* 1968, *113,* 283—294.

Ling, D., and Doehring, D. G. Learning limits of deaf children for coded speech. *Journal of Speech and Hearing Research,* 1969, *12,* 83—94.

Ling, D., and Druz, W. S. Transposition of high frequency sounds by partial vocoding of the speech spectrum: Its use by deaf children. *Journal of Auditory Research,* 1967, *7,* 133—144.

Ling, D., and Maretic, H. Frequency transposition in the teaching of speech to deaf children. *Journal of and Hearing Research,* 1971, *14,* 37—46.

Luterman, D. M., Welsh, O. L., and Melrose, J. Responses of aged males to time-altered speech stimuli. *Journal of Speech and Hearing Research,* 1966, *9,* 226—230.

McLain, J. R., A comparison of two methods of producing rapid speech. *International Journal for the Education of the Blind,* 1962, *12,* 40—43.

Maki, J. E., Beasley, D. S., and Orchik, D. J. Children's perception of time-compressed speech using two measures of speech discrimination. *Journal of Speech and Hearing Disorders*, 1975, in press.

Miller, G. A. The magical number seven, plus or minus two: Some limits to our capacity for processing information. *Psychological Review*, 1956, *63*, 81—97.

Miller, G. A., and Licklider, J. C. R. The intelligibility of interrupted speech. *Journal of the Acoustical Society of America*, 1950, *22*, 167—173.

Miscik, J., Smith, J., Hamm, N., Deffenbacher, K., and Brown, E. Short-term retention of auditory sequences as a function of stimulus duration, interstimulus interval, and encoding technique. *Journal of Experimental Psychology*, 1972, *96*, 147—151.

Nelson, H. The effect of variations of rates on the recall by radio listeners of straight newscasts. *Speech Monographs*, 1948, *15*, 178—180.

Orchik, D., and Oeschlager M. Time-compressed speech discrimination in children: Its relationship to articulation ability. Paper presented at the Annual Convention of the American Speech and Hearing Association, Las Vegas, Nevada, November 5—8, 1974.

Osgood, C. E. Motivational dynamics of language behavior. In M. P. Jones (Ed.), *Nebraska Symposium on Motivation*. Lincoln: Univ. of Nebraska Press, 1957. Pp. 348—424.

Pantalos, J., Schuckers, G. H., and Hipskind, N. Sentence length duration relationships in an auditory assembly task. *Journal of Communication Disorders*, 1975, *8*, 61—74.

Peterson, G. E., and Barney, H. L. Control methods used in a study of the vowels. *Journal of the Acoustical Society of America*, 1952, *24*, 175—184.

Picard, M., and Bode, D. L. Slow-played speech with and without time restoration: A phonemic analysis. Paper presented at the Meeting of the Acoustical Society of America, Los Angeles, California, October 30—November 2, 1973.

Pimonow, L. The application of synthetic speech to aural rehabilitation. *Journal of Auditory Research*, 1963, *3*, 73—82.

Powers, G. L., and Speaks, C. Intelligibility of temporally interrupted speech. *Journal of the Acoustical Society of America*, 1973, *54*, 661—667.

Raymond, T. H., and Proud, G. O. Audiofrequency conversion. *Archives Oto-Laryngology*, 1962, *76*, 436—446.

Rintelmann, W. F., and Beasley, D. S. Time-altered speech discrimination test. Unpublished manuscript, Michigan State University, 1974.

Rintelmann, W., Beasley, D., Linn, G., Forman, B., and Ciliax, D. Performance of individuals with central auditory lesions on time-compressed CNC monosyllables. Unpublished manuscript, Michigan State University, 1974.

Rintelmann, W. F., and Jetty, B. Unpublished manuscript, Michigan State University, 1968.

Ross, M., and Lerman, J. A picture identification test for hearing-impaired children. *Journal of Speech and Hearing Research*, 1970, *13*, 44—53.

Schill, M. J., and Schuckers, G. H. Auditory assembly of non-prosodic sentences by children. *Journal of Communication Disorders*, 1973, *6*, 303—314.

Schroeder, M. R. Vocoders: Analysis and synthesis of speech. *I.E.E.E. Transactions on Audio-Electroacoustics*, 1966, *AU—54*, 720—734.

Schuckers, G. H., Shriner, T. H., and Daniloff, R. G. Auditory reassembly of segmented sentences by children. *Journal of Speech and Hearing Research*, 1973, *16*, 116—127.

Seidel, S. J. The PICSI Test: Picture identification for children—a standardized index. Unpublished Master's thesis, Indiana University, 1963.

Shriner, T. H., Beasley, D. S., and Zemlin, W. R. The effects of frequency division on speech identification in children. *Journal of Speech and Hearing Research*, 1969, *12*, 413—422.

Shriner, T. H., and Daniloff, R. G. Reassembly of segmented CVC syllables by children. *Journal of Speech and Hearing Research*, 1970, *13*, 537—547.

Shriner, T., and Sprague, R. Effects of time-compressed speech signals on children's identification accuracy and latency measures. *Journal of Experimental Child Psychology*, 1969, *7*, 532—540.

Slawson, A. Vowel quality and musical timbre as functions of spectrum envelope and fundamental frequence. *Journal of the Acoustical Society of America*, 1968, *43*, 87—101.

Speaks, C., and Jerger, J. Method for measurement of speech identification. *Journal of Speech and Hearing Research*, 1965, *8*, 185—194.

Speaks, C., and Trooien, T. T. Interaural alternation and speech intelligibility. *Journal of the Acoustical Society of America*, 1974, *56*, 640—644.

Sticht, T. G. Learning by listening in relation to aptitude, reading and rate-controlled speech. *HumRRO Technical Report 69—23*, Dept. of the Army, 1969.

Sticht, T. G. Learning by listening in relation to aptitude, reading and rate-controlled speech: Additional Studies. *HumRRO Technical Report 71—75*, Dept. of the Army, 1971.

Sticht, T. G., and Gray, B. B. The intelligibility of time-compressed words as a function of age and hearing loss. *Journal of Speech and Hearing Research*, 1969, *12*, 443—448.

Takefuta, Y., and Swigart, E. Intelligibility of speech signals spectrally compressed by a sampling-synthesizing technique. *I.E.E.E. Transactions on Audio-Electroacoustics*, 1968, *AU—16*, 271—274.

Thompson, N. W. Comprehension of rate-controlled speech of varying linguistic complexity by normal children. Paper presented at the Annual Convention of the American Speech and Hearing Association, Detroit, Michigan, October 12—15, 1973.

Tiffany, W. R., and Bennett, D. N. The intelligibility of slow-played speech. *Journal of Speech and Hearing Research*, 1961, *4*, 248—258.

Tillman, T., and Carhart, R. An expanded test for speech discrimination using CNC monosyllabic words (N.U. Auditory Test No. 6). Technical Report No. *SAM-RT-66-55*, U.S.A. Air Force School of Aerospace Medicine, Brooks Air Force Base, Texas, June, 1966.

Vilbig, F., and Haase, K. H. Some systems for speech band-compression. *Journal of the Acoustical Society of America*, 1956, *28*, 573—577.

Voiers, W. D. The present state of digital vocoding technique: A diagnostic evaluation. *I.E.E.E. Transactions on Audio-Electroacoustics*, 1968, *AU—16*, 275—279.

Williams, C. E., and Hecker, M. H. L. Relation between intelligibility scores for four test methods and three types of speech distortion. *Journal of the Acoustical Society of America*, 1968, *44*, 1002—1006.

Wingfield, A., and Wheale, J. Interaural alternation, information load, and speech intelligibility. *Journal of the Acoustical Society of America*, 1975, *57*, 1219—1220.

Zemlin, W. R. The use of bandwidth and time compression for the hard of hearing handicapped. In E. Foulke (Ed.), *Proceedings of Louisville Conference on Time-Compressed Speech*. Louisville: Univ. of Louisville, 1967.

Zemlin, W. R., Daniloff, R. G., and Shriner, T. H. The difficulty of listening to time-compressed speech. *Journal of Speech and Hearing Research*, 1968, *11*, 875—881.

chapter 13

Perceptual Psychophysics: Speech and Hearing

John F. Brandt

University of Kansas, Lawrence

A student of the various areas of speech and hearing science spends much time reading the literature. If the reader is literally a *student*, he reads primarily what is assigned. If the student is at the faculty level or is an active professional worker, the reading content often becomes more variable. In each case, what is read is determined largely by the reader's special interests.

What are the determining factors? There are two major influences. The first is personal. The personality and special interest of the student are important, but what is read or studied may be determined by the personality and specific interests of the student's major professor. The following is a rather self-evident example of this personal influence. Somewhere, at an earlier time, a colleague of mine consistently described his professional interest as *vowel perception*. For many years his research and teaching emphasized the use of a sound spectrograph and the acoustic descriptions of vowels. Indeed, most of the literature assigned to students for study in the professor's experimental phonetics course concerned spectrographic data. The literature provides no indication that his interest has gone beyond *vowel perception*. Indeed, there are indications that the personal influence of this professor has affected at least one of his recent, but now graduated, students who described his own professional interests and expertise to a group of colleagues as being primarily *vowel perception*.

A second influence which often determines the special interest of a student is *the system*, which will remain undefined for the moment. This is slightly broader in scope than *vowel perception*. It can, of course, be influenced by the personality factors just described. The *system* influence can be broad in the sense of hearing science versus speech science, speech pathology versus audiology, and so forth. Examine your academic training program, whether it lies in the past or is current. The hearing courses are probably separate from the speech courses. This separation may emphasize the biases of the various disciplines or produce student factions; hearing versus speech, science versus clinic, and so on.

Examine your professional organizations. It is likely that the convention programs consist of technical sessions with speech and hearing programs scheduled concurrently. Additionally, the basic science and the clinical sessions are kept separate in some way. Your professional organization even may publish separate journals for the various disciplines.

These two influences—*personal* and *system*—can be good if they exist for only a short time and are present only for efficiency, or bad, if they produce total disregard for the various disciplines. The speech, hearing, and language sciences have produced so much data in the past few years that it is impossible for a *student* to be a generalist with somewhat equal facility in these three areas. If one were to assimilate small, but equal, amounts of data from these three areas, probably he would be accused of knowing a little about a lot and not enough of anything in particular. However, these two influences often result in compartmentalization; one is a speech scientist *or* a hearing scientist *or* a language scientist. Yet it is the *total process* of human communication that we hope to understand. A more scientific outlook would be to suggest that each of the three disciplines is only part of the total model of human communication.

A model of human communication always must include speech and hearing and language. Examine Figure 13.1. It is the *speech chain* described by many (viz., Denes and Pinson, 1973); an interactive model, it demonstrates the almost never-ending sequence of physical, physiological, or psychological activities which contribute to the

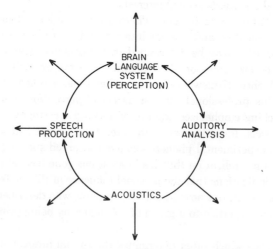

Figure 13.1   A representation of the processes of human speech communication. The acoustic signal is the input to the auditory system and can result from speech production. The brain–language system is interactive for both speech production and auditory analysis. The arrows extending outward represent the *or* scientist who selects a single interest area and often fails to take account of the interactive nature of the several processes of speech communication.

human communication process. The outward-extending arrows represent the *or* scientist—the student who is a *specialist in vowel perception* who escapes from the total picture and lives outside the communication process in his own little world.

However, regardless of the influences, the issue is that the general student too often is of the *or* variety. The issue is evidenced in a statement taken not too far out of context from a thought-provoking article by Rees (1973). This article is re-commended reading for all persons interested in this issue. Particularly pertinent are such statements as: "First, to infer anything about the perception of speech from data on the perception of nonspeech is *unjustifiable*. Speech perception *cannot* be predicted from analyses of the acoustic properties of spoken utterances *plus* the characteristics of the human auditory system" (p. 308, emphasis added).

Can the understanding of the total human communication process lack knowledge of the characteristics of the auditory system? All process models include the auditory signal and the auditory system. Certainly speech perception requires these processes. What follows in this chapter is an academic exercise in attempting to explain just how the author's last experiment in speech science evolved from his background in hearing science. The emphasis is upon the phenomenon of pitch as it clearly transcends speech, hearing, and language.

Hearing Science and Pitch

Hearing scientists generally have studied pitch perception with reference to the nature of the processes responsible for the mediation of pitch. In the simplest sense, data are interpreted to support two mechanisms of pitch perception: a place mech-anism *and* a neural mechanism. The emphasis upon *and* is made in spite of the fact that certain data can be explained best by a place mechanism and other data can be explained best (or only) by a neural mechanism. The diversity between place theo-rists and neural theorists within hearing science is sometimes as great as that between the hearing scientist and speech scientist.

Place Mechanism

In its simplest form, the place mechanism is a cochlear mechanism. Such a mechanism takes advantage of the fact that the cochlea or, more precisely, the basilar membrane and the structures thereon, exhibit mechanical responses to sinusoidal acoustic signals that vary in place (location) along the cochlea. This mechanical activity is located toward the basal end of the cochlea for high-frequency sinusoids and toward the apical end of the cochlea for low-frequency sinusoids. Thus, the mechanical activity of the cochlea has a specific location that is dependent upon the stimulus frequency.

Such a place mechanism also takes advantage of the fact that afferent auditory nerve fibers originate from the base of the hair cells located along the basilar mem-brane. Fibers originating from the basal end of the cochlea are stimulated by high-frequency mechanical activity. Fibers originating from the apical end of the cochlea are stimulated by low-frequency mechanical activity. Further, the low-frequency fibers and the high-frequency fibers can be traced through several levels of the auditory nervous system. This spatial organization is known as *tonotopic organization*. The result is that the frequency—place relationship of the cochlea is preserved in the nervous system. While certainly an oversimplification, the place mechanism implies that each location along the basilar membrane has its own specific nerve fiber that is responsive to its own specific frequency.

Pitch is coded by the place mechanism in a manner shown in Figure 13.2. A high-frequency stimulus produces mechanical activity at the basal end of the cochlea. Nerve fibers are stimulated, and the presence of this neural activity ultimately produces the perception of a high pitch. A low-frequency stimulus produces neural activity in the apical end of the cochlea, and this neural activity is coded as a low pitch. Where no mechanical (place) activity occurs, no neural activity is generated, and thus there is no pitch. In its simplest form, the presence of neural activity in any fiber signifies pitch.

Neural Mechanism

A neural mechanism does not depend totally upon the place—frequency arrangement of the cochlea and the nervous system. Rather, the important elements for frequency analysis lie in the neural discharge rates and patterns of several nerve fibers. A neural mechanism recognizes that a single nerve fiber receives stimulation from several hair cells spread over a limited area of the basilar membrane. Addition-

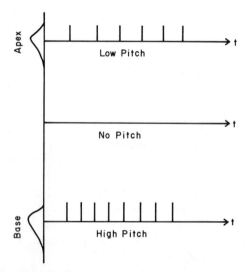

Figure 13.2 A representation of pitch coding by a place mechanism of hearing. Mechanical activity along the basilar membrane results in neural activity which carries the appropriate pitch information. Absence of mechanical activity produces no pitch information. The presence of neural activity is represented at various locations along the cochlea as a function of time (*t*).

ally, a single hair cell may innervate several nerve fibers. Although the area of mechanical stimulation is broad, the location of membrane stimulation is still determined by the place—frequency arrangement.

Perhaps the most common example of the neural mechanism is the volley activity of groups of neurons shown schematically in Figure 13.3. Two neurons are stimulated by the place activity. Both neurons are firing at the same discharge rate but at different cycles of the stimulus waveform. The nervous system sums the slow discharge rates of the two neurons and produces an effective neural discharge equal in frequency to the temporal waveform frequency. Thus, the neural discharge of several neurons carries the appropriate pitch information.

Periodicity Pitch

The existence of two mechanisms for pitch perception is well documented, but, while described as separate mechanisms, both are actually place mechanisms when simple acoustic stimuli, such as sinusoids, are analyzed. The place mechanism implies that frequency is coded from the place—frequency arrangement of the cochlea and that neural activity, per se, from the appropriate place, mediates pitch. The nervous system is viewed as a transmitter, and not as an analyzer, of pitch information. On the other hand, the neural mechanism implies that pitch is mediated by an analysis of total neural discharge. While the neural stimulus is determined by place activity, it takes into account the anatomical arrangements of several fibers and hair cells spread over a somewhat broad area and certain limitations of individual nerve cell firing rates. At high stimulus frequencies (above about 3000 Hz), the neural volleying breaks down, and simple place mechanisms are used to account for very high pitches.

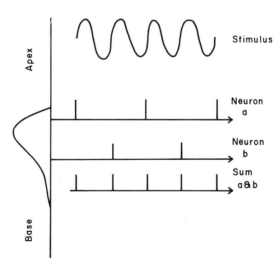

Figure 13.3 A representation of the neural coding of frequency by a volley principle. Several neurons respond at their own rate to mechanical activity. The sum of the neural activity of several fibers (pitch) is identical to the frequency of mechanical activity.

When a complex acoustic stimulus is presented to a listener, (e.g., a 2200 Hz sinusoid interrupted 150 times a second), a different situation exists that presents great difficulty for a simple place mechanism. Such a stimulus is heard as having a low pitch. Said another way, this complex, high-frequency stimulus is heard not as a high pitch but as a low pitch (equivalent to the pitch of a 150 Hz sinusoid) which corresponds to the interruption rate. Analysis of the acoustic signal with its high-frequency energy predicts place activity at the basal end of the cochlea and, because of the absence of energy at the low frequency, no place activity is present in the apical regions of the cochlea. A place theory would predict a high pitch, yet the listener assigns a low pitch to the complex sound.

Figure 13.4 diagrams the situation. The physical energy produces basal place activity, and the nervous system shows neural activity which is synchronous with the periodicity of the waveform envelope. The neural activity occurs at the low (interruption) rate and is coded as a low pitch. No place activity, and thus no neural activity, occurs at the apical end of the cochlea. The low pitch is originating from the *wrong* place.

Several experiments exist in the psychoacoustic literature dealing with the phenomenon of periodicity pitch and presumed pitch analyzers (Small, 1970; Wightman, 1973a, b). That periodicity pitch is coded from neural activity of the basal regions of the cochlea is shown best by masking experiments (Small and Campbell, 1961). A place activity resulting from a low-frequency narrowband of masking noise is located in the apical regions of the cochlea. This narrowband noise should mask out the low pitch if the analyzer is located in the apical regions of the cochlea. The Small and Campbell data show that no reasonable amount of masking noise will eliminate

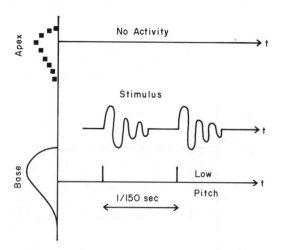

Figure 13.4 A representation of the coding of neural information leading to periodicity pitch. The stimulus is a train of damped high-frequency sine waves. Mechanical activity of the basilar membrane at the basal end of the cochlea would, by a place theory, dictate the perception of a high pitch. The nervous system, however, responds to the low repetition rate of the signal, which results in the perception of a low pitch. No neural activity is generated in the low-frequency region of the cochlea.

the low pitch. On the other hand, if the narrow-band noise is located at the basal regions of the cochlea, the low pitch is eliminated (masked out) with a very small amount of noise energy. The explanation of the experimental results centers around the fact that the nervous system is unable to synchronize adequately the neural firing rate with the envelope waveform because of the presence of the noise. The same fibers must also fire randomly to the continuous masking noise activity; thus temporal synchrony is lost.

The presence of neural activity, which is synchronous with the temporal characteristics of the acoustic stimulus, has been somewhat illusive (Plomp and Smoorenburg, 1970). Glattke (1969), however, using nonspeech signals, has demonstrated that the proper acting neurons do exist in the cochlear nucleus of the cat. These fibers apparently originate from the basal regions of the cochlea. No fibers that were synchronized with the waveform were found originating from apical regions. More recently, Kiang and Moxon (1974) demonstrated neural discharge rates in cats which were synchronous with major peaks in a vowel /æ/ waveform in both low-frequency and high-frequency 8th nerve fibers. Importantly, low-frequency masking noise obscured changes in gross discharge rate in low-frequency fibers and reduced the synchrony of discharges in high-frequency fibers.

Moore and Cashin (1974) recorded single unit responses from the cochlear nucleus of the guinea pig that were evoked by excerpts from human-produced vowels. A male speaker produced a CV utterance containing one of 10 vowels beginning with the consonant /b/. Segments beginning about 50 msec into the sustained vowel were used as stimuli. "These segments consisted of a single pitch period of the vowel (approximately 8 msec in duration)." The samples were stored in computer memory and then "regenerated in strings of five vowel sounds, each vowel consisting of five repetitions of the pitch period excerpted from the original analog signal of that vowel" (p. 1566).

Moore and Cashin described four different classes of neuron response which were based upon examination of PST histograms. The striking aspect of their data was the clear temporal nature of the neuronal responses. Almost all of the histograms showed a relatively clear periodicity of neural responses of about the rate of the pitch period of the vowel stimuli. Even more interesting was the result that additional energy placed in high-frequency inhibitory regions of the neuron tended to "sharpen" the responses in the *temporal* domain, producing more clearly defined response patterns to the fundamental frequency of the vowel stimuli.

It appears that a basic response of neurons in the 8th nerve and in the regions of the cochlear nucleus to human speech signals is related to the fundamental frequency of the speech signals. Further, inhibitory activity can modify the temporal characteristics of neural activity.

Another way to avoid spectral cues and minimize specific place analysis is to examine the periodicity pitch which comes from interrupted white noise (Small, 1955). A rather weak periodicity pitch corresponds to the interruption rate. Since the spectrum of interrupted noise is continuous rather than selective, as for interrupted sinusoids, the cue for pitch must be temporal in nature.

Jittered Pulses

How synchronous must the neural activity and the stimulus waveform envelope be for periodicity pitch perception? As was suggested above in reference to the masking experiments, the neural activity loses its synchrony with the waveform envelope because the nerve fibers also must fire asynchronously to a masking stimulus. In effect, the pitch analyzer is unable to separate the necessary synchronized neural activity from the unsynchronized activity. Considered in another way, the neural activity exhibits *jitter*. How much asynchrony or jitter in firing rate can be tolerated before periodicity pitch perception is destroyed? Rosenberg (1966) and Cardozo and Ritsma (1968), in various ways, asked listeners to determine the just-noticeable difference of pulse trains that varied in the amount of jitter around a mean pulse period. Both investigations used normally distributed interpulse periods, although Cardozo and Ritsma used quasi-Gaussian and Poisson distributions as well. The listeners apparently heard a relatively clear periodicity pitch if the mean pulse period did not vary by more than 10%. However, if the pulse period varied (jittered) by more than about 10%, the listeners described the stimuli as having lost their pitch. Said another way, the pitch analyzer will tolerate approximately a 10% variation in pulse periods and will assign a pitch which is about equal to the mean (or perhaps modal) pulse period. The pitch analyzer must be using the statistical (distribution) characteristics of the instantaneous pulse periods and thus is able to tolerate some jitter (asynchrony) in neural firing rates.

Pitch of Noise

Certain pitch phenomena are not easily explained by either a strict place or neural mechanism. For example, a noise stimulus results in a perception of pitch under certain conditions. If one listens to a narrow band of noise which increases in center frequency from low to high, one perceives the change in center frequency as an increase in pitch. The pitch quality is best with narrow bands of noise (e.g., 100 Hz or less), but it can be heard even with octave bands of noise. Similarly, if one listens to a wide band of noise and the low-frequency cutoff is increased, one hears an increase in pitch that is clearly dependent upon the increasing cutoff frequency. If one listens to wideband noise and changes the high-frequency cutoff, the pitch is related to the cutoff frequency when it exceeds about 600 Hz (Small and Daniloff, 1967). Von Bekesy (1963) demonstrated that an octave band of noise elicited two pitches, each corresponding to the cutoff frequencies of the noise. On the other hand, Ekdahl and Boring (1934) had shown earlier that narrow bands of tonal masses (eight sinusoids spaced at regular but inharmonic intervals) elicited a pitch corresponding to the center frequency of the masses.

To summarize the pitch characteristics of continuous noise, we find that narrow bands of noise, or narrow, inharmonic, tonal masses, elicit a pitch corresponding to the center of the band, while noises with cutoff frequencies generate pitch perceptions corresponding to the edges (cutoff frequencies) of the acoustic spectrum. Remembering that our description of a neural mechanism for pitch analysis required some sort of regular firing rate, which corresponded either to the temporal characteristics of a sinusoid or to the periodicity in a complex wave, we can predict that this mechanism will not adequately extract pitch information from random neural impulses such as those produced by random noises. The place mechanism also would have great difficulty in extracting pitch information because it depends more or less upon frequency-specific, mechanical, basilar membrane activity. The place of maximal activity determines pitch. If a noise produces a broad maximum, the place mechanism should produce the perception of several pitches, not simply a pitch corresponding to the cutoff frequencies. A combination of the place and neural mechanisms provides a first approximation to explain the pitch of noise (von Bekesy, 1960, 1963). Mechanical (place) activity along the membrane shows maximum activity within the noise band, but a decreasing amount of activity at the edges of the band near the cutoff frequency of the acoustic spectrum. The nervous system monitors the edge of the excitation pattern and, perhaps through some funneling or sharpening activity, extracts a relatively specific pitch. Since the cutoff frequency is at the edge of the mechanical excitation, the pitch corresponds best to that region. The point of this brief description is that noise stimuli can produce pitch sensations and that more complex pitch analyzers are required for explanations.

Pitch of Frequency-Modulated Signals

Hearing scientists have used frequency-modulated (FM) auditory signals in many kinds of experiments. Investigations of frequency differential thresholds (Brandt, 1967), phase perception (Goldstein, 1967), and certain pitch perceptions related to the fine structure of the acoustic waveform (Fischler, 1967) are found in the literature. Some of the more interesting experiments using FM signals relate to the limited-resolution Fourier analysis performed by the auditory system (Plomp and Mimpen, 1968; McClelland and Brandt, 1969).

One thing is certain in all such experiments: An FM auditory signal elicits a variety of pitch perceptions which are dependent upon the acoustic characteristics of the particular signal employed and the analysis capabilities of the auditory system.

More importantly for our present purposes, a free-response experiment, in which the listener is free to find any pitch he hears in an FM signal, results in the perception of not one (single) pitch, but many pitches. McClelland and Brandt (1969) presented 300, 1000, and 3000 Hz sinusoids, frequency modulated at modulation frequencies of 20 and 200 Hz, to listeners who were instructed to match the pitch of a single sinusoid to the pitch of the FM signal. Each of 200 pitch matches was recorded for each stimulus condition. The nature of the distributions of these pitch matches was dependent upon the frequency spacing of the individual spectral components and the limited filter analysis provided by the auditory system. Pitch matches occurred to individual spectral components when their spacing exceeded critical bandwidths. When the spacings of the components were less than critical bandwidths, pitch matches that resulted were appropriate to the center of the critical bands, located randomly within the bands, or at the sharp edges of the bands of spectral energy. These matches suggest that the ear is able to perform a long-term spectral analysis upon complex, ongoing auditory signals, provided the spacing of the components exceeds the resolving power (critical bandwidths) of the auditory system. The several pitches found in sinusoidally frequency-modulated signals are thus predictable. If the individual component spacings cannot be resolved, the pitch matches are predictable only when the edges of the spectrum are very sharp. Such matches are similar to the pitch perceptions of bandpassed, or high- or low-passed noises (Small and Daniloff, 1967). If the spectral edges are not sharp, the several pitches appear to be randomly distributed within the energy band.

Pitch of Signals with Frequency Transitions

Another type of signal used by both speech and hearing scientists is the stimulus which often begins with a fixed frequency (burst) and, following a transition period, ends at a different frequency. Their difference from sinusoidal FM signals described above lies in the constant termination frequencies rather than a constantly increasing and decreasing frequency.

Several experiments have examined the various parameters of the signal, including the duration of the bursts (both initial and final), the extent of frequency transition, and the rates of change in frequency (Brady, House, and Stevens, 1961; Pollack, 1968; Tsumura, Sone, and Nimura, 1973). A particularly valuable series of experiments, because of their contribution to both speech and hearing science, has been reported by Nábělek and Hirsh (1969) and Nábělek, Nábělek, and Hirsh (1970, 1973).

Nábělek and Hirsh (1969) asked listeners to detect the just-noticeable difference in frequency transition in tone bursts having linear increases or decreases in the early portions of the burst followed by a constant frequency portion at the end of each burst. Their data support the conclusion that the auditory system, when appropriate, makes use of one of two mechanisms to discriminate rates of change in frequency. If the rate of frequency change is rapid and the frequency change is slow, especially when the frequency difference is small, the cue for detection seems to be some minimum duration of change. The same conclusions have been arrived at independently by Pollack (1968) and Tsumura et al. (1973).

The cues for differential sensitivity of frequency change, however, say little about pitch, per se. In a second study, Nábělek et al. (1970) asked listeners to match the pitch of a constant frequency tone burst to the pitch of the transition bursts. Thus, some of the test bursts were changing constantly in frequency, and some bursts had, along with a frequency transition, initial and terminal frequencies. The burst durations ranged from 12 to 500 msec. Five or six pitch matches were made to each test stimulus. The data show that tone bursts with a linear change in frequency over the entire burst produce two kinds of pitch perceptions. If the burst durations are short and the frequency change is small, the pitch generally corresponds to a frequency in the center of the range. If the frequency change is large or the rate of change is slow, the pitch takes a value in the direction of, but not as high as, the terminal frequency.

When the frequency transition is preceded or followed by a constant frequency, the pitch judgments tend to be toward the frequency portion with the longest duration.

If, for example, the burst consisted of a transition region of increasing frequency for 10 msec followed by 30 msec of a fixed frequency, the pitch would take the value of the terminal frequency. If, however, the burst consisted of a 30-msec portion of constant frequency followed by a 10-msec portion of increasing frequency, the pitch would generally be at, or close to, the initial frequency. When the frequency transition was in the center of the burst (i.e., bracketed by fixed initial and final frequencies), subjects tended to provide pitch judgments which corresponded to both the initial and final frequencies. Apparently, they would choose either, and sometimes both, of the frequencies for pitch cues. One listener chose pitches which randomly distributed between the endpoints. If the bursts were quite short, the pitch judgments tended to be toward the frequency regions having the longest duration. Their data make it clear that tone bursts with frequency transitions can produce varied pitch judgments that are dependent upon the stimulus parameters. Several pitches can be detected, and sometimes only a single pitch is heard.

The stimuli used in the study mentioned above always consisted of continuous connections of tone. In a third experiment, Nábělek *et al.* (1973) asked how important was the continuous presence of sound for the occurrence of the different types of pitch judgments. What would the pitch percept be if only differing initial and final frequencies were presented? These investigators asked listeners to adjust the steady frequency of a test burst to equal the pitch of test bursts with a continuous or a discontinuous change in frequency. Those bursts with a discontinuous frequency transition were designated as *pause-bursts*, while those bursts with a continuous frequency transition were called *glide-bursts*.

The results of the experiment demonstrate that a frequency transition is not necessary for fusion (one pitch) or separation (two pitches). If the frequency difference is small (e.g., 60 Hz), the pitch percept falls at a frequency about midway between the initial and final frequencies of the burst. If the frequency difference between the initial and final frequencies is large (e.g., 120 Hz), the pitch percept will correspond to the initial frequency and the final frequency; that is, two pitches can be detected. If the frequency transition falls between 60 and 120 Hz, with both frequencies situated around 750 Hz, the pitch percept can take almost any frequency between the initial and final frequencies of the burst.

Summary: Hearing Science and Pitch

We have described, rather simplistically, two mechanisms of pitch perception: a place mechanism and a neural mechanism. The argument continues concerning the relative importance of each. Certain data (for example, pitch and sine waves) can be explained easily by place or mechanical analysis within the cochlea. Other data (for example, periodicity pitch) can be explained better by additional analysis of a neural mechanism. It is certain that both must operate simultaneously. Without mechanical (frequency) analysis along the basilar membrane, there will be no neural activity. Additionally, the data we have summarized point toward temporal and/or frequency analyzing mechanisms.

Speech Science and Pitch

Most hearing science experiments concerning pitch have been aimed at describing the nature of the processes responsible for mediating pitch and discrimination of auditory signals on the basis of pitch differences. In order to relate the acoustic characteristics of the signal to psychological (pitch) characteristics, most hearing scientists have used detailed signal analysis techniques in order to specify the important frequency, time, intensity, and phase characteristics. They have used exquisite psychophysical procedures which hopefully minimize extraneous effects. The classic experiments of Stevens, Volkmann, and Newman (1937), followed by the Stevens and Volkmann (1940) investigation, represent the broader psychological aspects of pitch. The mel scale and the techniques devised to generate the scale demonstrated clearly that frequency and pitch of sine waves are not equal. The furor that followed over a period of years seems to be, in large part, a result of emphasis upon stimulus analysis, heavily controlled experimental technique, and definitions of pitch or the lack thereof, on the one hand, and a truly psychological experiment, on the other hand.

Speech science, however, has borrowed the techniques of hearing science and signal analysis methods to investigate pitch. But the definition and importance of the pitch characteristics of speech signals within the communication process are broad. Pitch seems to be everything. As we shall see below, aspects of pitch are used to define vocal registers, jitter, voicing, stress and intonation, emotional characteristics, pathology, vocal effort, syntactic hypotheses, phoneme differences and, of course, the characteristics of the vocal mechanism.

Voice Pitch

Pitch is typically defined as "that attribute of auditory sensation in terms of which sounds may be ordered on a scale extending from low to high. Pitch depends primarily upon the sound pressure and waveform of the stimulus" (*American Standard Acoustical Terminology*, 1960, p. 44). This definition (12.1) continues with a note describing the pitch of a sound by the frequency or frequency level of a simple tone. In definition 13.2 (p. 47), "Simple tone is a sound sensation characterized by its singleness of pitch." This definition is followed by the note: "Whether or not a listener hears a tone as simple or complex is dependent upon ability, experience, and listening attitude" (p. 47). A complex tone is later described (13.3) as being periodic in nature and as a sound sensation characterized by more than one pitch.

We have seen already that these various definitions appear to be true in the hearing science experiments. We have seen the single pitch of a sine wave (a simple tone) matched to the pitch of complex periodic signals. These pitches were sometimes determined by the waveform. Sometimes a complex signal took on a single pitch characteristic and sometimes the characteristics of several pitches. In all of these experiments and definitions, periodicity of the acoustic signal provided the underlying influence.

While voice pitch has no totally adequate definition in speech research, it is generally associated with the fundamental frequency of sounds generated by the laryngeal mechanism. The speaking fundamental frequency (*SFF*) indeed can be high or low, and the concomitant percepts of pitch can be scaled from high to low. However, holding SFF constant does not produce a truly periodic signal, but rather one that is described as quasi-periodic. The glottal waveform varies in period from moment to moment around some mean SFF. Further, the distributions of these waveform periods are generally skewed, sometimes upward (positive) and sometimes downward (negative). Individual speaker differences are easily shown by measures of the skewness characteristics of vocal period and SFF (Mikheev, 1971; Horii, 1973). In spite of the lack of specific periodicity, a single pitch generally is assigned to voiced sounds. This fact should not be surprising since jittered pulses, narrow band of noise, and signals with frequency transitions have been shown above to evoke single pitch judgments by listeners.

Pitch of Vowels

Perhaps the best known speech signal is the vowel. Many authors have described the acoustic characteristics of the vowels and the primary determiner of vowel identification, the formant structure, is well established. The vowel is also the speech signal with a periodic envelope that is closest to nonspeech signals. From a hearing science point of view, the pitch of a vowel should correspond closely to either the fundamental frequency or the formant structure of the particular vowel. If the formants are widely spaced (outside critical bandwidth), multiple pitches may be heard, each corresponding to a formant region. If two formants are closely spaced in frequency, there may be a single pitch corresponding to frequency between the formant peaks.

Farnsworth (1937) presented several pure tones to listeners and asked them to assign a vowel label to each pure tone. There were no pitch matches to the vowels but rather listeners linked vowels (pitch) to the pitch of the sine waves. The vowel /i/ was ranked high and judged to correspond to a pitch of approximately 2000 Hz. The vowel /u/ was ranked low and judged to correspond to a pitch of approximately 400 Hz. The vowel /æ/ was judged to have a pitch of approximately 900 Hz. Thus, the vowels were judged low if the first and second formants were closely spaced and located at a low frequency. The vowels with somewhat equally spaced formants, with the second formant located in the middle-frequency range, generally were assigned a middle-frequency pitch. The ranking of pitch resemblance did not allow much quantification of the pitch of vowels. For example, the sine wave frequencies, and presumably their respective pitches, did not correspond to either the fundamental frequency or any of the formant frequency locations.

More recent data suggest that a single pitch will be assigned to vowels that correspond to the fundamental frequency of the signal. Wood and Michel (1971) have reported the results of a large experiment investigating various parameters of vowel production and perception. They asked listeners to match the pitch of a sine wave to the pitch of several different vowels. In every case, the pitch assigned to two-second samples removed from sustained vowels corresponded to the speaker's fundamental frequency. When the SFF changed, the assigned pitch also changed appropriately.

The absence of pitch matches to the formant regions suggests that the pitch of vowels is not mediated by a place mechanism. Obviously, since the selected pitch of vowels corresponds to the fundamental frequency, the mechanism mediating such a pitch must detect the information provided by the SFF in some form. Two kinds of information are possible: place information in the form of physically present low-frequency energy and the periodicity of the waveform which corresponds to the SFF.

Certain published data and some, as yet, unpublished data (Brandt) suggest that low-frequency place information is not necessary for the perception of the fundamental frequency of the pitch of vowels. Klatt (1973) demonstrated that the discrimination of the SFF of synthetic vowels was unaffected by high-pass filtering. Indeed, the discrimination was better with high-pass filtering than for unfiltered stimuli. High-pass filtered natural vowels presented to listeners at sensation levels less than 20 dB also elicit pitch judgments corresponding to the SFF (Brandt, unpublished data). Such evidence, taken with well-known limitations in low-frequency sensitivity of the auditory system, clearly suggests that low-frequency place information is unlikely to be of critical importance in mediating the pitch of vowels.

For the sake of the current argument, the remaining cue for the pitch of vowels appears to lie in the waveform periodicity. Klatt (1973) measured the differential thresholds for fundamental frequency of high-pass filtered and unfiltered samples of a synthetically produced vowel, /ɛ/, and a consonant vowel combination, /ja/. Each of the examples incorporated a linearly decreasing frequency transition. The differential thresholds were better (smaller) for the filtered samples than for the unfiltered samples. It would appear that the changes in fundamental frequency were discriminated by a mechanism which detected changes in the periodicity of the waveform. Additional evidence from speech science, that the cue provided by the fundamental frequency in voiced—voiceless distinctions does not depend upon physically present low-frequency energy but upon the pitch sensation, has been reported by Haggard, Ambler, and Callow (1970). This mechanism is the same as described above in the section on periodicity pitch. Differential thresholds for periodicity pitch-type signals are mediated by high-frequency neural activity (Campbell, 1963; Purvis and Brandt, 1973; Waryas, 1974).

One might reject such high-frequency analysis by the auditory system for vowels by recognizing that the acoustic spectrum of vowels shows that the amplitudes of the third and fourth formants are always much lower than those, for example, of the first formant, particularly for the back vowels. The third formant of /u/ has been reported by Peterson and Barney (1952) as being 40 dB lower than the first formant. The amplitudes of place information corresponding to the high-frequency region (above about 2000 Hz) are too low and therefore inadequate as a cue for pitch perception. An extremely important paper has been presented by Niemoeller, McCormick, and Miller (1973); it demonstrates that the conductive mechanism of the auditory system, mainly head diffraction and ear canal resonance, may serve to amplify the frequency region of interest, 2000 to 4000 Hz, to amplitudes within 5—10 dB of the maximum levels in the low-frequency region.

Several years ago we conducted an experiment using a vowel-shaped noise to mask sinusoids (Brandt and Thomas, 1967). To obtain the vowel-shaped noises, we substituted a white noise generator for the typical buzz source used in a static vowel synthesizer. The masking audiograms indicated the frequency region of the first

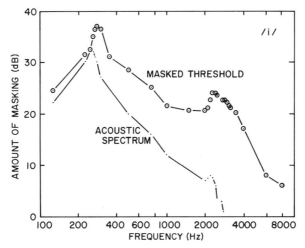

Figure 13.5 The amount of masking of sinusoids produced by a vowel-shaped thermal noise /i/ of 70 dB SPL, re: .0002 dynes/cm².

formant clearly, but in the vowel sounds of /i/ and /æ/, the masking audiograms showed only one large peak rather than the two expected from the second and third formants, respectively (Figures 13.5 and 13.6). The three peaks corresponding to the first three formants of /u/ were easily detectable from the masking audiograms (Figure 13.7). Additionally, while the frequency regions were represented in the masking audiograms, the amplitude relations between the formants were not. It appeared that the masked threshold did not follow the spectrum of the masker very well at frequencies above about 1500 Hz. More masking was seen than was predicted

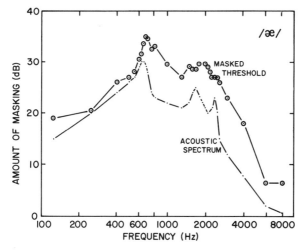

Figure 13.6 The amount of masking of sinusoids produced by a vowel-shaped thermal noise /æ/ of 70 dB SPL, re: .0002 dynes/cm².

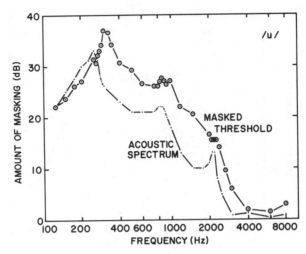

Figure 13.7 The amount of masking of sinusoids produced by a vowel-shaped thermal noise /u/ of 70 dB SPL, re: .0002 dynes/cm².

by the energy in the masker. We attributed this upward spread of masking in a *gestalt* hearing science manner by suggesting that such a result is due to ordinary upward spread of masking, as it is for pure tone and narrow-band noise masking. In recent months we have wondered whether *upward spread of masking by the auditory system* is totally appropriate. The masking data of hearing science imply that the upward spread of masking is cochlear or neural. Very little consideration is given to the possibility of selective amplification of the higher-frequency region, as suggested by Niemoeller *et al.* (1973). These data suggest that it is probable that high-frequency energy in the regions of the third and fourth formants is quite adequate for periodicity pitch analysis of the SFF. Could it be that the reasons for the relatively unchanging third and fourth formant regions, and the particular conductive characteristics of the auditory system which emphasize those frequency regions, are by design?

Pitch of Whispered Vowels

Perhaps the only way to minimize or eliminate the periodicity of the voice would be to utilize whispered vowels. The cues for the pitch of vowels would lie in the spectral envelope, and the concomitant place information in the ear of the listener. Thomas (1969) required listeners to match the pitch of a sine wave to the pitch of whispered vowels by male and female speakers. Almost all of the listeners identified the pitch of whispered vowels as corresponding closely to the frequency of the second formant. Two listeners were able to assign a pitch related to the first formant of /ɑ/ and /ɔ/ when the suggestion was made to find additional pitches. All other vowels were assigned a second formant pitch by these listeners. Thomas noted that during his experiment "the listeners, after perceiving the pitch of a stimulus, frequently whistled the pitch and then adjusted the oscillator to match the whistle" (p. 470). Because the ranges of whistling and of the second formant are virtually the same, it is difficult to evaluate the Thomas data as representative of the pitch of whispered vowels.

In an unpublished study (Brandt), we asked listeners to match the pitch of a sine wave to the vowel-shaped masking noises referred to above. In every case, the listeners assigned a pitch to the first formant of /i/, /u/, and /æ/. The formant structure of the spectrum corresponded to the structure of voiced vowels specified by Peterson and Barney (1952), and the amplitudes decreased with formant number. Since the first formant always provided the largest amplitude, it was not surprising that a place pitch was assigned to the various vowel-shaped noises.

The spectrum envelope in whispered vowels is different relative to normal voiced vowels (Meyer-Eppler, 1957; Thomas, 1969). The first and second formant amplitudes are more equal. According to Thomas, "if a particular formant frequency is to be heard as a perceived pitch, the formant amplitude must be comparable to, if not greater than, the amplitudes of other formants" (p. 470). In the absence of temporal information, this restatement of place theory of the auditory system may be quite appropriate. In the Brandt unpublished study of pitch of vowel-shaped noise, the amplitude of the first formant was always greater than other formant amplitudes. In the Thomas study, the first and second formants were approximately equal in amplitude. Taken with the suggestions that the region of the second formant can be amplified by the conduction characteristics of the auditory system, the spectra of the vowels whispered by live speakers in the Thomas study could indeed provide the necessary amount of second formant amplitude and frequency information to produce a pitch appropriate to the second formant.

Pitch of Continuous Speech

Assigning a pitch defined by a sine wave frequency to the pitch of a vowel is relatively easy. The vowel may be short, long, or sustained, and the signal analysis techniques for measuring the spectral characteristics and waveform periodicity are relatively simple, compared to the signal analysis of continuous speech. Large speech samples require advanced analysis methods by computers (Flanagan, 1972). Lacking adequate signal analysis techniques for continuous speech, we continue to have difficulty in determining the acoustic cues used by the ear to extract vocal pitch.

It appears from the pitch of vowels that the ear probably uses the periodicity of the waveform corresponding to the fundamental frequency of the laryngeal source, even though it is physically absent to the ear. Consider telephone circuits which typically do not transmit or receive low-frequency energy in the range of speaking fundamental frequencies. Radios and tape recorders, particularly uncalibrated ones with small loudspeakers, do not reproduce low frequencies very well. Yet, speech and music are perceived as having low pitches, and changes in pitch can be appreciated by the listener.

At least one attempt to study the pitch characteristics of continuous speech has been made (Brandt, 1973). Listeners were asked to match a periodicity pitch-type variable stimulus to the pitch of sentence material spoken at different fundamental frequencies. The periodicity pitch stimulus resulted from filtering a dc pulse train with a $\frac{1}{3}$ octave filter centered at a frequency of 2200 Hz. To insure the absence of low-frequency physical energy, this stimulus was additionally high-pass filtered at 1500 Hz. The pitch of this stimulus was controlled by varying the repetition rate of the pulse train. Three samples of the sentence, *According to the present information, the profits are high*, were extracted from a larger stimulus set previously tape-recorded for other experiments (Brandt, 1972; Brandt, Ruder, and Shipp, 1969). The three sentence samples have SFFs of 116, 138, and 179 Hz, as measured by hand from data obtained from wave-by-wave analysis after low-pass filtering.

The listeners were able to alternate between the comparison stimulus and the speech samples, which were also high-pass filtered, as often as necessary at any time during the sentence. The listeners tended to listen to most of each sentence (apparently *averaging* the vocal pitch) and then adjusted the pulse train for equality in pitch. Several replications were obtained. The listeners also matched the pitch of the pulse train to sinusoids of various low frequencies appropriate to the SFFs (e.g., 100–250 Hz). This control condition was included so that the listeners' pitch detection behavior could be compared for speech and nonspeech signals. The listeners always set the repetition rate of the pulse train to the frequency of the sinusoid for equal pitch. The control condition clearly demonstrated that the listeners assigned the pitch of the complex periodic signal primarily on the basis of the rate of signal envelope variation, that is, the missing fundamental frequency.

The listeners also detected changes in the SFF. When the SFF was low, the repetition rate of the pulse train was generally appropriate to the missing fundamental frequency. When the SFF was high, the listeners increased the repetition rate of the pulses appropriately. Certain bias appeared in the perception of SFF that did not occur with the periodic signal (control condition), where the pulse train repetition rate was always equal to the frequency of the sinusoid. When the mean SFF was lower than normal (for the speaker), the listeners tended to overestimate the pitch of continuous speech. That is, the repetition rate of the pulse train was set higher than the SFF. When the SFF was higher than normal, the listeners set the repetition rate of the pulse train lower than the SFF (underestimated the pitch). When the SFF was normal for the speaker, the listeners set the repetition rate equal to the missing SFF.

Brandt considered that the bias in pitch perception of continuous speech samples occurring around the normal SFF lies in the quasi-periodic nature of the speech signals. During phonation of sentence material, the instantaneous fundamental frequency is changing constantly. In comparison, and by definition, this is not the case for sinusoids. In order to extract a single vocal pitch, the listeners had to *average* these instantaneous pitch periods over a portion of the entire sentence. During repeated measures, the listener undoubtedly chooses different voice samples over which to average. This phenomenon forces the mechanism for pitch extraction to sample the stimulus envelope over some interval of time. Distribution characteristics of the SFFs were skewed positively in all three cases, but the skew was very small for the sample of the normal SFF of the speaker. The SFF distribution characteristic that was most closely related to the pitch of each of the three speech samples was the total range of SFFs. Specifically, the average pitch was approximately equal to a bisection of the total range of each sample. It appeared that the listeners were detecting the highest

SFF during the first half of the sentence and lowest SFF during the last half of the sentence, and then assigning a *pitch* which was equal to the bisected range. The results suggest that a listener's pitch extractor samples the envelope variation and computes some form of *average* pitch. This pitch, however, may not necessarily be the traditional *mean speaking fundamental frequency* of voice.

Wood and Michel (1971) reported that the pitch assigned to two-second samples removed from sustained vowels always corresponded to the fundamental frequency. The range of SFFs of sustained vowels is extremely small and perhaps functionally unimportant. Because the listener's pitch extractor in sampling the vowel waveform sees no important variations in SFF, the pitch match for vowels corresponds to the mean SFF. However, the pitch extractor operating on sentence material sees a constantly changing SFF and must select one of several values which corresponds to the proper pitch. At least for the speech samples used in the Brandt (1973) experiment that was described above, the assigned pitch and the mean SFF do not correspond exactly.

It was pointed out earlier that, under certain conditions, several nonspeech signals produce pitch matches that correspond to a midpoint or bisection of a range of frequencies. If a periodicity pitch signal is jittered slightly, the pitch corresponds to the midpoint of the instantaneous pulse periods. A band of noise appropriately filtered can result in a pitch perception that corresponds to a point midway between the cutoff frequencies (i.e., the range of place activity). Often when the spectrum of frequency-modulated signals cannot be resolved into discrete components, a pitch results which corresponds to center of the modulation range. Signals with continuous frequency transitions (bursts) sometimes correspond to the center of the frequency range or midway between initial and final frequencies in bursts consisting of two discrete frequencies. Thus, it appears that a pitch extractor that evaluates distribution characteristics such as a range of frequencies does indeed exist.

Most of the elegant hypotheses that describe the current status of the perception of periodicity pitch would find a pitch extractor operating upon range cues entirely too simple and probably incorrect. For the sake of argument, however, the following facts about the continuous speech signal or even sustained vowels pertain: The SFF is constantly changing, i.e., jitter; the frequency region which is three to five times the fundamental pitch period is occupied by a formant structure that often is in transition; the power spectrum is constantly changing; combination tones are not heard in speech; backward and forward masking effects are quite real; and, more importantly, periodicity is always present in the real speech signal. Where, then, is the cue for the perception of the pitch of the speaking fundamental frequency?

Since it appears that the listener searches for the highest and lowest periodicity of the SFF in assigning a pitch to continuous speech, we propose that the process is ruled-based. Simply, the pitch extractor "searches" for the highest periodicity and the lowest periodicity. The "search" is not haphazard. A plot of SFF as a function of time (in 100-msec intervals) showed the highest SFF occurring in the first half of the sentence (indeed during the initial word *according*), while the lowest SFF occurred either at the end of the first half of the sentence (the word *information*) or the end of the sentence (the word *high*). It would be easy to impose the rule that SFF will be highest early in a declarative sentence and lowest either at the end of a phrase or the end of the sentence. Support for such a notion has been provided recently by Olive (1975) in his study of fundamental frequency contours of naturally spoken simple declarative English sentences. He developed rules for synthesis that are quite simple and, while not at all intended to suggest a sensory process, agree remarkably well with the pitch-matching data obtained from listeners. Additional research is, of course, warranted.

The overall pitch contour is not continuous over time because of consonant production. We might propose that the consonant sounds, per se, are irrelevant for the pitch extractor in determining the general pitch of voice. The voiceless consonants, being basically aperiodic, would not provide pitch information. The voiced stop consonants, in some languages, often show short increases or decreases in fundamental frequency at onset (Haggard, Ambler, and Callow, 1970). It is not clear what effects these small, short-duration changes in SFF have on the perception of the average SFF, other than perhaps being necessary for natural-sounding synthetic speech. They may be more important phonemically.

It was pointed out earlier that the temporal nature of single nerve cells in the cochlear nucleus can be sharpened considerably by the addition of energy in high-frequency inhibitory regions (Moore and Cashin, 1974). The simple presence of high-frequency consonant energy may be important in neural coding of the speech information. The experiment that examines neural activity in response to vowel stimuli preceded or followed by consonant sounds has, to our knowledge, not been conducted as yet. The experiment should include all of the speech signal rather than only a sample of the vowel.

Formant transitions are important in speech and language as perceptual cues. These rapid frequency transitions probably are detected as place information and may not have an effect upon the extraction of the general vocal pitch. Thus, the pitch extractors of the auditory system use both periodicity information and place information: periodicity for the vocal pitch, and frequency transitions for identifications of phoneme classes, etc.

Additional Aspects of Vocal Pitch

Vocal Registers. The concept of vocal registers continues to interest several contemporary investigators. Although an argument continues about nomenclature (Hollien, 1972), at least three registers—vocal fry, modal, and falsetto—can be identified. Further, the experimental procedure used to investigate vocal registers forces the trichotomy to be a function of vocal pitch, although the ranges of the various registers are defined in terms of SFF. Speakers are instructed to match the pitch of a standard stimulus, a sine wave, with the pitch of the vowel /ɑ/. (The effect on register data of changing the vowel stimulus is not yet clear. The range of SFFs identified as particular registers may change from vowel to vowel.) Hollien and Michel (1968, p. 600) stated that a register "is a series or range of consecutive (vocal) fundamental frequencies of similar quality; in addition, there should be little or no overlap in fundamental frequency between adjacent registers . . ." After each speaker has produced the vowel sample over his total fundamental frequency range, the tape-recorded samples are often presented to listeners for categorization into the three (and sometimes more) registers. Hollien and Michel (1968) report the vocal fry register for males to range from fundamental frequencies of 24 to 52 Hz; the modal register ranges from 94 to 287 Hz; the falsetto register for males ranges from 275 to 634 Hz. It should be noted that the modal and falsetto registers overlap in frequency. The overlap has been confirmed by McGlone and Brown (1969) and others. The vocal fry and modal registers do not overlap.

The gross nature of pitch scaled from low to high determines which SFF is modal or falsetto. The region of overlap, in terms of samples of speech being found in both registers with equal SFF, produces the categorization of registers in terms of something other than, or in addition to, pitch. Apparently pitch becomes multidimensional. Perhaps changes in formant frequency, duty cycle of the laryngeal tone, or changes in period distribution (skewness) help to cue the categorization. Vocal intensity has recently been judged important (Colton, 1973). The vocal fry register seems to be not a pitch phenomenon, but rather a detection of intermittency of glottal pulses. This is not surprising; Flanagan and Guttman (1960) demonstrated that periodic signals with very low interruption (pulse) rates were judged by listeners on the basis of pulse rate. Pulses presented at higher rates were judged on the basis of fundamental frequency. The low pulse rates in the Flanagan and Guttman study incorporate the SFFs of vocal fry easily.

Miscellaneous (But Important) Aspects of Vocal Pitch. The multidimensional aspects of pitch become particularly important when the SFF takes on functional significance for the listeners of a given language. While hearing and speech scientists have avoided the multidimensional percepts of pitch by using nonspeech signals or limited speech signals (such as the vowel), changes in SFF become important in sentences. An increase in SFF can signal strong stress (Bolinger, 1958; Hadding-Koch, 1961). The intended meaning of an utterance, whether a statement or a question, is determined by SFF (Hadding-Koch and Studdert-Kennedy, 1964; Majewski and Blasdell, 1969). An increasing SFF denotes a question, while a constant or slightly decreasing SFF denotes a statement. A decrease in SFF usually occurs at the end of each major syntactic constituent; an increase in SFF occurs near the beginning of the following constituent. Sentence boundaries seem to be accompanied by large SFF increases and long pauses. Thus, SFF can be used to cue many aspects of syntactic structure (Lea, 1973). Many of the important prosodic features of speech and language are reviewed by Fry (1968).

Often we have had listeners with hearing losses who have participated in our experiments ask, "Are you telling me or asking me?" or, "I'm not sure what you mean." Many of these listeners have mild hearing losses, particularly at high frequencies, and often show speech discrimination scores of 100% correct on traditional audiological tests. The ambiguity shown by these listeners is not to be attributed to instructions in the experimental setting; they often show the same difficulty outside the laboratory.

Much of the ambiguity could be explained if the mechanism mediating the perception of SFF was impaired. Purvis and Brandt (1973) reported data that demonstrated that high-frequency hearing loss was likely to result in an inability to perceive periodicity pitch. Speech discrimination can be normal, at least in the ways shown by conventional audiological testing. Since we have suggested that the discrimination of SFF is the same as the nonspeech-like periodicity pitch, the data of Purvis and Brandt explain the ambiguity in comprehension of speech and language. The cues for syntax and meaning provided by changes in SFF are not fully available, and the communication process is impaired.

Emotions in Speech. Williams and Stevens (1972) summarized the gross acoustic attributes associated with various emotions of speech. The clearest aspect of the speech signal that provides an indication of the emotional state of the talker was the contour of SFF versus time. Normal unemotional speech was characterized by smooth, slow, and continuous changes in SFF. The SFF in speech denoting anger, fear, or sorrow changed markedly over time. The emotion *anger* produced SFFs that were much higher than normal, with a larger total range. Lieberman and Michaels (1962) had also noted these gross attributes of emotion. They further emphasized the fine structure (perturbations or jitter) of the SFF. Both investigations are multidimensional in nature. Lieberman and Michaels asked listeners to categorize various stimuli on the basis of perceived emotion. Williams and Stevens determined the acoustic characteristics of known emotional speech. It would be interesting to determine whether the listeners detect the SFF cues, per se. Does the emotion *anger* produce high pitch judgements, and *sorrow*, low pitch judgements? The variability of pitch matches should also be large for *anger* and small for *sorrow*.

Summary: Speech Science and Pitch

The strict definitions of pitch and development of mechanisms of pitch extraction used by the hearing scientist have been applied to broad definitions of pitch within speech and language science. The result was a definition of voice pitch as a percept of the speaking fundamental frequency. The mechanisms of auditory pitch extraction must be the same for speech and nonspeech acoustic signals. With a common definition and a common mechanism for pitch extraction, speech *and* hearing science come closer together and the investigators of each of these specialties come closer to an investigation of the communication process.

A Return to the Issue

Perhaps the most efficient way to gain experience and knowledge is to select a narrow, well-defined problem area and investigate. The problem area may be vowel perception, periodicity pitch, signal detection theory, or multidimensional scaling techniques. The areas may be defined as clinical or research. They are still pieces of the big jigsaw puzzle that is *human communication*. All of the pieces eventually must fit together.

We have reacted to the apparent direction of investigators and students of the communication process toward an increased fragmentation of research efforts. We speak of interdisciplinary research efforts as being the most profitable in the long run. Yet, at the same time, interdisciplinary research is commonly made up of a speech scientist, a hearing scientist, a language scientist, and some clinicians, all pursuing their own interests. The pieces have a lack of cohesiveness. Perhaps a few more pieces of the puzzle could be fitted together, however, if we learned from each other. A common definition and a common mechanism for analysis would help. It may not be found here, but to rephrase a quotation and thus reject a particular point of view: to infer something about the perception of speech from data on the perception of nonspeech *is* justifiable. Speech perception *may* be predicted from the analysis of the acoustic properties of spoken utterances *and* the characteristics of the human auditory system.

ACKNOWLEDGMENTS

The preparation of this chapter was supported in part by a grant from the National Institutes of Health. The author is particularly indebted to Professor John Michel for his suggestions, and especially to Lynne Marshall and her fellow students, who offered constructive criticisms and suggestions as the chapter progressed.

REFERENCES

American Standard Acoustical Terminology (S1.1—1960). New York: American Standards Association Inc., 1960.

Bolinger, D. L. A theory of pitch accent in English. *Word*, 1958, *14*, 109—149.

Brady, P. T., House, A. S., and Stevens, K. N. Perception of sounds characterized by a rapidly changing resonant frequency. *Journal of the Acoustical Society of America*, 1961, *33*, 1357—1362.

Brandt, J. F. Frequency discrimination following exposure to noise. *Journal of the Acoustical Society of America*, 1967, *41*, 448—457.

Brandt, J. F. Effect of stimulus bandwidth on listener judgments of vocal loudness and effort. *Journal of the Acoustical Society of America*, 1972, *52*, 705—707.

Brandt, J. F. Perception of the fundamental frequency of continuous speech. Paper presented at the Eight-Sixth Meeting of the Acoustical Society of America, October 30—November 2, 1973, Los Angeles, California.

Brandt, J. F., Ruder, K. F., and Shipp, T. Vocal loudness and effort in continuous speech. *Journal of the Acoustical Society of America*, 1969, *46*, 1543—1548.

Brandt, J. F., and Thomas, W. G. Auditory analysis of vowel-shaped thermal noise. Paper presented at the Communication Sciences Laboratory Seminar on Speech Perception, September 8, 1967, Univ. of Florida, Gainesville, Florida.

Campbell, R. A. Frequency discrimination of pulsed tones. *Journal of the Acoustical Society of America*, 1963, *35*, 1193—1200.

Cardozo, B. L., and Ritsma, R. J. On the perception of imperfect periodicity. *I.E.E.E. Transactions on Audio and Electroacoustics*, 1968, *AU—16*, 159—164.

Colton, R. H. Vocal intensity in the modal and falsetto registers. *Folia Phoniatrica*, 1973, *25*, 62—70.

Denes, P. B., and Pinson, E. N. *The speech chain.* Garden City, New York: Doubleday, 1973

Ekdahl, A. G., and Boring, E. G. The pitch of tonal masses. *American Journal of Psychology*, 1934, *46*, 452—455.

Farnsworth, P. R. An approach to the study of vocal resonance. *Journal of the Acoustical Society of America*, 1937, *9*, 152—154.

Fischler, H. Model of the *secondary* residue effect in the perception of complex tones. *Journal of the Acoustical Society of America*, 1967, *42*, 759—764.

Flanagan, J. *Speech analysis, synthesis, and perception.* (Second Edition). Berlin, Germany: Springer-Verlag, 1972.

Flanagan, J. L., and Guttman, N. On the pitch of periodic pulses. *Journal of the Acoustical Society of America*, 1960, *32*, 1308—1319.

Fry, D. B. Prosodic phenomena. In B. Malmberg (Ed.), *Manual of phonetics.* Amsterdam: North-Holland Publ., 1968. Pp. 365—410.

Glattke, T. J. Unit response of the cat cochlear nucleus to amplitude-modulated stimuli. *Journal of the Acoustical Society of America*, 1969, *45*, 419—425.

Goldstein, J. L. Auditory nonlinearity. *Journal of the Acoustical Society of America*, 1967, *41*, 676—689.

Hadding-Koch, K. Acoustico-phonetic studies in the intonation of Southern Swedish. *Transactions of the Institute of Phonetics, III*, 1961, cited in Fry (1968).

Hadding-Koch, K., and Studdert-Kennedy, M. An experimental study of some intonation contours. *Phonetica*, 1964, *11*, 175—185.

Haggard, M., Ambler, S., and Callow, M. Pitch as a voicing cue. *Journal of the Acoustical Society of America*, 1970, *47*, 613—617.

Hollien, H. Three major vocal registers: A proposal. In A. Rigault, and R. Charbonneau (Eds.), *Proceedings of the Seventh International Congress of Phonetic Sciences*. The Hague: Mouton, 1972. Pp. 320—331.

Hollien, H., and Michel, J. F. Vocal fry as a phonational register. *Journal of Speech and Hearing Research*, 1968, *11*, 600—604.

Horii, Y. Skewness characteristics of vocal period and fundamental frequency distributions. *Purdue University Contributed Papers (PUCP)*, 1973, *2*, 57—61.

Houtsma, A. J. M., and Goldstein, J. L. The central origin of the pitch of complex tones: Evidence from musical interval recognition. *Journal of the Acoustical Society of America*, 1972, *51*, 520—529.

Kiang, N. Y. S., and Moxon, E. C. Tails of tuning curves of auditory-nerve fibers. *Journal of the Acoustical Society of America*, 1974, *55*, 620—630.

Klatt, D. H. Discrimination of fundamental frequency contours in synthetic speech: Implications for models of pitch perception, *Journal of the Acoustical Society of America*, 1973, *53*, 8—16.

Lea, W. A. An approach to syntactic recognition without phonemics. *I.E.E.E. Transactions on Audio and Electroacoustics*, 1973, *AU—21*, 249—258.

Lieberman, P., and Michaels, S. B. Some aspects of fundamental frequency and envelope amplitude as related to the emotional content of speech. *Journal of the Acoustical Society of America*, 1962, *34*, 922—927.

Majewski, W., and Blasdell, R. Influence of fundamental frequency cues on the perception of some synthetic intonation contours. *Journal of the Acoustical Society of America*, 1969, *45*, 450—457.

McClelland, K. D., and Brandt, J. F. Pitch of frequency-modulated sinusoids. *Journal of the Acoustical Society of America*, 1969, *45*, 1489—1498.

McGlone, R. E., and Brown, W. S. Identification of the *shift* between vocal registers. *Journal of the Acoustical Society of America*, 1969, *46*, 1033—1036.

Meyer-Eppler, W. Realization of prosodic features in whispered speech. *Journal of the Acoustical Society of America*, 1957, *29*, 104—106.

Mikheev, Y. V. Statistical distribution of the periods of the fundamental tone of Russian speech. *Soviet Physics—Acoustics*, 1971, *16*, 474—477.

Moore, T. J., and Cashin, J. L., Jr. Response patterns of cochlear nucleus neurons to excerpts from sustained vowels. *Journal of the Acoustical Society of America*, 1974, *56*, 1565—1576.

Nábělek, I., and Hirsh, I. J. On the discrimination of frequency transitions. *Journal of the Acoustical Society of America*, 1969, *45*, 1510—1519.

Nábělek, I. V., Nábělek, A. K., and Hirsh, I. J. Pitch of bursts of changing frequency. *Journal of the Acoustical Society of America*, 1970, *48*, 536—553.

Nábělek, I. V., Nábělek, A. K., and Hirsh, I. J. Pitch of sound bursts with continuous or discontinuous change of frequency. *Journal of the Acoustical Society of America*, 1973, *53*, 1305—1312.

Niemoeller, A. F., McCormick, L., and Miller, J. D. On the spectrum of spoken English. Paper presented at the Eighty-Sixth Meeting of the Acoustical Society of America, October 30—November 2, 1973, Los Angeles, California.

Olive, J. P. Fundamental frequency rules for the synthesis of simple declarative English sentences. *Journal of the Acoustical Society of America*, 1975, *57*, 476—482.

Peterson, G. E., and Barney, H. L. Control methods used in the study of the vowels. *Journal of the Acoustical Society of America*, 1952, *24*, 175—184.

Plomp, R., and Mimpen, A. M. The ear as a frequency analyzer. II. *Journal of the Acoustical Society of America*, 1968, *43*, 764—767.

Plomp, R., and Smoorenburg, G. G. (Eds.) *Frequency analysis and periodicity detection in hearing.* Leiden, The Netherlands: Sijthoff, 1970.

Pollack, I. Detection of rate of change of auditory frequency. *Journal of Experimental Psychology*, 1968, *77*, 535—541.

Purvis, G. O., and Brandt, J. F. Periodicity pitch perception of hearing-impaired listeners. Paper presented at the Eighty-Sixth meeting of the Acoustical Society of America, October 30—November 2, 1973, Los Angeles, California.

Rees, N. S. Auditory processing factors in language disorders: The view from Procrustes' bed. *Journal of Speech and Hearing Disorders*, 1973, *38*, 304—315.

Rosenberg, A. E. Pitch discrimination of jittered pulse trains. *Journal of the Acoustical Society of America*, 1966, *39*, 920—928.

Small, A. M. Some parameters influencing the pitch of amplitude modulated signals. *Journal of the Acoustical Society of America*, 1955, *27*, 751—760.

Small, A. M. Periodicity pitch. In J. V. Tobias (Ed.), *Foundations of modern auditory theory*, Vol. I. New York: Academic Press, 1970. Pp. 3—54.

Small, A. M., and Campbell, R. A. Masking of pulsed tones by bands of noise. *Journal of the Acoustical Society of America*, 1961, *33*, 1570—1576.

Small, A. M., and Daniloff, R. G. Pitch of noise bands. *Journal of the Acoustical Society of America*, 1967, *41*, 506—512.

Stevens, S. S., and Volkmann, J. The relation of pitch to frequency. *American Journal of Psychology*, 1940, *53*, 329—353.

Stevens, S. S., Volkmann, J., and Newman, E. B. A scale for the measurement of the psychological magnitude of pitch. *Journal of the Acoustical Society of America*, 1937, *8*, 185—190.

Thomas, I. B. Perceived pitch of whispered vowels. *Journal of the Acoustical Society of America*, 1969, *46*, 468—470.

Tsumura, T., Sone, T., and Nimura, T. Auditory detection of frequency transition. *Journal of the Acoustical Society of America*, 1973, *53*, 17—25.

von Békésy, G. *Experiments in hearing.* New York: McGraw-Hill, 1960.

von Békésy, G. Hearing theories and complex sounds. *Journal of the Acoustical Society of America*, 1963, *35*, 588—601.

Waryas, P. A. Periodicity pitch perception by retarded children. Unpublished doctoral dissertation, Univ. of Kansas, 1974.

Wightman, F. L. Pitch and stimulus fine structure. *Journal of the Acoustical Society of America*, 1973, *54*, 397—406. (a)

Wightman, F. L. The pattern-transformation model of pitch. *Journal of the Acoustical Society of America*, 1973, *54*, 407—416. (b)

Williams, C. E., and Stevens, K. N. Emotions and speech: some acoustical correlates. *Journal of the Acoustical Society of America*, 1972, *52*, 1238—1250.

Wood, C., and Michel, J. F. The fundamental frequency of sustained vowels under different production conditions. Paper presented at the Eighty-First Meeting of the Acoustical Society of America, April 20—23, 1971, Washington, D.C.

Subject Index